The
Hub

A PLACE FOR READING
AND WRITING

Dear Instructor,

During the last six years, developmental writing and reading courses at colleges across the country have undergone immense changes: corequisite models such as the Accelerated Learning Program (ALP) are spreading quickly, reading and writing are being integrated, faculty are implementing active learning approaches, and instructors are more frequently choosing to address

Photo courtesy of Donna Crivello

the challenges students face in balancing school, work, and life issues. These seismic changes in the way we teach developmental writing and reading are the primary reasons for the creation of *The Hub: A Place for Reading and Writing*.

As faculty members at the Community College of Baltimore County, we pioneered ALP to meet the needs of our students. Our model took shape through many brainstorming sessions, conferences by active learning specialists, and continuous research around our students' outcomes and our courses. It emerged as the best model we could create to support our students, and better still, as further research by our faculty and others confirmed, it works.

Based on my experience developing ALP, and on my thirty-six years of experience teaching writing, I developed *The Hub: A Place for Reading and Writing* to bring students and instructors all of the materials and support they need to succeed in the composition classroom. I have designed *The Hub* around a series of carefully scaffolded multipart reading and writing projects that offer abundant opportunities for students to develop rhetorical knowledge, genre awareness, and critical reading and writing skills. At the same time, *The Hub* provides ideas, topics, activities, and other resources to support underprepared students and help accelerate their development into confident and successful college readers and writers.

The Hub is the result of all of the research and classroom work I've spent my career doing. The inquiry-based, active learning pedagogy you'll find in *The Hub* is thoroughly classroom-tested. The advice for instructors is based on the best practices for corequisite composition courses, as validated by outcomes research. I firmly believe it will help your students learn and succeed, just as it helped mine. So, welcome to *The Hub*! I hope you'll find it the place—your place—for reading and writing.

—*Peter*

Balancing School, Work, and Life

Reading/Writing Projects

The Hub

A PLACE FOR READING AND WRITING

Research and Documentation

Writing

Reading

Peter Adams

Community College of Baltimore County, Emeritus

bedford/st.martin's
Macmillan Learning

Boston | New York

For Bedford/St. Martin's

Vice President, Editorial, Macmillan Learning Humanities: Leasa Burton
Program Director for English: Stacey Purviance
Senior Program Manager: Karita F. dos Santos
Marketing Manager: Lauren Arrant
Market Development Manager: Azelie Fortier
Director of Content Development, Humanities: Jane Knetzger
Senior Development Editor: Gillian Cook
Assistant Editor: Paola Garcia-Muniz
Senior Digital Content Project Manager: Ryan Sullivan
Lead Digital Asset Archivist and Workflow Manager: Jennifer Wetzel
Production Supervisor: Brianna Lester
Advanced Media Project Manager: Rand Thomas
Media Editor: Angela Beckett
Senior Manager of Publishing Services: Andrea Cava
Editorial Services: Lumina Datamatics, Inc.
Composition: Lumina Datamatics, Inc.
Text Permissions Manager: Kalina Ingham
Text Permissions Researcher: Mark Schaefer, Lumina Datamatics, Inc.
Photo Permissions Editor: Angela Boehler
Photo Researcher: Krystyna Borgen, Lumina Datamatics, Inc.
Director of Design, Content Management: Diana Blume
Text Design: Claire Seng-Niemoeller
Cover Design: William Boardman
Cover Image: Cavan Images/Getty Images
Printing and Binding: King Printing Co., Inc.

Manufactured in the United States of America.

2   3   4   5   6   24   23   22   21   20

For information, write: Bedford/St. Martin's, 75 Arlington Street, Boston, MA 02116

ISBN 978-1-319-24072-1 (Student Edition Paperback)
ISBN 978-1-319-28463-3 (Student Edition Loose-Leaf)
ISBN 978-1-319-32942-6 (Instructor's Edition)

Acknowledgments

Text acknowledgments and copyrights appear at the back of the book on pages 757–59, which constitute an extension of the copyright page. Art acknowledgments and copyrights appear on the same page as the art selections they cover.

At the time of publication all internet URLs published in this text were found to accurately link to their intended website. If you do find a broken link, please forward the information to TheHub@macmillan.com so that it can be corrected for the next printing.

Preface for Instructors

The Hub: A Place for Reading and Writing consists of a series of carefully curated, inquiry-based reading/writing projects supported by crucial instruction and activities related to reading, writing, research, and life issues. It is available both in print and in a powerful digital format: *Achieve with Adams, The Hub.* For corequisite composition courses, it can serve as the complete "text" for both the composition course and the paired developmental section.

One Text for Two Courses

The breadth and depth of content in *The Hub* allows instructors the opportunity to select those elements that make the most sense for their students, their teaching styles, and the context in which they are teaching. Experienced instructors, for example, can select just the materials they want and assemble them into a powerful syllabus. Less experienced instructors (or those with less time to prepare) can choose from suggested schedules in the Instructor's Manual that combine selections of the materials into effective teaching plans for a variety of course types.

The Hub addresses the major topics typically covered in a composition rhetoric or reader: the rhetorical situation, thesis and unity, developing an argument, supporting assertions, diction, editing to reduce the frequency and severity of sentence-level errors, and research and documentation. (See the WPA Outcomes correlation chart on p. xiv for more details.) But it also addresses important issues that are not covered by other texts or digital products currently on the market:

- It features a strong and innovative approach to integrating reading and writing.

- It tackles the noncognitive issues that so often cause students to give up on college (e.g., life issues such as those related to finances, housing, health, child care, and so on, as well as affective issues like stress and impostor syndrome).

- It emphasizes active learning in small groups, which allows students to discover ideas about writing for themselves rather than simply read about them.

- It places more emphasis on the importance of inquiry and critical thinking.

One reason so many students drop out of college before they complete their developmental coursework is that the classes make them feel like they are back in seventh grade. *The Hub* does not do this. The materials in this collection ask students to read college-level essays, to complete college-level activities, and to write college-level essays. However, the additional materials provided for corequisite students offer the option of proceeding at a slower pace with more scaffolding, more support, and more opportunity for revisions.

Uniquely Flexible Content

Ideal for corequisite composition courses, *The Hub* was conceived of and designed as an in-depth suite of digital materials accompanied by a printed companion text. Seven multipart reading/writing projects on high-interest topics form the base of *The Hub*, with additional reading, writing, life skills, and research topics available in Parts 2–5. As your students work on readings and assignments in any of the projects, this rich library of additional content allows you to easily find and assign the exact materials and activities your students need when they need them. Whether it's detailed writing instruction on thesis development, a concise explanation of reading strategies like previewing or annotation, or advice on time management, it's all available for you to select from and combine in whatever order makes sense for your students.

To maximize the effectiveness of this unique resource, use *Achieve with Adams, The Hub* (see macmillanlearning.com for details). Achieve puts student writing at the center of your course and keeps revision at the core, with a dedicated composition space that guides students through draft, review, source check, and revision. In Achieve, students can read the complete text of *The Hub*, watch presentations on key topics narrated by the author, link to relevant websites, complete short writing assignments and reflection activities, get feedback from peers, and work on the end-of-project essay assignments.

Organization

The Hub consists of five parts:

Part 1: Reading/Writing Projects. This is the core of *The Hub* and consists of seven thematically organized projects of different lengths on a variety of high-interest topics, such as freedom of speech, what constitutes fake news, and choosing a career. These projects can be used in any order, and each takes 3–6 weeks to complete.

Part 2: Writing. This section of *The Hub* contains eleven Topics (8–18), each made up of several units that address essential writing issues, including the following: the rhetorical situation; the writing process; finding a focus; developing and organizing support; thesis, unity, and coherence; types of writing; argument; reducing sentence-level errors; and more. It includes several student essays, some annotated, and a series of drafts of an essay that illustrate the revision process.

Part 3: Reading. Three Topics (19–21), also made up of subunits, discuss active and critical reading strategies. These include purposes for reading, constructing meaning, activating schema, previewing, annotating, evaluating, identifying biases and assumptions, making inferences, distinguishing between facts and opinions, decoding difficult language, reading as a believer and doubter, and more.

Part 4: Research and Documentation. Topic 22 provides coverage of the research process: finding and evaluating sources; quoting, paraphrasing, and summarizing; conducting interviews and surveys; and avoiding plagiarism. Topics 23 and 24 provide detailed information on MLA and APA documentation, with numerous examples and a sample student paper in each.

Part 5: Balancing School, Work, and Life. An important feature of *The Hub* is the attention devoted to noncognitive issues, which can significantly impact student success. Topics 25–28 cover a broad range of issues students can find challenging: finances, health care, time management, goal setting, responding to setbacks, college terminology, asking for help, and more.

Elements and Features

The Hub contains a variety of important structural elements and features designed to support the overall pedagogical approach:

Reading/Writing Projects. Following best practices for teaching composition, each of the seven high-interest projects involves a variety of activities—reading articles, watching videos, engaging in class discussions, writing short papers, creating group responses to readings, analyzing data, interviewing someone who has knowledge or experience of the topic, and more. This approach inspires deep and prolonged thinking, encouraging students to articulate, analyze, and evaluate both their ideas and those of the authors they are reading, and to synthesize these ideas in their writing. In the end, the work students do for all of the shorter activities and assignments forms the basis of a longer paper or multimodal composition.

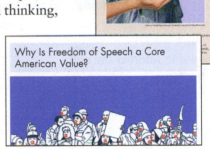

PROJECT 3
Freedom of Speech

Why Is Freedom of Speech a Core American Value?

3.10 Writing

Explaining the Senate's Reservations

Write a short paper—about a page—in which you explain the reservations that the US Senate registered in the document that can be found in the US Senate Response to the International Convention on the Elimination of All Forms of Racial Discrimination (3.9, p. 93). What were the government's reservations about the International Convention on the Elimination of All Forms of Racial Discrimination and why did it have those reservations?

Integration of Reading and Writing. Throughout the projects in Part 1, reading and writing are seamlessly integrated: when students read, they are asked to preview, annotate, paraphrase, summarize, analyze, evaluate, discuss, reflect on, and write in response to reading, and finally to draw on everything they have read to write a culminating essay or create a multimodal composition.

Top photo: (*statue*) Bryan Busovicki/Shutterstock; (*hand*) DenisNata/Shutterstock. Middle photo: rob zs/Shutterstock

Emphasis on Critical Thinking.
Group activities, discussion prompts, short writing assignments, readings from a variety of genres, and videos on related topics all challenge students to

> **3.11** Activity
> **Defining *Hate Speech***
> Much of current discussion about freedom of speech revolves around what is referred to as *hate speech*. Working in your group, write a definition of *hate speech*, explaining what your group agrees it is and what it isn't. If you need a refresher on how to

question what they read in any medium; evaluate the credentials, assumptions, and biases of authors; fact-check to distinguish between facts and opinions, truth and lies; and explore their own thinking.

> **19.1** Presentation
> **Reading Is Thinking**
> To watch this presentation, which discusses the importance of thinking, questioning, and extracting meaning from a text as you read, go to *Achieve for The Hub*, Topic 19, and open Unit 19.1.

Focus on Active Learning. *The Hub* uses an array of activity types to engage students' interest, promote critical thinking, and teach fundamental reading and writing skills: group and individual reading assignments, videos, narrated presentations, class discussions, small-group and whole-class exercises, short writing assignments, data analysis, interviewing, surveying, researching in class and out, essay assignments, peer review, and more.

Emphasis on Group Work. Students are frequently asked to work together in small groups to practice reading and writing skills, discuss readings, explore and debate ideas, brainstorm solutions to challenging life issues, and determine grammar rules.

Strategies to Address Life and Affective Issues. An important component of the ALP approach is the focus on helping students cope with challenging work and personal and affective issues. Topics 25–28, in Part 5, contain activities that aid students in identifying issues and brain-

> **26.7** Activity
> **Time Management: Strategies**
> Working together as a group, make a list of time-management strategies. To get you started, here's one strategy:
>
> **Do the hardest task first.** Sometimes a difficult task gets pushed to later in the day or even later in the week. Then you spend time dreading it, which makes you less effective at completing other tasks. There's nothing more satisfying than taking on that hard task first, preferably earlier in the day when you are at your most alert, and getting it done.

storming solutions to them in a group setting. In addition, the instructor-facing support for these activities provides suggestions to faculty on how to address these issues in the classroom as well as information on resources students could access and use.

Inductive Approach to Grammar. In contrast to traditional approaches, *The Hub* teaches grammar inductively. Grammar activities encourage students to work with peers to infer grammar rules from pairs and groups of sentences that illustrate correct and incorrect usage, work with them to articulate and record these rules, and apply what they have learned in the context of their own writing.

Instructor Support for Teaching with *The Hub*

Very few faculty have received preparation to teach an ALP or corequisite course, to address noncognitive issues, or to help students develop as readers.

> **16.27 Activity**
>
> **Subject-Verb Agreement 1**
>
> In the following pairs, the sentence in black is correct, and the sentence in blue has an error. Study these sentences and figure out the grammar rule they demonstrate.
>
> **Pair 1**
> ✓ One student rides a motorcycle to school.
> ✗ One student ride a motorcycle to school.
>
> **Pair 2**
> ✓ Two students ride motorcycles to school.
> ✗ Two students rides motorcycles to school.
>
> **Pair 3**
> ✓ A tree grows in Brooklyn.
> ✗ A tree grow in Brooklyn.
>
> **Pair 4**
> ✓ Many trees grow in Brooklyn.

Recognizing this problem, *The Hub* provides extensive assistance for instructors. In *Instructor's Manual for The Hub*, every activity, assignment, or reading in Projects 1–7 has a corresponding unit of suggestions, tips, and answers for instructors. In addition, there is specific guidance on teaching every unit in the Topics in Parts 2–5.

Two sections in the Instructor's Manual, Chapter 2 and Teaching Part 3: Reading (in Section 3: Teaching the Topics), address reading issues in some depth, and these pages will be extremely helpful for instructors with little preparation to encourage students to develop as readers. Also included are chapters for faculty explaining the history and development of ALP and corequisite models, how to teach integrated reading and writing, how to integrate group work and inductive learning, how to address noncognitive issues in the classroom, and how to use *The Hub* to design a syllabus for a composition or corequisite course.

Bedford/St. Martin's Puts You First

From day one, our goal has been simple: to provide inspiring resources that are grounded in best practices for teaching reading and writing. For more than 35 years, Bedford/St. Martin's has partnered with the field, listening to teachers, scholars, and students about the support writers need. We are committed to helping every writing instructor make the most of our resources.

How can we help *you*?

- Our editors can align our resources to your outcomes through correlation and transition guides for your syllabus. Just ask us.

- Our sales representatives specialize in helping you find the right materials to support your course goals.

- Our *Bits* blog on the Bedford/St. Martin's English Community site (community.macmillan.com) publishes fresh teaching ideas weekly. You'll also find easily downloadable professional resources and links to author webinars on our community site.

Contact your Bedford/St. Martin's sales representative or visit macmillanlearning .com to learn more.

Print and Digital Options for *The Hub*

Choose the format that works best for your course, and ask about our packaging options that offer savings for students.

Print

- *Paperback.* To order the paperback edition, use ISBN 978-1-319-24072-1. To order the paperback edition packaged with *Achieve with Adams, The Hub,* use ISBN 978-1-319-33951-7.
- *Loose-leaf edition.* This format does not have a traditional binding; its pages are loose and hole-punched to provide flexibility and a lower price to students. To order this version of *The Hub,* use ISBN 978-1-319-28463-3. To order the loose-leaf packaged with Achieve, use ISBN 978-1-319-33954-8.

Digital

- *Achieve with Adams, The Hub.* For details, visit macmillanlearning.com.
- *Popular e-book formats.* For details about our e-book partners, visit macmillanlearning.com/ebooks.
- *Inclusive Access.* Enable every student to receive their course materials through your LMS on the first day of class. Macmillan Learning's Inclusive Access program is the easiest, most affordable way to ensure all students have access to quality educational resources. Find out more at macmillanlearning.com/ inclusiveaccess.

Your Course, Your Way

No two writing programs or classrooms are exactly alike. Our Curriculum Solutions team works with you to design custom options that provide the resources your students need. (Options below require enrollment minimums.)

- *ForeWords for English.* Customize any print resource to fit the focus of your course or program by choosing from a range of prepared topics, such as Sentence Guides for Academic Writers.

- *Macmillan Author Program (MAP).* Add excerpts or package acclaimed works from Macmillan's trade imprints to connect students with prominent authors and public conversations. A list of popular examples or academic themes is available upon request.

- *Bedford Select.* Build your own print handbook or anthology from a database of more than 800 selections, and add your own materials to create your ideal text. Package with any Bedford/St. Martin's text for additional savings. Visit macmillanlearning.com/bedfordselect.

Instructor Resources

You have a lot to do in your course. We want to make it easy for you to find the support you need—and to get it quickly.

The Instructor's Edition for *The Hub: A Place for Reading and Writing* is available in print (ISBN 978-1-319-32942-6) and includes a sixteen-page insert that provides concise information on how to use *The Hub*, as well as sample schedules for teaching the ENG 101 and corequisite sections for three of the reading/writing projects.

Instructor's Manual for The Hub is available both in print (ISBN 978-1-319-32943-3) and as a PDF that can be downloaded from macmillanlearning .com. Section 1 provides detailed information on how to teach corequisite composition courses—discussing how to integrate reading and writing, use group work and inductive learning to create an active learning environment, and address noncognitive issues—as well as providing information on how to design a syllabus using content from *The Hub*. Section 2 includes sample schedules for using the projects in conjunction with content from Parts 2–5 of *The Hub* in composition and corequisite classes, and both Sections 2 and 3 provide unit-by-unit teaching tips, suggestions, and answers to exercises.

Acknowledgments

I am grateful to my colleagues at the Conference (now, Council) on Basic Writing for their support of my early thinking about corequisites (or, as we called it then, "mainstreaming" basic writers): Suellynn Duffey, Greg Glau, Barbara Gleason, Sugie Goen-Salter, Carolyn Kirkpatrick, Bill Lalicker, Rebecca Mlynarczyk, Deborah Mutnick, and Karen Uehling. I owe equal gratitude to my colleagues at the Community College of Baltimore County: Linda De La Ysla, Susan Gabriel, Jamey Gallagher, Sarah Gearhardt, Terry Hirsch, Patrick Kelleher, Donna McKusick, Bob Miller, Anne Roberts, Jackie Scott, and Monica Walker. The corequisite idea also received important support from Tom Bailey at the Community College

Research Center, from Bruce Vandal at Complete College America, and from David Bartholomae, whose "Tidy House" presentation at the CBW conference in 1992 provided reassurance that corequisite developmental writing was not a crazy idea.

For the development of *The Hub*, I was fortunate to have a faculty advisory board who provided insights, suggestions, corrections, and examples that have greatly improved the final manuscript under extremely tight time constraints. Warm thank-yous to Paul Beehler, *University of California–Riverside*; Mark Blaauw-Hara, *North Central Michigan College*; Brian Dickson, *Community College of Denver*; Jacqueline Gray, *St. Charles Community College*; Angelique Johnston, *Monroe Community College*; Meridith Leo, *Suffolk County Community College*; Angelina Oberdan, *Central Piedmont Community College*; Kelli Prejean, *Marshall University*; Sarah Snyder, *Western Arizona College*; and Christina Tarabicos, *Delaware Technical Community College*.

I also want to thank colleagues across the country who found time to review the manuscript and to participate in focus groups:

Susan Achziger, *Community College of Aurora*; Nancy Alexander, *Methodist University*; Eric Atchison, *Mississippi Institutions of Higher Learning*; Patricia Biebelle, *New Mexico State University*; Janice Brantley, *University of Arkansas at Pine Bluff*; Erin Breaux, *South Louisiana Community College*; Elizabeth Burton, *Hopkinsville Community College*; Katawna Caldwell, *Eastfield College*; Helen Ceraldi, *Cedar Valley College*; Mollie Chambers, *Lorain Community College*; Nancy Cheeks, *California State University–Northridge*; Emily Cosper, *Delgado Community College*; Jill Darley-Vanis, *Clark College*; Lacy Davis, *New Mexico State University–Carlsbad*; Darren DeFrain, *Wichita State University*; Elizabeth Donley, *Clark College*; Summer Doucet, *Baton Rouge Community College*; Amy Drees, *Northwest State Community College*; Karen Dulweber, *Kilgore College*; Margot Edlin, *Queensborough Community College*; Jennifer Ferguson, *Cazenovia College*; Jennifer Garner, *Howard Community College*; Tracie Grimes, *Bakersfield College*; Sharon Hayes, *Baltimore County Community College–Essex*; Cynthia Herrera, *Lone Star College*; Jennifer Hewerdine, *The University of Tennessee–Knoxville*; Josh Hite, *Hagerstown Community College*; Elizabeth Hope, *Delgado Community College*; Daniel Hutchinson, *Arkansas State University Mid-South*; Lisa Joslyn, *Community College of Denver*; Julia Laffoon-Jackson, *Hopkinsville Community College*; Rebekah Maples, *California Polytechnic State University*; Jennifer Martin, *Salem Community College*; April Brook Mayo, *Ashville-Buncombe Technical Community College*; Jeffrey Miller, *St. Charles Community College*; Elizabeth Newman, *Texas Southmost College*; Karen O'Donnell, *Finger Lakes Community College*; Pam Ortega, *Amarillo College*; Denise Parker, *Baltimore County Community College–Catonsville*; Stephanie Paterson,

California State University–Stanislaus; Jim Richey, *Tyler Junior College*; Elvis Robinson, *Jackson State University*; Laurie Rowland, *Cleveland State Community School*; Heather Sinnes, *Boise State University*; Daniel Stanford, *Pittsburgh Community College*; Lisa Tittle, *Harford Community College*; Charlie Warnberg, *Brookhaven College*; Kyle Warner, *Craven Community College*; Jonathan Warnock, *Tri-County Technical College–Pendleton*; Audrey Wick, *Blinn College*; Tina Willhoite, *San Jacinto College–South*; and Jason Ziebart, *Central Carolina Community College*.

It has been a great pleasure to work with the team at Bedford/St. Martin's. Their knowledge of the fields of composition and basic writing, their experience in textbook development, their willingness to talk through complex issues, and the breadth of their expertise have meant that working on this project for five years has been an exhilarating experience for me. I, first, want to thank my senior development editor, and friend, Gillian Cook, who guided and inspired my work with her wit, her expertise, her insight, and her encouragement. Her brilliance and hard work are present on every page. Karita dos Santos, Senior Program Manager for the project, managed it so gracefully that I seldom realized I was being managed. Ryan Sullivan, Senior Digital Content Project Manager, coordinated all the moving parts masterfully, and was very ably assisted by Andrea Cava, Senior Manager of Publishing Services. Heartfelt thanks to Paola Garcia-Muniz, Assistant Editor, for her dedication to this project. Leasa Burton, Vice President, Editorial, Macmillan Learning Humanities; Stacey Purviance, Program Director for English; and Edwin Hill, former Vice President, Editorial, Macmillan Learning Humanities, provided the kind of advice, support, and encouragement any author would hope for.

Thanks also to Lauren Arrant, Marketing Manager, and Azelie Fortier, Market Development Manager, who brilliantly organized meetings, brochures, letters, and blogs to spread the word about *The Hub*. I am also grateful to the digital experts—Adam Whitehurst, Director of Media Editorial, Humanities; Doug Silver, Product Manager; Rand Thomas, Advanced Media Product Manager; and Angela Beckett, Media Editor—for making my dream of a digital publication into a reality. My thanks also to William Boardman, Senior Design Manager, for *The Hub*'s delightful cover design.

Finally, I want to express my loving gratitude to my wife, Donna, and my mother-in-law, Rosemarie, who have provided the kind of environment that allowed me to hole up in my office for the past three years to work on this book and who were always ready with thoughtful suggestions when I needed them. I also owe thanks to my daughters, Melia and Emily, who have kept me connected to a younger generation, and to my grandchildren, Casey and Nick, who have provided the same connections to an even younger generation.

How *The Hub* Supports WPA Outcomes for First-Year Composition

This chart aligns *The Hub* with the latest WPA Outcomes Statement, ratified in July 2014.

WPA Outcomes	Most Relevant Features of *The Hub*
Rhetorical Knowledge	
Learn and use key rhetorical concepts through analyzing and composing a variety of texts.	• **Topic 9: Preparing to Write** discusses key rhetorical concepts as they apply to writing. • In **Topic 20: Reading Strategies**, Unit 20.2 discusses key rhetorical concepts as they apply to reading. • In **Projects 1–7**, as part of previewing texts, students are asked to analyze the rhetorical situation for each.
Gain experience reading and composing in several genres to understand how genre conventions shape and are shaped by readers' and writers' practices and purposes.	• The readings in **Projects 1–7** represent a range of genres including essays; editorials; newspaper, magazine, and research articles; nonfiction books; arguments; web pages; videos; and historical writings. • **Topic 18: Writing Strategies** provides strategies for composing arguments and writing using description, narration, process, comparison/contrast, cause/effect, definition, and classification as their purpose for writing requires. • Essay assignments in **Projects 1–7** ask students to write in a wide variety of genres.
Develop facility in responding to a variety of situations and contexts calling for purposeful shifts in voice, tone, level of formality, design, medium, and/or structure.	Throughout **Projects 1–7**, students encounter, analyze, discuss, and write in response to a wide variety of genres, using a variety of formats ranging from reflective, to short response, to full-length essays or multimodal compositions. Assignments also call for writing editorials, proposals, brochures, op-eds, and more.
Understand and use a variety of technologies to address a range of audiences.	The range of texts and technologies students interact with in the print and digital versions of *The Hub* helps them understand the variety of technologies they can use to address their own audiences.

WPA Outcomes	Most Relevant Features of *The Hub*
Match the capacities of different environments (e.g., print and electronic) to varying rhetorical situations.	• **Topic 18: Writing Strategies** provides information on writing using a variety of patterns, which can be modified according to the writing task or environment. • In **Projects 1–7,** students analyze web and blog sites, watch videos, and use online sites to find information, allowing them to see how environment influences text and rhetorical devices.
Critical Thinking, Reading, and Composing	
Use composing and reading for inquiry, learning, critical thinking, and communicating in various rhetorical contexts.	The **seven inquiry-based reading/writing projects in Part 1,** each consisting of several thematic readings from a variety of genres and accompanied by group and individual activities, are designed to develop critical thinking and reading skills, challenge students to learn new concepts and ideas, model rhetorical options, and provide content for writing thoughtful essays.
Read a diverse range of texts, attending especially to relationships between assertion and evidence, to patterns of organization, to the interplay between verbal and nonverbal elements, and to how these features function for different audiences and situations.	• **Topic 19: Active Reading** discusses reading as a thinking process, optimizing reading and recall, using different reading techniques based on the text and purpose for reading it, and how to construct meaning from a text. • **Topic 20: Reading Strategies** explains what to do before, during, and after reading, covering activating schema, previewing, predicting, annotating, keeping a reading journal, decoding difficult language, reading as a believer and doubter, and using graphic organizers. • **Topic 21: Critical Reading** addresses how to evaluate the author and source of a text; distinguish between facts and opinions, assertions and evidence; make inferences; and recognize assumptions and biases.
Locate and evaluate (for credibility, sufficiency, accuracy, timeliness, bias, and so on) primary and secondary research materials, including journal articles and essays, books, scholarly and professionally established and maintained databases or archives, and informal electronic networks and internet sources.	• In **Topic 22: Research, Units 22.1–22.3** address the research process, **Unit 22.4** is a presentation on finding online sources, **Unit 22.5** discusses how to locate books and articles in libraries and use databases, **Unit 22.6** covers evaluating sources, **Unit 22.10** describes how to conduct interviews, and **Unit 22.11** addresses how to conduct surveys. • **Project 4: Truth, Lies, and Fake News** contains readings that discuss issues related to truth, lies, facts, opinions, the ways statistics can be misused, and how to fact-check. It is designed to provide students with the tools to make thoughtful, informed decisions about what they read, see, and hear.

WPA Outcomes	Most Relevant Features of *The Hub*
Use strategies—such as interpretation, synthesis, response, critique, and design/redesign—to compose texts that integrate the writer's ideas with those from appropriate sources.	• **Units 18.23–18.26** discuss how to accurately summarize text. • **Unit 22.8: Quoting and Paraphrasing** explains and shows how to accurately and ethically paraphrase and quote sources. • **Unit 22.14: Synthesis** explains and shows how to interpret, synthesize, and integrate sources with the writer's own ideas.
Processes	
Develop a writing project through multiple drafts.	• **Topic 8: The Writing Process** discusses the stages of the writing process and shows the recursive nature of good writing in the **Unit 8.2** narrated presentation. • In **Projects 1–7**, students participate in low-stakes writing they can use in the final assignments, write and revise definitions based on new information (e.g., in **Project 7: What Is Art?**), and complete full-length writing assignments.
Develop flexible strategies for reading, drafting, reviewing, collaborating, revising, rewriting, rereading, and editing.	**Part 2: Writing** covers all aspects of the writing process: process (**Topic 8**); rhetorical situation, audience and purpose, planning (**Topic 9**); invention strategies, topic and thesis development (**Topic 10**); developing support (**Topic 11**); organizing ideas (**Topic 12**); language denotation/connotation, concrete and figurative (**Topic 13**); thinking while writing (**Topic 14**); revision strategies (**Topic 15**); editing for grammar and sentence structure (**Topic 16**); titles, introductions, and conclusions (**Topic 17**); and writing strategies, including argumentation, modes, summary, proposal, and reflection (**Topic 18**).
Use composing processes and tools as a means to discover and reconsider ideas.	**Topic 14: Thinking While Writing** contains units that encourage students to think deeply and broadly about their topic, finding new ideas and deepening their understanding of their original ones.
Experience the collaborative and social aspects of writing processes.	*The Hub* has an active learning, collaborative, group-work focus, and students have numerous opportunities to write together.
Learn to give and to act on productive feedback to works in progress.	• **Unit 8.4: Peer Review** is a tutorial on how to give and receive feedback on works in progress. • In **Projects 1–7**, students often work in groups to write together and provide feedback on each other's work.

WPA Outcomes	Most Relevant Features of *The Hub*
Adapt composing processes for a variety of technologies and modalities.	• Students are exposed to a wide range of print modalities in **Projects 1–7**, and they also visit and evaluate websites and blog posts and watch videos and narrated PowerPoint presentations, learning how content is adapted for different purposes and modalities. • Culminating assignments for each of **Projects 1–7** include a "real world essay" (e.g., a proposal, op-ed piece, article, etc.), "academic essay" (suitable for an English or content course), and a multimodal composition, for which students can produce a document with graphics, a PowerPoint presentation, blog, website, etc.
Reflect on the development of composing practices and how those practices influence their work.	• Low-stakes writing assignments throughout **Projects 1–7** ask students to reflect on what they've read, how it's written, rhetorical purpose, etc. • A **reflection activity** at the end of each of **Projects 1–7** asks students to report on what they've learned and how it will influence them in the future.
Knowledge of Conventions	
Develop knowledge of linguistic structures, including grammar, punctuation, and spelling, through practice in composing and revising.	• **Topic 16: Editing** contains 49 units covering issues in grammar (e.g., fragments, comma splices, subject-verb agreement, pronoun reference issues), punctuation, and sentence development. • A **unique inductive approach to grammar** prompts students working in small groups to discover important grammar rules for themselves and express them in language they understand and remember. • **Units 13.7–13.9** discuss dictionary usage, diction, and the spelling of confusing words.
Understand why genre conventions for structure, paragraphing, tone, and mechanics vary.	Throughout **Projects 1–7** students are exploring readings from a variety of sources and genres on many levels, including author, purpose, audience, topic, and context, leading to discussion of differences in structure, tone, paragraphing, and mechanics.
Gain experience negotiating variations in genre conventions.	Students read a wide variety of texts in **Projects 1–7**, ranging from straightforward news articles to excerpts from research papers and Aristotle's "Nicomachean Ethics." Annotations and scaffolded instruction explain and illustrate variations in genre conventions.

WPA Outcomes	Most Relevant Features of *The Hub*
Learn common formats and/or design features for different kinds of texts.	Throughout **Projects 1–7**, students are reading, analyzing, and discussing text presented in a variety of formats, including PowerPoints, videos, and web and blog sites.
Explore the concepts of intellectual property (such as fair use and copyright) that motivate documentation conventions.	• **Unit 22.13: Avoiding Plagiarism** explains what plagiarism is and why and how to avoid it. • **Unit 22.8: Quoting and Paraphrasing** provides information on how to accurately and ethically quote and paraphrase sources. • **Topics 23 and 24** explain MLA and APA documentation conventions.
Practice applying citation conventions systematically in their own work.	• **Topic 23: MLA Documentation** explains how to provide in-text citations and create a works cited list and includes an annotated essay. • **Topic 24: APA Documentation** explains how to provide in-text citations and create a references list and includes annotated examples.

Contents

PART 1

Reading/Writing Projects 1

Project 1: The Marshmallow Test 2

Photo by J. Adam Fenster,
University of Rochester

Getting Started: What Was the Marshmallow Test? 5

1.1 Video The Marshmallow Test 6 | **1.2 Activity** Thinking about the Marshmallow Video 6

Exploring What Mischel Learned in His Study 6

1.3 Activity Previewing "Delay of Gratification in Children" 7 | Working Together to Preview and Predict 7

1.4 Reading "Delay of Gratification in Children," *Walter Mischel, Yuichi Shoda, and Monica L. Rodriguez* 9 | **1.5 Activity** Explaining "Delay of Gratification in Children" 12

1.6 Reading *The Marshmallow Test, Walter Mischel* 13 | **1.7 Activity** Thinking about Mischel's Marshmallow Test Writings 16

Analyzing an Alternative Interpretation of the Marshmallow Test 17

1.8 Reading "The Marshmallow Study Revisited," *Celeste Kidd* 17 | **1.9 Writing** Summarizing "The Marshmallow Study Revisited" 21 | **1.10 Activity** Analyzing Summaries 21 | **1.11 Activity** Analyzing "The Marshmallow Study Revisited" 22

1.12 Writing Experiencing Delayed Gratification 22 | **1.13 Activity** Discussing Experiencing Delayed Gratification Papers 23

| KEY | | *Units that work together are placed in groups.* | | *Boxed units provide reinforcement for other items in each group.* |

See page xl for more information on the unit types in this book.

Project 2: Choosing a Career 29

ProStockStudio/Shutterstock

Project 3: Freedom of Speech 69

(Statue of Liberty) Bryan Busovicki/ Shutterstock; (hand) DenisNata/ Shutterstock

Project 4: Truth, Lies, and Fake News 124

Illustration Courtesy of New York Magazine

Project 5: Language and Power 197

Rawpixel.com/Shutterstock

Project 6: In Pursuit of Happiness 236

oneinchpunch/Shutterstock

Project 7: What Is Art? 270

Everett - Art/Shutterstock

PART 2 Writing 315

Topic 16: Editing 435

PART 3 Reading 561

Topic 21: Critical Reading 601

PART 4 Research and Documentation 617

Topic 22: Research 619

PART 5   Balancing School, Work, and Life 731

Topic 26: Life Issues 735

Topic 27: Staying the Course 745

Topic 28: College Knowledge 749

Definitions of Terms Used in *The Hub*	
Academic Essay	At the end of each reading/writing project, there are three writing assignments. One of the three is a traditional academic essay.
Activity	A unit designed for students to do some thinking, usually in a group, but most of these can be assigned as individual work if preferred.
Multimodal Composition	At the end of each reading/writing project, there are three writing assignments, one of which asks students to produce a multimodal composition.
Part	One of the five major divisions of *The Hub*—Part 1: Reading/Writing Projects, Part 2: Writing, Part 3: Reading, Part 4: Research and Documentation, and Part 5: Balancing School, Work, and Life. Each part contains a series of Topics on major subjects relevant to the part.
Presentation	A five-minute video narrated by the author.
Project	One of the seven reading/writing projects that constitute Part 1.
Reading	A reading can be an essay, newspaper article, journal article, blog post, excerpt from a nonfiction or fiction text, chapter from a book, legal statute, set of college policies, and more. These readings are the primary material in the reading/writing projects in Part 1. Students are expected to read them in preparation for class.
Real World Essay	At the end of each reading/writing project, there are three writing assignments. The "Real World Essay" asks students to write an essay that addresses an audience outside their classroom (e.g., next year's students, the community, visitors to an art museum, a career counselor, a college committee, or readers of a newspaper).
Topic	One of the major sections of each of Parts 2–5 (equivalent to a chapter). Each Topic contains a series of units that address relevant subjects.
Tutorial	Instructional text that discusses issues and strategies for writing, reading, and research, designed to be read in preparation for class.
Unit	Each topic consists of a series of units that provide instruction (tutorials and presentations), practice (activities), and reading and writing opportunities (readings, writing prompts, and essay assignments).
Video	A short video, almost always less than five minutes, and usually available on YouTube.
Writing	The word *Writing* is used in the titles of units in the Contents to indicate the many short writing assignments. These usually call for a page or so of writing, but sometimes even less. The idea, especially in Part 1, is that some of this writing may later be incorporated into the major writing projects, such as those at the end of each reading/writing project.

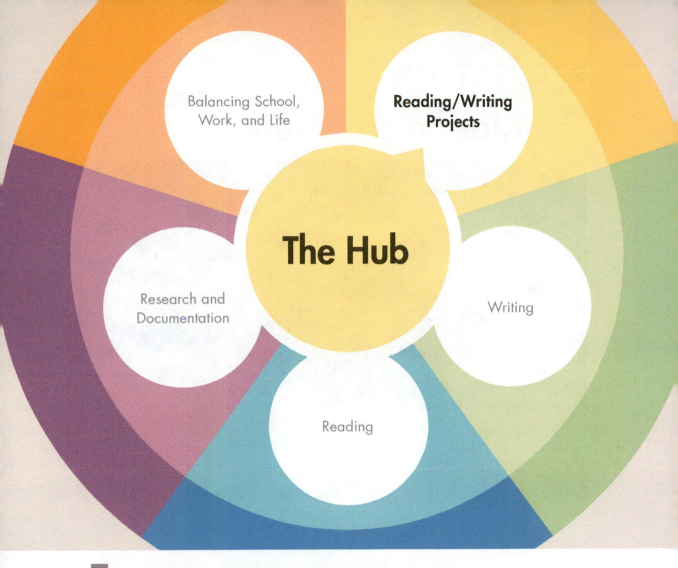

Balancing School, Work, and Life

Reading/Writing Projects

The Hub

Research and Documentation

Writing

Reading

1 Reading/Writing Projects

PROJECT 1

The Marshmallow Test

Photo by J. Adam Fenster, University of Rochester

Walter Mischel's "Marshmallow Test" is one of the most widely known psychological studies of the twentieth century. Mischel's work seemed to demonstrate just how important the ability to delay immediate pleasure is in order to gain a greater benefit later. He studied a group of four-year-old children, dividing them into two groups: those who were able to delay gratification and those who were not. He then followed them for more than thirty years. The results were startling and have had a major influence in the field of psychology that has lasted into the twenty-first century. The Marshmallow Test was even featured on *Sesame Street*, although cookies were substituted for marshmallows. Recently, however, a young graduate student named Celeste Kidd has raised serious questions about Mischel's conclusions. In this project we will explore this modern psychological controversy.

Getting Started: What Was the Marshmallow Test?

Project 1 starts with a video. A group of adorable and funny four-year-olds wrestle with whether to eat their marshmallows or not, and you will be asked to think about what you see in the video and what you think it means.

Exploring, Thinking, and Writing about Ideas

In this section, after reading two articles by Mischel, one written in 1989 and one written twenty-five years later, you will discuss the differences between the two texts and think about the significance of the conclusions he draws. Mischel's study presents data arguing that how much self-control children have at age four can determine much about the trajectory of their lives for years: how positive their lives will be in school, in their careers, and even in their health.

Then you will meet a young graduate student, Celeste Kidd, who has a remarkable thought one day while working at a homeless shelter in Santa Anna, California. What Kidd learns from watching a bully steal a lollipop from a little girl causes her to question Mischel's conclusions and upset decades of established psychological thinking.

These readings and discussions will ask you to think about research and data and how we "know" something to be true. They will ask you to wonder about how science makes discoveries. In addition, because researchers are still investigating the effects of being able to delay gratification and what influences people's ability to delay gratification, you will be asked to locate more recent articles to see what has been said since Celeste Kidd's discovery. You will also think about delayed gratification in your own life.

As you work through these materials, you will discuss your thoughts and findings with your classmates, reflect in writing on what you have read, and write in response to specific articles. You will also complete activities related to the readings that ask you to practice specific skills, such as previewing, actively reading, analyzing, evaluating, researching, preparing to write, generating ideas, organizing those ideas, and revising. According to directions from your instructor, you will work independently and/or in small groups to complete them. In addition, your instructor will assign relevant topics from other parts of *The Hub* that relate to writing, reading, research, and life issues that will address other important skills.

Bringing It All Together

Project 1 concludes with three assignments that ask you to use the tools and ideas you encountered in this project to write a persuasive argument expressing your ideas about delayed gratification. Your instructor may assign the first, second, or third option; may give you a choice among the three; or may even ask you to write more than one.

The first asks you to write an article to be handed out to next year's incoming students about the importance of delayed gratification while in college. The second assignment asks you to write an academic essay exploring the concept as it has been studied for the past fifty years. Think of this second essay as writing that would be appropriate in a college course on economics, political science, sociology, business, or something similar. The third assignment is to compose a multimodal composition—a narrated PowerPoint, a video, a podcast, a blog, or a website—that explains the importance of delayed gratification to next year's incoming students.

The final writing assignment, Reflecting on Project 1: The Marshmallow Test, asks you to reflect on what you have learned as you have worked through this reading/writing project.

Navigating Project 1

Below is the table of contents for Project 1, which you can use to easily locate the units you have been assigned to work on by your instructor. Several of these units ask you to connect to the internet to watch videos or explore websites. If you find that any of these search terms do not work, there is a list of URLs available at https://bit.ly/33IIHtf.

Getting Started: What Was the Marshmallow Test?

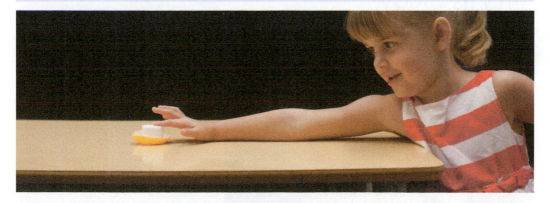

▲ How much information do you think you can find out about a person based on how long they can wait to eat a marshmallow when they are four years old? Can waiting less than two minutes or as many as four really be significant?

Photo by J. Adam Fenster, University of Rochester

1.1   Video

The Marshmallow Test

FloodSanDiego videotaped a re-enactment of the famous experiment conducted by Walter Mischel at Stanford University back in the early 1970s, in which children were told that if they could wait for a short while and not eat a marshmallow the researcher gave them, they could have a second marshmallow and eat both. To watch the video, type "the marshmallow experiment-instant gratification floodsandiego. com" into your browser. (If these search terms do not work, there is a list of URLs available at https://bit.ly/33IIHtf.)

1.2   Activity

Thinking about the Marshmallow Video

Working in groups, make a list of thoughtful observations about the Marshmallow Test video that you watched in "The Marshmallow Test" (1.1). After ten minutes or so, the groups will be asked to report out to the class.

Exploring What Mischel Learned in His Study

◀ How long do you think you could have waited to eat a marshmallow when you were four years old?

CDM Wild/Alamy

1.3 Activity

Previewing "Delay of Gratification in Children"

The Marshmallow Test video you watched showed a re-enactment of a famous experiment conducted by Walter Mischel at Stanford University. Mischel reported the results of that experiment in an article he wrote in 1989 for the journal *Science*, published by the American Association for the Advancement of Science. Your next assignment will be to read Mischel's 1989 article.

However, before you start reading the text itself, spend a few minutes previewing, or preparing to read, which is highly recommended before you dive into any challenging reading. Below is an activity that will help you to know what to look for and do before immersing yourself in a text.

Working Together to Preview and Predict

Careful review of a text you are about to read requires a fairly lengthy process of previewing and predicting. Often you won't have time for this elaborate a preview, but doing the complete process outlined below will familiarize you with a range of previewing options from which you will be able to select when you have time for only a more abbreviated process.

For this activity, work in groups to examine the text as outlined in section 1. Then answer the questions listed in sections 2 and 3. Later, working by yourself, answer the questions in section 4.

1. **Examine the text.** Working in your group, examine the items listed below and answer this question about each one: What did this item tell you about the text? This is a list you could use for longer works than the one you'll be reading, so some will not apply.

    - Take a look at the title.
    - If the text is a book, look over the front and back covers and the table of contents, if there is one.
    - Read any introductory material, such as a preface.
    - If the text starts with an abstract or executive summary, read it.
    - If the text has headings for different parts, read these.
    - Read the opening paragraph.
    - Read the final paragraph.
    - Take a look at any illustrations, charts, tables, or associated videos.
    - Look to see if there are citations, endnotes, or a works cited list.
    - Check to see how long the text is.

2. **Analyze the rhetorical situation.** As long ago as classical Greece—300 BC or so—thinkers have been aware that every text has four important components: the *author* of the text, the *audience* for the text, the *topic* the text is about, and the *purpose* of the text. These components make up the "rhetorical situation," the context in which the writing takes place. You don't need to remember the term *rhetorical situation*, but thinking about author, audience, topic, and purpose should be part of your previewing and predicting process. (For more details, see The Rhetorical Situation [9.3, p. 327].)

Now, working in your group, write brief answers to the following questions.

- **Author.** You don't simply want to find out the name of the author. What else can you learn about him or her? What evidence is there that the author really has some expertise? What biases might the author have? Is the author part of an organization? A corporation? What else has the author written?

- **Audience.** Whom does it appear that the author intended to be the reader or readers of this text? Whom was he or she addressing? Were there other, secondary, audiences?

- **Topic.** What is this text about?

- **Purpose.** What does it appear that the author intended or, at least, hoped would happen as a result of this piece of writing? What did the author want the effect of this text on its audience to be?

3. **Predict what the text is about.** Predicting what a text might discuss, using background knowledge or personal experiences or information from previous reading, can also prepare you to better understand the content. While not every text will reveal information about all of the following questions, every text will provide answers to some of them. Before launching into reading a text, use the steps listed above to preview it to help you answer as many of these questions as you can.

- What is this text "about"? What is the major topic or subject?

- Does the author take a stand on this topic?

- Does the author seem to make any assumptions about the subject?

- What do I know about the publishers of the text or sponsors of the website? Does the text appear in a reputable and reliable source?

- What evidence is there that the author of the text has at least some expertise about his or her subject?

4. **Think about yourself in relation to the text.** A final way to preview a text is to think about how the subject of the text relates to you individually. Of course, this

personal kind of previewing is not appropriate for group work, so working individually, answer the following questions.

- What do you already know about the topic?
- Have you had experiences that are related to this topic?
- Have you read other texts about this same topic?
- What have you heard or seen about this topic (on the radio, TV, internet, podcasts, YouTube, other classes, etc.)?
- How do you feel about the text's stand on the topic?
- What is your purpose for reading this text?
- How similar or different are you from the intended audience for the text?
- How difficult will the text be to read?
- How much time will you need to read it?

1.4 Reading

"Delay of Gratification in Children," Walter Mischel, Yuichi Shoda, and Monica L. Rodriguez

Below you will find an excerpt from the article psychologist Walter Mischel and his colleagues wrote in 1989 about his marshmallow experiment. This experiment has become a classic of twentieth-century psychology.

Delay of Gratification in Children

WALTER MISCHEL, YUICHI SHODA, AND MONICA L. RODRIGUEZ

Born in Vienna, Austria, in 1930, Walter Mischel fled the Nazi occupation with his parents when he was eight years old. He spent the remainder of his childhood in Brooklyn, New York. After receiving a PhD in clinical psychology from Ohio State University, he taught at Colorado University, Harvard University, Stanford University, and Columbia University, where he worked in the Department of Psychology until his death in 2018. Ironically, this advocate of delayed gratification was a smoker of three packs of cigarettes a day throughout his life.

Science
MAY 26, 1989

ABSTRACT: To function effectively, individuals must voluntarily postpone immediate gratification and persist in goal-directed behavior for the sake of

▶

later outcomes. The present research program analyzed the nature of this type of future-oriented self-control and the psychological processes that underlie it. Enduring individual differences in self-control were found as early as the preschool years. Those 4-year-old children who delayed gratification longer in certain laboratory situations developed into more cognitively and socially competent adolescents, achieving higher scholastic performance and coping better with frustration and stress. Experiments in the same research program also identified specific cognitive and attentional processes that allow effective self-regulation early in the course of development. The experimental results, in turn, specified the particular types of preschool delay situations diagnostic for predicting aspects of cognitive and social competence later in life.

---

1   For almost a century the infant has been characterized as impulse-driven, pressing for tension reduction, unable to delay gratification, oblivious to reason and reality, and ruled entirely by a pleasure principle that demands immediate satisfaction.[1] The challenge has been to clarify how individuals, while remaining capable of great impulsivity, also become able to control actions for the sake of temporally distant consequences and goals, managing at least sometimes to forgo more immediate gratifications to take account of anticipated outcomes. The nature of this future-oriented self-control, which develops over time and then coexists with more impetuous behaviors, has intrigued students of development, who have made it central in theories of socialization and in the very definition of the "self."[2] Such goal-directed self-imposed delay of gratification is widely presumed to be important in the prevention of serious developmental and mental health problems, including those directly associated with lack of resilience, conduct disorders, low social responsibility, and a variety of addictive and antisocial behaviors.

2   As efforts at self-reform so often attest, however, decisions to forgo immediate gratification for the sake of later consequences (for example, by dieting) are readily forgotten or strategically revised when one experiences the frustration of actually having to execute them. Because intentions to practice self-control frequently dissolve in the face of more immediate temptations, it is also necessary to go beyond the study of initial decisions to delay gratification and to examine how young children become able to sustain delay of gratification as they actually try to wait for the outcomes they want. For this purpose, a second method was devised and used to test preschool children in the Stanford University community.[3, 4]

3   In this method, the experimenter begins by showing the child some toys, explaining they will play with them later (so that ending the delay leads to uniform positive consequences). Next, the experimenter teaches a game in which he or she has to leave

the room and comes back immediately when the child summons [him or her] by ringing a bell. Each child then is shown a pair of treats (such as snacks, small toys, or tokens) which differ in value, established through pretesting to be desirable and of age-appropriate interest (for example, one marshmallow versus two; two small cookies versus five pretzels). The children are told that to attain the one they prefer they have to wait until the experimenter returns but that they are free to end the waiting period whenever they signal; if they do, however, they will get the less preferred object and forgo the other one. The items in the pair are selected to be sufficiently close in value to create a conflict situation for young children between the temptation to stop the delay and the desire to persist for the preferred outcome when the latter requires delay. After children understand the contingency, they are left on their own during the delay period while their behavior is observed unobtrusively, and the duration of their delay is recorded until they terminate or the experimenter returned (typically after 15 minutes). With this method, "self-imposed delay of gratification" was investigated both as a psychological process in experiments that varied relevant features in the delay situation and as a personal characteristic in studies that examined the relation between children's delay behavior and their social and cognitive competencies.

4   A recent follow-up study of a sample of these children found that those who had waited longer in this situation at 4 years of age were described more than 10 years later by their parents as adolescents who were more academically and socially competent than their peers and more able to cope with frustration and resist temptation. At statistically significant levels, parents saw these children as more verbally fluent and able to express ideas; they used and responded to reason, were attentive and able to concentrate, to plan, and to think ahead, and were competent and skillful. Likewise they were perceived as able to cope and deal with stress more maturely and seemed more self-assured.[5, 6] In some variations of this laboratory situation, seconds of delay time in preschool also were significantly related to their Scholastic Aptitude Test (SAT) scores when they applied to college.[7] The demonstration of these enduring individual differences in the course of development, as well as the significance attributed to purposeful self-imposed delay of gratification theoretically, underline the need to understand and specify the psychological processes that allow the young child to execute this type of self-regulation in the pursuit of desired outcomes.

Endnotes

1.   S. Freud, Collected Papers (Basic Books, New York, 1959), vol. 4, pp. 13–21.

2.   S. Harter, in *Handbook of Child Psychology*, P. H. Mussen, Ed. (Wiley, New York, 1983), vol. 4, pp. 275–385.

▶

3. W. Mischel and E. B. Ebbesen, *J. Pers. Soc. Psychol.* 16, 329 (1970).

4. ——— A. R. Zeiss, ibid. 21, 204 (1972).

5. W. Mischel, Y. Shoda, P. K. Peake, ibid. 54, 687 (1988).

6. Studies following children's development over many years, using other measures of self-control requiring different types of delay of gratification, also found evidence of enduring psychological qualities.

7. Y. Shoda, W. Mischel, P. K. Peake, in preparation.

↳ **1.5** **Activity**

Explaining "Delay of Gratification in Children"

Below are three passages from Walter Mischel's "Delay of Gratification in Children." Working together with your group, write a brief explanation in more ordinary language of what each passage says.

1. "To function effectively, individuals must voluntarily postpone immediate gratification and persist in goal-directed behavior for the sake of later outcomes."

2. "Enduring individual differences in self-control were found as early as the preschool years."

3. "The challenge has been to clarify how individuals, while remaining capable of great impulsivity, also become able to control actions for the sake of temporally distant consequences and goals."

The following passage appears near the end of the article. Discuss in your group whether you are convinced that such long-lasting and wide-ranging effects can be forecasted based on a simple test. How could it be that the ability to delay gratification at the age of four would predict all these effects?

> A recent follow-up study of a sample of these children found that those who had waited longer in this situation at 4 years of age were described more than 10 years later by their parents as adolescents who were more academically and socially competent than their peers and more able to cope with frustration and resist temptation. At statistically significant levels, parents saw these children as more verbally fluent and able to express ideas; they used and responded to reason, were attentive and able to concentrate, to plan, and to think ahead, and were competent and skillful. Likewise they were perceived as able to cope and deal with stress more maturely and seemed more self-assured. In some

variations of this laboratory situation, seconds of delay time in preschool also were significantly related to their Scholastic Aptitude Test (SAT) scores when they applied to college.

The Marshmallow Test, Walter Mischel

The excerpt below is from Walter Mischel's best-selling book *The Marshmallow Test,* which was written twenty-five years after his original scholarly article (see "Delay of Gratification in Children" [1.4, p. 9]). This book was intended to bring his theories about delayed gratification to a much larger audience and to give, not just children, but all of us, advice about how to improve our willpower and apply it to such everyday problems as weight gain, smoking, and overcoming heartbreak.

Before you read this selection, take a few minutes to preview it using the list you used in Previewing "Delay of Gratification in Children" (1.3, p. 7). Be sure to read the editorial reviews of *The Marshmallow Test,* which follow the selection, as part of your previewing process.

The Marshmallow Test: Mastering Self-Control (excerpt)

WALTER MISCHEL

Born in Vienna, Austria, in 1930, Walter Mischel fled the Nazi occupation with his parents when he was eight years old. He spent the remainder of his childhood in Brooklyn, New York. After receiving a PhD in clinical psychology from Ohio State University, he taught at Colorado University, Harvard University, Stanford University, and Columbia University, where he worked in the Department of Psychology until his death in 2018. Ironically, this advocate of delayed gratification was a smoker of three packs of cigarettes a day throughout his life.

1   It began in the 1960s with preschoolers at Stanford University's Bing Nursery School, in a simple study that challenged them with a tough dilemma. My students and I gave the children a choice between one reward (for example, a marshmallow) that they could have immediately, and a larger reward (two marshmallows) for which they would have to wait, alone, for up to 20 minutes. We let the children select the rewards they wanted most from an assortment that included marshmallows, cookies, little pretzels, mints, and so on. "Amy," for example, chose marshmallows. She sat alone at a table facing the one marshmallow that she could have immediately, ▶

as well as the two marshmallows that she could have if she waited. Next to the treats was a desk bell she could ring at any time to call back the researcher and eat the one marshmallow. Or she could wait for the researcher to return, and if Amy hadn't left her chair or started to eat the marshmallow, she could have both. The struggles we observed as these children tried to restrain themselves from ringing the bell could bring tears to your eyes, have you applauding their creativeness and cheering them on, and give you fresh hope for the potential of even young children to resist temptation and persevere for their delayed rewards.

*   *   *

2   More than 550 children who were enrolled in Stanford University's Bing preschool between 1968 and 1974 were given the Marshmallow Test. We followed a sample of these participants and assessed them on diverse measures about once every decade after the original testing. In 2010, they reached their early to mid-forties, and in 2014, we are continuing to collect information from them, such as their occupational, marital, physical, financial, and mental health status. The findings surprised us from the start, and they still do.

3   In the first follow-up study, we mailed small bundles of questionnaires to their parents and asked them to "think about your child in comparison to his or her peers, such as classmates and other same-age friends. We would like to get your impression of how your son or daughter compares to those peers." They were to rate their children on a scale of 1 to 9 (from "Not at all" to "Moderately" to "Extremely"). We also obtained similar ratings from their teachers about the children's cognitive and social skills at school.

4   Preschoolers who delayed longer on the Marshmallow Test were rated a dozen years later as adolescents who exhibited more self-control in frustrating situations; yielded less to temptation; were less distractible when trying to concentrate; were more intelligent, self-reliant, and confident; and trusted their own judgment. When under stress they did not go to pieces as much as the low delayers did, and they were less likely to become rattled and disorganized or revert to immature behavior. Likewise, they thought ahead and planned more, and when motivated they were more able to pursue their goals. They were also more attentive and able to use and respond to reason, and they were less likely to be sidetracked by setbacks. In short, they managed to defy the widespread stereotype of the problematic, difficult adolescent, at least in the eyes and reports of their parents and teachers.

5   To measure the children's actual academic achievement, we asked parents to provide their children's SAT verbal and quantitative scores, when available. The SAT is the test in the United States that students routinely take as part of their application

for college admission. To assess the reliability of the scores reported by the parents, we also contacted the Educational Testing Service, which administered the test. Preschoolers who delayed longer on the whole earned much better SAT scores. When the SAT scores of children with the shortest delay times (bottom third) were compared with those of children with longer delay times (top third), the overall difference in their scores was 210 points.

6   Around age twenty-five to thirty, those who had delayed longer in preschool self-reported that they were more able to pursue and reach long-term goals, used risky drugs less, had reached higher educational levels, and had a significantly lower body mass index. They were also more resilient and adaptive in coping with interpersonal problems and better at maintaining close relationships. As we continued to follow the participants over the years, the findings from the Bing study became more surprising in their sweep, stability, and importance: if behavior on this simple Marshmallow Test in preschool predicted (at statistically significant levels) so much for so long about how well lives turned out, the public policy and educational implications had to be considered.

Editorial Reviews

"The discoveries that grew out of the marshmallow studies add up to one of the most insightful research stories in the history of psychology. Whatever it is now, your view of human nature will change profoundly as you read this brilliant book."

—Daniel Kahneman, author of *Thinking Fast and Slow*

"The book we've all been waiting for. . . . [Mischel] illustrates with solid research and insightful anecdote the most important claim of the book: that self-control can be taught and mastered."

—Angela Lee Duckworth, Associate Professor, Department of Psychology, University of Pennsylvania, and a 2013 MacArthur Foundation Fellow

"A charmingly told scientific story, makes clear the test is not just about youngsters, but is helpful to us all in the marshmallow moments we face through life. Mischel has written a wonderful book, engaging, enlightening, and profound."

—Daniel Goleman, author of *Emotional Intelligence and Focus*

"This marvelous book is unique, and beautifully written from beginning to end. The range that Walter Mischel covers—from creative cognitive science to neuroscience to genetics—is breathtaking. This speaks for science at its best. Bravo!"

—Eric R. Kandel, MD, Winner of the Nobel Prize in Physiology or Medicine, University Professor, Department of Neuroscience, Columbia University, author of *The Age of Insight* and *In Search of Memory*

"Walter Mischel is one of the most influential psychologists of the twentieth century, and *The Marshmallow Test* will make him one of the most influential in this century, too."

—Steven Pinker, Johnstone Professor of Psychology, Harvard University, and the author of *The Better Angels of Our Nature*

"Walter Mischel has changed psychologists' view of human potential, and *The Marshmallow Test* will change yours. The book is full of insights about self-control and how to master it, though it does create one impulse that is hard to resist—the desire to read the book cover to cover. It is both a fascinating story of a brilliant researcher at work and a recipe for how to change one's life."

—Timothy Wilson, Sherrell J. Aston Professor of Psychology, University of Virginia, author of *Redirect*

1.7 Activity

Thinking about Mischel's Marshmallow Test Writings

You've now read two articles written by the same person—Walter Mischel—that discuss the same topic, his marshmallow experiment. Working in your group, answer the following questions about these two articles.

1. What are the differences between these two texts? Describe the differences.
2. Why do you think they are so different?
3. Which is better writing? Why?

After all the groups have reported on their answers, the class will discuss the following question.

4. Mischel finds a surprisingly strong relationship between the ability to delay gratification as a four-year-old and a number of positive outcomes for an individual later in life. Does this relationship surprise you? Why or why not?

Analyzing an Alternative Interpretation of the Marshmallow Test

◀ What factors besides an ability to delay gratification might affect how long a child can wait? Why might some children not wait?

pchyburrs/Getty Images

1.8 Reading

"The Marshmallow Study Revisited," Celeste Kidd

The following article about Celeste Kidd's research raises interesting questions about Mischel's Marshmallow Test.

The Marshmallow Study Revisited

UNIVERSITY OF ROCHESTER

OCTOBER 11, 2012

1　　For the past four decades, the "Marshmallow Test" has served as a classic experimental measure of children's self-control: will a preschooler eat one of the fluffy white confections now or hold out for two later?

2　　Now a **new study** demonstrates that being able to delay gratification is influenced as much by the environment as by innate ability. Children who experienced reliable interactions immediately before the marshmallow task waited on average four times longer—12 versus three minutes—than youngsters in similar but unreliable situations.

3　　"Our results definitely temper the popular perception that marshmallow-like tasks are very powerful diagnostics for self-control capacity," says Celeste Kidd, a doctoral candidate in brain and cognitive sciences at the University of Rochester and lead author on the study to be published online October 11 in the journal *Cognition*.

4　　"Being able to delay gratification—in this case to wait 15 difficult minutes to earn a second marshmallow—not only reflects a child's capacity for self-control, it also reflects their belief about the practicality of waiting," says Kidd. "Delaying gratification is only the rational choice *if* the child believes a second marshmallow is likely to be delivered after a reasonably short delay."

5　　The findings provide an important reminder about the complexity of human behavior, adds coauthor Richard Aslin, the William R. Kenan Professor of brain and cognitive sciences at the University. "This study is an example of both nature and nurture playing a role," he says. "We know that to some extent, temperament is clearly inherited, because infants differ in their behaviors from birth. But this experiment provides robust evidence that young children's actions are also based on rational decisions about their environment."

6　　The research builds on a long series of marshmallow-related studies that began at

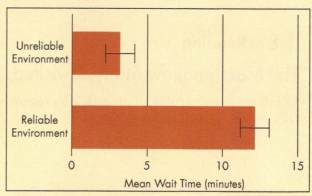

▲ Children who experienced unreliable interactions with an experimenter waited for a mean time of three minutes and two seconds on the subsequent marshmallow task, while youngsters who experienced reliable interactions held out for 12 minutes and two seconds. Error bars show 95% confidence intervals, meaning that the findings statistically are highly reliable.　Credit: University of Rochester

Stanford University in the late 1960s. Walter Mischel and other researchers famously showed that individual differences in the ability to delay gratification on this simple task correlated strongly with success in later life. Longer wait times as a child were linked years later to higher SAT scores, less substance abuse, and parental reports of better social skills.

7   Because of the surprising correlation, the landmark marshmallow studies have been cited as evidence that qualities like self-control or emotional intelligence in general may be more important to navigating life successfully than more traditional measures of intelligence, such as IQ.

8   The Rochester team wanted to explore more closely why some preschoolers are able to resist the marshmallow while others succumb to licking, nibbling, and eventually swallowing the sugary treat. The researchers assigned 28 three- to five-year-olds to two contrasting environments: unreliable and reliable. The study results were so strong that a larger sample group was not required to ensure statistical accuracy and other factors, like the influence of hunger, were accounted for by randomly assigning participants to the two groups, according to the researchers. In both groups the children were given a create-your-own-cup kit and asked to decorate the blank paper that would be inserted in the cup.

9   In the unreliable condition, the children were provided a container of used crayons and told that if they could wait, the researcher would return shortly with a bigger and better set of new art supplies for their project. After two and a half minutes, the researcher returned with this explanation: "I'm sorry, but I made a mistake. We don't have any other art supplies after all. But why don't you use these instead?" She then helped to open the crayon container.

10   Next a quarter-inch sticker was placed on the table and the child was told that if he or she could wait, the researcher would return with a large selection of better stickers to use. After the same wait, the researcher again returned empty handed.

11   The reliable group experienced the same set up, but the researcher returned with the promised materials: first with a rotating tray full of art supplies and the next time with five to seven large, die-cut stickers.

12   The marshmallow task followed, with the explanation that the child could have "one marshmallow right now. Or—if you can wait for me to get more marshmallows from the other room—you can have *two* marshmallows to eat instead." The researcher removed the art supplies and placed a single marshmallow in a small dessert dish four inches from the table's edge directly in front of the child. From an adjoining room, the researchers and the parent observed through a computer video camera until the first taste or 15 minutes had lapsed, whichever came first. All children then received three additional marshmallows.

▶

13   "Watching their strategies for waiting was quite entertaining," says Holly Palmeri, coauthor and coordinator of the Rochester Baby Lab. Kids danced in their seats, sang, and took pretend naps. Several took a bite from the bottom of the marshmallow then placed it back in the dessert cup so it looked untouched. A few then nibbled off the top, forgetting they could then no longer hide the evidence since both ends were eaten, she said.

14   "We had one little boy who grabbed the marshmallow immediately and we thought he was going to eat it," recalled Kidd. Instead he sat on it. "Instead of covering his eyes, he covered the marshmallow."

15   Children who experienced unreliable interactions with an experimenter waited for a mean time of three minutes and two seconds on the subsequent marshmallow task, while youngsters who experienced reliable interactions held out for 12 minutes and two seconds. Only one of the 14 children in the unreliable group waited the full 15 minutes, compared to nine children in the reliable condition.

16   "I was astounded that the effect was so large," says Aslin. "I thought that we might get a difference of maybe a minute or so. . . . You don't see effects like this very often."

17   In prior research, children's wait time averaged between 6.08 and 5.71 minutes, the authors report. By comparison, manipulating the environment doubled wait times in the reliable condition and halved the time in the unreliable scenario. Previous studies that explored the effect of teaching children waiting strategies showed smaller effects, the authors report. Hiding the treat from view boosted wait times by 3.75 minutes, while encouraging children to think about the larger reward added 2.53 minutes.

18   The robust effect of manipulating the environment, conclude the authors, provides strong evidence that children's wait times reflect rational decision making about the probability of reward. The results are consistent with other research showing that children are sensitive to uncertainty in future rewards and with population studies showing children with absent fathers prefer more immediate rewards over larger but delayed ones.

19   The findings, says Kidd, are reassuring. She recalls reading about the predictive power of these earlier experiments years ago and finding it "depressing." At the time she was volunteering at a homeless shelter for families in Santa Ana, California. "There were lots of kids staying there with their families. Everyone shared one big area, so keeping personal possessions safe was difficult," she says. "When one child got a toy or treat, there was a real risk of a bigger, faster kid taking it away. I read about these studies and I thought, 'All of these kids would eat the marshmallow right away.'"

20   But as she observed the children week after week, she began to question the task as a marker of innate ability alone. "If you are used to getting things taken away

from you, not waiting *is* the rational choice. Then it occurred to me that the marshmallow task might be correlated with something else that the child already knows—like having a stable environment."

21 So does that mean that if little ones gobble up dessert without waiting, as is typical of preschoolers, parents should worry that they have failed to be role models of reliability every minute?

22 Not necessarily, say the researchers. "Children do monitor the behavior of parents and adults, but it is unlikely that they are keeping detailed records of every single action," says Aslin. "It's the overall sense of a parent's reliability or unreliability that's going to get through, not every single action."

23 Adds Kidd: "Don't do the Marshmallow Test on your kitchen table and conclude something about your child. It especially would not work with a parent, because your child has all sorts of strong expectations about what a person who loves them very much is likely to do."

1.9 Writing

Summarizing "The Marshmallow Study Revisited"

You probably have a sense of what it means to write a summary. You write something short that summarizes the main content of something longer that you have read.

For this assignment, you are going to try your hand at summary writing. After you've read the article "The Marshmallow Study Revisited" (1.8, p. 17) and perhaps made some notes, write a short paper—a half page would be plenty—in which you summarize the text.

1.10 Activity

Analyzing Summaries

Your instructor will distribute to each group a selection of the summaries that you wrote for Summarizing "The Marshmallow Study Revisited" (1.9). Your group's task is to read over the summaries and make two lists: one of what you found that worked well in one or more of the summaries and one of what weaknesses or mistakes you found in one or more of the summaries. After a half hour or so, the groups will report out on their lists.

Analyzing "The Marshmallow Study Revisited"

Working in groups, answer the following questions based on your reading of "The Marshmallow Study Revisited."

1. Here is the second paragraph from the article.

    > Now a new study demonstrates that being able to delay gratification is influenced as much by the environment as by innate ability. Children who experienced reliable interactions immediately before the marshmallow task waited on average four times longer—12 versus three minutes—than youngsters in similar but unreliable situations.

    What do you think the article means when it says children are influenced as much by the "environment" as by innate ability? What does the article seem to mean by the word "environment"?

2. The article also talks about "reliable interactions" and "unreliable situations." What does it mean by "reliable" and "unreliable"? How did you figure out the answer to these questions?

3. What questions does this article raise about the original Marshmallow Study by Walter Mischel?

Be prepared to report out after about thirty minutes.

1.12 **Writing**

Experiencing Delayed Gratification

Think about a time when you had an experience with delaying gratification, a time when you had to choose between doing something enjoyable right away or doing something less enjoyable but with benefits in the future.

Write a one-page paper about this experience to be read by the students in the class. Here are some questions you may want to think about, but don't try to answer all of them and don't use them to organize your paper.

1. What made the short-term choice so tempting? What would be so enjoyable about it?

2. What were the benefits of choosing the less enjoyable option?

3. If you chose the short-term, enjoyable option, how did that work out? Was it really a mistake? Was it as enjoyable as you expected? Did it cost you anything in the longer term?

4. If you chose the less enjoyable but more-beneficial-in-the-long-term option, why did you make this decision? How did you convince yourself to give up the more enjoyable option? Did you really benefit in the long term?

If you prefer, you can write about someone else who faced such a choice, not you yourself. Remember that your paper may be shared with the entire class.

↳ **1.13** Activity

Discussing Experiencing Delayed Gratification Papers

Your instructor will divide the class into groups of three or four. Take about ten minutes to read all the papers written by members of your group for Experiencing Delayed Gratification (1.12, p. 22). Next designate each member of the group as note taker for one of the questions. Then, for about a half hour, discuss the following questions.

1. What kinds of strategies seem to work best when people want to delay gratification?
2. What kinds of strategies don't seem to work when people want to delay gratification?
3. Are there times when delaying gratification may not be the best strategy?
4. Is it possible sometimes to find a middle ground between delaying gratification and instant gratification?

Bringing It All Together

◀ How much weight should be given to studies like Mischel's Marshmallow Test? Is it surprising that it took so long for his results to be questioned? Do the new interpretations seem logical? Might they also be overturned in time?

Natali Zakharova/Shutterstock.com

1.14 Writing

Researching Delayed Gratification

For this activity, you will locate at least three recent articles on the subject of delayed gratification, at least one of which discusses the findings of Celeste Kidd. Kidd's article was published in 2013, so you should look for articles published since then.

When you use Google to locate an article in a scholarly journal, you will often find that to read the article, you will need to pay a fee. You are not expected to do this. Instead, go to your library or to your library's website. There you will find that your library subscribes to a number of databases filled with scholarly articles. These are usually organized by subject matter. Select the one that seems most likely to cover the topic you are researching. In this case, the most likely databases are JSTOR, Pro-Quest Central, Psychology Journals, or Social Science Database.

If you would like some help with conducting this search, see Finding Sources Online (22.4, p. 626) and Finding Sources in the Library (22.5, p. 626).

Questions for Evaluating Sources

Answer the following questions about each of the articles you find. If you would like a little guidance on evaluating articles, see Evaluating Sources (22.6, p. 631).

1. Who was the author(s)? What can you find out about the author(s)? What level of expertise does the author have on the subject?

2. Where was the article published? In what kind of journal, book, or website did it appear, and is that source reliable, accurate, and up-to-date?

3. Does the author or the publisher of the article have a particular bias? Does that bias make the article less valuable as a resource?

4. Who seems to be the intended audience for this article?

5. Does the article provide convincing evidence to support its thesis?

6. Which of the three articles would be the best resource for you to quote from in an essay? Why?

1.15 Activity

Audience Analysis

Before you do any actual writing on the essays assigned in An Article on Delayed Gratification for Incoming Students (1.16, p. 25) and The Evolution of Thinking on Delayed Gratification (1.17, p. 26), your instructor will form the class into groups of four or so. In your group, discuss who the audience will be for this writing. Who will be the readers of this essay? What do you know about them? Is there only one audience for your writing? If you think there is more than one, what do you know about the second audience? Who might they be? How much does each audience you identify know about delayed gratification? How much are they likely to agree or disagree with your point? What will be the most effective stance for you to take? Can you pull off being an expert? Or should you emphasize that you are "just a student"?

After fifteen minutes or so, the groups will report out.

1.16 Real World Essay

An Article on Delayed Gratification for Incoming Students

For this assignment, you will write a three- to four-page essay that grows out of your reading, your discussion, and your thinking about delayed gratification. Your audience for this paper is students who will be arriving at your institution next year. Your essay, if accepted by the college's New Student Orientation Committee, will be included in a packet of information new students will receive to help them understand how to be more successful in college.

Think deeply about delayed gratification—what it is, when it is a good strategy, and how one might be successful at doing it. Support your argument with information from the articles you have read or others you locate yourself and/or with examples from your own life or from the lives of people you know.

If you want to use your sources most effectively to support your argument, it's not enough to simply include them as a series of unrelated sources; you need to tie them together, explain their relationships with each other, and express your conclusions about them. This process is called *synthesizing*, and it is discussed in more detail in Synthesis (22.14, p. 648).

Because your essay is an argument, you will want to follow the conventions for arguments. You may want to review these conventions in What Is an Argument? (18.1, p. 513), The Features of Effective Arguments (18.3, p. 513), and How to Answer Counterarguments (18.5, p. 514).

Documentation. If you do quote, paraphrase, or summarize material from the articles you have read, be sure to provide appropriate documentation and to include a works cited list or list of references at the end of your essay. If you need to review how to provide this documentation, refer to MLA Documentation (Topic 23, p. 650) or APA Documentation (Topic 24, p. 687).

1.17   Academic Essay

The Evolution of Thinking on Delayed Gratification

For this assignment, you will write an academic essay suitable for a class in psychology, sociology, education, or even first-year composition. In this essay, you will discuss the evolution of thinking over the past fifty years about delayed gratification. You will need to explain Mischel's contribution, then explore more recent thoughts on the subject, and, finally, present your own thoughts about the issue.

If you want to use your sources most effectively to support your argument, it's not enough to simply include them as a series of unrelated sources; you need to tie them together, explain their relationships with each other, and express your conclusions about them. This process is called *synthesizing*, and it is discussed in more detail in Synthesis (22.14, p. 648).

Documentation.   In Researching Delayed Gratification (1.14, p. 24)—if you did that unit—you located at least three additional articles on delayed gratification, so now you have at least six articles discussing the topic. As you write this essay, you will want to include information from these articles by quoting, paraphrasing, or summarizing relevant passages. When you do this, be sure to provide appropriate citations for any words you quote, paraphrase, or summarize from the websites and to include a works cited list or list of references at the end of your essay. If you need to review how to provide this documentation, refer to MLA Documentation (Topic 23, p. 650) or APA Documentation (Topic 24, p. 687).

1.18   Multimodal Composition

A Message on Delayed Gratification for Incoming Students

For this assignment, as in the assignment for An Article on Delayed Gratification for Incoming Students (1.16, p. 25), you will be composing a message for next year's incoming students at your college. For this assignment, however, you are invited to deliver that message, not as an essay, but as a narrated PowerPoint, video, podcast, blog, or website.

Your composition should grow out of your reading, your discussion, your writing, and your thinking about delayed gratification. Your audience for this composition is students who will be arriving at your institution next year. Your composition is intended to give new students advice about delayed gratification—what it is, when it is a good strategy, and how one might be successful at doing it. Support your argument with information from the articles you have read or others you locate yourself and/or with examples from your own life or from the lives of people you know.

Your composition, if accepted by the college's New Student Orientation Committee, will be presented to new students arriving next year, to help them understand how to be more successful in college.

Documentation. If you do quote, paraphrase, or summarize material from the articles you have read, be sure to provide appropriate documentation and to include a works cited list or list of references at the end of your essay. If you need to review how to provide this documentation, refer to MLA Documentation (Topic 23, p. 650) or APA Documentation (Topic 24, p. 687).

1.19 Activity

Getting Started on Your Essay or Composition

During this class period, you and your classmates will begin working on your assignment (see An Article on Delayed Gratification for Incoming Students [1.16, p. 25], The Evolution of Thinking on Delayed Gratification [1.17, p. 26], or A Message on Delayed Gratification for Incoming Students [1.18, p. 26]). You may use this time to start brainstorming or to begin your research online. You may want to write an opening paragraph or two, or you may want to review what you've already read and written in this project. You may want to compare notes with a couple of classmates or ask your instructor a question or two. The idea is that you will at least get a start on the assignment.

1.20 Writing

Reflecting on Project 1: The Marshmallow Test

Reflective writing is different from most writing you do in college. Reflective writing asks you to think back, to "reflect" on an experience—an essay you have written, a major change in your life, a time when you didn't have success at something you wanted to do, a semester's work in a course—and to examine how you now think and feel about that experience. What effect has the experience had on you? How have you changed? Reflective writing then asks you to look forward. How will you be different in the future? (If you'd like a little more explanation of this type of writing, visit Strategies for Writing a Reflection [18.29, p. 555].)

Now you're going to reflect on all the reading, thinking, discussing, and writing you have done in this project on delayed gratification. To do this, you may want to review any short reflective writing you did as you worked through the project. Then, in a short paper—a page or so—reflect on this experience.

1. Report on what you learned about delayed gratification. What were the most important or most useful ideas you encountered?

2. Describe how you feel about the experience and what you *think* about what you have learned.

3. Report on what you learned that will make a difference for you in the future and why.

PROJECT 2

Choosing a Career

ProStockStudio/Shutterstock

The career you choose to prepare for in college will make an enormous difference in your life. It will have a major effect on how happy you are, how satisfied you are, how much money you make, how good or bad you feel about what you spend your life doing, and how proud you are to tell others what you do for a living. On average, you will spend 36 percent of your waking hours at work, so choosing a career is a big decision; yet most of us make it without enough information, without enough investigation, without enough thought.

In this project you will think about the kinds of careers you're interested in; gather information and investigate various career options; and write about what you find, which jobs most appeal to you, and why.

Getting Started: Exploring Career Opportunities

Project 2 begins with an activity that asks you and your classmates to develop a list of all the benefits you would like to receive from a career. Then you will explore several websites that provide information about salaries, employment outlooks, and educational requirements for a wide range of careers. As you explore these websites, you will select three different careers that you might want to pursue and write brief summaries of what you learned about each of the three.

Exploring, Thinking, and Writing about Ideas

In this section, you will read an article about a woman who has chosen the lowest-paying major in the nation, an article that raises important questions about what motivates people to choose a major besides the amount of money they will make. You will also read several short articles that explore the relationship between people's majors and the jobs they end up doing, as well as an article that provides fascinating data about which careers provide the highest salaries and which are the most meaningful. Finally, you will read an article with a surprising attitude about the common advice that you should "do what you love."

As you work through these materials, you will discuss your thoughts and findings with your classmates, reflect in writing on what you have read, and write short papers in response to specific articles. You will also complete activities related to the readings that ask you to practice specific skills, such as previewing, annotating, summarizing, analyzing, thinking critically, researching, synthesizing sources, and more. According to directions from your instructor, you will work independently and/or in small groups to complete them. In addition, your instructor will assign relevant topics from other parts of *The Hub* that relate to writing, reading, research, and life issues that will address other important skills.

Bringing It All Together

This project concludes with three assignments that ask you to use the tools and ideas you encountered in the project to make some tentative decisions about career directions. Your instructor may assign the first, the second, or the third; may give you the choice among the three; or may even ask you to complete more than one.

The first assignment asks you to select one of the three possible careers you identified in Investigating Career Opportunities (2.3) and to imagine you have an appointment with a career counselor. The essay will be addressed to the counselor and will explain why you have chosen the career you have selected. The second assignment asks you to write an academic essay, appropriate for a class in education, business, or sociology. In this essay you will suggest what a student should consider when choosing a career.

The third assignment is a multimodal composition—perhaps a narrated Power-Point, a website, a blog, or a video—that will report in detail the steps you took to arrive at the one career you are considering pursuing at the end of this project. This composition will be made available to students who are trying to make their own decisions about careers. Because this composition will be a narrative—telling the story of how you made your decision—it should follow the normal conventions for narrative. You may want to review these in Strategies for Writing Narratives (18.10, p. 526).

The final writing assignment, Reflecting on Project 2: Choosing a Career, asks you to reflect on what you have learned as you have worked through this reading/writing project.

Navigating Project 2

Below is the table of contents for Project 2, which you can use to easily locate the units you have been assigned to work on by your instructor. Several of these units ask you to connect to the internet to watch videos or explore websites. If you find that any of the search terms provided do not work, there is a list of URLs available at https://bit.ly/33IIHtf.

Getting Started: Exploring Career Opportunities

▲ What do you know about possible career opportunities?   ProStockStudio/Shutterstock

2.1 Activity

What's Important to You in a Career?

To start this activity, your instructor will give you some time to think about what you hope to get out of your career. Salary is certainly important. So are job opportunities in the field. What else matters to you? What else do you want to get out of your life's work besides salary and job security? Make a list of what's important to you about your career.

Next, your instructor will organize the class into groups of three or four. For the next ten minutes or so, each group will consolidate these individual lists, adding any new ideas they come up with.

At the end of this activity, your instructor will collect all the group lists, consolidate them, and give everyone in the class a copy. With the benefit of all this discussion and after looking at all the ideas from your class, make a new, more thoughtful list of what *you* consider important about a career *you* might follow. This list will be helpful when you work on Average Salaries for Different College Degrees (2.2, p. 34) and Investigating Career Opportunities (2.3, p. 37).

2.2 Activity

Average Salaries for Different College Degrees

Have you ever wondered what the average salary of an architect is? Or of a chef? Or of someone with a two-year associate's degree?

Where to Go and What to Do

In this activity you're going to explore a chart that gives information about the average salaries for people with a variety of college degrees. You are going to work by yourself, and your instructor will let you know when and how to turn in the results of your work.

1. To access the chart, type "hamilton project career earnings by major" into your browser. (If these search terms do not work, there is a list of URLs available at https://bit.ly/33IIHtf.)

2. When you arrive at a website like this, one of the first things to do is find out who owns the website.

   Questions: What can you find out about who owns the Hamilton Project website? What kinds of biases might you expect on this website? What kind of an audience does it seem aimed at?

3. Now you're going to explore how the website works. For this activity, you're going to look only at the chart at the top of the page, the one titled "Annual Earnings." (If you are interested, you can take a look at the chart at the bottom of the page, the one titled "Lifetime Earnings" as well, but all the questions in this activity refer to the "Annual Earnings" chart.)

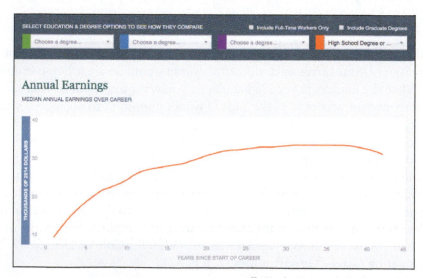

The Hamilton Project at the Brookings Institution

There is a series of small gray numbers across the bottom of the chart, starting with zero and increasing by fives.

Questions: What do these numbers indicate? Along the left edge of the chart is another series of small gray numbers. What do these numbers indicate?

4. Before going any further, go to the top of the screen and check the box labeled "Include Full-Time Workers Only." This means you will see the salaries only for people with full-time jobs. Do not check the box labeled "Include Graduate Degrees." This means the salaries you will see will not include those people with graduate degrees.

5. Across the top of the chart are four boxes, each with a different color tab on the left. Go to the box on the right and use the drop-down menu to select "High School Degree or GED." (It may already be selected when you arrive at the website.) Notice the orange line on the chart. This line represents the average annual income for a person with a high school diploma. As you move your cursor around in the chart, a blue line appears and a box telling you what the average annual salary (in thousands of dollars) is for a high school graduate each year since they started working.

6. Now go to the second box from the right at the top of the chart, the one with a purple tab, and use the drop-down menu to select "Associates Degree." Notice a purple line appears on the chart indicating annual salaries for people with an associate's degree.

The Hamilton Project at the Brookings Institution

Question: After five years of working, how much higher is the average annual salary of someone with an associate's degree compared to that of a high school graduate?

7. Now go to the box at the top with a blue tab and use the drop-down menu to select "All Majors." This is the setting for people who have a four-year college degree in any major.

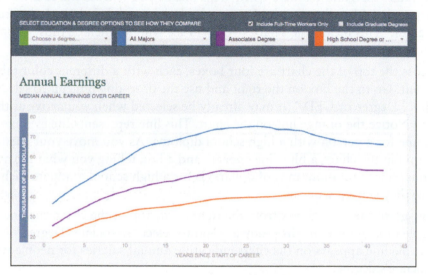

The Hamilton Project at the Brookings Institution

Question: After ten years of working, how much higher is the salary of a graduate with a four-year degree than that of someone with an associate's degree?

8. Next, explore the salaries for various careers using the left-most box, the one with a green tab. Using the drop-down menu in the green box, select aerospace engineer as a major. You will see that the average aerospace engineer, after working 33 years, will be earning $134,000 annually.

    •   Explore the list of majors in this box, and find at least five majors for which average salaries will be more than $100,000 at some time during a worker's career.

    •   Next, find at least five majors for which average salaries will *never* be more than $60,000 during the course of a career.

    Question: What do you think these statistics reveal about our society?

2.3 Writing

Investigating Career Opportunities

For this activity you are going to use two US government websites to investigate three careers that you might be interested in pursuing. As you investigate, be sure to take notes. Later, you will be asked to do a short writing assignment summarizing what you learned about the three occupations you investigated.

Exploring the *Occupational Outlook Handbook* Website

1. To complete this activity, you will need to visit the *Occupational Outlook Handbook* website sponsored by the US Department of Labor. Start by typing "occupational outlook handbook" into your browser.

2. One way to locate careers on this website is to use the list of Occupation Groups on the left side of the page.

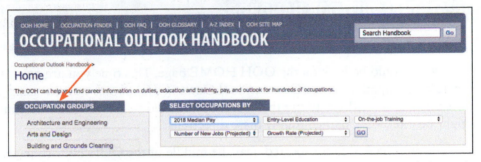

U.S. Bureau of Labor Statistics

Select one of these clusters that you might be interested in and click on it. On the left side of the next page is a list of occupations in the cluster you selected, a brief job summary, a list of the education level required, and an indication of the median annual pay. Here is an example of what the Arts and Design Occupations page looks like:

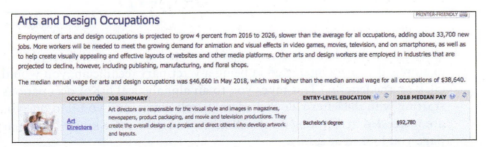

U.S. Bureau of Labor Statistics

3. Scroll down and select a specific occupation you might be interested in and click on it. This takes you to the summary page for that occupation, where you will see a lot of brief nuggets of information about the occupation.

4. Notice, also, at the top of page, a series of tabs:

Clicking on these tabs will lead you to much more information about the occupation you are investigating.

5. At any time, you can return to the home page of the *Occupational Outlook Handbook* website by clicking on OOH HOME marked with a red arrow below. Do this now.

Now you should be back on the OOH HOME page. This time you are going to locate an occupation on the *Occupational Outlook Handbook* website using a different search method. To use this method, you need to know a job title you might be interested in; then follow these directions:

- Locate the A-Z Index located near the middle of the OOH HOME page. It looks like this:

- Click on the first letter of the occupation you want to investigate. (For example, if you are interested in being a veterinary technician, you would click on the letter *v*.) This takes you to an alphabetical list of occupations starting with the letter you clicked on. Scroll down until you find one you are interested in. Clicking on it will take you to the same kind of summary page you looked at earlier.

This would be a good time to look at the lists that you and the class constructed during What's Important to You in a Career? (2.1, p. 33). Now that you are familiar with how the *Occupational Outlook Handbook* website works, take some time to explore careers you think you might be interested in.

Exploring the My Next Move Website

Now you're going to explore a second website that may help you identify potential careers—My Next Move, also sponsored by the US Department of Labor. Start by typing "mynextmove" into your browser.

1. In the middle of the home page for My Next Move, you will see three boxes, which will take you to three different sections of the website.

You're going to use the one on the right, labeled "Tell us what you like to do."

2. Click the start button, which will lead you to the O*NET Interest Profiler, a series of questions designed to identify the kinds of careers you might like to pursue. After clicking through four screens of instructions, you will arrive at a survey. Answer these questions as honestly as you can. The entire survey, sixty questions, should take no more than ten minutes.

3. When you have answered all the questions, the next screen allows you to go back and review your answers if you want to or to review the questions you responded to that you were "unsure" about. You can change any answers at this time.

4. Once you are sure about your answers, click Next, and the next screen gives you your Interest Profiler Results in a chart that looks something like the one that follows on page 40. The Profiler analyzes your responses to the survey

in six areas of interest: realistic, investigative, artistic, social, enterprising, and conventional. Your score for each area is represented by a number and a bar on the bar chart at the top. The higher the number or the higher the bar, the more interest you have in that area.

Realistic	1
Investigative	25
Artistic	29
Social	13
Enterprising	25
Conventional	5

5. Next the website wants to know how much preparation you plan on putting in before starting your chosen career in a series of questions in the Interest + Job Zones = Careers section. The website analyzes preparation in terms of five "zones," ranging from "little or no preparation" to "extensive preparation." Preparation includes education but also experience and training. The website suggests you answer in terms either of how much preparation you have at this moment or how much you plan to have in the future. For the purposes of this activity, answer in terms of how much preparation you plan to have in the future.

6. Click through the three screens explaining these zones and explore them as much as you would like. Then select the preparation zone you are most likely to achieve. The website will then combine your interests and the amount of preparation you are likely to make and identify a series of jobs that someone with your interests and preparation is likely to succeed at.

7. Read over the list and click on the jobs that sound interesting to you. That will take you to a page of information about that career, including salary, education needed, what people in the career do, and job outlooks. Near the bottom of the page is a link labeled "See more details at O*NET OnLine." Be sure to click on that link for even more information including specifics about salary and job outlook in your state.

Activity: Summarizing Three Potential Occupations

As you explored these websites, you may have identified more than three occupations you are interested in. Select just three of these occupations and write a summary of what you learned about each of them.

What Matters Most When Choosing a Career: Salary?

▲ Does it make sense that careers in child development, early childhood education, child and family studies, human services, and elementary education are the lowest paid careers? Why are services that are so important to society so undervalued in terms of salary? Cayla Calfee

2.4 Activity

Analyzing Author, Audience, Topic, and Purpose in "What It's Like to Graduate from College with the Lowest-Paying Major"

As long ago as classical Greece—300 BC or so—thinkers have been aware that four important components exist for every text: the *author* of the text, the *audience* for the text, the *topic* of the text, and the *purpose* of the text. Thinking about author, audience, topic, and purpose should help you prepare to read a text.

- **Author.**   Don't simply find the name of the author. What else can you learn about him or her? What evidence is there that the author really has some expertise? What biases might the author have? Is the author part of an organization? A corporation? What else has the author written?

- **Audience.**   Whom does it appear that the author intended to be the reader or readers of this text? Whom was he or she addressing? Were there other, more secondary, audiences?

- **Topic.**   What is this text about?

- **Purpose.**   What does it appear that the author intended or, at least, hoped would happen as a result of this piece of writing? What did the author want the effect of this text to be on its audience?

Analyzing Author, Audience, Topic, and Purpose

Working in your group, write a brief response—a paragraph is plenty—about each of these components—author, audience, topic, and purpose—for "What It's Like to Graduate from College with the Lowest-Paying Major" (2.6, p. 44).

2.5   Activity

Previewing "What It's Like to Graduate from College with the Lowest-Paying Major"

When you set out to read a book, an article, an essay, a blog, or a web page—when you set out to read any text—your strategy may be simply to dive in, to start reading at the beginning and plow your way through to the end. With the limited time in most of our busy lives, simply diving in can seem like the quickest way to get something read.

Here's a different approach. Most experienced readers have found that taking a few minutes before diving into a text to get a sense of what the text is about and how it is organized will actually save them time and make their reading more effective. This does not mean you have to spend hours previewing and predicting; just a few minutes will be very helpful when you start to read.

Working Together to Preview

For this activity, work in groups to examine the text as outlined in step 1. Then answer the questions listed in steps 2 and 3. Later, working by yourself, answer the questions in step 4.

Step 1: Examine the Text

Every text is slightly different—some may be significantly different—so not all of the following items will apply to all texts, but look for as many of them as you can when you read Danielle Paquette's article "What It's Like to Graduate from College with the Lowest-Paying Major" (2.6, p. 44).

- Take a look at the title.
- If the text is a book, look over the front and back covers and the table of contents, if there is one.
- If the text has headings for different parts, read these.
- If the text starts with an abstract or executive summary, read it.
- Read any introductory material.
- Read the opening paragraph.
- Read the final paragraph.
- Take a look at any illustrations, charts, tables, or videos.
- Look to see if there are citations, endnotes, or a works cited list.
- Check to see how long the text is.

Step 2: Analyze the Rhetorical Situation: Author, Audience, Topic, and Purpose

As long ago as classical Greece—300 BC or so—thinkers have been aware that every text has four important components: the *author* of the text, the *audience* for the text, the *topic* of the text, and the *purpose* of the text. These components make up the "rhetorical situation," the context in which the writing takes place. You don't need to remember the term *rhetorical situation*, but thinking about author, audience, topic, and purpose should be part of your previewing and predicting process. (For more details, see The Rhetorical Situation [9.3, p. 327].)

- **Author.**   Don't simply find out the name of the author. What else can you learn about him or her? What evidence is there that the author really has some expertise about the subject? What biases might the author have? Is the author part of an organization? A corporation? What else has the author written?
- **Audience.**   Whom does it appear that the author intended to be the reader or readers of this text? Whom was he or she addressing? Were there other, more secondary, audiences?
- **Topic.**   What is this text about?
- **Purpose.**   What does it appear that the author intended or, at least, hoped would happen as a result of this piece of writing? What did the author want the effect of this text on its audience to be?

Step 3: Predict What the Text Is About

Predicting what a text might discuss, using background knowledge or personal experiences or information from previous reading, can also prepare you to better understand the content. While not every text will reveal information about all of the following questions, every text will provide answers to some of them. Before launching into reading a text, use the steps listed above to preview the text to help you answer as many of these questions as you can.

1. What is this text "about"? What is the major topic or subject?
2. Does the text take a stand on this topic?
3. Does the author seem to make any assumptions about the subject?
4. What evidence is there that the author of the text has at least some expertise about his or her subject?
5. What do I know about the publishers of the text or the sponsors of the website?
6. How difficult will the text be to read?
7. How much time will I need to read it?

Step 4: Think about Yourself in Relation to the Text

Another way to connect to a text is to consider what you already know about the subject—that is, your prior knowledge. Thinking about what you know before you read helps you to understand and remember the material better and can make it more interesting to read. Ask yourself the following questions.

1. How much do I already know about the topic?
2. Have I had experiences that are related to this topic?
3. Have I read other texts about the same topic?
4. How do I feel about the text's stand on the topic?
5. What is my purpose for reading this text?
6. How similar or different am I from the intended audience for the text?

2.6 Reading

"What It's Like to Graduate from College with the Lowest-Paying Major," Danielle Paquette

In the following article, which appeared in the *Washington Post*, Danielle Paquette thinks about what it's like to graduate from college with the lowest-paying major. First, take a few minutes to preview Paquette's article; then read it.

What It's Like to Graduate from College with the Lowest-Paying Major

DANIELLE PAQUETTE

Danielle Paquette graduated from Indiana University with a BA in journalism in 2012. She was a crime reporter for the *Tampa Bay Times* in St. Petersburg, Florida, before becoming a journalist at the *Washington Post* in 2014, where she focuses on national labor issues. Her articles have appeared in the *Huffington Post*, the *Los Angeles Times*, the *Independent*, the *Chicago Tribune*, and a number of other newspapers and media outlets.

◀ Preschool teacher Cayla Calfee would not trade her dream job for one that pays more.

Cayla Calfee

SEPTEMBER 29, 2014

1   The preschool teacher walked a 4-year-old student to his apartment in Rogers Park, a neighborhood in Chicago where many straddle the poverty line. On this September evening, Cayla Calfee, 23, met the boy's mother, a full-time nanny for two families. They discussed the boy's goals, the application process for a competitive kindergarten.

2   The boy, comfortable between the women, handed his teacher a motocross toy. The toy was a casualty of play, with snapped handlebars. He was eager to share now. When class started four weeks ago at the Howard Area Community, he barely held eye contact.

3   These moments, however slight, are why Calfee keeps education theory textbooks on her coffee table. It's why she signed up for the 12-hour workday, why her biggest splurge now is a carton of frozen yogurt.

▶

4   The sacrifice of this lifestyle, she said, is a privilege. Not everyone can afford to be a preschool teacher.

5   Calfee graduated last year from Indiana University with a bachelor's degree in early childhood education—the major with the lowest lifetime pay, according to a new study.

6   Researchers at the Brookings Institution's Hamilton Project recently set out to answer: As student debt rises—and devours our wealth—how do the high school students of today, feverishly applying to colleges this fall, decide what they can *afford* to study?

7   A college degree, in any major, significantly increases your lifetime earning potential, the study found. Some do more than others. But all do more than Calfee's.

8   The financial stakes have never been higher: About 70 percent of workers with bachelor's degrees have some amount of student debt, said co-author Brad Hershbein, a labor economist at Upjohn Institute for Employment Research and a visiting fellow at Hamilton. The average student with debt graduates with $33,000 in loans, according to a recent analysis by Edvisors.

9   Calfee, who grew up in a Chicago suburb, has no debt. Her family financed her college education. Students in early childhood education at Indiana, she said, were not allowed to hold jobs during unpaid student-teaching semesters.

10   "I was lucky to be able to pursue my dream career," Calfee said. "Economic barriers keep talented students out of this field. It's hard to pay for school, housing and food on your own."

11   And she was fully aware of the average annual pay after graduation: $27,000.

12   The Hamilton Project researchers analyzed career earnings for 80 undergraduate majors from the Census Bureau's American Community Survey and found that, at every career stage, college graduates as a group fare better than workers whose educations didn't continue after high school. What's less obvious, and perhaps more useful when picking a major: Median lifetime pay for college graduates varies greatly, depending on what they studied.

13   Hershbein hopes high school and college students will snoop through the project's salary database, which is being released Monday.

14   "The intent is not to induce people to pick a certain major or deter them from another one," Hershbein said. "Study what you like, what you're good at—and then plan for how much money you'll make, how you'll be able to pay off student debt."

15   One year after graduation, Calfee makes $48,000 per year, which puts her in the top 10 percent of earners in her field. She lives with her boyfriend in Evanston, Ill., pays $900 per month in rent and bikes nine miles to work each day. She's saving to buy a car.

16   After reading Jonathan Kozol's *Savage Inequalities,* which details the challenges students face in low-income areas, Calfee pledged to spend her career helping inner-city kids shape brighter futures.

17   "Your Zip code or the color of your skin should not determine the quality of your education," she said.

18   The value of her college education should not be measured in dollar signs, Calfee said. Her coursework inspired her teaching philosophy—the same teaching philosophy she says helped the 4-boy-old boy ease out of his shell.

19   Calfee hopes that more scholarships become available for college students who want to study early childhood education but can't shoulder tuition costs. The work will always be a privilege, she says. It shouldn't, however, be restricted to the privileged.

↳   ## 2.7 Activity

Thinking about "What It's Like to Graduate from College with the Lowest-Paying Major"

For this activity, your instructor will let you know which parts you should do at home and which parts you will do in groups in class.

After you've read the article "What It's Like to Graduate from College with the Lowest-Paying Major" (2.6, p. 44), answer the following questions.

1. At the end of paragraph 1, Paquette reports that she discussed with one of her student's mother "the application process for a competitive kindergarten." Explain what this means. What is a competitive kindergarten? What do you suppose the application process is like?

2. In paragraph 2, Paquette tells us that her student made "eye contact" with her when she was visiting his home and that he hadn't four weeks earlier. What's the point of this talk about "eye contact"?

3. In the fourth paragraph, Paquette laments that "[N]ot everyone can afford to be a preschool teacher." What does she mean by this assertion?

4. In paragraph 17, Calfee asserts that "Your Zip code or the color of your skin should not determine the quality of your education." It seems that when she says this, she is thinking that sometimes your Zip code or race *does* determine the quality of your education. In the article, does she provide any support for this opinion?

5. What do you learn about Cayla Calfee in this article?

6. What is the thesis of this article?

What Matters Most When Choosing a Career: Your Major?

▲ Graduation day is one of joy and celebration for students and their families. But what comes next? Will the subject you majored in actually prepare you for the job you end up in, or will it have little to no relationship to that job?
Lev Dolgachov/Alamy

2.8 Reading

"Six Reasons Why Your College Major Doesn't Matter," Ashley Stahl

Below is a short article followed by a graphic representation of some data from the Census Bureau that examines the relationship between what you study in college and what career you end up in.

Be sure to take a few minutes to preview before you dive into reading this article. (For a refresher on previewing strategies, look at Previewing a Text [20.2, p. 575].)

Six Reasons Why Your College Major Doesn't Matter

ASHLEY STAHL

Ashley Stahl graduated from the University of Redlands with a BA in a triple major: French, government, and history. She earned master's degrees at the University of Santa Barbara (spiritual psychology) and King's College, London (war studies). After working as a counterterrorism professional, she became an entrepreneur, launching businesses related to her passion for career leadership. As well as being a career coach, she founded CAKE Publishing, which helps produce content to inspire the customers of companies and influencers, and the Job Offer Academy, an online business that helps people around the world find jobs.

Forbes Website

AUGUST 12, 2015

1   "So, what's it going to be?"

2   My advisor looked at me expectantly, as if I was simply at a McDonald's needing to make the simple choice between a Big Mac or a Quarter Pounder.

3   "Let's run through the options," she continued. "Government is a solid choice if you're thinking about law school. English would be a smart decision if you're interested in publishing or teaching. Communications is useful in most fields. . . ."

4   "Women's studies?" I ventured, hoping she would run off a list of career doors that would open to me if I chose this particular field of study.

5   Instead, she cocked her head to the side, chewed her pen cap and looked at me as if I was a unicorn.

6   Next, her eyes lit up: "You can always find a job as a nanny!"

7   That meeting took my stress levels to unprecedented heights. In hindsight, I realize that she had all of the best intentions with her "let's choose a major that increases your employability" approach. It seemed reasonable enough at the time, but after helping thousands of job-seekers land multiple offers through my online coaching program, I've come to realize that your declared major has nothing to do with your success.

8   Unfortunately, that realization hasn't caught on in the mainstream yet.

9   According to a recent study, 82% of 2015 graduates researched their field of choice before determining what major to pursue in college. When you look at this statistic through the lens of student loans and the 2008 recession, it comes as no surprise that students want to pursue careers that will enable them to pay off their hefty debt.

10   If your degree alone guaranteed a job, this kind of strategic long-term planning would make sense. And yes, there *are* certain jobs that require the skills affiliated with specified degrees, such as engineering, architecture, and computer science. But

▶

by and large, your college major is unlikely to have any bearing on your career success. I've coached math majors who later chose to pursue careers in comedy, and I've seen plenty of Elle Woodses come through my door, so I know firsthand that a fashion merchandising degree doesn't affect your ability to get accepted to law school.

11   Plus, look at me: I'm a political science graduate and counterterrorism professional turned career coach.

12   Here are a few points to consider about why our attachment to the idea that majors matter should be put to rest.

1. **Your degree is a prerequisite for the competitive workforce; the topic is irrelevant.** It used to be important and special for someone to have a degree, and now it just stands as a prerequisite in the workforce. While your job will most likely require a Bachelor's degree, it probably won't matter what field it is in. According to recent research, 62% of recent college graduates are working in jobs that require a degree, yet only 27% of college graduates are working in a job that even relates to their major.

2. **Certain fields yield higher incomes, but your major does not need to align with the industry.** The individuals who dedicate their undergrad years to their field of choice (business, medicine, law) don't necessarily end up achieving greater success in the field than those who arrived there with a completely unrelated major. For example, history majors who pursued careers in business ended up earning as much as business majors, according to one study. You don't have to study English to be a writer, you don't have to study business to be a consultant, and you don't have to study political science to go into government. The real world doesn't care about your degree as much as your work ethic and attitude.

3. **Your experience, be it on the job or off the job, is what people notice.** Take advantage of the opportunities you have as an undergraduate to pursue interesting internships, get involved in student organizations, and volunteer for causes you are passionate about. These lines on your resume are so much more powerful than your major because they tell employers that you are motivated, passionate, and involved. Best of all, they allow you to "create" your experience that employers request of you.

4. **Think soft skills, not major topics.** Employers want to know that you will be able to learn quickly, fit into the workplace environment, and be responsive to the task at hand. For these reasons, 93% of employers believe that critical thinking, communication, and problem-solving skills are more

important than a job candidate's undergraduate field of study. Furthermore, 95% of employers are looking for candidates whose skills translate into out-of-the-box thinking and innovation, as many of the jobs being filled today come with challenges that are more complex than in the past. Perhaps this explains why Silicon Valley is starting to favor employees who studied liberal arts, versus those who took the more "typical" tech path as software engineers. Soft skills are the skills of the future.

5. **You're a better performer when you're aligned with your purpose.** As a career coach, I hear from countless clients who feel energetically zapped by their jobs. When I help them get more clear on their purpose, it's as though a new, powerful energy takes them over. . . . Why? Because purpose gives you unprecedented energy. If you major in a field you're truly interested in, you will give it the effort, attention and enthusiasm that translates into success. Stellar performance—in any field—is what translates into career success. Studies show that a happy brain is engaged, motivated, and productive. In other words, our happiness drives our success, so think twice before committing to that math major: Many roads lead to business school, so you might as well take the one that will make you the happiest.

6. **Your network matters way more than your college major.** You can choose a major that correlates with a high-paying job in the real world . . . you can hunker down and score A's in your classes and graduate with a perfect GPA . . . but without a solid network of contacts, you're missing a huge piece of the puzzle. If no one knows *who* you are, no one will care how smart you are. This is why it is so important that people who truly want to be successful put just as much effort, if not more, into networking as they do into their studies. You can start doing this right now, simply by building relationships with your professors, participating in internships and volunteer activities, and even by reaching out to strangers who fascinate you. I've seen it with my own clients, many of whom have received multiple job offers: authentic flattery goes a long way.

13 Your major is not going to pave a yellow brick road for career success. Scoring straight A's in your prelaw coursework is not always the golden ticket to a million-dollar payday. . . . If you don't believe me, ask a lawyer.

14 Whatever you choose to study, make your own personal development the true goal of your undergraduate career. Use your undergraduate years to learn about yourself—your unique brilliance and your passions—not to learn everything there is ▶

to know about the branches and functions of foreign governments that don't interest you in the belief that doing so will land you a job in politics.

15   We've all worked with the genius intern with the perfect resume who couldn't make it to the office on time (ever); the one who spoke six languages but teamwork wasn't one of them. Likewise, we've all known the colleague from the never-heard-of-it college who hustled harder than anyone else on the team and flew up the ladder with *blink and you'll miss her* speed.

16   As Arthur C. Clarke said, "It has yet to be proven that intelligence has any survival value."

17   What *has* been proven is that the most successful leaders are motivated by a purpose.

Share of College Graduates Working in a Job Requiring a College Degree or Related to Their College Major

As the chart below shows, we find that close to two-thirds of college graduates in the labor force work in a job requiring a college degree, while a little more than a quarter work in a job that is directly related to their college major.

College Degree Match

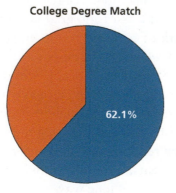

62.1%

College Major Match

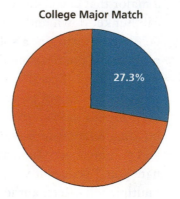

27.3%

Data from U.S. Bureau of the Census, 2010 American Community Survey; authors' calculations.

Note: Individuals with graduate degrees are not included in the calculation of college major matching because the information available on majors relates to the undergraduate degree.

Source: Jaison R. Abel and Richard Deitz, "Do Big Cities Help College Graduates Find Better Work?" *Liberty Street Economics*, May 20, 2013.

↳ ## 2.9 Activity

Looking for Facts in "Six Reasons Why Your College Major Doesn't Matter"

The article "Six Reasons Why Your College Major Doesn't Matter" and the graphic from the Census Bureau that accompanies it (2.8, p. 52) present information about the relationship between college majors and careers. For this activity, working in your group, read the article and examine the graphic chart with one specific purpose: to find out what percentage of people working today are working in a field related to their college major. Once you've answered that question, evaluate the credibility of the data you find. Do you know where the data came from? How recent it is? Who produced it?

NOTE: Before doing this activity, you may want to take a look at Purposes for *Your* Reading (19.5, p. 565), which discusses different approaches to reading depending on your purpose.

2.10 Reading

"Want to Do What You Love and Get Paid for It?" Christopher Ingraham

Read this *Washington Post* article "Want to Do What You Love and Get Paid for It?" Don't forget to spend some time previewing the article before you dive into reading it. (For a refresher on previewing strategies, look at Previewing a Text [20.2, p. 575].)

Want to Do What You Love and Get Paid for It? Choose One of These Majors

CHRISTOPHER INGRAHAM

Christopher Ingraham graduated from Cornell University with a BA in religious studies and worked at the Brookings Institution and the Pew Research Center before becoming a reporter for the *Washington Post*. He writes about topics related to data and makes "charts, maps, and interactive things" to illustrate information, such as the geographic distribution of rejected absentee ballots in Georgia or who controls redistricting. He is particularly interested in gun and drug policies.

▶

OCTOBER 2, 2014

1   We often think of our careers as a tradeoff between doing something we love, and doing something that pays the bills. But new survey data released by salary firm PayScale.com shows that some college majors lead to careers where you really can have it all—while others might land you a job providing neither good pay nor a sense of purpose.

2   Careers in healthcare and engineering ranked high in both meaningfulness and average pay. At the other end of the spectrum, people who had majored in art and design or humanities fields reported low pay, little sense of purpose, and they were relatively unlikely to say that they'd recommend their major to others. Somewhere in between, the bulk of college degrees resulted in some degree of tradeoff between working to live, and living to work.

3   For a sense of the relationship between meaningfulness and salary, look at the following graphic. I've plotted PayScale's 207 bachelor's degree categories by respondents' mid-career salaries, the percent of respondents saying their job is meaningful, and the percent who say they'd recommend their major to others.

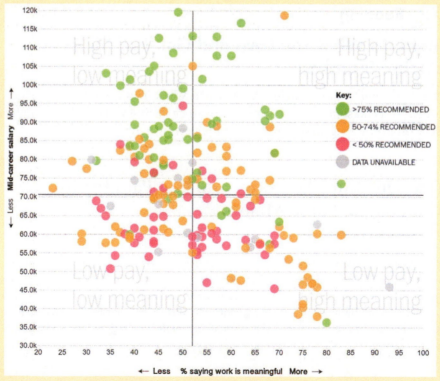

PayScale, Inc.

4   The dark lines mark the median mid-career salary and the median share of respondents saying their job is meaningful. This divides the chart into four quadrants—majors that lead to high pay and high meaning, high pay and low meaning, low pay and high meaning, and, worst of all, little pay and little sense of meaning. There's a degree of arbitrariness at play here—there's probably little practical difference between a reading that's a few points above or a few points below the median. But the divisions provide a useful framework for exploring the relationship between salary and sense of purpose.

5   As you might expect, there's a slight negative relationship—college majors that lead to more meaningful jobs generally don't pay as well by your mid-career. But the relationship isn't particularly tight.

6   PayScale surveyed 1.4 million college graduates who provided information on the school they attended, their choice of major, and their current job and salary. It asked respondents whether their job makes the world a better place, and whether they'd recommend their undergraduate major to others. While the survey respondents are all PayScale users, and hence a somewhat self-selective sample, it's worth nothing that PayScale's earnings figures comport closely with separate research released by the Brookings Institution's Hamilton Project . . . , which is reassuring.

7   93 percent of pastoral ministry graduates said their work was meaningful—even if, on average, they only make about $46,000 by the middle of their careers. Nurses, on the other hand, report a mid-career salary of $73,600—slightly above

The 10 Most Meaningful Majors

Rank	Major	% High Meaning
1	Pastoral Ministry	93%
2	Nursing	83%
2	Clinical Laboratory Science	83%
4	Child Development	80%
5	Athletic Training	78%
5	Early Childhood Education	78%
5	Sports Medicine	78%
5	Medical Technology	78%
9	Special Education	77%
9	Therapeutic Recreation	77%

PayScale, Inc.   ▶

the median. 83 percent of them say their job is meaningful, and 85 percent would recommend the degree to others.

8 "Finding a career path at the intersection of high pay and high meaning is kind of the holy grail, and we've generally seen that often you have to give up one to get the other," PayScale's Lydia Frank told me. "Of course, there are always exceptions, and healthcare seems to be a big one. Careers in healthcare can be very lucrative and workers in the field also tend to have a strong sense of purpose."

9 Another notable exception? Engineering. The upper-right quadrant of the chart is dominated by engineering fields—nuclear, chemical, aerospace and the like. These jobs pay exceedingly well, and people are generally happy with them. One of them—petroleum engineering—pays so well ($176,000 by mid-career, on average) that I had to omit it from the chart. 70 percent of petroleum engineers say their work is meaningful, and 85 percent would recommend it to others.

10 Aside from actuarial mathematics, every one of the top 10 best-paying majors is in engineering.

The 10 Best-Paying Majors

Rank	Major	Early Career Salary	Mid-Career Salary
1	Petroleum Engineering	$102,300	$176,300
2	Actuarial Mathematics	$60,800	$119,600
3	Nuclear Engineering	$67,000	$118,800
4	Chemical Engineering	$69,600	$116,700
5	Electronics & Communications Engineering	$64,100	$113,200
6	Electrical & Computer Engineering (ECE)	$66,500	$113,000
7	Computer Science (CS) & Engineering	$66,700	$112,600
8	Computer Engineering (CE)	$67,300	$108,600
9	Aerospace Engineering	$64,700	$107,900
9	Electrical Engineering (EE)	$65,900	$107,900

PayScale, Inc.

11 On the other hand, there are a fair number of jobs that pay well, but that may not give you a great sense of purpose. Statisticians and computer scientists, for instance, report 6-figure paychecks, but less than 40 percent of them say their work is meaningful. Only half of government majors say their work is meaningful, even though they tend to make well above average.

The 10 Least-Meaningful Majors

Rank	Major	% High Meaning
207	Film Production	23%
206	Fashion Design	27%
204	Fashion Merchandising	29%
204	Graphic Communication	29%
203	Advertising	30%
202	Pre-law	31%
200	Classics	32%
200	Marketing & International Business	32%
199	Radio/Television & Film Production	33%
196	Art & Design	34%

PayScale, Inc.

12   The least meaningful major, according to PayScale? Film production. Only 23 percent said their work made the world a better place. Artists and graphic designers also reported a surprisingly low sense of purpose.

13   Finally, in the lower-left quadrant we come to majors that provide the worst of both worlds: low pay, and little sense of purpose. Art, design and media majors dominate this section. Liberal arts and humanities majors also make a strong showing. Accounting and business majors also show up in this quadrant, but just barely.

14   But by and large, the lowest-*paying* majors don't show up in this quadrant. Majors at the absolute bottom of the pay scale are at least somewhat compensated by the sense of purpose they bring. As Danielle Paquette reported in *Storyline* this week, many people who've chosen these career paths say they're well worth it, and that the financial sacrifice is a privilege.

15   It's also important to put these numbers in context—for the vast majority of people who graduate college, regardless of degree, the financial returns are well worth it. Recent research from the Brookings Institution's Hamilton Project concludes that "a college degree—in any major—is important for advancing one's earnings potential."

▶

The 10 Lowest-Paying Majors

Rank	Major	Early Career Salary	Mid-Career Salary
207	Child Development	$32,200	$36,400
206	Early Childhood Education	$29,700	$38,000
205	Child & Family Studies	$31,200	$38,600
204	Early Childhood & Elementary Education	$32,300	$40,400
203	Human Services (HS)	$33,800	$41,300
202	Elementary Education	$33,600	$45,500
201	Athletic Training	$35,000	$45,900
200	Pastoral Ministry	$36,300	$46,000
199	Social Work (SW)	$32,800	$46,600
198	Special Education	$34,500	$46,800

PayScale, Inc.

16   But the PayScale data comports with the Hamilton Project's other main finding, which is that earnings potential varies wildly by degree. And they shed some light on an aspect of college education that often gets overlooked in abstract discussion about earnings and returns-on-investment: the sense of fulfillment that some careers provide relative to others.

↳ **2.11 Activity**

Thinking about "Want to Do What You Love and Get Paid for It?"

Working in groups, discuss these questions about Christopher Ingraham's article, "Want to Do What You Love and Get Paid for It?" (2.10, p. 53).

1. In the first paragraph, Ingraham suggests that one reason to select a particular career is because you love it. The other reason is because it pays well. By the end of that paragraph he has substituted another concept for what he first called *love*. He talks about a career that provides a *sense of purpose*. And in the next paragraph he switches to the term *meaningful*. Do you think these three terms—a career you *love*, a career that provides a *sense of purpose*, and a career that is *meaningful*—mean the same thing?

2. Ingraham seems to argue that there are two reasons to select a career: for the salary or for the fuzzy idea of meaningfulness. Do you agree that these are the two biggest goals for a career, or would you suggest something else?

3. In the article, Ingraham provides charts listing the ten most "meaningful" majors and the ten least "meaningful" careers based on a survey of 1.4 million college graduates by PayScale.com. Based on the information in those charts, what does he seem to think makes a career "meaningful"?

What Matters Most When Choosing a Career: Doing What You're Passionate About?

▲ What makes you happy? Can you pursue a career that allows you to do what you most care about? How important is it to have a job doing what you love? Should personal happiness be a factor in considering a career? Gustavo Frazao/Shutterstock

"Introduction: Life by Design," Bill Burnett and Dave Evans

Below is an excerpt from the book *Designing Your Life: How to Build a Well-Lived, Joyful Life*. In it, Bill Burnett and Dave Evans discuss how to apply Stanford University's principles of design to find a meaningful career and build a satisfying life by approaching challenges and major decisions the way a designer would. Take a moment to preview it before you start to read. (For a refresher on previewing strategies, look at Previewing a Text [20.2, p. 575].)

Introduction: Life by Design

BILL BURNETT AND DAVE EVANS

Bill Burnett graduated from Stanford University with a BSE and MSE in product design and mechanical engineering. He worked at Apple as a program manager and at D2M Inc. as president and senior fellow. He has worked at Stanford University as a consulting assistant professor for thirty-five years and as the executive director of the Design Program there for twelve years.

Dave Evans also obtained his BSE and MSE in product design and mechanical engineering from Stanford University and worked at Apple as a manufacturing engineer. He was director of design at Lytro Inc. and Playground.Global and is now an adjunct lecturer at Stanford University and vice president of design at Essential in Palo Alto, California.

1   Ellen liked rocks. She liked collecting them, sorting them, and categorizing them according to size and shape, or type and color. After two years at a prestigious university, the time came for Ellen to declare her major. She had no idea what she wanted to do with her life or who she wanted to be when she grew up, but it was time to choose. Geology seemed like the best decision at the time. After all, she really, really liked rocks.

2   Ellen's mother and father were proud of their daughter, *the geology major, a future geologist*. When Ellen graduated, she moved back home with her parents. She began babysitting and dog walking to make a little money. Her parents were confused. This is what she had done in high school. They had just paid for an expensive college education. When was their daughter going to turn magically into a geologist? When was she going to begin her career? This is what she had studied for. This is what she was *supposed* to do.

3   The thing is—Ellen had realized she didn't want to be a geologist. She wasn't all that interested in spending her time studying the earth's processes, or materials, or history. She wasn't interested in fieldwork, or in working for a natural-resource

company or an environmental agency. She didn't like mapping or generating reports. She had chosen geology by default, because she had liked rocks, and now Ellen, diploma in hand, frustrated parents in her ear, had absolutely no idea how to get a job and what she should do with the rest of her life.

4   If it was true, as everyone had told her, that her college years were the best four years of her life, Ellen had nowhere to go but down. She did not realize that she was hardly alone in not wanting to work in the field in which she had majored. In fact, in the United States, only 27 percent of college grads end up in a career related to their majors.

* * *

5   Many people operate under the dysfunctional belief that they just need to find out what they are passionate about. Once they know their passion, everything else will somehow magically fall into place. We hate this idea for one very good reason: most people don't know their passion. Our colleague William Damon, director of the Stanford Center on Adolescence, found that only one in five young people between twelve and twenty-six have a clear vision of where they want to go, what they want to accomplish in life, and why. Our experience suggests, similarly, that 80 percent of people of all ages don't really know what they are passionate about.

6   So conversations with career counselors often go like this:

Career Counselor: "What are you passionate about?"

Job Seeker: "I don't know."

Career Counselor: "Well, come back when you figure it out."

7   Some career counselors will give people tests to assess people's interests or strengths, or to survey their skills, but anyone who has taken such tests knows that the conclusions are often far from conclusive. Besides, finding out that you could be a pilot, an engineer, or an elevator repairman isn't very helpful or actionable. So we're not very passionate about finding your passion. We believe that people actually need to take time to develop a passion. And the research shows that, for most people, passion comes after they try something, discover they like it, and develop mastery— not before. To put it more succinctly: passion is the result of a good life design, not the cause.

8   Most people do not have that *one thing* they are passionate about—that singular motivator that drives all of their life decisions and infuses every waking moment with a sense of purpose and meaning. If you've found that studying the mating habits and evolution of mollusks from the Cambrian period until the present day is your purpose for living—we salute you. Charles Darwin spent thirty-nine   ▶

years studying earthworms; we salute Charles Darwin. What we don't salute is a method of approaching life design that leaves out 80 percent of the population. In truth, most people are passionate about many different things, and the only way to know what they want to do is to prototype some potential lives, try them out, and see what really resonates with them. We are serious about this: you don't need to know your passion in order to design a life you love. Once you know how to prototype your way forward, you are on the path to discovering the things you truly love, passion or not.

2.13 Activity

Annotating "Introduction: Life by Design"

In Unit 2.12 (p. 60) you are asked to read an article entitled "Introduction: Life by Design." For this activity, you will need to print out the article and then annotate it—add comments, questions, symbols, underlining, and highlighting to indicate your reactions, thoughts, and questions about the text.

To annotate is more than just highlighting the important ideas. It is an activity that automatically increases your engagement with the text you are reading. When annotating you mark what seems important, but you also may mark words you don't know, mark passages you find puzzling, ask questions about the text, argue with the text, and mark places you think are well written. If you need a little refresher on the concept, take a look at Annotation Explained (20.6, p. 583).

2.14 Activity

Thinking about "Introduction: Life by Design"

Your instructor will let you know whether you will be working in groups or working individually on this activity. Either way, answer the following questions about the excerpt from "Introduction: Life by Design" (2.12, p. 60).

1. What was the most interesting idea or information you found in the text?

2. How do *you* fit into this article? Have you, like Ellen, chosen a program or major to follow in college without really knowing what kind of work that program or major will lead to? Is there some one thing that you are passionate about? Do you believe that you should try to find that one thing you could be passionate about so you can move forward in your life?

3. In the last sentence of the article, Burnett and Evans claim, "Once you know how to prototype your way forward, you are on the path to discovering the things you truly love, passion or not." What do you think they mean by the word *prototype*, which they use as a verb?

Bringing It All Together

▲ Once you have an idea of the kind of job you would like after graduation, how do you find out more about it? What do you need to know? Who can you ask? Where can you look for information? Tashatuvango/Shutterstock

2.15 Writing

Research into What It's Like to Be a _____

In earlier activities in Project 2, you investigated the practical issues involved in various careers: employment outlook, salaries, necessary education. But you haven't really looked at the "what it's like to be a _____" question. For example, if you've been thinking about being a physical therapist, how could you learn more about what it's like to be a physical therapist?

Activity: Gathering Information on a Potential Career

For this activity, you're going to try to do just that, to gather some information about what it's like to be a person working in the career you are considering pursuing. There are several ways you might be able to gather this information:

- Interview someone working in the field.

- Interview a faculty member who teaches in the field.

- Find out if your school has an office for career guidance or career counseling. If so, visit that office and see if the staff could put you in touch with someone working in the field.

- Look in the library for books or articles about working in the field.

- Look on the internet for sites set up for people in the field. See it you can get in touch with someone to interview through these sites.

Preparing for an Interview

If you decide to conduct an interview, be aware that the person you are interviewing probably has lots of other things to do. He or she is being generous to agree to an interview. It's important that you keep this in mind and do everything possible to respect your interviewee's time. Follow the following guidelines.

1. **Set up a time for the interview well in advance.** Nothing is more inconsiderate than asking someone for an interview and telling them you need to do it tomorrow because the paper is due the next day.

2. **Be flexible about how and where the interview is conducted.** The most common approach is for you to go to the interviewee's office and ask him or her questions face-to-face, but interviews can also be conducted in another place (a coffee shop, a quiet room on campus, etc.), on the phone, or even through an email exchange. Find out what the person you are planning to interview prefers.

3. **Ask in advance whether it is okay to record the interview.** If it is, come prepared and check that your recording device is working before you arrive.

4. **Research your subject.** Find out as much as you can about the interviewee before the interview, so you don't have to waste time asking for his or her job title or where he or she went to college. This information is probably available on a website.

5. **Plan what you will ask.** Make a list of questions ahead of time so you don't waste time at the interview and you don't forget to ask about something important.

Of course, during the interview, you may ask follow-up questions depending on what you learn during the conversation, but you should arrive with a thoughtful list of the main questions you plan to ask.

6. **Make notes.** Especially if you were not able to record the interview, try to sit down and write up your notes as soon as you can afterward.

Writing about What Your Chosen Career Would Be Like

After you've completed your research, write a short essay—a page is plenty—in which you discuss what it would be like to work in the career you've researched. Include in your essay the advantages and the disadvantages of working in that career.

↳ **2.16** Activity

Class Discussion of Possible Careers

This class will consist of a discussion of the short writings about possible careers that you turned in, focusing particularly on what you and your classmates identified as strengths and weaknesses of various careers.

2.17 Real World Essay

The Advantages and Disadvantages of a Specific Career

This essay will build on the work you have been doing exploring careers.

Essay Assignment. In Investigating Career Opportunities (2.3, p. 37), you summarized three occupations, careers, you were interested in. At this point, focus on one career that you might want to pursue. Don't worry. This is not a permanent decision; in fact, one perfectly reasonable outcome of writing this paper might be that you decide this is *not* the career for you!

For this essay, you will discuss the advantages and disadvantages for you of the career you have chosen. Think back to the list of what's important in a career that you compiled in What's Important to You in a Career? (2.1, p. 33). That should help you think about what you want to discuss.

Think or your audience as a career counselor. You have an appointment in a week or two, and she has asked you to write an essay explaining what career you currently are thinking about pursuing. She will use your essay to help you with advice and guidance, so it is important that you write as thoroughly as you can about your current thinking. Be sure you use the information you acquired about the career you choose to support your decision.

If you want to use your sources most effectively to support your argument, it's not enough to simply include them as a series of unrelated sources; you need to tie them together, explain their relationships with each other, and express your conclusions about them. This process is called *synthesizing*, and it is discussed in more detail in Synthesis (22.14, p. 648).

Because your essay is an argument, you will want to follow the conventions for arguments. You may want to review these conventions in What Is an Argument? (18.1, p. 513), The Features of Effective Arguments (18.3, p. 513), and How to Answer Counterarguments (18.5, p. 514).

Documentation.　If you do quote, paraphrase, or summarize material from the texts you have read for this project, be sure to provide appropriate in-text citations and include a works cited list or list of references at the end of your essay. If you need to review how to provide this documentation, refer to MLA Documentation (Topic 23, p. 650) or APA Documentation (Topic 24, p. 687).

2.18　Academic Essay

Priorities for Students Making Career Decisions

This essay will build on the work you have been doing exploring careers.

Essay Assignment.　Building on the reading, writing, discussing, and thinking you've been doing about career decision-making, in this essay you will propose and defend what should be the highest priorities for students making a decision about careers. Think of this as an academic essay you might write for a class in education, business, or sociology.

First, make a list of what you think are the ten most important things students should consider when making career decisions. Then explain and argue for the list you have compiled. For each of the ten items, you will explain why it is important and then give advice about how a student might carry it out.

If you want to use your sources most effectively to support your argument, it's not enough to simply include them as a series of unrelated sources; you need to tie them together, explain their relationships with each other, and express your conclusions about them. This process is called *synthesizing*, and it is discussed in more detail in Synthesis (22.14, p. 648).

Because your essay is an argument, you will want to follow the conventions for arguments. You may want to review these conventions in What Is an Argument? (18.1, p. 513), The Features of Effective Arguments (18.3, p. 513), and How to Answer Counterarguments (18.5, p. 514).

Documentation.   In this essay, be sure to provide appropriate citations for any words you quote, paraphrase, or summarize from the texts you read and include a works cited list or list of references at the end of your essay. If you need to review how to provide this documentation, refer to MLA Documentation (Topic 23, p. 650) or APA Documentation (Topic 24, p. 687).

2.19   Multimodal Composition
A Process for Students Making Career Decisions

Building on the reading, writing, discussing, and thinking you've been doing about career decision making, in this assignment you will narrate the process you followed to make your tentative career decision.

Assignment.   This assignment will be multimodal—perhaps a narrated PowerPoint, a website, a blog, or a video—your choice. It is designed for students who are already competent at PowerPoint, website design, blogging, or making a video.

In this multimodal composition, you will describe in detail the process you followed to arrive at the career you are considering pursuing now that you are at the end of this project. The audience for the composition is students who are trying to make their own decisions about careers. The idea is that by describing the process you followed, you will help them figure out a process they will follow.

Because this composition will be explaining a process, it should follow the normal conventions for process writing. You may want to review these in Strategies for Process Writing (18.12, p. 530).

Documentation.   Be sure to provide appropriate citations for any words you quote, paraphrase, or summarize from the texts you read and include a works cited list or list of references at the end of your essay. If you need to review how to provide this documentation, refer to MLA Documentation (Topic 23, p. 650) or APA Documentation (Topic 24, p. 687).

2.20 Activity

Getting Started on Your Essay or Composition

During this class period, you and your classmates will begin working on your assignments (see Real World Essay: The Advantages and Disadvantages of a Specific Career [2.17, p. 65], Academic Essay: Priorities for Students Making Career Decisions [2.18, p. 66], or Multimodal Composition: A Process for Students Making Career Decisions [2.19, p. 67]).

You may use this time to start brainstorming or to begin your research online. You may want to write an opening paragraph or two, or to review what you've already read and written in this project. You may want to compare notes with a couple of classmates or ask a question or two of your instructor. If you are composing a multimodal project, you may want to talk to others who are doing the same to compare approaches. The idea is that you will use this period to, at least, get a start on the essay.

2.21 Writing

Reflecting on Project 2: Choosing a Career

Reflective writing is different from most writing you do in college. Reflective writing asks you to think back, to "reflect" on an experience—an essay you have written, a major change in your life, a time when you didn't have success at something you wanted to do, a semester's work in a course—and to examine how you now think and feel about that experience. What effect has the experience had on you? How have you changed? How will you be different in the future?

Now you're going to reflect on all the reading, thinking, discussing, and writing you have done in this project on choosing a career. To do this, you may want to review any short reflective writing you did as you worked through the project. Then, in a short paper—a page or so—reflect on this experience:

1. Report on what you learned about choosing a career. What were the most important or most useful ideas you encountered?

2. Describe how you feel about the experience and what you *think* about what you have learned.

3. Report on what you learned that will make a difference for you in the future and why.

PROJECT 3
Freedom of Speech

(Statue of Liberty) Bryan Busovicki/Shutterstock; (hand) DenisNata/Shutterstock

In this Project, you will explore the topic of freedom of speech, which is guaranteed in the First Amendment to the US Constitution:

> Congress shall make no law respecting an establishment of religion, or prohibiting the free exercise thereof; or abridging the freedom of speech, or of the press; or the right of the people peaceably to assemble, and to petition the government for a redress of grievances.

In addition, you'll explore the tension between a broad commitment to free speech as set forth in the First Amendment and the need for some restrictions.

Getting Started: First Thoughts on *Freedom of Speech*

To begin this project, you'll do some thinking about just what freedom of speech is and what it is not. In this section, you'll also gain an understanding of why freedom of speech is such a strong concept in our culture and in our laws.

Exploring, Thinking, and Writing about Ideas

After exploring free speech in an abstract way, you will examine how it works in some concrete situations. First, you will read, discuss, and write about documents related to a conflict between the US commitment to free speech and our desire to support a United Nations treaty on combating racism. In the next section, you will explore how several writers have grappled with the tensions between our belief in free speech and our desire to limit hate speech. Finally, you'll focus these questions down to the college level. How can colleges and universities construct policies that respect free speech but also protect people from having to endure a hostile environment?

As you work through these materials, you will discuss your thoughts and findings with your classmates, reflect in writing on what you have read, and write in response to specific articles. You will also complete activities related to the readings that ask you to practice specific skills such as active reading, note-taking, researching, analyzing, summarizing, evaluating, and reflecting on what you have learned. According to directions from your instructor, you will work independently and/or in small groups to complete them. In addition, your instructor will assign relevant topics from other parts of *The Hub* that relate to writing, reading, research, and life issues that will address other important skills.

Bringing It All Together

Project 3 concludes with three assignments that ask you to think deeply about freedom of speech. Your instructor may ask you to complete the first, second, or third assignment; may give you a choice among the three; or may even ask you to complete more than one.

The first assignment asks you to write a brief proposal for what the college's policy should be on one specific aspect of free speech and then to write an essay in which you defend that proposal to a committee that is formulating your school's free speech policy. The second assignment asks you to write an academic essay explaining freedom of speech in America. Think of this second essay as writing that would be appropriate in a college course on political science, sociology, government, law, or something similar. The third assignment asks you to compose a multimodal composition—a narrated PowerPoint, a video, a podcast, a blog, or a website—that, first, presents your proposal for the college's policy on one specific aspect of free speech and, second, defends that proposal.

The final writing assignment, Reflecting on Project 3: Freedom of Speech, asks you to reflect on what you have learned as you have worked through this reading/writing project.

Navigating Project 3

Below is the table of contents for Project 3, which you can use to easily locate the units you have been assigned to work on by your instructor. Several of these units ask you to connect to the internet to watch videos or explore websites. If you find that any of these search terms do not work, there is a list of URLs available at https://bit.ly/33IIHtf.

Getting Started: First Thoughts on *Freedom of Speech*

AMENDMENTS TO THE CONSTITUTION [1]

Religious and Political Freedom

background of or press, assembly, and petition. Congress shall make no law re-
ll of Rights specting an establishment of religion, or prohibiting the free exer-
see p. 152. cise thereof; or abridging the freedom of speech, or of the press;
or the right of the people peaceably to assemble, and to petition
the government for a redress of grievances.

Congress must not interfere with freedom of religion, speech

le II. Right to B... rms. A well-regulated militia being nec-
...ary to the security of a ...e State, the right of the people to keep
a... bear arms [i.e., for mili... purposes] shall not be infringed.

The people may be a...

...arily quartered or ...he ...ouse with...

Quartering of Troops

...ldiers may not be a... ...be quartered in ... ...in a mann...
... in time of pea... ... time of war,
...ner, no...

▲ Free speech is protected by the First Amendment to the US constitution. It is a right most Americans take for granted. So what constitutes *free speech*? What does the term mean to you? James E. Knopf/Shutterstock

3.1 Writing

Defining *Speech*

The First Amendment to the Constitution declares that "the Congress shall make no law . . . abridging the freedom of speech." For this assignment, you will need to do some research into exactly what counts as *speech*. Does speech have to be spoken? Can it be written? Can it be in the form of financial contributions to candidates? What else counts as speech?

Write a short paper—about a page—in which you discuss, under the First Amendment, what the word *speech* has been interpreted as including.

3.2 Activity

Listing Exceptions to Freedom of Speech

The First Amendment to the Constitution declares that "the Congress shall make no law . . . *abridging the freedom of speech* [emphasis added]." However, through the years, the courts have specified a number of exceptions to this rule. The courts have declared that certain kinds of speech can, in fact, be limited by Congress.

Working in your group and making use of the internet, create a list of as many of these exceptions as you can find. A sentence or two to explain each exception should be fine.

Why Is Freedom of Speech a Core American Value?

▲ Freedom of speech is the opposite of censorship. Many people believe that the only way for society to improve is for all voices to be heard. But aren't there times when people should not be allowed to speak? For example, are hate speech and racial slurs acceptable? Where would you draw the line? rob zs/Shutterstock

Activity

Previewing "Speech Overview"

When you set out to read a book, an article, an essay, a blog, a web page—when you set out to read any text—your usual strategy may be simply to dive in, to start reading at the beginning and plow your way through to the end. With the limited time in most of our busy lives, simply diving in can seem like the quickest way to get something read.

Here's a different approach. Most experienced readers have found that taking a few minutes before diving in to get a sense of the text they are about to read will actually save them time and help them read more effectively. This does not mean spending hours previewing; just a few minutes will be very helpful when you start to read. Give it a try. You may find that previewing will actually save you time because it will make the reading itself easier. And you'll get more out of the reading because you will have prepared yourself to be an engaged reader.

Working Together to Preview and Predict

Working in your group, preview Rodney A. Smolla's essay "Speech Overview" (3.5, p. 79). For this activity, work in groups to examine the text as outlined in step 1 below. Then answer the questions listed in steps 2 and 3. Later, working by yourself, answer the questions in step 4.

1. **Examine the text.** Working in your group, complete the tasks listed below and answer this question about each one: What did this task tell you about the text? Keep in mind that this is a list you could use for larger works than the one you'll be reading, so some of the items listed will not apply.

    - Take a look at the title.
    - If the text is a book, look over the front and back covers and the table of contents, if there is one.
    - Read any introductory material, such as a preface or headnote.
    - If the text starts with an abstract or executive summary, read it.
    - If the text has headings for different parts, read these.
    - Read the opening paragraph.
    - Read the final paragraph.
    - Take a look at any illustrations, charts, tables, or associated videos.
    - Look to see if there are citations, endnotes, or a works cited list.
    - Check to see how long the text is.

2. **Analyze the rhetorical situation.** As long ago as classical Greece—300 BC or so—thinkers have been aware that every text has four important components—the *author* of the text, the *audience* for the text, the *topic* of the text, and the *purpose* of the text. These components make up the *rhetorical situation*, the context in which the writing takes place. You don't need to remember the term *rhetorical situation*, but thinking about author, audience, topic, and purpose should be part of your previewing and predicting process.

Now, working in your group, write brief answers to the following questions.

- **Author.** You don't simply want to find out the name of the author. What else can you learn about him? What evidence is there that the author really has some expertise? What biases might the author have? Is the author part of an organization? A corporation? What else has the author written?

- **Audience.** Whom does it appear that the author intended to be the reader or readers of this text? Whom was he addressing? Were there other, secondary, audiences?

- **Topic.** What is this text about?

- **Purpose.** What does it appear that the author intended or, at least, hoped would happen as a result of this piece of writing? What did the author want the effect of this text on its audience to be?

3. **Predict what the text is about.** Predicting what a text might discuss, using background knowledge or personal experiences or information from previous reading, can also prepare you to better understand the content. While not every text will reveal information about all of the following questions, every text will provide answers to some of them. Before reading, use the steps listed above to preview the text to help you answer as many of the questions as you can.

- What is this text "about"? What is the major topic or subject?

- Does the author take a stand on this topic?

- Does the author seem to make any assumptions about the subject?

- What do I know about the publishers of the text or sponsors of the website? Does the text appear in a reputable and reliable source?

- What evidence is there that the author of the text has at least some expertise about the subject?

4. **Think about yourself in relation to the text.** A final way to preview a text is to think about how the subject of the text relates to you individually. Of course, this personal kind of previewing is not appropriate for group work, so, working individually, answer the following questions.

- What do you already know about the topic?
- Have you had experiences that are related to this topic?
- Have you read other texts about this same topic?
- What have you heard or seen about this topic (on the radio, TV, internet, podcasts, YouTube, other classes, etc.)?
- How do you feel about the text's stand on the topic?
- What is your purpose for reading this text?
- How similar or different are you from the intended audience for the text?
- How difficult will the text be to read?
- How much time will you need to read it?

3.4 Activity

Dealing with Challenging Vocabulary in "Speech Overview"

The text that follows consists of the first five paragraphs from the essay that appears in Rodney A. Smolla's "Speech Overview" (3.5, p. 80). A number of words that may be unfamiliar to you are underlined.

Finding the Meanings of Unfamiliar Words

When, in your reading, you encounter a word you are not familiar with, you can use one of the following six strategies to work out its meaning.

1. Derive the meaning from context.
2. Analyze the parts of the word.
3. Back up and re-read the passage.
4. Keep reading to see if the writer explains the difficult passage.
5. Decide the word is not important and just keep reading.
6. Look the word up in a dictionary.

If you are not familiar with any of these strategies, you may want to refer to Dealing with Difficult Language (20.9, p. 594), where they are discussed in detail.

Decoding Unfamiliar Words in "Speech Overview"

For this unit, working in your group, use one or more of the strategies listed above to deal with the difficulty presented by each of the underlined words. Keep track of which strategy your group used for each word.

Excerpt from "Speech Overview"

Rodney A. Smolla

1   The First Amendment to the Constitution of the United States declares that "Congress shall make no law . . . <u>abridging</u> the freedom of speech." What does and should this mean? Justice Oliver Wendell Holmes, in his famous *Abrams v. United States* (1919) <u>dissenting opinion</u>, began what may be the single most poetic paragraph ever written by a Supreme Court justice on the meaning of freedom of speech. Here is that <u>improbable</u> opening line: "<u>Persecution</u> for the expression of opinions seems to me perfectly logical." What could Holmes have been thinking?

2   Perhaps Holmes was expressing the view that all of us, individually and collectively, have within us a kind of censorship-impulse. Governments are especially prone to censor. As Holmes went on to put it: "If you have no doubt of your <u>premises</u> or your power and want a certain result with all your heart you naturally express your wishes in law and sweep away all opposition." Censorship is thus a kind of social instinct. As caring and responsible citizens of society, *especially* good and decent citizens of a good and decent society, we are likely to want *many* results with all our hearts. We want security, we want freedom from fear, we want order, civility, racial and religious tolerance, we want the well-being of our children. We want these things with all our hearts, and when others express opinions that seem to threaten these <u>aspirations</u>, who can blame us for being tempted to express our wishes in law and sweep away the opposition? It is perfectly logical. And that is what, at bottom, freedom of speech is all about.

3   Over the course of roughly the last 50 years the U.S. Supreme Court has set our nation on a remarkable experiment, often <u>construing</u> the First Amendment in a manner that <u>strenuously</u> defies the natural and logical <u>impulse</u> to censor. In <u>scores</u> of decisions, the Supreme Court has interpreted the First Amendment in a manner that to most of the world seems positively radical. Those decisions are numerous and cover a vast and various <u>terrain</u>, but consider some highlights. Americans have the right to:

- <u>Desecrate</u> the national flag as a symbol of protest.
- Burn the cross as an expression of racial bigotry and hatred.
- Espouse the violent overthrow of the government as long as it is mere abstract advocacy and not an immediate incitement to violence.
- Traffic in sexually explicit erotica as long as it does not meet a rigorous definition of "hard core" obscenity.
- <u>Defame</u> public officials and public figures with falsehoods provided they are not published with knowledge of their falsity or reckless disregard for the truth.
- <u>Disseminate</u> information invading personal privacy if the revelation is deemed "newsworthy."

- Engage in countless other forms of expression that would be outlawed in many nations but are regarded as constitutionally protected here.

4   Such First Amendment decisions reject the impulse to censor; they are therefore striking as legal doctrines. Perhaps more striking, however, is that these decisions have gained widespread currency within American culture as a whole. The Supreme Court is not alone in its commitment to the free-speech project. While undoubtedly any one decision will often be controversial with the public, which may be deeply divided on topics such as flag-burning or sex on the Internet, on balance what is extraordinary about the evolution of freedom of speech in America over the last 50 years is that it has taken such a strong hold on the American consciousness, a hold that seems to cut across party labels such as "Democrat" or "Republican" or ideological labels such as "liberal" or "conservative." On the Supreme Court itself, for example, justices with hardy conservative credentials such as Antonin Scalia or Clarence Thomas have often been as committed to expansive protection for freedom of speech as justices famous for their liberal views, such as William Brennan or Thurgood Marshall. Appointees of Republican presidents, such as Anthony Kennedy or David Souter, have been as stalwart as appointees of Democratic presidents, such as Stephen Breyer or Ruth Bader Ginsburg, in their articulation of strong free-speech doctrines. So too, in the political arena, views on free-speech issues often do not track along traditional party lines or classic ideological divisions.

5   This is not to say that in some simplistic sense everybody in America believes in freedom of speech, and certainly it is not to say that everybody in America believes that freedom of speech means the same thing. But it is to say that in a sense both deep and wide, "freedom of speech" is a value that has become powerfully internalized by the American polity. Freedom of speech is a core American belief, almost a kind of secular religious tenet, an article of constitutional faith.

3.5   Reading

"Speech Overview," Rodney A. Smolla

This essay appears on the website of the Freedom Forum Institute. If you want to read it there, type "speech overview, freedom forum institute" into your search engine. (If these search terms do not work, there is a list of URLs available at https://bit.ly/33IIHtf.) The links in blue throughout the essay online will take you to various legal cases affecting free speech. You are welcome to follow them if you are interested, but doing so is not required.

Be sure to do a little "previewing" before you dive into reading this essay. If you need more information on previewing, go to Previewing a Text (20.2, p. 575).

Speech Overview

RODNEY A. SMOLLA

Rodney A. Smolla, an award-winning author and First Amendment scholar, obtained a bachelor's degree from Yale University and a law degree from Duke University. He is currently dean and professor of law at the Delaware Law School of Widener University, in Wilmington, Delaware; formerly served as the eleventh president of Furman University; and prior to that was dean and faculty member at several different institutions. He is an expert on constitutional law, civil rights, freedom of speech, and mass media, and he has authored numerous books on these topics.

1   The First Amendment to the Constitution of the United States declares that "Congress shall make no law . . . abridging the freedom of speech." What does and should this mean? Justice Oliver Wendell Holmes, in his famous *Abrams v. United States* (1919) dissenting opinion, began what may be the single most poetic paragraph ever written by a Supreme Court justice on the meaning of freedom of speech. Here is that improbable opening line: "Persecution for the expression of opinions seems to me perfectly logical." What could Holmes have been thinking?

2   Perhaps Holmes was expressing the view that all of us, individually and collectively, have within us a kind of censorship-impulse. Governments are especially prone to censor. As Holmes went on to put it: "If you have no doubt of your premises or your power and want a certain result with all your heart you naturally express your wishes in law and sweep away all opposition." Censorship is thus a kind of social instinct. As caring and responsible citizens of society, *especially* good and decent citizens of a good and decent society, we are likely to want *many* results with all our hearts. We want security, we want freedom from fear, we want order, civility, racial and religious tolerance, we want the well-being of our children. We want these things with all our hearts, and when others express opinions that seem to threaten these aspirations, who can blame us for being tempted to express our wishes in law and sweep away the opposition? It is perfectly logical. And that is what, at bottom, freedom of speech is all about.

3   Over the course of roughly the last 50 years the U.S. Supreme Court has set our nation on a remarkable experiment, often construing the First Amendment in a manner that strenuously defies the natural and logical impulse to censor. In scores of decisions, the Supreme Court has interpreted the First Amendment in a manner that to most of the world seems positively radical. Those decisions are numerous and cover a vast and various terrain, but consider some highlights. Americans have the right to:

- Desecrate the national flag as a symbol of protest.
- Burn the cross as an expression of racial bigotry and hatred.

- Espouse the violent overthrow of the government as long as it is mere abstract advocacy and not an immediate incitement to violence.

- Traffic in sexually explicit erotica as long as it does not meet a rigorous definition of "hard core" obscenity.

- Defame public officials and public figures with falsehoods provided they are not published with knowledge of their falsity or reckless disregard for the truth.

- Disseminate information invading personal privacy if the revelation is deemed "newsworthy."

- Engage in countless other forms of expression that would be outlawed in many nations but are regarded as constitutionally protected here.

4   Such First Amendment decisions reject the impulse to censor; they are therefore striking as legal doctrines. Perhaps more striking, however, is that these decisions have gained widespread currency within American culture as a whole. The Supreme Court is not alone in its commitment to the free-speech project. While undoubtedly any one decision will often be controversial with the public, which may be deeply divided on topics such as flag-burning or sex on the Internet, on balance what is extraordinary about the evolution of freedom of speech in America over the last 50 years is that it has taken such a strong hold on the American consciousness, a hold that seems to cut across party labels such as "Democrat" or "Republican" or ideological labels such as "liberal" or "conservative." On the Supreme Court itself, for example, justices with hardy conservative credentials such as Antonin Scalia or Clarence Thomas have often been as committed to expansive protection for freedom of speech as justices famous for their liberal views, such as William Brennan or Thurgood Marshall. Appointees of Republican presidents, such as Anthony Kennedy or David Souter, have been as stalwart as appointees of Democratic presidents, such as Stephen Breyer or Ruth Bader Ginsburg, in their articulation of strong free-speech doctrines. So too, in the political arena, views on free-speech issues often do not track along traditional party lines or classic ideological divisions.

5   This is not to say that in some simplistic sense everybody in America believes in freedom of speech, and certainly it is not to say that everybody in America believes that freedom of speech means the same thing. But it is to say that in a sense both deep and wide, "freedom of speech" is a value that has become powerfully internalized by the American polity. Freedom of speech is a core American belief, almost a kind of secular religious tenet, an article of constitutional faith.

6   How do we account for the modern American reverence for freedom of speech? Why is this value so solidly entrenched in our constitutional law, and why is it so

▶

widely embraced by the general public? Over the years many philosophers, historians, legal scholars and judges have offered theoretical justifications for strong protection of freedom of speech, and in these justifications we may also find explanatory clues.

7   An obvious starting point is the direct link between freedom of speech and vibrant democracy. Free speech is an indispensable tool of self-governance in a democratic society. Concurring in *Whitney v. California* (1927), Justice Louis Brandeis wrote that "freedom to think as you will and to speak as you think are means indispensable to the discovery and spread of political truth."

8   On a communal level, free speech facilitates majority rule. It is through talking that we encourage consensus, that we form a collective will. Whether the answers we reach are wise or foolish, free speech helps us ensure that the answers usually conform to what most people think. Americans who are optimists (and optimism is a quintessentially American characteristic) additionally believe that, over the long run, free speech actually *improves* our political decision-making. Just as Americans generally believe in free markets in economic matters, they generally believe in free markets when it comes to ideas, and this includes politics. In the long run the best test of intelligent political policy is its power to gain acceptance at the ballot box.

9   On an individual level, speech is a means of participation, the vehicle through which individuals debate the issues of the day, cast their votes, and actively join in the processes of decision-making that shape the polity. Free speech serves the individual's right to join the political fray, to stand up and be counted, to be an active player in the democracy, not a passive spectator.

10   Freedom of speech is also an essential contributor to the American belief in government confined by a system of checks and balances, operating as a restraint on tyranny, corruption and ineptitude. For much of the world's history, governments, following the impulse described by Justice Holmes, have presumed to play the role of benevolent but firm censor, on the theory that the wise governance of men proceeds from the wise governance of their opinions. But the United States was founded on the more cantankerous revolutionary principles of John Locke, who taught that under the social compact sovereignty always rests with the people, who never surrender their natural right to protest, or even revolt, when the state exceeds the limits of legitimate authority. Speech is thus a means of "people-power," through which the people may ferret out corruption and discourage tyrannical excesses.

11   Counter-intuitively, influential American voices have also often argued that robust protection of freedom of speech, *including speech advocating crime and revolution,* actually works to make the country more stable, increasing rather than decreasing our ability to maintain law and order. Again the words of Justice

Brandeis in *Whitney v. California* are especially resonant, with his admonition that the framers of the Constitution "knew that order cannot be secured merely through fear of punishment for its infraction; that it is hazardous to discourage thought, hope and imagination; that fear breeds repression; that repression breeds hate; that hate menaces stable government; that the path of safety lies in the opportunity to discuss freely supposed grievances and proposed remedies; and that the fitting remedy for evil counsels is good ones." If a society as wide-open and pluralistic as America is not to explode from festering tensions and conflicts, there must be valves through which citizens with discontent may blow off steam. In America we have come to accept the wisdom that openness fosters resiliency, that peaceful protest displaces more violence than it triggers, and that free debate dissipates more hate than it stirs.

12   The link between speech and democracy certainly provides some explanation for the American veneration of free speech, but not an entirely satisfying or complete one. For there are many flourishing democracies in the world, but few of them have adopted either the constitutional law or the cultural traditions that support free speech as expansively as America does. Moreover, much of the vast protection we provide to expression in America seems to bear no obvious connection to politics or the democratic process at all. Additional explanation is required.

13   Probably the most celebrated attempt at explanation is the "marketplace of ideas" metaphor, a notion that is most famously associated with Holmes' great dissent in *Abrams,* in which he argued that "the best test of truth is the power of the thought to get itself accepted in the competition of the market." The marketplace of ideas metaphor does not posit that truth *will* emerge from the free trade in ideas, at least not instantly. That would be asking too much. It merely posits that free trade in ideas is the best *test* of truth, in much the same way that those who believe in laissez-faire economic theory argue that over the long haul free economic markets are superior to command-and-control economies. The American love of the marketplace of ideas metaphor stems in no small part from our irrepressible national optimism, the American "constitutional faith" that, given long enough, good will conquer evil. As long as this optimism is not blind naiveté, but is rather a motive force that encourages us to keep the faith in the long view of history, it can be a self-fulfilling prophecy. Just as we often have nothing to fear but fear, hope is often our best hope. Humanity may be fallible, and truth illusive, but the hope of humanity lies in its faith in progress. The marketplace metaphor reminds us to take the long view. Americans like to believe, and largely *do* believe, that truth has a stubborn and incorrigible persistence. Cut down again and again, truth will still not be extinguished. Truth will out, it will be rediscovered and rejuvenated. It will prevail.

▶

14   The connection of freedom of speech to self-governance and the appeal of the marketplace of ideas metaphor still, however, do not tell it all. Freedom of speech is linked not merely to such grandiose ends as the service of the democracy or the search for truth. Freedom of speech has value on a more personal and individual level. Freedom of speech is part of the human personality itself, a value intimately intertwined with human autonomy and dignity. In the words of Justice Thurgood Marshall in the 1974 case *Procunier v. Martinez*, "The First Amendment serves not only the needs of the polity but also those of the human spirit—a spirit that demands self-expression."

15   Many Americans embrace freedom of speech for the same reasons they embrace other aspects of individualism. Freedom of speech is the right to defiantly, robustly and irreverently speak one's mind just because it is one's mind. Freedom of speech is thus bonded in special and unique ways to the human capacity to think, imagine and create. Conscience and consciousness are the sacred precincts of mind and soul. Freedom of speech is intimately linked to freedom of thought, to that central capacity to reason and wonder, hope and believe, that largely defines our humanity.

16   If these various elements of our culture do in combination provide some insight into why freedom of speech exerts such a dominating presence on the American legal and cultural landscape, they do not by any means come close to explaining the intense and seemingly never-ending legal and cultural debates over the *limits* on freedom of speech.

17   There *are* limits. The major labor of modern First Amendment law is to articulate the points at which those limits are reached. This ongoing process is often contentious and difficult, and no one simple legal formula or philosophical principle has yet been discovered that is up to the trick of making the job easy. Americans thus continue to debate in political forums and litigate in legal forums such issues as the power of society to censor offensive speech to protect children, the power to arrest speakers spreading violent or hateful propaganda for fear that it will foment crime or terrorism, the permissibility of banning speech that defeats protection of intellectual property, the propriety of curbing speech to shelter personal reputation and privacy, the right to restrict political contributions and expenditures to reduce the influence of money on the political process, and countless other free-speech conflicts.

18   Yet while the country continues to struggle mightily to define the limits and continues to debate vigorously the details, there is surprisingly little struggle and debate over the core of the faith. Americans truly *do* embrace the central belief that freedom of thought, conscience and expression are numinous values, linked to our defining characteristics as human beings. While limits must exist, American culture and law approach such limits with abiding caution and skepticism, embracing freedom of speech as a value of transcendent constitutional importance.

↳ <mark>3.6</mark> **Writing**

Analyzing "Speech Overview"

In his essay "Speech Overview" (3.5, p. 80), Rodney A. Smolla explains why, compared to most countries, the United States places so much value on freedom of speech. For this writing assignment, list as many explanations as you can find in Smolla's essay for Americans' devotion to free speech.

The Impact of the First Amendment on an International Treaty

▲ One hundred and thirty-five countries, including the United States, ratified the United Nations Geneva Convention on the elimination of racial discrimination in the late 1960s that specified the steps members would perform to prevent racial injustice. However, the United States had reservations about the convention based on the freedom of speech clause of the First Amendment. What do you think those reservations might have been? ChomPoo019/Shutterstock

International Convention on the Elimination of All Forms of Racial Discrimination

The document below is an excerpt from the United Nations Geneva Convention, approved in 1969, that specifies what steps the countries that sign the agreement will perform to eliminate racial discrimination. Be sure to spend some time previewing before you dive into the document. (If you need more information on previewing, go to Previewing a Text [20.2, p. 575].)

The entire document can be found on the United Nations Human Rights website. If you want to read it, just type the title below into your browser. (If these search terms do not work, there is a list of URLs available at https://bit.ly/33IIHtf.)

International Convention on the Elimination of All Forms of Racial Discrimination

Adopted and opened for signature and ratification by General Assembly resolution 2106(XX) of 21 December 1965

Entry into force 4 January 1969, in accordance with Article 19

1 The States Parties to this Convention,

2 Considering that the Charter of the United Nations is based on the principles of the dignity and equality inherent in all human beings, and that all Member States have pledged themselves to take joint and separate action, in co-operation with the Organization, for the achievement of one of the purposes of the United Nations which is to promote and encourage universal respect for and observance of human rights and fundamental freedoms for all, without distinction as to race, sex, language or religion,

3 Considering that the Universal Declaration of Human Rights proclaims that all human beings are born free and equal in dignity and rights and that everyone is entitled to all the rights and freedoms set out therein, without distinction of any kind, in particular as to race, colour or national origin,

4 Considering that all human beings are equal before the law and are entitled to equal protection of the law against any discrimination and against any incitement to discrimination,

5   Considering that the United Nations has condemned colonialism and all practices of segregation and discrimination associated therewith, in whatever form and wherever they exist, and that the Declaration on the Granting of Independence to Colonial Countries and Peoples of 14 December 1960 (General Assembly resolution 1514 (XV)) has affirmed and solemnly proclaimed the necessity of bringing them to a speedy and unconditional end,

6   Considering that the United Nations Declaration on the Elimination of All Forms of Racial Discrimination of 20 November 1963 (General Assembly resolution 1904 (XVIII)) solemnly affirms the necessity of speedily eliminating racial discrimination throughout the world in all its forms and manifestations and of securing understanding of and respect for the dignity of the human person,

7   Convinced that any doctrine of superiority based on racial differentiation is scientifically false, morally condemnable, socially unjust and dangerous, and that there is no justification for racial discrimination, in theory or in practice, anywhere,

8   Reaffirming that discrimination between human beings on the grounds of race, colour or ethnic origin is an obstacle to friendly and peaceful relations among nations and is capable of disturbing peace and security among peoples and the harmony of persons living side by side even within one and the same State,

9   Convinced that the existence of racial barriers is repugnant to the ideals of any human society,

10   Alarmed by manifestations of racial discrimination still in evidence in some areas of the world and by governmental policies based on racial superiority or hatred, such as policies of apartheid, segregation or separation,

11   Resolved to adopt all necessary measures for speedily eliminating racial discrimination in all its forms and manifestations, and to prevent and combat racist doctrines and practices in order to promote understanding between races and to build an international community free from all forms of racial segregation and racial discrimination,

12   Bearing in mind the Convention concerning Discrimination in respect of Employment and Occupation adopted by the International Labour Organisation in 1958, and the Convention against Discrimination in Education adopted by the United Nations Educational, Scientific and Cultural Organization in 1960,

13   Desiring to implement the principles embodied in the United Nations Declaration on the Elimination of All Forms of Racial Discrimination and to secure the earliest adoption of practical measures to that end,

▶

Have agreed as follows:

Article 1

Part I

1. In this Convention, the term "racial discrimination" shall mean any distinction, exclusion, restriction or preference based on race, colour, descent, or national or ethnic origin which has the purpose or effect of nullifying or impairing the recognition, enjoyment or exercise, on an equal footing, of human rights and fundamental freedoms in the political, economic, social, cultural or any other field of public life.

2. This Convention shall not apply to distinctions, exclusions, restrictions or preferences made by a State Party to this Convention between citizens and non-citizens.

3. Nothing in this Convention may be interpreted as affecting in any way the legal provisions of States Parties concerning nationality, citizenship or naturalization, provided that such provisions do not discriminate against any particular nationality.

4. Special measures taken for the sole purpose of securing adequate advancement of certain racial or ethnic groups or individuals requiring such protection as may be necessary in order to ensure such groups or individuals equal enjoyment or exercise of human rights and fundamental freedoms shall not be deemed racial discrimination, provided, however, that such measures do not, as a consequence, lead to the maintenance of separate rights for different racial groups and that they shall not be continued after the objectives for which they were taken have been achieved.

Article 2

1. States Parties condemn racial discrimination and undertake to pursue by all appropriate means and without delay a policy of eliminating racial discrimination in all its forms and promoting understanding among all races, and, to this end:

   (a) Each State Party undertakes to engage in no act or practice of racial discrimination against persons, groups of persons or institutions and to ensure that all public authorities and public institutions, national and local, shall act in conformity with this obligation;

   (b) Each State Party undertakes not to sponsor, defend or support racial discrimination by any persons or organizations;

(c) Each State Party shall take effective measures to review governmental, national and local policies, and to amend, rescind or nullify any laws and regulations which have the effect of creating or perpetuating racial discrimination wherever it exists;

(d) Each State Party shall prohibit and bring to an end, by all appropriate means, including legislation as required by circumstances, racial discrimination by any persons, group or organization;

(e) Each State Party undertakes to encourage, where appropriate, integrationist multiracial organizations and movements and other means of eliminating barriers between races, and to discourage anything which tends to strengthen racial division.

2. States Parties shall, when the circumstances so warrant, take, in the social, economic, cultural and other fields, special and concrete measures to ensure the adequate development and protection of certain racial groups or individuals belonging to them, for the purpose of guaranteeing them the full and equal enjoyment of human rights and fundamental freedoms. These measures shall in no case entail as a consequence the maintenance of unequal or separate rights for different racial groups after the objectives for which they were taken have been achieved.

Article 3

States Parties particularly condemn racial segregation and apartheid and undertake to prevent, prohibit and eradicate all practices of this nature in territories under their jurisdiction.

Article 4

States Parties condemn all propaganda and all organizations which are based on ideas or theories of superiority of one race or group of persons of one colour or ethnic origin, or which attempt to justify or promote racial hatred and discrimination in any form, and undertake to adopt immediate and positive measures designed to eradicate all incitement to, or acts of, such discrimination and, to this end, with due regard to the principles embodied in the Universal Declaration of Human Rights and the rights expressly set forth in article 5 of this Convention, inter alia:

(a) Shall declare an offence punishable by law all dissemination of ideas based on racial superiority or hatred, incitement to racial discrimination, as well as all acts of violence or incitement to such acts against any race or group

▶

of persons of another colour or ethnic origin, and also the provision of any assistance to racist activities, including the financing thereof;

(b) Shall declare illegal and prohibit organizations, and also organized and all other propaganda activities, which promote and incite racial discrimination, and shall recognize participation in such organizations or activities as an offence punishable by law;

(c) Shall not permit public authorities or public institutions, national or local, to promote or incite racial discrimination.

Article 5

In compliance with the fundamental obligations laid down in article 2 of this Convention, States Parties undertake to prohibit and to eliminate racial discrimination in all its forms and to guarantee the right of everyone, without distinction as to race, colour, or national or ethnic origin, to equality before the law, notably in the enjoyment of the following rights:

(a) The right to equal treatment before the tribunals and all other organs administering justice;

(b) The right to security of person and protection by the State against violence or bodily harm, whether inflicted by government officials or by any individual group or institution;

(c) Political rights, in particular the right to participate in elections-to vote and to stand for election-on the basis of universal and equal suffrage, to take part in the Government as well as in the conduct of public affairs at any level and to have equal access to public service;

(d) Other civil rights, in particular:

    i.   The right to freedom of movement and residence within the border of the State;

    ii.   The right to leave any country, including one's own, and to return to one's country;

    iii. The right to nationality;

    iv. The right to marriage and choice of spouse;

    v.   The right to own property alone as well as in association with others;

    vi. The right to inherit;

vii.   The right to freedom of thought, conscience and religion;

viii. The right to freedom of opinion and expression;

ix.   The right to freedom of peaceful assembly and association;

(e) Economic, social and cultural rights, in particular:

i.   The rights to work, to free choice of employment, to just and favourable conditions of work, to protection against unemployment, to equal pay for equal work, to just and favourable remuneration;

ii.   The right to form and join trade unions;

iii. The right to housing;

iv.   The right to public health, medical care, social security and social services;

v.   The right to education and training;

vi.   The right to equal participation in cultural activities;

(f) The right of access to any place or service intended for use by the general public, such as transport hotels, restaurants, cafes, theatres and parks.

Article 6

States Parties shall assure to everyone within their jurisdiction effective protection and remedies, through the competent national tribunals and other State institutions, against any acts of racial discrimination which violate his human rights and fundamental freedoms contrary to this Convention, as well as the right to seek from such tribunals just and adequate reparation or satisfaction for any damage suffered as a result of such discrimination.

Article 7

States Parties undertake to adopt immediate and effective measures, particularly in the fields of teaching, education, culture and information, with a view to combating prejudices which lead to racial discrimination and to promoting understanding, tolerance and friendship among nations and racial or ethnical groups, as well as to propagating the purposes and principles of the Charter of the United Nations, the Universal Declaration of Human Rights, the United Nations Declaration on the Elimination of All Forms of Racial Discrimination, and this Convention.

↳ **3.8** Activity

Responding to the International Convention on the Elimination of All Forms of Racial Discrimination

Working in your group, answer the following questions about the International Convention on the Elimination of All Forms of Racial Discrimination (3.7, p. 86).

1. What kind of a document is this?

2. Who were the originators of it?

3. What was its purpose?

4. The document uses a couple of terms that you may not be familiar with: *convention* and *states parties*. Can you figure out what these words mean in this text just by studying the context in which they are used?

5. Read Article 4 carefully. Write a summary of what it says parties are required to do under this article.

6. The spelling of the words *colour*, *favourable*, and *labour* may look strange to you. Can you figure out any reason they are spelled this way?

3.9 Reading

US Senate Response to the International Convention on Racism

The following document is an excerpt from the report of the Senate Foreign Relations Committee recommending that the United States sign the Geneva Convention on Racism with certain reservations.

The section of this document that is most central to the issue of free speech and the one you will be writing about in Explaining the Senate's Reservations (3.10, p. 96) is paragraphs 13 and 14, entitled "Reservations." Skim the background material (paragraphs 1 to 12) that precedes the "Reservations" section, and then read carefully the "Reservations" section.

(By the way, Senator Pell, who chaired the Foreign Relations Committee in 1994 and who wrote this report, is the same Senator Pell who proposed Pell Grants for students.)

US Senate Response to the International Convention on the Elimination of All Forms of Racial Discrimination

JUNE 2, 1994

Mr. Pell from the Committee on Foreign Relations
Submitted the Following Report

1   The Committee on Foreign Relations to which was referred the International Convention on the Elimination of All Forms of Racial Discrimination, adopted unanimously by the United Nations General Assembly on December 21, 1965, and signed on behalf of the United States on September 28, 1966, having considered the same, reports favorably thereon and recommends that the Senate give its advice and consent to ratification thereof subject to 3 reservations, 1 understanding, 1 declaration, and 1 proviso as set forth in this report and the accompanying resolution of ratification.

I. Purpose

2   The purpose of the Convention is to forbid racial and ethnic discrimination in all fields of public life. The Convention obligates States Parties to condemn racial discrimination, to undertake to pursue by all appropriate means a policy of eliminating racial discrimination in all of its forms and promoting racial understanding, and to guarantee the right of everyone, without distinction as to race, color, or national or ethnic origin, equality before the law in the enjoyment of a broad spectrum of legal, civil, political and economic rights.

3   The Convention also establishes a Committee on the Elimination of Racial Discrimination to oversee compliance, examine complaints concerning noncompliance made by one Party against another, and facilitate the settlement of disputes.

II. Background

4   The International Convention on the Elimination of All Forms of Racial Discrimination is one of several instruments designed by the international community to implement the human rights articles of the United Nations Charter. It was adopted unanimously by the United Nations General Assembly on December 21, 1965, and entered into force on January 4, 1969. Today, more than 135 States are party to the Convention.

5   The United States played a leading role in the formulation of the Convention. The United States signed the Convention on September 28, 1966. The Carter Administration transmitted the Convention to the Senate on February 23, 1978, with four proposed U.S. conditions. In his letter of transmittal, President Carter stated:

▶

The Racial Discrimination Convention deals with a problem which in the past has been identified with the United States; ratification of this treaty will attest to our enormous progress in this field in recent decades and our commitment to ending racial discrimination.

6 The Committee on Foreign Relations held hearings on this, and three other human rights treaties submitted by the Carter Administration, on November 14, 15, 16, and 19, 1979. Domestic and international events at the end of 1979, including the Soviet invasion of Afghanistan and the hostage crisis in Iran, prevented the Committee from moving to a vote on the Convention. Neither the Reagan nor Bush Administration supported ratification.

7 The Clinton Administration supports ratification of the Convention with a limited package of reservations, understandings, and declarations, similar to those suggested by the Carter Administration. In a letter to Senator Claiborne Pell, the Chairman of the Committee on Foreign Relations, dated April 26, 1994, Acting Secretary of State Strobe Talbott "writing on behalf of the President" urged the Committee "to give its prompt attention to and approval of this Convention."

8 In his letter, the Acting Secretary stated that ratification would "underscore our national commitment" to the promotion of values and principles embodied in the Convention, "enhance our ability to take effective steps within the international community to confront and combat the increasingly destructive discrimination which occurs against minorities around the world on national racial and ethnic grounds," and "permit" the United States to "play an even more active and effective role in the struggle against racial discrimination throughout the world."

9 The Convention is rooted in Western legal and ethical traditions. For the most part, its provisions are consistent with existing U.S. law.

* * *

III. Committee Action

10 On May 11, 1994, the Committee on Foreign Relations held a public hearing on the Convention and the Clinton Administration's proposed reservations, understandings, and declarations for ratification of the Convention. John Shattuck, Assistant Secretary of State for Democracy, Human Rights and Labor; Conrad K. Harper the Department of State's Legal Adviser; and Deval L. Patrick, Assistant Attorney General in the Civil Rights Division of the Department of Justice testified on behalf of the Administration. The following public witnesses also testified: Robert F. Drinan, S.J., Georgetown University Law Center, on behalf of the American Bar

Association; Mr. William T. Lake, Partner at Wilmer, Cutler & Pickering, on behalf of the International Human Rights Law Group; Mr. Wade Henderson, Director, Washington Bureau of the National Association for the Advancement of Colored People; and Dr. Robert C. Henderson, Secretary General, National Spiritual Assembly of the Baha'is of the United States.

11   The Committee met to consider the Convention on May 25, 1994. The Committee adopted by voice vote an amendment offered by Senator Helms to the proposed resolution of ratification. The Helms amendment added a proviso, to be included in the resolution of ratification but not in the instrument of ratification, clarifying the relationship of the Convention to the U.S. Constitution. The Committee then voted unanimously by voice vote to report favorably the Convention with a resolution of ratification to the Senate for its advice and consent.

12   The resolution of ratification reported by the Committee contains the reservations, understandings and declarations proposed by the Clinton Administration and the Helms proviso.

*   *   *

Reservations

13   *Freedom of Speech, Expression and Association.* Articles 4 and 7 of the Convention reflect the view that penalizing and prohibiting the dissemination of ideas based on racial superiority are key elements in the international struggle against racial discrimination. Article 4 requires States Parties not only to condemn all propaganda and organizations based on ideas or theories of racial superiority but also to "eradicate all incitement to, or acts of, such discrimination by: (a) punishing the dissemination of such ideas and acts of violence or incitement to acts of violence; (b) prohibiting organizations and activities promoting and inciting racial discrimination and violence; and (c) preventing public authorities or institutions from promoting or inciting racial discrimination." Article 7 requires the Parties to take measures to combat prejudice and promote tolerance in various fields.

14   The U.S. Government's ability to restrict or prohibit the expression of certain ideas is limited by the First Amendment, which protects opinions and speech without regard to content. In that Article 4 is inconsistent with the First Amendment and that the Committee on the Elimination of Racial Discrimination has given a broad interpretation to Article 4, the Administration recommends a reservation to make it clear that the United States accepts no obligations under this Convention which have the effect of limiting individual speech, expression, and association guaranteed by the Constitution and U.S. law.

↳ ## 3.10 Writing

Explaining the Senate's Reservations

Write a short paper—about a page—in which you explain the reservations that the US Senate registered in the document that can be found in the US Senate Response to the International Convention on the Elimination of All Forms of Racial Discrimination (3.9, p. 93). What were the government's reservations about the International Convention on the Elimination of All Forms of Racial Discrimination and why did it have those reservations?

Freedom of Speech versus Hate Speech

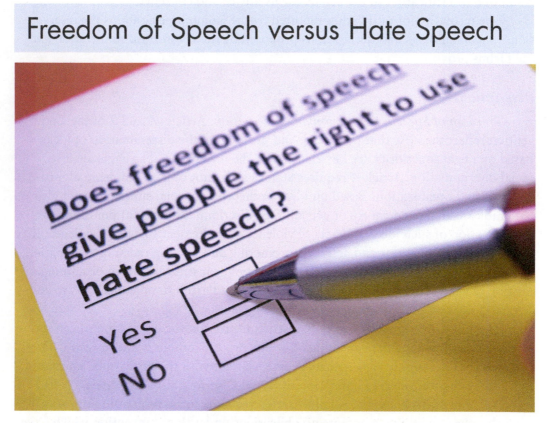

▲ Does freedom of speech mean that people have an automatic right to use hate speech without any consequences? Why or why not?   Yeexin Richelle/Shutterstock

3.11 Activity

Defining *Hate Speech*

Much of current discussion about freedom of speech revolves around what is referred to as *hate speech*. Working in your group, write a definition of *hate speech*, explaining what your group agrees it is and what it isn't. If you need a refresher on how to write a definition, see Strategies for Writing Definitions (18.18, p. 540). If your group can't agree on a single definition, write two.

3.12 Reading

Excerpt from *The Harm in Hate Speech*, Jeremy Waldron

The selection below is an excerpt from the beginning of Jeremy Waldron's book *The Harm in Hate Speech*. Be sure you take a few minutes to preview before you dive into reading it. (If you need a refresher on previewing, see Previewing a Text [20.2, p. 575].)

Excerpt from *The Harm in Hate Speech*

JEREMY WALDRON

Born in New Zealand in 1953, Jeremy Waldron now lives in New York City and teaches law at New York University School of Law. Since receiving his doctorate in philosophy at Oxford University in 1986, Waldron has taught legal and political philosophy at a number of prestigious schools including Berkeley, Princeton, Columbia, and Cornell. He is considered one of the world's leading legal and political philosophers and has published fifteen books on topics like equality, torture, property, and the theory of rights.

Dignity and Assurance

1   A man out walking with his seven-year-old son and his ten-year-old daughter turns a corner on a city street in New Jersey and is confronted with a sign. It says: "Muslims and 9/11! Don't serve them, don't speak to them, and don't let them in." The daughter says, "What does it mean, papa?" Her father, who is a Muslim—the whole family is Muslim—doesn't know what to say. He hurries the children on, hoping they will not come across any more of the signs. Other days he has seen them on the streets: a large photograph of Muslim children with the slogan "They are all called Osama," and a poster on the outside wall of his mosque which reads "Jihad Central."

▶

2   What is the point of these signs? We may describe them loosely as "hate speech," putting them in the same category as racist graffiti, burning crosses, and earlier generations of signage that sought to drive Jews out of fashionable areas in Florida with postings like "Jews and Dogs Prohibited." Calling these signs hate speech makes it sound as though their primary function is expressive—a way in which one or another racist or Islamophobic element "lets off steam," as it were, venting the hatred that is boiling up inside. But it is more than that. The signs send a number of messages. They send a message to the members of the minority denounced in the posters and pamphlets:

> Don't be fooled into thinking you are welcome here. The society around you may seem hospitable and nondiscriminatory, but the truth is that you are not wanted, and you and your families will be shunned, excluded, beaten, and driven out, whenever we can get away with it. We may have to keep a low profile right now. But don't get too comfortable. Remember what has happened to you and your kind in the past. Be afraid.

And they send a message to others in the community, who are not members of the minority under attack:

> We know some of you agree that these people are not wanted here. We know that some of you feel that they are dirty (or dangerous or criminal or terrorist). Know now that you are not alone. Whatever the government says, there are enough of us around to make sure these people are not welcome. There are enough of us around to draw attention to what these people are really like. Talk to your neighbors, talk to your customers. And above all, don't let any more of them in.

3   That's the point of these signs—that's the point of hate speech—to send these messages, to make these messages part of the permanent visible fabric of society so that, for the father walking with his children in our example, there will be no knowing when they will be confronted by one of these signs, and the children will ask him, "Papa, what does it mean?"

4   Many of my colleagues who are not Muslim say that they detest these signs and others like them (the racist slogans, the anti-Semitic signage). But they say that people like us, who detest hate speech, should learn to live with it. Less often, and only under pressure, they will say that the father in our example (who is not a First Amendment scholar) and his children and others like them should also learn to live with these signs. But they say that uneasily. They are more often confident in their own liberal bravado, calling attention to their ability to bear the pain of this vicious invective: "I hate what you say but I will defend to the death your right to say it."

5   That is the most important thing, in their opinion. The signs that we have been talking about, the bigoted invective that defiles our public environment, should be no concern of the law, they say. People are perfectly within their rights, publishing stuff like this. There is nothing to be regulated here, nothing for the law to concern itself with, nothing that a good society should use its legislative apparatus to suppress or disown. The people who are targeted should just learn to live with it. That is, they should learn to live their lives, conduct their business, and raise their children in the atmosphere that this sort of speech gives rise to.

6   I disagree. I think there is something socially and legally significant at stake. We can describe what is at stake in two ways. First, there is a sort of public good of inclusiveness that our society sponsors and that it is committed to. We are diverse in our ethnicity, our race, our appearance, and our religions. And we are embarked on a grand experiment of living and working together despite these sorts of differences. Each group must accept that the society is not *just* for them; but it *is* for them too, along with all of the others. And each person, each member of each group, should be able to go about his or her business, with the assurance that there will be no need to face hostility, violence, discrimination, or exclusion by others. When this assurance is conveyed effectively, it is hardly noticeable; it is something on which everyone can rely, like the cleanness of the air they breathe or the quality of the water they drink from a fountain. This sense of security in the space we all inhabit is a public good, and in a good society it is something that we all contribute to and help sustain in an instinctive and almost unnoticeable way.

7   Hate speech undermines this public good, or it makes the task of sustaining it much more difficult than it would otherwise be. It does this not only by intimating discrimination and violence, but by reawakening living nightmares of what this society was like—or what other societies have been like—in the past. In doing so, it creates something like an environmental threat to social peace, a sort of slow-acting poison, accumulating here and there, word by word, so that eventually it becomes harder and less natural for even the good-hearted members of the society to play their part in maintaining this public good.

8   The second way of describing what's at stake looks at it from the point of view of those who are meant to benefit from the assurance that is thrown in question by the hate speech. In a sense we are all supposed to benefit. But for the members of vulnerable minorities, minorities who in the recent past have been hated or despised by others within the society, the assurance offers a confirmation of their membership: they, too, are members of society in good standing; they have what it takes to interact on a straightforward basis with others around here, in public, on the streets, in the shops, in business, and to be treated—along with everyone else—as proper objects of society's

▶

protection and concern. This basic social standing, I call their *dignity*. A person's dignity is not just some Kantian aura. It is their social standing, the fundamentals of basic reputation that entitle them to be treated as equals in the ordinary operations of society. Their dignity is something they can rely on—in the best case implicitly and without fuss, as they live their lives, go about their business, and raise their families.

9   The publication of hate speech is calculated to undermine this. Its aim is to compromise the dignity of those at whom it is targeted, both in their own eyes and in the eyes of other members of society. And it sets out to make the establishment and upholding of their dignity—in the sense that I have described—much more difficult. It aims to besmirch the basics of their reputation, by associating ascriptive characteristics like ethnicity, or race, or religion with conduct or attributes that should disqualify someone from being treated as a member of society in good standing.

10   As the book goes on, we will look at a number of examples of this, of the way in which hate speech is both a calculated affront to the dignity of vulnerable members of society and a calculated assault on the public good of inclusiveness. I offer a characterization of these concerns at this early stage in order to give readers a sense of what I think is at stake in the discussion of hate speech, a sense of what legislation limiting it or regulating it might be trying to safeguard. The case will be made in detail as the book goes on, and various objections confronted and answered.

11   The argument is not easy, and many readers will be inclined to dismiss it at the outset, because they just "know" that these sorts of publications must be protected as free speech and that we must defend to the death their authors' right to publish them. Most people in the United States assume that that's where the argument must end up, and they are puzzled (not to say disappointed) that I am starting off down this road. I think it is a road worth exploring, even if no one's mind is changed. It's always good to get clear about the best case that can be made for a position one opposes.

↳ | **3.13** | **Writing**

Summarizing the Excerpt from *The Harm in Hate Speech*

You probably have a sense of what it means to write a summary: You write something short that summarizes the main content of something longer that you have read.

For this assignment, try your hand at summary writing. After you've read the excerpt from *The Harm in Hate Speech* (3.12, p. 97) and perhaps made some notes, write a short paper—a half page would be plenty—in which you summarize the text.

3.14 Activity

Analyzing Summaries

Your group will receive a selection of the summaries that the class wrote for summarizing the excerpt from *The Harm in Hate Speech* (3.13, p. 100). Your group's task is to read over these summaries and make two lists: one of what you found that worked well in one or more of the summaries and one of the weaknesses or mistakes you found in one or more of the summaries. After a half hour or so, the groups will report out on their lists.

3.15 Reading

"'Freedom' Is Best Response to White Supremacy Hatemongers," Gene Policinski

The excerpt below is taken from the website of the Newseum Institute, an interactive museum located in Washington, DC, that is dedicated to helping the public better understand the importance of a free press and the First Amendment. The Newseum is a 501(c)(3) nonprofit organization funded by private individuals, corporations, and foundations.

Be sure you take a few minutes to preview before you dive into reading it. (If you need a refresher on previewing, see Previewing a Text [20.2, p. 575].)

"Freedom" Is Best Response to White Supremacy Hatemongers

GENE POLICINSKI

Gene Policinski is the president and chief operating officer of the Newseum Institute and the chief operating officer of the Freedom Forum Institute (the principal funder of the Newseum) and the Institute's First Amendment Center. He graduated with a degree in journalism from Ball State University in 1972. He was a founding editor of *USA Today* in 1982; has worked in print, television, radio, and online; and is an adjunct faculty member at Winthrop University in South Carolina. He is a strong proponent of a free press and writes and speaks regularly on topics related to journalism ethics, reporting, and diversity in the newsroom. He was also a contributing author to the book *Whistleblowers, Leaks and the Media*, published in 2014.

POSTED ON AUGUST 15, 2017

1   Let them march in Charlottesville. Let them speak.   ▶

2   Hate-propagating neo-Nazis and bottom-dwelling white supremacists—the dregs of our open society—have and should have First Amendment rights to speak and march in public.

3   We need to see them for what they are: a disappointing collection of the disaffected; some parading around in silly costumes, often ignorant of the real meaning and history of the symbols they display, carrying torches meant as much to intimidate as to illuminate.

4   We need to hear them for what they say: advocacy of discredited ideas involving racial purity and intolerance, couched in misrepresentations of U.S. history and the American experience.

5   We need to understand them for what they are: betrayers of what President Lincoln called "our better angels," of the principles of equality, justice and the rule of law—painfully worked out over time and sometimes imperfectly at the outset, through the self-correcting processes of speaking and writing freely, of assembling and petitioning peaceably for change.

6   Granted, it is tempting after events like those of last weekend to take another view. While there is only a small fraction of our fellow citizens who hold such repellent views on white supremacy and racial hatred, there is the very real danger that a few more, and then a few more than that, will be seduced by false pretentions and misleading presentations of patriotism, economic security and personal safety.

7   History tells us of the rise at various times in our nation of groups preaching hate and bigotry and violence, using their rights of speech, press and assembly to inflame rather than inform, incite rather than inspire, and indoctrinate rather than educate. Nativists, the Ku Klux Klan, neo-Nazis and others at various times have used fear, prejudice and ignorance to flourish and gain public accommodation or support—sometimes for decades—before crawling back under the social rocks from whence they came.

8   It's tempting to believe that if only such domestic terrorists were silenced by government, their views would dissipate; that "out of sight" truly would mean "out of mind." But such censoring, suppressing and silencing is a betrayal of our core principles—along with being ineffective and often counterproductive. If it ever was possible, never mind desirable, to counter such anti-American sentiments by silencing its proponents, it is now a lost cause in the Age of the Internet and social media. A few provocative tweets or a viral video can reach a global audience that dwarfs anything possible in earlier human history.

9   But, the desire "to do something" when we witness demonstrations of hate and regressive ideologies can tempt us to take actions that ultimately erode our freedoms.

10   More than a decade ago, when the hatemongering Westboro Baptist Church group began appearing at the funerals of U.S. military personnel who died in combat, the tiny assembly gained far more visibility than it could have purchased otherwise through its well-publicized fights with municipal authorities seeking to shut down or shunt to remote locations its offensive messages about gays and others.

11   Defenders of free expression sometimes are the target of those who espouse what the late First Amendment advocate Nat Hentoff described as *Free Speech for Me, but not for Thee.*" The ACLU of Virginia is being vehemently attacked online for representing in court the white supremacist group that successfully challenged the Charlottesville government's initial decision to ban the group from gathering in a centrally-located city park, in favor of a more isolated park about a mile away. What other stand should the ACLU, which has been protecting the free speech rights of opposing groups for nearly a century, have taken?

12   The First Amendment protects us all from government actions based solely on our views or the content of our expression. There is no national authority on what's right or acceptable—no "national nanny" to rap knuckles over offensive, disgusting or repugnant views. U.S. District Judge Glen Conrad, in rejecting the government ban on the alt-right rally in Charlottesville, was not validating the views of those who gathered. Rather, Conrad was upholding the nation's commitment to free speech, and the view of the nation's founders that their descendants would, over time and when left to freely discuss and consider all options, arrive at the best solution for the greatest number of people.

13   Hate speech, racial prejudice and policies rooted in white supremacy beliefs were accepted in much of the nation for decades, until confronted by a modern civil rights movement that finally touched a nation's conscience—and altered its law books—by using all five of the First Amendment freedoms. And the right of free expression stood strong to counter public officials of that era who also cited "public safety" as justification to oppose or arrest those calling for racial justice.

14   We don't want to hand our government, at any level, the authority to restrain free expression on the mere supposition that it may provoke violence—or worse, because many or even most in a locale oppose it. Over time, we have developed and been well-served by legal doctrines narrowly defining when officials can act to suppress speeches, rallies or marches; doctrines rooted in specific evidence of real, immediate threats to public safety. From schools to sidewalks, those laws focus applying restrictions on conduct rather than suppressing the ideas behind those actions.

15   Let's concede that this system is not neat and tidy, nor effective in all cases. It requires both great effort and great restraint on the part of police and elected officials charged with public safety.

▶

16   We are debating the limits of free expression in other areas of life today. On college campuses, some argue that their right to be "free from" exposure to some views is greater than the freedom for others to express those views. There is also much debate over the extent to which social media platforms and the internet should now be considered "public spaces" rather than private property, and thus subject to the First Amendment. And the speed and rapidity of the web challenges a legal structure built around communications that moved much more slowly, and less pervasively.

17   In the wake of the tragedy in Charlottesville, we must remain committed to our core belief that we're better off—and ultimately, more secure—when we may freely discuss, debate and decide.

18   For those who repudiate hate groups and the ugly messages they work to spread, let's keep in mind another adage of the First Amendment community: "Sunlight is the best disinfectant."

↳ **3.16** Activity

Listing Hate Speech Arguments

You've now read two different arguments about restricting hate speech: one that argues that the public good requires that we limit hate speech (Excerpt from *The Harm in Hate Speech* [3.12, p. 97]) and the other that argues that freedom of speech should apply to all speech, even speech we find hateful ("'Freedom' Is Best Response to White Supremacy Hatemongers" [3.15, p. 101]).

Working in your group, list the main arguments each of the two essays makes to support its position. In addition, add any arguments the group comes up with that were not mentioned in either essay. Be prepared to report out on your lists.

↳ **3.17** Writing

Alternative Responses to Hate Speech

In the articles you have read, the remedy often proposed for hate speech has been to pass a law forbidding it. For this writing assignment, assume that passing a law is not an option.

Write a short essay—about a page—in which you discuss other possible responses to hate speech. How might a society that strongly believes in freedom of speech take steps other than passing laws to reduce the frequency of such speech or to lessen its effects?

Free Speech on Campus

▲ The image above shows the Free Speech Movement Café at the University of California's Berkeley Campus. Universities and colleges take pride in encouraging students to speak openly, to express differing points of view, and to evaluate and argue for and against positions they do not agree with. Students are often at the forefront of political movements. Should there be limits on what students can say, write, or do on campus? Allstar Picture Library/Alamy

3.18 Activity

What Are Reasonable Limits on Students' Freedom of Speech?

The American Association of University Professors (AAUP) offers two statements that seem to sum up the legal and constitutional status of students' free speech rights in the classroom:

1. Scholars disagree on whether students have a legal right to academic freedom at all.

2. Courts discuss student academic freedom most commonly as some type of First Amendment right, although few have addressed the issue directly. However, many courts have used language and reasoning that seems to support at least some kind of First Amendment right of academic freedom for students.

According to the AAUP, we are not going to find clarity about the free speech rights of students in classrooms. In this activity, working in your group, come up with a list of restrictions or limits on student speech that your group thinks would be reasonable.

3.19 Reading

AAUP Statement "On Freedom of Expression and Campus Speech Codes"

The American Association of University Professors (AAUP) is an organization of about 47,000 faculty on over 500 campuses. The AAUP's mission is "to define fundamental professional values and standards for higher education, advance the rights of academics, particularly as those rights pertain to academic freedom and shared governance, and promote the interests of higher education teaching and research."

The text that follows is the AAUP's policy statement on speech codes, rules that some colleges have adopted to protect students from language that offends because it is racist, sexist, homophobic, or ethnically demeaning. Be sure you take a few minutes to preview before you dive into reading it. (If you need a refresher on previewing, see Previewing a Text [20.2, p. 575].)

On Freedom of Expression and Campus Speech Codes

AAUP STATEMENT

1   Freedom of thought and expression is essential to any institution of higher learning. Universities and colleges exist not only to transmit knowledge. Equally, they interpret, explore, and expand that knowledge by testing the old and proposing the new. This mission guides learning outside the classroom quite as much as in class, and often inspires vigorous debate on those social, economic, and political issues that arouse the strongest passions. In the process, views will be expressed that may seem to many wrong, distasteful, or offensive. Such is the nature of freedom to sift and winnow ideas.

2   On a campus that is free and open, no idea can be banned or forbidden. No viewpoint or message may be deemed so hateful or disturbing that it may not be expressed.

3   Universities and colleges are also communities, often of a residential character. Most campuses have recently sought to become more diverse, and more reflective of the larger community, by attracting students, faculty, and staff from groups that were historically excluded or underrepresented. Such gains as they have made are recent, modest, and tenuous. The campus climate can profoundly affect an institution's continued diversity. Hostility or intolerance to persons who differ from the majority (especially if seemingly condoned by the institution) may undermine the confidence of new members of the community. Civility is always fragile and can easily be destroyed.

4   In response to verbal assaults and use of hateful language, some campuses have felt it necessary to forbid the expression of racist, sexist, homophobic, or ethnically demeaning speech, along with conduct or behavior that harasses. Several reasons are offered in support of banning such expression. Individuals and groups that have been victims of such expression feel an understandable outrage. They claim that the academic progress of minority and majority alike may suffer if fears, tensions, and conflicts spawned by slurs and insults create an environment inimical to learning.

5   These arguments, grounded in the need to foster an atmosphere respectful of and welcoming to all persons, strike a deeply responsive chord in the academy. But, while we can acknowledge both the weight of these concerns and the thoughtfulness of those persuaded of the need for regulation, rules that ban or punish speech based upon its content cannot be justified. An institution of higher learning fails to fulfill its mission if it asserts the power to proscribe ideas—and racial or ethnic slurs, sexist epithets, or homophobic insults almost always express ideas, however repugnant. Indeed, by proscribing any ideas, a university sets an example that profoundly disserves its academic mission.

6   Some may seek to defend a distinction between the regulation of the content of speech and the regulation of the manner (or style) of speech. We find this distinction untenable in practice because offensive style or opprobrious phrases may in fact have been chosen precisely for their expressive power. As the United States Supreme Court has said in the course of rejecting criminal sanctions for offensive words:

> [W]ords are often chosen as much for their emotive as their cognitive force. We cannot sanction the view that the Constitution, while solicitous of the cognitive content of individual speech, has little or no regard for that emotive function which, practically speaking, may often be the more important element of the overall message sought to be communicated.

▶

The line between substance and style is thus too uncertain to sustain the pressure that will inevitably be brought to bear upon disciplinary rules that attempt to regulate speech.

7   Proponents of speech codes sometimes reply that the value of emotive language of this type is of such a low order that, on balance, suppression is justified by the harm suffered by those who are directly affected, and by the general damage done to the learning environment. Yet a college or university sets a perilous course if it seeks to differentiate between high-value and low-value speech, or to choose which groups are to be protected by curbing the speech of others. A speech code unavoidably implies an institutional competence to distinguish permissible expression of hateful thought from what is proscribed as thoughtless hate.

8   Institutions would also have to justify shielding some, but not other, targets of offensive language—proscribing uncomplimentary references to sexual but not to political preference, to religious but not to philosophical creed, or perhaps even to some but not to other religious affiliations. Starting down this path creates an even greater risk that groups not originally protected may later demand similar solicitude—demands the institution that began the process of banning some speech is ill equipped to resist. Distinctions of this type are neither practicable nor principled; their very fragility underscores why institutions devoted to freedom of thought and expression ought not to adopt an institutionalized coercion of silence.

9   Moreover, banning speech often avoids consideration of means more compatible with the mission of an academic institution by which to deal with incivility, intolerance, offensive speech, and harassing behavior:

1.   Institutions should adopt and invoke a range of measures that penalize conduct and behavior, rather than speech—such as rules against defacing property, physical intimidation or harassment, or disruption of campus activities. All members of the campus community should be made aware of such rules, and administrators should be ready to use them in preference to speech-directed sanctions.

2.   Colleges and universities should stress the means they use best—to educate—including the development of courses and other curricular and co-curricular experiences designed to increase student understanding and to deter offensive or intolerant speech or conduct. These institutions should, of course, be free (indeed encouraged) to condemn manifestations of intolerance and discrimination, whether physical or verbal.

3.   The governing board and the administration have a special duty not only to set an outstanding example of tolerance, but also to challenge boldly and condemn immediately serious breaches of civility.

4. Members of the faculty, too, have a major role; their voices may be critical in condemning intolerance, and their actions may set examples for understanding, making clear to their students that civility and tolerance are hallmarks of educated men and women.

5. Student-personnel administrators have in some ways the most demanding role of all, for hate speech occurs most often in dormitories, locker rooms, cafeterias, and student centers. Persons who guide this part of campus life should set high standards of their own for tolerance and should make unmistakably clear the harm that uncivil or intolerant speech inflicts.

10 To some persons who support speech codes, measures like these—relying as they do on suasion rather than sanctions—may seem inadequate. But freedom of expression requires toleration of "ideas we hate," as Justice Holmes put it. The underlying principle does not change because the demand is to silence a hateful speaker, or because it comes from within the academy. Free speech is not simply an aspect of the educational enterprise to be weighed against other desirable ends. It is the very precondition of the academic enterprise itself.

↳ **3.20** **Writing**

Summarizing AAUP Statement "On Freedom of Expression and Campus Speech Codes"

Write a short paper—a page or less—in which you summarize the AAUP statement on speech codes (3.19, p. 106). If you need to refresh your understanding of what makes a good summary, take a look at What Makes a Good Summary? (18.23, p. 547).

3.21 **Reading**

Two College Policies on Controversial Speakers

Below are excerpts from policy statements regarding freedom of speech and controversial speakers from the University of Colorado and the University of Chicago. If you want to read the entire policies, type the titles into your browser. (If these search terms do not work, there is a list of URLs available at https://bit.ly/33IIHtf.)

Be sure you take a few minutes to preview before you dive into reading them. (If you need a refresher on previewing, see Previewing a Text [20.2, p. 575].)

Policy 1: University of Colorado Legal Origins, Guiding Principles, and Principles of Ethical Behavior

UNIVERSITY OF COLORADO

Policy 1.D: Freedom of Expression

1   *1.D.1*   As required by Regent Law, the University of Colorado shall protect the freedom of expression of its students, faculty, and staff on campus and in its programs and activities.

2   *1.D.2*   This policy addresses speech that occurs on University of Colorado campuses, but not speech occurring in the course of research or in the classroom instructional environment. Speech in research and teaching is governed by Regent Articles 5.D and 7.C.

3   *1.D.3*   Use of University Grounds, Buildings, and Facilities:

(A) No campus shall designate any area as a free speech zone or otherwise limit free expression to a predetermined and designated area of campus. Generally accessible outdoor areas on the campuses shall be available to members of the university community for free expression in accordance with campus policies authorized by this section.

(B) The president of the university shall adopt, in accordance with university policy and applicable external law, regulations and procedures governing the use of university grounds, buildings, and facilities not located upon any university campus.

(C) The chancellor of each campus shall adopt, in accordance with university policy and applicable external law, regulations and procedures governing the use of university grounds, buildings, and facilities on that campus.

    (1) The use of university grounds, buildings, and facilities shall be limited to members of the university community, except as the use by others is specifically authorized under regulations adopted in accordance with university policy and applicable law.

    (2) The use of university grounds, buildings, and facilities may be subject to requirements that govern the time, place, and manner of expression, including scheduling requirements, but all such requirements must be:

        (a) Reasonable;

        (b) Justified without reference to the content of the expression;

(c) Narrowly tailored to protect the university environment, prevent disruption of university activities, or serve another significant university interest;

(d) Leave open ample alternate channels for communication of the information or message.

(3) The use of university grounds, buildings, and facilities by members of the university community may be conditioned upon the payment of reasonable expenses incurred by the campus in hosting an event. Any such fees shall be determined based upon the campus's good faith estimate, based upon the application of objective criteria, of the actual expenses it shall incur in hosting an event. In no instance shall a campus assess any such expenses in a manner that is based upon disapproval of the substantive message that the speaker expresses.

(4) Nothing in this section grants members of the university community the right to materially disrupt previously scheduled or reserved activities occurring on university grounds, buildings, and facilities.

(D) **Freedom of Expression by University of Colorado Faculty**

(1) When engaged in teaching and research, faculty enjoy the associated rights and observe the associated responsibilities of academic freedom as expressed in Article 5, Part D.

(2) University faculty are members of our communities and members of a learned profession. When university faculty speak or write as citizens, not in furtherance of their university duties or in the course and scope of their university employment, on matters of political, academic, artistic, or social concern, the university shall not censor their expression, initiate disciplinary action against them, or otherwise subject the faculty members to adverse employment actions because it disapproves of the substance of their expression.

(3) When university faculty speak or write in their personal capacities, not in furtherance of their university duties or in the course and scope of their university employment, they must make every effort to indicate that their expression is their own and does not represent the opinion or position of the university.

▶

(4) The freedom of expression recognized in this section does not grant university faculty the right to refuse to perform official duties, to materially disrupt the university environment or university activities, or to disregard the standards of ethical conduct as expressed in Article 1, Part D, of the Laws of the Regents or Regent Policy 1.C.

(E) **Freedom of Expression by University of Colorado Staff**

(1) All staff of the university are members of our communities. When staff of the university speak or write in their personal capacities, not in furtherance of their university duties or in the course and scope of their university employment, on matters of political, academic, artistic, or social concern, the university shall not censor their expression, initiate disciplinary action against them, or otherwise subject the staff members to adverse employment actions because it disapproves of the substance of their expression.

(2) When staff of the university speak or write as citizens, they must make every effort to indicate that their expression is their own and does not represent the opinion or position of the university.

(3) The freedom of expression recognized in this section does not grant staff of the university the right to refuse to perform official duties, to materially disrupt the university environment or university activities, or to disregard the standards of ethical conduct as expressed in Article 1, Part D, of the Laws of the Regents or Regent Policy 1.C.

(F) **Freedom of Expression by University Students**

(1) When engaged in educational activities, university students enjoy the associated rights and observe the associated responsibilities of academic freedom as expressed in Article 7, Part C, of the Laws of the Regents.

(2) University students are members of our communities. When university students speak or write in their personal capacities on matters of political, academic, artistic, or social concern, not in furtherance of their studies or in the course of their academic duties, the university shall not censor their expression, initiate disciplinary action against them, or otherwise subject the students to adverse academic actions because it disapproves of the substance of their expression.

(3) The freedom of expression recognized in this section does not grant university students the right to materially disrupt the university environment or university activities or to disregard the standards of conduct as promulgated under Article 7, Part C, of the Laws of the Regents.

Report of the Committee on Freedom of Expression

UNIVERSITY OF CHICAGO

If you want to see the full statement, type the complete title above into your browser. (If these search terms do not work, there is a list of URLs available at https://bit.ly/33IlHtf.)

The Committee on Freedom of Expression at the University of Chicago was appointed in July 2014 by President Robert J. Zimmer and Provost Eric D. Isaacs "in light of recent events nationwide that have tested institutional commitments to free and open discourse." The Committee's charge was to draft a statement "articulating the University's overarching commitment to free, robust, and uninhibited debate and deliberation among all members of the University's community."

The Committee has carefully reviewed the University's history, examined events at other institutions, and consulted a broad range of individuals both inside and outside the University. This statement reflects the long-standing and distinctive values of the University of Chicago and affirms the importance of maintaining and, indeed, celebrating those values for the future.

1 From its very founding, the University of Chicago has dedicated itself to the preservation and celebration of the freedom of expression as an essential element of the University's culture. In 1902, in his address marking the University's decennial, President William Rainey Harper declared that "the principle of complete freedom of speech on all subjects has from the beginning been regarded as fundamental in the University of Chicago" and that "this principle can neither now nor at any future time be called in question."

2 Thirty years later, a student organization invited William Z. Foster, the Communist Party's candidate for President, to lecture on campus. This triggered a storm of protest from critics both on and off campus. To those who condemned the University for allowing the event, President Robert M. Hutchins responded that "our students . . . should have freedom to discuss any problem that presents itself." He insisted that the "cure" for ideas we oppose "lies through open discussion rather than through inhibition." On a later occasion, Hutchins added that "free inquiry is indispensable to the good life, that universities exist for the sake of such inquiry, [and] that without it they cease to be universities."

3 In 1968, at another time of great turmoil in universities, President Edward H. Levi, in his inaugural address, celebrated "those virtues which from the beginning and until now have characterized our institution." Central to the values of the

▶

University of Chicago, Levi explained, is a profound commitment to "freedom of inquiry." This freedom, he proclaimed, "is our inheritance."

4   More recently, President Hanna Holborn Gray observed that "education should not be intended to make people comfortable, it is meant to make them think. Universities should be expected to provide the conditions within which hard thought, and therefore strong disagreement, independent judgment, and the questioning of stubborn assumptions, can flourish in an environment of the greatest freedom."

5   The words of Harper, Hutchins, Levi, and Gray capture both the spirit and the promise of the University of Chicago. Because the University is committed to free and open inquiry in all matters, it guarantees all members of the University community the broadest possible latitude to speak, write, listen, challenge, and learn. Except insofar as limitations on that freedom are necessary to the functioning of the University, the University of Chicago fully respects and supports the freedom of all members of the University community "to discuss any problem that presents itself."

6   Of course, the ideas of different members of the University community will often and quite naturally conflict. But it is not the proper role of the University to attempt to shield individuals from ideas and opinions they find unwelcome, disagreeable, or even deeply offensive. Although the University greatly values civility, and although all members of the University community share in the responsibility for maintaining a climate of mutual respect, concerns about civility and mutual respect can never be used as a justification for closing off discussion of ideas, however offensive or disagreeable those ideas may be to some members of our community.

7   The freedom to debate and discuss the merits of competing ideas does not, of course, mean that individuals may say whatever they wish, wherever they wish. The University may restrict expression that violates the law, that falsely defames a specific individual, that constitutes a genuine threat or harassment, that unjustifiably invades substantial privacy or confidentiality interests, or that is otherwise directly incompatible with the functioning of the University. In addition, the University may reasonably regulate the time, place, and manner of expression to ensure that it does not disrupt the ordinary activities of the University. But these are narrow exceptions to the general principle of freedom of expression, and it is vitally important that these exceptions never be used in a manner that is inconsistent with the University's commitment to a completely free and open discussion of ideas.

8   In a word, the University's fundamental commitment is to the principle that debate or deliberation may not be suppressed because the ideas put forth are thought by some or even by most members of the University community to be offensive, unwise, immoral, or wrong-headed. It is for the individual members of the University community, not for the University as an institution, to make those judgments for themselves, and to act on those judgments not by seeking to suppress speech, but by openly and vigorously contesting the ideas that they oppose. Indeed, fostering the ability of members of the University community to engage in such debate and deliberation in an effective and responsible manner is an essential part of the University's educational mission.

9   As a corollary to the University's commitment to protect and promote free expression, members of the University community must also act in conformity with the principle of free expression. Although members of the University community are free to criticize and contest the views expressed on campus, and to criticize and contest speakers who are invited to express their views on campus, they may not obstruct or otherwise interfere with the freedom of others to express views they reject or even loathe. To this end, the University has a solemn responsibility not only to promote a lively and fearless freedom of debate and deliberation, but also to protect that freedom when others attempt to restrict it.

10   As Robert M. Hutchins observed, without a vibrant commitment to free and open inquiry, a university ceases to be a university. The University of Chicago's long-standing commitment to this principle lies at the very core of our University's greatness. That is our inheritance, and it is our promise to the future.

↳ **3.22** Activity

Evaluating Two College Policies on Controversial Speakers

You have just read the policy statements from the University of Colorado and the University of Chicago regarding the free speech rights of speakers in Two College Policies on Controversial Speakers (3.21, p. 110). Now, working in your group, answer the following questions about these two policy statements.

1. What are the major differences between the policies of the two schools?
2. Which statement does your group prefer?
3. Why?

    Be prepared to report out.

Bringing It All Together

▲ The people in this photo are exercising their right to express their opinions, in this case, against the rising tide of racism around the world. Should Americans have the right to march in the streets and protest when they do not like decisions made by federal or state governments? Or in solidarity with groups they support? Or against those they disagree with? Should students be able to hold sit-ins or other types of protest actions on campus?   Steve Parkins/Shutterstock

3.23 Real World Essay

Proposing a College Policy on Freedom of Speech

For this assignment, you will write an essay that is informed by your reading, discussions, and thinking about the topic in this reading/writing project as well as the additional information you have found through research.

Assignment. Imagine your campus has been experiencing considerable controversy about the issue of free speech. The administration has formed a task force of administrators, faculty, and students to develop a broad series of policies to address the problem. The task force has invited the college community to submit policy proposals to be included in a policy document, and you have decided to submit a proposal. You will first draft a policy for your college to address one free speech issue on campus, using articles you have researched. You will then write a three- to four-page essay defending your proposed policy.

- **Part 1: Write your proposed policy.** You are not going to try to write a complete "free speech" policy covering every aspect of the issue. That would require twenty or thirty pages—or more. Instead, you are going to focus on one issue involving free speech and write a short statement—no more than a page—of your proposed policy. If selected, your proposed policy would become part of a much larger document spelling out the college's policy on a multitude of free speech issues.

    Here are some example topics, but you can also come up with your own:

    - The adoption of a speech code to restrict hate speech
    - A policy on outside speakers who have controversial views
    - The rights of students to protest speakers they find offensive
    - The rights of students to protest limits on free speech
    - The rights of faculty speech in the classroom
    - Limits on what students can say in class
    - Limits on what students can write in their essays
    - Limits on the display of images, symbols, posters, or flags that may offend some students
    - Limits on sexist language
    - Students' right not to be exposed to statements (by other students? by their instructors?) that offend their deeply held beliefs

    Work hard in this "policy statement" to be precise, to define exactly what your proposed policy is allowing and what it is restricting.

- **Part 2: Research your topic.** Before you write the essay to defend your proposal, you will need to do a little research. Either in the library or online, locate three articles or books that discuss the free speech issue you are addressing. (If you would like some help with conducting this search, see Finding Sources Online [22.4, p. 626] and Finding Sources in the Library [22.5, p. 626].)

When you use Google to locate an article in a scholarly journal, you will often find that to read the article, you will need to pay a fee. You are not expected to do this. Instead, go to your library or to your library's website. There you will find that your library subscribes to a number of databases filled with scholarly articles. These are usually organized by subject matter. Select the one that seems most likely to cover the topic you're researching. In this case, the most likely databases are JSTOR, ProQuest Central, or Social Science Database.

Answer the following questions about each of the articles you find.

1. Who is the author(s)? What can you find out about the author(s)? How expert is the author on the subject?

2. What kind of journal, book, or website did it appear in, and is that source reliable, accurate, and up-to-date?

3. Does the author or the publisher of the article have a particular bias? Does that bias make the article less valuable as a resource?

4. Who seems to be the audience this article was intended for?

5. Does the article provide convincing evidence to support its thesis?

6. Which of the three articles would be the best resource for you to quote from in an essay? Why?

7. Does the article contain information you may be able to use in your essay?

- **Part 3: Defend your proposal.**   For the third part of this assignment, you will write a three- to four-page essay defending your proposed policy. In this essay, make use of ideas and quotations from the many articles you have read as part of this project and the ones you located in any additional research you have done. When you refer to your sources to support your argument, it's not enough to simply include them as a series of unrelated sources; you need to tie them together, explain their relationships with each other, and express your conclusions about them. This process is called *synthesizing*, and it is discussed in more detail in Synthesis (22.14, p. 648). This essay will accompany your policy proposal, and in it, you will attempt to convince the committee that your policy proposal should be included in the comprehensive document.

Documentation.   Be sure to provide appropriate citations for any words you quote, paraphrase, or summarize from the websites and to include a works cited list or list of references at the end of your essay. If you need to review how to provide this documentation, refer to MLA Documentation (Topic 23, p. 650) or APA Documentation (Topic 24, p. 687).

3.24 Academic Essay

Explaining Freedom of Speech in America

For this assignment, you will write a three- to four-page academic essay that relates to freedom of speech in America.

Assignment. In your essay, you will discuss what freedom of speech means in America through your focus on a specific topic like one of the following or a related topic of your choice.

- The origins of the principle of freedom of speech at the time the country was forming

- Reservations about freedom of speech when it was proposed

- Changes in the principle of freedom of speech over time

- Threats to free speech over the years

- Controversies that have arisen involving free speech

- How the American version of free speech is different from that of other countries

Your essay will be informed by your reading, discussions, writing, and thinking about the topic in this reading/writing project as well as by additional information you have found. Think of this essay as writing that would be appropriate in a college course on history, political science, law, or something similar.

Research. Once you've settled on a topic to write about, you are going to do some research. Locate at least three articles on your topic. (If you would like some help with conducting this search, see Finding Sources Online [22.4, p. 626] and Finding Sources in the Library [22.5, p. 626].)

Note that when you use Google to locate an article in a scholarly journal, you will often find you will need to pay a fee in order to read it. You are not expected to do this. Instead, go to your library or to your library's website. There you will find that your library subscribes to a number of databases filled with scholarly articles. These are usually organized by subject matter. Select the one that seems most likely to cover the topic you're researching. In this case, the most likely databases are JSTOR, ProQuest Central, or Social Science Database.

Once you have your articles, write a brief evaluation of each using the questions that follow.

1. Who was the author(s)? What can you find out about the author(s)? What level of expertise does the author have on the subject?

2. Where was the article published? What kind of journal, book, or website did it appear in, and is that source reliable, accurate, and up-to-date?

3. Does the author or the publisher of the article have a particular bias? Does that bias make the article less valuable as a resource?

4. Who seems to be the audience this article was intended for?

5. Does the article provide convincing evidence to support its thesis?

6. Which of the three articles would be the best resource for you to quote from in an essay? Why?

When you do include quotations, paraphrases, or summaries of articles to support your argument, it's not enough to simply include them as a series of unrelated sources; you need to tie them together, explain their relationships with each other, and express your conclusions about them. This process is called *synthesizing*, and it is discussed in more detail in Synthesis (22.14, p. 648).

Documentation.   Be sure to provide appropriate citations for any words you quote, paraphrase, or summarize from the websites and to include a works cited list or list of references at the end of your essay. If you need to review how to provide this documentation, refer to MLA Documentation (Topic 23, p. 650) or APA Documentation (Topic 24, p. 687).

3.25 Multimodal Composition

Proposing a College Policy on Freedom of Speech

This assignment is similar to the one in Unit 3.23 except that you are not limited to a formal *written* document. Instead, you are invited to use any skills you have developed that make use of other media—images, video, PowerPoint with narration, graphs, charts, even a website—to convey your argument. You might, for example, produce a paper document that includes images, charts, or graphs. Or, if you are comfortable working with PowerPoint, you could produce a PowerPoint presentation with recorded narration, or, if your instructor gives you the okay, one that you narrate to the class. If you are skilled at website development, you could present your argument as a website.

Assignment.   Imagine your campus has been experiencing considerable controversy about the issue of free speech. The administration has formed a Free Speech Task Force of administrators, faculty, and students to develop a broad series of policies to address the problem. They have invited the college community to submit policy proposals to this task force to be included in their document. You have decided to submit a proposed policy.

- **Part 1: Compose your policy.**   You are not going to try to compose a complete "free speech" policy covering every aspect of the issue. That would require twenty or thirty pages—or more. You are going to focus on one issue involving free speech and compose a short statement presenting your proposed policy. This statement will then be included at the beginning of your multimodal composition. For example, if you are composing a PowerPoint, this statement would appear on the first slide after any title slide. If you are designing a website, this policy statement would be appropriate for the "landing" page, the page students first land on when they visit your website.

  If selected, your proposed policy would then become part of a much larger document spelling out the college's policy on a multitude of free speech issues.

  Here are some example topics, but you can also come up with your own:

  - The adoption of a speech code to restrict hate speech
  - A policy on outside speakers who have controversial views
  - The rights of students to protest speakers they find offensive
  - The rights of students to protest limits on free speech
  - The rights of faculty speech in the classroom
  - Limits on what students can say in class
  - Limits on what students can write in their essays
  - Limits on the display of images, symbols, posters, or flags that may offend some students
  - Limits on sexist language
  - Students' right not to be exposed to statements (by other students? by their instructors?) that offend their deeply held beliefs

Work hard in this "policy statement" to be precise, to define exactly what your proposed policy is allowing or restricting.

- **Part 2: Research your topic.**   Before you formulate your policy statement, you will need to do a little research. Either in the library or online, locate three articles or books that discuss the free speech issue you are addressing. (If you would like some help with conducting this search, see Finding Sources Online [22.4, p. 626] and Finding Sources in the Library [22.5, p. 626].)

  When you use Google to locate an article in a scholarly journal, you will often find that to read the article, you will need to pay a fee. You are not expected to do this. Instead, go to your library or to your library's website. There you will find that your library subscribes to a number of databases filled with scholarly articles. These are usually organized by subject matter. Select the one that seems most likely to cover the topic you're researching.

In this case, the most likely databases are JSTOR, ProQuest Central, or Social Science Database.

Once you have your articles, answer the questions that follow about each of them.

1. Who is the author(s)? What can you find out about the author(s)? How expert is the author on the subject?
2. What kind of journal, book, or website did it appear in, and is that source reliable, accurate, and up-to-date?
3. Does the author or the publisher of the article have a particular bias? Does that bias make the article less valuable as a resource?
4. Who seems to be the audience this article was intended for?
5. Does the article provide convincing evidence to support its thesis?
6. Which of the three articles would be the best resource for you to quote from in an essay? Why?
7. Does the article contain information you may be able to use in your essay?

- **Part 3: Defend your proposal.**   The third part of this assignment is to compose a multi-media presentation defending your proposed policy statement. This could simply be a written document supplemented with images, charts, or tables, or, it could take the form of a video, website, or PowerPoint suitable for presentation to the Free Speech Task Force. In this presentation, make use of ideas and quotations from the many articles you have read as part of this project and the ones you located in Part 2, above. If you want to use your sources most effectively to support your argument, it's not enough to simply include them as a series of unrelated quotations, paraphrases, or summaries; you need to tie them together, explain their relationships with each other, and express your conclusions about them. This process is called *synthesizing*, and it is discussed in more detail in Synthesis (22.14, p. 648).

   The idea here is that this multimodal composition will be presented to the committee in order to convince them that your proposal should be included in the comprehensive document on free speech at your college or university.

Documentation.   Be sure to provide appropriate citations for any words you quote, paraphrase, or summarize from the websites and to include a works cited list or list of references to accompany your composition. If you need to review how to provide this documentation, refer to MLA Documentation (Topic 23, p. 650) or APA Documentation (Topic 24, p. 687).

⮕ **3.26** Activity

Getting Started on Your Essay or Composition

During this class period, you and your classmates will begin working on your essay (see Real World Essay: Proposing a College Policy on Freedom of Speech [3.23, p. 116], Academic Essay: Explaining Freedom of Speech in America [3.24, p. 119], or Multimodal Composition: Proposing a College Policy on Freedom of Speech [3.25, p. 120]).

You may use this time to start brainstorming or to begin your research online. You may want to write an opening paragraph or two, or to review what you've already read and written in this project. You may want to compare notes with a couple of classmates or ask a question or two of your instructor. If you are composing a multimodal project, you may want to talk to others who are doing the same to compare approaches. The idea is that you will at least get a start on the essay or composition.

3.27 Writing

Reflecting on Project 3: Freedom of Speech

Reflective writing is different from most writing you do in college. Reflective writing asks you to think back, to "reflect" on an experience—an essay you have written, a major change in your life, a time when you didn't have success at something you wanted to do, a semester's work in a course—and to examine how you now think and feel about that experience. What effect has the experience had on you? How have you changed? How will you be different in the future? If you'd like a little more explanation of reflective writing, visit Strategies for Writing a Reflection (18.29, p. 555).

Now you're going to reflect on all the reading, thinking, discussing, and writing you have done in this project on freedom of speech. Then, in a short paper—a page or so—reflect on this experience:

1. Report on what you learned about the concept of freedom of speech and the issues related to it. What were the most important or most useful ideas you encountered?

2. Describe how you feel about the experience and what you *think* about what you have learned.

3. Report on what you learned that will make a difference for you in the future.

PROJECT 4

Truth, Lies, and Fake News

Illustration Courtesy of New York Magazine

The way news washes over us from our televisions, from social media, and from newspapers and magazines, it is often difficult to distinguish between the truth, outright lies, half-truths, and exaggeration. It is easy to simply feel like sheep lining up in orderly rows. Some claim that what we see on the evening news or read in newspapers is "fake news." Others argue that the press is essential to democracy and can play a crucial role in exposing corruption and wrongdoing at all levels of society by revealing "the truth." Meanwhile, the FBI and CIA have reported that the Russians used social media to spread deceptive stories during the 2016 election with the goal of changing the outcome, and the Trump administration denies this happened. It's becoming hard to know what the truth is. In this project you will explore the concepts of truth, lies, and fake news... and how to recognize the differences between them.

Getting Started: Discovering What You Know

This project starts with two activities—Thinking about Key Terms and Applying Key Terms—that will help you get in touch with what you already know about these issues through thinking about and answering questions like "How do you define key terms, such as *truth*, *lie*, *fact*, and *opinion*?" and asking how you apply these key terms to a real-world situation.

Exploring, Thinking, and Writing about Ideas

In this section, you will read articles and excerpts from newspapers, a website, and books that discuss various issues involving truth, lies, facts, and opinions. You will also watch a video, "Can a Divided America Heal?" which discusses how tribalism—behavior, attitudes, and beliefs that derive from identifying with a particular group—is currently dominating American politics and culture.

These readings and the video ask you to think about how language and statistics can be used to deceive, the importance of facts, the meaning of truth, and the consequences of "tribalism." They ask you to grapple with a number of questions: Is it possible for the news to be unbiased? Who is an expert? How do fact checkers work? What constitutes "fake news"? All are challenging. Preview them first, and then, as you read, think carefully and analyze what the authors are saying and why, annotating important, interesting, or confusing ideas and opinions.

As you work through these materials, you will discuss your thoughts and findings with your classmates, reflect in writing on what you have read, and write in response to specific articles. You will also complete activities related to the readings that ask you to practice specific skills, such as previewing, actively reading, analyzing, evaluating, researching, preparing to write, generating ideas, organizing those ideas, and revising. According to directions from your instructor, you will work independently and/or in small groups to complete them. In addition, your instructor will assign relevant topics from other parts of *The Hub* that relate to writing, reading, research, and life issues that will address other important skills.

Bringing It All Together

This project concludes with three assignments that ask you to use the tools and ideas you have encountered as you worked through this project to research a topic about which there has been much fake news—raising the minimum wage. Your instructor may assign the first, second, or third option; may give you a choice among the three; or may even ask you to write more than one.

The first assignment asks you to write an essay suitable for publication on the op-ed page of your local newspaper recommending what the minimum wage should be in your city or state. The second assignment asks you to write an academic essay taking a stand on the same issue—the appropriate minimum wage in your city or state.

Think of this second essay as writing that would be appropriate in a college course on economics, political science, sociology, business, or something similar. The third assignment asks you to create a multimodal composition to influence public opinion on the issue of the minimum wage, using a website, blog, narrated PowerPoint, or video, in which you make your argument for what the minimum wage should be in your city or state.

The final writing assignment, Reflecting on Project 4: Truth, Lies, and Fake News, asks you to reflect on what you have learned as you have worked through this reading/writing project.

Navigating Project 4

Below is the table of contents for Project 4, which you can use to easily locate the units you have been assigned to work on by your instructor. Several of these units ask you to connect to the Internet to watch videos or explore websites. If you find that any of these search terms do not work, there is a list of URLs available at https://bit.ly/33IIHtf.

Getting Started: Discovering What You Know

▲ How do you know that what you see is true? Evgeny Murtola/Shutterstock

4.1 Activity

Thinking about Key Terms

As you begin working through this reading/writing project on truth, lies, and fake news, start by exploring the meaning of some key terms. Working in your group, write a definition of the following words:

- truth
- lie
- fact
- opinion

→ | **4.2** | **Activity**

Applying Key Terms

Keeping in mind the definitions you arrived at for the terms *truth*, *lie*, *fact*, and *opinion*, work in your group to answer the following questions related to the terms *truth* and *lie*:

1. *Two people witness a traffic accident involving a bright red Toyota RAV4 and a dark blue Toyota Prius. One witness, Allison, tells the investigating police officer she saw the Prius driving very fast and failing even to slow down for a stop sign. The other witness, Miguel, tells police the Prius approached the stop sign very slowly and came to a complete stop before driving through.*

   - Assume that both witnesses are honest; neither is lying. Even though they contradict each other, is the statement that each of them made true? (Notice you are not being asked if anyone was lying. You're not being asked about the witnesses but only about their statements.)

   - Suppose a videotape of the accident was made by a nearby security camera. The tape reveals that a blue Prius approached the intersection at 50 mph and didn't slow down at all for the stop sign.

   What is "the truth" in this situation? Is there such a thing as absolute truth?

2. Can you speak the truth, but be wrong? If you speak what you are certain is true, and it later turns out not to have been true, did you tell the truth? Did you lie?

3. Think of as many examples as you can of facts that have changed over the years (e.g., How many planets are there?). Are there some kinds of facts that cannot change?

4. Listed below are a series of statements that may be facts, opinions, or statements most experts agree on. Working in your group, decide which category each of the following items falls into. If you need more clarification of the distinctions between them, see Distinguishing among Facts, Statements Most Experts Agree On, and Opinions (21.3, p. 604).

   a. A square has four equal sides.
   b. All birds have feathers.
   c. Louisville is the capital of Kentucky.
   d. The American school system is in bad shape.
   e. The Mississippi River flows into the Gulf of Mexico.
   f. Thomas Jefferson owned slaves.
   g. Texas is the largest state.
   h. French fries are not good for your health.

i.   Smoking is not good for your health.

j.   The United States gave the Panama Canal to Panama.

k.   Men are usually taller than women.

l.   Egyptian hieroglyphics were the earliest writing system.

m.   Gustave Eiffel designed the Eiffel Tower and the Statue of Liberty.

n.   America was discovered by Christopher Columbus in 1492.

o.   Taxes are too high in America.

p.   Glass is made from sand.

q.   People in the Midwest are nicer than people who live on the East or West Coast.

r.   The murder rate has gone up dramatically in the past twenty years.

s.   Ivory-billed woodpeckers are extinct.

t.   It's rude to check your twitter feed during a college class.

Exploring the Concept of Facts

◀ Scientific studies became available in the early 1950s that clearly established the link between smoking and cancer, and yet the tobacco companies managed to resist regulation and to combat their unhealthy image for decades. How did they do this? Why didn't the "facts" about smoking and cancer bring an end to the cigarette industry?

Lightspring/Shutterstock

4.3 Activity

Previewing "The Problem with Facts"

In this reading, Tim Harford, an economics writer for the *Financial Times* of London, discusses how difficult it is to successfully confront lies by using facts. Like other readings in this project, it contains a lot of information, ideas, and opinions, and it requires careful reading.

Previewing

When you set out to read a book, an article, an essay, a blog, or a web page—when you set out to read any text—your usual strategy may be simply to dive in, to start reading at the beginning and plow your way through to the end. With the limited time in most of our busy lives, simply diving in can seem like the quickest way to get something read.

Here's a different approach. Most experienced readers have found that taking a few minutes to preview to get a sense of the text they are about to read *before* diving in actually saves them time and helps them read more effectively. This does not mean spending hours previewing; just a few minutes can be very helpful before you start to read.

Give it a try. It's likely you'll find that previewing will actually save you time because it will make the reading easier to understand. And you'll get more out of the reading, because you will have prepared yourself to be an engaged reader. (For additional details on what's involved in previewing, refer to Previewing a Text [20.2, p. 575].)

Previewing "The Problem with Facts"

Working in your group, preview the essay "The Problem with Facts" (4.4, p. 132) by taking a quick look at the following parts of the essay:

- The headnote, which contains information about the author
- The title
- The opening paragraph
- The final paragraph
- Any information in boxes, illustrations, or charts

Then answer the following questions based on your previewing:

1. Who is the author?
2. What are his credentials?
3. Is he a reliable source of information on the topic?
4. What seems to be the main topic of this essay?
5. What did you learn from the opening and closing paragraphs?
6. Did you notice anything that might make this essay a challenge to understand?
7. What seems like it will be the main point of the essay?

"The Problem with Facts," Tim Harford

This article by economics writer Tim Harford originally appeared in the *Financial Times*, an international newspaper published in London that focuses on business news. In it, he discusses how difficult it is to successfully confront lies by using facts. Like other readings in this project, it contains a lot of information, ideas, and opinion, and it requires careful reading.

Some of the terminology used in this British newspaper may be unfamiliar to an American audience, so definitions are provided in the following box.

> *Brexit:* The nickname for the decision by Britain to leave, or "exit," the European Union
>
> *UK:* The acronym for the United Kingdom, the nation comprised of England, Northern Ireland, Scotland, and Wales
>
> *EU:* The acronym for the European Union, a political and economic organization of 28 nations, mostly in Europe
>
> *£350m:* 350 million pounds, the British currency (approximately $453 million)
>
> *The "Leave" side:* Those in Britain who favored Britain "leaving" the European Union
>
> *"Remain" campaigners:* Those in Britain who favored Britain "remaining" in the European Union

Be sure to preview before you dive into reading this essay. (For a refresher on previewing strategies, look at Previewing a Text [20.2, p. 575].)

The Problem with Facts

TIM HARFORD

Tim Harford is the economics writer for the *Financial Times,* a global newspaper covering world financial issues. Harford's book *The Undercover Economist* is a *Business Week* bestseller and a *Sunday Times* bestseller, and was number one on Amazon.co.uk.

FT Magazine

MARCH 9, 2017

1   Just before Christmas 1953, the bosses of America's leading tobacco companies met John Hill, the founder and chief executive of one of America's leading public

relations firms, Hill & Knowlton. Despite the impressive surroundings—the Plaza Hotel, overlooking Central Park in New York—the mood was one of crisis.

2   Scientists were publishing solid evidence of a link between smoking and cancer. From the viewpoint of Big Tobacco, more worrying was that the world's most read publication, *The Reader's Digest*, had already reported on this evidence in a 1952 article, "Cancer by the Carton." The journalist Alistair Cooke, writing in 1954, predicted that the publication of the next big scientific study into smoking and cancer might finish off the industry.

3   It did not. PR guru John Hill had a plan—and the plan, with hindsight, proved tremendously effective. Despite the fact that its product was addictive and deadly, the tobacco industry was able to fend off regulation, litigation and the idea in the minds of many smokers that its products were fatal for decades.

4   So successful was Big Tobacco in postponing that day of reckoning that their tactics have been widely imitated ever since. They have also inspired a thriving corner of academia exploring how the trick was achieved. In 1995, Robert Proctor, a historian at Stanford University who has studied the tobacco case closely, coined the word "agnotology". This is the study of how ignorance is deliberately produced; the entire field was started by Proctor's observation of the tobacco industry. The facts about smoking—indisputable facts, from unquestionable sources—did not carry the day. The indisputable facts were disputed. The unquestionable sources were questioned. Facts, it turns out, are important, but facts are not enough to win this kind of argument.

5   Agnotology has never been more important. "We live in a golden age of ignorance," says Proctor today. "And Trump and Brexit are part of that."

6   In the UK's EU referendum, the Leave side pushed the false claim that the UK sent £350m a week to the EU. It is hard to think of a previous example in modern western politics of a campaign leading with a transparent untruth, maintaining it when refuted by independent experts, and going on to triumph anyway. That performance was soon to be eclipsed by Donald Trump, who offered wave upon shameless wave of demonstrable falsehood, only to be rewarded with the presidency. The Oxford Dictionaries declared "post-truth" the word of 2016. Facts just didn't seem to matter anymore.

7   The instinctive reaction from those of us who still care about the truth—journalists, academics and many ordinary citizens—has been to double down on the facts. Fact-checking organizations, such as Full Fact in the UK and PolitiFact in the US, evaluate prominent claims by politicians and journalists. I should confess a personal bias: I have served as a fact checker myself on the BBC radio programme *More or Less*, and I often rely on fact-checking websites. They judge what's true rather than faithfully reporting both sides as a traditional journalist would. Public, ▶

transparent fact checking has become such a feature of today's political reporting that it's easy to forget it's barely a decade old.

8   Mainstream journalists, too, are starting to embrace the idea that lies or errors should be prominently identified. Consider a story on the NPR website about Donald Trump's speech to the CIA in January: "He falsely denied that he had ever criticized the agency, falsely inflated the crowd size at his inauguration on Friday . . . —" It's a bracing departure from the norms of American journalism, but then President Trump has been a bracing departure from the norms of American politics.

9   Facebook has also drafted in the fact checkers, announcing a crackdown on the "fake news" stories that had become prominent on the network after the election. Facebook now allows users to report hoaxes. The site will send questionable headlines to independent fact checkers, flag discredited stories as "disputed," and perhaps downgrade them in the algorithm that decides what each user sees when visiting the site.

10   We need some agreement about facts or the situation is hopeless. And yet: will this sudden focus on facts actually lead to a more informed electorate, better decisions, a renewed respect for the truth? The history of tobacco suggests not. The link between cigarettes and cancer was supported by the world's leading medical scientists and, in 1964, the US surgeon general himself. The story was covered by well-trained journalists committed to the values of objectivity. Yet the tobacco lobbyists ran rings round them.

11   In the 1950s and 1960s, journalists had an excuse for their stumbles: the tobacco industry's tactics were clever, complex and new. First, the industry appeared to engage, promising high-quality research into the issue. The public were assured that the best people were on the case. The second stage was to complicate the question and sow doubt: lung cancer might have any number of causes, after all. And wasn't lung cancer, not cigarettes, what really mattered? Stage three was to undermine serious research and expertise. Autopsy reports would be dismissed as anecdotal, epidemiological work as merely statistical, and animal studies as irrelevant. Finally came normalization: the industry would point out that the tobacco-cancer story was stale news. Couldn't journalists find something new and interesting to say?

12   Such tactics are now well documented—and researchers have carefully examined the psychological tendencies they exploited. So we should be able to spot their re-emergence on the political battlefield.

13   "It's as if the president's team were using the tobacco industry's playbook," says Jon Christensen, a journalist turned professor at the University of California, Los Angeles, who wrote a notable study in 2008 of the way the tobacco industry tugged on the strings of journalistic tradition.

14   One infamous internal memo from the Brown & Williamson tobacco company, typed up in the summer of 1969, sets out the thinking very clearly: "Doubt is our

product." Why? Because doubt "is the best means of competing with the 'body of fact' that exists in the mind of the general public. It is also the means of establishing a controversy." Big Tobacco's mantra: keep the controversy alive.

15   Doubt is usually not hard to produce, and facts alone aren't enough to dispel it. We should have learnt this lesson already; now we're going to have to learn it all over again.

16   Tempting as it is to fight lies with facts, there are three problems with that strategy. The first is that a simple untruth can beat off a complicated set of facts simply by being easier to understand and remember. When doubt prevails, people will often end up believing whatever sticks in the mind. In 1994, psychologists Hollyn Johnson and Colleen Seifert conducted an experiment in which people read an account of an explosive warehouse fire. The account mentioned petrol cans and paint but later explained that petrol and paint hadn't been present at the scene after all. The experimental subjects, tested on their comprehension, recalled that paint wasn't actually there. But when asked to explain facts about the fire ("why so much smoke?"), they would mention the paint. Lacking an alternative explanation, they fell back on a claim they had already acknowledged was wrong. Once we've heard an untrue claim, we can't simply unhear it.

17   This should warn us not to let lie-and-rebuttal take over the news cycle. Several studies have shown that repeating a false claim, even in the context of debunking that claim, can make it stick. The myth-busting seems to work but then our memories fade and we remember only the myth. The myth, after all, was the thing that kept being repeated. In trying to dispel the falsehood, the endless rebuttals simply make the enchantment stronger.

18   With this in mind, consider the Leave campaign's infamous bus-mounted claim: "We send the EU £350m a week." Simple. Memorable. False. But how to rebut it? A typical effort from *The Guardian* newspaper was headlined, "Why Vote Leave's £350m weekly EU cost claim is wrong," repeating the claim before devoting hundreds of words to gnarly details and the dictionary definition of the word "send." This sort of fact-checking article is invaluable to a fellow journalist who needs the issues set out and hyperlinked. But for an ordinary voter, the likely message would be: "You can't trust politicians but we do seem to send a lot of money to the EU." Doubt suited the Leave campaign just fine.

19   This is an inbuilt vulnerability of the fact-checking trade. Fact checkers are right to be particular, to cover all the details and to show their working out. But that's why the fact-checking job can only be a part of ensuring that the truth is heard.

20   Andrew Lilico, a thoughtful proponent of leaving the EU, told me during the campaign that he wished the bus had displayed a more defensible figure, such as £240m. But Lilico now acknowledges that the false claim was the more effective one. ▶

"In cynical campaigning terms, the use of the £350m figure was perfect," he says. "It created a trap that Remain campaigners kept insisting on jumping into again and again and again."

21   Quite so. But not just Remain campaigners—fact-checking journalists too, myself included. The false claim was vastly more powerful than a true one would have been, not because it was bigger, but because everybody kept talking about it.

22   Proctor, the tobacco industry historian turned agnotologist, warns of a similar effect in the US: "Fact checkers can become Trump's poodle, running around like an errand boy checking someone else's facts. If all your time is [spent] checking someone else's facts, then what are you doing?"

23   There's a second reason why facts don't seem to have the traction that one might hope. Facts can be boring. The world is full of things to pay attention to, from reality TV to your argumentative children, from a friend's Instagram to a tax bill. Why bother with anything so tedious as facts?

24   Last year, three researchers—Seth Flaxman, Sharad Goel and Justin Rao— published a study of how people read news online. The study was, on the face of it, an inquiry into the polarization of news sources. The researchers began with data from 1.2 million internet users but ended up examining only 50,000. Why? Because only 4 per cent of the sample read enough serious news to be worth including in such a study. (The hurdle was 10 articles and two opinion pieces over three months.) Many commentators worry that we're segregating ourselves in ideological bubbles, exposed only to the views of those who think the same way we do. There's something in that concern. But for 96 per cent of these web surfers the bubble that mattered wasn't liberal or conservative, it was: "Don't bother with the news."

25   In the war of ideas, boredom and distraction are powerful weapons. A recent study of Chinese propaganda examined the tactics of the paid pro-government hacks (known as the "50 cent army", after the amount contributors were alleged to be paid per post) who put comments on social media. The researchers, Gary King, Jennifer Pan and Margaret Roberts, conclude: "Almost none of the Chinese government's 50c party posts engage in debate or argument of any kind . . . they seem to avoid controversial issues entirely . . . the strategic objective of the regime is to distract and redirect public attention."

26   Trump, a reality TV star, knows the value of an entertaining distraction: simply pick a fight with Megyn Kelly, *The New York Times* or even Arnold Schwarzenegger. Isn't that more eye-catching than a discussion of healthcare reform?

27   The tobacco industry also understood this point, although it took a more highbrow approach to generating distractions. "Do you know about Stanley Prusiner?" asks Proctor.

28   Prusiner is a neurologist. In 1972, he was a young researcher who'd just encountered a patient suffering from Creutzfeldt-Jakob disease. It was a dreadful degenerative condition then thought to be caused by a slow-acting virus. After many years of study, Prusiner concluded that the disease was caused instead, unprecedentedly, by a kind of rogue protein. The idea seemed absurd to most experts at the time, and Prusiner's career began to founder. Promotions and research grants dried up. But Prusiner received a source of private-sector funding that enabled him to continue his work. He was eventually vindicated in the most spectacular way possible: with a Nobel Prize in Medicine in 1997. In his autobiographical essay on the Nobel Prize website, Prusiner thanked his private-sector benefactors for their "crucial" support: RJ Reynolds, maker of Camel cigarettes.

29   The tobacco industry was a generous source of research funds, and Prusiner wasn't the only scientist to receive both tobacco funding and a Nobel Prize. Proctor reckons at least 10 Nobel laureates are in that position. To be clear, this wasn't an attempt at bribery. In Proctor's view, it was far more subtle. "The tobacco industry was the leading funder of research into genetics, viruses, immunology, air pollution," says Proctor. Almost anything, in short, except tobacco. "It was a massive 'distraction research' project." The funding helped position Big Tobacco as a public-spirited industry but Proctor considers its main purpose was to produce interesting new speculative science. Creutzfeldt-Jakob disease may be rare, but it was exciting news. Smoking-related diseases such as lung cancer and heart disease aren't news at all.

30   The endgame of these distractions is that matters of vital importance become too boring to bother reporting. Proctor describes it as "the opposite of terrorism: trivialism". Terrorism provokes a huge media reaction; smoking does not. Yet, according to the US Centers for Disease Control, smoking kills 480,000 Americans a year. This is more than 50 deaths an hour. Terrorists have rarely managed to kill that many Americans in an entire year. But the terrorists succeed in grabbing the headlines; the trivialists succeed in avoiding them.

31   Tobacco industry lobbyists became well-practiced at persuading the media to withhold or downplay stories about the dangers of cigarettes. "That record is scratched," they'd say. Hadn't we heard such things before?

32   Experienced tobacco watchers now worry that Trump may achieve the same effect. In the end, will people simply start to yawn at the spectacle? Jon Christensen, at UCLA, says: "I think it's the most frightening prospect."

33   On the other hand, says Christensen, there is one saving grace. It is almost impossible for the US president not to be news. The tobacco lobby, like the Chinese government, proved highly adept at pointing the spotlight elsewhere. There are reasons to believe that will be difficult for Trump.

▶

34   There's a final problem with trying to persuade people by giving them facts: the truth can feel threatening, and threatening people tends to backfire. "People respond in the opposite direction," says Jason Reifler, a political scientist at Exeter University. This "backfire effect" is now the focus of several researchers, including Reifler and his colleague Brendan Nyhan of Dartmouth.

35   In one study, conducted in 2011, Nyhan, Reifler and others ran a randomised trial in which parents with young children were either shown or not shown scientific information debunking an imaginary but widely feared link between vaccines and autism. At first glance, the facts were persuasive: parents who saw the myth-busting science were less likely to believe that the vaccine could cause autism. But parents who were already wary of vaccines were actually less likely to say they'd vaccinate their children after being exposed to the facts—despite apparently believing those facts.

36   What's going on? "People accept the corrective information but then resist in other ways," says Reifler. A person who feels anxious about vaccination will subconsciously push back by summoning to mind all the other reasons why they feel vaccination is a bad idea. The fear of autism might recede, but all the other fears are stronger than before.

37   It's easy to see how this might play out in a political campaign. Say you're worried that the UK will soon be swamped by Turkish immigrants because a Brexit campaigner has told you (falsely) that Turkey will soon join the EU. A fact checker can explain that no Turkish entry is likely in the foreseeable future. Reifler's research suggests that you'll accept the narrow fact that Turkey is not about to join the EU. But you'll also summon to mind all sorts of other anxieties: immigration, loss of control, the proximity of Turkey to Syria's war and to Isis, terrorism and so on. The original lie has been disproved, yet its seductive magic lingers.

38   The problem here is that while we like to think of ourselves as rational beings, our rationality didn't just evolve to solve practical problems, such as building an elephant trap, but to navigate social situations. We need to keep others on our side. Practical reasoning is often less about figuring out what's true, and more about staying in the right tribe.

39   A more recent study [examined this] idea in the context of political tribes. The researchers showed students footage of a demonstration and spun a yarn about what it was about. Some students were told it was a protest by gay-rights protesters outside an army recruitment office against the military's (then) policy of "don't ask, don't tell." Others were told that it was an anti-abortion protest in front of an abortion clinic.

40   Despite looking at exactly the same footage, the experimental subjects had sharply different views of what was happening—views that were shaped by their political loyalties. Liberal students were relaxed about the behavior of people they thought were gay-rights protesters but worried about what the pro-life protesters

were doing; conservative students took the opposite view. As with "They Saw a Game", this disagreement was not about the general principles but about specifics: did the protesters scream at bystanders? Did they block access to the building? We see what we want to see—and we reject the facts that threaten our sense of who we are.

41 When we reach the conclusion that we want to reach, we're engaging in "motivated reasoning". Motivated reasoning was a powerful ally of the tobacco industry. If you're addicted to a product, and many scientists tell you it's deadly, but the tobacco lobby tells you that more research is needed, what would you like to believe? Christensen's study of the tobacco public relations campaign revealed that the industry often got a sympathetic hearing in the press because many journalists were smokers. These journalists desperately wanted to believe their habit was benign, making them ideal messengers for the industry.

42 On a politically charged issue such as climate change, it feels as though providing accurate information about the science should bring people together. The opposite is true, says Dan Kahan, a law and psychology professor at Yale and one of the researchers on the study into perceptions of a political protest. Kahan writes: "Groups with opposing values often become more polarized, not less, when exposed to scientifically sound information."

43 When people are seeking the truth, facts help. But when people are selectively reasoning about their political identity, the facts can backfire.

44 All this adds up to a depressing picture for those of us who aren't ready to live in a post-truth world. Facts, it seems, are toothless. Trying to refute a bold, memorable lie with a fiddly set of facts can often serve to reinforce the myth. Important truths are often stale and dull, and it is easy to manufacture new, more engaging claims. And giving people more facts can backfire, as those facts provoke a defensive reaction in someone who badly wants to stick to their existing world view. "This is dark stuff," says Reifler. "We're in a pretty scary and dark time."

↳ 4.5 Activity

Analyzing "The Problem with Facts"

Now that you have previewed and read "The Problem with Facts" (4.4, p. 132), work in your group to answer the following questions:

1. Describe the strategy the tobacco companies followed to resist any move to limit the sales of cigarettes.

2. Harford proposes several reasons why using facts in an argument or in a campaign may not work. Discuss these reasons.

3. What is your response to the story of Stanley Prusiner? Why do you think Harford included it in his article?

4. Explain this statement, taken from paragraph 43 of Harford's article: "When people are seeking the truth, facts help. But when people are selectively reasoning about their political identity, the facts can backfire."

↳ **4.6** Writing

Evaluating Fact-Checking Sites

Because of the growing trend in recent years of people misusing facts, or even deliberately distorting or ignoring them, in political and advertising campaigns, on social media, and through some media outlets, a number of websites have been created to "fact check" statements in the news. Reliable, unbiased sites can provide an important resource when you are trying to determine what is true and what is not when you are reading print and online newspapers or blogs, listening to radio programs or podcasts, watching TV news or YouTube videos, or checking your favorite social media sites.

Reliable Fact-Checking Sites

Five sites that don't favor the views of either the Democratic or the Republican parties are listed below. You can access these sites by typing their names into your browser. (If this does not work, there is a list of URLs available at https://bit.ly/33IIHtf.)

1. **Politifact** is sponsored by the *Tampa Bay Times* and was awarded a Pulitzer Prize for its coverage of the 2008 presidential campaign. Politifact rates the accuracy of statements by politicians and advocacy groups as "True," "Mostly True," "Half True," "False," and "Pants on Fire" and provides detailed explanations of its ratings.

2. **Factcheck.org**, founded in 2003, is the oldest of the fact-checking sites. Factcheck.org is sponsored by the Annenberg Public Policy Center of the University of Pennsylvania and primarily reviews TV ads, debates, speeches, interviews, and news releases.

3. **Ask FactCheck** is a website sponsored by Fastcheck.org that specializes in investigating false or misleading rumors that circulate on the internet.

4. **The Washington Post Fact Checker** is a blog written by journalist Glenn Kessler and rates the truth of statements by politicians and advocacy groups by awarding "Pinocchios." Four "Pinocchios" go to the most dishonest statements; none to statements that are true.

5. **Snopes.com**, founded in 1995, specializes in debunking myths and rumors originating from memes, fake news stories, and satirical websites.

Activity: Evaluate and Write about a Statement or Rumor Currently in the News

For this short writing assignment, use at least three of the websites listed above to evaluate a statement or rumor that is currently in the news or circulating on the internet. Then write a short paper, approximately one page, in which you report what you learned about the news item you were investigating and what you learned about the usefulness of these fact-checking websites.

Thinking about Statistics

◀ "There are three kinds of lies: lies, damned lies, and statistics." —Mark Twain

ranjith ravindran/Shutterstock

4.7 Reading

"Dishonest Numbers: Evaluating the Accuracy of Statistics," Daniel Levitin

"Dishonest Numbers: Evaluating the Accuracy of Statistics," by Daniel Levitin, focuses on how numbers can be manipulated to confuse or mislead people. Just as "facts" can be distorted, so can numbers; therefore, evaluating statistical and other numerical information is important in discovering "the truth" in what you hear, read, and watch.

Be sure to do a little "previewing" before you dive into reading this essay. (For a refresher on previewing strategies, look at Previewing a Text [20.2, p. 575].)

Dishonest Numbers: Evaluating the Accuracy of Statistics

DANIEL LEVITIN

This reading is excerpted from Daniel Levitin's A Field Guide to Lies: Critical Thinking in the Information Age, *a book that explores strategies for learning the truth in a world full of lies. Levitin is a neuroscientist, a cognitive psychologist, and a bestselling author. He has served on the faculty at Minerva School of KGI, the Haas School of Business at UC Berkeley, and at McGill University.*

1   Statistics, because they are numbers, appear to us to be cold, hard facts. It seems that they represent facts given to us by nature and it's just a matter of finding them. But it's important to remember that *people* gather statistics. People choose what to count, how to go about counting, which of the resulting numbers they will share with us, and which words they will use to describe and interpret those numbers. Statistics are not facts. They are interpretations. And your interpretation may be just as good as, or better than, that of the person reporting them to you.

2   Sometimes, the numbers are simply wrong, and it's often easiest to start out by conducting some quick plausibility checks. After that, even if the numbers pass plausibility, three kinds of errors can lead you to believe things that aren't so: how the numbers were collected, how they were interpreted, and how they were presented graphically.

3   In your head or on the back of an envelope you can quickly determine whether a claim is plausible (most of the time). Don't just accept a claim at face value; work through it a bit.

4   When conducting plausibility checks, we don't care about the exact numbers. That might seem counterintuitive, but precision isn't important here. We can use common sense to reckon a lot of these: If Bert tells you that a crystal wineglass fell off a table and hit a thick carpet without breaking, that seems plausible. If Ernie says it fell off the top of a forty-story building and hit the pavement without breaking, that's not plausible. Your real-world knowledge, observations acquired over a lifetime, tells you so. Similarly, if someone says they are two hundred years old, or that they can consistently beat the roulette wheel in Vegas, or that they can run forty miles an hour, these are not plausible claims.

5   What would you do with this claim?

In the thirty-five years since marijuana laws stopped being enforced in California, the number of marijuana smokers has doubled every year.

6   Plausible? Where do we start? Let's assume there was only one marijuana smoker in California thirty-five years ago, a very conservative estimate (there were half a million marijuana arrests nationwide in 1982). Doubling that number every year for thirty-five years would yield more than 17 billion—larger than the population of the entire world. (Try it yourself and you'll see that doubling every year for twenty-one years gets you to over a million: l; 2; 4; 8; 16; 32; 64; 128; 256; 512; 1,024; 2,048; 4,096; 8,192; 16,384; 32,768; 65,536; 131,072; 262,144; 524,288; 1,048,576.) This claim isn't just implausible, then. It's impossible. Unfortunately, many people have trouble thinking clearly about numbers because they're intimidated by them. But as you see, nothing here requires more than elementary school arithmetic and some reasonable assumptions.

7   Here's another. You've just taken on a position as a telemarketer, where agents telephone unsuspecting (and no doubt irritated) prospects. Your boss, trying to motivate you, claims:

> Our best salesperson made 1,000 sales a day.

Is this plausible? Try dialing a phone number yourself—the fastest you can probably do it is five seconds. Allow another five seconds for the phone to ring. Now let's assume that every call ends in a sale—clearly this isn't realistic, but let's give every advantage to this claim to see if it works out. Figure a minimum of ten seconds to make a pitch and have it accepted, then forty seconds to get the buyer's credit card number and address. That's one call per minute (5 + 5 + 10 + 40 = 60 seconds), or 60 sales in an hour, or 480 sales in a very hectic eight-hour workday with no breaks. The 1,000 just isn't plausible, allowing even the most optimistic estimates.

8   Some claims are more difficult to evaluate. Here's a headline from *Time* magazine in 2013:

> More people have cell phones than toilets.

What to do with this? We can consider the number of people in the developing world who lack plumbing and the observation that many people in prosperous countries have more than one cell phone. The claim seems *plausible*—that doesn't mean we should accept it, just that we can't reject it out of hand as being ridiculous; we'll have to use other techniques to evaluate the claim, but it passes the plausibility test.

9   Sometimes you can't easily evaluate a claim without doing a bit of research on your own. Yes, newspapers and websites really ought to be doing this for you, but

▶

they don't always, and that's how runaway statistics take hold. A widely reported statistic some years ago was this:

In the U.S., 150,000 girls and young women die of anorexia each year.

Okay—let's check its plausibility. We have to do some digging. According to the U.S. Centers for Disease Control, the annual number of deaths *from all causes* for girls and women between the ages of fifteen and twenty-four is about 8,500. Add in women from twenty-five to forty-four and you still only get 55,000. The anorexia deaths in one year cannot be three times the number of *all* deaths.

10　　In an article in *Science,* Louis Pollack and Hans Weiss reported that since the formation of the Communication Satellite Corp.,

The cost of a telephone call has decreased by 12,000 percent.

If a cost decreases by 100 percent, it drops to zero (no matter what the initial cost was). If a cost decreases by 200 percent, someone is paying *you* the same amount you used to pay *them* for you to take the product. A decrease of 100 percent is very rare; one of 12,000 percent seems wildly unlikely. An article in the peer-reviewed *Journal of Management Development* claimed a 200 percent reduction in customer complaints following a new customer care strategy. Author Dan Keppel even titled his book *Get What You Pay For: Save 200% on Stocks, Mutual Funds, Every Financial Need.* He has an MBA. He should know better.

11　　Of course, you have to apply percentages to the same baseline in order for them to be equivalent. A 50 percent reduction in salary cannot be restored by increasing your new, lower salary by 50 percent, because the baselines have shifted. If you were getting $1,000/week and took a 50 percent reduction in pay, to $500, a 50 percent increase in that pay only brings you to $750. Percentages seem so simple and incorruptible, but they are often confusing. If interest rates rise from 3 percent to 4 percent, that is an increase of 1 percentage point, or 33 percent (because the 1 percent rise is taken against the baseline of 3, so 1/3 = .33). If interest rates fall from 4 percent to 3 percent, that is a decrease of 1 percentage point, but not a decrease of 33 percent—It's a decrease of 25 percent (because the 1 percentage point drop is now taken against the baseline of 4). Researchers and journalists are not always scrupulous about making this distinction between percentage point and percentages clear, but you should be.

12　　The *New York Times* reported on the closing of a Connecticut textile mill and its move to Virginia due to high employment costs. The *Times* reported that employment costs, "wages, worker's compensation and unemployment insurance—are 20 times higher in Connecticut than in Virginia." Is this plausible? If it were true, you'd think that there would be a mass migration of companies out of Connecticut and into Virginia—not just this one mill—and that you would have heard of it by now. In fact, this was not true and the *Times* had to issue a correction. How did this happen? The reporter simply misread a company report. One cost, unemployment insurance, was in fact twenty times higher in Connecticut than in Virginia, but when factored in with other costs, total employment costs were really only 1.3 times the cost in Connecticut, not 20 times higher. The reporter did not have training in business administration and we shouldn't expect her to. To catch these kinds of errors requires taking a step back and thinking for ourselves—which anyone can do (and she and her editors should have done).

13   New Jersey adopted legislation that denied additional benefits to mothers who have children while already on welfare. Some legislators believed that women were having babies in New Jersey simply to increase the amount of their monthly welfare checks. Within two months, legislators were declaring the "family cap" law a great success because births had already fallen by 16 percent. According to the *New York Times*:

> After only two months, the state released numbers suggesting that births to welfare mothers had already fallen by 16 percent, and officials began congratulating themselves on their overnight success.

Note that they're not counting pregnancies, but births. What's wrong here? Because it takes nine months for a pregnancy to come to term, any effect in the first two months cannot be attributed to the law itself but is probably due to normal fluctuations in the birth rate (birth rates are known to be seasonal).

14   Even so, there were other problems with this report that can't be caught with plausibility checks:

> . . . over time, that 16 percent drop dwindled to about 10 percent as the state belatedly became aware of births that had not been reported earlier. It appeared that many mothers saw no reason to report the new births since their welfare benefits were not being increased.

15   This is an example of a problem in the way statistics were collected. We're not actually surveying all the people that we think we are. Some errors in reasoning are sometimes harder to see coming than others, but we get better with practice.

4.8 Activity

Evaluating the Plausibility of Statistical Statements

Using what you learned in the essay "Dishonest Numbers: Evaluating the Accuracy of Statistics" (4.7, p. 141), work in your group to check the *plausibility* of each of the statements below. Remember, all you are being asked is whether each statement is *plausible*, not whether it is exactly correct.

1. Two years ago, unemployment dropped from 8.0 to 6.0, a drop of 25%. This year it fell another 25% to 4.5%.

2. Announcing our 50% sale. Buy two pairs of shoes, and the second pair is 50% off.

3. The Hispanic population in Baltimore, Maryland, is more than 600,000.

4. The number of people with cataracts is greater in Arizona than in California.

5. Forty percent of senators in Washington support a requirement that a background check be required for all gun purchases, 30% support no background check requirement, and 45% support the current policy which doesn't require a background check for purchases at gun shows.

6. The average American male watched more than 3,000 hours of sports on television last year.

7. The average age of a college student today is 21.

8. If there are five equally weighted grades in this course and you have gotten two Bs and a C so far, it is impossible for you to get an A for the course.

9. Because your company was having a budgetary crisis, your salary was reduced by 10% on January 1, 2018. A year later you learned that you would be receiving a 10% raise on January 1, 2019. Your boss tells you that this means in 2019 you will be making the same salary you were making in 2017.

10. If you have invested $1,000 at an interest rate of 3% per year, in ten years, your investment will be worth less than $1,300.

Diving into the Concept of Truth

▲ How hard is it to find the truth? How complicated is the concept of truth? Either something is true or it isn't. Or is it? Olivier Le Moal/Shutterstock

4.9 Reading

"The Nature of Truth," Julian Baggini

In this excerpt from his book *A Short History of Truth*, Julian Baggini explores the nature of truth, its importance to society, and the role we each have to play in discovering it. Be sure to preview before you dive into reading this essay. (For a refresher on previewing strategies, look at Previewing a Text [20.2, p. 575].) Also, as you read, think about what you have learned from previous readings. How does this reading complement or contradict what the other authors have said?

The Nature of Truth

JULIAN BAGGINI

Julian Baggini is an English philosopher who has published more than a dozen books on philosophy, many of them, such as *The Ethics Toolkit* and *A Short History of Truth*, written for a general audience. He received his PhD in philosophy from University College London in 1996. This essay is an excerpt from his book *A Short History of Truth: Consolations for a Post-Truth World* (pages 1–10 and 21–31), in which he explores how the idea of truth has been viewed differently over history and how it has frequently been abused or distorted.

1   When I was growing up, I discovered *The Plain Truth*. It was something of a novelty, the only free magazine stacked in pavement dump bins in my small home town. The title was worthy of a marketing award, with an extra commendation for its strapline: "A Magazine of Understanding." Who wouldn't want to know the truth, to understand the world? I picked one up and in time sent off for a free subscription. I wasn't alone. At its peak in 1986 the monthly had a circulation of 8.2 million copies, 2.3 million more than *Time*.

2   The promise of "The Truth" has always been alluring. The most quoted gospel verse on evangelical posters and literature is John 14:6, in which Jesus proclaims, "I am the way, the truth and the life." It resonates because we all have a sense that truth is not merely an abstract property of propositions but somehow essential to living well. If your life turns out to have been built on nothing but lies, it is as though it has not been real. Whether you believe Jesus shows the way or not, John's promise that "The truth shall make you free" (8:32) rings true.

3   Looking back now at *The Plain Truth*, however, I find the adjective in the title at least as interesting as the noun, with its supremely definite article. "Plain" and "simple" are among the most common descriptors of truth, because that is often exactly how the truth seems. Paris is the capital of France, George Washington was the first President of the United States, water is H_2O: there are innumerable truths like this, which only idiots or obtuse academics (often thought to be the same thing) would deny. Sometimes it is hard to uncover the truth, but that is not because we don't understand what truth itself means.

* * *

4   Somehow, however, the truth has ceased to be plain or simple. Indeed, it is not uncommon to hear people deny that there is any such thing as the truth at all, only opinions, what is "true-for-you" or "true-for-me." Scanning millions of books and written texts, Google's N-Gram viewer reveals that the word "truth" was used only

a third as much at the turn of the millennium as it was 150 years previously. The decline in plain and simple truths is even more precipitous.

* * *

5   Our problem is not primarily with what truth means but *how and by whom truth is established*. Truth used to seem simple because it was easy to assume that most of what we thought to be true really was true, that things were as they seemed, that the wisdom passed down the generations was timeless. This simplicity has been eroded by a variety of different forces. Science showed us that much of what we think about how the world works is false and that we are even mistaken about the workings of our own minds. The pace of its development has left us questioning whether today's orthodoxy will be tomorrow's outdated fallacy. In addition, the more the world shrinks through globalization, the more we have reason to question whether what we take to be true in our cultures really is so or merely a local prejudice. The openness of democratic societies has also allowed the free press to expose more and more of what goes on in the corridors of power, making us more aware of the ways in which we are deceived. And the growth of psychology has enabled more people to master myriad techniques of manipulation, and more people to understand how they work, in a kind of arms race of deception in which truth is the main casualty.

6   Truth has become much less plain and simple, but I see no evidence at all that most people have ceased to believe in it. People remain as outraged by lies as they have ever done, which would make no sense if they did not believe they were untrue.

7   That's why talk of a "post-truth" society is premature and misguided. The same data that shows a century-and-a-half decline in the use of the word "truth" also points to a twenty-first century revival in the concept. We wouldn't even be talking about post-truth if we didn't think truth mattered. The world is neither ready nor willing to say goodbye to truth, even in politics where it sometimes seems as though it has already taken its leave. . . . In fact, lies can still land politicians in very hot water indeed. Loss of interest in political truth is quite tightly focused on their policy promises and the evidence used to back them up. The electorate increasingly takes the view that manifesto commitments, supported by cherry-picked or invented facts and numbers, are not worth the paper they are no longer even printed on.

8   Underpinning this world-weary cynicism is a kind of defeatism, an acceptance that we do not have the resources to discern who's telling the truth and who's just trying it on. Feeling unable to distinguish truth from falsehood, electorates choose their politicians on other, more emotional factors. Losing trust in our brains, we tend to go with our guts and hearts instead.

▶

9   The antidote is not a return to the comfort of simple truths. *The Plain Truth* disappeared in its original form, surely in part because it presented no such thing. It was the mouthpiece of an eccentric evangelical Christian sect led by its bullying, autocratic founder, Herbert W. Armstrong. Its promise of simple truth was seductive but false, like the pledges of populist politicians today. They tap into an understandable disenchantment with political elites and peddle the reassuring message that we don't need to listen to experts, only the will of the people. They promise a world that is not so much post-truth as post-complexity, and that is a powerful message in a disconcertingly uncertain world.

10   To rebuild belief in the power and value of truth, we can't dodge its complexity. Truths can be and often are difficult to understand, discover, explain, verify. They are also disturbingly easy to hide, distort, abuse or twist. Often we cannot claim with any certainty to know the truth. We need to take stock of the various kinds of real and supposed truths out there and understand how to test their authenticity. If we can do this then we might not be at the start of a post-truth era but rather at a temporary post-truth moment, a kind of cultural convulsion born of a despair that will give way in time to measured hope.

*   *   *

11   Secular expertise also grants authority, as indicated by the fact that experts are often described as leading authorities on their subjects. No one thinks this odd and for good reason. There are many things of which most of us know very little and understand even less, so we accept we have to defer to the authority of experts. Those who believe this is rational but that it is foolish to defer to the authority of spiritual experts have no quarrel with the principle of deference to authority per se.

12   The question is when is it right to accept (or at least give weight to) an authority's version of the truth?

*   *   *

13   Then . . . our question [is] whether a *particular* expert is to be trusted. This [question] has to take account of the fact that not all expert views are equal. If my electrician warns me that touching a wire will electrocute me, I have no reason to doubt her. If a doctor tells me I should lose a little weight, my knowledge of the incomplete state of nutritional science might justify at least a little hesitancy. If my doctor is a trained physician but a known maverick, we need to be even more careful. If one economist predicts there will be no recession in the coming year, it might be sensible not to do anything differently at all as a result.

*   *   *

14 Every culture accepts some people as authorities. Truth becomes a victim of this only when such authority is either unwarranted or exceeds its scope. It is unwarranted when there are no truths to be had or someone is in no position to claim special knowledge of them. It exceeds its scope when people are taken as authorities on matters outside of their expertise. So, for example, . . . scientists don't have any authority to give the last word on the ethics of their science because their expertise is scientific rather than ethical.

15 The principle that authority must be warranted and not exceed its scope is simple enough, but putting it into practice is extremely difficult.

* * *

16 This sums up beautifully the core problem of truth by authority. We *need* to defer to experts but not everyone who claims to be an expert is one. If we decide which experts to defer to on the basis of expert opinion, we paradoxically have to choose which experts to trust in order to decide which experts to trust. So inevitably our choice of experts is at bottom based on our own judgement, even though we know that it is not fully informed. In other words, we accept the authority of our own judgement in order to decide whose authority of judgement to accept.

17 There is no way out of this. Reason's dirty secret is that we have to rely on our own judgement without being able rationally to justify it completely. This is not a counsel of despair. By attending to justifications and evidence we can minimize the role of our own insight and maximize the role of facts, evidence and sound inference. But we shouldn't kid ourselves we can rely solely on logically following the facts.

18 Getting the balance right between our own judgement and the expert testimony of others is difficult, and the post-truth world doesn't try too hard to walk the tightrope. Our current predicament is that authorities of expertise are routinely dismissed, with the authority of the gut, intuition, the people and/or God taking its place. There is not enough emphasis given to the wisdom of genuine experts who have devoted their lives to the study of their subjects. This is not a completely different world to a more rational one, simply one where things have become unbalanced. If we care about the truth, we can neither reject nor too enthusiastically embrace the authorities who appear to guide us towards it. Rather, we have to take more care as to whom we grant authority, and on what basis.

19 But we cannot escape the exercise of our own woefully under-informed judgement. That is what lies behind Kant's Enlightenment injunction "Dare to know." And daring it is, because it always carries the risk of error. Don't think *by* yourself but do think *for* yourself, not because you're wiser or smarter than other people but because ultimately that's what you have to do. No one can make up your mind for you, unless you make up your mind to let them.

↳  **Writing**

Summarizing "The Nature of Truth"

For this assignment, write a short paper—a page would be plenty—in which you summarize "The Nature of Truth" (4.9, p. 147).

You probably have a sense of what it means to write a summary: You write something short that summarizes the main content of something longer that you have read. For this assignment, do not look for additional information on how to draft a summary. Rely on what you already know, and do the best you can.

↳ **4.11** **Activity**

Analyzing Summaries

Your group will receive a selection of the summaries that the class wrote of "The Nature of Truth" (4.9, p. 147). Your group's task is to read over these summaries and make two lists: (1) what you found that worked well in one or more of the summaries and (2) the weaknesses or mistakes you found in one or more of the summaries. After a half hour or so, the groups will report out on their lists.

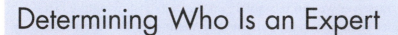

Determining Who Is an Expert

◄ How do you know if someone is a *real* expert?

iQoncept/Shutterstock

"Identifying Expertise," Daniel Levitin

In this excerpt from Daniel Levitin's book *A Field Guide to Lies: Critical Thinking in the Information Age* (pages 129–51), he explores strategies for learning the truth in a world full of lies. He also discusses what an "expert" is and how to identify one. As with other excerpts and articles in this project, this reading will add to your knowledge of what constitutes truth and how to determine whether what you are reading, seeing, or hearing is accurate.

Be sure to preview before you dive into reading this essay. (For a refresher on previewing strategies, see Previewing a Text [20.2, p. 575].)

Identifying Expertise

DANIEL LEVITIN

Daniel Levitin is a neuroscientist, a cognitive psychologist, and a bestselling author. He has served on the faculty at Minerva School of KGI, the Haas School of Business at UC Berkeley, and at McGill University.

1   The first thing to do when evaluating a claim by some authority is to ask who or what established their authority. If the authority comes from having been a witness to some event, how credible a witness are they?

2   Venerable authorities can certainly be wrong. The U.S. government was mistaken about the existence of weapons of mass destruction (WMDs) in Iraq in the early 2000s, and, in a less politically fraught case, scientists thought for many years that humans had twenty-four pairs of chromosomes instead of twenty-three. Looking at what the acknowledged authorities say is not the last step in evaluating claims, but it is a good early step.

* * *

3   The term *expert* is normally reserved for people who have undertaken special training, devoted a large amount of time to developing their expertise (e.g., MDs, airline pilots, musicians, or athletes), and whose abilities or knowledge are considered high relative to others'. As such, expertise is a social judgment—we're comparing one person's skill to the skill level of other people in the world. Expertise is relative. Einstein was an expert on physics sixty years ago; he would probably not be considered one if he were still alive today and hadn't added to his knowledge base what Stephen Hawking and so many other physicists now know. Expertise also

▶

falls along a continuum. Although John Young is one of only twelve people to have walked on the moon, it would probably not be accurate to say that Captain Young is an *expert* on moonwalking, although he knows more about it than almost anyone else in the world.

*   *   *

4   In science, technology, and medicine, experts' work appears in peer-reviewed journals (more on those in a moment) or on patents. They may have been recognized with awards such as a Nobel Prize, an Order of the British Empire, or a National Medal of Science. In business, experts may have had experience such as running or starting a company, or amassing a fortune (Warren Buffett, Bill Gates). Of course, there are smaller distinctions as well—salesperson of the month, auto mechanic of the year, community "best of" awards (e.g., best Mexican restaurant, best roofing contractor).

Expertise Is Typically Narrow

5   Dr. Roy Meadow, the pediatrician who testified in the case of the alleged baby killer Sally Clark, had no expertise in medical statistics or epidemiology. He *was* in the medical profession, and the prosecutor who put him on the stand undoubtedly hoped that jurors would assume he had this expertise. William Shockley was awarded a Nobel Prize in physics as one of three inventors of the transistor. Later in life, he promoted strongly racist views that took hold, probably because people assumed that if he was smart enough to win a Nobel, he must know things that others don't. Gordon Shaw, who "discovered" the now widely discredited Mozart effect, was a physicist who lacked training in behavioral science; people probably figured, as they did with Shockley, "He's a physicist—he must be really smart." But intelligence and experience tend to be domain-specific, contrary to the popular belief that intelligence is a single, unified quantity. The best Toyota mechanic in the world may not be able to diagnose what's wrong with your VW, and the best tax attorney may not be able to give the best advice for a breach-of-contract suit. A physicist is probably not the best person to ask about social science.

*   *   *

Source Hierarchy

6   Some publications are more likely to consult true experts than others, and there exists a hierarchy of information sources. Some sources are simply more consistently reliable than others. In academia, peer-reviewed articles are generally more accurate than books, and books by major publishers are generally more accurate than self-published books (because major publishers are more likely

to review and edit the material and have a greater financial incentive to do so). Award-winning newspapers such as the *New York Times,* the *Washington Post,* and the *Wall Street Journal* earned their reputations by being consistently accurate in their coverage of news. They strive to obtain independent verifications for any news story. If one government official tells them something, they get corroboration from another. If a scientist makes a claim, they contact other scientists who don't have any stake in the finding to hear independent opinions. They do make mistakes; even *Times* reporters have been found guilty of fabrications, and the "newspaper of record" prints errata every day. Some people, including Noam Chomsky, have argued that the *Times* is a vessel of propaganda, reporting news about the U.S. government without a proper amount of skepticism. But again, like with auto mechanics, it's a matter of averages—the great majority of what you read in the *New York Times* is likelier to be true than what you read in, for example, the *New York Post.*

7   Reputable sources want to be certain of facts before publishing them. Many sources have emerged on the Web that do not hold to the same standards, and in some cases, they can break news stories and do so accurately before the more traditional and cautious media do. Many of us learned of Michael Jackson's death from TMZ.com before the traditional media reported it. TMZ was willing to run the story based on less evidence than were the *Los Angeles Times* or NBC. In that particular case, TMZ turned out to be right, but you can't count on this sort of reporting.

8   A number of celebrity death reports that circulated on Twitter were found to be false. In 2015 alone, these included Carlos Santana, James Earl Jones, Charles Manson, and Jackie Chan. A 2011 fake tweet caused a sell-off of shares for the company Audience, Inc., during which its stock lost 25 percent. Twitter itself saw its shares climb 8 percent—temporarily—after false rumors of a takeover were tweeted, based on a bogus website made to look a great deal like Bloomberg.com's. As the *Wall Street Journal* reported, "The use of false rumors and news reports to manipulate stocks is a centuries-old ruse. The difference today is that the sheer ubiquity and amount of information that courses through markets makes it difficult for traders operating at high speeds to avoid a well-crafted hoax." And it happens to the best of us. Veteran reporter (and part of a team of journalists that was awarded a 1999 Pulitzer Prize) Jonathan Capehart wrote a story for the *Washington Post* based on a tweet by a nonexistent congressman in a nonexistent district.

9   We don't want to blindly believe everything we encounter from a good source, nor do we want to automatically reject everything from a questionable source. You shouldn't trust everything you read in the *New York Times,* or reject everything you   ▶

read on TMZ. Where something appears goes to the credibility of the claim. And, as in a court trial, you don't want to rely on a single witness, you want corroborating evidence.

The Website Domain

10   The three-digit suffix of the URL indicates the domain. It pays to familiarize yourself with the domains in your country because some of the domains have restrictions, and that can help you establish a site's credibility for a given topic. In the United States, for example, .edu is reserved for nonprofit educational institutions like Stanford.edu (Stanford University); .gov is reserved for official government agencies like CDC.gov (the Centers for Disease Control); .mil for U.S. military organizations, like army.mil. The most famous is probably .com, which is used for commercial enterprises like GeneralMotors.com. Others include .net, .nyc, and .management, which carry no restrictions(!). *Caveat emptor* (Latin for "Let the buyer beware"). BestElectricalService.nyc might actually be in New Jersey (and their employees might not even be licensed to work in New York); AlphaAndOmegaConsulting.management may not know the first or the last thing about management.

11   Knowing the domain can also help to identify any potential bias. You're more likely to find a neutral report from an educational or nonprofit study (found on a .edu, .gov, or .org site) than on a commercial site, although such sites may also host student blogs and unsupported opinions. And educational and nonprofits are not without bias: They may present information in a way that maximizes donations or public support for their mission. Pfizer.com may be biased in their discussions about drugs made by competing companies, such as GlaxoSmithKline, and Glaxo of course may be biased toward their own products.

12   Note that you don't always want neutrality. When searching for the owner's manual for your refrigerator, you probably want to visit the (partisan) manufacturer's website (e.g., Frigidaire.com) rather than a site that could be redistributing an outdated or erroneous version of the manual. That .gov site may be biased toward government interests, but a .gov site can give you the most accurate info on laws, tax codes, census figures, or how to register your car. CDC.gov and NIH.gov probably have more accurate information about most medical issues than a .com because they have no financial interest in them.

Who Is Behind It?

13   Could the website be operating under a name meant to deceive you? The Vitamin E Producers Association might create a website called NutritionAndYou. info, just to make you think that their claims are unbiased. The president of the

grocery chain Whole Foods was caught masquerading as a customer on the Web, touting the quality of his company's groceries. Many rating sites, including Yelp! and Amazon, have found their ratings ballot boxes stuffed by friends and family of the people and products being rated. People are not always who they appear to be on the Web. Just because a website is named U.S. Government Health Service, that doesn't mean it is run by the government; a site named Independent Laboratories doesn't mean that it is independent—it could well be operated by an automobile manufacturer who wants to make its cars look good in not-so-independent tests.

＊　＊　＊

14　　Knowing the domain name is helpful but hardly a foolproof verification system. MartinLutherKing.org sounds like a site that would provide information about the great orator and civil rights leader. Because it is a .org site, you might conclude that there is no ulterior motive of profit. The site proclaims that it offers "a true historical examination" of Martin Luther King. Wait a minute. Most people don't begin an utterance by saying, "What I am about to tell you is true." The BBC doesn't begin every news item saying, "This is true." Truth is the default position and we assume others are being truthful with us. An old joke goes, "How do you know that someone is lying to you? Because they begin with the phrase *to be perfectly honest*." Honest people don't need to preface their remarks this way.

15　　What MartinLutherKing.org contains is a shameful assortment of distortions, anti-Semitic rants, and out-of-context quotes. Who runs the site? Stormfront, a white-supremacy, neo-Nazi hate group. What better way to hide a racist agenda than by promising "the truth" about a great civil rights leader?

Institutional Bias

16　　Are there biases that could affect the way a person or organization structures and presents the information? Does this person or organization have a conflict of interest? A claim about the health value of almonds made by the Almond Growers' Association is not as credible as one made by an independent testing laboratory.

Peer-Reviewed Journals

17　　In peer-reviewed publications, scholars who are at arm's length from one another evaluate a new experiment, report, theory, or claim. They must be expert in the domain they're evaluating. The method is far from foolproof, and peer-reviewed findings are sometimes overturned, or papers retracted. Peer review is not the only system to rely on, but it provides a good foundation in helping us to draw our own conclusions, and like democracy, it's the best such system we have. If something appears in *Nature, The Lancet,* or *Cell,* for example, you can be sure it went through ▶

rigorous peer review. As when trying to decide whether to trust a tabloid or a serious news organization, the odds are better that a paper published in a peer-reviewed journal is correct.

18   In a scientific or scholarly article, the report should include footnotes or other citations to peer-reviewed academic literature. Claims should be justified, facts should be documented through citations to respected sources. Ten years ago, it was relatively easy to know whether a journal was reputable, but the lines have become blurred with the proliferation of open-access journals that will print anything for a fee, in a parallel world of pseudo-academia. Reference librarians can help you distinguish the two. Journals that appear on indexes such as PubMed (maintained by the U.S. National Library of Medicine) are selected for their quality; articles you return from a regular search are not. Scholar.Google.com is more restrictive than Google or other search engines, limiting search results to scholarly and academic papers, although it does not vet the journals and many pseudo-academic papers are included. It does do a good job of weeding out things that don't even *resemble* scholarly research, but that's a double-edged sword: That can make it more difficult to know what to believe because so many of the results appear to be valid. Jeffrey Beall, a research librarian at the University of Colorado, Denver, has developed a blacklist of what he calls predatory open-access journals (which often charge high fees to authors). His list has grown from twenty publishers four years ago to more than three hundred today. Other sites exist that help you to vet research papers, such as the Social Science Research Network (ssrn.com).

Regulated Authority

19   On the Web, there is no central authority to prevent people from making claims that are untrue, no way to shut down an offending site other than going through the costly procedure of obtaining a court injunction.

20   Off the Web, the lay of the land can be easier to see. Textbooks and encyclopedias undergo careful peer review for accuracy (although that content is sometimes changed under political pressure by school boards and legislatures). Articles at major newspapers in democratic countries are rigorously sourced compared to the untrustworthy government-controlled newspapers of Iran or North Korea, for example.

*   *   *

Is the Information Current? Discredited?

21   Unlike books, newspapers, and conventional sources, Web pages seldom carry a date; graphs, charts, and tables don't always reveal the time period they apply to. You can't assume that the "Sales Earnings Year to Date" you read on a Web page today actually covers today in the "To Date," or even that it applies to this year.

22   Because Web pages are relatively cheap and easy to create, people often abandon them when they're done with them, move on to other projects, or just don't feel like updating them anymore. They become the online equivalent of an abandoned storefront with a lighted neon sign saying "open" when, in fact, the store is closed.

23   For the various reasons already mentioned—fraud, incompetence, measurement error, interpretation errors—findings and claims become discredited. Individuals who were found guilty in properly conducted trials become exonerated. Vehicle airbags that underwent multiple inspections get recalled. Pundits change their minds. Merely looking at the newness of a site is not enough to ensure that it hasn't been discredited. New sites pop up almost weekly claiming things that have been thoroughly debunked. There are many websites dedicated to exposing urban myths, such as Snopes.com, or to collating retractions, such as RetractionWatch.com.

24   During the fall of 2015 leading up to the 2016 U.S. presidential elections, a number of people referred to fact-checking websites to verify the claims made by politicians. Politicians have been lying at least since Quintus Cicero advised his brother Marcus to do so in 64 B.C.E. What we have that Cicero didn't is real-time verification. This doesn't mean that all the verifications are accurate or unbiased, dear reader—you still need to make sure that the verifiers don't have a bias for or against a particular candidate or party.

25   Politifact.com, a site operated by the *Tampa Bay Times,* won a Pulitzer Prize for their reporting, which monitors and fact-checks speeches, public appearances, and interviews by political figures, and uses a six-point meter to rate statements as True, Mostly True, Half True, Mostly False, False, and—at the extreme end of false—Pants on Fire, for statements that are not accurate and completely ridiculous (from the children's playground taunt "Liar, liar, pants on fire"). The *Washington Post* also runs a fact-checking site with ratings from one to four Pinocchios, and awards the prized Geppetto Checkmark for statements and claims that "contain the truth, the whole truth, and nothing but the truth."

26   As just one example, presidential candidate Donald Trump spoke at a rally on November 21, 2015, in Birmingham, Alabama. To support his position that he would create a Muslim registry in the United States to combat the threat of terrorism from within the country, he recounted watching "thousands and thousands" of Muslims in Jersey City cheering as the World Trade Center came tumbling down on 9/11/2001. ABC News reporter George Stephanopoulos confronted Trump the following day on camera, noting that the Jersey City police denied this happened. Trump responded that he saw it on television, with his own eyes, and that it was very well covered. Politifact and the *Washington Post* checked all records of television broadcasts and

▶

news reports for the three months following the attacks and found no evidence to support Trump's claim. In fact, Paterson, New Jersey, Muslims had placed a banner on the city's main street that read "The Muslim Community Does Not Support Terrorism." Politifact summarized its findings, writing that Trump's recollection "flies in the face of all evidence we could find. We rate this statement Pants on Fire." The *Washington Post* gave it their Four-Pinocchio rating.

27   During the same campaign, Hillary Clinton claimed "all of my grandparents" were immigrants. According to Politifact (and based on U.S. census records), only one grandparent was born abroad; three of her four grandparents were born in the United States.

↳ **4.13** **Writing**

Analyzing What Constitutes an "Expert"

The essay below reports on what some experts have to say about a variety of issues concerning shooters in schools. Read this essay, paying close attention to the way Hartocollis and Fortin use the word *expert*. Having read "The Nature of Truth" (4.9, p. 147) and "Identifying Expertise" (4.12, p. 153), both of which discuss what constitutes an "expert," you are now something of an expert on "expert."

After you have read this article, put your expertise to work by writing a short paper—a page is plenty—in which you analyze how Hartocollis and Fortin use the word *expert* and how clear they are about who they consider to be an expert. In addition to the people referred to as "the experts," do the authors make use of any other experts? If so, what gives you the idea that these people are experts?

Should Teachers Carry Guns? Are Metal Detectors Helpful? What Experts Say

ANEMONA HARTOCOLLIS AND JACEY FORTIN

The New York Times

FEBRUARY 22, 2018

1   Paul Hankins keeps a box of smooth, colorful river stones—he calls them "fidgets"—in his classroom for students to hold when they need to soothe their nerves.

2   The stones also have a different purpose, as do the billiard balls and the plank from the old gym floor. They can all be used as weapons in an emergency.

3   "Before we go to the corner where everybody gets invisible, grab one of those," he tells his students at Silver Creek High School in Sellersburg, Ind. "We could cause one hell of a ruckus if we need to."

4   Mr. Hankins does not begrudge teachers who argue that they should be allowed to carry guns to class, especially in the wake of attacks like last week's shooting that killed 17 at Marjory Stoneman Douglas High School in Parkland, Fla.

5   For him, stones are better.

6   They put the fight in "Run, hide, fight," the mantra that he and countless other teachers are learning as lockdown drills become routine.

7   Yet experts are as divided as Mr. Hankins and his colleagues on how to protect students from violence or whether, for that matter, there is anything that can be done to prevent a determined attacker.

8   The latest shooting has intensified the debate over what tactics to use to protect against imminent danger: whether teachers should carry guns, or hide with their students; whether schools should invest in fancy security devices like door jammers or put more resources into crisis teams that could identify and intervene with troubled students. What follows is some of the discussion.

What about teachers carrying guns?

9   Most law enforcement experts argue that teachers should not carry guns. Civilians may be able to hit a bull's-eye at the shooting range, but they lack the tactical knowledge of handling weapons that trained law enforcement personnel get.

10   Accidents happen. Guns can fall out of holsters, be taken from the classroom or accidentally discharge.

11   "You don't want to have a gun that's available to a student or another worker who may have mental health issues," said Maureen S. Rush, vice president for public safety and superintendent of the Police Department at the University of Pennsylvania.

12   But some disagree.

13   Dave Workman, the senior editor of *The Gun Mag* and communications director of the Citizens Committee for the Right to Keep and Bear Arms, said arming guards or teachers could act as a deterrent so that no one had to draw a weapon in the first place.

14   "I understand the debate out there: 'Should this be the job of a teacher?'" he said.

15   "Why not? The teacher is going to be there," Mr. Workman said. "They become the first responder sometimes. It does take a while for police to respond to an incident."

16   The Parkland school had an armed sheriff's deputy who never encountered the gunman.

▶

Are metal detectors helpful?

17   Metal detectors are unlikely to stop a gunman, experts say. But they can be useful in certain contexts, if, for instance, the school is in a neighborhood with high crime or gang activity where students may try to bring guns or knives into school to defend themselves.

What is the purpose of a lockdown drill?

18   In a lockdown drill, everyone in the school practices responding seamlessly to the presence of an intruder. Teachers and students go to a secure location, like a classroom, closet or storage area that can be locked, and move out of sight, away from windows or doors.

19   Speed is important. The typical gunman is like water, the experts said, following the path of least resistance. Typically, a gunman will not try to kick in a closed door, but will look for one with a crack of light showing.

20   "Within 20 or 30 seconds, I, as a bad guy, should have very little easy access to anybody," said David R. Connors, head of Connors Security Consulting Services in Spencerport, N.Y., and a former police officer. The locks or barricades on the doors do not need to be very strong, just enough to last until help can arrive.

21   The point of a lockdown drill is to know what to do automatically, without having to think.

22   "When something's going down, you will not respond from your head, you will respond from your stomach," Ms. Rush said. "You need to get that in your stomach. You need to know what instinctively you will do. That's got to be part of your psyche. So it requires constant training."

23   Different schools or districts may have different protocols. The important thing is that everyone, from teachers to students to parents, know what they are. "It has to be something that goes like clockwork," said Dr. Irwin Redlener, a professor of pediatrics and public health and the director of the National Center for Disaster Preparedness at Columbia University.

If someone knocks on a locked door, should they be allowed in?

24   It may be heart-wrenching, but don't open the door, experts say. A teacher has to think of the lives of the many who have moved to a safe place over the one person outside in the hallway who may bring danger in.

25   "You don't open that door until you know the police are on the other side," Ms. Rush said, adding, "You're doing it for the masses of kids."

What should students be told?

26 It depends on their age. "We don't have to scare the heck out of these kids," Mr. Connors said. "In a kindergarten through third-grade building, you might tell the kids, come over here and sit down next to the wall. Be nice and quiet. I'm going to read you a book. That's all the kids have to know."

27 Mr. Connors does not believe in making drills too realistic. "You don't have to have someone come over and try to kick in the door. I don't think that's constructive. With staff, yes. But not with kids."

Is it a good idea to let students use cellphones?

28 Phones should be put on silent, not even vibrating. "Texting is fine," Ms. Rush said. "You want to be invisible, and you want silence."

29 Ms. Rush said she was alarmed by the students who took videos while hiding from the gunman in Parkland, not because she disapproved of the video, but because it changed their mentality. "That could be taking them out of their survivor mode," she said.

What about identifying a troubled student?

30 The experts vary on whether this is possible. Some say that students who become violent are often not the ones who seem most troubled or who make the most noise. "The perpetrators are very often not the bullies or the guys roughing people up," Mr. Connors said. "Quite often, it's the guy who is quiet. In hindsight, they'll go back and find that there's some family or mental health issue."

31 Others say that schools can do more to enlist students to help identify troubled classmates. Social media can be an early warning system, the experts say. Students may express their violent thoughts there, as did Nikolas Cruz, who has been charged in the Florida shooting, according to law enforcement officials.

32 "These kids are begging us to stop them," said Amy Klinger, a co-founder of the Educator's School Safety Network, who consults on school safety from the perspective of the former teacher and principal that she is. "We just have to be better at picking up the warning signs."

33 The schools alone cannot do it. Arguably, Dr. Klinger said, the failure to identify Mr. Cruz as troubled was a failure of the entire community, along with law enforcement agencies that had been warned about him.

34 "A school can identify the individual of concern, but they didn't create that individual," Dr. Klinger said. "So yeah, there is a role that the community and parents and our society has to play in identifying and dealing with those individuals as well." ▶

What about investing in security devices?

35   Law enforcement experts suggest hardening the perimeter, that is, putting up security cameras, door buzzers, gates, and other barricades or high-tech devices.

36   But they say that buzzers are not enough, especially at arrival and dismissal times when hundreds of students may be milling around.

37   "After Sandy Hook, a lot of schools got very panicky and bought $5,000 buzzer systems," Dr. Klinger said. "They bought the system that was breached by the intruder in the first 30 seconds of Sandy Hook. He shot out the door and walked into the school. So your buzzer system did absolutely no good."

38   Ms. Rush said that everyone at the front office should be informed when a student has been suspended or expelled. A photo should be posted, and they should call 911 if the person appears.

39   "This happens in corporate America all the time," she said. "Workplace violence, where the person comes back and wants to kill the boss."

40   Dr. Klinger said that schools should invest in teachers who mingle with students in the lobby or in hallways as a way to learn about troubling behavior that may be brewing.

41   Even in a large school, the experts said, doors need to be manned by someone who knows the students and will recognize anyone who looks out of place. Dr. Klinger said that this should be a teacher, who relates to the students, not a security guard.

42   "If you want to take this to the extreme, you can ensure the safety of kids by locking them in a cell, but that's a prison," Dr. Klinger said. "This is not a prison. It's not a shopping mall."

What if you can't run or hide?

43   Cultivate the survivor mentality, experts said. Fight. "If he's coming no matter what, if you got that one guy who starts breaking the door out, you take every object in the room and you beat the hell out of him to disarm him, because you're going to die if you don't," Ms. Rush said. "So you might as well take your chances of trying to fight."

44   Ms. Rush gave the example of a professor who, as a gunman approached, took his phone out to look at pictures of his children one last time before he died. "But a female student jumped and ran and locked the door. She had survivor instinct."

Recognizing Fake News

▲ What you're seeing and what you're reading, it's true. Or is it? How can you tell? Andrew Aitchison/In Pictures Ltd./Corbis/Getty Images

4.14 Activity

Understanding Slippery Words

The terms listed below—often used in the news, in advertising, and in political speeches—could be called "slippery." Their meanings aren't clear. They change depending on how they are used, who uses them, and the context in which they appear. They seem to imply something without actually saying it, or they seem to promise something that they really aren't promising.

Your instructor will assign a set of the following words to your group. Working together, discuss what makes each of these terms "slippery."

Set 1

- according to experts
- research shows
- self-proclaimed
- regime (used instead of government)

Set 2

- doctor recommended
- up to 50 percent off
- the number one Italian restaurant in town
- it is well established that

Set 3

- everyone agrees
- the number one selling product
- best-selling
- so-called

Set 4

- studies have shown
- award-winning
- clinical trials show
- save up to $500 or more

4.15 | Writing

Taking Focused Notes on "How to Spot Fake News"

Most people take notes by jotting down everything in a text they find interesting, important, or puzzling, and you probably already have a system for taking notes when you are reading or, especially, studying a text. Focused note-taking, however, is slightly different. You don't note everything that is interesting, important, or puzzling. Instead, you take notes with a particular question or theme in mind, noting only those places where the text addresses that theme or question.

For this activity, you will take notes focused on the different strategies for identifying fake news suggested by Eugene Kiely and Lori Robertson in their article "How to Spot Fake News" (4.16). When you finish, you should have a list of the strategies suggested in the article.

4.16 Reading

"How to Spot Fake News," Eugene Kiely and Lori Robertson

Following on from other readings in this project that have discussed the difficulty of refuting lies using facts, how statistics can be manipulated, the nature of truth, and what constitutes a reliable expert, this article, "How to Spot Fake News" by Eugene Kiely and Lori Robertson, provides useful advice for evaluating what you read, see, and hear in the media in this age of deliberate deception.

Be sure to preview before you dive into reading this essay. (For a refresher on previewing strategies, read Previewing a Text [20.2, p. 575].)

How to Spot Fake News

EUGENE KIELY AND LORI ROBERTSON

This reading, which appears on the FactCheck.org website, is designed to help readers to distinguish between real news and fake news. FactCheck.org is a nonpartisan, nonprofit "consumer advocate" for voters that aims to reduce the level of deception and confusion in US politics. "We monitor the factual accuracy of what is said by major U.S. political players in the form of TV ads, debates, speeches, interviews, and news releases. Our goal is to apply the best practices of both journalism and scholarship, and to increase public knowledge and understanding." FactCheck.org is a project of the Annenberg Public Policy Center of the University of Pennsylvania.

POSTED ON NOVEMBER 18, 2016

1   Fake news is nothing new. But bogus stories can reach more people more quickly via social media than what good old-fashioned viral emails could accomplish in years past.

2   Concern about the phenomenon led Facebook and Google to announce that they'll crack down on fake news sites, restricting their ability to garner ad revenue. Perhaps that could dissipate the amount of malarkey online, though news consumers themselves are the best defense against the spread of misinformation.

3   Not all of the misinformation being passed along online is complete fiction, though some of it is. Snopes.com has been exposing false viral claims since the

▶

mid-1990s, whether that's fabricated messages, distortions containing bits of truth and everything in between. Founder David Mikkelson warned in a Nov. 17 article not to lump everything into the "fake news" category. "The fictions and fabrications that comprise fake news are but a subset of the larger *bad news* phenomenon, which also encompasses many forms of shoddy, unresearched, error-filled, and deliberately misleading reporting that do a disservice to everyone," he wrote.

4   A lot of these viral claims aren't "news" at all, but fiction, satire and efforts to fool readers into thinking they're for real.

5   We've long encouraged readers to be skeptical of viral claims, and make good use of the delete key when a chain email hits their inboxes. In December 2007, we launched our Ask FactCheck feature, where we answer readers' questions, the vast majority of which concern viral emails, social media memes and the like. Our first story was about a made-up email that claimed then-House Speaker Nancy Pelosi wanted to put a "windfall" tax on all stock profits of 100 percent and give the money to, the email claimed, "the 12 Million Illegal Immigrants and other unemployed minorities." We called it "a malicious fabrication"—that's "fake news" in today's parlance.

6   In 2008, we tried to get readers to rid their inboxes of this kind of garbage. We described a list of red flags—we called them Key Characteristics of Bogusness—that were clear tip-offs that a chain email wasn't legitimate. Among them: an anonymous author; excessive exclamation points, capital letters and misspellings; entreaties that "This is NOT a hoax!"; and links to sourcing that does not support or completely contradicts the claims being made.

7   Those all still hold true, but fake stories—as in, completely made-up "news"— have grown more sophisticated, often presented on a site designed to look (sort of) like a legitimate news organization. Still, we find it's easy to figure out what's real and what's imaginary if you're armed with some critical thinking and fact-checking tools of the trade.

8   Here's our advice on how to spot a fake:

9   ***Consider the source.***   In recent months, we've fact-checked fake news from abcnews.com.co (not the actual URL for ABC News), WTOE 5 News (whose "about" page says it's "a fantasy news website"), and the *Boston Tribune* (whose "contact us" page lists only a gmail address). Earlier this year, we debunked the claim that the Obamas were buying a vacation home in Dubai, a made-up missive that came from WhatDoesItMean.com, which describes itself as "One Of The Top Ranked Websites In The World for New World Order, Conspiracy Theories and Alternative News" and further says on its site that most of what it publishes is fiction.

10   Clearly, some of these sites do provide a "fantasy news" or satire warning, like WTOE 5, which published the bogus headline, "Pope Francis Shocks World,

Endorses Donald Trump for President, Releases Statement." Others aren't so upfront, like the *Boston Tribune*, which doesn't provide any information on its mission, staff members or physical location—further signs that maybe this site isn't a legitimate news organization. The site, in fact, changed its name from Associated Media Coverage, after its work had been debunked by fact-checking organizations.

11 Snopes.com, which has been writing about viral claims and online rumors since the mid-1990s, maintains a list of known fake news websites, several of which have emerged in the past two years.

12 ***Read beyond the headline.*** If a provocative headline drew your attention, read a little further before you decide to pass along the shocking information. Even in legitimate news stories, the headline doesn't always tell the whole story. But fake news, particularly efforts to be satirical, can include several revealing signs in the text. That abcnews.com.co story that we checked, headlined "Obama Signs Executive Order Banning The Pledge Of Allegiance In Schools Nationwide," went on to quote "Fappy the Anti-Masturbation Dolphin." We have to assume that the many readers who asked us whether this viral rumor was true hadn't read the full story.

13 ***Check the author.*** Another tell-tale sign of a fake story is often the byline. The pledge of allegiance story on abcnews.com.co was supposedly written by "Jimmy Rustling." Who is he? Well, his author page claims he is a "doctor" who won "fourteen Peabody awards and a handful of Pulitzer Prizes." Pretty impressive, if true. But it's not. No one by the name of "Rustling" has won a Pulitzer or Peabody award. The photo accompanying Rustling's bio is also displayed on another bogus story on a different site, but this time under the byline "Darius Rubics." The Dubai story was written by "Sorcha Faal, and as reported to her Western Subscribers." The Pope Francis story has no byline at all.

14 ***What's the support?*** Many times these bogus stories will cite official—or official-sounding—sources, but once you look into it, the source doesn't back up the claim. For instance, the *Boston Tribune* site wrongly claimed that President Obama's mother-in-law was going to get a lifetime government pension for having babysat her granddaughters in the White House, citing "the Civil Service Retirement Act" and providing a link. But the link to a government benefits website doesn't support the claim at all.

15 The banning-the-pledge story cites the number of an actual executive order—you can look it up. It doesn't have anything to do with the Pledge of Allegiance.

16 Another viral claim we checked a year ago was a graphic purporting to show crime statistics on the percentage of whites killed by blacks and other murder statistics by race. Then-presidential candidate Donald Trump retweeted it, telling Fox News commentator Bill O'Reilly that it came "from sources that are very credible." But almost every figure in the image was wrong—FBI crime data is publicly

▶

available—and the supposed source given for the data, "Crime Statistics Bureau — San Francisco," doesn't exist.

17   Recently, we've received several questions about a fake news story on the admittedly satirical site Nevada County Scooper, which wrote that Vice President-elect Mike Pence, in a "surprise announcement," credited gay conversion therapy for saving his marriage. Clearly such a "surprise announcement" would garner media coverage beyond a website you've never heard of. In fact, if you Google this, the first link that comes up is a Snopes.com article revealing that this is fake news.

18   *Check the date.*   Some false stories aren't completely fake, but rather distortions of real events. These mendacious claims can take a legitimate news story and twist what it says—or even claim that something that happened long ago is related to current events.

19   Since Trump was elected president, we've received many inquiries from readers wanting to know whether Ford had moved car production from Mexico to Ohio, because of Trump's election. Readers cited various blog items that quoted from and linked to a CNN Money article titled "Ford shifts truck production from Mexico to Ohio." But that story is from August 2015, clearly not evidence of Ford making any move due to the outcome of the election. (A reminder again to check the support for these claims.)

20   One deceptive website didn't credit CNN, but instead took CNN's 2015 story and slapped a new headline and publication date on it, claiming, "Since Donald Trump Won The Presidency . . . Ford Shifts Truck Production From Mexico To Ohio." Not only is that a bogus headline, but the deception involves copyright infringement.

21   If this Ford story sounds familiar, that's because the CNN article has been distorted before.

22   In October 2015, Trump wrongly boasted that Ford had changed its plans to build new plants in Mexico, and instead would build a plant in Ohio. Trump took credit for Ford's alleged change of heart and tweeted a link to a story on a blog called Prntly.com, which cited the CNN Money story. But Ford hadn't changed its plans at all, and Trump deserved no credit.

23   In fact, the CNN article was about the transfer of some pickup assembly work from Mexico to Ohio, a move that was announced by Ford in March 2014. The plans for new plants in Mexico were still on, Ford said. "Ford has not spoken with Mr. Trump, nor have we made any changes to our plans," Ford said in a statement.

24   *Is this some kind of joke?*   Remember, there is such thing as satire. Normally, it's clearly labeled as such, and sometimes it's even funny. Andy Borowitz has been writing a satirical news column, the Borowitz Report, since 2001, and it

has appeared in the *New Yorker* since 2012. But not everyone gets the jokes. We've fielded several questions on whether Borowitz's work is true.

25   Among the headlines our readers have flagged: "Putin Appears with Trump in Flurry of Swing-State Rallies" and "Trump Threatens to Skip Remaining Debates If Hillary Is There." When we told readers these were satirical columns, some indicated that they suspected the details were far-fetched but wanted to be sure.

26   And then there's the more debatable forms of satire, designed to pull one over on the reader. That "Fappy the Anti-Masturbation Dolphin" story? That's the work of online hoaxer Paul Horner, whose "greatest coup," as described by *The Washington Post* in 2014, was when Fox News mentioned, as fact, a fake piece titled, "Obama uses own money to open Muslim museum amid government shutdown." Horner told the *Post* after the election that he was concerned his hoaxes aimed at Trump supporters may have helped the campaign.

27   The posts by Horner and others—whether termed satire or simply "fake news"—are designed to encourage clicks, and generate money for the creator through ad revenue. Horner told *The Washington Post* he makes a living off his posts. Asked why his material gets so many views, Horner responded, "They just keep passing stuff around. Nobody fact-checks anything anymore."

28   ***Check your biases.***   We know this is difficult. Confirmation bias leads people to put more stock in information that confirms their beliefs and discount information that doesn't. But the next time you're automatically appalled at some Facebook post concerning, say, a politician you oppose, take a moment to check it out.

29   Try this simple test: What other stories have been posted to the "news" website that is the source of the story that just popped up in your Facebook feed? You may be predisposed to believe that Obama bought a house in Dubai, but how about a story on the same site that carries this headline: "Antarctica 'Guardians' Retaliate Against America With Massive New Zealand Earthquake." That, too, was written by the prolific "Sorcha Faal, and as reported to her Western Subscribers."

30   We're encouraged by some of the responses we get from readers, who—like the ones uncertain of Borowitz's columns—express doubt in the outrageous and just want to be sure their skepticism is justified. But we are equally discouraged when we see debunked claims gain new life.

31   We've seen the resurgence of a fake quote from Donald Trump since the election—a viral image that circulated last year claims Trump told *People* magazine in 1998: "If I were to run, I'd run as a Republican. They're the dumbest group of voters in the country. They believe anything on Fox News. I could lie and they'd still eat it up. I bet my numbers would be terrific." We found no such quote in *People*'s archives from 1998, or any other year. And a public relations representative

▶

for the magazine confirmed that. *People*'s Julie Farin told us in an email last year: "We combed through every Trump story in our archive. We couldn't find anything remotely like this quote—and no interview at all in 1998."

32   Comedian Amy Schumer may have contributed to the revival of this fake meme. She put it on Instagram, adding at the end of a lengthy message, "Yes this quote is fake but it doesn't matter."

33   ***Consult the experts.***   We know you're busy, and some of this debunking takes time. But we get paid to do this kind of work. Between FactCheck.org, Snopes.com, *The Washington Post* Fact Checker and PolitiFact.com, it's likely at least one has already fact-checked the latest viral claim to pop up in your news feed.

34   FactCheck.org was among a network of independent fact-checkers who signed an open letter to Facebook's Mark Zuckerberg suggesting that Facebook "start an open conversation on the principles that could underpin a more accurate news eco-system on its News Feed." We hope that conversation happens, but news readers themselves remain the first line of defense against fake news.

↳ 4.17 Activity

Evaluating Fake News

Working in your group and using the list of strategies for recognizing fake news that you compiled while reading the article "How to Spot Fake News" (4.16, p. 167), search for each of the articles listed below, using the search terms provided, and determine whether it is providing fake news or factual information. (If you find that any of the search terms provided do not work, there is a list of updated URLs available at https://bit.ly/33IIHtf.)

1. "California Soon to Be the First State to Teach LGBT History in Public Schools," cnsnews.com (Type "california first LGBT school cnsnews" into your browser to locate this article.)

2. "White House Releases Obama's Birth Certificate," CNN Political Unit. (Type the entire title of this article into your browser in order to access this article.)

3. "PDF Layers in Obama's Birth Certificate," Nathan Goulding. (Type "pdf layers Obama Goulding" into your browser to locate this article.)

4. "Ginsburg: 'I Am Mentally Fit Enough to Serve through the End of Eisenhower's Term.'" (Type the entire title of this article into your browser in order to access this article.)

5. "Vice President Mike Pence: Our Agenda Is Working for Philadelphia," Mike Pence. (Type "pence philadelphia opinion" into your browser to locate this article.)

Considering Objective versus Subjective Reporting

▲ Reporters are supposed to report the news objectively, focusing on the facts, not their personal opinions. Are they successful? Should this be their goal?

FrameStockFootages/Shutterstock

4.18 Reading

"When Reporters Get Personal," Margaret Sullivan

Other readings in this project have focused on facts, lies, fake news, and experts. This one takes a different approach. In this article, which appeared on the *New York Times* website on January 5, 2013, Margaret Sullivan explores the question of whether news reporters should aim to be objective in their reporting (basing their writing on facts, avoiding bias, and striving not to be influenced by their personal feelings) or should simply be honest with readers about their biases and opinions.

Before you dive into reading this, take a few minutes to do some previewing. (For a refresher on previewing strategies, read Previewing a Text [20.2, p. 575].)

When Reporters Get Personal

MARGARET SULLIVAN

Born in Lackawanna, New York, Margaret Sullivan graduated from Georgetown University and received a master's degree in journalism from Northwest University. She served as public editor for the *New York Times* from 2012 to 2016. A public editor writes a regular column in a newspaper exploring issues with the paper's coverage and policies. This public editor article discusses objectivity in news reporting.

The New York Times

JANUARY 5, 2013

1   Bill Grueskin remembers being an editor at *The Wall Street Journal* in 2004 when Farnaz Fassihi's e-mail, meant for a few friends' eyes only, began to circle the globe. Ms. Fassihi, an Iranian-American, was a reporter for *The Journal*, and the exposure of her views about the deteriorating situation in Iraq, provocative and incisive, was shocking. Published outside the normal bounds of painfully balanced journalism, her missive gave readers an unfiltered blast of reality.

2   "It was startling to read it, and the reaction was explosive," said Mr. Grueskin, now the academic dean at Columbia University's Graduate School of Journalism.

3   Since then, the debate about whether reporters should expose their personal views has only gathered power and velocity. The debate—in a different form—flared again a few weeks ago when I wrote on my blog about *The Times*'s Jerusalem bureau chief, Jodi Rudoren. Ms. Rudoren, writing on Facebook, had expressed personal thoughts about Palestinians in a way she later regretted. But some observers saw an important lesson in the situation.

4   "Journalists' thoughts and beliefs DO matter, enough of this 'objectivity' myth," Jillian York, a free-speech advocate, wrote on Twitter.

5   The message from some readers: We don't want a reporter's personal beliefs covered up, even if we disagree. One who commented on my blog, Mark from Sydney, wrote: "I think the instinct to maintain the old fiction that professional journalists can free themselves of their personal views and habits of mind is doomed to failure."

6   In an increasingly polarized society, this is an increasingly important subject, and a complex one. Does objectivity matter? Is the idea of impartiality worth preserving? Let's acknowledge upfront that it is a two-headed beast: partly about the personal biases that reporters may bring into their work, and partly about the middle-ground reporting that muddies the truth in the name of fairness.

7   Jay Rosen, a New York University journalism professor, believes that traditional notions about impartial reporting are fundamentally flawed. For starters, he thinks journalists should just come out and tell readers more about their beliefs.

8   "The grounds for trust are slowly shifting," he told me recently. "The View from Nowhere is slowly getting harder to trust, and 'Here's where I'm coming from' is more likely to be trusted."

9   Pushing back are editors like Philip B. Corbett, *The Times*'s associate managing editor for standards. "I flatly reject the notion that there is no such thing as impartial, objective journalism—that it's some kind of pretense or charade, and we should just give it up, come clean and lay out our biases," he said. "We expect professionals in all sorts of fields to put their personal opinions aside, or keep them to themselves, when they do their work—judges, police officers, scientists, teachers. Why would we expect less of journalists?"

10   Neither of these thoughtful journalists, though, is black-and-white on the subject.

11   Mr. Rosen won't go so far as to say that *The Times*'s Washington bureau chief, for example, should have a Web page summarizing whom he voted for, whether he believes in abortion rights, and what political party he is registered with. While he believes that is the right direction for journalists, "I also understand that there are lots of practical problems, including the simple fact that the Washington bureau chief will get attacked for saying that."

12   And for his part, Mr. Corbett doesn't expect reporters and editors to be faceless, impersonal entities. He encourages them to take part in Web-based chats where readers can get to know the people behind the bylines. He supports *Times* journalists' use of Facebook, Twitter and other social media platforms to communicate in a more personal way.

13   But that's a far cry from making public declarations of political opinions, a practice he believes would "erode our credibility and feed the false notion that there are no real facts, no impartial reporting or analysis—just spin and polemic."

14   I agree with Mr. Corbett that *The Times*'s credibility would be damaged if its reporters began declaring their partisan beliefs. As he notes, readers already have a hard time accepting that reporting is fair-minded.

15   But I also appreciate an element of Mr. Rosen's philosophy. In his view, objectivity is problematic when it involves "taking the midpoint between opposing sides and calling that neither/nor position 'impartial.'" He's dead right about that.

16   As I've written before, what readers really want is reporting that gets to the bottom of a story without having to give opposing sides equal weight. They also want

▶

reporters to state established truths clearly, without hedging or always putting the words in a source's mouth.

17 They're most interested in truth. Smart journalists may reasonably differ on how to get there. Mr. Rosen says, "Tell us where you're coming from." Mr. Corbett says, "Check your personal beliefs at the door."

18 I'll offer these conclusions:

- The idea that "transparency is the new objectivity," as the author David Weinberger puts it, has merit. Journalists can let readers get to know their backgrounds, their personalities and how they do their jobs. *The Times* has embraced that move toward transparency, through social media, Web-based chats with journalists, and even its employment of a public editor who explains the paper to readers.

- But there should be limits, especially for news reporters, as opposed to opinion writers. *The Times* should continue to enforce its rules that bar journalists from the most visible forms of partisanship: contributing to campaigns, joining rallies or making public shows of support for candidates or causes. It would be hard for readers to believe that a reporter who contributed to a campaign or carried a sign in an abortion-related rally could report without bias.

- If "impartiality" means an even split between opposing beliefs in every article, the concept deserves to be tossed out. Get at the truth, above all. But getting at the truth can require setting aside personal views to evaluate evidence fairly. If that's impartiality, it remains not only worthwhile but crucially necessary.

↳ **4.19** Activity

Analyzing "When Reporters Get Personal"

A good way to really engage with a reading and think through what an author says is to work in a group to find and discuss answers to questions about it. Working in your assigned group, answer the following questions about "When Reporters Get Personal."

1. In paragraph 6 of the article, Sullivan points out that the topic of objectivity is a "two-headed beast," that there are two different issues that should be discussed in reference to objectivity by reporters. What are these two issues?

2. In paragraph 16, Margaret Sullivan says, "As I've written before, what readers really want is reporting that gets to the bottom of a story without having to give opposing sides equal weight. They also want reporters to state established truths clearly, without hedging or always putting the words in a

source's mouth." How do you feel about this as a summary of what reporters should aim to do?

3. In the second bullet of paragraph 18, Sullivan writes, "But there should be limits, especially for news reporters, as opposed to opinion writers." What is the difference between "news reporters" and "opinion writers"? Sections of newspapers are often labeled with one of these terms: *editorial*, *op-ed*, and *news analysis*. What do these terms mean? While you're exploring journalism lingo, think about a couple more: What is the difference between a *news show* and a *talk show* on television? What do these phrases mean: "according to sources" and "alleged"?

4. Do you agree or disagree with Sullivan's assertion in the final bullet of paragraph 18 that "If 'impartiality' means an even split between opposing beliefs in every article, the concept deserves to be tossed out"?

Understanding Tribalism

▲ What's happening to America?   TeddyandMia/Shutterstock

"America Wasn't Built for Humans," Andrew Sullivan

Now that you have a working sense of what constitutes truth and lies, and what the difference is between news and fake news, read this essay, "America Wasn't Built for Humans" by Andrew Sullivan. It discusses the dire consequences of people taking extreme positions on either side of the political spectrum, only listening to those they already agree with and in the process becoming so polarized they can no longer communicate or work together effectively. Andrew Sullivan looks at how American society got to where it is now, why this is dangerous, and what we can do to change the dialogue and the direction of our political system.

Sullivan's essay appeared in *New York Magazine* on September 18, 2017. The original article was thirteen pages long; this version omits sections (marked with asterisks) that referred to issues that seemed important in 2017, but which might not be current at the time you are reading the essay. If you'd like to read the entire article, type "can our democracy survive tribalism?" into your browser. (If the search terms do not work, there is an updated list of URLs at https://bit.ly/33IIHtf.)

As with most reading you do, annotating the text as you read it will help you to start a dialogue with the author, think more deeply about his ideas, and become clearer about your own views on the topic. Remember that annotating means a lot more than just highlighting everything that seems important. You may want to read Annotation Explained (20.6, p. 583). In addition, if you want more information on previewing, look at Previewing a Text (20.2, p. 575).

America Wasn't Built for Humans

ANDREW SULLIVAN

Andrew Sullivan, born in England in 1963 and now an American citizen living in Washington, DC, is an author, editor, and blogger. His conservative views grew out of his Roman Catholic background, but in 2003, he announced he could not support the American conservative movement because of the Republican Party's rightward movement on social issues, which started during the presidency of George W. Bush. Today he remains an openly gay Roman Catholic. Sullivan has published six books and has written blogs for *Time Magazine,* the *Atlantic,* and the *Daily Beast.*

New York Magazine

SEPTEMBER 18, 2017

1   From time to time, I've wondered what it must be like to live in a truly tribal society. Watching Iraq or Syria these past few years, you get curious about how the

collective mind can come so undone. What's it like to see the contours of someone's face, or hear his accent, or learn the town he's from, and almost reflexively know that he is your foe? How do you live peacefully for years among fellow citizens and then find yourself suddenly engaged in the mass murder of humans who look similar to you, live around you, and believe in the same God, but whose small differences in theology mean they must be killed before they kill you? In the Balkans, a long period of relative peace imposed by communism was shattered by brutal sectarian and ethnic warfare, as previously intermingled citizens split into irreconcilable groups. The same has happened in a developed democratic society—Northern Ireland—and in one of the most successful countries in Africa, Kenya.

*   *   *

2   But then we don't really have to wonder what it's like to live in a tribal society anymore, do we? Because we already do. Over the past couple of decades in America, the enduring, complicated divides of ideology, geography, party, class, religion, and race have mutated into something deeper, simpler to map, and therefore much more ominous. I don't just mean the rise of political polarization (although that's how it often expresses itself), nor the rise of political violence (the domestic terrorism of the late 1960s and '70s was far worse), nor even this country's ancient black-white racial conflict (though its potency endures).

3   I mean a new and compounding combination of all these differences into two coherent tribes, eerily balanced in political power, fighting not just to advance their own side but to provoke, condemn, and defeat the other.

4   I mean two tribes whose mutual incomprehension and loathing can drown out their love of country, each of whom scans current events almost entirely to see if they advance not so much their country's interests but their own. I mean two tribes where one contains most racial minorities and the other is disproportionately white; where one tribe lives on the coasts and in the cities and the other is scattered across a rural and exurban expanse; where one tribe holds on to traditional faith and the other is increasingly contemptuous of religion altogether; where one is viscerally nationalist and the other's outlook is increasingly global; where each dominates a major political party; and, most dangerously, where both are growing in intensity as they move further apart.

5   The project of American democracy—to live beyond such tribal identities, to construct a society based on the individual, to see ourselves as citizens of a people's republic, to place religion off-limits, and even in recent years to embrace a multiracial and post-religious society—was always an extremely precarious endeavor. It rested, from the beginning, on an 18th-century hope that deep divides can be bridged by a culture of compromise, and that emotion can be defeated by reason. It failed once, ▶

spectacularly, in the most brutal civil war any Western democracy has experienced in modern times. And here we are, in an equally tribal era, with a deeply divisive president who is suddenly scrambling Washington's political alignments, about to find out if we can prevent it from failing again.

6   Tribalism, it's always worth remembering, is not one aspect of human experience. It's the *default* human experience. It comes more naturally to us than any other way of life. For the overwhelming majority of our time on this planet, the tribe was the only form of human society. We lived for tens of thousands of years in compact, largely egalitarian groups of around 50 people or more, connected to each other by genetics and language, usually unwritten. Most tribes occupied their own familiar territory, with widespread sharing of food and no private property. A tribe had its own leaders and a myth of its own history. It sorted out what we did every day, what we thought every hour.

*   *   *

7   Comparatively few actual tribes exist today, but that doesn't mean that humans are *genetically* much different.

*   *   *

8   Successful modern democracies do not abolish this feeling; they co-opt it. Healthy tribalism endures in civil society in benign and overlapping ways. We find a sense of belonging, of unconditional pride, in our neighborhood and community; in our ethnic and social identities and their rituals; among our fellow enthusiasts. There are hip-hop and country-music tribes; bros; nerds; Wasps; Dead Heads and Packers fans; Facebook groups. (Yes, technology upends some tribes and enables new ones.) And then, most critically, there is the *Über*-tribe that constitutes the nation-state, a megatribe that unites a country around shared national rituals, symbols, music, history, mythology, and events, that forms the core unit of belonging that makes a national democracy possible.

9   None of this is a problem. Tribalism only destabilizes a democracy when it calcifies into something bigger and more intense than our smaller, multiple loyalties; when it rivals our attachment to the nation as a whole; and when it turns rival tribes into enemies. And the most significant fact about American tribalism today is that all three of these characteristics now apply to our political parties, corrupting and even threatening our system of government.

*   *   *

10   And in the first half of the 20th century, with immigration sharply curtailed after 1924, the world wars acted as great unifiers and integrators. Our political parties became less polarized by race, as the FDR Democrats managed to attract more

black voters as well as ethnic and southern whites. By 1956, nearly 40 percent of black voters still backed the GOP.

11   But we all know what happened next. The re-racialization of our parties began with Barry Goldwater's presidential campaign in 1964, when the GOP lost almost all of the black vote. It accelerated under Nixon's "southern strategy" in the wake of the civil-rights revolution. By Reagan's reelection, the two parties began to cohere again into the Civil War pattern, and had simply swapped places.

* * *

12   Then there were other accelerants: The arrival of talk radio in the 1980s, Fox News in the '90s, and internet news and MSNBC in the aughts; the colossal blunder of the Iraq War, which wrecked the brief national unity after 9/11; and the rise of partisan gerrymandering that allowed the GOP to win, in 2016, 49 percent of the vote but 55 percent of House seats. (A recent study found that a full fifth of current districts are more convoluted than the original, contorted district that first gave us the term *gerrymander* in 1812.) The greatest threat to a politician today therefore is less a candidate from the opposing party than a more ideologically extreme primary opponent. The incentives for cross-tribal compromise have been eviscerated, and those for tribal extremism reinforced.

13   Add to this the great intellectual sorting of America, in which, for generations, mass college education sifted countless gifted young people from the heartland and deposited them in increasingly left-liberal universities and thereafter the major cities, from which they never returned, and then the shifting of our economy to favor the college-educated, which only deepened the urban-rural divide. The absence of compulsory military service meant that our wars would be fought disproportionately by one tribe, and the rise of radical Islamic terrorism only inflamed tribal suspicions. Then there's the post-1965 wave of mass immigration, which disorients in ways that cannot be wished or shamed away; the decision among the country's intellectual elite to junk the "melting pot" metaphor as a model for immigration in favor of "multiculturalism"; and the decline of Christianity as a common cultural language for both political parties—which had been critical, for example, to the success of the civil-rights movement.

14   The myths that helped us unite as a nation began to fray. We once had a widely accepted narrative of our origins, shared icons that defined us, and a common pseudo-ethnicity—"whiteness"—into which new immigrants were encouraged to assimilate. Our much broader ethnic mix and the truths of history make this much harder today—as, of course, they should. But we should be clear-eyed about the consequence. We can no longer think of the Puritans without acknowledging the

▶

genocide that followed them; we cannot celebrate our Founding Fathers without seeing that slavery undergirded the society they constructed; we must tear down our Confederate statues and relitigate our oldest rifts. Even the national anthem now divides those who stand from those who kneel. We dismantled many of our myths, but have not yet formed new ones to replace them.

15   The result of all this is that a lopsided 69 percent of white Christians now vote Republican, while the Democrats get only 31. In the last decade, the gap in Christian identification between Democrats and Republicans has increased by 50 percent. In 2004, 44 percent of Latinos voted Republican for president; in 2016, 29 percent did. Forty-three percent of Asian-Americans voted Republican in 2004; in 2016, 29 percent did. Since 2004, the most populous urban counties have also swung decisively toward the Democrats, in both blue and red states, while rural counties have shifted sharply to the GOP. When three core components of a tribal identity—race, religion, and geography—define your political parties, you're in serious trouble.

* * *

16   And so by 2017, 41 percent of Republicans and 38 percent of Democrats said they disagreed not just with their opponents' political views but with their values and goals beyond politics as well. Nearly 60 percent of all Americans find it stressful even to talk about Trump with someone who disagrees with them. A Monmouth poll, for good measure, recently found that 61 percent of Trump supporters say there's nothing he could do to make them change their minds about him; 57 percent of his opponents say the same thing. *Nothing* he could do.

17   One of the great attractions of tribalism is that you don't actually have to think very much. All you need to know on any given subject is which side you're on. You pick up signals from everyone around you, you slowly winnow your acquaintances to those who will reinforce your worldview, a tribal leader calls the shots, and everything slips into place. After a while, your immersion in tribal loyalty makes the activities of another tribe not just alien but close to incomprehensible. It has been noticed, for example, that primitive tribes can sometimes call their members simply "people" while describing others as some kind of alien. So the word *Inuit* means people, but a rival indigenous people, the Ojibwe, call them Eskimos, which, according to lore, means "eaters of raw meat."

18   When criticized by a member of a rival tribe, a tribalist will not reflect on his own actions or assumptions but instantly point to the same flaw in his enemy. The most powerful tribalist among us, Trump, does this constantly. When confronted with his own history of sexual assault, for example, he gave the tiniest of apologies and immediately accused his opponent's husband of worse, inviting several of Bill Clinton's accusers to

a press conference. But in this, he was only reflecting the now near-ubiquitous trend of "whataboutism," as any glance at a comments section or a cable slugfest will reveal. The Soviets perfected this in the Cold War, deflecting from their horrific Gulags by pointing, for example, to racial strife in the U.S. It tells you a lot about our time that a tactic once honed in a global power struggle between two nations now occurs within one. What the Soviets used against us we now use against one another.

* * *

19 Conservative dissent therefore becomes tribal blasphemy. Free speech can quickly become "hate speech," "hate speech" becomes indistinguishable from a "hate crime," and a crime needs to be punished. Many members of the academic elite regard opposing views as threats to others' existences, and conservative speakers often can only get a hearing on campus under lockdown.

20 There is, of course, an enormous conservative intellectual counter-Establishment, an often incestuous network of think tanks, foundations, journals, and magazines that exists outside of universities. It, too, has fomented its own orthodoxies, policed dissent, and punished heresy.

21 Conservatism thrived in America when it was dedicated to criticizing liberalism's failures, engaging with it empirically, and offering practical alternatives to the same problems. It has since withered into an intellectual movement that does little but talk to itself and guard its ideological boundaries.

* * *

22 And so, among tribal conservatives, the Iraq War remained a taboo topic when it wasn't still regarded as a smashing success, tax cuts were still the solution to every economic woe, free trade was all benefit and no cost, and so on. Health care was perhaps the most obvious example of this intellectual closure. Republican opposition to the Affordable Care Act was immediate and total. Even though the essential contours of the policy had been honed at the Heritage Foundation, even though a Republican governor had pioneered it in Massachusetts, and even though that governor became the Republican nominee in 2012, the anathematization of it defined the GOP for seven years. After conservative writer David Frum dared to argue that a moderate, market-oriented reform to the health-care system was not the ideological hill for the GOP to die on, he lost his job at the American Enterprise Institute. When it actually came to undoing the reform earlier this year, the GOP had precious little intellectual capital to fall back on, no alternative way to keep millions insured, no history of explaining to voters outside their own tribe what principles they were even trying to apply.

* * *

▶

23   Total immersion within one's tribe also leads to increasingly extreme ideas. The word "hate," for example, has now become a one-stop replacement for a whole spectrum of varying, milder emotions involved with bias toward others: discomfort, fear, unease, suspicion, ignorance, confusion. And it has even now come to include simply defending traditional Christian, Jewish, and Muslim doctrine on questions such as homosexuality.

* * *

24   Liberals should be able to understand this by reading any conservative online journalism and encountering the term "the left." It represents a large, amorphous blob of malevolent human beings, with no variation among them, no reasonable ideas, nothing identifiably human at all. Start perusing, say, townhall.com, and you will soon stumble onto something like this, written recently by one of my favorite right-tribalists, Kurt Schlichter: "They hate you. Leftists don't merely disagree with you. They don't merely feel you are misguided. They don't think you are merely wrong. They hate you. They want you enslaved and obedient, if not dead. Once you get that, everything that is happening now will make sense." And, yes, everything will. How does Schlichter describe the right? "Normals." It's the Inuit and the Eskimos all over again.

* * *

25   Tribalism is not a static force. It feeds on itself. It appeals on a gut level and evokes emotions that are not easily controlled and usually spiral toward real conflict. And there is no sign that the deeper forces that have accelerated this—globalization, social atomization, secularization, media polarization, ever more multiculturalism—will weaken. The rhetorical extremes have already been pushed further than most of us thought possible only a couple of years ago, and the rival camps are even more hermetically sealed. In 2015, did any of us anticipate that neo-Nazis would be openly parading with torches on a college campus or that antifa activists would be proudly extolling violence as the only serious response to the Trump era?

26   As utopian as it sounds, I truly believe all of us have to at least try to change the culture from the ground up. There are two ideas that might be of help, it seems to me. The first is individuality. I don't mean individualism. Nothing is more conducive to tribalism than a sea of disconnected, atomized individuals searching for some broader tribe to belong to. I mean valuing the unique human being—distinct from any group identity, quirky, full of character and contradictions, skeptical, rebellious, immune to being labeled or bludgeoned into a broader tribal grouping. This cultural antidote to tribalism, left and right, is still here in America and ready to be rediscovered. That we expanded the space for this to flourish is one of the greatest achievements of the West.

27   Perhaps I'm biased because I'm an individual by default. I'm gay but Catholic, conservative but independent, a Brit but American, religious but secular. What tribe would ever have me? I may be an extreme case, but we all are nonconformist to some degree. Nurturing your difference or dissent from your own group is difficult; appreciating the individuality of those in other tribes is even harder. It takes effort and imagination, openness to dissent, even an occasional embrace of blasphemy.

28   And, at some point, we also need mutual forgiveness. It doesn't matter if you believe, as I do, that the right bears the bulk of the historical blame. No tribal conflict has ever been unwound without magnanimity. Yitzhak Rabin had it, but it was not enough. Nelson Mandela had it, and it was. In Colombia earlier this month, as a fragile peace agreement met public opposition, Pope Francis insisted that grudges be left behind: "All of us are necessary to create and form a society. This isn't just done with the 'pure-blooded' ones, but rather with everyone. And here is where the greatness of the country lies, in that there is room for all and all are important." If societies scarred by recent domestic terrorism can aim at this, why should it be so impossible for us?

29   But this requires, of course, first recognizing our own tribal thinking. So much of our debates are now an easy either/or rather than a complicated both/and. In our tribal certainties, we often distort what we actually believe in the quiet of our hearts, and fail to see what aspects of truth the other tribe may grasp.

30   Not all resistance to mass immigration or multiculturalism is mere racism or bigotry; and not every complaint about racism and sexism is baseless. Many older white Americans are not so much full of hate as full of fear. Equally, many minorities and women face genuine blocks to their advancement because of subtle and unsubtle bias, and it is not mere victim-mongering. We also don't have to deny African-American agency in order to account for the historic patterns of injustice that still haunt an entire community. We need to recall that most immigrants are simply seeking a better life, but also that a country that cannot control its borders is not a country at all. We're rightly concerned that religious faith can easily lead to intolerance, but we needn't conclude that having faith is a pathology. We need not renounce our cosmopolitanism to reengage and respect those in rural America, and we don't have to abandon our patriotism to see that the urban mix is also integral to what it means to be an American today. The actual solutions to our problems are to be found in the current no-man's-land that lies between the two tribes. Reentering it with empiricism and moderation to find different compromises for different issues is the only way out of our increasingly dangerous impasse.

31   All of this runs deeply against the grain. It's counterintuitive. It's emotionally unpleasant. It fights against our very DNA. Compared with bathing in the affirming balm of a tribe, it's deeply unsatisfying. But no one ever claimed that living in a republic was going to be easy—if we really want to keep it.

→ **4.21** Writing

Thinking about Tribalism

In his essay "America Wasn't Built for Humans" (4.20, p. 178), Andrew Sullivan explains why tribalism has come to dominate American society and why he thinks this is a problem. In this short writing assignment, discuss what Sullivan's solution to the problem is. What does he think can be done to reduce the level of tribalism in this country?

4.22 Video

"Can a Divided America Heal?"

You have just read Andrew Sullivan's article "America Wasn't Built for Humans" (4.20, p. 178), in which he discusses the origins and consequences of tribalism. Now you are going to watch a video of social psychologist Jonathan Haidt discussing how tribalism is dominating the political and social culture in America.

To access the video of Haidt's TED Talk from November 2016, type "ted talk haidt divided america" into your browser. (If these search terms do not work, there is a list of URLs available at https://bit.ly/33IIHtf.)

While you are welcome to watch the entire video (20 minutes), for this assignment, you are only expected to watch up to minute 3:50, after Haidt introduces the terms *drawbridge uppers* and *drawbridge downers*.

→ **4.23** Activity

Are You a Tribalist?

In "America Wasn't Built for Humans" (4.20, p. 178) and the video "Can a Divided America Heal?" (4.22), you read an author and heard a psychologist arguing that America is becoming a nation made up of tribes of people who believe so strongly in their tribe's positions that they cannot listen to differing views and view members of other tribes as not just mistaken, but evil and dangerous.

Discussing Tribalism

Working in your group, discuss your responses to the questions below.

1. Sullivan points out the following:

    Healthy tribalism endures in civil society in benign and overlapping ways. We find a sense of belonging, of unconditional pride, in our neighborhood and community; in our ethnic and social identities and their rituals; among our fellow enthusiasts. There are hip-hop and country-music tribes; bros; nerds; Wasps; Dead Heads and Packers fans; Facebook groups. (Yes, technology upends some tribes and enables new ones.)

What tribes do members of your group belong to?

2. In addition to these small-scale tribes, Sullivan argues the following:

Over the past couple of decades in America, the enduring, complicated divides of ideology, geography, party, class, religion, and race have mutated into something deeper, simpler to map, and therefore much more ominous. I don't just mean the rise of political polarization (although that's how it often expresses itself), nor the rise of political violence (the domestic terrorism of the late 1960s and '70s was far worse), nor even this country's ancient black-white racial conflict (though its potency endures).

I mean a new and compounding combination of all these differences into two coherent tribes, eerily balanced in political power, fighting not just to advance their own side but to provoke, condemn, and defeat the other.

I mean two tribes whose mutual incomprehension and loathing can drown out their love of country, each of whom scans current events almost entirely to see if they advance not so much their country's interests but their own. I mean two tribes where one contains most racial minorities and the other is disproportionately white; where one tribe lives on the coasts and in the cities and the other is scattered across a rural and exurban expanse; where one tribe holds on to traditional faith and the other is increasingly contemptuous of religion altogether; where one is viscerally nationalist and the other's outlook is increasingly global; where each dominates a major political party; and, most dangerously, where both are growing in intensity as they move further apart.

Do you agree with Sullivan about the existence of these two major tribes in America today? Do you belong to one of them?

3. Describe a time when you had a successful conversation with someone in an tribe opposed to yours.

Bringing It All Together

▲ What is a fair wage? How should it be determined? Who should determine it? David Grossman/Alamy

4.24 Writing

Research into the Truth

During the course of this project you have read, watched, discussed, and written about truth, lies, facts, and opinions. You have thought about what constitutes an expert, learned about options for fact-checking and for identifying fake news. These experiences have prepared you for this activity.

Think of an issue you would like to know the truth about, or choose one of the following:

- Whether we are winning the war in Afghanistan
- Whether drug companies overcharge

- Whether immigrants increase the amount of crime in America

- Whether universal health insurance in England results in long wait lists

- Whether coffee is harmful to your health

- Whether organic foods are beneficial to your health

- Whether the murder rate in America has increased in the past ten years

Do some investigating to find out what the truth is about the topic you have chosen. Then write a short paper—a page would be plenty—in which you describe *how* you went about learning the truth. Note that you are not being asked to argue your position on the issue in this paper, but rather to explain how you decided what the truth is. Where appropriate, discuss how the concepts you have been exploring in this unit helped you—concepts such as *facts, opinions, dishonest numbers, objectivity, fact checkers, expert, slippery words, fake news, peer-reviewed journals,* and *tribal thinking*.

4.25 Real World Essay

An Op-Ed on the Minimum Wage

The one thing Democrats and Republicans, liberals and conservatives, seem to agree on is that the other side is spreading a lot of fake news, making statements that are not true. In this environment, it is important that people be able to make well-reasoned, evidence-based decisions on important national issues. Project 4 is designed to help you develop the skills to make informed and thoughtful decisions about what you believe to be the truth by providing the following useful information.

Tools for Making Informed and Thoughtful Decisions about "Truth"

- An understanding of key terms like *truth, lie, opinion,* and *fact*

- An awareness of how fact checkers can be useful

- An awareness of how numbers can be used to deceive

- Ways to identify and evaluate "experts"

- An awareness of "slippery words" and how they can slant a report

- A method for detecting fake news

- An understanding of bias and objectivity in news reporting

- An awareness of "tribal" thinking

- Recognition of the importance of peer-reviewed journals

You may be surprised to learn that, after all this work on truth, lies, and fake news, you are now being asked to write about raising the minimum wage, a topic that wasn't discussed at all during this project. However, raising the minimum wage is a topic about which there has been a great deal of discussion, some of it factual and some "fake news." Now that you have developed insights and skills for distinguishing between facts and "fake news," you are going to write about a topic that will allow you to demonstrate your ability to apply these insights and skills.

Essay Assignment.   One way you might be able to influence public opinion on an issue like the minimum wage is to publish your argument on the editorial page of your local newspaper. For this assignment, write a three- to four-page editorial in which, based on your evaluation of a number of websites, you make a recommendation on what the minimum wage should be in your city or state. To reach your conclusion on this issue, you will need to evaluate each of the websites, making use of some of the tools listed above. You will probably want to include your evaluation of the websites as you support the position you are taking.

This kind of essay, in which you take a position and provide evidence to support that position, is known as an "argument." You may want to review these conventions in What Is an Argument? (18.1, p. 513), The Features of Effective Arguments (18.3, p. 513), and How to Answer Counterarguments (18.5, p. 514).

Documentation.   Be sure to provide appropriate citations for any words you quote, paraphrase, or summarize from the websites and to include a works cited list or list of references at the end of your essay. If you need to review how to provide this documentation, refer to MLA Documentation (Topic 23, p. 650) or APA Documentation (Topic 24, p. 687).

If you want to use your sources most effectively to support your argument, it's not enough to simply include them as a series of unrelated sources; you need to tie them together, explain their relationships with each other, and express your conclusions about them. This process is called *synthesizing*, and it is discussed in more detail in Synthesis (22.14, p. 648).

Sources.   The websites you will evaluate will include the five listed below as well as two additional sites that you locate. The websites listed below all explore the effect of raising the minimum wage on jobs, as should the two you locate.

Additional Information.   You may be a little worried that you simply don't have enough information to make these evaluations. Don't worry. Unless you have a doctorate in economics, you, like most of us, don't have nearly as much information as you would like. Nevertheless, you need to make decisions. At some point, you may need to vote on raising the minimum wage where you live. Perhaps the best advice is what Julian Baggini says at the end of "The Nature of Truth": "[W]e cannot escape the exercise of our own woefully under-informed judgement. . . . Don't think *by* yourself but do think *for* yourself, not because you're wiser or smarter than other people but because ultimately that's what you have to do. No one can make up your mind for you, unless you make up your mind to let them."

Websites.   Here are the five websites. Remember, you need to locate two more that also address the effect of raising the minimum wage on employment. You can access these sites by typing their titles into your browser. (If you cannot find a site using its title, there is an updated list of URLs available at https://bit.ly/33IIHtf.)

1. "Increase in Minimum Wage Kills Jobs," Employment Policies Institute, OpEd
2. "Minimum Wage and Job Loss: One Alarming Seattle Study Is Not the Last Word," Arindrajit Dube, *New York Times*
3. "New Minimum Wage Hikes Set to Kill Jobs in 2018," Brendan Pringle, *Washington Examiner*
4. "The Controversial Study Showing High Minimum Wages Kills Jobs, Explained," Jeff Guo, *Vox*
5. "Study: Seattle's $15 Minimum Wage WORKED," David Pakman, *HuffPost*

4.26 Academic Essay

Searching for the Truth about the Minimum Wage

The one thing Democrats and Republicans, liberals and conservatives, seem to agree on is that the other side is spreading a lot of fake news, making statements that are not true. In that environment, it is important that people be able to make well-reasoned, evidence-based decisions on important national issues. Project 4 is designed to help you develop the skills to make informed and thoughtful decisions about what you believe to be the truth by providing the following useful information.

Tools for Making Informed and Thoughtful Decisions about "Truth"

- An understanding of key terms like *truth*, *lie*, *opinion*, and *fact*
- An awareness of how fact checkers can be useful
- An awareness of how numbers can be used to deceive
- Ways to identify and evaluate "experts"

- An awareness of "slippery words" and how they can slant a report
- A method for detecting fake news
- An understanding of bias and objectivity in news reporting
- An awareness of "tribal" thinking
- Recognition of the importance of peer-reviewed journals

You may be surprised to learn that, after all this work on truth, lies, and fake news, you are being asked to write about raising the minimum wage, a topic that wasn't discussed at all during this project. However, raising the minimum wage is a topic about which there has been a great deal of discussion, some of it factual and some "fake news." Now that you have developed insights and skills for distinguishing between facts and "fake news," you are going to write about a topic that will allow you to demonstrate your ability to apply them.

Essay Assignment. For this assignment, you are going to construct as argument to convince others of your position on the minimum wage, writing a three- to four-page academic essay that would be appropriate for a course on economics, political science, sociology, business, or something similar. You will visit seven websites addressing the issue of raising the minimum wage—five are listed below and two you will find. You will evaluate each of the websites making use of some or all of the tools listed above. You will probably want to include your evaluation of the websites as you support the position you are taking. Finally, you will recommend what the minimum wage should be in your city or state based on the research you have done.

This kind of essay, in which you take a position and provide evidence to support that position, is known as an "argument." You may want to review these conventions in What Is an Argument? (18.1, p. 513), The Features of Effective Arguments (18.3, p. 513), and How to Answer Counterarguments (18.5, p. 514).

Documentation. Be sure to provide appropriate citations for any words you quote, paraphrase, or summarize from the websites and include a works cited list or list of references at the end of your essay. If you need to review how to provide this documentation, refer to MLA Documentation (Topic 23, p. 650) or APA Documentation (Topic 24, p. 687).

If you want to use your sources most effectively to support your argument, it's not enough to simply include them as a series of unrelated sources; you need to tie them together, explain their relationships with each other, and express your conclusions about them. This process is called *synthesizing*, and it is discussed in more detail in Synthesis (22.14, p. 648).

Additional Information. You may be a little worried that you simply don't have enough information to make these evaluations. Don't worry. Unless you have a doctorate in economics, you, like most of us, don't have nearly as much information as you would like. Nevertheless, you need to make decisions. At some point, you may need to vote on raising the minimum wage where you live. Perhaps the best advice is what Julian Baggini says at the end of "The Nature of Truth": "[W]e cannot escape the exercise of our own woefully under-informed judgement. . . . Don't think *by* yourself but do think *for* yoursef, not because you're wiser or smarter than other people but because ultimately that's what you have to do. No one can make up your mind for you, unless you make up your mind to let them."

Websites. Here are the five websites. Remember, you need to locate two more that also address the effect of raising the minimum wage on employment. You can access these sites by typing their titles into your browser. (If you cannot find a site using its title, there is an updated list of URLs available at https://bit.ly/33IIHtf.)

1. "Increase in Minimum Wage Kills Jobs," Employment Policies Institute, OpEd
2. "Minimum Wage and Job Loss: One Alarming Seattle Study Is Not the Last Word," Arindrajit Dube, *New York Times*
3. "New Minimum Wage Hikes Set to Kill Jobs in 2018," Brendan Pringle, *Washington Examiner*
4. "The Controversial Study Showing High Minimum Wages Kills Jobs, Explained," Jeff Guo, *Vox*
5. "Study: Seattle's $15 Minimum Wage WORKED," David Pakman, *HuffPost*

4.27 Multimodal Composition

Searching for the Truth about the Minimum Wage

The one thing Democrats and Republicans, liberals and conservatives, seem to agree on is that the other side is spreading a lot of fake news, making statements that are not true. In that environment, it is important that people be able to make well-reasoned, evidence-based decisions on important national issues. Project 4 is designed to help you develop the skills to make informed and thoughtful decisions about what you believe to be the truth by providing the following useful information.

Tools for Making Informed and Thoughtful Decisions about "Truth"

- An understanding of key terms like *truth*, *lie*, *opinion*, and *fact*
- An awareness of how fact checkers can be useful
- An awareness of how numbers can be used to deceive
- Ways to identify and evaluate "experts"
- An awareness of "slippery words" and how they can slant a report
- A method for detecting fake news
- An understanding of bias and objectivity in news reporting
- An awareness of "tribal" thinking
- Recognition of the importance of peer-reviewed journals

You may be surprised to learn that, after all this work on truth, lies, and fake news, you are being asked to express your opinions about raising the minimum wage, a topic that wasn't discussed at all during this project. However, raising the minimum wage is a topic about which there has been a great deal of discussion, some of it factual and some "fake news." Now that you have developed insights and skills for distinguishing between facts and "fake news," you are going to create a multimodal composition about the topic that will allow you to demonstrate your ability to apply them.

Multimodal Assignment.   Another way you might be able to influence public opinion on an issue like the minimum wage is to develop a digital presentation—a website, a blog, a narrated PowerPoint, a video, or podcast—in which you make your argument for what the minimum wage should be in your city or state. You will visit seven websites addressing the issue of raising the minimum wage—five are listed below and two you will find. You will evaluate each of the websites making use of some or all of the tools listed above. You will probably want to include your evaluation of the websites as you support the position you are taking. Finally, you will recommend what the minimum wage should be in your city or state based on the research you have done.

This kind of composition, in which you take a position and provide evidence to support that position, is known as an "argument." You may want to review these conventions in What Is an Argument? (18.1, p. 513), The Features of Effective Arguments (18.3, p. 513), and How to Answer Counterarguments (18.5, p. 514).

Documentation.   Be sure to provide appropriate citations for any words you quote, paraphrase, or summarize from the websites and to include a works cited list or list of references to accompany your composition. If you need to review how to provide this documentation, refer to MLA Documentation (Topic 23, p. 650) or APA Documentation (Topic 24, p. 687).

If you want to use your sources most effectively to support your argument, it's not enough to simply include them as a series of unrelated sources; you need to tie them together, explain their relationships with each other, and express your conclusions about them. This process is called *synthesizing*, and it is discussed in more detail in Synthesis (22.14, p. 648).

Additional Information.   You may be a little worried that you simply don't have enough information to make these evaluations. Don't worry. Unless you have a doctorate in economics, you, like most of us, don't have nearly as much information as you would like. Nevertheless, you need to make decisions. At some point, you may need to vote on raising the minimum wage where you live. Perhaps the best advice is what Julian Baggini says at the end of the excerpt from *A Short History of Truth*: "[W]e cannot escape the exercise of our own woefully under-informed judgement. . . . Don't think *by* yourself but do think *for* yourself, not because you're wiser or smarter than other people but because ultimately that's what you have to do. No one can make up your mind for you, unless you make up your mind to let them."

Websites.   Here are the five websites. Remember, you need to locate two more that also address the effect of raising the minimum wage on employment. You can access these sites by typing their titles into your browser. (If you cannot find a site using its title, there is an updated list of URLs available at https://bit.ly/33IIHtf.)

1. "Increase in Minimum Wage Kills Jobs," Employment Policies Institute, OpEd

2. "Minimum Wage and Job Loss: One Alarming Seattle Study Is Not the Last Word," Arindrajit Dube, *New York Times*

3. "New Minimum Wage Hikes Set to Kill Jobs in 2018," Brendan Pringle, *Washington Examiner*

4. "The Controversial Study Showing High Minimum Wages Kills Jobs, Explained" Jeff Guo, Vox

5. "Study: Seattle's $15 Minimum Wage WORKED," David Pakman, *HuffPost*

 **4.28**   **Activity**

Getting Started on Your Essay or Multimodal Composition

You have received the final assignments for this project: An Op-Ed on the Minimum Wage (4.25, p. 189), Searching for the Truth about the Minimum Wage (4.26, p. 191), or Searching for the Truth about the Minimum Wage (multimodal composition; 4.27, p. 193).

In this class period, you will have time to get started on your assignment(s) by doing some of the following:

- Making sure you understand the assignment

- Thinking about the audience and purpose for your assignment (you may want to review Thinking about Audience [9.4, p. 328] and Thinking about Purpose [9.6, p. 331])

- Exploring the websites provided in the assignment

- Searching for other websites, especially websites related to the minimum wage in your city or state

- Brainstorming a list of ideas you may want to include in your final product

- Talking with your classmates or your instructor about the assignment

- Talking to others who are considering a multimodal composition

4.29 Writing

Reflecting on Project 4: Truth, Lies, and Fake News

Reflective writing is different from most writing you do in college. Reflective writing asks you to think back, to "reflect" on an experience—an essay you have written, a major change in your life, a time when you didn't have success at something you wanted to do, a semester's work in a course—and to examine how you now think and feel about that experience. What effect has the experience had on you? How have you changed? How will you be different in the future? If you'd like a little more explanation of this type of writing, visit Strategies for Writing a Reflection (18.29, p. 555).

Now you're going to reflect on all the reading, thinking, discussing, and writing you have done in this project on truth, lies, and fake news. To do this, you may want to review any short reflective writing you did as you worked through the project. Then, in a short paper—a page or so—reflect on this experience:

1. Report on what you learned. What were the most important or most useful ideas you encountered?

2. Describe how you feel about the experience and what you *think* about what you have learned.

3. Report on what you learned that will make a difference for you in the future and why.

PROJECT 5

Language and Power

Rawpixel.com/Shutterstock

Language gives people power. Those who speak a version of English that is thought of as "standard" are likely to be more successful in education and in their careers. Why is this the way it is? Why do people who speak (and write) a version different from the standard version have less power? Who decided what is considered standard? Where did they get the power to make that decision? How can those who speak a different version of English gain power? Do they have to convert to the "standard" way of speaking and writing to be successful? Do they have to give up their own language and, in the process, some of their own culture? Or is there some hope the situation can change? Should it change? These are the kinds of questions you'll be exploring in this reading/writing project.

This project will primarily deal with language issues involving African American Vernacular English (AAVE) and Standard Written English (SWE), but there are many groups in addition to African Americans who use a version of English that differs from Standard Written English—groups like Latinx, English Language Learners, many working-class Americans, speakers of Hawai'ian Creole, speakers of Nigerian English or Sri Lankan English, and people from certain geographical regions.

Each of these groups encounters issues unique to itself, but, luckily, they also face many issues in common. So the decision to focus on issues with AAVE and SWE, in the interest of keeping this project to a reasonable length, will mean you will be exploring issues most of these groups face in common.

Getting Started: Can English Be "Good" or "Bad"?

This project starts with two key questions:

1. Does the requirement that students write in Standard Written English make it harder for students who have grown up using a different version of English to succeed in college writing courses?

2. If colleges don't help students learn to write in Standard Written English, will it be harder for them to succeed in the American workplace?

Next you examine the thinking behind the terms *good English* and *bad English* and then look at some examples that explore how powerful and logical language that departs from Standard Written English can be. This section closes with a formal statement on student language issues from a national organization of college writing faculty.

Exploring, Thinking, and Writing about Ideas

In the first activity of this project you addressed two questions that raise important issues about attitudes toward language in the writing classroom. In this section you will read articles by four leading scholars on these language issues, scholars who propose several different answers to these two important questions. You will write several short papers that ask you to summarize several of the articles and to respond with your own ideas to others.

You will also complete activities related to the readings that ask you to practice specific skills, such as previewing, annotating, summarizing, analyzing, thinking critically, researching, synthesizing sources, and more. Following instructions from your instructor, you will work independently and/or in small groups to complete them. In addition, your instructor will assign relevant topics from other parts of *The Hub* that relate to writing, reading, research, and life issues to address other important skills.

Bringing It All Together

This project concludes with three assignments that ask you to combine what you've learned about these language issues as you've worked through the project with your own thinking about these issues. Your instructor may assign the first, second, or third assignment; may give you a choice among the three; or may even ask you to complete more than one.

The first assignment asks you write a proposal to the English Department at your school spelling out what you believe the department's policy on these language issues should be and supporting your proposal with evidence from the readings and with your own reasoning. The second assignment asks you to write an academic essay taking a stand on the language issue in higher education. Think of this second essay as writing that would be appropriate in a college course in education, political science, English, or something similar. A third option is much like the first except you are not limited to a written essay. Instead, you are invited to produce a multimodal composition—a narrated PowerPoint, a video, a podcast, a blog, or a website—that would be appropriate to communicate your proposal to the entire college community and to convince them to support it.

The final writing assignment, Reflecting on Project 5: Language and Power, asks you to reflect on what you have learned as you have worked through this reading/writing project.

Navigating Project 5

Below is the table of contents for Project 5, which you can use to easily locate the units you have been assigned to work on by your instructor. Several of these units ask you to connect to the Internet to watch videos or explore websites. If you find that any of the search terms provided do not work, there is a list of URLs available at https://bit.ly/33IIHtf.

Getting Started: Can English Be "Good" or "Bad"?

▲ Words are just words, aren't they? What makes them good or bad? Who decides? On what basis? Could "good English" for one person be "bad English" for another person?   pathdoc/Shutterstock

5.1 **Activity**

Two Key Questions about Standard Written English (SWE)

Scholars working on questions about language and race use several terms to describe the version of English you find in newspapers and published books, the version often expected in papers written in college courses: *Standard Written English*, *Standard Edited American English*, the *Language of Power*, and *White English*, to name a few.

In this project, the term *Standard Written English*, sometimes abbreviated as SWE, will be used.

These scholars also use several terms for the version of English used by many African Americans: *Black English, Ebonics, Black English Vernacular*, and *African American Vernacular English*. For this version of English, the term *African American Vernacular English*, sometimes abbreviated as AAVE, will be used.

You might want to photocopy this helpful chart, as the authors of the articles in this project frequently use different terms and sometimes use only the acronym.

Names and Acronyms for Types of Formal Written English	Names and Acronyms for the Versions of English Used by Many African Americans
Standard Written English (SWE)	African American Vernacular English (AAVE)
Standard English (SE)	Black English Vernacular (BEV)
Standardized English (SE)	Black English (BE)
Standard Edited American English (SEAE)	African American English (AAE)
The Language of Wider Communication (LWC)	Ebonics
Metropolitan English (ME)	African American Language (AAL)
The Language of Power	
White English	

Answering Two Key Questions

Having gotten some terminology out of the way, here's what to do for this activity: working in your group, write short answers to these two questions:

1. Does the requirement that students write in Standard Written English make it harder for students who have grown up using a different version of English to succeed in college writing courses?

2. If colleges don't help students learn to write in Standard Written English, will it be harder for them to succeed in the American workplace?

5.2 Activity

"Good" and "Bad" English

You've probably heard people talk about *good English* and *bad English*. You may have even used these terms yourself. This activity asks you to think about these terms in more depth.

Your instructor will organize the class into groups. In your group, discuss these questions:

1. What is the difference between "good" English and "bad" English?
2. Why do people consider "bad" English "bad"?
3. Who speaks and writes mostly in "good" English?
4. Why should someone want to become proficient in "good" English?

After about fifteen minutes of discussion, when your instructor gives you the word, divide up the questions among yourselves so that one of you writes a brief answer to each one. A paragraph on each one is plenty. You'll be discussing these paragraphs with the whole class.

5.3 Activity

Logic and Power in Language

Working in your group, study each of the following pairs of sentences to determine, first, which version is more logical and, second, which is more powerful. Be ready with reasons to explain and support your decisions.

1. a. I'm gonna explain how I got ovah.
   b. I'm going to explain how I outsmarted the system.
2. a. Mark hit his brother upside the head.
   b. Mark hit his brother in the head.
3. a. When you leave the room, please turn off the lights.
   b. When you leave the room, please close the lights.
4. a. This is a CD that will get you dancing.
   b. This is a CD that's bound to put some dips in your hips.
5. a. I've been a-studying about how to say "no" till I've nigh wearied myself to death.
   b. I've been thinking about how to say "no" until I have almost worried myself to death.

6. a. The new Nike sneakers take coolness to a whole 'nuther level.

   b. The new Nike sneakers are more stylish than any before.

7. a. The dude is also hella down to earth.

   b. The man is very down to earth.

5.4 **Writing**

Interpreting "Students' Right to Their Own Language"

The following brief statement was adopted in 1974 as an official policy of the Conference on College Composition and Communication, the largest national organization of college-level writing teachers.

Students' Right to Their Own Language

We affirm the students' right to their own patterns and varieties of language—the dialects of their nurture or whatever dialects in which they find their own identity and style. Language scholars long ago denied that the myth of a standard American dialect has any validity. The claim that any one dialect is unacceptable amounts to an attempt of one social group to exert its dominance over another. Such a claim leads to false advice for speakers and writers, and immoral advice for humans. A nation proud of its diverse heritage and its cultural and racial variety will preserve its heritage of dialects. We affirm strongly that teachers must have the experiences and training that will enable them to respect diversity and uphold the right of students to their own language.

Write a short essay—less than a page—in which you explain what you think this statement means.

Diversity and the Culture of Power

▲ What if the way one person speaks and writes is considered "better" than the way another person does? If both are equally intelligent and thoughtful but express themselves differently, is it fair that one should have a significantly better chance of success than the other?   lolloj/Shutterstock

5.5   Activity

Analyzing Author, Audience, Topic, and Purpose in "The Silenced Dialogue"

As long ago as classical Greece—300 BC or so—thinkers have been aware that four important components exist for every text: the *author* of the text, the *audience* for the text, the *topic* of the text, and the *purpose* of the text. Thinking about author, audience, topic, and purpose should help you prepare to read a text.

Author

You don't simply want to find out the name of the author. What else can you learn about him or her? What evidence is there that the author really has some expertise? What biases might the author have? Is the author part of an organization? A corporation? What else has the author written?

Audience

Whom does it appear that the author intended to be the reader or readers of this text? Whom was the author addressing? Were there other, more secondary, audiences?

Topic

What is the text about? What subject is the text focused on?

Purpose

What does it appear that the author intended or, at least, hoped would happen as a result of this piece of writing? What did the author want the effect of this text on its audience to be?

Analyzing Author, Audience, Topic, and Purpose

Working in your group, write a brief response—a paragraph is plenty—about each of these components—author, audience, topic, and purpose—for "The Silenced Dialogue" (5.7, p. 209).

5.6 Activity

Previewing "The Silenced Dialogue"

When you set out to read a book, an article, an essay, a blog, a web page—when you set out to read any text—your usual strategy may be simply to dive in, to start reading at the beginning and plow your way through to the end. With the limited time in most of our busy lives, simply diving in can seem like the quickest way to get something read.

Here's a different approach. Most experienced readers have found that taking a few minutes before diving in to get a sense of the text they are about to read will actually save them time and help them read more effectively. This does not mean spending hours previewing; just a few minutes will be very helpful when you start to read.

Give it a try. You may find that previewing will actually save you time because it will make the reading itself easier. And you'll get more out of the reading, because you will have prepared yourself to be an engaged reader.

Working Together to Preview and Predict

Working in your group, preview "The Silenced Dialogue" by Lisa Delpit (5.7, p. 209). A full preview of a text requires a fairly lengthy process of previewing and predicting. Often you won't have time for this elaborate a preview, but doing the complete process outlined below will familiarize you with a range of previewing options from which you will be able to select when you only have time for a more abbreviated process.

For this activity, work in groups to examine the text as outlined in step 1. Then answer the questions listed in steps 2 and 3. Later, working by yourself, answer the questions in step 4.

Step 1: Examine the text.   Working in your group, examine the items listed below and answer this question about each one: What did this item tell you about the text?

- Take a look at the title.
- If the text is a book, look over the front and back covers and the table of contents, if there is one.
- Read any introductory material, such as a preface.
- If the text starts with an abstract or executive summary, read it.
- If the text has headings for different parts, read them.
- Read the opening paragraph.
- Read the final paragraph.
- Take a look at any illustrations, charts, tables, or associated videos.
- Look to see if there are citations, endnotes, or a works cited list.
- Check to see how long the text is.

Step 2: Analyze the rhetorical situation.   As long ago as classical Greece—300 BC or so—thinkers have been aware that every text has four important components: the *author* of the text, the *audience* for the text, the *topic* of the text, and the *purpose* of the text that make up the *rhetorical situation*, the context in which the writing takes place. You don't need to remember the term *rhetorical situation*, but thinking about author, audience, topic, and purpose should be part of your previewing and predicting process.

Now, working in your group, write brief answers to the following questions.

- **Author.**   You don't simply want to find out the name of the author. What else can you learn about him or her? What evidence is there that the author really has some expertise? What biases might the author have? Is the author part of an organization? A corporation? What else has the author written?

- **Audience.** Whom does it appear that the author intended to be the reader or readers of this text? Whom was the author addressing? Were there other, secondary, audiences?

- **Topic.** What is the text about? What subject is the text focused on?

- **Purpose.** What does it appear that the author intended or, at least, hoped would happen as a result of this piece of writing? What did the author want the effect of this text on its audience to be?

Step 3: Predict what the text is about. Predicting what a text might discuss, using background knowledge or personal experiences or information from previous reading, can also prepare you to better understand the content. While not every text will reveal information about all of the following questions, every text will provide answers to some of them. Before launching into reading a text, use the steps listed above to preview it to help you answer as many of these questions as you can.

- What is this text "about"? What is the major topic or subject?

- Does the author take a stand on this topic?

- Does the author seem to make any assumptions about the subject?

- What do I know about the publishers of the text or sponsors of the website? Does the text appear in a reputable and reliable source?

- What evidence is there that the author of the text has at least some expertise about his or her subject?

Step 4: Think about yourself in relation to the text. A final way to preview a text is to think about how the subject of the text relates to you individually. Of course, this personal **kind of previewing is not appropriate for group work, so, working individually,** answer the following questions.

- What do you already know about the topic?

- Have you had experiences that are related to this topic?

- Have you read other texts about this same topic?

- What have you heard or seen about this topic (on the radio, TV, internet, podcasts, YouTube, other classes, etc.)?

- How do you feel about the text's stand on the topic?

- What is your purpose for reading this text?
- How similar or different are you from the intended audience for the text?
- How difficult will the text be to read?
- How much time will you need to read it?

5.7 Reading

"The Silenced Dialogue," Lisa Delpit

◀ Lisa Delpit

Luckett Portrait Studio/
Courtesy of The New Press

The following excerpt, "The Silenced Dialogue," is taken from Lisa Delpit's book *Other People's Children: Cultural Conflict in the Classroom*, which was first published by the New Press in 1995 and reprinted with a new introduction by the author in 2005. The book posits that many of the academic problems experienced by children of color relate to miscommunication and cultural assumptions and biases inherent within the system. Promoting literacy is a major focus of the book.

Before you start reading, take a moment to preview. (If you need a refresher on previewing, see Previewing a Text [20.2, p. 575].)

The Silenced Dialogue

LISA DELPIT

Born in Baton Rouge, Louisiana, in 1952, Lisa Delpit received her PhD from the School of Education at Harvard University. She has taught in Alaska; Papua, New Guinea; and Florida at the Florida International University. In addition to writing five books, she won a MacArthur Fellowship in 1990. She currently lives, teaches, and writes in Miami, Florida.

1   I suggest that students must be *taught* the codes needed to participate fully in the mainstream of American life, not by being forced to attend to hollow, inane, decontextualized subskills, but rather within the context of meaningful communicative endeavors; that they must be allowed the resource of the teacher's expert knowledge, while being helped to acknowledge their own "expertness" as well; and that even while students are assisted in learning the culture of power, they must also be helped to learn about the arbitrariness of those codes and about the power relationships they represent.

2   Now you may have inferred that I believe that because there is a culture of power, everyone should learn the codes to participate in it, and that is how the world should be. Actually, nothing could be further from the truth. I believe in a diversity of style, and I believe the world will be diminished if cultural diversity is ever obliterated. Further, I believe strongly, as do my liberal colleagues, that each cultural group should have the right to maintain its own language style. When I speak, therefore, of the culture of power, I don't speak of how I wish things to be but of how they are.

3   I further believe that to act as if power does not exist is to ensure that the power status quo remains the same. To imply to children or adults (but of course the adults won't believe you anyway) that it doesn't matter how you talk or how you write is to ensure their ultimate failure. I prefer to be honest with my students. I tell them that their language and cultural style is unique and wonderful but that there is a political power game that is also being played, and if they want to be in on that game there are certain games that they too must play.

4   But don't think that I let the onus of change rest entirely with the students. I am also involved in political work both inside and outside of the educational system, and that political work demands that I place myself to influence as many gatekeeping points as possible. And it is there that I agitate for change, pushing gatekeepers to open their doors to a variety of styles and codes. What I'm saying, however, is that I do not believe that political change toward diversity can be effected from the bottom up, as do some of my colleagues. They seem to believe that if we accept and

encourage diversity within classrooms of children, then diversity will automatically be accepted at gatekeeping points.

5   I believe that will never happen. What will happen is that the students who reach the gatekeeping points—like Amanda Branscornbe's student who dropped out of high school because he failed his exit exam—will understand that they have been lied to and will react accordingly. No, I am certain that if we are truly to effect societal change, we cannot do so from the bottom up, but we must push and agitate from the top down. And in the meantime, we must take the responsibility to *teach*, to provide for students who do not already possess them, the additional codes of power.

6   But I also do not believe that we should teach students to passively adopt an alternate code. They must be encouraged to understand the value of the code they already possess as well as to understand the power realities in this country. Otherwise they will be unable to work to change these realities.

5.8 Writing

Summarizing "The Silenced Dialogue"

For this assignment, try your hand at summary writing. You probably have a sense of what it means to write a summary. You write something short that summarizes the main content of something longer that you have read.

Write a short paper—a page would be plenty—in which you summarize the "The Silenced Dialogue" (5.7, p. 209).

5.9 Activity

Analyzing Summaries

Your instructor will distribute to each group a selection of the summaries that you wrote for Summarizing "The Silenced Dialogue" (5.8). Your group's task is to read over these summaries and make two lists: one of what you found that worked well in one or more of the summaries and one of the weaknesses or mistakes you found in one or more of the summaries. After a half hour or so, the groups will report out on their lists.

Each group will then compare their lists of strengths and weaknesses to the guidance found in What Makes a Good Summary? (18.23, p. 547). Each group will report out on the differences between their lists and the guidance they found.

↳ **5.10** **Writing**

Responding to "The Silenced Dialogue"

For this assignment, you are going to write a short paper—a page or so—in which you respond to "The Silenced Dialogue" (5.7, p. 209) by answering the following questions.

1. After reading "The Silenced Dialogue," what do you feel is the most important point in the article?
2. What are the primary benefits of what Delpit proposes?
3. What are the risks/costs of what she proposes?

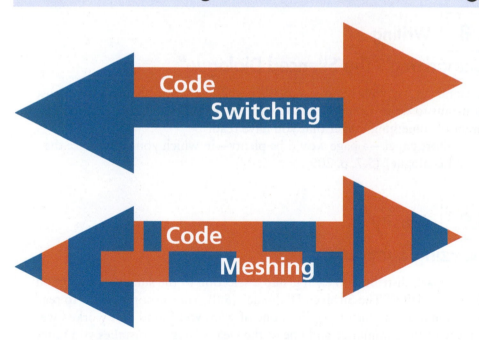

Code Switching versus Code Meshing

Code Switching

Code Meshing

▲ Code switching requires changing from one way of communicating—for example, Standard Written English—to a different one—such as African American Vernacular English. Code meshing means integrating different types of speech into new ways of communicating. What might be the advantages and disadvantages of these two options?

Smitherman Meshes Code

Geneva Smitherman, a respected scholar among teachers of composition and chair of the committee that formulated "Students' Right to Their Own Language" (5.4, p. 204), was criticized in the journal *College English* by Jean Hunt and Walter Myers. Smitherman's response to Hunt and Myers appears below.

> Tellin kids they lingo is cool but it ain cool enough for where it really counts (i.e., in the economic world) is just like tellin them it ain cool at all. If the problem is not the kid's dialect but *attitudes* toward that dialect, then why not work to change those attitudes? See, we all time talkin bout preparin people for the mainstream but never talkin bout changin the course of that stream.

> — Geneva Smitherman, "Response to Hunt, Myers," *College English*, vol. 35, no. 6, p. 731.

Note that much of her response is written in African American Vernacular English, but not all of it is. Consider the sentence "If the problem is not the kid's dialect but *attitudes* toward that dialect, then why not work to change those attitudes?" It is written in Standard Written English, as is the phrase in parentheses, "i.e., in the economic world." Writing in this way, combining language from one version of English, in this case AAVE, with another, SWE, is referred to as *code meshing*. You'll discuss code meshing in "Toward Multilingual Writing Models" (5.14, p. 219) and Responding to Canagarajah (5.15, p. 224).

Rewriting African American Vernacular English

Working in your group, rewrite the short Smitherman passage above so it is all in Standard Written English. Then discuss which version, the original or your group's "translation," is more effective writing.

5.12 Writing

Responding to Smitherman's Response to Hunt, Myers

Write a short paper—a page or so—in which you explain what Smitherman is proposing in the excerpt from Smitherman's "Response to Hunt, Myers" below. What would it mean to change "the course of that stream"? Then explain your response to her proposal. Is such change possible? Desirable?

Tellin kids they lingo is cool but it ain cool enough for where it really counts (i.e., in the economic world) is just like tellin them it ain cool at all. If the problem is not the kid's dialect but *attitudes* toward that dialect, then why not work to change those attitudes? See, we all time talkin bout preparin people for the mainstream but never talkin bout changin the course of that stream.

— Geneva Smitherman, "Response to Hunt, Myers," *College English*, vol. 35, no. 6, p. 731.

5.13 | Activity

Exploring Canagarajah's Vocabulary in "Toward Multilingual Writing Models"

The excerpt that follows comes from a longer article, "The Place of World Englishes in Composition: Pluralization Continued," by Suresh Canagarajah, who was born in Sri Lanka, an island nation located south and east of the southernmost tip of India.

Canagarajah's article contains a fairly challenging vocabulary, so in this activity, you are being asked to use a range of strategies to make sure you understand these challenging words. Remember that looking words up in a dictionary is only one strategy and usually not the best first choice. Here are six strategies to use when encountering words or phrases you aren't familiar with:

1. Derive the meaning from context.
2. Analyze the parts of the word.
3. Back up and re-read the passage.
4. Keep reading to see if the writer explains the difficult passage.
5. Decide the word is not important and just keep reading.
6. Look the word up in a dictionary.

(If you'd like more advice about dealing with words you don't know, see Dealing with Difficult Language [20.9, p. 594].)

Understanding Challenging Words

In Canagarajah's essay, which follows, challenging words are underlined. Working in your group, decide on a strategy for decoding each of these words and then determine the meaning of each one. Use the chart below to record your strategies and the meanings you discover. In the case of words you decide are not important, just write "Meaning not important" in the right-hand column. The first two are completed as examples.

Words	Strategy Used	Meaning
pragmatic	From context	Practical
Englishes	Analyzed parts of word	Plural of English
ethnography		
ESOL		
vernacular		
utilitarian		
mimic		
unidirectional monolingualist paradigm		
invoke		
code		
rhetorically compelling ways		
bilingualism		
multidialectalism		
monodialectalism		
multilingualism		
pluralization		
dominant codes		
flaunt		
nonlegitimized codes		
extratextual power		
nativized varieties		
intrasentential level		
pluralizing		

Toward Multilingual Writing Models

SURESH CANAGARAJAH

Suresh Canagarajah was born and grew up in Sri Lanka, an island nation located south and east of the southernmost tip of India. Sri Lanka became a British colony, called Ceylon, early in the nineteenth century and gained independence in 1948. The country changed its name to Sri Lanka in 1972. The two official languages in Sri Lanka are Sinhalese and Tamil, although English is also recognized in the Constitution as a "bridge" language.

▶

Canagarajah received his bachelor's degree from the University of Kelaniya in Sri Lanka. He came to America for his graduate study, receiving a PhD from the University of Texas in 1990. Author of eight books and hundreds of articles, Canagarajah is currently a professor of applied linguistics, English, and Asian studies at Pennsylvania State University.

Much of Canagarajah's work examines World Englishes, the many forms of English spoken in Sri Lanka, India, Nigeria, Jamaica, and elsewhere. In this article, he uses his insights into these World Englishes to consider the situation of students whose home language is African American Vernacular English in a society that privileges Standard Written English.

1   I am glad that some composition scholars are disturbed by the inconsistencies in the current practices and attitudes toward English in composition pedagogies. Peter Elbow would go further and call this state of affairs a "contradiction" ("Vernacular Literacies" 126). He is among the few who have started thinking and writing actively to resolve the dilemmas present in implementing SRTOL [Students' Right to Their Own Language]. Mindful of the concern that minority students shouldn't be further disadvantaged by being excluded from attaining proficiency in established traditional varieties of English while being empowered to use their own (a criticism raised by minority scholars themselves), Elbow adopts a two-pronged approach: "A good strategy for handling contradiction is to introduce the dimension of time: to work for the long-range goal of changing the culture of literacy, and the short-range goal of helping students now" ("Vernacular Literacies" 126). He proposes to accomplish this by letting minority students use their own varieties for their early drafts but teaching them copy editing skills and/or getting them help from copy editors so that their final product conforms to the expectations in the academy. This way, he would help students to acquire SWE [Standard Written English] in order to prosper in the dominant culture of literacy and succeed in education and society. However, by keeping other varieties alive in the composition classroom and helping students develop written competence in them in low-stakes activities, he would be working toward the long-term goal of full acceptance for all dialects.

2   Though this is a <u>pragmatic</u> resolution that is sensitive to the competing claims in this debate—i.e., the importance of challenging the inequalities of languages and the need to master the dominant codes for social and educational success—I have experienced certain difficulties in implementing this approach. I have found that minority students are reluctant to hold back their <u>Englishes</u> even for temporary reasons. In my <u>ethnography</u> of both African American and <u>ESOL</u> students, I have discovered the strategies students covertly adopt to bring their Englishes into formal academic writing in a curriculum that encourages their varieties in everything other than formal graded assignments. . . . The desire to use one's <u>vernacular</u> even in formal

texts is easy to understand. Everything [we know about language acquisition] teaches us that to use a language meaningfully is to appropriate it and make it one's own. . . . Proficiency requires adapting the new language for one's own values and interests. To use a language without any personal engagement, even for temporary <u>utilitarian</u> and pragmatic reasons, is to <u>mimic</u> not speak. It means "acting white" for my African American students and "putting a show" for Sri Lankan students.

3   In the light of such student resistance, we become alert to some ambiguities in Elbow's model. Despite its attempts to accommodate diversity, the model still falls under the dominant <u>unidirectional monolingualist paradigm</u> in writing. Other varieties of English are accepted only as tentative, dispensable moves toward ME [ME stands for "Metropolitan English," Canagarajah's term for Standard Written English] norms. The editing of the other Englishes in the final product may also lump these varieties into the category of "errors" to be avoided, in the eyes of students, and lead to the gradual loss of their home language. What I propose is a modification of Elbow's proposal. In the place of his notion of time, I like to <u>invoke</u> the notion of space. I am interested in exploring how we can accommodate more than one <u>code</u> within the bounds of the same text. In an essay that is written in ME, I would also teach students to bring in their preferred varieties for relevant purposes. In textual terms, this strategy will result in a hybrid text that contains divergent varieties of English. To use another metaphor to capture the difference, while Elbow . . . propose[s] a model of *code switching*, I propose a model of *code meshing*. While they separate the codes and prioritize ME for formal purposes, I consider merging the codes. Code meshing is not new to academic writing. As I will illustrate with a close textual analysis in the next section, some African American scholars have already used AAVE [African American Vernacular English] in <u>rhetorically compelling ways</u> in academic texts that feature SWE. . . . Though code meshing was used in classical rhetoric as a highbrow activity (i.e., inserting Greek or Latin without translation into English texts), I am presenting this notion as a popular communicative strategy in multilingual communities and developing it even for cases outside such elite <u>bilingualism</u>.

4   Code meshing calls for <u>multidialectalism</u> not <u>monodialectalism</u>. Holding that knowledge of the vernacular is solely sufficient for minority students would ignore the reality of <u>multilingualism</u> demanded by globalization. It would also segregate minority students into vernacular speech ghettos. My proposal demands more, not less, from minority students. They have to not only master the dominant varieties of English, but also know how to bring in their preferred varieties in rhetorically strategic ways. It is not even sufficient to learn different English

▶

varieties and use them in appropriate contexts (as proposed by code switching models); now minority students have to learn to bring them together to serve their interests.

* * *

5   It could be objected that this approach is yet another temporary strategy that defers the full <u>pluralization</u> of academic texts and legitimization of WE [World Englishes, Canagarajah's term for the variety of forms of English spoken in Sri Lanka, India, Nigeria, Jamaica, and elsewhere] for a later time. I can hear my South Asian colleagues saying: "But your approach is looking like the very same one as Elbow's, no?" I agree. "However," I would reply, "there are small, small differences that make big, big significance." The advantage in my proposal is that minority students get to see their own variety of English written in academic texts. They don't have to edit out all vernacular expressions. Furthermore, we satisfy the desire of minority students to engage with the <u>dominant codes</u> when they write, and make a space for their own varieties of English in formal texts. Elbow's approach keeps these codes separate and unequal, and compels minority students to postpone critical literacy practices. Moreover, my approach enables students to personally engage in the process of textual change, not to wait for time to do the trick for them.

* * *

Conclusion

6   It is time now to . . . ask what difference these activities will make in pluralizing composition. . . . [C]ode meshing in English writing has a politics of its own. Though not directly confrontational as to reject the dominant codes or to <u>flaunt</u> the vernacular codes in established contexts, multilingual students will resist ME from the inside by inserting their codes within the existing conventions. This activity serves to infuse not only new codes, but also new knowledge and values, into dominant texts. . . . There is value in making gradual cultural and ideological changes in the notions of textuality and language among educationists and policy makers, building a coalition of disparate social groups and disciplinary circles, and winning small battles in diverse institutions toward an acceptance of hybrid texts, before we mount a frontal assault by using <u>nonlegitimized codes</u> in high-stakes writing. In making this sobering concession, we have to keep in mind that textual resistance cannot by itself sustain the larger institutional changes needed to legitimize WE [World Englishes]. Even the ability to initiate textual changes is often dependent on the <u>extratextual power</u> authors bring with them. We have to admit that Smitherman [see 5.11, p. 213] is able to use AAVE so confidently in her writing because of her standing as a distinguished scholar

in academic circles and her achieved status as a spokesperson for language rights in professional associations. Many other black scholars and students cannot succeed in using AAVE if they don't enjoy the relative status in their contexts of communication. Despite the authority she brings to writing, Smitherman herself is strategic in making qualified uses of AAVE in her texts and in taking measured steps of meshing in her writing career.

* * *

7   Talking of time, this is the moment for me to come clean about my own evolving positions on [World Englishes] in writing. Having criticized the field of composition and other progressive scholars for their limitations in accepting WE in academic writing, I must confess that I have myself held such positions in the past. The extent to which my radicalism extended previously was to argue for alternative tone, styles, organization, and genre conventions in formal academic writing. I have steered clear of validating <u>nativized varieties</u> at the <u>intrasentential level</u>. In retrospect, it occurs to me that I was playing it safe in my argument. I didn't want to jeopardize my case for <u>pluralizing</u> academic writing by extending it to the controversial terrain of grammar. But a combination of developments in theoretical discourses, social changes, communicative advances, and pedagogical rethinking (reviewed in this article) tell me that now is the time to take my position to its logical conclusion. The moment is ripe to extend my argument of pluralizing English and academic writing into the "deep structure" of grammar. Still, I must confess that I am myself unsure how to practice what I preach (other than the few instances where I shamelessly copy Smitherman's strategies above). Throughout my life, I have been so disciplined about censoring even the slightest traces of Sri Lankan English in my own academic writing that it is difficult to bring them into the text now. Therefore, this article is only a statement of intent, not a celebration of accomplishment. It only aims to make some space for pedagogical rethinking and textual experimentation on the place of [World Englishes] in composition. As for practice, I am hereby humbly announcing that I'll be joining my esteemed students in the classroom for learning how to accommodate local Englishes in academic writing.

5.14   Reading

"Toward Multilingual Writing Models," Suresh Canagarajah

Be sure to do a little "previewing" before you dive into reading this essay. If you need more information on previewing, go to Previewing a Text (20.2, p. 575).

Toward Multilingual Writing Models

SURESH CANAGARAJAH

▲ Suresh Canagarajah

Suresh Canagarajah was born and grew up in Sri Lanka, an island nation located south and east of the southernmost tip of India. Sri Lanka was a British colony called Ceylon beginning in the nineteenth century and gained independence in 1948. The two official languages in Sri Lanka are Sinhalese and Tamil, although English is also recognized in the Constitution as a "bridge" language.

Canagarajah received his bachelor's degree from the University of Kelaniya in Sri Lanka. He came to America for his graduate study, receiving a PhD from the University of Texas in 1990. Author of eight books and hundreds of articles, Canagarajah is currently a professor of applied linguistics, English, and Asian studies at Pennsylvania State University.

Much of Canagarajah's work examines World Englishes, the many forms of English spoken in Sri Lanka, India, Nigeria, Jamaica, and elsewhere. In this article, he uses his insights into these World Englishes to consider the situation of students whose home language is African American Vernacular English in a society that privileges Standard Written English.

1   I am glad that some composition scholars are disturbed by the inconsistencies in the current practices and attitudes toward English in composition pedagogies. Peter Elbow would go further and call this state of affairs a "contradiction" ("Vernacular Literacies" 126). He is among the few who have started thinking and writing actively to resolve the dilemmas present in implementing SRTOL [Students' Right to Their Own Language]. Mindful of the concern that minority students shouldn't be further disadvantaged by being excluded from attaining proficiency in established traditional varieties of English while being empowered to use their own (a criticism raised by minority scholars themselves), Elbow adopts a two-pronged approach: "A good strategy for handling contradiction is to introduce the dimension of time: to work for the long-range goal of changing the culture of literacy, and the short-range goal of helping students now" ("Vernacular Literacies" 126). He proposes to accomplish this by letting minority students use their own varieties for their early drafts but teaching them copy editing skills and/or getting them

help from copy editors so that their final product conforms to the expectations in the academy. This way, he would help students to acquire SWE [Standard Written English] in order to prosper in the dominant culture of literacy and succeed in education and society. However, by keeping other varieties alive in the composition classroom and helping students develop written competence in them in low-stakes activities, he would be working toward the long-term goal of full acceptance for all dialects.

2   Though this is a pragmatic resolution that is sensitive to the competing claims in this debate—i.e., the importance of challenging the inequalities of languages and the need to master the dominant codes for social and educational success—I have experienced certain difficulties in implementing this approach. I have found that minority students are reluctant to hold back their Englishes even for temporary reasons. In my ethnography of both African American and ESOL students, I have discovered the strategies students covertly adopt to bring their Englishes into formal academic writing in a curriculum that encourages their varieties in everything other than formal graded assignments. . . . The desire to use one's vernacular even in formal texts is easy to understand. Everything [we know about language acquisition] teaches us that to use a language meaningfully is to appropriate it and make it one's own. . . . Proficiency requires adapting the new language for one's own values and interests. To use a language without any personal engagement, even for temporary utilitarian and pragmatic reasons, is to mimic not speak. It means "acting white" for my African American students and "putting a show" for Sri Lankan students.

3   In the light of such student resistance, we become alert to some ambiguities in Elbow's model. Despite its attempts to accommodate diversity, the model still falls under the dominant unidirectional monolingualist paradigm in writing. Other varieties of English are accepted only as tentative, dispensable moves toward ME [ME stands for "Metropolitan English," Canagarajah's term for Standard Written English] norms. The editing of the other Englishes in the final product may also lump these varieties into the category of "errors" to be avoided, in the eyes of students, and lead to the gradual loss of their home language. What I propose is a modification of Elbow's proposal. In the place of his notion of time, I like to invoke the notion of space. I am interested in exploring how we can accommodate more than one code within the bounds of the same text. In an essay that is written in ME, I would also teach students to bring in their preferred varieties for relevant purposes. In textual terms, this strategy will result in a hybrid text that contains divergent varieties of English. To use another metaphor to capture the difference, ▶

while Elbow . . . propose[s] a model of *code switching,* I propose a model of *code meshing.* While they separate the codes and prioritize ME for formal purposes, I consider merging the codes. Code meshing is not new to academic writing. As I will illustrate with a close textual analysis in the next section, some African American scholars have already used AAVE in rhetorically compelling ways in academic texts that feature SWE. . . . Though code meshing was used in classical rhetoric as a highbrow activity (i.e., inserting Greek or Latin without translation into English texts), I am presenting this notion as a popular communicative strategy in multilingual communities and developing it even for cases outside such elite bilingualism.

4   Code meshing calls for multidialectalism not monodialectalism. Holding that knowledge of the vernacular is solely sufficient for minority students would ignore the reality of multilingualism demanded by globalization. It would also segregate minority students into vernacular speech ghettos. My proposal demands more, not less, from minority students. They have to not only master the dominant varieties of English, but also know how to bring in their preferred varieties in rhetorically strategic ways. It is not even sufficient to learn different English varieties and use them in appropriate contexts (as proposed by code switching models); now minority students have to learn to bring them together to serve their interests.

*   *   *

5   It could be objected that this approach is yet another temporary strategy that defers the full pluralization of academic texts and legitimization of WE [World Englishes, Canagarajah's term for the variety of forms of English spoken in Sri Lanka, India, Nigeria, Jamaica, and elsewhere] for a later time. I can hear my South Asian colleagues saying: "But your approach is looking like the very same one as Elbow's, no?" I agree. "However," I would reply, "there are small, small differences that make big, big significance." The advantage in my proposal is that minority students get to see their own variety of English written in academic texts. They don't have to edit out all vernacular expressions. Furthermore, we satisfy the desire of minority students to engage with the dominant codes when they write, and make a space for their own varieties of English in formal texts. Elbow's approach keeps these codes separate and unequal, and compels minority students to postpone critical literacy practices. Moreover, my approach enables students to personally engage in the process of textual change, not to wait for time to do the trick for them.

*   *   *

Conclusion

6   It is time now to . . . ask what difference these activities will make in pluralizing composition. . . . [C]ode meshing in English writing has a politics of its own. Though not directly confrontational as to reject the dominant codes or to flaunt the vernacular codes in established contexts, multilingual students will resist ME from the inside by inserting their codes within the existing conventions. This activity serves to infuse not only new codes, but also new knowledge and values, into dominant texts. Such subtle Gramscian "wars of position" are important in order to gain spaces for a more direct "war of maneuver." There is value in making gradual cultural and ideological changes in the notions of textuality and language among educationists and policy makers, building a coalition of disparate social groups and disciplinary circles, and winning small battles in diverse institutions toward an acceptance of hybrid texts, before we mount a frontal assault by using nonlegitimized codes in high-stakes writing. In making this sobering concession, we have to keep in mind that textual resistance cannot by itself sustain the larger institutional changes needed to legitimize [World Englishes]. Even the ability to initiate textual changes is often dependent on the extratextual power authors bring with them. We have to admit that Smitherman [see 5.11, p. 213] is able to use AAVE so confidently in her writing because of her standing as a distinguished scholar in academic circles and her achieved status as a spokesperson for language rights in professional associations. Many other black scholars and students cannot succeed in using AAVE if they don't enjoy the relative status in their contexts of communication. Despite the authority she brings to writing, Smitherman herself is strategic in making qualified uses of AAVE in her texts and in taking measured steps of meshing in her writing career.

*   *   *

7   Talking of time, this is the moment for me to come clean about my own evolving positions on [World Englishes] in writing. Having criticized the field of composition and other progressive scholars for their limitations in accepting [World Englishes] in academic writing, I must confess that I have myself held such positions in the past. The extent to which my radicalism extended previously was to argue for alternative tone, styles, organization, and genre conventions in formal academic writing. I have steered clear of validating nativized varieties at the intrasentential level. In retrospect, it occurs to me that I was playing it safe in my argument. I didn't want to jeopardize my case for pluralizing academic writing by extending it to the controversial terrain of grammar. But a combination of developments in theoretical discourses, social changes, communicative advances,

▶

and pedagogical rethinking (reviewed in this article) tell me that now is the time to take my position to its logical conclusion. The moment is ripe to extend my argument of pluralizing English and academic writing into the "deep structure" of grammar. Still, I must confess that I am myself unsure how to practice what I preach (other than the few instances where I shamelessly copy Smitherman's strategies above). Throughout my life, I have been so disciplined about censoring even the slightest traces of Sri Lankan English in my own academic writing that it is difficult to bring them into the text now. Therefore, this article is only a statement of intent, not a celebration of accomplishment. It only aims to make some space for pedagogical rethinking and textual experimentation on the place of [World Englishes] in composition. As for practice, I am hereby humbly announcing that I'll be joining my esteemed students in the classroom for learning how to accommodate local Englishes in academic writing.

↳ **5.15** **Writing**

Responding to Canagarajah

Canagarajah proposes replacing the approach of Peter Elbow and Lisa Delpit (see "The Silenced Dialogue" [5.7, p. 209]), which he calls "code switching," with an approach he calls "code meshing."

In a short paper—a page more or less—respond to the following questions.

1. Explain the difference between code switching and code meshing.
2. Explain why Canagarajah prefers code meshing.
3. Explain what Canagarajah is saying in the final paragraph of the excerpt.

Addressing Inequality

▲ This image was used in 2018 as the symbol for the European Day of Languages, an event that is sponsored by the Council of Europe to celebrate linguistic diversity, and that has been celebrated in forty-seven member states since 2001.

How do you think your college could balance the responsibility of teaching all students how to communicate in Standard Written English—so essential to post-college success—with the responsibility to help students from different ethnic and cultural backgrounds to communicate and succeed using the language they are most confident using?   Council of Europe

5.16   Activity

Analyzing Inequality in Excerpt from *Antiracist Writing Assessment Ecologies*, Asao Inoue

Remember this question, which you wrestled with back in Two Key Questions about Standard Written English (5.1, p. 202):

Does the requirement that students write in Standard Written English make it harder for students who have grown up using a different version of English to succeed in college writing courses?

Asao Inoue, a respected English scholar and chair of the Conference on College Composition, the national organization for college-level composition teachers, raises the same question in the following excerpt from his book, *Antiracist Writing Assessment Ecologies*. He also points out that students of color consistently have higher failure rates in writing classes than white students.

After reading this excerpt, work in your group to answer the following questions.

1. What possible explanations does Inoue offer for the higher failure rates for students of color?

2. Can you think of any other possible explanations?

Excerpt from *Antiracist Writing Assessment Ecologies*

ASAO INOUE

1   Why do more Blacks, Latinos, and multilingual students relatively speaking perform worse on writing assessments than their white peers in writing classrooms? At Fresno State, for instance, between 2009 [and] 2012, the average failure rate for Blacks in the first-year writing program was 17.46%, while the average failure rate for whites for the same years was 7.3%. . . . Whites have the lowest failure rates of all racial formations, and this is after the program revised itself completely in part to address such issues. That is, these are better numbers than in the years before. I realize that there are many ways to fail a writing class beyond being judged to write poorly, but these internally consistently higher numbers that are consistent with other writing programs suggest more, suggest that we cannot let such numbers pass us by just because we can assume that teachers are not biased.

2   I'm not saying we assume bias or prejudice. I'm saying let's assume there is no bias, no prejudice. Now, how do we read those numbers? What plausible assumptions can we make that help us make sense of these data, what rival hypotheses can be made? Do we assume that more Blacks, Latinos/as, and Asians at Fresno State are lazier or worse writers than their white peers? Is it the case that on average Blacks, Latinos/as, and Asians at Fresno State simply do not write as well as their white peers, that there is some inherent or cultural problem with the way these racial formations write? Or could it be that the judgments made on all writing are biased toward a discourse that privileges whites consistently because it is a discourse of whiteness?

↳ **5.17** Writing

Responding to "Contract Grading," Asao Inoue

Having concluded that a grading system based on a professor evaluating students' writing gives an advantage to students who grow up speaking a version of English close to Standard Written English and disadvantages students who come from a culture that uses a different version of English, Asao Inoue (who you read in Analyzing Inequality [5.16, p. 225]) devised a startlingly different way of determining grades: he bases it on a contract that he distributes to students at the beginning of the semester.

Excerpts from that contract, taken from his book *Antiracist Writing Assessment Ecologies,* follow. In that book, explaining his use of grading contracts based on labor, Inoue makes a surprising statement: "[G]rading students' writing on its quality is a racist practice, despite the fact that it is important for students to learn (about) dominant discourses" (185).

Writing in Response to Inoue's Concept of Contract Grading

For this short writing assignment—a page would be plenty—read the following passage and then explain your response to Inoue's system of contract grading. If you can, include in your response your thoughts about the statement quoted in the paragraph just above this one.

Contract Grading

ASAO INOUE

Asao Inoue is director of the University Writing Program and the Writing Center and professor of Interdisciplinary Arts and Sciences at the University of Washington in Tacoma. He has published extensively in academic journals on the subjects of writing assessment, the impact of race on learning and assessment, and the teaching of composition. He coedited *Race and Writing Assessment* (2012) and wrote *Antiracist Writing Assessment Ecologies* (2015), both of which won awards from the Conference of College Composition and Communication.

1   This contract is based on a simple principle and a few important assumptions, which are not typical in most classrooms. First, the principle: how much *labor* you do is more important to your learning and growth as a reader and writer than the quality of your writing. Our grading contract calculates grades by how much *labor* you do and the manner in which you do it. The more you work, the better your grade—no matter what folks think of the product of your labor—but we assume that you'll be striving in your labors to improve, learn, and take risks. The other ▶

important assumption that this principle depends upon for success is that we must assume that all students will try their hardest, work their hardest, and not deceive anyone, when it comes to their labor. If we ask for an hour of writing at home, and someone says they did that and produced X, then we must believe them. This is a culture of trust. We must trust one another, and know that deception and lying hurts mostly the liar and his/her learning and growth.

*   *   *

2   The default grade, then, is a "B." In a nutshell, if you do all that is asked of you in the manner and spirit it is asked, if you work through the processes we establish and the work we assign ourselves during the semester, then you'll get a "B." If you miss class, turn in assignments late, or forget to do assignments, etc., your grade will be lower.

*   *   *

3   Below is a table that shows the main components that affect your successful compliance with our contract:

Table 1: The break-down of labor that calculates your final course grade.

	# of Absences	# of Late Assigns.	# of Missed Assigns.	# of Ignored Assigns.
A	4 or less	5	0	0
B	4 or less	5	0	0
C	5	6	1	0
D	6	7	2	1
F	7	8 or more	2	2

"A" Grades

4   All grades in this course depend upon how much *labor* you do. If you do all that is asked of you in the manner and spirit asked, and meet the guidelines in this contract, specifically the "Break-Down" section at the end of this contract, then you get a "B" course grade. Grades of "A," however, depend on doing advanced projects for both Project 1 and 2, which equates to about twice the work or length of the final project documents. Thus you earn a B if you put in good time and effort, do all the work, and do both projects in an acceptable fashion. But you earn an "A" if you do more work in the two projects—that is, do more in-depth projects (described on the Project handout and in the Syllabus).

5   While you do not have to worry about anyone's judgments or standards of excellence to meet the grading contract, you are obligated to listen carefully to and address your colleagues' and my concerns in all your work of the class. This means that when you receive feedback you'll use that feedback to help you continually improve your writing. So while others' judgments of your work is not important to your course grade, it is important to your learning and development.

5.18 Video

"Acting White," Barack Obama

In this unit, you are going to first watch a brief video (it's only about a minute long) in which President Barack Obama talks about "acting white." In the video clip, Obama acknowledges that sometimes young black men who read too much or who speak formally correct English are accused of "acting white." To watch this video, type "youtube Obama acting white has to go" into your browser. (If these search terms do not work, there is an updated list of URLs available at https://bit.ly/33IIHtf.)

Has the term *acting white* ever been applied to you? If you're not African American, you probably answered in the negative. Sometimes people from other groups are also criticized for going to college by members of their own group: People from Appalachia who go off to college are sometimes accused of "trying to get ahead of their rearin'." Sometimes students who go to college discover they have trouble "fitting in" with their old high school friends, who accuse them of "putting on airs."

Responding to the Term *Acting White*

Many African-American students who have gone to college have been accused of "acting white" by their friends back home, but other students have also received this kind of criticism from friends and even family who have not gone to college. For this assignment, write a short paper—a page is plenty—in which you discuss this phenomenon. What do you think about putting people down for getting educated? Is it a different problem for African Americans? Why do some people have this attitude toward their friends who have gone to college? How does one cope with it? Should you try to avoid "putting on airs" with your old friends? What would that mean? Should you simply find some new friends?

Even if you've never experienced this situation yourself or even observed it happening to others, you can still write about it. For example, you could analyze why you've never experienced it. Or you could strategize about what your reaction would be if you did.

Don't try to answer all of these questions, or even any of them. These questions are just here to get you thinking. All you need to do is write a thoughtful paper that expresses your thinking in some way about this topic.

Bringing It All Together

▲ What have you learned about the power of language and strategies for integrating different ways of communicating in writing that you could share with the group of students in this photo? Rawpixel.com/Shutterstock

5.19 Writing

Researching Language and Power

In Units 5.20 (p. 231), 5.21 (p. 232), and 5.22 (p. 233), you are asked to write an essay or create a multimodal composition taking a position on the language requirement colleges expect: that academic writing always conforms to the conventions of Standard Written English. Before you work on your assignment, you are going to do a little research. First, look over the writing assignment options and decide which option you are going to respond to. Then, either in a library or online, locate three articles or books that discuss the topic you have decided to address and answer the questions below about each of the three. (For more on finding and evaluating sources, see Research [Topic 22, p. 617].)

1. Who is the author(s)? What can you find out about the author(s)? How expert is the author on the subject?
2. Where was the article or book published? In what kind of journal, book, or website?
3. Does the author or the publisher have a particular bias? Does that bias make the article or book less valuable as a resource?
4. Who seems to be the audience this article or book was intended for?
5. Does the article or book provide convincing evidence to support its position?
6. Does the article or book contain information you may be able to use in your essay?

5.20 Real World Essay

A Proposal to the English Department about Requiring Standard Written English

At the beginning of this project, in Two Key Questions about Standard Written English (5.1, p. 201), you were asked these questions:

1. Does the requirement that students write in Standard Written English make it harder for students who have grown up using a different version of English to succeed in college writing courses?
2. If colleges don't help students learn to write in Standard Written English, will it be harder for them to succeed in the American workplace?

Talk about the perfect "rock and a hard place." If the college requires all students to master Standard Written English, it is making success less likely for African American students, but if the college doesn't help those students to master Standard Written English, it is not preparing them to succeed in the real world. Luckily, it is not necessary to choose between these two opposite solutions. You have been reading and thinking about positions that are not completely at either extreme, but somewhere in between: solutions like code switching, code meshing, and contract grading.

Assignment. For this essay, you should think over all the ideas raised in the readings, in the short writings you have done, and in the discussions in your group, and decide what you think the policy of the English Department at your school should be. Then write a three- to four-page proposal to the English faculty at your school recommending what the department's policy should be on this tough issue.

The two essential components of a proposal are a convincing argument that there is a problem and a clear and effective presentation of a solution that will address that problem. In addition, proposals often include many of these elements:

- Background information about the problem
- Examples of the negative effects of the problem
- Evidence that the solution is feasible
- Evidence that the proposed solution will solve or, at least, reduce the problem
- Argument that the proposed solution is a better response than other solutions

For more about writing proposals, see Strategies for Writing a Proposal (18.27, p. 552).

Option.   In this project, we have focused primarily on language and power issues as they affect African American students. If you would prefer to discuss these same issues as they apply to a different group—Hispanic students, Appalachian students, students from working-class backgrounds, students for whom English is a second language, students who speak a World English, students who speak a Pidgin or Creole—that would be fine.

Documentation.   Your instructor will provide specific requirements about including quotations, citations, and the documentation style to use. Be sure to provide appropriate citations for any words you quote, paraphrase, or summarize from readings in this project or articles that you have found through your research and to include a works cited list or list of references at the end of your essay. If you need to review how to provide this documentation, refer to MLA Documentation (Topic 23, p. 650) or APA Documentation (Topic 24, p. 687).

When you do include quotations, paraphrases, or summaries to support your argument, you need to tie them together, explain their relationships with each other, and express your conclusions about them (see Synthesis [22.14, p. 648]).

5.21 Academic Essay

Taking a Stand on Standard Written English

At the beginning of this project, in Two Key Questions about Standard Written English (5.1, p. 201), you were asked these questions:

1. Does the requirement that students write in Standard Written English make it harder for students who have grown up using a different version of English to succeed in college writing courses?

2. If colleges don't help students learn to write in Standard Written English, will it be harder for them to succeed in the American workplace?

Throughout this project, you have read, discussed, and written about the issues raised by these questions and explored some of the possible solutions to them. Now it is your turn to express and support your position on this topic.

Assignment. For this assignment, you will write a college essay—three to four pages long—that is suitable for a course in education, political science, social sciences, or even English. In your essay, you will argue for one of the following positions.

1. Students should be required to write essays in college courses that conform to the conventions of Standard Written English.

2. Students should be allowed to write college essays making use of the version of English they are comfortable with.

3. A position of your choice on the issue of acceptable language in college essays that is different from either of the first two options.

Option. This project has primarily focused on language and power issues as they affect African American students. If you would like to include in your essay a discussion of how these issues affect other groups—Hispanic students, Appalachian students, students from working-class backgrounds, students for whom English is a second language, students who speak a World English, students who speak a Pidgin or Creole—that would be fine too.

Documentation. Your instructor will provide specific requirements about including quotations, citations, and the documentation style to use. Be sure to provide appropriate citations for any words you quote, paraphrase, or summarize from readings in this project or articles that you have found through your research and to include a works cited list or list of references at the end of your essay. If you need to review how to provide this documentation, refer to MLA Documentation (Topic 23, p. 650) or APA Documentation (Topic 24, p. 687).

When you do include quotations, paraphrases, or summaries to support your argument, you need to tie them together, explain their relationships with each other, and express your conclusions about them (see Synthesis [22.14, p. 648]).

5.22 Multimodal Composition

A Proposal to Your College or University Regarding Standard Written English

At the beginning of this project, in Two Key Questions about Standard Written English (5.1, p. 201), you were asked two key questions:

1. Does the requirement that students write in Standard Written English make it harder for students who have grown up using a different version of English to succeed in college writing courses?

2. If colleges don't help students learn to write in Standard Written English, will it be harder for them to succeed in the American workplace?

Talk about the perfect "rock and a hard place." If the college requires all students to master Standard Written English, it is making success less likely for African American students, but if the college doesn't help those students to master Standard Written English, it is not preparing them to succeed in the real world. Luckily, it is not necessary to choose between these two opposite solutions. You have been reading and thinking about positions that are not completely at either extreme, but somewhere in between: solutions like code switching, code meshing, and contract grading.

Assignment. For this assignment, you should think over all the ideas raised in the readings, in the short writings you have done, and in the discussions in your group, and decide what you think the policy of the English Department at your school should be. You will then develop a proposal to present to the entire college that recommends what the department's policy should be on this tough issue.

This assignment is similar to the academic assignment in Unit 5.21 (p. 232) except that you have a broader audience and are not limited to a formal *written* document. Instead, you are invited to use any skills you have developed that make use of other media—images, video, PowerPoint with narration, graphs, charts, even a website—to convey your argument. You might produce a paper document that includes images, charts, or graphs. If you are comfortable working with PowerPoint, you could produce a PowerPoint presentation with recorded narration or, if your instructor gives you the okay, one that you narrate to the class. If you are skilled at website or video development, you could present your argument as a website or video.

Option. This project has primarily focused on language and power issues as they affect African American students. If you would prefer to discuss these issues as they apply to a different group—Hispanic students, Appalachian students, students from working-class backgrounds, students for whom English is a second language, students who speak a World English, students who speak a Pidgin or Creole—that would be fine too.

Documentation. Your instructor will give you any requirements about including quotations, citations, or works cited lists. Be sure to provide appropriate citations for any words you quote, paraphrase, or summarize from readings in this project or articles that you have found through your research and to include a works cited list or list of references at the end of your essay. If you need to review how to provide this documentation, refer to MLA Documentation (Topic 23, p. 650) or APA Documentation (Topic 24, p. 687).

When you do include quotations, paraphrases, or summaries to support your argument, you need to tie them together, explain their relationships with each other, and express your conclusions about them (see Synthesis [22.14, p. 648]).

5.23 Activity

Getting Started on Your Essay or Composition

During this class period, you and your classmates will begin working on your essay (see Real World Essay: A Proposal to the English Department about Requiring Standard Written English [5.20, p. 231], Academic Essay: Taking a Stand on Standard Written English [5.21, p. 232], or Multimodal Composition: A Proposal to Your College or University Regarding Standard Written English [5.22, p. 233]).

You may use this time to start brainstorming or to begin your research online. You may want to write an opening paragraph or two, or you may want to review what you've already read and written in this project. You may want to compare notes with a couple of classmates or ask a question or two of your instructor. If you are composing a multimodal project, you may want to talk to others who are doing the same to compare approaches. The idea is that you will at least get a start on the essay.

5.24 Writing

Reflecting on Project 5: Language and Power

Reflective writing is different from most writing you do in college. Reflective writing asks you to think back, to "reflect" on an experience—an essay you have written, a major change in your life, a time when you didn't have success at something you wanted to do, a semester's work in a course—and to examine how you now think and feel about that experience. What effect has the experience had on you? How have you changed? How will you be different in the future? (For more on reflective writing, visit Strategies for Writing a Reflection [18.29, p. 555].)

Now you're going to reflect on all the reading, thinking, discussing, and writing you have done in this project on language and power. Then, in a short paper—a page or so—reflect on this experience:

1. Report on what you learned about the complexities of language and power. What were the most important or most useful ideas you encountered?

2. Describe how you feel about the experience and what you *think* about what you have learned.

3. Report on what you learned that will make a difference for you in the future and why.

PROJECT 6

In Pursuit of Happiness

oneinchpunch/Shutterstock

It seems odd that Thomas Jefferson and the other writers of the Declaration of Independence declared that certain rights—life and liberty—were "inalienable," but not happiness. Only the *pursuit* of happiness was declared inalienable, as if the writers recognized that happiness was more of a goal than a right. In this project, we will question what happiness actually is, whether it is worth our pursuit, and what path might lead us to it.

Getting Started: Defining *Happiness*

In this first section, you'll explore what happiness means to a variety of people. You'll start by writing a short statement of what it means to you and then explore in a group what you think would be essential to your happiness in the future. Based on these activities, the class will conduct a survey of other people to discover the range of meanings *happiness* has.

Exploring, Thinking, and Writing about Ideas

In this section, you will explore a wide range of thinking about happiness. Will Storr proposes there are two kinds of happiness: *hedonistic* happiness, which is focused on the pursuit of pleasure for the individual, and *eudemonic* happiness, which is connected to a life with meaning. Eudemonic happiness aims for excellence and connection to something larger. The Greek philosopher Aristotle, writing almost 2,000 years earlier, identified two similar kinds of happiness, and Sri Lankan graduate student Rashmi suggests that happiness may be something much simpler. Emily Esfahani Smith questions whether happiness should even be a goal, while Gen Kelsang Nyema, a Buddhist monk, argues that you cannot achieve happiness by pursuing it.

As you read these differing views on happiness, you will also write about them and engage in many discussions about them with your classmates. In addition, you will complete activities related to the readings that ask you to practice specific skills, such as reviewing, critical thinking, analyzing, annotating, thinking as a doubter and believer, and finding and evaluating sources. According to directions from your instructor, you will work independently and/or in small groups to complete them. Finally, your instructor will assign relevant topics from other parts of *The Hub* that relate to writing, reading, research, and life issues that will address other important skills.

Bringing It All Together

Project 6 concludes with three assignments that ask you to combine what you've learned about how other people view happiness with your own thinking about the topic. Your instructor may assign the first, second, or third assignment; may give you a choice among the three; or may even ask you to complete more than one.

The first assignment asks you to write something on happiness that has an audience outside the college classroom—either an article on happiness for a national magazine or an essay urging incoming students to think about what will make them happy as they make a variety of educational decisions. The second assignment asks you to write an academic essay that explores the concept of happiness. Think of this second essay as writing that would be appropriate for a course in philosophy or American history. The third option is much like the first, except you are not limited to a written essay. Instead, you are invited to produce a multimodal project—a narrated PowerPoint, a video, a podcast, a blog, or a website—that would be appropriate to communicate your thoughts about happiness either to a national audience or to incoming students to your school.

The final writing assignment, Reflecting on Project 6: In Pursuit of Happiness, asks you to reflect on what you have learned as you worked through this reading/writing project.

Navigating Project 6

Below is the table of contents for Project 6, which you can use to easily locate the units you have been assigned to work on by your instructor. Several of these units ask you to connect to the Internet to watch videos or explore websites. If you find that any of the search terms provided do not work, there is a list of URLs available at https://bit.ly/33IIHtf.

Getting Started: Defining *Happiness*

▲ As a student (and maybe also as a husband or wife, mother or father, worker or volunteer), what makes you happy? How do you define the term *happiness*? How important is happiness to you? oneinchpunch/Shutterstock

6.1 Writing

In Pursuit of Happiness

The most often quoted words in the Declaration of Independence are the following:

> We hold these truths to be self-evident, that all men are created equal, that they are endowed by their Creator with certain unalienable Rights, that among these are Life, Liberty and the pursuit of Happiness.

Write a short paper—no more than a page—in which you explain what happiness means to you.

6.2　Activity

What Would Make You Happy?

For this activity, think about yourself far in the future. Think about yourself thirty or forty years from now. Working in your group, make a list of the things that members of the group say would be essential at that stage of their lives in order for them to feel happy, to feel that they had led a "good life."

6.3　Activity

The "Happiness Survey"

In What Would Make You Happy? (6.2), you worked in groups to compile lists of items that you and your classmates thought would be important to achieving happiness. Your instructor has turned that list into a survey document. Working with the other members of your group, have at least twenty people who are not in the class fill out this "Happiness Survey."

6.4　Writing

Analyzing the "Happiness Survey"

Your instructor will distribute the results of the "Happiness Survey" you and your classmates conducted for Unit 6.3. Using this compilation, write a short paper—a page or so will be plenty—in which you report on what you learned about the attitudes toward happiness from the people your class surveyed. In this report, don't just report the data; do some analysis of that data. What does the data reveal about the way the surveyed people think about happiness? What surprised you? What seemed problematic? What seemed contradictory? Were there patterns in how certain groups of people answered the survey?

Can Happiness Improve Your Health?

▲ This is an image of an urban garden in Malacca, Malaysia. What does it suggest to you? Who might have created it? Why? Is it useful? Meaningful? Beautiful? Could it make its creators happy? Why?   Jakob Fischer/Shutterstock

6.5 Activity

Analyzing Author, Audience, Topic, and Purpose in "A Better Kind of Happiness"

As long ago as classical Greece—300 BC or so—thinkers have been aware that four important components exist for every text: the *author* of the text, the *audience* for the text, the *topic* of the text, and the *purpose* of the text. Thinking about author, audience, topic, and purpose should help you prepare to read a text.

- **Author.** You don't simply want to find out the name of the author. What else can you learn about him or her? What evidence is there that the author really has some expertise? What biases might the author have? Is the author part of an organization? A corporation? What else has the author written?

- **Audience.**   Whom does it appear that the author intended to be the reader or readers of this text? Whom was the author addressing? Were there other, more secondary, audiences?

- **Topic.**   What is the text about? What is the subject?

- **Purpose.**   What does it appear that the author intended or, at least, hoped would happen as a result of this piece of writing? What did the author want the effect of this text on its audience to be?

Analyzing Author, Audience, Topic, and Purpose

For this activity, working in your group, examine "A Better Kind of Happiness" (p. 245) and together write a brief response—a paragraph is plenty—about each of these components: author, audience, topic, and purpose.

6.6   Activity

Previewing "A Better Kind of Happiness"

When you set out to read a book, an article, an essay, a blog, a web page—when you set out to read any text—your strategy may be simply to dive in, to start reading at the beginning and plow your way through to the end. With the limited time in most of our busy lives, simply diving in can seem like the quickest way to get something read.

Here's a different approach. Most experienced readers have found that taking a few minutes before diving in to get a sense of what it is they are about to read actually saves them time and makes their reading more effective. This does not mean you have to spend hours previewing; just a few minutes will be very helpful when you start to read.

Working in your group, preview "A Better Kind of Happiness" (p. 245) as outlined in step 1. Then answer the questions listed in steps 2 and 3. Later, working by yourself, answer the questions in step 4.

1. **Examine the text.**   Working in your group, examine the items listed below.

    a.   The title

    b.   The first and last paragraphs

    c.   Any section headings

    d.   Graphic images, if any

    e.   Any introductory material such as an abstract, introduction, or author biography

2. **Analyze the rhetorical situation.** As long ago as classical Greece—300 BC or so—thinkers have been aware that every text has four important components: the *author* of the text, the *audience* for the text, the *topic* of the text, and the *purpose* of the text that make up the *rhetorical situation*, the context in which the writing takes place. You don't need to remember the term *rhetorical situation*, but thinking about author, audience, topic, and purpose should be part of your previewing and predicting process.

   Now, working in your group, write brief answers to the following questions.

   a. **Who is the author?** This does not mean simply finding out the name of the author. What else can you learn about him or her? What evidence is there that the author really has some expertise? What biases might the author have? Is the author part of an organization? A corporation? What else has the author written?

   b. **Who is the author's audience?** Whom does it appear that the author intended to be the reader or readers of this text? Whom was the author addressing? Were there other, more secondary, audiences?

   c. **Topic.** What is the text about? What is the subject?

   d. **What is the author's purpose?** What does it appear that the author intended or, at least, hoped would happen as a result of this piece of writing? What did the author want the effect of this text to be on its audience?

3. **Predict what the text is about.** Predicting what a text might discuss, using background knowledge or personal experiences or information from previous reading, can also prepare you to better understand the content. While not every text will reveal information about all of the following questions, every text will provide answers to some of them. Before launching into reading the text, use the steps listed above to preview it to help you answer as many of the following questions as you can.

   - Does the author take a stand on his or her main topic?
   - Does the author seem to make any assumptions about the subject?
   - What do you know about the publishers of the text?
   - What evidence is there that the author of the text has at least some expertise about his or her subject?

4. **Think about yourself in relation to the text.** A final way to preview a text is to think about how the subject of the text relates to you individually. Of course, this personal kind of previewing is not appropriate for group work, so, working individually, answer the following questions.

- What do I already know about the topic?
- Have I had experiences that are related to this topic?
- Have I read other texts about this same topic?
- What have I heard or seen about this topic (on the radio, TV, internet, podcasts, YouTube, other classes, etc.)?
- How do I feel about the text's stand on the topic?
- What is my purpose for reading this text?
- How similar or different am I from the intended audience for the text?
- How difficult will the text be to read?
- How much time will I need to read it?

6.7 Reading

"A Better Kind of Happiness," Will Storr

In the article below, which originally appeared in the *New Yorker* magazine in 2016, Will Storr discusses happiness. If you haven't already done so, take a few minutes to preview it before you start reading. (If you need a refresher on previewing, see Previewing a Text [20.2, p. 575].)

A Better Kind of Happiness

WILL STORR

Will Storr is an investigative journalist who has written for national newspapers in England, Australia, and the United States. He has won numerous awards for his reporting, including the Australian Food Media Award for Best Investigative Journalism, the One World Press Award and the Amnesty International Award for his writing about sexual violence against men, and the Association for International Broadcasting Award for his 2013 BBC radio series *An Unspeakable Act*. He has written a number of books investigating topics as diverse as the supernatural (*Will Storr vs. The Supernatural: One Man's Search for the Truth*), heretics (*The Heretics: Adventures with the Enemies of Science*), and the current obsession with self (*Selfie: How the West Became Self-obsessed*). In addition, he is a successful novelist and photojournalist.

JULY 7, 2016

1   Nearly two and a half millennia ago, Aristotle triggered a revolution in happiness. At the time, Greek philosophers were trying hard to define precisely what this   ▶

state of being was. Some contended that it sprang from hedonism, the pursuit of sensual pleasure. Others argued from the perspective of tragedy, believing happiness to be a goal, a final destination that made the drudge of life worthwhile. These ideas are still with us today, of course, in the decadence of Instagram and gourmet-burger culture or the Christian notion of heaven. But Aristotle proposed a third option. In his Nicomachean Ethics, he described the idea of eudaemonic happiness, which said, essentially, that happiness was not merely a feeling, or a golden promise, but a practice. "It's living in a way that fulfills our purpose," Helen Morales, a classicist at the University of California, Santa Barbara, told me. "It's flourishing. Aristotle was saying, 'Stop hoping for happiness tomorrow. Happiness is being engaged in the process.'" Now, thousands of years later, evidence that Aristotle may have been onto something has been detected in the most surprising of places: the human genome.

2   The finding is the latest in a series of related discoveries in the field of social genomics. In 2007, John Cacioppo, a professor of psychology and behavioral neuroscience at the University of Chicago, and Steve Cole, a professor of medicine at the University of California, Los Angeles, among others, identified a link between loneliness and how genes express themselves. In a small study, since repeated in larger trials, they compared blood samples from six people who felt socially isolated with samples from eight who didn't. Among the lonely participants, the function of the genome had changed in such a way that the risk of inflammatory diseases increased and antiviral response diminished. It appeared that the brains of these subjects were wired to equate loneliness with danger, and to switch the body into a defensive state. In historical and evolutionary terms, Cacioppo suggested, this reaction could be a good thing, since it helps immune cells reach infections and encourages wounds to heal. But it is no way to live. Inflammation promotes the growth of cancer cells and the development of plaque in the arteries. It leads to the disabling of brain cells, which raises susceptibility to neurodegenerative disease. In effect, according to Cole, the stress reaction requires "mortgaging our long-term health in favor of our short-term survival." Our bodies, he concluded, are "programmed to turn misery into death."

3   In early 2010, Cole spoke about his work at a conference in Las Vegas. Among the audience members was Barbara Fredrickson, a noted positive psychologist from the University of North Carolina at Chapel Hill, who had attended graduate school with Cole. His talk made her wonder: If stressful states, including loneliness, caused the genome to respond in a damaging way, might sustained positive experiences have the opposite result? "Eudaemonic and hedonic aspects of well-being had previously been linked to longevity, so the possibility of finding beneficial effects seemed plausible," Fredrickson told me. The day after the conference, she sent Cole an e-mail, and by autumn of that year they had secured funding for a collaborative project.

Fredrickson's team would profile a group of participants, using questionnaires to determine their happiness style, then draw a small sample of their blood. Cole would analyze the samples and see what patterns, if any, emerged.

4   Fredrickson believed that hedonism would prove more favorable than eudaemonia—that discrete feelings of happiness would register on the genome more powerfully than abstract notions of meaning and purpose. Cole, meanwhile, was skeptical about the possibility of linking happiness and biology. He had worked with all kinds of researchers, trying to find a genomic response to everything from yoga to meditation to tai chi. Sometimes he made quite interesting findings, but more often the data provoked only a shrug. "Day after day, I see null results," he told me. "Nothing there, nothing there, nothing there." Fredrickson and Cole's first study wasn't huge, containing usable results from eighty people, but, because Cole had been studying misery for so long, he knew what to look for in the blood samples. "By this time, we had a pretty clear sense of the kinds of shifts in gene expression we see when people are threatened or uncertain," he said. "We were in a good position, even in a relatively small study, to say, 'These are the outcomes I'm going to look at.'"

5   When they parsed the data, they saw that Fredrickson's prediction appeared to be wrong. "This whole hedonic well-being stuff—just how happy are you, how satisfied with life?—didn't really correlate with gene expression at all," Cole said. Then he checked the correlation with eudaemonic happiness. "When we looked at that, things actually looked quite impressive," he said. The results, while small, were clearly significant. "I was rather startled." The study indicated that people high in eudaemonic happiness were more likely to show the opposite gene profile of those suffering from social isolation: inflammation was down, while antiviral response was up. Since that first test, in 2013, there have been three successful replications of the study, including one of a hundred and eight people, and another of a hundred and twenty-two. According to Cole, the kind of effect sizes that are being found indicate that lacking eudaemonia can be as damaging as smoking or obesity. They also suggest that, although people high in eudaemonic happiness often experience plenty of the hedonic stuff, too, the associated health benefits tend to surface only in those who lead what Aristotle might have called a good life.

6   But what, precisely, is this quasi-mythical good life? What do we mean when we talk about eudaemonia? For Aristotle, it required a combination of rationality and *arete*—a kind of virtue, although that concept has since been polluted by Christian moralizing. "It did mean goodness, but it was also about pursuing excellence," Morales told me. "For Usain Bolt, some of the training it takes to be a great athlete is not pleasurable, but fulfilling your purpose as a great runner brings happiness." Fredrickson, meanwhile, believes that a key facet of eudaemonia is connection. "It

►

refers to those aspects of well-being that transcend immediate self-gratification and connect people to something larger," she said. But Cole noted that connectedness doesn't appear to be an absolute precondition. "It seems unlikely that Usain Bolt is doing what he does to benefit humanity in any simply pro-social sense," he said. "If that's the case, is eudaemonic well-being mostly about the stretched goal, doing something you personally think is amazing or important? Or does it involve something more around pro-social behavior?" For Cole, the question remains open.

7   A further tantalizing clue might come from a distant corner of the academy. Since the early nineteen-seventies, the psychologist Brian R. Little has been interested in what he calls personal projects. He and his colleagues at Cambridge University, he told me, have "looked at literally tens of thousands of personal projects in thousands of participants." Most people, Little's work suggests, have around fifteen projects going at any time, ranging from the banal, like trying to get your wife to remember to switch off your computer once she's used it (that's one of mine), to the lofty, like trying to bring peace to the Middle East. Little refers to this second category as the "core" projects. One of his consistent findings is that, in order to bring us happiness, a project must have two qualities: it must be meaningful in some way, and we must have efficacy over it. (That is, there's little use trying to be the fastest human in the world if you're an overweight, agoraphobic retiree.) When I described Cole and Fredrickson's research, Little noted that it was remarkably congruent with his ideas. As with eudaemonia, though, the precise definition of a core project is malleable. "Core projects *can* increase the possibilities for social connection, but not necessarily," Little said. It all depends on an individual's needs. "A Trappist monk's core projects don't require the same kind of connection as an everyday bloke from Birmingham."

8   Indeed, this malleability is perhaps the most encouraging quality of both Little's core project and Aristotle's eudaemonia, because it makes finding happiness a real possibility. Even the most temperamentally introverted or miserable among us has the capacity to find a meaningful project that suits who we are. Locating it won't just bring pleasure; it might also bring a few more years of life in which to get the project done.

6.8 Activity

Annotating "A Better Kind of Happiness"

For this activity, you will read "A Better Kind of Happiness" (6.7, p. 245) and then annotate it—add comments, questions, symbols, underlining, and highlighting to indicate your reactions, thoughts, and questions about the text.

As with most reading you do, annotating the text as you read it will help you to start a dialogue with the author, think more deeply about his ideas, and become clearer about your own views on the topic. Remember that annotating means a lot more than just highlighting everything that seems important. You may want to read Annotation Explained (20.6, p. 583) before you start this activity.

↳ 6.9 Activity

Thinking about "A Better Kind of Happiness"

Working in your group, answer the following questions about "A Better Kind of Happiness" (6.7, p. 245).

1. In this article, Storr discusses two kinds of happiness: *eudaemonic* and *hedonic*. What does each of these terms mean?

2. Storr reports on a series of studies that suggest a connection between happiness and biology or, at least, genetics. Explain the connection he is suggesting.

3. In the final third of the article, Storr tries to answer these questions: "But what, precisely, is this quasi-mythical good life? What do we mean when we talk about eudaemonia?" How does he answer these questions? Does your group agree with his answer?

↳ 6.10 Writing

Believing and Doubting "A Better Kind of Happiness"

The believing and doubting game simply asks you to read a text two different ways. It asks you to read it once as a "believer," someone who agrees with the author and is reading because you want to understand exactly what the author's point is and why the author came to that conclusion. Then it asks you to read the text a second time from the point of view of a skeptic, someone who doubts that the central argument of the text is correct. This time you are reading to find flaws in the argument, weaknesses in the logic, and reasons to refute the conclusions. Many readers find this believing and doubting approach leads them into a deeper understanding of the text.

Read "A Better Kind of Happiness" (6.7, p. 245) and first try to agree with and "believe" what Storr is saying. Make notes as you read, in which you indicate the points you most strongly agree with and give reasons for your agreement. Then read the essay again and this time try to doubt or question the author's ideas as you do so. Again, make notes, as you are reading, of the parts of the essay you have doubts about and why you have those doubts.

Aristotle on Happiness

▲ More than 2,000 years ago the Greek philosopher Aristotle was thinking about happiness. He would probably be amazed to learn that all these years later we are still reading his ideas and being influenced by them. How relevant do you think the writings of a person who has been dead for over 2,000 years are to people living today? What can we learn, if anything, from them? thelefty/Shutterstock

6.11 Activity

Previewing Excerpt from "Nicomachean Ethics"

Working in your group, preview Aristotle's "Nicomachean Ethics" (6.12, p. 251) and look for the following items. (If you need a refresher on previewing, take a look at Previewing a Text [20.2, p. 575].)

- The title
- Any biographical information about the author
- Any introductory material
- The first paragraph
- The last paragraph

As you preview, answer the following questions.

1. **Author.** Beyond his name, what else can you learn about Aristotle? What evidence is there that he really has some expertise? What biases might he have? What else has he written?

2. **Audience.** Whom does it appear that Aristotle intended to be the reader or readers of this text? Whom was he addressing? Were there other, more secondary, audiences?

3. **Topic.** What is the text "about"? What seems to be the main focus?

4. **Purpose.** What does it appear that the author intended or, at least, hoped would happen as a result of this piece of writing? What did he want the effect of this text to be on its audience?

Deciphering Aristotle's Writing

Previewing can help you to prepare to read a text, and the information you've gained from answering the previous questions should help you as you work on "Nicomachean Ethics." However, because this text is quite challenging, you are going to tackle the first chunk of it in class. Here is the beginning of the first paragraph:

> To judge from the lives that men lead, most men, and men of the most vulgar type, seem (not without some ground) to identify the good, or happiness, with pleasure; which is the reason why they love the life of enjoyment. For there are, we may say, three prominent types of life—that just mentioned, the political, and thirdly the contemplative life. Now the mass of mankind are evidently quite slavish in their tastes, preferring a life suitable to beasts, but they get some ground for their view from the fact that many of those in high places share the tastes of Sardanapallus.

Working in your group, attempt to write one or two sentences that sum up the main ideas of this small excerpt from Aristotle's "Nicomachean Ethics."

6.12 Reading

Excerpt from "Nicomachean Ethics," Aristotle

This is not an easy text to read. It is an English translation of a lecture given by the Greek philosopher Aristotle. It is not in Greek but in a very stilted style of English. Nevertheless, while challenging, it is possible to read, and it is interesting as one of the earliest known discussions of happiness.

The essay is on the left below. Comments and explanations of the terms in bold on the left are provided on the right, which should help you work your way through this challenging text.

Excerpt from "Nicomachean Ethics"

ARISTOTLE

The Greek philosopher and scientist Aristotle lived from 384 to 348 BC. He is considered one of the "Fathers" of Western philosophy and his writings cover numerous topics ranging from physics and biology to logic, poetry, and politics. His writings and philosophy have had a profound impact on Western thought from his own times through the Middle Ages to the Renaissance and up to the modern era, and he influenced both Islamic thought and Christian theology. A significant feature of his thinking is that knowledge, and the hypotheses drawn from it, is based on perception, on information derived from the senses. Therefore, he placed emphasis on the importance of evidence obtained by observation and carefully documented.

Aristotle's lectures were written down by his followers and later edited, first by Aristotle himself and later by his son Nicomachus—hence the name "Nicomachean Ethics."

1 To judge from the lives that **men** lead, most men, and men of the most vulgar type, seem (not without some ground) to identify the good, or **happiness,** with pleasure; which is the reason why they love the life of enjoyment. For there are, we may say, three prominent types of life—that just mentioned, the **political**, and thirdly the contemplative life. Now the mass of mankind are evidently quite slavish in their tastes, preferring a life suitable to beasts, but they get some ground for their view from the fact that many of those in high places share the tastes of **Sardanapallus**. A consideration of the prominent types of life shows that people of superior refinement and of active disposition identify happiness with honor; for this is, roughly speaking, the **end** of the political life. But it seems too superficial to be what we are looking for, since it is thought to depend on those who bestow honor rather than on him who receives it, but the good we divine to be something of one's own and not easily taken from one. Further, men seem to pursue honor in order that they may be assured of their merit; at least it is by men of practical wisdom that they seek to be honored, and among those who know them, and on the ground of their **virtue**; clearly, then, according to them, at any rate, virtue is better. And perhaps one might even suppose

Greek society was male dominated; women had very little public role.

The Greek word translated here as "happiness" is "eudaimonia," which is closer in meaning to something like "well-being."

"Polis" was the Greek word for "city," but it referred more to the citizenry of the city rather than its physical nature. So, to act "politically" was to act in a way that was responsible to the city, to act in a socially responsible way.

Sardanapallus was the Greek name for the Assyrian King Ashurbanipal, whom the Greeks viewed as a man completely dedicated to a life of sensual pleasure.

Think of "end" as meaning something like "goal" or "purpose."

"Virtue" is a translation of the Greek word "arete," which can also be translated as moral excellence and is also associated with bravery.

this to be, rather than honor, the end of the political life. But even this appears somewhat incomplete; for possession of virtue seems actually compatible with being asleep, or with lifelong inactivity, and, further, with the greatest sufferings and misfortunes; but a man who was **living so** no one would call happy, unless he were **maintaining a thesis at all costs**. But enough of this; for the subject has been sufficiently treated even in the popular discussions. Third comes the contemplative life, which we shall consider later.

2   The life of money-making is one undertaken under compulsion, and wealth is evidently not the good we are seeking; for it is merely useful and for the sake of something else. And so one might rather take the aforenamed objects to be ends; for they are loved for themselves. But it is evident that not even these are the end; yet many arguments have been wasted on the support of them. Let us leave this subject, then.

* * *

3   Now we call that which is in itself worthy of pursuit more final than that which is worthy of pursuit for the sake of something else, and that which is never desirable for the sake of something else more final than the things that are desirable both in themselves and for the sake of that other thing, and therefore we call final without qualification that which is always desirable in itself and never for the sake of something else.

4   Now such a thing happiness, above all else, is held to be; for this we choose always for itself and never for the sake of something else, but honor, pleasure, reason, and every virtue we choose indeed for themselves (for if nothing resulted from them we should still choose each of them), but we choose them also for the sake of happiness, judging that through them we shall be happy. Happiness, on the other hand, no one chooses for the sake of these, nor, in general, for anything other than itself.

Here, "living so" means "living in such a way." In this case, it means living a life of sleeping or of inactivity.

Think of "maintaining a thesis at all costs" as defending your argument no matter what it costs you to do so—for example, by defending something ridiculous.

↳ **6.13** **Activity**

Thinking about the Excerpt from "Nicomachean Ethics"

Working in your group, answer the following questions.

1. In a paragraph or less, sum up what the group thinks is the main idea of the excerpt from "Nicomachean Ethics" (6.12, p. 251).

2. What reasons does Aristotle give for not considering wealth or honor to be the primary goal for life?

3. What do you think Aristotle means by the word *happiness*?

Alternate Views of Happiness

▲ There are many paths to happiness. Finding meaning in life, setting and completing challenging goals, and seeking enlightenment through meditation and spiritual retreat are just some ways people pursue it. Based on your reading so far and the results of the "Happiness Survey," what new ways to find happiness have you learned about that appeal to you?   Lucky Business/Shutterstock

6.14 Writing

Responding to "Happiness in Sri Lanka?" Rashmi

Here's a story from Rashmi, a graduate student from Sri Lanka, an island country located off the southern tip of India. Read the story and then write a short paper—a page or so is plenty—in which you discuss what this story reveals about happiness. Could you be happy if you were a member of Rashmi's family in Sri Lanka?

Happiness in Sri Lanka?

RASHMI

1   I was born into a poor family in a poor village in a rural section of Sri Lanka, far from Colombo, my country's capital. We lived in a small house with mud floors, a thatched roof, one electric light bulb, no glass in our windows, and no running water. Everyone else in our village lived in similar circumstances, except one family: the wealthy family, who owned all the land in the village and lived in a mansion outside of the village. Everyone in the village worked for them.

2   At the end of the eighth grade in our little village school, we were all given a test designed by the national government. I scored one of the highest scores in all Sri Lanka, so I was selected to attend a prestigious boarding school in Colombo for high school. Four years later, I took another test as I graduated from high school and again scored among the top scores in the country. This time I was offered a full scholarship to attend Oxford University in England. After four years at Oxford, I again received a full scholarship to pursue a Ph.D. at the University of Massachusetts. I am on my way to a career as an engineer.

3   My brothers and sisters and the rest of my family still live in our small house in our little village in Sri Lanka. I get to visit them every three years.

4   People often say to me, "You must be very happy. You escaped such poverty and gained such a wonderful education and are on your way to a very rewarding career." I always respond that I am not so sure. When I visit my family, I see that they are very happy. They don't experience any of the stress I do, they don't worry about "being successful," they don't envy their neighbors because they all live similar, simple lives. There is plenty to eat. They are surrounded by family and friends. They really seem to be much happier than I am.

"There's More to Life Than Being Happy," Emily Esfahani Smith

In the article below, which originally appeared in the *Atlantic Monthly* magazine in 2013, Emily Esfahani Smith discusses happiness. The level of happiness in America may have declined somewhat in the troubled years since 2013, but Smith's central point still seems relevant. Be sure to do some previewing before diving in to this article. (If you need a refresher on previewing, take a look at Previewing a Text [20.2, p. 575].)

There's More to Life Than Being Happy

EMILY ESFAHANI SMITH

Emily Esfahani Smith was born in Zurich, Switzerland; grew up in Montreal, Canada; and now lives in Washington, DC. She earned a master's degree in applied psychology from the University of Pennsylvania, and in her writing, she draws on psychology, philosophy, and literature as she explores how people find meaning in a world of struggle and difficulty. She is a journalist who has written for the *New York Times*, the *Wall Street Journal*, and the *Atlantic*, and she is the author of the book *The Power of Meaning: Crafting a Life That Matters*.

JANUARY 29, 2013

1   In September 1942, Viktor Frankl, a prominent Jewish psychiatrist and neurologist in Vienna, was arrested and transported to a Nazi concentration camp with his wife and parents. Three years later, when his camp was liberated, most of his family, including his pregnant wife, had perished—but he, prisoner number 119104, had lived. In his bestselling 1946 book, *Man's Search for Meaning*, which he wrote in nine days about his experiences in the camps, Frankl concluded that the difference between those who had lived and those who had died came down to one thing: Meaning, an insight he came to early in life. When he was a high school student, one of his science teachers declared to the class, "Life is nothing more than a combustion process, a process of oxidation." Frankl jumped out of his chair and responded, "Sir, if this is so, then what can be the meaning of life?"

2   As he saw in the camps, those who found meaning even in the most horrendous circumstances were far more resilient to suffering than those who did not. "Everything can be taken from a man but one thing," Frankl wrote in *Man's Search*

for Meaning, "the last of the human freedoms—to choose one's attitude in any given set of circumstances, to choose one's own way."

3   Frankl worked as a therapist in the camps, and in his book, he gives the example of two suicidal inmates he encountered there. Like many others in the camps, these two men were hopeless and thought that there was nothing more to expect from life, nothing to live for. "In both cases," Frankl writes, "it was a question of getting them to realize that life was still expecting something from them; something in the future was expected of them." For one man, it was his young child, who was then living in a foreign country. For the other, a scientist, it was a series of books that he needed to finish. Frankl writes:

> This uniqueness and singleness which distinguishes each individual and gives a meaning to his existence has a bearing on creative work as much as it does on human love. When the impossibility of replacing a person is realized, it allows the responsibility which a man has for his existence and its continuance to appear in all its magnitude. A man who becomes conscious of the responsibility he bears toward a human being who affectionately waits for him, or to an unfinished work, will never be able to throw away his life. He knows the "why" for his existence, and will be able to bear almost any "how."

4   In 1991, the Library of Congress and Book-of-the-Month Club listed *Man's Search for Meaning* as one of the 10 most influential books in the United States. It has sold millions of copies worldwide. Now, over twenty years later, the book's ethos—its emphasis on meaning, the value of suffering, and responsibility to something greater than the self—seems to be at odds with our culture, which is more interested in the pursuit of individual happiness than in the search for meaning. "To the European," Frankl wrote, "it is a characteristic of the American culture that, again and again, one is commanded and ordered to 'be happy.' But happiness cannot be pursued; it must ensue. One must have a reason to 'be happy.'"

5   According to Gallup, the happiness levels of Americans are at a four-year high—as is, it seems, the number of best-selling books with the word "happiness" in their titles. At this writing, Gallup also reports that nearly 60 percent of all Americans today feel happy, without a lot of stress or worry. On the other hand, according to the Center[s] for Disease Control, about 4 out of 10 Americans have not discovered a satisfying life purpose. Forty percent either do not think their lives have a clear sense of purpose or are neutral about whether their lives have purpose. Nearly a quarter of Americans feel neutral or do not have a strong sense of what makes their lives meaningful. Research has shown that having purpose and meaning in life increases overall well-being and life satisfaction, improves mental and

▶

physical health, enhances resiliency, enhances self-esteem, and decreases the chances of depression. On top of that, the single-minded pursuit of happiness is ironically leaving people less happy, according to recent research. "It is the very pursuit of happiness," Frankl knew, "that thwarts happiness."

*   *   *

6   This is why some researchers are cautioning against the pursuit of mere happiness. In a new study, which will be published . . . in the *Journal of Positive Psychology*, psychological scientists asked nearly 400 Americans aged 18 to 78 whether they thought their lives were meaningful and/or happy. Examining their self-reported attitudes toward meaning, happiness, and many other variables—like stress levels, spending patterns, and having children—over a month-long period, the researchers found that a meaningful life and happy life overlap in certain ways, but are ultimately very different. Leading a happy life, the psychologists found, is associated with being a "taker" while leading a meaningful life corresponds with being a "giver." "Happiness without meaning characterizes a relatively shallow, self-absorbed or even selfish life, in which things go well, needs and desire are easily satisfied, and difficult or taxing entanglements are avoided," the authors write.

7   How do the happy life and the meaningful life differ? Happiness, they found, is about feeling good. Specifically, the researchers found that people who are happy tend to think that life is easy, they are in good physical health, and they are able to buy the things that they need and want. While not having enough money decreases how happy and meaningful you consider your life to be, it has a much greater impact on happiness. The happy life is also defined by a lack of stress or worry.

8   Most importantly from a social perspective, the pursuit of happiness is associated with selfish behavior—being, as mentioned, a "taker" rather than a "giver." The psychologists give an evolutionary explanation for this: happiness is about drive reduction. If you have a need or a desire—like hunger—you satisfy it, and that makes you happy. People become happy, in other words, when they get what they want. Humans, then, are not the only ones who can feel happy. Animals have needs and drives, too, and when those drives are satisfied, animals also feel happy, the researchers point out.

9   "Happy people get a lot of joy from receiving benefits from others while people leading meaningful lives get a lot of joy from giving to others," explained Kathleen Vohs, one of the authors of the study, in a recent presentation at the University of Pennsylvania. In other words, meaning transcends the self while happiness is all about giving the self what it wants. People who have high meaning in their lives are more likely to help others in need. "If anything, pure happiness is linked to not

helping others in need," the researchers, which include Stanford University's Jennifer Aaker and Emily Garbinsky, write.

10   What sets human beings apart from animals is not the pursuit of happiness, which occurs all across the natural world, but the pursuit of meaning, which is unique to humans, according to Roy Baumeister, the lead researcher of the study and author, with John Tierney, of the recent book *Willpower: Rediscovering the Greatest Human Strength*. Baumeister, a social psychologist at Florida State University, was named an ISI [Institute for Scientific Information] highly cited scientific researcher in 2003.

11   The study participants reported deriving meaning from giving a part of themselves away to others and making a sacrifice on behalf of the overall group. In the words of Martin E. P. Seligman, one of the leading psychological scientists alive today, in the meaningful life "you use your highest strengths and talents to belong to and serve something you believe is larger than the self." For instance, having more meaning in one's life was associated with activities like buying presents for others, taking care of kids, and arguing. People whose lives have high levels of meaning often actively seek meaning out even when they know it will come at the expense of happiness. Because they have invested themselves in something bigger than themselves, they also worry more and have higher levels of stress and anxiety in their lives than happy people. Having children, for example, is associated with the meaningful life and requires self-sacrifice, but it has been famously associated with low happiness among parents, including the ones in this study. In fact, according to Harvard psychologist Daniel Gilbert, research shows that parents are less happy interacting with their children than they are exercising, eating, and watching television.

12   "Partly what we do as human beings is to take care of others and contribute to others. This makes life meaningful but it does not necessarily make us happy," Baumeister told me in an interview.

13   Meaning is not only about transcending the self, but also about transcending the present moment—which is perhaps the most important finding of the study, according to the researchers. While happiness is an emotion felt in the here and now, it ultimately fades away, just as all emotions do; positive affect and feelings of pleasure are fleeting. The amount of time people report feeling good or bad correlates with happiness but not at all with meaning.

14   Meaning, on the other hand, is enduring. It connects the past to the present to the future. "Thinking beyond the present moment, into the past or future, was a sign of the relatively meaningful but unhappy life," the researchers write. "Happiness is not generally found in contemplating the past or future." That is, people who thought more about the present were happier, but people who spent more time thinking

▶

about the future or about past struggles and sufferings felt more meaning in their lives, though they were less happy.

15   Having negative events happen to you, the study found, decreases your happiness but increases the amount of meaning you have in life. Another study from 2011 confirmed this, finding that people who have meaning in their lives, in the form of a clearly defined purpose, rate their satisfaction with life higher even when they were feeling bad than those who did not have a clearly defined purpose. "If there is meaning in life at all," Frankl wrote, "then there must be meaning in suffering."

* * *

16   Which brings us back to Frankl's life and, specifically, a decisive experience he had before he was sent to the concentration camps. It was an incident that emphasizes the difference between the pursuit of meaning and the pursuit of happiness in life.

17   In his early adulthood, before he and his family were taken away to the camps, Frankl had established himself as one of the leading psychiatrists in Vienna and the world. As a 16-year-old boy, for example, he struck up a correspondence with Sigmund Freud and one day sent Freud a two-page paper he had written. Freud, impressed by Frankl's talent, sent the paper to the *International Journal of Psychoanalysis* for publication. "I hope you don't object," Freud wrote the teenager.

18   While he was in medical school, Frankl distinguished himself even further. Not only did he establish suicide-prevention centers for teenagers—a precursor to his work in the camps—but he was also developing his signature contribution to the field of clinical psychology: logotherapy, which is meant to help people overcome depression and achieve well-being by finding their unique meaning in life. By 1941, his theories had received international attention and he was working as the chief of neurology at Vienna's Rothschild Hospital, where he risked his life and career by making false diagnoses of mentally ill patients so that they would not, per Nazi orders, be euthanized.

19   That was the same year when he had a decision to make, a decision that would change his life. With his career on the rise and the threat of the Nazis looming over him, Frankl had applied for a visa to America, which he was granted in 1941. By then, the Nazis had already started rounding up the Jews and taking them away to concentration camps, focusing on the elderly first. Frankl knew that it would only be time before the Nazis came to take his parents away. He also knew that once they did, he had a responsibility to be there with his parents to help them through the trauma of adjusting to camp life. On the other hand, as a newly married man with his visa in hand, he was tempted to leave for America and flee to safety, where he could distinguish himself even further in his field.

20   As Anna S. Redsand recounts in her biography of Frankl, he was at a loss for what to do, so he set out for St. Stephan's Cathedral in Vienna to clear his head. Listening to the organ music, he repeatedly asked himself, "Should I leave my parents behind? Should I say goodbye and leave them to their fate?" Where did his responsibility lie? He was looking for a "hint from heaven."

21   When he returned home, he found it. A piece of marble was lying on the table. His father explained that it was from the rubble of one of the nearby synagogues that the Nazis had destroyed. The marble contained the fragment of one of the Ten Commandments—the one about honoring your father and your mother. With that, Frankl decided to stay in Vienna and forgo whatever opportunities for safety and career advancement awaited him in the United States. He decided to put aside his individual pursuits to serve his family and, later, other inmates in the camps.

22   The wisdom that Frankl derived from his experiences there, in the middle of unimaginable human suffering, is just as relevant now as it was then: "Being human always points, and is directed, to something or someone, other than oneself—be it a meaning to fulfill or another human being to encounter. The more one forgets himself—by giving himself to a cause to serve or another person to love—the more human he is."

23   Baumeister and his colleagues would agree that the pursuit of meaning is what makes human beings uniquely human. By putting aside our selfish interests to serve someone or something larger than ourselves—by devoting our lives to "giving" rather than "taking"—we are not only expressing our fundamental humanity, but are also acknowledging that that there is more to the good life than the pursuit of simple happiness.

↳ **6.16** **Activity**

Thinking about "There's More to Life Than Being Happy"

Working in your group, answer the following questions about "There's More to Life Than Being Happy" (6.15, p. 256).

1. Does Smith think that happiness is not something we should desire? Why or why not?

2. In paragraph 5 (p. 258) of the essay, Smith speaks of "overall well-being and life satisfaction." What seems to be the relationship between "overall well-being and life satisfaction" and "happiness"? What is the relationship between "overall well-being and life satisfaction" and living a "meaningful" life?

3. If someone wanted to live a "meaningful" life, what would that mean? What gives a life "meaning"?

4. Can you think of anything one could do to give his or her life "meaning" that would *not* help others?

6.17 Video

"Happiness Is All in Your Mind," Gen Kelsang Nyema

Set aside fifteen minutes to watch a video of the TED Talk "Happiness Is All in Your Mind" by Gen Kelsang Nyema, which suggests a very different path to happiness. To access the video, type "ted talk happiness nyema" into your browser. (If you find that these search terms do not work, there is an updated list of URLs available at https://bit.ly/33IIHtf.)

Gen Kelsang Nyema is an American Buddhist nun. After years as the resident teacher at the Kadampa Meditation Centre in South Carolina, she is now the resident teacher at the Vajrayogini Buddhist Center in Washington, DC. If you would like to know more about her, you can read the article "Unzipped, a Year Later: Gen Kelsang Nyema" by typing the title into your browser.

6.18 Writing

Thinking about "Happiness Is All in Your Mind"

Write a short paper—a page is plenty—in which you report your understanding of what Gen Kelsang Nyema says about happiness in her TED Talk (6.17).

Bringing It All Together

▲ Now that you've completed most of this reading/writing project, have your ideas about what constitutes happiness changed? If so, how? Why?   Rawpixel.com/Shutterstock

6.19 Writing

Happiness Redefined

At the beginning of this project you explored what happiness means to you and other people you know. For this assignment, write a short paper—a page would be plenty—in which you explain how your understanding of happiness has changed as you have worked your way through this project, exploring a variety of perspectives on the topic and thinking, discussing, and writing about them.

6.20 Writing

Finding and Evaluating Sources

In the following three writing assignments—Real World Essay: Getting Personal about Happiness (6.21, p. 264), Academic Essay: Defining Happiness (6.22, p. 266), and Multimodal Composition: Pursuing Happiness (6.23, p. 267)—there are several options to write about. Decide which option you are going to choose. Either in the library or online, locate three articles or books that are relevant to the option you have selected and answer the questions below about each of them. (For more on finding and evaluating sources, see Research [Topic 22, p. 617].)

1. Who is the author(s)? What can you find out about the author(s)? How expert is the author on the subject?

2. Where was the article or book published? What kind of journal, book, or website did the article appear in?

3. Does the author or the publisher of the article or book have a particular bias? Does that bias make the article or book less valuable as a resource?

4. Who seems to be the audience this article or book was intended for?

5. Does the article or book provide convincing evidence to support its thesis?

6. Does the article or book have information you may be able to use in your essay?

7. Which of the three articles or books would be the best resource for you to quote from in an essay? Why?

6.21 Real World Essay

Getting Personal about Happiness

For this assignment, you will write a three- to four-page essay that grows out of your reading, discussions, and thinking about happiness. There are two options for this essay.

Option 1: What Happiness Means to You

For this assignment, you are going to present your ideas about "the pursuit of happiness" in relation to your own life. Think about what you have read or watched; the conversations you've had with your classmates; the attitudes you discovered from the survey your class conducted; the discussion by Gen Kelsang Nyema, the Buddhist nun (6.17, p. 262); and the thoughts of Rashmi, the graduate student from Sri Lanka (6.14, p. 255).

Audience.   In this project, you read articles from the *Atlantic* (6.15, p. 256) and the *New Yorker* (6.7, p. 245), popular magazines that publish thoughtful essays aimed at a general audience. Think of the essay you are about to write as being like the essays you read from these magazines—thoughtful, but not highly technical, and aimed at a general audience, not specialists. Your assignment, then, is to write a three- to four-page essay in the style of an article from the *Atlantic* or the *New Yorker* in which you explain and defend your attitude toward happiness.

Documentation.   Your instructor will provide specific requirements about including quotations, citations, or the documentation style to use. Be sure to provide appropriate citations for any words you quote, paraphrase, or summarize from readings in this project or articles that you have found through your research and to include a works cited list or list of references at the end of your essay. If you need to review how to provide this documentation, refer to MLA Documentation (Topic 23, p. 650) or APA Documentation (Topic 24, p. 687).

If you want to use your sources most effectively to support your argument, it's not enough to simply include them as a series of unrelated sources; you need to tie them together, explain their relationships with each other, and express your conclusions about them. This process is called *synthesizing*, and it is discussed in more detail in Synthesis (22.14, p. 648).

Option 2: Considering Happiness When Making Decisions in College

As new students arrive at college, they are faced with many decisions: how many courses to take, what courses to take, what major or program to enroll in, how many hours a week to work, where to live, whether to take out a student loan, among others. As they make these decisions, students have to weigh factors like whether they are good at math or not, the chances of finding a job in the career they are thinking about, what the fastest way is to finish college, and what their parents want them to do. One factor students don't often consider is what will make them happy.

Audience.   For this assignment, write an essay intended for next year's incoming students in which you argue that they should also consider what choices will make them happy as they make decisions about college. To accomplish this, you will need to explain what you mean by *happiness*. Draw on what you have read or watched; the conversations you've had with your classmates; the attitudes you discovered from the survey your class conducted; the discussion by Gen Kelsang Nyema, the Buddhist nun (6.17, p. 262); and the thoughts of Rashmi, the graduate student from Sri Lanka (6.14, p. 255).

Documentation.   Your instructor will provide specific requirements about including quotations, citations, or the documentation style to use. Be sure to provide appropriate citations for any words you quote, paraphrase, or summarize from readings in this project or articles that you have found through your research and to include a works cited list or list of references at the end of your essay. If you need to review how to provide this documentation, refer to MLA Documentation (Topic 23, p. 650) or APA Documentation (Topic 24, p. 687).

If you want to use your sources most effectively to support your argument, it's not enough to simply include them as a series of unrelated sources; you need to tie them together, explain their relationships with each other, and express your conclusions about them. This process is called *synthesizing*, and it is discussed in more detail in Synthesis (22.14, p. 648).

6.22 Academic Essay

Defining Happiness

For this assignment, you will write a three- to four-page essay that grows out of your reading, discussions, and thinking about happiness. There are two options for this essay.

Option 1: What Happiness Means to You

Think about what you have read or watched; the conversations you've had with your classmates; the attitudes you discovered from the survey your class conducted; the discussion by Gen Kelsang Nyema, the Buddhist nun (6.17, p. 262); and the thoughts of Rashmi, the graduate student from Sri Lanka (6.14, p. 255). Then write a three- to four-page essay in which you define what you think happiness is and why you think of it the way you do. Think of this as an essay appropriate for a college class in philosophy, sociology, psychology, or even freshman composition. Because this assignment asks you to *define* happiness, you may want to take a look at Strategies for Writing Definitions (18.18, p. 540).

Documentation.   Your instructor will provide specific requirements about including quotations, citations, or the documentation style to use. Be sure to provide appropriate citations for any words you quote, paraphrase, or summarize from readings in this project or articles that you have found through your research and to include a works cited list or list of references at the end of your essay. If you need to review how to provide this documentation, refer to MLA Documentation (Topic 23, p. 650) or APA Documentation (Topic 24, p. 687).

If you want to use your sources most effectively to support your argument, it's not enough to simply include them as a series of unrelated sources; you need to tie them together, explain their relationships with each other, and express your conclusions about them. This process is called *synthesizing*, and it is discussed in more detail in Synthesis (22.14, p. 648).

Option 2: Your Definition of Happiness versus That of the Declaration of Independence

Think about what you have read or watched; the conversations you've had with your classmates; the attitudes you discovered from the survey your class conducted; the discussion by Gen Kelsang Nyema, the Buddhist nun (6.17, p. 262); and the thoughts of Rashmi, the graduate student from Sri Lanka (6.14, p. 255). Then write a three- to four-page essay in which you discuss what the writers of the Declaration of Independence meant by the term *happiness* (see 6.1, p. 240) and what you think would have been a better definition of the term. Then explain why your kind of happiness would have been preferable to theirs. Think of this as an essay appropriate for a college class in American history or even freshman composition. Because this assignment asks you to *define* happiness, you may want to take a look at Strategies for Writing Definitions (18.18, p. 540).

Documentation. Your instructor will provide specific requirements about including quotations, citations, or the documentation style to use. Be sure to provide appropriate citations for any words you quote, paraphrase, or summarize from readings in this project or articles that you have found through your research and to include a works cited list or list of references at the end of your essay. If you need to review how to provide this documentation, refer to MLA Documentation (Topic 23, p. 650) or APA Documentation (Topic 24, p. 687).

If you want to use your sources most effectively to support your argument, it's not enough to simply include them as a series of unrelated sources; you need to tie them together, explain their relationships with each other, and express your conclusions about them. This process is called *synthesizing*, and it is discussed in more detail in Synthesis (22.14, p. 648).

6.23 Multimodal Composition

Pursuing Happiness

As new students arrive at college, they are faced with many decisions: how many courses to take, what courses to take, what major or program to enroll in, how many hours a week to work, where to live, whether to take out a student loan, among others. As they make these decisions, students have to weigh factors like whether they are good at math or not, the chances of finding a job in a career they are thinking about, what the fastest way is to finish college, and what their parents want them to do. One factor students don't often consider is what will make them happy.

Assignment. Compose a multimodal project intended for next year's incoming students in which you argue that they should also consider what choices will make them happy. Draw on what you have read or watched; the conversations you've had with your classmates; the attitudes you discovered from the survey your class conducted; the discussion by Gen Kelsang Nyema, the Buddhist nun (6.17, p. 262); and the thoughts of Rashmi, the graduate student from Sri Lanka (6.14, p. 255). You will need to define what you mean by *happiness* and apply that concept to making decisions about college. Because this assignment asks you to *define* happiness, you may want to take a look at Strategies for Writing Definitions (18.18, p. 540).

Format. This assignment is similar to the one in Unit 6.21 (p. 264), except that you are not limited to a formal *written* document. Instead, you are invited to use any skills you have that make use of other media—images, video, PowerPoint with narration, graphs, charts, even a website—to convey your argument. You might, for example, produce a paper document that includes images, charts, or graphs. If you are comfortable working with PowerPoint, you could produce a PowerPoint presentation with recorded narration, or, if your instructor gives you the okay, one that you narrate to the class. If you are skilled at website or video development, you could present your argument as a website or video.

Documentation. Your instructor will provide specific requirements about including quotations, citations, or the documentation style to use. Be sure to provide appropriate citations for any words you quote, paraphrase, or summarize from readings in this project or articles that you have found through your research and to include a works cited list or list of references to accompany your composition. If you need to review how to provide this documentation, refer to MLA Documentation (Topic 23, p. 650) or APA Documentation (Topic 24, p. 687).

If you want to use your sources most effectively to support your argument, it's not enough to simply include them as a series of unrelated sources; you need to tie them together, explain their relationships with each other, and express your conclusions about them. This process is called *synthesizing*, and it is discussed in more detail in Synthesis (22.14, p. 648).

6.24 Activity

Getting Started on Your Essay or Composition

During this class period, you and your classmates will begin working on your assignment (see Real World Essay: Getting Personal about Happiness [6.21, p. 264], Academic Essay: Defining Happiness [6.22, p. 266], or Multimodal Composition: Pursuing Happiness [6.23, p. 267]).

You may use this time to start brainstorming or to begin your research online. You may want to write an opening paragraph or two, or you may want to review what you've already read and written in this project. You may want to compare notes with a couple of classmates or ask a question or two of your instructor. If you are composing a multimodal project, you may want to talk to others who are doing the same to compare approaches. The idea is that you will at least get a start on the assignment.

6.25   Writing

Reflecting on Project 6: In Pursuit of Happiness

Reflective writing is different from most writing you do in college. Reflective writing asks you to think back, to "reflect" on an experience—an essay you have written, a major change in your life, a time when you didn't have success at something you wanted to do, a semester's work in a course—and to examine how you now think and feel about that experience. What effect has the experience had on you? How have you changed? How will you be different in the future? (If you'd like a little more explanation of reflective writing, visit Strategies for Writing a Reflection [18.29, p. 555].)

Now you're going to look back on all the reading, thinking, discussing, and writing you have done in this project on the pursuit of happiness. Then, in a short paper—a page or so—reflect on this experience:

1. Report on what you learned about happiness. What were the most important or most useful ideas you encountered?

2. Describe how you feel about the experience and what you *think* about what you have learned.

3. Report on what you learned that will make a difference for you in the future and why.

PROJECT 7

What Is Art?

▲ Paul Gauguin, *The Siesta*, 1892, Metropolitan Museum of Art, New York City   Everett - Art/Shutterstock

What is art? You are being asked a question that no one in thousands of years has been able to answer. In the readings in this project, you will encounter many attempts at answering it, all quite different. The fact that it is a hard question, however, makes your job easier. There is no "correct answer," which means there are many "good answers."

If art is something you've never thought much about before, if you've never had a chance or perhaps an inclination to visit an art museum, don't worry. This project is not designed for artists or art specialists or art historians. It is designed to ask you to think, read, discuss, and write as a novice about a challenging question. You will encounter some experts in the readings and have a chance to decide what you think about their ways of defining this elusive term.

Getting Started: Discovering Your Definition of *Art*

This project begins with an activity in which you are asked to look at some images of paintings from the Metropolitan Museum of Art in New York City and, working in your group, to draft a preliminary definition of what *art* is. Then you will look at some images of less conventional art. As you and your group decide which of these you think are art and which you think are not art, you will revise your original definition.

Exploring, Thinking, and Writing about Ideas

In this section you will read and analyze essays by three writers who are considered to be experts on art (and who agree that defining the term is not easy). As you work through these materials, you will discuss your thoughts and findings with your class-mates, reflect in writing on what you have read, and write in response to specific arti-cles. As you do all this you will grapple with questions like, Does art have to be created by a human being? Is bad art "art"? Is an iPhone art? Finally, you will be asked to answer a series of probing questions to help you tighten up your definition of *art*.

You will also complete activities related to the readings that ask you to practice specific skills, such as previewing, defining, thinking critically, evaluating, analyzing, summarizing, and researching. According to directions from your instructor, you will work independently and/or in small groups to complete them. In addition, your instructor will assign relevant topics from other parts of *The Hub* that relate to writ-ing, reading, research, and life issues.

Bringing It All Together

Project 7 concludes with three possible assignments that ask you to use the under-standings about art that you have arrived at through the reading, writing, thinking, and discussing you have been doing. Your instructor may assign the first, second, or third option; may give you a choice among the three; or may even ask you to com-plete more than one.

The first assignment asks you to write an essay to be handed out to first-time visitors to a museum explaining why the works in the museum are considered art. The second asks you to write an academic essay in which you give your final defini-tion of *art*, defend it, and apply it to some specific works of art. Think of this second essay as writing that would be appropriate in a college course on art history, art appreciation, or philosophy. The third invites you to develop a narrated PowerPoint or a video explaining the art in a museum to first-time visitors.

The final writing assignment, Reflecting on Project 7: What Is Art? asks you to reflect on what you have learned as you have worked through this reading/writing project.

Navigating Project 7

Below is the table of contents for Project 7, which you can use to easily locate the units you have been assigned to work on by your instructor.

Getting Started: Discovering Your Definition of *Art*

▲ Most of us spent time drawing when we were children. Was what we produced "art"? Melia Wilkinson

7.1 **Writing**

Defining *Art*

While it's clear that art can take many forms—almost everyone would agree that sculpture, architecture, and even photography, video, and other media can be art—in this activity, to make things a little simpler, we are going to limit our thinking about art to the form of painting.

To start, take a look at the five paintings reproduced below. These works are all located in the Metropolitan Museum of Art in New York City, so it seems clear that they are considered art by many people. Working in your group, write a definition of *art* based on your study of these five paintings.

▲ Edouard Manet, *Boating*, 1874, Metropolitan Museum of Art, New York City   Everett - Art/Shutterstock

▲ Auguste Renoir, *By the Seashore*, 1883, Metropolitan Museum of Art, New York City   Everett - Art/Shutterstock

▲ Duccio di Buoninsegna, *Madonna and Child*, 1290, Metropolitan Museum of Art, New York City   New York Daily News Archive/Getty Images

▲ Paul Cézanne, *The Card Players*, 1890, Metropolitan Museum of Art, New York City   Everett - Art/Shutterstock

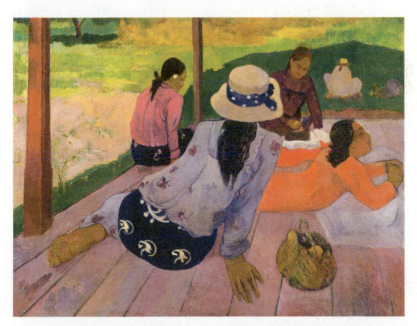

▲ Paul Gauguin, *The Siesta*, 1892, Metropolitan Museum of Art, New York City   Everett - Art/Shutterstock

7.2 Activity

Are These Items Art?

In Defining *Art* (7.1, p. 273), you looked at five examples of art from the Metropolitan Museum of Art in New York City. In this activity, you will examine some additional examples of what many people consider art. These works are all located in art museums around the world, but you may have reservations about them. You may even think that several of them are not only not art, but also that they have no right to be in an art museum.

Working in your group, look them over and decide which you think are art and which you think are not art. Make a list of reasons for your group's decisions.

▲ Francisco Goya, *Kronos Devouring His Son*, 1819–1823, Prado Museum, Madrid, Spain   Art Media/Print Collector/Getty Images

▲ Unknown artist, *Textile: African Print Fabric*, Twentieth Century   kirkchai benjarusameeros/Shutterstock

▲ Unknown artist, Prehistoric cave painting, Lascaux, France, c. 15,000 BC

France: Upper Paleolithic cave painting of animals from the Lascaux Cave complex, Dordogne, France, estimated to be c. 17,300 years old/Pictures from History/Bridgeman Images

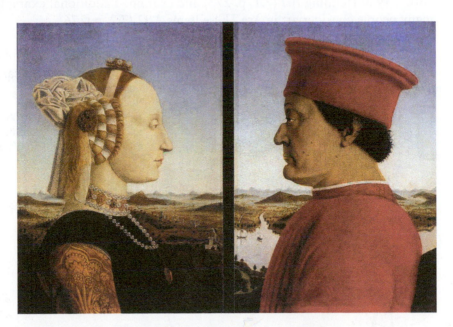

▲ Piero della Francesca, Portraits of Federico da Montefeltro and his wife, Battista Sforza, 1465, Uffizi, Florence, Italy   classicpaintings/Alamy

7.3 Writing

Defining *Art*, Second Draft

In Defining *Art* (7.1, p. 273), you encountered a group of fairly traditional art works from the Metropolitan Museum of Art. In Are These Items Art? (7.2, p. 276), you discovered a group of works of art from a variety of museums and were asked to think about whether you considered each of them to be art or not.

In this activity, return to your group's first draft of a definition of *art*, the one you wrote together for Defining *Art* (7.1). This time make the definition your own. Decide how it needs to be revised to account for the works in Are These Items Art? (7.2). If you decided some of those works were not art, does your definition need to be revised to exclude them? If you decided some of the works are art, does your group's first draft definition need to be revised so they are not excluded?

7.4 Activity

Can These Items Be Art?

You have looked at five examples of art from the Metropolitan Museum of Art in New York City in Defining *Art* (7.1, p. 273) and examined additional examples of what many people consider art in Are These Items Art? (7.2, p. 276).

The works here do not hang in art museums. Many people would not consider them art. Your group's job is to look them over and decide whether *you* think any of them are art or not and what you base your judgments on. Examine them carefully and answer the questions related to each one.

◀ A drawing by Melia Wilkinson, age 5, located in her father's collection of his children's art.

Melia Wilkinson

Is children's art "art"?

First think about whether the sunset itself is art; then think about whether the photograph of the sunset is art. What are your conclusions?

First think about whether the stilt as it appeared in the water that day was art; then think about this photo of it. Is it art?

These two leaves are certainly beautiful, but does that make them art? This image is quite tricky. Use the following questions to think about it.

1. When the photographer first saw the two leaves on the cobblestones, were they art?

2. What about the photograph of the leaves? Is it art?

3. What if you were told that the leaves weren't originally arranged like this? When the photographer found them, they were further apart. He moved them together and pointed their stems in opposite directions. Does that make them art? Does it make the photo art?

Certainly this is a stylish geometric tie with a subtly patterned gray shirt, but does that make it art? What if the shirt and tie were designed by a famous clothing designer like Giorgio Armani?

This is a complicated image. What if this is the shirt and tie of a man who gave a lecture at your college? You admired the combination of shirt and tie so much that you took this picture. Were the shirt and tie he wore that day art? How about your photo of it? What if this is really a photo advertising a national line of clothing and it appeared in *Esquire* magazine? Now is it art? Again, why or why not?

7.5 Writing

Defining *Art*, Third Draft

In Can These Items Be Art? (7.4, p. 278), you examined a group of works most people don't consider to be art. For this short writing assignment, revise the definition of *art* you wrote in Defining *Art*, Second Draft (7.3, p. 278), taking into consideration the examples you have just reviewed in Can These Items Be Art? (7.4). Keep in mind your reactions to and thoughts about the paintings from the Metropolitan Museum of Art in Defining *Art* (7.1, p. 273) and the variety of museum works you examined in Are These Items Art? (7.2, p. 276).

Analyzing What "Experts" Say Art Is

▲ Can a building be art?

Chartres Cathedral, France, 1194–1260.   Radu Razvan/Shutterstock

What Is Art? John Canady

The following text is excerpted from the preface to *What Is Art?* by John Canady, formerly the art critic for the *New York Times* and author of several volumes of art history and criticism. Because Canady was writing a book for a general audience and not for art history scholars, he wrote in a clear, jargon-free, and lucid style that requires no background in art history to understand. In this essay, Canady, after admitting the difficulty of defining the term *art*, identifies a number of characteristics that seem to indicate that something *is* a work of art. As you read, think about which of these characteristics you agree with and which you don't.

Be sure to do some previewing before reading. If you're not sure what previewing is or if you need a little refresher on it, see Previewing a Text (20.2, p. 575).

What Is Art?

JOHN CANADY

John Canady was born in Fort Scott, Kansas, in 1907. He earned a BA in French and English literature from the University of Texas and an MA in painting and art history from Yale. He taught at several universities, served in the US Marine Corps during World War II, worked as chief of the educational division at the Philadelphia Museum of Art, and was a respected art critic for the *New York Times* for seventeen years. He wrote a number of influential books on art and art history as well as seven crime novels under the pen name Matthew Head.

1   The only way to begin this book is to make clear that we are not going to arrive at any single answer to the question, what is art? Art has so many aspects, takes so many directions, serves so many purposes in such a variety of ways, that the question is almost as big as the biggest of all, what is life?

2   The two questions, in fact, overlap. The popular phrase "art for art's sake" implies that art can be an escape from life, but this—fortunately—is a delusion. Rather than an escape, art is an enrichment, and the underlying premise of this book is that art and living are inseparable and mutually sustaining, and always have been, ever since the appearance of human beings on our planet. "Creativity of man as distinguished from the world of nature" is the dictionary definition (one of many) that comes closest to answering our first question. This creativity and an awareness of history are the two characteristics most frequently cited as distinguishing human beings from animals.

3   For most people who enjoy it without knowing much about it, art's first function is to be ❲"pleasing to the eye"❳—a sound enough idea as far as it goes. Art has served life as an embellishment from the day our prehistoric ancestors first smeared magical signs on their bodies with colored clays up to this moment, when no one reading this page is likely to be in a position to look away from it without seeing dozens of embellishments in one or another form of art—the patterns of rugs, book bindings, and upholstery; the shapes of moldings, ashtrays, and knickknacks; the color and design of clothing—blue jeans being just as much an embellishment as are embroidered robes—and whatever pictures hang on the walls. Presuming that these objects were chosen because they were more attractive than others, the eye that chose them is pleased. But to stop with this pleasure is to deny ourselves the further ones of understanding why the eye is pleased and how these various forms and patterns evolved over the centuries and millennia of art history. The genealogy of virtually any painting or sculpture, no matter how modern, can be traced back to the ancient world or even to savage and prehistoric peoples.

4   The idea that art is created to please the eye leaves unanswered the question as to how an object like *Nourrice Profuse* by the modern French artist Jean Dubuffet can please art critics even though it grates on eyes habituated to the beauties of more conventional sculpture. To such eyes, *Nourrice Profuse* looks like a lump of slag iron—which is exactly what it is. But it is not *only* a lump of slag iron. Nor can this ugly object—we will call it ugly for the moment, since we will be seeing it again—be very easily explained by a definition of the function of art widely accepted by estheticians, which is "to bring order to the chaotic material of human experience."

▲ Jean Dubuffet, *Nourrice Profuse* (Profuse Wet Nurse), 1954, Hirshhorn, Washington, DC   Photo by Cathy Carver. Hirshhorn Museum and Sculpture Garden; © 2019 Artists Rights Society (ARS), New York/ADAGP, Paris

▶

5   This definition is applicable enough when we test it on the Parthenon, a work of art so perfectly ordered that even in ruins it is the consummate affirmation that life is a reasonable affair, that its goals can be formulated and achieved, that all confusion and ugliness can be vanquished in the creation of an ultimate harmony, a vital clarity.

▲ The Parthenon, 438 BC, Athens, Greece
Goodshoot/Getty Images

6   But what becomes, then, of Michelangelo's thunderous *Last Judgment* in the Sistine Chapel, which is all turbulence and terror? Even the martyrs, the saints, and the blessed on their way to Paradise seem to share the convulsions of the damned. On purely esthetic grounds we can rationalize that the *Last Judgment* is a carefully organized painting and thus "brings order" to its chaotic subject; but primarily this scene of universal damnation intensifies our experience of desperation and terror by investing these familiar human emotions with awesome grandeur.

7   So we extend the idea of bringing order to the chaotic material of human experience to form the second premise upon which this book is built, which is: The function of art is to clarify, intensify, or otherwise enlarge our experience of life. "Otherwise enlarge" affords a necessary catch-all that overlaps clarification and intensification but reaches into fields ranging from Dubuffet's *Nourrice Profuse* to the most acutely realistic paintings and sculptures ever created, with some of the most conventionally eye-pleasing in between.

▲ Michaelangelo, *Last Judgment*, 1541, Sistine Chapel, Rome   Art Library/Alamy

8   Finally, every interpretation or analysis of a work of art in this book will be made within the all-embracing conviction that painting, sculpture, and architecture are the truest and most complete witnesses to the nature of the times and places that produced them.

*　*　*

9   As a more profound record of its time, art rarely depends on topical reference, distilling instead the essence of the faith or philosophy by which people of that time lived, or tried to live. New art forms seem almost literally to invent themselves in response to changing ideals.

10   As an example: Around the middle of the twelfth century a miraculous process of germination seemed to be taking place in the soil of Europe, beginning in France, then spreading through the continent and into England. Churches began to rise as if gigantic seeds of stone had sprouted and thrust new and wonderful forms into the light, growing higher and higher and more and more elaborate in competition with one another, becoming eventually the piers and columns of the Gothic cathedrals, slender stalks flowering at last into vaults supported by webs of ribs like the veins of leaves or petals. On the exterior, this upward striving was continued in spires that rose higher than any structures ever before imagined, tapering and finally disappearing in points that merged with the sky.

▲ Chartres Cathedral, France, 1194–1260
Radu Razvan/Shutterstock

11   The Gothic cathedral summarized the spiritual aspirations of an age that had at the very least its full share of human evils—cruel wars, torture, superstition, ignorance, filthy poverty, political and religious persecution, and mass hysteria. Some of these abominations were perversions of the forces of faith, terrible facts that historians have recorded. But the cathedrals rise above terrible facts as witnesses to a glorious truth, the mystical faith symbolized by the soaring forms.

*　*　*

12   Beginning with the premise of revelation, medieval philosophers constructed logical systems to prove God's existence, even while architect-engineers were constructing vaults to create the space that, for the Middle Ages, was the symbol

▶

of God, crystallizing the coincidence of medieval cathedral architecture with medieval thought. Integrating architecture with the arts then still subservient to it, the cathedrals were encrusted with sculptures expounding theological and scientific doctrines, while painting was represented by tapestries, murals, and the ultimate glory of walls of stained glass telling the history of the world as the Middle Ages conceived it.

13   We have considered Gothic cathedral architecture at some length in this introduction because it exemplifies so well our premise that the forms art takes are inevitably determined, as if self-invented, by forces within the times that demand appropriate expression. The more complex a civilization becomes, the less possible it is for a single work of art to summarize its culture. Regarded as a single work of art combining architecture, sculpture, and (as it originally did) color, the Parthenon is such a summary, created when Athens was a small city (100,000 people) with a corresponding unity and clarity of goals, in contrast with the modem city that now sprawls out around the Acropolis. There is no single Gothic cathedral that can be called the perfect summary of its time (Chartres comes closest), but the Gothic cathedral generically is that summary.

*   *   *

14   As for our own time, our wonderful and terrible century, is there a work of art or assemblage of works of art that represents us at our best, as the Parthenon represents ancient Greece, the cathedrals the medieval world?

15   Perhaps the question belongs at the end of this book, but let us anticipate it and propose that the spectacle of New York City from the air at night is that composite work of art. We can even make a direct comparison with what we have said about the Middle Ages, a far from ideal period in terms of daily life that produced a glorious expression of faith. Similarly, New York seen from the air rises above the dross that surrounds us.

16   New York at street level (like the rest of our civilization) is often ugly, violent, sordid, dirty, noisy, confused, corrupt, and inhumane. It is a city where good living is the prerogative of those who can pay for it. But none of this is any more true of New York today than it has been of the representative metropolises of the past—ancient Rome, medieval Paris, seventeenth-century Rome, eighteenth-century London, and nineteenth-century Paris, which held its own well into the twentieth century. As the supermetropolis of the latter half of our century, New York has a vitality about it that for many people, even some of those who suffer most from the difficulties the city imposes, makes living there an indispensable condition of existence.

*   *   *

17   While none of our efforts, some foolish and others serious, to create new art forms appropriate to our times can be more than fragmentary expressions of our inconceivably complex culture, all of them are fused in the single compound work of art called

New York City—not as experiments and not as art forms, but in satisfaction of demands peculiar to our times that had to be met in practical terms.

18   Manhattan is a small island transformed by the works of man. Seen from the air at night, it is an anonymous manmade work of art, a phenomenon possible only in this century, the century of the airplane, glass-and-steel construction, the automobile, and electric light. Seen from above in daylight, the skyscrapers are spectacular enough[,] their towering clusters transformed from architecture into titanic sculptures—or titanic natural forms of a newly discovered planet. At night they dissolve in their own light; neon signs become scattered jewels; the blazing crisscross pattern of streets surrounds a large, dark rectangle through which wind a few wavering lines of light—Central Park. The spectacle is doubly kinetic: its masses shift as our aerial point of vision moves across the island, and on the island itself the traffic flows in liquid light. Everything sordid, ugly, and trivial disappears in an astounding affirmation that the values our society lives by are ultimately valid, whatever their distortions at close range.

▲ New York City at Night   Yukinori Hasumi/Getty Images

↳ 7.7 Writing

Summarizing Canady's *What Is Art?*

Canady begins his essay with an admission that he is "not going to arrive at any single answer to the question, what is art?" After working on the first six units of this project, you probably have also discovered that *art* is not an easy term to define. What Canady does is not really answer the question; instead, he gives a series of assertions about what art does, what its functions are.

You probably have a sense of what it means to write a summary. You write something short that recaps the main content of something that you have read. For this assignment, write a brief summary—a half page would be fine—in which you provide a concise restatement of the main content of Canady's preface to *What Is Art?* (7.6, p. 282). In your summary, be sure to include each of the functions of art that he outlines. (For more information, see Strategies for Writing a Summary [18.25, p. 547].)

"What Is Art?" Albert Elsen

The following is a short essay taken from Albert Elsen's book *Purposes of Art*, a text often used in college art history courses. For a short little text like this, you can still do a quick preview. If you need to refresh your understanding of previewing, see Previewing a Text (20.2, p. 575). Elsen occasionally uses words you may not be familiar with. Strategies for dealing with difficult words are discussed in Dealing with Difficult Language (20.9, p. 594).

What Is Art?

ALBERT ELSEN

Born in New York City in 1928, Elsen received his doctorate from Columbia University and taught at Stanford University for twenty-eight years. A recognized expert on modern sculpture, especially the work of French sculptor Auguste Rodin, Elsen was responsible for Stanford's impressive sculpture garden. Elsen died in 1995. In this article, he not only takes a stab at defining *art*, but he also explains how and why the definition of *art* underwent such dramatic change in the twentieth century.

1   **What Is Art?** The short answer to this question is: What artists make with the intention that it be art. Validation of the result depends primarily upon artists, and then art dealers, critics, curators, collectors, and historians. That the question is so often posed today by the public is a recent phenomenon in history. Its cause comes from critical thinking by artists.

2   In our own century, for the first time, there has been a prolonged questioning by artists of what art is. Many individuals and groups have attempted either to push back its traditional limits or to go beyond them, while not claiming that what they have done is art. The 20th century has witnessed a drastic shrinkage of what is *not* art. In the decade of the 1960s artists began to build upon premises established by Duchamp (who questioned that anything manmade was not art), Picasso, the Dadaists, and Dubuffet, to name a few, with results that seem to have stripped the word "art" of all meaning. When painters set aside the picture frame and sculptors eschewed the pedestal and base so as to make their works more tangible or concrete as aesthetic objects, we saw the contravening of art's tradition of illusion and preciousness.

3   Many young artists today speak of "demythologizing" art, taking it out of the realm of "inspired genius" where it was put during the Renaissance, and renouncing "miracles" of the hand. We have defined "art" as the skillful interpretation of human experience in a man-made object capable of producing an aesthetic response. When an artist like Picasso minimizes his skill, when a sculptor like Judd turns the execution of his work over to industrial metalworkers, it is evident that the viewer's enjoyment of skill or craft is not something the artist desires or anticipates. The interpretation of human experience, with its connotations of symbolism, metaphor, and analogy, has been increasingly set aside by many young artists who make "specific" objects to be taken literally and at face value. The desirability of inducing an aesthetic response or appealing to taste has also fallen before the onslaught of countless artists throughout the world, who see beauty as something "irrelevant," "elitist," and smacking of "class" or "establishment" snobbery. Beauty, to them, is less interesting than what they are doing. One can be interested or deeply moved by an artist's work even though it is not beautiful, as Picasso, Pollock, and De Koening have taught us. In the case of these three artists, however, it could be argued that in their search for truth in art they have established a new aesthetic of the brutal or violent.

4   The work of art as an object that is permanent, negotiable, and precious because of its uniqueness and the skill lavished on it no longer interests the artist preoccupied with motion, concepts, and the ephemeral. Artists who use technology to produce works that actually move or who employ machines and systems for their effects—works that plug into a wall socket or depend on the postal service, medical check-ups, and earth movers, for example—have no patience with the hard and fast. The premise that a work of art must be visible is rejected by conceptual artists who believe that art comes into being in the artist's mind and that the intermediary with an audience can be a diagram or words. Artists who place more value on the making or the process of assembling vernacular materials that may or may not be keyed to a certain site set no store by a finished art object. After the artist has stopped or the show is over, the work is disassembled or destroyed. Order or composition leading to "good form," which was one of the last ties to traditional art, is scrupulously avoided by certain artists who refuse either to arrange their materials consciously or to repeat themselves, for the latter would imply the development of a style. Obviously, what has been described is usually unsalable, uncollectable, and even hard to document photographically.

↳ **7.9** **Activity**

Analyzing Elsen's "What Is Art?"

Working in your group, answer these questions about Elsen's essay "What Is Art?" (7.8, p. 288).

1. Elsen defines *art* in different ways in this essay. What are they?

2. Elsen's essay focuses primarily on how our sense of what art is has changed in the twentieth century. How does he say it changed?

3. Elsen doesn't really give much explanation for *why* our sense of art changed so dramatically. Can you think of any reasons for this change?

4. Elsen asserts that "countless artists throughout the world . . . see beauty as something 'irrelevant,' 'elitist,' and smacking of 'class' or 'establishment' snobbery." Do you think that traditional art—art up until the twentieth century—was elitist? Was art something intended for and enjoyed primarily by those who were rich and powerful? Can you think of exceptions to this description—times or places or kinds of art that were created for ordinary people who were neither rich nor powerful?

5. Elsen writes, "The premise that a work of art must be visible is rejected by conceptual artists who believe that art comes into being in the artist's mind and that the intermediary with an audience can be a diagram or words." Can you think of any examples of this kind of "conceptual" art?

7.10 **Reading**

"Working Towards a Definition of Art," Arthur Danto

In this excerpt from Arthur Danto's book *What Art Is*, the skeleton of his argument has been pulled out. In the process, many fascinating, but distracting, digressions about modern art have been omitted. The goal is to provide the essence of Danto's attempt to define art in a way that includes much of contemporary art.

Don't worry if, at times, the argument seems hard to follow; it is. Just do your best to understand what Danto thinks defines art in the twenty-first century. Before beginning to read, take a few minutes to preview. If you need to refresh your understanding of previewing, see Previewing a Text (20.2, p. 575). Danto occasionally uses words you may not be familiar with. Strategies for dealing with difficult words are discussed in Dealing with Difficult Language (20.9, p. 594).

Working Towards a Definition of Art

ARTHUR DANTO

Born in Ann Arbor, Michigan in 1924, Arthur Danto studied art history at Wayne State University and then received a doctorate in philosophy at Columbia University. In 1951, Danto returned to teach at Columbia and also served as long-time art critic for *The Nation*. He struggled to identify the characteristic that makes an object art in an era when the kind of objects accepted into art museums has expanded far beyond traditional ideas about what is art. In this book, Danto has a tendency to wander away from his main argument onto many side issues. For this reading, those wanderings have been left out in order to provide just the main stream of his argument. The asterisks mark the many places where material unrelated to the main argument has been omitted.

1   It is widely accepted that Plato defined art as imitation, though whether this was a theory or merely an observation is difficult to say, since there was nothing else by way of art in Athens in his time. All that seems clear is that imitation in Plato meant pretty much what it means in English: looks like the real thing but isn't the real thing.

*   *   *

2   In any case, no one can deny that art as practiced consisted in imitations or capturing appearances, to paraphrase modern art historians. How different from the present situation! "I am very interested in how one approaches that topic—What is Art," writes my friend the artist Tom Rose in a personal note. "The question that comes up in every class and in every context." It is as if imitation disappeared, and something else took its place. In the eighteenth century, when aesthetics was invented or discovered, the thought was that art contributed beauty, hence gave pleasure to those with taste.

*   *   *

3   Small wonder the question of what is art came up "in every class and every context." So—what is art? What we know from the cacophony of artistic argument is that there is too much art that is non-imitational for us to read Plato except for the sake of his views. This was a first step.

4   My thought is that if some art is imitation and some art is not, neither term belongs to the definition of art as philosophically understood. A property is part of the definition only if it belongs to every work of art there is. With the advent of Modernism, art backed away from mirror images, or, better, photography set the standard of fidelity. Its advantage over mirror images is that it is able to preserve images, though of course photographic images are liable to fade.

5   There are degrees of fidelity in imitation, so Plato's definition of art remained in place, with little to argue about until it stopped capturing the seeming essence of art.   ▶

How could this have happened? Historically it happened with the advent of Modernism, so this book begins with certain revolutionary changes that took place in France, mainly in Paris. Plato had had an easy run, from the sixth century BC until AD 1905–7, with the so-called Fauves—Wild Beasts—and Cubism. In my view, to get a definition better than Plato's you have to look to more recent artists, since they are most likely to subtract from their theories properties that were earlier thought to be essential to art, like beauty. . . . After that, everything was feasible. Anything went, leaving it uncertain whether a definition of art is any longer possible. Anything cannot be art.

* * *

6   Andy Warhol's contribution to the definition of art was made not through a text, but through a remarkable body of sculptures, which constituted his first project upon taking possession of the Silver Factory in 1963, and was shown the following spring at the Stable Gallery, which is today the business entrance on 74th Street of the Whitney Museum of Art. The *Brillo Box* became a kind of philosophical Rosetta Stone, since it allowed us to deal with two languages—the language of art and the language of reality. The partial definition of art that I developed in *The Transfiguration of the Commonplace* was the result of reflections on the questions this remarkable object raised.

* * *

7   Socrates' definition of art crumples totally when abstraction and then ready-mades [pieces] of art that are everyday objects found by the artist and then converted into art, for example, Duchamp's *Fountain* (urinal), which come along in the twentieth century. Beyond question, most works of art in the West have been mimetic, to use the word derived from the Greek, and Western artists have become more and more adept at it. When the camera was invented, it took some decades before the human face could be rendered lifelike, but the camera did not invalidate as art early efforts at imitation, like those of Giotto or Cimabue. But imitation can no longer be part of the definition of art, since Modern and contemporary art is full of counterexamples. But one cannot be expected to know what art will be like in two millennia! Only if art has reached an end can that be. Socrates, for all his sharpness, has little to say about the future of art. He seems to imagine that things basically will go on as they are, so far as art is concerned. Abstraction and readymades make it increasingly difficult to find *a* definition of art. That is why the question "What is art?" has been raised more frequently and often more heatedly. The nice thing about imitation is that people in general are able to identify art in cultures such as the one in which Socrates offered his definition of art.

* * *

8   In the sixties the philosopher George Dickie developed a theory known as the Institutional Theory of art. It more or less overpowered earlier theories of art. Basically, it states that determining what is art is altogether a matter to be decided by his designation of the Art World, which he defines . . . [as] a sort of social network, consisting of curators, collectors, art critics, artists (of course), and others whose life is connected to art in some way. Something is a work of art, then, if the Art World decrees that it is.

9   Abstraction proves that imitation does not belong to the essence of art—and neither does abstraction. We don't really know what belongs and what does not. My view, though, is that Warhol helps us see what is likely to belong to the essence of art for as long as art is made. The problem is that philosophers, of all people, conclude that art is an open concept because they cannot find a set of common *visual* properties. I think they stopped looking [too soon], since I know of at least two properties inherent in artworks, and these then belong to the definition of art. All we need to do is hunt around a bit and find a property that works of art have in common.

*   *   *

[*At this point, Danto bases his discussion on Andy Warhol's* Brillo Boxes, *which you can see below. When Danto talks of "Factory" with a capital* F, *he is referring to the building in New York where Warhol constructed his art. When he talks of "factory" with a lower-case* f, *he is talking about the actual factory where Brillo pads are manufactured and boxed.*]

*   *   *

10   The individual boxes looked as much like actual commercial containers as Andy and his helpers could make them. They were fabricated in a woodworking shop to Andy's specifications. Real cartons were photographed, and the labels then stenciled onto the fabricated boxes.

11   The question, then, was, in what way did Andy's Factory-made boxes differ from the factory-made boxes? That is, what differentiating visible properties separated them? The Factory-made boxes were wood, while the factory-made boxes were fashioned from corrugated cardboard.

▲ Andy Warhol, *Brillo Boxes*, 1964, Philadelphia Museum of Art   Philadelphia Museum of Art: Acquired with funds contributed by the Committee on Twentieth-Century Art and as a partial gift of the Andy Warhol Foundation for the Visual Arts, Inc., 1994-79-1–3; © 2019 The Andy Warhol Foundation for the Visual Arts, Inc./Licensed by Artists Rights Society (ARS), New York

▶

12   But the difference between them could have been reversed. The Factory-made boxes were painted white, with the design stenciled onto four sides and the top, but so were many of the factory-made boxes. Other factory-made boxes were unpainted except for the logo—they were the normal brown of unpainted corrugated cardboard. The commercial boxes contained scouring pads, while Andy's boxes had no such contents, but he could have filled his boxes with the pads and they would still be art. Could members of the Art World differentiate them as art? Maybe—but they would be guessing. Externally, both sets were alike.

13   My sense is that, if there were no visible differences, there had to have been *invisible* differences—not invisible like the Brillo pads packed in the Brillo boxes, but properties that were *always* invisible. I've proposed two such properties that are invisible in their nature. In my first book on the philosophy of art I thought that works of art are *about* something, and I decided that works of art accordingly have meaning. We infer meanings, or grasp meanings, but meanings are not at all material. . . . [T]he meanings are *embodied* in the object that had them.

*   *   *

14   I must admit that I have done relatively little to analyze embodiment, but my intuition was this: The artwork is a material object, some of whose properties belong to the meaning, and some of which do not. What the viewer must do is interpret the meaning-bearing properties in such a way as to grasp the intended meaning they embody.

15   The explanation that an embodied meaning is what makes an object a work of art applies . . . to Warhol's. In fact, it applies to everything that is art. When philosophers supposed that there is no property that artworks share, they were looking only at visible properties. It is the invisible properties that make something art.

16   From that perspective, it is worth considering the Brillo box's style, designed by James Harvey, whose day job was as a commercial designer, although he was also an artist, an abstract expressionist.

> [*Danto then describes what a good design the Brillo box of the commercial world is.*]

17   So how does art criticism come in? It comes in because commercial art through its ordinariness was in some way what Warhol's art was about. He had a view of the ordinary world as aesthetically beautiful, and admired greatly the things Harvey and his Abstract Expressionist heroes would have ignored or condemned. Andy loved the surfaces of daily life, the nutritiousness and

predictability of canned goods, the poetics of the commonplace. . . . This approach shows a philosophical shift from the rejection of industrial society . . . to endorsement, which is what one might expect from someone born into poverty and who might therefore be in love with the warmth of a kitchen in which all the new products were used.

18   Although I would have hoped for the contrast to be between art and reality, it is hard to deny that Harvey's Brillo box is art. It is art, but it is commercial art. Once the design is set, the cartons are manufactured by the thousands. They are made of corrugated cardboard to protect the contents while still being light enough to be lifted and moved, and to allow for easy opening. None of that is true of Andy's boxes; only a few were made, and their purpose was purely to be seen and understood as art. It is pure snobbishness to deny that commercial art is art just because it is utilitarian. And besides, cardboard boxes are part of the Lebenswelt. Andy's box is not. It is part of the Art World. Harvey's box belongs to visual culture, as that is understood, but Andy's boxes belong to high culture.

↳ **7.11** **Activity**

Analyzing Danto's "Working Towards a Definition of Art"

Working in your group, answer the following questions about Arthur Danto's "Working Towards a Definition of Art" (7.10, p. 290).

1. What does it mean to say art is *imitational*?

2. What does Danto suggest caused art to move away from attempting to imitate reality?

3. What does Danto suggest replaced the idea of art as imitation of reality in the eighteenth century?

4. Danto talks about two forms of art that challenge traditional definitions: *abstractions* and *readymades*. What do these two terms mean?

5. What does Danto mean by the "Institutional Theory" of art?

6. What does Danto argue is the "embodied meaning" in the Warhol *Brillo Boxes*?

7. In the final paragraph, Danto discusses the "artness" of commercial Brillo boxes and Warhol's *Brillo Boxes*. What does Danto conclude about these two? What do you think of his conclusion?

↳ 7.12 **Activity**

Asking Deeper Questions about Art

For this activity, your group is going to do some "pondering," some thinking, about a series of questions designed to invite you to dig deeper into what you think art is. Working in your group, answer the following questions.

1. Is "bad" art still art?
2. Can a piece of art also be useful? Or does a utilitarian purpose disqualify it as art?
3. Is art an elitist concept? Has art been primarily for the rich and powerful?
4. Does art have to be created by a human being?
5. Can art be simply a concept? Does it have to result in a physical object?
6. Is flower arranging an art?
7. Is commercial art *art*? Is an iPhone art? How about an Alpha Romeo car?

Bringing It All Together

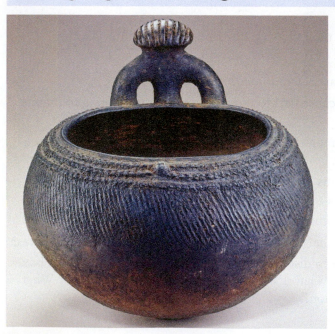

◀ Can something useful like this pot also be art?

Photograph by Franko Khoury, National Museum of African Art, Smithsonian Institution

7.13 Real World Essay

Handout Explaining Art to First-Time Visitors to a Museum

After all the thinking, reading, writing, and arguing that you've been doing about what the word *art* actually means, you've become somewhat of an expert, or at least a "novice expert," on art.

Assignment.   For this essay, you will need to imagine an art museum in your town whose collection includes the nine works that follow these instructions. The museum has told you that in the past first-time visitors to the museum have not responded well to the museum's collection. They have asked, "What is this stuff doing in an art museum? This isn't art."

In this essay, you will have three tasks: first, to define the word *art*; second, to provide an argument to explain and defend that definition; and, third, to use your definition to analyze six of the nine possible works of art that follow these instructions. Choose the works you think other viewers would have the hardest time accepting as art, although, of course, you aren't expected to defend a work you don't think is art. For each of the six works you choose to discuss, explain why—according to your definition—it is or **is not** art. Also, in each case, you are not being asked to discuss whether a *photo* of an object or painting is art, but whether the *original object* is art.

Because your essay is an argument, you will want to follow the conventions for arguments. You may want to review these conventions in What Is an Argument? (18.1, p. 513), The Features of Effective Arguments (18.3, p. 513), and How to Answer Counterarguments (18.5, p. 514).

Documentation.   If you quote, paraphrase, or summarize from the articles you have read, be sure to provide appropriate citations and include a works cited list or list of references at the end of your essay. If you need to review how to provide this documentation, refer to MLA Documentation (Topic 23, p. 650) or APA Documentation (Topic 24, p. 687).

If you want to use your sources most effectively to support your argument, it's not enough to simply include them as a series of unrelated sources; you need to tie them together, explain their relationships with each other, and express your conclusions about them. This process is called *synthesizing*, and it is discussed in more detail in Synthesis (22.14, p. 648).

1. Wassily Kandinsky, *On White II*, 1923, Georges Pompidou Center, Paris

Gianni Dagli Orti/Shutterstock

2. Ikebana, Ohara School of Ikebana. Japanese flower arranging dates to the seventh century. It began as a way of arranging flowers as offerings in a Buddhist temple.

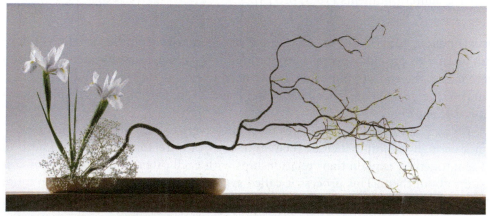

MIGUEL GARCIA SAAVEDRA/Shutterstock

3. Unknown artist, Embroidered sampler, late nineteenth century, Cooper Hewitt, Smithsonian Design Museum

Cooper Hewitt, Smithsonian Design Museum/Art Resource, NY

4. Jimmie Durham, *Still Life with Spirit and Xitle*, 2007, Hirshhorn Museum, Washington, DC

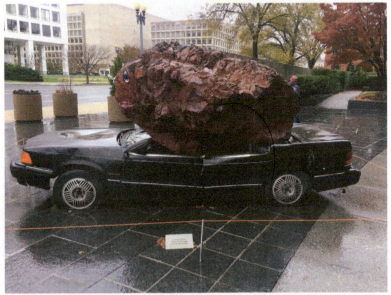

Peter Adams

5. Unknown artist, Bamileke bowl, early twentieth century, National Museum of African Art, Washington, DC. Used to hold water, food, or a condiment.

Photograph by Franko Khoury, National Museum of African Art, Smithsonian Institution

6. Giotto, Crucifix, 1289, Santa Maria Novella, Florence, Italy

DEA PICTURE LIBRARY/DeAgostini/Getty Images

7. Unknown artist, Frescoed wall from the House of Livia, first century BC, National Roman Museum, Rome, Italy

AGTravel/Alamy

8. Kara Walker, *The Emancipation Approximation (Scene #18)*, 1999–2000, University of Massachusetts Fine Arts Museum

"Explaining Art to First-Time Visitors to a Museum." Kara Walker, The Emancipation Approximation, Scene #18 (2000), permission by Sikkema Jenkins & Co.

9. *Emily's Bike*, a painting by author Peter Adams's eleven-year-old daughter

Emily Chamberlin

7.14 Academic Essay

Defining *Art* and Applying the Definition

For this reading/writing project you have been thinking, reading, and arguing about what the word *art* actually means. As you have seen, even the experts don't agree on a definition, so there is clearly not a "right" answer.

Assignment.   In this essay, you will have three tasks: first, to define the word *art*; second, to provide an argument to explain and defend that definition; and, third, to use your definition to analyze six of the nine possible works of art that follow these instructions. Choose the works you think other viewers would have the hardest time accepting as art, although, of course, you aren't expected to defend a work you don't think is art. For each of the six works you choose to discuss, explain why—according to your definition—it is or is not art. Also, in each case, you are not being asked to discuss whether a *photo* of an object or painting is art, but whether the *original object* is art.

Since your first task is to write a definition, you may want to review Strategies for Writing Definitions (18.18, p. 540).

Audience.   This is the kind of essay you might be asked to write in an art history class, so imagine you are taking such a class and are writing this essay for your instructor.

Because your essay is an argument, you will want to follow the conventions for arguments. You may want to review these conventions in What Is an Argument? (18.1, p. 513), The Features of Effective Arguments (18.3, p. 513), and How to Answer Counterarguments (18.5, p. 514).

Documentation.   If you quote, paraphrase, or summarize from the articles you have read, or others you find on the topic, be sure to provide appropriate citations and include a works cited list or list of references at the end of your essay. If you need to review how to provide this documentation, refer to MLA Documentation (Topic 23, p. 650) or APA Documentation (Topic 24, p. 687).

If you want to use your sources most effectively to support your argument, it's not enough to simply include them as a series of unrelated sources; you need to tie them together, explain their relationships with each other, and express your conclusions about them. This process is called *synthesizing*, and it is discussed in more detail in Synthesis (22.14, p. 648).

1.   Wassily Kandinsky, *On White II*, 1923, Georges Pompidou Center, Paris

Gianni Dagli Orti/Shutterstock

2. Ikebana, Ohara School of Ikebana. Japanese flower arranging dates to the seventh century. It began as a way of arranging flowers as offerings in a Buddhist temple.

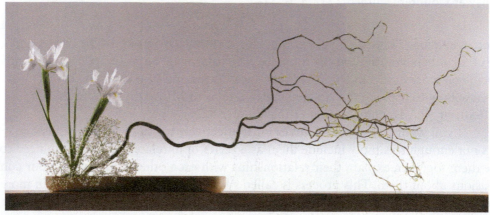

MIGUEL GARCIA SAAVEDRA/Shutterstock

3. Unknown artist, Embroidered sampler, late nineteenth century, Cooper Hewitt, Smithsonian Design Museum

Cooper Hewitt, Smithsonian Design Museum/Art Resource, NY

4. Jimmie Durham, *Still Life with Spirit and Xitle*, 2007, Hirshhorn Museum, Washington, DC

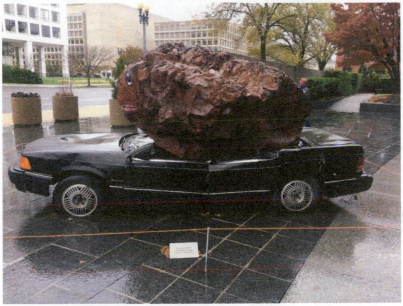

Peter Adams

5. Unknown artist, Bamileke bowl, early twentieth century, National Museum of African Art, Washington, DC. Used to hold water, food, or a condiment.

Photograph by Franko Khoury, National Museum of African Art, Smithsonian Institution

6. Giotto, Crucifix, 1289, Santa Maria Novella, Florence, Italy

DEA PICTURE LIBRARY/DeAgostini/Getty Images

7. Unknown artist, Frescoed wall from the House of Livia, first century BC, National Roman Museum, Rome, Italy

AGTravel/Alamy

8. Kara Walker, *The Emancipation Approximation (Scene #18)*, 1999–2000, University of Massachusetts Fine Arts Museum

"Explaining Art to First-Time Visitors to a Museum." Kara Walker, The Emancipation Approximation, Scene #18 (2000), permission by Sikkema Jenkins & Co.

9. *Emily's Bike*, a painting by author Peter Adams's eleven-year-old daughter

Emily Chamberlin

7.15 Multimodal Composition

Explaining Art to First-Time Visitors to a Museum

After all the thinking, reading, writing, and arguing that you've been doing about what the word *art* actually means, you've become somewhat of an expert, or at least a "novice expert," on art.

Assignment. For this assignment, you will need to imagine an art museum in your town whose collection includes the nine works that follow these instructions. The museum has told you that, in the past, first-time visitors to the museum have not responded well to the museum's collection. They have asked, "What is this stuff doing in an art museum? This isn't art."

The museum has asked you to compose a narrated PowerPoint presentation or a video for first-time visitors who have never been to an art museum before. For this PowerPoint or video, select six of the possible nine works that follow these directions and explain to these first-time visitors why they *are* art. Choose the works you think other viewers would have the hardest time accepting as art, although, of course, you aren't expected to defend a work you don't think is art. Use all the ideas you have encountered in the essays you have read in this project, the ideas you heard in your group discussions, and the ideas you came up with in the writing you have been doing. Also, remember that in each case, you are not being asked to discuss whether the *photo* is art, but whether the *original object* is art.

Audience. Think about the audience you are composing this presentation for. How can you explain to them, first-time visitors to the museum, what you have defined as *art*? How can you explain your reasons for defining *art* that way? How can you explain why certain works are not art? What is your reasoning for that definition? Then you might explain and defend your definition. Finally, use the six works you have selected to show how they satisfy your definition or how they don't.

Documentation. If you quote, paraphrase, or summarize from the articles you have read, be sure to provide appropriate citations and include a works cited list or list of references to accompany your composition. If you need to review how to provide this documentation, refer to MLA Documentation (Topic 23, p. 650) or APA Documentation (Topic 24, p. 687).

If you want to use your sources most effectively to support your argument, it's not enough to simply include them as a series of unrelated sources; you need to tie them together, explain their relationships with each other, and express your conclusions about them. This process is called *synthesizing*, and it is discussed in more detail in Synthesis (22.14, p. 648).

1. Wassily Kandinsky, *On White II*, 1923, Georges Pompidou Center, Paris

Gianni Dagli Orti/Shutterstock

2. Ikebana, Ohara School of Ikebana. Japanese flower arranging dates to the seventh century. It began as a way of arranging flowers as offerings in a Buddhist temple.

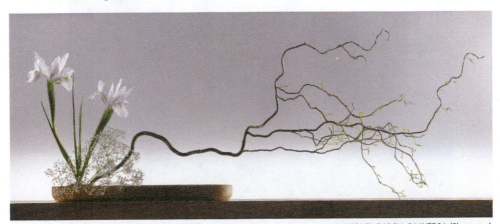

MIGUEL GARCIA SAAVEDRA/Shutterstock

3. Unknown artist, Embroidered sampler, late nineteenth century, Cooper Hewitt, Smithsonian Design Museum

Cooper Hewitt, Smithsonian Design Museum/Art Resource, NY

4. Jimmie Durham, *Still Life with Spirit and Xitle*, 2007, Hirshhorn Museum, Washington, DC

Peter Adams

5. Unknown artist, Bamileke bowl, early twentieth century, National Museum of African Art, Washington, DC. Used to hold water, food, or a condiment.

Photograph by Franko Khoury, National Museum of African Art, Smithsonian Institution

6. Giotto, Crucifix, 1289, Santa Maria Novella, Florence, Italy

DEA PICTURE LIBRARY/DeAgostini/Getty Images

7. Unknown artist, Frescoed wall from the House of Livia, first century BC, National Roman Museum, Rome, Italy

AGTravel/Alamy

8. Kara Walker, *The Emancipation Approximation (Scene #18)*, 1999–2000, University of Massachusetts Fine Arts Museum

"Explaining Art to First-Time Visitors to a Museum." Kara Walker, The Emancipation Approximation, Scene #18 (2000), permission by Sikkema Jenkins & Co.

9. *Emily's Bike*, a painting by author Peter Adams's eleven-year-old daughter

Emily Chamberlin

7.16 Activity

Getting Started on Your Essay or Composition

During this class period, you and your classmates will begin working on your assignment (see Real World Essay: Handout Explaining Art to First-Time Visitors to a Museum [7.13, p. 297], Academic Essay: Defining *Art* and Applying the Definition [7.14, p. 302], and Multimodal Composition: Explaining Art to First-Time Visitors to a Museum [7.15, p. 308]). You may use this time to start brainstorming or to begin your research online. You may want to write an opening paragraph or two, or to review what you've already read and written in this project. You may want to compare notes with a couple of classmates or ask a question or two of your instructor. If you are composing a multimodal project, you may want to talk to others who are doing the same to compare approaches. The idea is that you will at least get a start on the assignment.

7.17 Writing

Reflecting on Project 7: What Is Art?

Reflective writing is different from most writing you do in college. Reflective writing asks you to think back, to "reflect" on an experience—an essay you have written, a major change in your life, a time when you didn't have success at something you wanted to do, a semester's work in a course—and to examine how you now think and feel about that experience. What effect has the experience had on you? How have you changed? How will you be different in the future? (If you'd like a little more explanation of reflective writing, visit Strategies for Writing a Reflection [18.29, p. 555].)

Now you're going to reflect on all the reading, thinking, discussing, and writing you have done in this project on the nature of art. To do this, you may want to review any short reflective writing you did as you worked through the project, the definitions you worked on, and the essay you wrote. Then, in a short paper—a page or so—reflect on this experience:

1. Report on what you learned about art and the issues that trying to define it raises. What were the most important or most useful ideas you encountered?

2. Describe how you feel about the experience and what you *think* about what you have learned.

3. Report on what you learned that will make a difference for you in the future and why.

The Hub

Balancing School, Work, and Life

Reading/Writing Projects

Research and Documentation

Writing

Reading

2 Writing

n Part 2, you will find an abundance of advice in tutorials, group activities, short writing assignments, and narrated presentations to help you with every facet of the writing process. After a narrated presentation on the writing process at the beginning of Topic 8, you will find a series of Topics related to effective writing, such as preparing to write, generating ideas and finding a focus, developing and organizing support, revising and editing, and thinking while writing.

TOPIC 8
The Writing Process

This Topic does not discuss what effective writing is; instead, it explores what you need to do to produce effective writing by examining the process that effective writers follow.

Navigating Topic 8

The tutorials and presentation listed below provide information about the writing process. You can work through the entire Topic on your own, learning about all the strategies and practicing them; work on items you've been assigned by your instructor; or choose just the ones you find helpful.

Introduction to the Writing Process

This Topic focuses on the writing process and begins with an activity asking about your current writing strategies. It's followed by a presentation that discusses the different elements of an effective writing process—prewriting strategies, finding a focus, developing and organizing ideas, drafting, revising and editing—and, very importantly, emphasizes how good writers move back and forth among these different steps in the process. Next, you will follow a student writer as she thinks through how to focus a topic and write for a specific assignment. Finally, you will learn about and practice peer review.

8.1 Activity

How Do *You* Write an Essay?

For this activity, you're going to do a short piece of informal writing. Your instructor will let you know whether you will write this in class or at home and when it should be turned in.

For this assignment, you will need to think back to a time when you had to write an essay, perhaps in high school, in another course, or even earlier in this course. Write a numbered list of the steps that you took to write the paper.

If it's been a while since you wrote an essay in a class and you cannot remember a specific essay you had to write, you can use the following assignment and make a list of the steps you would take today to write this essay.

Essay Assignment

Write a letter to the editor of the *New York Times* in which you discuss an event or an issue reported in the paper this week. A selection of letters written to the editor are published each day. They are seldom more than 250 words long. Your goal is to get your letter published in the *New York Times*.

8.2 Presentation

The Writing Process

To watch this presentation on the writing process and the steps involved in reading an assignment, narrowing a topic, deciding on a thesis, generating ideas, drafting, revising, and editing an essay, go to *Achieve for The Hub*, Topic 8, and open Unit 8.2.

8.3 Tutorial

How Effective Writers Go about Writing

Good writing takes time and effort. Developing a process that you can follow and change as needed based on a specific assignment will improve your writing. The chart below lists six major activities involved in the writing process.

| Preparing to Write | Finding a Focus | Developing Ideas | Organizing Ideas | Writing | Editing |

Thoughtful writers do not simply move through the steps listed in the chart, performing each activity once and then moving on to the next in the linear fashion shown in the following diagram.

Instead, as illustrated in the diagram below, they weave back and forth among these activities as they find new information, generate new ideas, revise their thesis, reorganize their ideas, add support, revise their writing, and edit their final draft. Their process is messy and involves lots of circling back to improve parts of the paper they worked on earlier—messy, yes, but very productive.

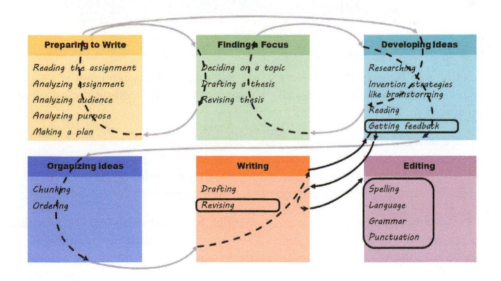

The diagram that follows represents the way one writer, named Juanita, carried out the recursive process of writing discussed above and in more detail on page 320.

Preparing to Write	Finding a Focus	Developing Ideas	Organizing Ideas	Writing	Editing
1 Reading the assignment	**6** Deciding on a topic	**2 8** Researching	Chunking	**9 12** Drafting	**14** Style
Analyzing assignment	Drafting a thesis **7**	**5 11** Invention strategies like brainstorming	Ordering	**13** Revising	Language
4 Analyzing audience	Revising **10** thesis	Reading			Grammar
3 Analyzing purpose					
Making a plan		Getting feedback			Punctuation

How Juanita Wrote Her Essay

In this example of one student's process while working on an assignment, you can see how recursive the writing process can be. Juanita starts by reading the assignment from her teacher:

> Write a letter to the editor of the *New York Times* in which you discuss an event or an issue reported in the paper this week. A selection of letters written to the editor are published each day. They are seldom more than 250 words long. Your goal is to get your letter published in the *New York Times*.

Once she understands what the assignment is, Juanita doesn't just start writing. She takes some steps to help her get ready to write. **She 1 reads the assignment** again carefully. Since she has never read a letter to the editor of the *Times* before, she goes online to see what the letters look like. **She 2 also** gets a sense of how they "sound" and the kinds of topics they are written about.

She returns to the assignment and sees that her essay should be fewer than 250 words and that **her 3 purpose** is to get it published in the *Times*. She thinks, at first, that **her 4 audience** is people who read the *Times*, and it is; but there is also another audience: the editors at the paper who decide which letters to publish. From the letters she reads in the library, she decides the editors at the *Times* seem to prefer letters that take a strong stand and back up their positions with thoughtful arguments.

Looking in the *New York Times* online, Juanita notices that just one day earlier there had been a shooting at a Burger King. An angry employee had returned to work with a pistol and shot the manager, two workers, and a customer. The manager died, and the other victims were in serious condition in the hospital. The shooter, who had been diagnosed as schizophrenic, was shot and killed by police as he fled the scene.

Juanita thinks maybe she could write a letter about the need for greater gun control laws, and she **starts** 5 **brainstorming**, making a list of ideas for her letter. After a few minutes, she discovers that her ideas about gun control are not very original; she is just repeating what she has heard lots of other people say. Then she remembers the struggles of her older half-brother Jake, who suffers from a bipolar disorder that often leads him to violent behavior. Jake has struggled for years to get help with his condition, but he has been continually sent back out onto the streets because he has no health insurance. Juanita **decides to** 6 **write** about the lack of treatment for people with mental illnesses in our society. Thinking about the shooting at Burger King, Juanita decides that, at least for now, her thesis—**the** 7 **point** of her letter—will be that neglecting to treat people with mental health issues in this country endangers us all.

Juanita **next** 8 **goes online** and finds a website that provides statistics on how many people arrested for violent crimes are suffering from mental illness. She **returns to her** 9 **draft** and starts writing, combining her brother's story with the statistics she has found.

At this point, Juanita pauses to read over what she has written and comes to a disappointing conclusion. There is no way she can say all she has to say in 250 words or less, so she decides **to** 10 **narrow** down her thesis to focus only on the treatment her brother received when he was in high school, where all his troubles began.

At this point, Juanita remembers a conversation with her school's guidance counselor, who had tried to help her brother but was overwhelmed by the number of troubled students she needed to help as she worked only two days per week. Juanita **decides to** 11 **add this information** to her argument.

She **returns** 12 **to her draft** and adds a few sentences about the overworked guidance counselor. Next, **she** 13 **reads the paper** over looking for places that might need revising—changing the order of ideas, providing more support for her assertions and adding coherence to her essay. Finally, she pours herself a fresh cup of coffee and 14 **reads the entire paper** several times looking for problems with spelling, grammar, punctuation, wording, and style.

How Juanita's Process Relates to You

Although every writer's process is different, and even the same writer's process is different for different writing tasks, the most effective writers carry out all the stages listed above and keep circling back to do them over and over. This kind of recursive process may take more time than you're used to devoting to an essay, but it produces consistently better results. In addition, following this kind of process will significantly improve the quality of the writing you submit for assignments.

8.4 Tutorial

Peer Review

After finishing a draft of a piece of writing, many writers like to ask a friend, a classmate, a coworker, or someone else to look their writing over and give them some feedback. Because this practice—asking someone else to review writing—is so common in the world outside college, many instructors in college writing courses ask their students to review each other's drafts, a process known as *peer review*. A *peer* is someone who has the same standing as you, someone like one of your classmates.

There are two ways you might participate in peer review this semester. Your instructor may organize a peer review session either in class or online. Or you may decide, on your own, to ask a classmate or a friend to look over a draft of your writing. In this tutorial, you will learn how to ask for and receive such feedback and get some ideas about how to give others feedback on their drafts. These ideas should be useful whether you are informally asking a friend for feedback or you are more formally asking for feedback in class or online.

Guidelines for Peer Review

Here are some suggestions for how to respond when you are asked to review someone else's writing.

1. **Make sure you understand the assignment for the piece of writing.** Be sure to check whether the writer is actually doing the kind of writing the assignment asks for.

2. **Determine where the writer is in the process of writing this paper.** If you are reviewing a very early rough draft, you will want to concentrate on the big issues. Is it clear what the point, the thesis, of the paper is? Does the paper include convincing evidence to support that thesis? On the other hand, if the writer is almost finished with a paper that has been revised several times, it probably makes more sense to focus on the little stuff: places where the writing is unclear, errors with grammar and punctuation, and spelling errors.

3. **Keep in mind that receiving criticism is not exactly fun.** The writer of the paper wants to hear what can be improved but is probably also dreading hearing your feedback. One way to make your comments easier for the writer to hear is to make sure you praise what you really like about the paper. Find a place where the writer has made a good point or expressed an idea in particularly powerful language. Be sure you are sincere in this praise; most writers can see right through empty compliments.

4. **Use a guide (rubric) if one has been assigned.** If you are reviewing a piece of writing because your instructor has required the class to do so, you may have received a list of topics or questions to guide your review. Be sure you follow this guide.

5. **If you are not given a guide (rubric) for your review, you might want to use the following suggestions.**

   a. *Comment on the focus of the writing.* Is the main argument—the thesis of the writing—clear? Does that thesis remain the focus of the whole paper or does the writer lose track and wander into other topics in some places? Is the main idea of the paper the same at the end of the paper as it was at the beginning? If there are problems with the thesis and unity, point out exactly where the problems occur and, if possible, suggest how they might be eliminated.

   b. *Comment on how well the writer provided convincing evidence to support the thesis.* Compliment the writer on evidence that really "works," but also point out where the writer has made assertions without convincing support or where evidence seems to be presented that doesn't really belong because it does not support the argument.

   c. *Comment on how well the writer has responded to possible opposing arguments.* Does the essay simply ignore obvious arguments that those who disagree with its thesis would raise? When the writer acknowledges arguments that opponents would make, does he or she provide effective counterarguments? Or, when it seems necessary, does the writer concede the point and then explain why the point is of minimal importance?

   d. *Comment on how easy it was to follow the paper's argument.* Are there places that confused you? Are there places where the paper seemed to jump from one point to the next and it was difficult to see the connection between the points? If possible, suggest changes to the organization that would make the argument easier to follow.

6. **Try to make your comments as specific as possible.** Don't just write, "You need more evidence to support your assertions." Instead, point out a specific assertion that needs more evidence and, if possible, give some suggestions about what kind of evidence might help.

7. **If you are reviewing an essay that you receive as a Word document, you may want to use the "Review" function in Word to make your comments.** The illustration below demonstrates how to do this.

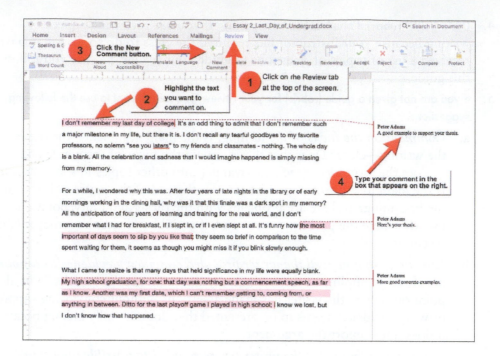

Guidelines for Responding to Peer Review

Here are some suggestions for how to respond when someone reviews your writing.

1. Ask your reviewer to address some specific things you'd like to know about your draft.

2. If your reviewer is giving feedback orally, be sure to take notes.

3. If your reviewer's comments are not clear, ask questions.

4. Don't get in an argument with your reviewer. If the reviewer is making criticisms or suggestions you don't agree with, listen carefully to what is said, but feel free to ignore comments you simply don't agree with. It's your paper.

8.5 Activity

Practicing Peer Review

Your instructor will give you instructions about working in pairs to review each other's drafts of an essay. If you need to refresh your understanding of peer review, see Peer Review (8.4, p. 322).

TOPIC 9
Preparing to Write

In this Topic, you'll learn about some important steps you can take before starting to write an essay, steps that will take only a few minutes but will greatly improve the effectiveness of what you write.

Navigating Topic 9

The tutorials listed below provide information on preparing to write. Each is followed by an opportunity to apply the skills you have just learned. You can work through the entire Topic on your own, learning about all the strategies and practicing them; work on items you've been assigned by your instructor; or choose just the ones you find helpful.

Introduction to Preparing to Write

Topic 9 starts by giving advice on how to read writing assignments and ensure you understand what they are asking you to do. Then it discusses the elements of the rhetorical situation (author, audience, topic, purpose, context, genre, and medium), providing more detailed information on audience and purpose, and ends by explaining how to create a plan for completing a writing assignment.

9.1 Tutorial

Reading an Assignment

To write effectively in a college class, it is essential that you carefully read each assignment and make sure you understand exactly what the instructor expects you to do. If possible, read the assignment when it's handed out in class and ask any questions you have about it then. When you are ready to start working on the assignment later, read it again slowly, perhaps marking it up with comments, reminders, and questions. If you do have questions, check whether your instructor is open to receiving them via email.

When reading an assignment, be particularly attentive to the verbs your instructor has used. Were you asked to *explain* something? To *define* something? To *propose* something? If you have already completed Terms for Writing Assignments (28.2, p. 750), you'll have a list of these terms and their definitions (if not, you might consider working on Unit 28.2 now). These kinds of words are important clues to the kind of writing your instructor expects. Also, you need to note the specific requirements of the assignment—length, format, type of citations required, due dates for drafts, and the due date for the final paper.

9.2 Activity

Analyzing an Assignment

Below is a writing assignment on the topic of grit (defined by Angela Duckworth as "perseverance and passion for long-term goals"). Working in your group, make a numbered list of everything this assignment asks you to do.

Assignment: The Significance of Grit

For this assignment, you will write a three- to four-page essay that grows out of your reading, discussion, and thinking about grit.

> You will write an academic essay suitable for a class in psychology, sociology, education, or even freshman composition. In this essay, you will explain the concept of grit, present the arguments on both sides of the controversy about grit, and take a position on the significance of grit, a position you support with evidence.

As you write this essay, you will want to include information from the three articles you have read in this project and at least one article you find on your own by quoting, paraphrasing, or summarizing relevant passages. When you do this, be sure to provide appropriate citations for any words you quote, paraphrase, or summarize and include a works cited list or list of references at the end of your essay. . . .

If you want to use your sources most effectively to support your argument, it's not enough to simply include them as a series of unrelated sources; you need to tie them together, explain their relationships with each other, and express your conclusions about them.

9.3 Tutorial

The Rhetorical Situation

As long ago as classical Greece—300 BC or so—thinkers have been aware that four important components exist for every text: the *author* of the text, the *audience* for the text, the *topic* of the text, and the *purpose* of the text. These four important elements are discussed from the point of view of the reader in Previewing a Text (20.2, p. 575). There readers are urged, before diving into reading a text, to take a few minutes to analyze the rhetorical situation, as it will help them to better understand and analyze what they are reading. These same four components are also important for a *writer* to think about before and during any writing project. You will need to analyze them as you prepare to write.

Traditional Components of Rhetorical Analysis

The following are the four traditional components of rhetorical analysis.

1. **Author.**   Of course, you know who the author is; it's you. But what version of *you* do you want your readers to encounter? Having done considerable research and thinking about your topic, do you want to take on the role of an expert? Or would it be a better strategy to be up front about the fact that you are "just a college student" and argue that being a college student gives you a valuable perspective on the topic? If you have been personally affected in some way by the topic, do you want your readers to see you as someone with personal experience of the issue?

2. **Audience.**   What do you know about your audience, the people who will read what you have written? Audience analysis is discussed more fully in Thinking about Audience (9.4, p. 328).

3. **Topic.** What will you be writing about? Early in the process your topic may be very broad, but before you start to write, you will need to narrow it down to something manageable. (See How to Use Invention Strategies to Select a Topic [10.3, p. 344].)

4. **Purpose.** What is your purpose for writing? What do you want to have happen as a result of people reading your essay? Read more about this in Thinking about Purpose (9.6, p. 331).

Additional Components of Rhetorical Analysis

In addition to the four traditional components of rhetorical analysis, before starting to write, you should also think about three additional elements that have come to be considered part of a rhetorical analysis in the modern world:

1. **Context.** *Where* does the writing you're doing fit into the world in which it will be read? Is your topic the center of a firestorm of public argument? Are you writing about a topic that most of the world views as already settled and not in need of more discussion? Are you writing about a topic that has been neglected, that most people have not been thinking about? Are you breaking new ground? Are you writing about a topic that has been much discussed already, but which you are addressing from a new perspective or as a result of new evidence? Thinking about where your writing fits into the broader conversation will help you to adopt the most effective tone and style.

2. **Genre.** What *kind* of writing are you doing? Is this going to be a memo, a formal report, an essay for publication, an application for a job, a letter to potential supporters of a project? What style and tone of writing is expected in this genre of writing? What length is expected? What kind of evidence? What kind of documentation of sources? Does the type of writing you're doing call for the use of a series of paragraphs, or would the use of bulleted or numbered lists be more effective?

3. **Medium.** Give some thought to what medium would be most effective for presenting your argument. Don't assume that a ten-page formal written report is your best option. Depending on the situation, your writing may be more effective if it's enriched with images, charts, and diagrams. Is a PowerPoint or web page an option? Considering your topic, purpose, and audience, what medium would be most effective?

9.4 Tutorial

Thinking about Audience

Before starting any writing task, most writers find it helpful to think about who their audience will be. Who will be reading what they are about to write? This knowledge will shape the tone of their writing, the content, the examples, and the amount of detail they provide.

Identify Your Audience

This task can actually be a little more complicated than it seems. Suppose the writing assignment you are responding to asks you to write to your college or university's Committee on the Student Code of Conduct to propose a change in its policy on bringing children on campus. As with most assignments in college English classes, your essay will have two different audiences. The first is the committee, but the second is your instructor. And if that's not complicated enough, your instructor will be reading and evaluating your essay based on how well he or she thinks it addresses the committee as audience.

Writing tasks in the workplace can just as easily have multiple audiences. Imagine that a company you work for has discovered a flaw in a product it sells. Your boss has asked you to write a letter to customers explaining what the flaw is and what steps the company will take to correct it. Your audience is, obviously, the people who bought the product, but remember that first your letter will be read by your boss. In addition, it may be sent to other offices, like the legal affairs office, for their approval.

Analyze Your Audience

Once you know who your audience is, you will need to think about them and answer questions such as the following.

- **How much does your audience already know about the subject you are writing about?** Do you need to provide some background information as context, such as a brief overview of events preceding a political crisis you are analyzing or the different ways people in the past have addressed a problem to which you are proposing a solution?

- **How technical should you be with this audience?** If you are writing for a general audience, you may need to define important terms and be careful not to assume your readers know more than they do. On the other hand, if you are writing for people knowledgeable about your topic, you may be able to use more technical language and assume that they are familiar with certain basic information.

- **Are they likely to agree or disagree with what you have to say?** How you think an audience might react to your writing can help you determine how to present your position. For those who agree, you might only need to present a well-researched and supported argument. For those who hold different opinions, you might also need to acknowledge their positions and provide well-supported counterarguments.

- **Are there characteristics about them you should take into account as you write?** Do most of them have children? Are most of them in school? Do most of them read a newspaper? Are there demographic characteristics (e.g., race, gender, sexual orientation, religion, economic status) you should be aware of? What style of writing is most likely to be successful with this group of readers?

9.5 Activity

Practice Thinking about Audience

Below is an assignment you might be asked to write about later in the course (see Unit 1.16, p. 25). For this activity, you're not going to write the paper; you're just going to do some thinking about audience.

Your instructor will form the class into groups of four or so. In your group, discuss who the audience will be for this writing assignment. Who will be the readers of this essay? What do you know about them? Is there only one audience for this assignment? If you think there is more than one, what do you know about the second audience? Who might they be?

How much does each audience know about the topic of delayed gratification? How much are they likely to agree or disagree with your point? What will be the most effective stance for you to take? Can you pull off being an expert? Or should you emphasize that you are "just a student"? Remember, you are not being asked to actually write a paper at this time.

NOTE: *Delayed gratification* is when you put off something that you'd like to do until later in order to achieve a more important goal. For example, you want to watch a football game on TV on Sunday afternoon, but instead, you tape it for later so you can finish your English essay. (If you'd like to know more, see Project 1: The Marshmallow Test [p. 2], which explores the subject of delayed gratification.)

> For this assignment, you will write a three- to four-page essay that grows out of your reading, discussion, and thinking about delayed gratification. Your audience for this paper is students who will be arriving at your institution next year. Your essay, if accepted by the college's New Student Orientation Committee, will be included in a packet of information new students will receive to help them understand how to be more successful in college.
>
> Think deeply about *delayed gratification*—what it is, when it is a good strategy, how one might be successful at doing it. Support your argument with information from the articles you have read or others you locate yourself and/ or with examples from your own life or from the lives of people you know.

9.6 Tutorial

Thinking about Purpose

Before starting any writing task, most writers find it helpful to think about the purpose of the writing they are about to do. Knowing what they want to accomplish will shape the tone of their writing, the examples they use, the amount of detail they include, and the way they present their ideas.

Traditionally, a small number of possible purposes for writing have been identified:

1. To persuade
2. To explain
3. To express (feelings or thoughts)
4. To entertain

However, you could add to the list some additional purposes for writing:

5. To request
6. To recommend
7. To reassure
8. To summarize

Lots of writing certainly does have one of these as its purpose, although more often a piece of writing will combine several of them.

Nonetheless, instead of thinking about purpose in terms of these very broad and general descriptions, you can think about purpose in another way: you can think more specifically and concretely about *your* purpose. To identify a specific focused purpose, think about this question: *What do you want to happen as a result of this writing?*

Realistically, most times when you write, you will have several different purposes. Consider the following example.

> One Saturday afternoon, Tanya Jennings was backing her car out of a parking space at a local mall when she heard a sickening crashing sound. She had backed into a car parked beside her. When she got out and saw the damage she had done, she was horrified. The other car's fender, taillight, and bumper were all damaged, although her own car was not even dented. She also noticed a small crowd had gathered and was watching her.
>
> Tanya was late for a doctor's appointment, so she decided to write a note to the owner of the other car and leave it under the windshield wiper.

The note she wrote had several different purposes, illustrating how complicated the purpose of a piece of writing can be:

1. To apologize to the owner of the car

2. To provide contact information so the owner of the car could reach her

3. To convince the people gathered around, who might read the note after she left, that she had really left contact information

4. To make the point that the other car was parked over the line into her parking space in case the accident ended up in court

This next example demonstrates how thinking carefully about purpose can help someone be a more effective writer.

> Imagine that you've heard about a job you would really like: an evening receptionist position in a hospital that's within walking distance of your college. Perfect. You make sure your résumé is up to date, and then you go to work on a cover letter to go with the résumé.

If you don't give it a lot of thought, the purpose of the cover letter may seem almost obvious: you want to be hired for the job. However, the actual purpose for a cover letter is slightly different. Seldom do employers hire someone based simply on a résumé and cover letter. They will invite some of the applicants in for an interview and then hire one person based on the interviews, the résumé and letter, and perhaps other factors like recommendations or college transcripts.

The purpose of the cover letter is to be invited for an interview, which you hope will lead to the job. If you keep this purpose in mind, you will probably close the letter by saying something like "I would be available for an interview any day next week." But if you do not realize what the true purpose of the letter is, you might close with something like "If you hire me, I can be available to start in one week." The latter closing is inappropriate in this scenario and could lead the employer to think you are not "savvy" enough about the working world to be considered for the job.

9.7 Activity

Practice Thinking about Purpose

For this activity, your instructor will divide the class into groups of three or four. Each group will read the following text. Working in your group, come up with a list of as many different possible purposes for the letter you would write about the experience described below as you can.

> A few weeks ago, you purchased a laptop computer at a local electronics store. When you got home and set up your computer, all that appeared on the screen was "Error Message 134," which informed you that your computer was damaged, and you would have to take it to an authorized repair shop.
>
> When you returned the computer to the store where you had purchased it, the salesperson said you must have damaged the computer while taking it home and refused to repair it for free. When you explained that you had taken it home in its factory packaging and had opened it up very carefully when you got there, he insisted that you must have done something to damage it. He argued that "Error Message 134" could only be the result of extreme carelessness. When you asked to see the manager, he informed you that he was the manager and suggested you were being unreasonably difficult.
>
> Before you completely lost your cool, you decided to leave the store. The salesperson yelled something at you as you left, but you couldn't hear what it was.
>
> When you arrived home, you decided to write a letter about your experience to the general manager of the store.

9.8 Tutorial

Making a Plan

Taking some time before you start to write to make a plan for a writing project is well worth it. If you have four weeks to complete an elaborate research project that culminates in a twelve-page research paper, you will clearly need to develop a work plan. Many students like to do this planning on a calendar like the one on page 334.

Sunday	Monday	Tuesday	Wednesday	Thursday	Friday	Saturday
3	4 Read assignment. Analyze audience and purpose.	5	6 Brainstorm for a topic.	7 Browse library and online resources.	8 Select a narrowed topic. Draft thesis.	9 Conduct research focused on topic. Start bibliog.
10 Brainstorm ideas for paper.	11	12 Chunk ideas and order them.	13 Revise thesis.	14	15 Identify ideas that need more sources.	16 Conduct research for missing sources.
17 Start first draft.	18	19 Continue work on draft.	20 Draft for peer review.	21 Revise.	22	23 Create works cited list.
24 Revise.	25 Edit MLA citations and works cited list.	26	27 Do a careful edit for the little stuff.	28 Research paper due!	29	30

Of course, you don't need an elaborate plan like this if you're writing something much shorter, but believe it or not, even if you are writing an in-class essay and have only an hour, it is still a good idea to take a minute to plan your time. A brief outline like the one that follows will remind you when it's time to move on to the next step in the process. In fact, some students even use the alarm on their phones to alert them to when they need to move on.

5 mins: Reading assignment and analyzing audience and purpose
5 mins: Brainstorming & ordering
30 mins: Drafting
10 mins: Revising
10 mins: Editing

TOPIC 10
Finding a Focus

In this Topic you'll learn to use various invention strategies to develop a focus for your writing and create a draft thesis.

Navigating Topic 10

The tutorials and presentation listed below discuss how to focus a broad subject, and the activities provide opportunities for practice. You can work through the entire Topic on your own, learning about all the strategies and practicing them; work on items you've been assigned by your instructor; or choose just the ones you find helpful.

Introduction to Finding a Focus

Topic 10 starts with an explanation of five different *invention strategies* (brainstorming, freewriting, browsing and reading, mapping, and outlining), sometimes known as *prewriting*, which is followed by a more detailed presentation on brainstorming. It then discusses how to use invention strategies to select and narrow a topic and develop a draft thesis. It ends with an activity to get you thinking about where you might place your thesis in an essay, based on your topic, purpose, and audience.

Invention Strategies

For many writers, getting started is the hardest part. In this tutorial, you will find many ideas and strategies to help you generate ideas and identify and narrow a topic.

Sometimes when you are asked to write in college, you are given complete freedom to write about a topic of your choosing or, at least, a very wide topic area in which to carve out a specific topic. Broad assignments might sound like this:

- Write a three-page essay in which you argue for a cause you believe in.
- Write a three- to four-page essay discussing an issue involving the labor movement in America.
- Write a fifteen-page research paper on American immigration policy over the past fifty years.
- Write a three-page essay discussing one issue raised by the book you read last week for this course.

Sometimes your professors will give you more specifics about what they want you to write about:

- Write a three-page essay in which you explain why the global-warming resisters are wrong.
- Write a four-page essay in which you agree or disagree with this statement: Public schools in America do not provide an equal education to all citizens.

At work, your boss might ask for writing that addresses certain situations:

- The copiers in the office are old and break down frequently. Investigate options for replacing them and have a proposal for new copiers on my desk by noon on Friday.
- Write a letter to customer X explaining why the television he ordered took three weeks to arrive and explaining what we will do to compensate him for the inconvenience.

Whether you have significant leeway in finding a topic or fairly narrow guidelines to work with, the following material offers some techniques, with examples, for generating ideas and then focusing in on a specific topic, including brainstorming, freewriting, browsing and reading, mapping, and outlining.

Brainstorming

To brainstorm, you have to turn your internal censor off. Just write down every idea that comes to you. Don't worry about writing complete sentences; phrases are fine.

Don't even worry about spelling. Just get every idea you can think of written down. When you run out of ideas, read over what you've written. That will often generate additional ideas. When you run out again, go get a cup of coffee or take a break. When you come back, more ideas may come to you.

Many people like to brainstorm on a blank sheet of paper; others prefer to do it in a blank document on a computer. Try both to see what works best for you, but keep in mind that the next step, organizing your list, is much easier to do on a computer, so you may want to choose that approach.

For an example of how brainstorming works, see the presentation in Brainstorming (10.2, p. 344).

Brainstorming Example

Tania was preparing to write an essay on disciplining her five- and seven-year-old daughters. Working on her computer, she began by typing short phrases as they popped into her head.

spanking

"time out"

no TV

chores

yelling

a formal sit-down talk

---

setting clear rules and limits that everyone understands

talking about the rules from time to time, not just when they are broken

explaining the reasons behind the rules

---

what kinds of rules?

rules about cleaning up after making a mess

rules about teasing your sister

rules about not eating snacks between meals

rules about going to be on time

rules about lying

rules about throwing balls in the house

do I need all these rules???

Something really interesting (and not that unusual) happened as Tania did this brainstorming. She started out thinking about how to discipline children, but at the point where she drew the first line, her focus seems to shift. Instead of thinking about what she might do when her daughters misbehave, she starts thinking about what she might do to reduce the times when a need for discipline comes up. Below the second line, Tania's focus shifts again. She starts listing all the rules she might need to discuss, and then pauses and wonders whether she really needs all these rules.

Brainstorming, as it did for Tania, often goes in directions the writer wasn't even thinking about when he or she started. Tania has ended up with some good ideas for three different topics:

1. What kind of discipline to use with her daughters
2. Steps she could take to reduce the need for discipline
3. Why does she need so many rules?

But now Tania will have to make a decision. She cannot write about three different topics, even though they are somewhat related. She'll have to settle on one of these and then do some more brainstorming on that topic.

Freewriting

Other writers use a system called freewriting when they are trying to find ideas. They just start writing about whatever comes to mind, and they keep writing for an extended time without worrying about whether what they are writing is coherent, whether it has unity, or whether it even makes sense. Some writers like to set themselves a goal: they will write for twenty minutes or until they have filled two pages. The idea is to write freely, hoping to generate a few good ideas surrounded, usually, by a lot of not-so-good stuff.

When they're finished, they read over what they've written, searching for a few good ideas. They may end up discarding a large percentage of what they wrote, but the effort will have been worthwhile if it produced a few good ideas.

Freewriting Example

When Alethea started working on a paper about racism for her political science class, she chose freewriting as her invention strategy.

> Racism . . . well, I know its bad. I know it involves treating people of some races badly and giving privileges to other people, usually white like me. And when it gets really ugly with terrible words like the n-word. That's clearly racism. But is racism always that obvious? How bout when I'm walking home at night and see a black man walking in my direction. Do I have a

different reaction cos he's black? What neighborhoods do I make sure I lock my car door in? Do I feel different when a couple of black dudes are talking, joking real loudly in the mall than if its a coupla white guys making a racket?

Alethea took a break at this point, but she had at least started on her paper. She'd raised some interesting questions. When she returned, she reread what she'd written and got some new ideas and even a new direction to take her paper in.

Those sentences are all about me . . . my feelings, actions. But does racism have to be about one person??? Can organizations be racist? Can structures be racist? What about the way schools are funded in America—property taxes. Doesn't that mean schools in places where people have big houses and lots of money get more $s than schools in neighborhoods where poorer people live? People of color? What about who goes to prison for long sentences? Don't black people get longer sentences? Why is that?

After her break, Alethea had moved in a new direction—structural racism instead of individual racism. She may end up needing to choose one or the other to write about, or she might end up writing about both in a paper that compares these two types of racism. In any case, she has a great start on her paper. Notice she didn't spend time correcting typos and grammar errors—this is freewriting, getting ideas down as fast as you can.

Browsing and Reading

Another great way to generate ideas to write about is through browsing and reading, either in the library or online. Using the card catalog or the computer database in the library, browse titles or subjects until something catches your eye. Using Google, start a search for a broad topic and then follow links to wherever they lead. Skim articles or browse books making lots of notes of ideas that hold promise. When you finish, you'll have a long list of ideas that need to be organized and focused.

Browsing and Reading Example

Lani knew she wanted to write about health care and the elderly. Her mother was in her late seventies, and it was clear she was not going to be able to live alone too much longer without some in-home support, so this topic was important to Lani. She first visited her college library, where she went to the computerized database for books and found listings for a couple that looked promising. She made a note of the titles, authors, and call numbers, in case she would decide to use these in her works cited list, and headed to the stacks to locate the actual books.

> *The Psychology of Aging: Theory, Research, and Practice* by Janet Belsky
> (BF724.55.A35 B44 1984)
>
> *Learning to Be Old: Gender, Culture, and Aging* by Margaret Cruikshank
> (BF724.55.A35 C78 2013)

When Lani found these two books on a shelf on the second floor of the library, she took them to a table and started browsing. In the Belsky book, Chapter 6 discusses cognition and aging. Lani had worried that her mother was getting a little forgetful and sometimes seemed confused, so that chapter caught her attention. The Cruikshank book didn't have a chapter on cognition, so Lani headed back to the shelf where she'd found the first two books. Lani returned the second book to the shelf, and when she looked a little farther down the shelf, she was really excited. There were three more books focused specifically on cognition and aging.

> *Aging and Cognition: Research Methodologies and Empirical Advances*,
> edited by Hayden B. Bosworth (BF724.55.C63 A47 2009)
>
> *Everyday Cognition in Adulthood and Late Life*, edited by Leonard W. Poon,
> David C. Rubin, Barbara A. Wilson (BF724.55.C63 P66 1989)
>
> *Adult Cognition and Aging: Developmental Changes in Processing,
> Knowing and Thinking* by John M. Rybas (BF724.55.C63 R93 1986)

Armed with these four books, Lani headed for the library's computer where databases for periodicals were available. She decided to use the ProQuest Nursing and Allied Health database. She typed in the words "aging and cognition" and was startled to learn 21,268 articles were available. She was greatly relieved to learn that she could search the titles from her computer at home and narrow her search criteria so she would get a smaller, more focused list of articles, which she could print out.

Lani's trip to the library was very productive. She not only focused her topic on a narrower topic—aging and cognition—but she was headed home with four books on the subject and access to lots of articles.

Mapping

Mapping is much like brainstorming, only more visual. Start by writing down a single idea in the center of a blank page and drawing an oval around it. Then add additional ideas and position them around the first idea. Draw lines to show connections among the ideas. Keep going until you run out of ideas or the page is full.

At this point, you might want to select one of the more promising ideas, write it in the middle of a fresh sheet of paper, and start an entirely new map with it.

Some writers like to do their mapping using sticky notes that can be rearranged as the map grows larger. Mapping can even be done in a word processing program. Most of them have a function under the "insert" menu called "text box." Click on it and then click in the center of your page to insert a text box, in which you can write your first idea. Then add additional ideas each in its own text box. These can be rearranged easily by dragging them around the screen. Lines showing connections among the boxes can be added by clicking on the "insert" menu, clicking on "shape," and selecting "line."

Mapping Example

John was interested in writing about the dangers of driving, so he created a map using text boxes in a Microsoft Word document. He placed "dangers of driving" at the center, and then added four boxes for what he considered the major categories of danger: other drivers, bad weather, road hazards, and driver error. For each of these categories, he added related ideas. Using this process, he came up with enough ideas that he could use any one of the four major topics as the basis for a paper.

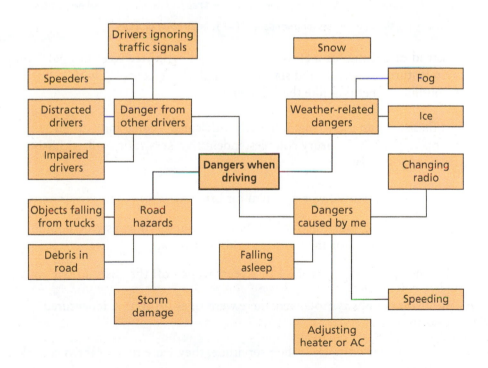

Outlining

Outlines range from quick lists of three or four ideas to highly structured documents complete with indentations, capital and lowercase letters, and Roman and Arabic numbers. For short writing assignments, or assignments when you don't have much time, such as an exam, a scratch outline can still be very helpful.

However, when you are working on an essay assignment, creating a more detailed outline can be really useful once you have narrowed your topic, drafted a working thesis statement, and generated some supporting evidence. An outline helps you to organize your ideas, decide on what order to present them, and identify where you need more support; it provides a road map for your essay that will guide your writing.

Outlining Example

When asked in a history class to write an in-class essay on the beginnings of slavery in America, Javier jotted down a few quick ideas before beginning to write.

- Indentured servitude brought many poor Europeans to the colonies in the 17th century
- How it worked
- First Africans brought to Virginia in 1619 — treated as indentured servants
- Slavery legalized in Massachusetts in 1641, in Virginia in 1661

If, instead of writing for a class test, Javier had had three weeks to work on his paper on indentured servitude and slavery, he might have come up with a much more elaborate outline, something like the following.

Draft Thesis: As an increasing number of Africans became indentured servants in the 17th-century colonies, indentured servitude evolved fairly quickly into slavery.

I. Indentured servitude was a system for bringing workers to the colonies.

    A. The earliest indentured servants were poor Europeans who couldn't afford to pay for their voyage to the Americas.

    B. They promised to work 4 to 7 years to pay off the cost of their voyage.

II. Although not always followed, there were rules protecting indentured servants.

    A. When they completed their servitude, they were then granted complete freedom.

B. Most were also given their "freedom dues" of something like 25 acres of land, seed for a year, fresh clothes, and a firearm.

III. Although initially classified as indentured servants, Africans were never treated the same way as Europeans.

    A. Most were captured in Africa and *forcibly* transported to the colonies.

    B. Beginning in 1619, Africans were brought to Virginia and categorized as indentured servants, but even then, their treatment was not the same as the treatment of the Europeans.

        1. Some Africans actually achieved freedom after serving out their period of indenture, but most of these were not given "freedom dues."

        2. By 1650, the total number of Africans in Virginia had risen to only 400; the total number of Europeans was nearly 19,000.

IV. Indentured servitude evolves into slavery.

    A. Slavery in England had been reserved for "non-Christians," and was not usually related to race.

    B. The number of freed Europeans in the colonies was growing and creating pressure on land ownership.

    C. The colonists began to see slavery as a more economically feasible option than indenture.

        1. Slaves could be enslaved for life.

        2. The children of slaves would become slaves as well.

        3. Slavery, originally based on religion—only non-Christians could be enslaved—had a problem: slaves could convert to Christianity and demand freedom.

        4. Gradually, the basis for slavery changed from religion to race, an unchangeable and easily identified category.

A formal outline like this is different in several ways from the scratch outline Javier used when he had to write a paper quickly.

1. It is much more detailed. Although he started with a brief outline, as Javier did more research and thinking, he added more and more detail.

2. An elaborate system of letters, numbers, and indentation is used to indicate where the ideas fit in the hierarchy of the argument.

3. Each entry is a complete sentence. This is only necessary in the most formal kind of outline—a sentence outline. In a less formal outline, each entry could just be a phrase.

4. At every level, where there is one entry, there is at least one more. For example, there are no 1's without 2's; no A's without B's.

Some instructors require that an outline like this one be turned in along with a research paper.

Most writers who use an outline to guide their writing consider it a very fluid document that is constantly revised, pruned, and added to. In many cases, as the writer fleshes out the outline, the draft thesis is revised significantly, paragraphs are reordered, new evidence is added, and support that is not relevant is deleted.

10.2 Presentation

Brainstorming

To watch this presentation on brainstorming, a particularly useful prewriting strategy that can help you to find and narrow a topic, develop a working thesis, and generate ideas to support it, go to *Achieve for The Hub*, Topic 10, and open Unit 10.2.

10.3 Tutorial

How to Use Invention Strategies to Select a Topic

Using invention strategies to come up with a topic to write about is often a two-stage process. In the first stage, you use one or more of the strategies described in Invention Strategies (10.1, p. 336) to develop a collection of potential ideas to write about. Then you read through your list, crossing out or deleting any ideas that no longer appeal to you, that don't match the assignment, or that you don't think you have much to say about. Now you should have a handful of ideas that might work as a topic for a paper. You might try them out on other people. Get their reactions and suggestions. Or you might select one of the ideas and try writing about it. If it seems to work, you may have your topic. If it doesn't, try another one.

Finally, with luck and perseverance, you will arrive at one topic that seems like it will work for your essay. Topics at this stage often look something like these:

- Solar energy
- Prison reform
- Transsexuals in the army

- Freedom of speech at college
- Religious freedom
- Right to die

The most common problem that students have with these early topics is that they are too broad. Most of those listed above would require many pages to discuss adequately. So, in the second stage, you take the broad topic you've selected and use an invention strategy to find more ideas that relate to it. If you had chosen, for example, "religious freedom," you might have brainstormed a list that looks something like this:

Freedom to worship the way your faith tells you to

Freedom to refuse to do anything your religious beliefs say you shouldn't do

Freedom to raise your children in accordance with your beliefs

Freedom to marry in accordance with your religious beliefs

Freedom to engage in rituals and ceremonies dictated by your religion

Freedom to refuse medical treatment for yourself and your children when your religion forbids such treatment

Once again, it's time to make a decision. Following the same technique that you did in the first stage, read through your list, deleting any ideas that no longer appeal to you, that don't match the assignment, or that you don't think you have much to say about. At this point, you should have a narrowed topic that you can address within the page limits of your assignment.

10.4 Activity

Using Brainstorming to Narrow a Topic

Use the following steps to narrow a broad topic to one you could write about in a paper of three to four pages in length.

1. Choose one of the broad topics listed below or one from the next essay assignment for this course and brainstorm a list of more focused topics you might write about.

- Patriotism
- Lying
- Success
- Religion
- The environment

- Race in America
- Drugs
- Education
- Transportation
- Criminal justice

2. After you've had enough time to do this brainstorming, your instructor will organize you into groups of three or four to compare the lists you have come up with. If you like some of the topics on a classmate's list, feel free to add them to your list.

3. Working individually, go over your list to eliminate any topics that don't seem very promising, that you don't know enough about, or that you simply aren't interested in writing about. Then review the remaining topics to see if any can be combined into one topic. Finally, select the one topic you could write an essay about.

4. Complete a second round of brainstorming. Make a list of all the ideas you might include in a paper about the topic you have chosen. If you run out of ideas, you might want to take a short break and relax for a few minutes. Then return to the brainstorming to see if you can come up with some more ideas, or try one of the other invention strategies listed in Unit 10.1 (p. 336).

5. As you did in step 4, review your list of ideas eliminating any that don't seem to fit under your topic, that you don't know enough to write about, or that you are not interested in writing about.

For information on how to further organize the ideas you have now listed for your topic, see Chunking and Ordering (12.5, p. 383).

10.5 Tutorial

Thesis Statements

Most successful college essays focus on a single idea or main point, which is referred to as a *thesis* or *thesis statement*. The thesis of an essay includes two major parts: (1) a statement of the subject or topic for the essay and (2) an assertion about that subject or topic.

Here are some examples:

- Global warming is a threat to the US economy.
- A police officer's life is frequently at risk.
- Today's automobiles are much safer than those of ten years ago.

Notice that each of these theses (*theses* is the plural form of thesis) has two parts:

A thesis statement must do these two things—identify the topic and make an assertion about that topic—but it can also do other things.

1. It can provide some background information about the topic of the paper.

- *Because it threatens our ability to produce enough food to feed our nation,* global warming is a threat to the US economy.
- A police officer's life is frequently at risk *as a result of the widespread ownership of handguns in America.*
- *Since computers have become widespread in our cars,* today's automobiles are much safer than those of ten years ago.

2. It can also give a preview of the organization of the argument to follow.

- Global warming is a threat to the US economy *because of its effect on agriculture, coastal cities, flooding, and wildfires.*
- A police officer's life is frequently at risk *from attacks by violent criminals, accidental shootings, and deranged individuals.*
- Today's automobiles are much safer than those of ten years ago *because they are fitted with a significant number of safety devices and include software that can alert drivers to potential dangers.*

Avoid These Common Mistakes

Avoid these common mistakes when creating a thesis.

- **Stating a fact.** A thesis that simply states a fact will not work well because there is not enough to write about; an essay is not necessary to prove something that is factually true. The theses here state a fact:

  - Newspapers provide news to many people.
  - Some foods are healthier than others.
  - Many children are born each year.

- **Taking an uncontested position.** A thesis that simply argues something that most people already agree with will not produce an interesting essay:

  - Drunk driving is a terrible thing.
  - Child abuse should not be tolerated.
  - Not showing up regularly for work will lead to losing your job.

- **Reusing language that is in the actual assignment.** If the assignment reads, "Write a three-page essay in which you discuss at least three causes of global warming," your thesis should not recycle the same language:

  - In this essay I will discuss three causes of global warming.

- **Making sweeping statements about what you are going to write about.**

  - In this essay, I will explain why America's groundwater is in danger.
  - This essay will prove that we need lower speed limits on interstate highways.

- **Stating your thesis as your opinion.**

  - In my opinion, we need a major revision of immigration laws in this country.
  - My belief is that racial justice should be the top priority.

A Thesis with More Than One Point

Some teachers insist that a thesis argue only a single point, but others recognize that it is possible, although more difficult, to write a fine essay that argues more than one point. Here are some examples:

- *America is in danger of spending too much on the military* and of not spending enough on education.
- *Children's television can have a positive effect on children's development,* but it can also have a very negative effect.
- *Americans who break some laws receive excessively harsh sentences,* while those who break other laws receive sentences that are far too light.

Check with your professor whether he or she will accept a more complex thesis statement like one of these.

10.6 Tutorial

Using Invention Strategies to Arrive at a Thesis

Once you have a topic, how do you turn it into a *thesis*? Using an invention strategy, or more than one, that works for you, you can come up with a variety of ideas about your topic. Freewriting, brainstorming, mapping, and reading about the topic can all help you to develop a thesis about that topic.

Here is the list of possible topics brainstormed for "religion" in Using Brainstorming to Narrow a Topic (10.4, p. 345):

Freedom to worship the way your faith tells you to

Freedom to refuse to do anything your religious beliefs say you shouldn't do

Freedom to raise your children in accordance with your beliefs

Freedom to marry in accordance with your religious beliefs

Freedom to engage in rituals and ceremonies dictated by your religion

Freedom to refuse medical treatment for yourself and your children when your religion forbids such treatment

At this point, the writer needs to make a choice. In most cases, a well-organized essay has only one thesis, so one topic will need to be selected. For this example, the writer decides on "freedom to marry in accordance with your religious beliefs" as his topic. He then chooses to brainstorm a list of possible theses:

> The government should not pass laws controlling who can marry whom.
>
> The government should not impose the beliefs of one religion about marriage on people who practice another religion.
>
> Marriage is a religious practice; the government should have no role and should not issue marriage licenses.
>
> The age at which people can marry should be set by their religion, not by the government.
>
> Two major world religions, Islam and Hinduism, as well as many smaller religions allow polygamy; the government should not outlaw polygamy.

Again, it's time to make a choice. The writer thinks about his list of potential theses and rereads the assignment to make sure they fulfill the requirements. Then he thinks about the audience for and purpose of the writing as detailed in the assignment and eliminates theses that would not address both sufficiently. He asks for opinions from friends or classmates to help him make a choice. As he focuses in on one of the theses, he decides to try freewriting about it to see whether that produces enough ideas for an essay. If it does, he's ready to start drafting. If not, he will try finding ideas for another thesis in his list.

The choice of a thesis is important, but it is not irrevocable. Later in the writing process, your thesis can be modified or even replaced, based on where your reading, research, or writing takes you.

10.7 Activity

Where Should the Thesis Be Located?

Read over the following short essays that were written to argue that the city of Baltimore should install a traffic light at the intersection of Northern Parkway and Chinquapin Parkway. These essays were intended to be sent as letters to the director of transportation for the city.

The three essays are quite similar, but they are organized in different ways. Working in groups, study them carefully, looking particularly at the location of the thesis in each. Discuss which way of organizing the essay your group thinks is most effective.

Essay 1

For the past six years, I've been living a few houses away from the intersection of Northern Parkway and Chinquapin Parkway, a busy intersection in a neighborhood where many families have children. I urge the city to install a traffic light at this intersection.

In the years I've lived here I've seen and heard far too many accidents at this intersection. In the last month, I have observed two, one of which involved serious personal injury. In the past year, I have personally witnessed twenty-one accidents. While I was out of town last summer, a terrible four-car accident occurred after which five people were admitted to the hospital. I know that two accidents at this busy intersection have resulted in loss of life. Something needs to be done.

This morning as I was leaving my house for work, I heard the squealing sound of the brakes of a large city bus trying to stop suddenly, followed by the sickening sound of that bus crashing into the side of a station wagon carrying three small children. As I ran to the station wagon, I saw that two children were scared but had been restrained by their seatbelts. The third child, unfortunately, had not been wearing her seatbelt. She flew through the windshield and landed in a forsythia bush on the opposite side of the intersection. Fortunately, the bush cushioned her impact. She was bleeding from many scratches and cuts, but did not suffer any serious injuries. We were lucky this time.

I checked with the Department of Transportation and learned that the minimum traffic requirement to trigger a new traffic light is at least 1,200 vehicles per hour on the more congested road at peak traffic periods and at least 50% of that volume on the less congested road. My neighbor and I sat near the intersection on three different work days last week. On Northern Parkway, I counted more than 1,500 vehicles per hour each day. My neighbor counted 855 vehicles per hour on Chinquapin Parkway. In addition to exceeding the minimum traffic requirements for a new traffic light, I'd like to point out that there is a large public school just a block away from this intersection, meaning that large numbers of children cross at this intersection every school day.

In light of the alarming number of accidents at this intersection and the fact that the traffic density exceeds the minimum requirements, I urge the Department of Transportation to install a traffic light at the intersection of Northern and Chinquapin Parkways.

Essay 2

This morning as I was leaving my house for work, I heard the squealing sound of the brakes of a large city bus trying to stop suddenly, followed by the sickening sound of that bus crashing into the side of a station wagon carrying three small children. As I ran to the station wagon, I saw that two children were scared but had been restrained by their seatbelts. The third child, unfortunately, had not been wearing her seatbelt. She flew through the windshield and landed in a forsythia bush on the opposite side of the intersection. Fortunately, the bush cushioned her impact. She was bleeding from many scratches and cuts, but did not suffer any serious injuries. We were lucky this time.

In the years I've lived here I've seen and heard far too many accidents at this intersection. In the last month, I have observed two, one of which involved serious personal injury. In the past year, I have personally witnessed twenty-one accidents. While I was out of town last summer, a terrible four-car accident occurred after which five people were admitted to the hospital. I know that two accidents at this busy intersection have resulted in loss of life. Something needs to be done.

For the past six years, I've been living a few houses away from the intersection of Northern Parkway and Chinquapin Parkway, a busy intersection in a neighborhood where many families have children. I urge the city to install a traffic light at this intersection.

I checked with the Department of Transportation and learned that the minimum traffic requirement to trigger a new traffic light is at least 1,200 vehicles per hour on the more congested road at peak traffic periods and at least 50% of that volume on the less congested road. My neighbor and I sat near the intersection on three different work days last week. On Northern Parkway, I counted more than 1,500 vehicles per hour each day. My neighbor counted 855 vehicles per hour on Chinquapin Parkway. In addition to exceeding the minimum traffic requirements for a new traffic light, I'd like to point out that there is a large public school just a block away from this intersection, meaning that large numbers of children cross at this intersection every school day.

In light of the alarming number of accidents at this intersection and the fact that the traffic density exceeds the minimum requirements, I urge the Department of Transportation to install a traffic light at the intersection of Northern and Chinquapin Parkways.

Essay 3

This morning as I was leaving my house for work, I heard the squealing sound of the brakes of a large city bus trying to stop suddenly, followed by the sickening sound of that bus crashing into the side of a station wagon carrying three small children. As I ran to the station wagon, I saw that two children were scared but had been restrained by their seatbelts. The third child, unfortunately, had not been wearing her seatbelt. She flew through the windshield and landed in a forsythia bush on the opposite side of the intersection. Fortunately, the bush cushioned her impact. She was bleeding from many scratches and cuts, but did not suffer any serious injuries. We were lucky this time.

In the years I've lived here I've seen and heard far too many accidents at this intersection. In the last month, I have observed two, one of which involved serious personal injury. In the past year, I have personally witnessed twenty-one accidents. While I was out of town last summer, a terrible four-car accident occurred after which five people were admitted to the hospital. I know that two accidents at this busy intersection have resulted in loss of life. Something needs to be done.

I checked with the Department of Transportation and learned that the minimum traffic requirement to trigger a new traffic light is at least 1,200 vehicles per hour on the more congested road at peak traffic periods and at least 50% of that volume on the less congested road. My neighbor and I sat near the intersection on three different work days last week. On Northern Parkway, I counted more than 1,500 vehicles per hour each day. My neighbor counted 855 vehicles per hour on Chinquapin Parkway. In addition to exceeding the minimum traffic requirements for a new traffic light, I'd like to point out that there is a large public school just a block away from this intersection, meaning that large numbers of children cross at this intersection every school day.

In light of the alarming number of accidents at this intersection and the fact that the traffic density exceeds the minimum requirements, I urge the Department of Transportation to install a traffic light at the intersection of Northern and Chinquapin Parkways.

Know Your Instructor's Preferences

There is some disagreement among English teachers about *where* a thesis statement should be located in an essay. Some insist that it appear in the first paragraph; some even specify a particular location in that paragraph, like the last sentence. Others recognize that the thesis can effectively be withheld until later in the paper, even until the final paragraph. Making sure you understand your instructor's preferences about thesis placement before you start writing is always a good idea. (For more on thesis placement, see Introductory Paragraphs [17.3, p. 503].)

TOPIC 11
Developing Ideas

One of the most effective ways to make an essay stronger is to provide more "development," more reasons for readers to agree with your thesis. In this Topic, you will learn a variety of strategies for providing support for your thesis and topic sentences.

Navigating Topic 11

The tutorials listed below provide information on how to generate support for an argument. You can work through the entire Topic on your own, learning about all the strategies and practicing them; work on items you've been assigned by your instructor; or choose just the ones you find helpful.

Introduction to Developing Ideas

Topic 11 is all about making your argument stronger and more convincing. It opens with an explanation of ways to make your essays more interesting, followed by an activity that gets you thinking about evidence and assertions, which leads to an overview of the kinds of support you could use in an essay, such as examples, statistics, interviews, expert testimony, and more. Group activities are designed to give you practice at providing support for a thesis and recognizing support in someone else's essay. The Topic also offers advice on three types of appeals and how to avoid logical fallacies.

11.1 **Tutorial**

Options for What to Include in an Essay

At its most basic, an essay consists of these three components:

- An introduction
- Body paragraphs that provide support for the thesis; for example, a series of paragraphs that provide, explain, and support reasons for an argument or position
- A conclusion

These three components can make a perfectly satisfactory essay, but many other components can make your essay more interesting, more convincing, and more appealing to the reader, as outlined below. Think about including some of these in your next essay. Also think about your audience. What will it take to win them over to your position? What is likely to be their primary reservation?

Ways to Make Essays More Interesting

1. **Add more arguments.** Just because you've come up with three reasons that support the position you have taken in your thesis, there is no reason to stop thinking. Most essays can be made more convincing if they include more reasons, more arguments, to support the thesis.

2. **Provide definitions of key terms.** If there are several words or phrases that are central to your argument, you may want to use a paragraph near the beginning of your essay to explain how you will be using them. For example, if you're writing about juvenile delinquency, you may want to explain what that term will mean in your discussion. It's not that you think your reader has never heard of the term; it's just that it has a wide range of meanings, and you want to make clear what you mean when you use the term. Does it, for example, include juveniles who commit murder? How about juveniles who spray paint graffiti?

3. **Recognize negative effects.** Your thesis may be a good idea, and you may have presented a number of positive outcomes that will result from it, but it is often

a good strategy also to admit that there are some negative outcomes that may result. Recognizing these can add to your credibility. They demonstrate that you are knowledgeable enough to be aware of these negatives and honest enough to admit they exist. Of course, it is a good idea if you can also explain why these negatives are less serious than they appear or how they can be mitigated.

4. **Recognize what opponents may say.**   Closely related to recognition of negative effects is the recognition of opponents' arguments, especially if those arguments are well known. Summarize them as objectively as you can and then answer, rebut, or counter them.

5. **Include some history of the topic you're writing about.**   How long has it been an issue? What positions have others taken about it?

6. **Make suggestions for implementation.**   If you are trying to convince your reader to agree with you about some issue, it can be a great idea to include some advice, toward the end of the essay, about what steps will be needed to implement the change you are proposing.

7. **Make a call to action.**   Even stronger than advice about implementation is a call to action, urging the reader not just to begin implementing some change, but to actually commit to some cause.

8. **Include background about who you are and/or why you decided to write about the topic.**   Especially if it makes you a more credible author or demonstrates you are an author with a particular viewpoint, it can be very helpful to take a paragraph or two to give the reader some information about who you are and why you are writing about the topic.

11.2   Activity

Evidence and Assertions

On October 15, 2018, police found a man unconscious on the sidewalk at the intersection of Charles and Lombard Streets in Baltimore, Maryland. They called an ambulance to take the man to the emergency room, but they also emptied his pockets into an evidence container to help them figure out who he was. The following items were found in his pockets and in his wallet.

Working in groups, make a list of observations about the man based on the contents of his pockets. You will have about fifteen minutes to complete your list.

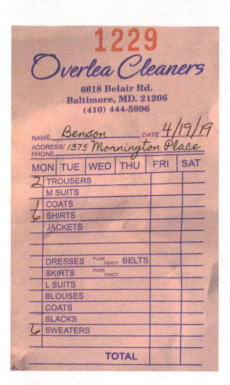

1229

Overlea Cleaners

6618 Belair Rd.
Baltimore, MD. 21206
(410) 444-5996

NAME Benson   DATE 4/19/19
ADDRESS 1375 Mornington Place
PHONE

	MON	TUE	WED	THU	FRI	SAT
2 TROUSERS						
M SUITS						
1 COATS						
6 SHIRTS						
JACKETS						
DRESSES PLAIN FANCY BELTS						
SKIRTS PLAIN FANCY						
L SUITS						
BLOUSES						
COATS						
SLACKS						
6 SWEATERS						
TOTAL						

Bank of America

Talk to an advisor about
what's ahead. Visit ML.com/prepare

5/13/18   IMDN4438

XXXXXXX0000
*CANTON SQUARE REMOTE
BALTIMORE   MD

Ser. No. 5595
Withdrawal $200.00
From PRIMARY   Checking
Available Balance $1,043.79

Member FDIC

ATM

Next time use your phone instead of your card.
Visit bankofamerica.com/CardlessATM

AAA
Roadside Assistance
1-800-

SAFEWAY CLUB

AAdvantage American Airlines

NCTE National Council of Teachers of English
www.ncte.org

123456   Membership Expires
                          2/23/2019
Mathew Benson   College Section

M E M B E R S H I P   C A R D

Nikolai's Roof
Address
City, State Zip Code
Phone Number

MERCH ID:
CASHIER: Manuela
TERMINAL: 11

        Visa

NAME: BENSON/MATHEW
NUMBER: XXXXXXXXXXXX
EXPIRE: XX/XX
AUTH: 09060D
AMOUNT: 101.11

CHECK: 118196
TABLE: 15

TOTAL: 101.11

GRATUITY: 25.00

TOTAL: 126.11

I agree to pay above total
amount according to my card
issuer agreement.

X

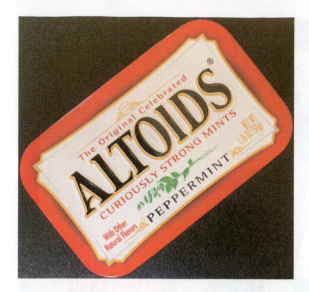

THE BALTIMORE MUSEUM OF ART
10 Art Museum Drive, Baltimore, MD 21218
443-573-1700 | artbma.org
Members Hotline: 443-573-1800
MEMBER

BALTIMORE MUSEUM OF ART BMA

012340

Expiration: 12/31/2019

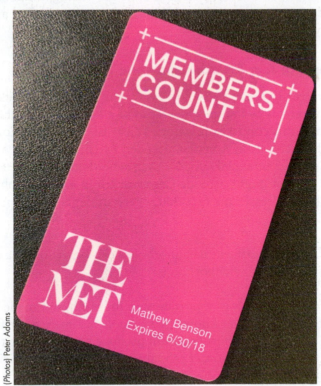

MEMBERS COUNT

THE MET

Mathew Benson
Expires 6/30/18

(Photos) Peter Adams

Development, Support, or Evidence

At one time or another, you've probably been told that something you've written needs more development, more support, or more evidence. These kinds of suggestions usually indicate that the reader feels that you've expressed an opinion or made an assertion that he or she finds unconvincing. Providing more development, support, or evidence will make it more likely that your readers will be persuaded to agree with your assertion. In this discussion, these words—development, support, and evidence—will be used interchangeably, although sometimes people do make fine distinctions among them.

One way to improve the evidence you provide to support your assertions is to think about your audience. What will it take to win them over to your position? What do they need to know in order to understand your point of view? What kinds of assumptions or biases might they have? Another way is to consider your purpose. What do you want to achieve through your writing? How can you choose evidence to support your goal?

When in doubt about whether you have been convincing, think harder to come up with more evidence to support your position. Below you will find a variety of types of evidence you might use.

Connecting Evidence to Your Topic Sentences and Thesis

It is usually quite clear to the *writer* of an essay why a particular piece of evidence is there and how it relates to the topic sentence of a paragraph or thesis of an essay, but sometimes this connection is not so clear to the *reader*. For example, in a paper arguing that schools in America attended by children from affluent families receive much greater financial support than schools that children from poorer families attend, a student might provide this evidence in a paragraph to support a topic sentence that addresses the fact that where students live impacts their education:

> The value of homes in affluent neighborhoods can be ten times as high as the value of those in poorer neighborhoods.

The writer knows why this is important support but hasn't made the connection clear to the reader. The writer knows that schools in America are funded by local property taxes, so wealthy neighborhoods will produce more revenue to support their schools than poorer ones. In order to make the connection explicit, she could have written this:

> Because property taxes are used to fund schools, neighborhoods with a greater proportion of wealthy families who pay higher taxes will have schools with more and better resources than neighborhoods with predominantly poorer residents who pay less.

In the same way, you want to make clear the connection between the evidence you discuss in each paragraph and your thesis. One way to do this is to ensure that each topic sentence clearly supports your main point: outlining before, during, and after drafting can help you to see the connections between the different parts of your essay. Delete or revise topic sentences that do not support your main argument. Once you are sure of your major support and how you want to present it, be sure to connect your evidence to your topic sentences, explaining how each piece supports your argument.

Types of Support

Suppose you wanted to argue that the country is not doing enough to address poverty. To support your opinion, you would need to provide evidence. As you can supply evidence to support an assertion in several different ways, similar kinds have been grouped together here. They include facts, examples, statistics or numerical evidence, expert testimony, and appeals.

Facts

It was John Adams who said that "facts are stubborn things," and indeed they are. Facts are based on reality; they are known to exist or to have happened because they have been experienced or observed. They don't leave room for argument. They establish the credibility of a writer who "knows the facts," and they can be assembled into a well-structured argument. An essay on poverty would be strengthened by the inclusion of facts like these:

- According to the US Census Bureau, a family of four earning less than $25,465 a year is living in poverty.
- According to the Center for Poverty Research at the University of California, Davis, 39.7 million Americans lived in poverty in 2017.
- According to the US Census Bureau, 13.9% of Americans were living in poverty in 2017.

For more discussion of facts, see Distinguishing among Facts, Statements Most Experts Agree On, and Opinions (21.3, p. 604).

Examples

One of the most common and most effective ways to provide support is to present examples, descriptions of situations that illustrate the point a writer is making. Examples can take several different forms such as a single brief example, an extended example with more detail, a story, or a report of the results of an interview:

- **Brief examples.** You might tell about a person you know who is living in extreme poverty. To make your argument more convincing, you might add three more examples of people living in poverty, or even add ten more. At some point, however, examples alone begin to lose their power to convince, and you need to use other types of evidence as well.

- **Extended examples.** Another way to add support to your argument might be to dig down into an example of living in poverty in greater detail: to describe what it's like to run out of food before your next payday, to be afraid to answer the phone because it might be a collection agency trying to pressure you into paying off a debt, to worry when there's a knock at the door that might mean you're being evicted, or to have to watch your daughter crying because you cannot afford the medicine to treat her earache.

- **Stories.** One of the oldest methods that human beings have used to convince an audience of a point is to tell a story. Sometimes a narrative will move a reader far more than cold statistics or expert testimony.

- **Interviews.** Another way to "dig down" into a subject is to interview one or more people who are living in poverty. Be sure to plan your interview(s) in advance, to choose relevant quotes that accurately represent your interviewee(s), and to report and document his or her words accurately. For more details on interviewing, see Conducting Interviews (22.10, p. 642).

Statistics or Numerical Evidence

Statistics are a powerful form of evidence because they represent many examples, not just one or two. Statistics as a subject is a branch of mathematics related to collecting, organizing, analyzing, and interpreting large quantities of numerical data. Statistical analysis is particularly useful for inferring general conclusions based on representative samples of people who have been asked to answer questions on specific topics. Statistical data are often presented in a visual format—a graph, chart, or infographic—that can make it easy to see trends or to compare sets of information:

- **Statistics.** Instead of adding examples to your essay on poverty one at a time, you might decide to make your argument more convincing by adding statistics that show the scale of the problem. You might do some research and report how many people in this country are living in poverty, or how many

African-American men under twenty-five live in poverty, or how many children live in poverty. You could also create graphics to illustrate and/or compare statistical information or incorporate graphs and charts from material you have researched, providing you clearly document your sources.

- **Survey results.** Sometimes it is possible to conduct a survey to support your position. If you are arguing that a large percentage of community college students are living in poverty, for example, you could conduct a survey at your college and present the information you gather. For more details on surveying, see Conducting Surveys (22.11, p. 644).

- **Analysis of trends.** When you analyze trends, you are not just looking at statistics at one point in time. You are showing how those statistics are changing over time. In the essay on poverty, for instance, you could bolster your argument by analyzing trends over time and demonstrating that the percentage of people living in poverty has increased dramatically in recent years. You could even project into the future: if nothing is changed, what percentage of Americans will be living in poverty in ten years?

Expert Testimony

On almost any topic, a little research will lead you to people who are recognized experts in their field. Supporting your argument with expert testimony, such as a quotation from economist Paul Krugman or conservative commentator David Brooks that points out that increasing levels of poverty are harmful to the nation, can make your argument more convincing. To determine whether individuals are experts in their fields, take note of their titles, publications, credentials, and how often other experts mention them. For more discussion on identifying experts, see Identifying Expertise (4.12, p. 153) and Distinguishing among Facts, Statements Most Experts Agree On, and Opinions (21.3, p. 604).

At some point in your argument about poverty, you might want to explain why your opinion is worthy of consideration, in what way you are an "expert" who should be listened to. For example, if you grew up in poverty, you may have insights that others don't have. If you worked for three years in a shelter for the homeless, you may have unique experiences. Explaining the source of your "expertise" is often a good way of supporting your argument.

Appeals

Writers often appeal to their readers to take a stand, to provide support, to express sympathy, or to change their behavior. Appeals can take many forms, including traditional appeals to ethos, logos, and pathos (see Three Types of Appeal [11.6, p. 372]), as well as appeals to people's values.

When you appeal to a reader's values, it is important that you know your audience or at least know them well enough to have some idea of their values. For example, if you are writing to a conservative and fairly wealthy audience, perhaps readers of the *Wall Street Journal*, you might want to discuss the longstanding belief in the American Dream, something many wealthy Americans support. Then you could point out that the American Dream is in danger of disappearing as more people become trapped in generational poverty.

11.4 Activity

Developing Strong Support for an Argument

Below is a thesis statement followed by a brainstormed list of the kinds of strong, convincing evidence that could be used to support it. Read the thesis and supporting evidence carefully. Then, using this example as a model, work with your group to select one of the following six theses and make a list of all the kinds of evidence that would help provide strong evidence to support it.

> **Thesis:** The United States should not attempt to overthrow rulers of Near Eastern countries, even if they are tyrannical dictators.
>
> - Examples of countries in which we have intervened with results that are disastrous (Iran, Somalia, Afghanistan, Iraq, Libya)
>
> - Statistics on the numbers of Americans who have died in several of our wars
>
> - Statistics on the number of civilians who died in the same wars
>
> - Ethical reason: It is morally wrong for one country to attempt to dictate who rules in another country.
>
> - Statements by respected officials like former Secretary of State Colin Powell, who has argued that we should not attempt such interventions

1. We need laws in this country that will make it less likely that guns will end up in the hands of violent or mentally unstable people.

2. Laws to limit people from buying guns will not keep guns out of the hands of violent or mentally unstable people.

3. The American people are losing their morality.

4. The American people are becoming more moral.

5. America is becoming more unfair than it used to be.

6. America is not perfect, but it is fairer than it used to be.

Recognizing Development Strategies in "Violence Vanquished," Steven Pinker

Read the following essay by Steven Pinker, a professor of psychology at Harvard University, and answer the questions below. This essay is adapted from his book *The Better Angels of Our Nature: Why Violence Has Declined*, published by Viking Press. The essay originally appeared in the *Wall Street Journal* on September 24, 2011.

1. Working together as a group—in a paragraph or two—describe the audience you think Pinker was writing for.

2. You'll notice that some words and phrases in the article are underlined. After you've read the article, working in your group, write a definition of each of the underlined words or phrases. Do not look them up in a dictionary; instead, use one of these five strategies for dealing with difficult language:

   a. Derive the meaning from context.

   b. Analyze the parts of the word.

   c. Back up and reread the passage.

   d. Keep reading to see if the writer explains the difficult passage.

   e. Decide the word is not important and just keep reading.

   If you'd like more information about these strategies, see Dealing with Difficult Language (20.9, p. 594).

3. Finally, after you've read the article, go back and highlight each example of evidence or support that you can find. Remember that evidence can be any of the following:

   - Examples
   - Extended examples
   - Stories
   - Interviews
   - Statistics
   - Survey results
   - Analysis of trends
   - Facts
   - Expert testimony

Violence Vanquished

STEVEN PINKER

SEPTEMBER 24, 2011

1   On the day this article appears, you will read about a shocking act of violence. Somewhere in the world there will be a terrorist bombing, a senseless murder, a bloody <u>insurrection</u>. It's impossible to learn about these catastrophes without thinking, "What is the world coming to?"

2   But a better question may be, "How bad was the world in the past?"

3   Believe it or not, the world of the past was *much* worse. Violence has been in decline for thousands of years, and today we may be living in the most peaceable era in the existence of our species.

4   The decline, to be sure, has not been smooth. It has not brought violence down to zero, and it is not guaranteed to continue. But it is a persistent historical development, visible on scales from <u>millennia</u> to years, from the waging of wars to the spanking of children.

5   This claim, I know, invites skepticism, <u>incredulity</u>, and sometimes anger. We tend to estimate the probability of an event from the ease with which we can recall examples, and scenes of <u>carnage</u> are more likely to be beamed into our homes and burned into our memories than footage of people dying of old age. There will always be enough violent deaths to fill the evening news, so people's impressions of violence will be disconnected from its actual likelihood.

6   Evidence of our bloody history is not hard to find. Consider the genocides in the Old Testament and the crucifixions in the New, the gory <u>mutilations</u> in Shakespeare's tragedies and Grimm's fairy tales, the British monarchs who beheaded their relatives and the American founders who dueled with their rivals.

7   Today the decline in these brutal practices can be quantified. A look at the numbers shows that over the course of our history, humankind has been blessed with six major declines of violence.

8   The first was a process of pacification: the transition from the anarchy of the hunting, gathering and <u>horticultural</u> societies in which our species spent most of its evolutionary history to the first agricultural civilizations, with cities and governments, starting about 5,000 years ago.

9   For centuries, social theorists like Hobbes and Rousseau speculated from their armchairs about what life was like in a "state of nature." Nowadays we can do better. Forensic archeology—a kind of "CSI: Paleolithic"—can estimate rates of violence from the proportion of skeletons in ancient sites with bashed-in skulls, <u>decapitations</u>

or arrowheads embedded in bones. And ethnographers can tally the causes of death in tribal peoples that have recently lived outside of state control.

10   These investigations show that, on average, about 15% of people in <u>prestate</u> eras died violently, compared to about 3% of the citizens of the earliest states. Tribal violence commonly <u>subsides</u> when a state or empire imposes control over a territory, leading to the various "<u>paxes</u>" (Romana, Islamica, Brittanica and so on) that are familiar to readers of history.

11   It's not that the first kings had a <u>benevolent</u> interest in the welfare of their citizens. Just as a farmer tries to prevent his livestock from killing one another, so a ruler will try to keep his subjects from cycles of raiding and feuding. From his point of view, such squabbling is a dead loss—forgone opportunities to extract taxes, tributes, soldiers and slaves.

12   The second decline of violence was a civilizing process that is best documented in Europe. Historical records show that between the late Middle Ages and the 20th century, European countries saw a 10- to 50-fold decline in their rates of homicide.

13   The numbers are consistent with narrative histories of the brutality of life in the Middle Ages, when highwaymen made travel a risk to life and limb and dinners were commonly enlivened by dagger attacks. So many people had their noses cut off that medieval medical textbooks speculated about techniques for growing them back.

14   Historians attribute this decline to the consolidation of a patchwork of feudal territories into large kingdoms with centralized authority and an infrastructure of commerce. Criminal justice was nationalized, and zero-sum plunder gave way to positive-sum trade. People increasingly controlled their impulses and sought to cooperate with their neighbors.

15   The third transition, sometimes called the Humanitarian Revolution, took off with the Enlightenment. Governments and churches had long maintained order by punishing nonconformists with mutilation, torture and gruesome forms of execution, such as burning, breaking, <u>disembowelment</u>, <u>impalement</u> and sawing in half. The 18th century saw the widespread abolition of judicial torture, including the famous prohibition of "cruel and unusual punishment" in the eighth amendment of the U.S. Constitution.

16   At the same time, many nations began to whittle down their list of capital crimes from the hundreds (including <u>poaching</u>, sodomy, witchcraft and counterfeiting) to just murder and treason. And a growing wave of countries abolished blood sports, dueling, witch hunts, religious persecution, absolute <u>despotism</u> and slavery.

17   The fourth major transition is the respite from major interstate war that we have seen since the end of World War II. Historians sometimes refer to it as the Long Peace.   ▶

18   Today we take it for granted that Italy and Austria will not come to blows, nor will Britain and Russia. But centuries ago, the great powers were almost always at war, and until quite recently, Western European countries tended to initiate two or three new wars every year. The cliché that the 20th century was "the most violent in history" ignores the second half of the century (and may not even be true of the first half, if one calculates violent deaths as a proportion of the world's population).

19   Though it's tempting to attribute the Long Peace to nuclear deterrence, non-nuclear developed states have stopped fighting each other as well. Political scientists point instead to the growth of democracy, trade and international organizations—all of which, the statistical evidence shows, reduce the likelihood of conflict. They also credit the rising valuation of human life over national grandeur—a hard-won lesson of two world wars.

20   The fifth trend, which I call the New Peace, involves war in the world as a whole, including developing nations. Since 1946, several organizations have tracked the number of armed conflicts and their human toll world-wide. The bad news is that for several decades, the decline of interstate wars was accompanied by a bulge of civil wars, as newly independent countries were led by <u>inept</u> governments, challenged by <u>insurgencies</u> and armed by the cold war superpowers.

21   The less bad news is that civil wars tend to kill far fewer people than wars between states. And the best news is that, since the peak of the cold war in the 1970s and '80s, organized conflicts of all kinds—civil wars, genocides, repression by autocratic governments, terrorist attacks—have declined throughout the world, and their death tolls have declined even more precipitously.

22   The rate of documented direct deaths from political violence (war, terrorism, genocide and warlord militias) in the past decade is an unprecedented few hundredths of a percentage point. Even if we multiplied that rate to account for unrecorded deaths and the victims of war-caused disease and famine, it would not exceed 1%.

23   The most immediate cause of this New Peace was the demise of communism, which ended the <u>proxy</u> wars in the developing world stoked by the superpowers and also discredited genocidal ideologies that had justified the sacrifice of vast numbers of eggs to make a utopian omelet. Another contributor was the expansion of international peacekeeping forces, which really do keep the peace—not always, but far more often than when adversaries are left to fight to the bitter end.

24   Finally, the postwar era has seen a <u>cascade</u> of "rights revolutions"—a growing revulsion against aggression on smaller scales. In the developed world, the civil rights movement obliterated lynchings and lethal <u>pogroms</u>, and the women's-rights movement has helped to shrink the incidence of rape and the beating and killing of wives and girlfriends.

25   In recent decades, the movement for children's rights has significantly reduced rates of spanking, bullying, paddling in schools, and physical and sexual abuse. And the campaign for gay rights has forced governments in the developed world to repeal laws criminalizing homosexuality and has had some success in reducing hate crimes against gay people.

*   *   *

26   Why has violence declined so dramatically for so long? Is it because violence has literally been bred out of us, leaving us more peaceful by nature?

27   This seems unlikely. Evolution has a speed limit measured in generations, and many of these declines have unfolded over decades or even years. Toddlers continue to kick, bite and hit; little boys continue to play-fight; people of all ages continue to <u>snipe</u> and bicker, and most of them continue to harbor violent fantasies and to enjoy violent entertainment.

28   It's more likely that human nature has always comprised inclinations toward violence and inclinations that counteract them—such as self-control, empathy, fairness and reason—what Abraham Lincoln called "the better angels of our nature." Violence has declined because historical circumstances have increasingly favored our better angels.

29   The most obvious of these pacifying forces has been the state, with its monopoly on the legitimate use of force. A disinterested judiciary and police can defuse the temptation of exploitative attack, inhibit the impulse for revenge and <u>circumvent</u> the self-serving biases that make all parties to a dispute believe that they are on the side of the angels.

30   We see evidence of the pacifying effects of government in the way that rates of killing declined following the expansion and consolidation of states in tribal societies and in medieval Europe. And we can watch the movie in reverse when violence erupts in zones of anarchy, such as the Wild West, failed states and neighborhoods controlled by mafias and street gangs, who can't call 911 or file a lawsuit to resolve their disputes but have to administer their own rough justice.

31   Another pacifying force has been commerce, a game in which everybody can win. As technological progress allows the exchange of goods and ideas over longer distances and among larger groups of trading partners, other people become more valuable alive than dead. They switch from being targets of demonization and dehumanization to potential partners in reciprocal altruism.

32   For example, though the relationship today between America and China is far from warm, we are unlikely to declare war on them or vice versa. Morality aside, they make too much of our stuff, and we owe them too much money.

33   A third peacemaker has been <u>cosmopolitanism</u>—the expansion of people's <u>parochial</u> little worlds through literacy, mobility, education, science, history, journalism and mass media. These forms of virtual reality can prompt people to take

▶

the perspective of people unlike themselves and to expand their circle of sympathy to embrace them.

34   These technologies have also powered an expansion of rationality and objectivity in human affairs. People are now less likely to privilege their own interests over those of others. They reflect more on the way they live and consider how they could be better off. Violence is often <u>reframed</u> as a problem to be solved rather than as a contest to be won. We devote ever more of our brainpower to guiding our better angels. It is probably no coincidence that the Humanitarian Revolution came on the heels of the Age of Reason and the Enlightenment, that the Long Peace and rights revolutions coincided with the electronic global village.

35   Whatever its causes, the implications of the historical decline of violence are profound. So much depends on whether we see our era as a nightmare of crime, terrorism, genocide and war or as a period that, in the light of the historical and statistical facts, is blessed by unprecedented levels of peaceful coexistence.

36   Bearers of good news are often advised to keep their mouths shut, lest they lull people into <u>complacency</u>. But this prescription may be backward. The discovery that fewer people are victims of violence can thwart cynicism among compassion-fatigued news readers who might otherwise think that the dangerous parts of the world are irredeemable hell holes. And a better understanding of what drove the numbers down can steer us toward doing things that make people better off rather than congratulating ourselves on how moral we are.

37   As one becomes aware of the historical decline of violence, the world begins to look different. The past seems less innocent, the present less sinister. One starts to appreciate the small gifts of coexistence that would have seemed utopian to our ancestors: the interracial family playing in the park, the comedian who lands a zinger on the commander in chief, the countries that quietly back away from a crisis instead of escalating to war.

38   For all the <u>tribulations</u> in our lives, for all the troubles that remain in the world, the decline of violence is an accomplishment that we can <u>savor</u>—and an <u>impetus</u> to cherish the forces of civilization and enlightenment that made it possible.

11.6   Tutorial

Three Types of Appeal: Logos, Ethos, and Pathos

Evidence is certainly essential to supporting your position in an essay, but there is another strategy, another way of thinking about strengthening your argument—*appeals*, an odd word. Think about a politician *appealing* for your vote or a nonprofit *appealing* for donations. In this sense, to appeal is to attempt to persuade, and more than 3,000 years ago, the Greek philosopher Aristotle identified three ways to make appeals to an audience. He called them *logos*, *ethos*, and *pathos*, and we still use these Greek terms today. When you consciously decide to appeal in one of these three ways, you are trying to figure out what sort of an argument will be most likely to convince your reader. It is also possible to use more than one appeal for your audience.

Logos. If you are using *logos* as your appeal to the reader, you are using reason and logic. In fact, the English word *logic* comes from the Greek word *logos*. Using logic, your goal is to demonstrate to your reader that your argument is sensible and reasonable, that the evidence you present is trustworthy, and that the evidence demonstrates the validity of your thesis.

Ethos. Using *ethos*, your goal is to convince your reader that you are trustworthy. To accomplish this, you need to convince your reader that you know what you're talking about, that you've "done your homework." It's also important to show the reader you have no ulterior motives, that you have integrity. (The English word *ethical* is derived from *ethos*.) If your reader detects any "stretching" of the truth, any distortion of the facts, or any exaggeration in your reporting of information, your credibility will be undermined, making it less likely that your reader will be persuaded.

Pathos. When you use *pathos* to convince readers, you are using emotions and feelings. You are trying to convince your readers of the validity of your argument by appealing to their values and beliefs. Giving moving details, designed to appeal more to the readers' hearts than their minds, is one way to employ *pathos*. Appeals to *pathos* may not be as effective as *logos* or *ethos*, but they often succeed when combined with *logos*.

11.7 Tutorial

Avoiding Logical Fallacies

There are ways of arguing that are widely seen as unfair, unethical, or dishonest. These kinds of argument, called *fallacies*, are based on illogical statements, manipulation, or deception and should be avoided. *Ethos*, discussed in Three Types of Appeal above, is impossible to achieve if your reader sees you as untrustworthy.

Common Rhetorical Fallacies

Some of the most common fallacies are described below, and you should avoid using them in your writing as they are more likely to alienate your readers than to convince them.

Ad Hominem.   Instead of challenging a person's position, the writer attacks his or her character.

> The senator's proposal for free community college tuition is a terrible idea because she is an elitist, East Coast liberal.

Bandwagon Fallacy.   Here, the position is that many people agree with your argument, so your readers should too. However, the majority opinion is not always the right or best one.

> Recent polls show that 60% of Americans want tougher laws on background checks before people buy guns, so you should support the proposal to make background checks mandatory.

Begging the Question.   Sometimes called *circular reasoning*, this involves arguing a position simply by stating it again in different words.

> Driving a motorcycle without a helmet is unsafe because it is dangerous.

False Analogy.   In this fallacy, the writer compares two things that have some similarities and assumes they are similar in other ways, even if they are not.

> Elections in America are like circuses, so we can't take them seriously.

False Choice.   This fallacy assumes that in an argument there are only two choices: the one the writer is proposing or something unacceptable, when, in fact, there are other choices.

> You must resist all gun control laws, or you are against the Second Amendment.

Hasty (or Sweeping) Generalizations.   Closely related to stereotyping, this dangerous fallacy makes assertions about everyone belonging to a group because of the characteristics of some people in the group.

> Millennials don't understand what hard work is.

Post Hoc Ergo Propter Hoc.   Latin for "After this, therefore because of this." In this fallacy, it is argued that because something happened right after something else, the first event *caused* the second.

> The budget for the Department of the Interior has been reduced by 15%; as a result, the population of wolves in Wyoming, Idaho, and Montana has dropped by 50%.

Slippery Slope.   This is an argument that says that if one thing is done, catastrophic events will inevitably follow.

> If the state passes a 1% tax increase, within five years our taxes will have tripled.

Straw Man.   The writer distorts an opponent's argument into something easily refuted and then argues against that argument instead of the opponent's actual argument.

> The Democrats don't want border security, so to protect the country, we need to elect a Republican Congress next year.

TOPIC 12
Organizing Ideas

This Topic discusses strategies for ensuring that when you write, your ideas are organized to have the maximum impact on the reader.

Navigating Topic 12

The tutorials and presentation listed below provide practical advice on how to logically organize ideas in your academic writing. After each strategy is presented, there is an activity allowing you to practice it. You can work through the entire Topic on your own, learning about all the strategies and practicing them; work on items you've been assigned by your instructor; or choose just the ones you find helpful.

Introduction to Organizing Ideas

Topic 12 starts with a discussion of how to ensure your writing is unified by checking that your support directly relates to your thesis statement and making sure you do not change the focus of your thesis as you move through your essay. It continues with an explanation of how to chunk and order ideas to support your argument and finishes with a series of examples of ways to ensure coherence (the smooth flow of ideas) in your essay through the use of logical organization, repetition of key words and pronouns, and the use of transitional words and phrases.

12.1 Tutorial

Unity

Unity is the quality of belonging to a whole. A football team has unity when all the parts—the linemen, the running backs, the defensive team, and even the coaches—are working together as a team. If the backfield thinks the linemen are missing their blocks, or if the offense thinks the defense is missing too many tackles, or if the coaches think the players aren't staying in shape—if the different parts of the team aren't working well together—the team isn't unified (and probably isn't winning a lot of games).

An essay is unified when all the parts work together. An essay has unity problems when parts of the essay do not work well with the other parts and do not support the thesis of the essay.

Unity Problems Caused by Unrelated Material

As an example, an essay might start out with a clear thesis, but then some parts of the essay wander away from that thesis and, in extreme cases, may even begin supporting a different thesis. The essay that follows has these kinds of unity problems.

Is It Possible to "Get Ahead" in America?

It has often been said that "in America, if you work hard you will get ahead," but I believe that <u>most Americans, even if they work hard, will not get ahead</u>.

One important reason many Americans can't work their way out of poverty is our unequal education system. Funding for schools is based on property taxes paid in each local school district. School systems located in poorer areas are underfunded because the property in those areas is of much lower value than property in wealthy suburbs. Lower funding leads to buildings that are often dilapidated, textbooks that are in short supply, and teachers who are paid lower salaries than their counterparts in wealthier areas. In many cases, the most effective teachers in poor schools leave after a few years for the higher salaries in wealthier school districts.

To make matters worse, many students from truly wealthy families are sent to private schools where they have beautiful surroundings, the best teachers, small class sizes, and access to guidance and counselling services. <u>Many of these kids have grown up in families that put pressure on them to succeed, which leads them to suffer from psychological problems. Depression, bipolar disorder, and even suicide are common among these students. Sometimes their families spend more on therapy and medication than they do on education.</u>

Young people who grow up in poverty usually don't have the kinds of connections that help them to obtain a good job. Their parents, too often, do not have the kinds of jobs in large corporations or offices where they can help their kids meet people who might hire them. They seldom have older brothers or sisters who can introduce them to people who can give them advice about how to move up in the world. In fact, sometimes, when they do get a job interview at a place where they have a chance of advancement, they are simply unfamiliar with the protocol for such meetings.

Here's the thesis.

This paragraph provides the first reason that lots of Americans won't get ahead even if they work hard: the education system is unequal.

Note that the underlined portion of this paragraph is no longer discussing the thesis of the essay but has wandered into a discussion of unrelated problems experienced by wealthy students.

This paragraph gives a second argument in support of the thesis: lack of social connections. No unity problem here.

In addition, young people who grow up in lower-income households frequently don't have role models to follow and to receive encouragement from. Many of these young students are the first in their families to attempt to go to college. They, too often, don't know someone who can "teach them the ropes." And frequently they are under pressure to get a job and start supporting a family.

<u>The belief that all it takes to "get ahead" is hard work results in people thinking that if they haven't gotten ahead, it's their fault: they didn't work hard enough. In fact, there are many causes why, despite hard work, many don't get ahead—an education system that doesn't treat them fairly, the struggle to find the right balance of time and money, a personal crisis, or a personal mistake.</u> **It takes more than hard work to get ahead in America. It takes luck . . . or being born into a middle-class family.**

Sometimes these young people give up on college and decide just to try to make it in the workplace. Starting in jobs that don't require a college education, they find, no matter how hard they work, that they just can't get a promotion. Often, they work more and more hours—60 or 70 a week—and they are, nevertheless, barely keeping themselves above water. Then a crisis hits. They become pregnant. They become sick. Their job is eliminated. Suddenly, they're deep in debt with no hope of digging themselves out. They worked hard, but it didn't pay off.

This paragraph gives a third reason to support the thesis: no role models. It supports the thesis.

This paragraph discusses a related issue but does not support the thesis, so it should be deleted, but the bolded sentence could make a powerful end to the essay.

Another paragraph that supports the thesis. Another reason why, even after working hard, some people don't "get ahead."

Unity Problems Caused by a Change of Focus

A different kind of unity problem occurs when writers start out with a good strong thesis and then, as they continue writing, change their mind about the thesis, so that by the end of the essay, they are arguing a different position.

Greg's brief essay, which appears below, illustrates this second kind of unity problem. It is also an essay that needs more development with evidence and examples. (See Development, Support, or Evidence [11.3, p. 362] for more on how to develop and support a thesis.)

Strengthen the Drunk Driving Laws!

Montana needs tougher laws against drunk driving. Everyone know that too many Montanans are being injured or even killed by people who are driving when impaired by alcohol.

A few years ago, my sister was in a crosswalk and was hit by a drunk driver. Margie was in the hospital for six weeks and still suffers from intense pain in her hip. Even though the driver of the other car was convicted of DWI, he was given probation before judgment.

When a jerk in my class in high school was found guilty of driving while intoxicated for the second time, the judge believed the "sob story" his lawyer told and gave him a sentence of only six months, which was then suspended.

When a little girl in my neighborhood was killed by a drunk driver, the judge, who has a reputation for being lenient, sentenced him to "time served."

After reading about these horrific cases, I hope you'll agree that judges in Montana need to start giving tougher sentences for drunk driving.

The clear thesis of this paper appears as the first sentence:

"Montana needs tougher laws against drunk driving."

But look at the closing sentence, in which the writer seems to intend to restate the thesis in different words:

"Judges in Montana need to start giving tougher sentences for drunk driving."

The problem is that the writer has changed his mind. He no longer believes that Montana needs "tougher laws," but that the state needs "tougher judges."

So how would you fix this unity problem? The most obvious (but least effective way) would be to change the final sentence so it agrees with the thesis in the first sentence. This would be ineffective because all the examples given in the essay illustrate problems with lenient judges, not lenient laws. Much more effective would be to change the first sentence so it agrees with the last sentence. Then the paper would be unified because the thesis would remain constant from beginning to end, with the evidence in the body of the essay all supporting that thesis.

There is, however, an additional problem with the essay. It doesn't present very convincing evidence to support the thesis. Three brief descriptions of personal experiences are one kind of evidence, but if the writer wants to argue that this is a major problem for the state of Montana, he needs to find evidence on a much larger scale—evidence that these lenient judges are prevalent throughout the state, data showing that large numbers of drunk drivers are getting away with slaps on their wrists, and evidence that some experts have agreed that lenient judges are a large problem.

12.2 Activity

Evaluating Thesis and Unity

Working in your group, read the following essay, identify the thesis, and identify any places where there are unity problems.

Motorcycle Helmets and Individual Freedom

Many states have laws requiring motorcyclists to wear helmets when riding their bikes. These laws violate the principle of individual freedom. Henry David Thoreau wrote in "Civil Disobedience," "That government is best that governs least," and Lincoln is reported to have said, "My freedom to swing my arms ends where your nose begins."

I agree with Thoreau that the government should pass as few laws as possible, thereby maximizing individual freedom. And I agree with Lincoln that we only need laws to prevent one person's freedom from harming another person. The law requiring motorcycle helmets is a violation of these principles and an attack on the individual freedom of Americans.

I recognize that some laws are necessary. We need a law that says I must drive on the right side of the road so I don't crash into people coming from the opposite direction. I understand laws that

---

say I can't fire a weapon in a public place because I could kill or injure someone. I understand laws that require people who own factories to provide necessary safety measures because, if they didn't, they could harm their workers.

But why do we need laws requiring employers to check the immigration status of their employees? These laws don't protect the employees from being harmed by their employer; they are a restriction on the employer's individual freedom. How about laws requiring that I get my children vaccinated? Don't I have individual freedom to make decisions about my own children's health?

Clearly the law requiring motorcycle helmets violates personal freedom. I understand that people think these helmets save lives, and I suppose they do. But if I choose to take chances with my own life, isn't that my choice? If I choose not to wear a helmet and then crash into a tree, I'm the only one who suffers. I haven't done harm to anyone else.

There is nothing more exhilarating than cruising down a highway on a spring afternoon with the wind blowing through my hair. I can smell the flowers blooming along the sides of the road and hear the songs of the birds. It's just not the same experience if I'm wearing a helmet.

I'm fine with the government passing laws requiring me to drive on the right side of the road, to have headlights that work, and to have brakes that work. Those laws are there to prevent me from harming other people. But laws like the helmet law—laws that protect me only from myself—are a gross violation of individual liberty.

12.3 Writing

One Unusual Thing

Write a brief, one-page essay in which you tell your instructor one unusual thing about your family or about your high school. He or she will be reading these papers to get to know each of you but also to begin a discussion of how to make your writing more effective. Please provide concrete examples to back up what you write about your family or school.

12.4 Activity

Thesis and Unity in One Unusual Thing

You may recall that most successful college essays focus on a single idea or main point, which is known as the thesis. The writing assignment in One Unusual Thing (12.3, p. 382) was "to tell your instructor *one* unusual thing about your family or about your high school." In other words, you were asked to write an essay with a thesis: the "one unusual thing" about your family or your high school.

Your instructor will organize the class into groups of three or four and give each group copies of some of the papers your class turned in for that assignment. Work together with your group to decide if each paper is about just "one unusual thing." If a paper discusses two or three different "unusual things," it would not be following the assignment, and it would not have a single, clear thesis. If it starts out discussing a particular "interesting thing," but changes its focus to something different by the end, again, it doesn't have a single, clear thesis. After about twenty minutes, the groups will report out on how well each of the essays is organized.

12.5 Presentation

Chunking and Ordering

To watch this presentation on chunking and ordering, which involves chunking ideas into related groups and ordering those groups to build the body of your essay, go to *Achieve for The Hub*, Topic 12, and open Unit 12.5.

12.6 Activity

Practice Chunking

Here's a brainstormed list on one of the suggested topics from Using Brainstorming to Narrow a Topic (10.4, p. 345)—religion. Chunk these items. In other words, organize them into logical groups or chunks of ideas that are related. Then give each chunk a label.

Is religion dying out?

How does someone choose a religion?

What do most religions have in common?

Religions provide guidance for how to lead a good life.

Definition of religion

What is not a religion?

Do religions have to believe in a god/gods?

Religions provide comfort when people experience tragedy or loss.

What do religions say about other religions?

What do people get out of religion?

Religion helps people to accept death.

Is Alcoholics Anonymous a religion?

Religions provide community and companionship.

Religions can motivate people to go to war.

Religion is the opiate of the people.

Religion motivates people to resist giving in to animal instincts.

How do religions start?

Religions provide support for the needy

12.7 Activity

Practice Ordering Ideas

In Practice Chunking (12.6, p. 383), you grouped brainstormed ideas into logical "chunks" and gave each "chunk" a name.

For this activity, you will decide on the order in which you would like to discuss your "chunks" of ideas in an essay. In the process, you may think of some ideas to add or decide to move some ideas from one "chunk" into another. When you finish, you will have a thoughtful and well-organized plan for an essay, almost an outline.

12.8 Tutorial

Coherence

Coherence is simply the connection of ideas within a piece of writing to make logical sense to the reader and ensure he or she can follow the writer's line of thought. When people read a coherent text, they easily understand the parts, how they fit together, and why they are in the order presented. A piece of writing is not coherent when the reader has trouble following the writer's argument because the ideas do not connect smoothly or obviously.

Three ways to improve the coherence of your writing are logical organization, repetition of key words and pronouns, and the use of transitions.

Logical Organization

One way to ensure coherence is to organize a sequence of ideas in a recognizably logical order—from general to specific, most important to least important (or vice versa), first to last (chronological), near to far (or back to front), bottom to top (or top to bottom), or left to right (or right to left).

General to Specific

Travel can be very educational. You learn all kinds of new information when you visit a place you've never been to before, but you also meet new people with new ways of looking at the world. Most enjoyable, you experience new kinds of food—tastes you never would have sampled at home.

Most Important to Least Important

The primary reason I am going to college is to gain the skills and credentials that will lead to a good job when I graduate. I also want to learn about ideas and people and ways of seeing the world that are different from what I experienced growing up in my hometown of Lawton, Oklahoma. It is also important to me that I understand political issues better. I sometimes listen to debates on television about issues I should care about, but I don't know enough to really have an opinion.

First to Last (Chronological)

When I first came to Lakeland Community College, I felt totally confused. I was supposed to pay my bill in the Bursar's Office, but I didn't even know what a bursar was. When I sat down in my first class and the instructor started explaining the syllabus, her policy on plagiarism, and office hours, I had the vague notion that these things were important, but I didn't really know what they were. Today, after two years at this school, I feel like an expert. I know my way around. In fact, this summer I will be working as a student guide for new students who come to orientation.

Near to Far

Out of my window, I see tree branches crisscrossing the panes of glass. They belong to the maple tree beside the front door, and now, in winter, they are bare except for a few withered brown leaves. Beyond the branches, behind a row of trees, stretches the front lawn, carpeted in snow, and scattered with branches from a recent storm. Far in back to the left, insulated with tarpaper and surrounded by an electric fence is the beehive, warm and still quietly humming despite the subzero temperatures.

Bottom to Top

I live in an eight-story building in downtown Denver. As you approach the building at street level, you'll see a series of small shops—a men's clothing store, a bookstore, a computer store, and, of course, a Starbucks. As you look up, you'll notice seven floors of apartments with large glass windows and little balconies cantilevered out into space. If you lean back and look all the way up to the top, you may get a glimpse of people sitting around in chairs while others swim in the rooftop pool.

Left to Right

It's a small room with slanted ceilings and windows facing south and east. On the left side there is a shelf filled with books, a window hung with glass ornaments and a shell wind chime, and a calendar. In the middle, in front of the south-facing window, is a desk and chair, a computer, a phone, and containers of pens and pencils. On the right side is another desk with drawers full of files and an odd-shaped closet, without a door, lined with shelves jammed with office supplies.

Repetition of Key Words and Pronouns

Coherence in a text can be enhanced by repetition of a key word, the use of synonyms for that word, and the repetition of pronouns referring to that word. In the following text, note the repetition of the term *scientist*, the use of *these experts* as a synonym for the word *scientists*, and the use of the pronoun *they* to refer to the scientists.

Scientists studying the warming of the planet are increasingly worried. They point to the melting of the Arctic ice cap as one alarming development. In a recent study by these scientists, it was announced that the rate of melting in 2012 was nearly four times the rate in 2003. When these experts looked at melting in Antarctica, they found that melting there is contributing more to rising sea levels than previously thought. In addition, other scientists suggest that the warming of the oceans is proceeding at a faster rate than predicted. If nothing is done, these experts predict that sea levels will rise by more than two feet, and 32 to 80 million people will experience coastal flooding within twenty years.

Use of Transitional Expressions

Another way to improve coherence is to use transitional expressions, words and phrases such as *for example*, *as a result*, and *finally*. These expressions serve as signposts, helping the reader follow the text and the connections being made within it. Here's a chart of the most common transitional expressions organized by their function.

To signal sequence	again, also, then, first, second, last, next, before, after
To signal time	later, subsequently, in the meantime, the next day, a week later, after a while, in a few days, within minutes, earlier that day
To signal examples	for example, for instance, specifically, such as, to illustrate, namely, specifically
To signal location	in front of, beside, behind, nearby, next to, adjacent to, below, beyond, elsewhere, to the left, to the right, near, far
To signal summary	hence, in summary, to summarize, in brief, in conclusion, as a result, as I have demonstrated
To signal comparison	in the same way, likewise, similarly, also
To signal contrast	in contrast, on the other hand, however, instead, nevertheless, regardless, but, yet, on the contrary
To signal causation	as a result, therefore, thus, so, accordingly, fortunately, consequently

The following two paragraphs demonstrate how much transitional expressions help make a piece of writing coherent. In Paragraph 1, the transitional expressions have been omitted. Read it first. With a little effort, you should be able to understand what it says. Then read Paragraph 2, in which transitional expressions have been inserted. The difference between these two paragraphs demonstrates how important transitional expressions are to coherence.

Paragraph 1

When Jeanine started her new job as a server at Ciao, a high-end Italian restaurant, she was a little nervous because of her lack of experience. She didn't know how to pronounce many of the Italian words on the menu. The more experienced servers were very helpful. They showed her how to put in a drink order at the bar and how to let the kitchen know if a customer had an allergy. She became more comfortable and more confident. She is one of those experienced servers who help out the newcomers, but she still has trouble pronouncing *bruschetta*.

Paragraph 2

When Jeanine started her new job as a server at Ciao, a high-end Italian restaurant, she was a little nervous because of her lack of experience. <u>For example</u>, she didn't know how to pronounce many of the Italian words on the menu. <u>Fortunately</u>, the more experienced servers were very helpful. <u>For instance</u>, they showed her how to put in a drink order at the bar and how to let the kitchen know if a customer had an allergy. <u>As a result</u>, she became more comfortable and more confident. <u>Today</u>, she is one of those experienced servers who help out the newcomers, but she still has trouble pronouncing *bruschetta*.

12.9 Activity

Editing for Coherence

Working in your group, revise the following essay by making the organization more logical, repeating key words and phrases, and adding transitional words and phrases.

Making Millions

I'm working on becoming a millionaire. It's a good thing I have lots of energy, because I'm going to need it. I'm only twenty-five but I'm handling a lot more than the average young adult. I juggle a 40-hour work week, 15 credit hours of school, and two kids on a daily basis. I'm not talking about your average Monday through Friday 9 to 5 type of job, either. It's more along the lines of 1:00 to 7:00 PM six days a week with a random day off. Oops, I almost forgot. There's one more complication. Sundays offer variety— often in the form of a migraine—with a schedule (for my convenience, of course) of 6:00 to 2:00 AM for those of us who need no sleep before our Monday morning classes. Monday morning, I need even more of it to get up and running.

After school and after work is when I really need a supply of it. Off I go to the Kiddie Academy in Brookdale (or to Hampton if it happens to be Saturday) to pick up my two gregarious children. I have one daughter, Lakia, age 5 (Kindergartener Extraordinaire) and one son, Blake, age 3 (The Accident King). Lakia, while good at heart, already has the curse of the brilliant child—boredom. This requires constant attention and a lot of work on my part. I need to be the source of all things entertaining on an around-the-clock basis or suffer the consequences of her overactive imagination. Even under the most intense supervision, my son Blake is an accident always happening. I thank God that he has "Super Powers" (although I object strongly to calling him Power Ranger Blake [the green one]) that allow him to feel no pain. I have never had to clean up so many spills or take so many trips to the emergency room as I do now. If only I had that "no fear" attitude toward doing things that I lost around the time of puberty.

Which brings me to my newly found hobby of returning to school. Amidst and in opposition to, multiple family members' warnings that I was "already too busy to take on any more responsibilities," I started back to school this semester. And I came back with a vengeance. I wasn't going to go to school part-time and have it take forever. I was slow in starting to begin with. So, five classes and 15 credits later, here I am, running a little low on enthusiasm. Besides, my boss was kind enough to let me come to work at one, as opposed to my pre-student hour of noon.

What it takes to be a full-time mom, student, and professional adult is phenomenal. Yet, somehow, I do it (without help) 24/7, 365 days a year with a reasonable amount of sanity. If I could figure out a way to bottle all that stuff—could you imagine the millions I would make?

TOPIC 13

Using Language Powerfully

It's not surprising that good writers carefully edit their writing to ensure there are no errors, that everything is grammatically correct. In this Topic, however, you will be working on a different issue—not just "Is my writing correct?" but also "Have I said this in the clearest, most exact, most powerful way I can?"

Navigating Topic 13

The tutorials listed below provide information about strategies for writing powerfully, and each contains, or is followed by, an opportunity to apply the skills you have just learned. You can work through the entire Topic on your own, learning about all the strategies and practicing them; work on items you've been assigned by your instructor; or choose just the ones you find helpful.

Introduction to Using Language Powerfully

This Topic focuses on strategies for enhancing your writing by using language more powerfully. Understanding the difference between connotation and denotation; including concrete, sensory details; choosing the right words for the writing occasion; using figurative language; and knowing how to use a dictionary to find the precise word you need and to determine the meanings of confusing words will all help you to communicate more effectively.

13.1 Tutorial

Connotation and Denotation

To use language effectively, you have to be careful to choose words that convey exactly what you mean to say. Take a look at the twelve words or phrases listed below.

mogul	fat cat	well-to-do person
billionaire	wealthy person	moneyed person
tycoon	person of means	loaded
magnate	affluent person	prosperous

In one sense, these words all *mean* the same thing. They all refer to someone who has a lot of money. But, in another sense, their meanings are quite different. If you say someone is *prosperous*, you are implying that they worked hard and earned a lot of money; if you say someone is *moneyed*, it is more likely you are suggesting they were born into wealth. To say someone is a *fat cat* means something very different from saying someone is a *person of means*. Describing someone as *loaded* is not the same as describing them as *wealthy*.

The basic meaning, shared by all these words, is that the persons referred to have a lot of money. This basic meaning of a word is known as its *denotation*. *Connotation* is the term used to refer to the secondary meanings that have come to be associated with words, meanings that often have cultural or emotional overtones. For example, the term *fat cat* is often used to refer to powerful businesspeople or politicians to indicate disapproval of the way they use their wealth or influence, while calling someone a *person of means* is more neutral but can suggest the person is not only wealthy but has inherited money as a result of belonging to the upper class. Saying someone is *loaded* is slang for saying they are *wealthy*: you might use the former when talking to friends but the latter in an academic essay.

When writing, be careful to select words with the precise denotative meaning you want to convey and be sure that any connotative meanings are in line with what you mean to communicate. Also take into account the writing situation: words that are appropriate in informal writing situations, such as emails or letters to friends, are not necessarily the right choice in college writing assignments or workplace writing like memos or reports.

Activity: Explaining Differences in Meaning

Working in your group, write an explanation of the differences in meaning among the following two sets of words.

Set 1

unusual	bizarre	abnormal
odd	weird	unnatural

Set 2

articulate	voluble	rambling
glib	prolix	verbose

13.2   Activity

Seeing How Concrete Language Works

Working in your group, read and discuss the following two versions of the same passage. After ten minutes, each group will report out their answers to these two questions:

1. Which is more effective?
2. Why?

Passage 1

On most days, when I enter the Capitol, a train carries me from the building where my office is located through a tunnel lined with flags and seals. The train halts and I make my way, past people, to the elevators that take me to the second floor. Stepping off, I walk around the press who normally gather there, say hello to the Capitol Police, and enter, through double doors, onto the floor of the U.S. Senate.

The Senate chamber is not the most beautiful space in the Capitol, but it is imposing nonetheless. The walls are set off by panels and columns. Overhead, the ceiling is an oval, with an American eagle in its center. Above the visitors' gallery are statues of the nation's first twenty vice-presidents.

Passage 2

On most days, I enter the Capitol through the basement. A small subway train carries me from the Hart Building, where my office is located, through an underground tunnel lined with the flags and seals of the fifty states. The train creaks to a halt and I make my way, past bustling staffers, maintenance crews, and the occasional tour group, to the bank of old elevators that takes me to the second floor. Stepping off, I weave around the swarm of press that normally gathers there, say hello to the Capitol Police, and enter, through a stately set of double doors, onto the floor of the U.S. Senate.

The Senate chamber is not the most beautiful space in the Capitol, but it is imposing nonetheless. The dun-colored walls are set off by panels of blue damask and columns of finely veined marble. Overhead, the ceiling forms a creamy white oval, with an American eagle etched in its center. Above the visitors' gallery, the busts of the nation's first twenty vice presidents sit in solemn repose.

—Barack Obama, *Audacity of Hope*, pages 13–14

13.3 Tutorial

Using Concrete Language to Bring Writing to Life

Abstract language is used to describe ideas and qualities that do not have a physical presence. For example, common abstract terms are words like *democracy*, *sexism*, *success*, *freedom*, *ideal*, or *love*, all of which convey concepts. All of them are open to different interpretations depending on how they are used, by whom, and in what context.

Concrete language refers to specific sensory details—descriptive words related to sight, sound, touch, smell, and taste—that bring writing to life. Examples of these types of words are *black velvet curtains, golden daffodils, knives and forks, sewage fumes, hurricane winds*, and *screeching brakes*, all of which relate to the physical world and can be perceived through the senses.

Here is a paragraph from *The Painted Drum* by Louise Erdrich. The narrator, Faye Travers, who handles estate sales, uses concrete and sensory language to describe an old house she is visiting to assess the contents.

The Tatro house is not grand anymore. The original nineteenth-century homestead has been renovated and enlarged so many times that its style is entirely obscured. Here a cornice, there a ledge. The building is now a great clapboard mishmash, a warehouse with aluminum-clad storm windows bolted over the old rippled glass and a screen porch tacked darkly across its front. The siding is painted the brown-red color of old blood. The overall appearance is rattling and sad, but the woman who greets me is cheerful enough, and the inside of the house is comfortable, but dim. The rooms are filled with an odor I have grown used to in my work. It is a smell that alerts me, an indefinable scent, really, composed of mothballs and citrus oil, of long settled dust and cracked leather. The smell of old things is what it is. My pulse ticks as I note that even on the ground floor an inordinate number of closets have been added during some period of expansion. Some run the length of whole walls, I estimate, roughly the room's proportions.

Erdrich uses concrete details to describe the look of the house: "nineteenth-century homestead," "[h]ere a cornice, there a ledge," "aluminum-clad storm windows," and siding "painted the brown-red color of old blood," a vivid image. She describes how it smells, an "indefinable scent . . . composed of mothballs and citrus oil, of long settled dust and cracked leather," and how it makes her feel, "my pulse ticks," indicating her rising excitement at the treasures she might find. As you read these descriptive details, you can see and smell and experience what the narrator is seeing, smelling, and experiencing.

Adding these kinds of details to your writing will not only make it more interesting for your readers but also make it more accurate and informative. Whether you are telling a story, providing an example, describing a scene, or making a persuasive case, including concrete details will add color and life to your words.

13.4 Activity

Adding Concrete Language

Working in your group, edit the following text to make it more concrete and specific. To do this, you will need to simply "make up" relevant concrete details.

When I got home from work last night, I was exhausted. All I wanted was a quick dinner, a bottle of beer, and an early bedtime. Then I opened the refrigerator and discovered that the meat I planned to cook had gone bad. Worse yet, my roommate had drunk my last bottle of beer. So off I went to the local store to purchase a few things. Coming out of the store with my supplies, I discovered I had a flat tire. After changing the tire and driving home, I was too tired to cook, so I headed straight to bed.

13.5 Activity

Words, Fancy and Plain

In this activity, you will be asked to think about the word choice that is most effective in a series of writing situations. You will be asked to think about when simple, clear language would work best and when more sophisticated language would be more effective. For most of the following items, there is room for argument about the best answer. In fact, that's the point of this activity: not to get you arguing but to get you thinking about the different options the English language offers.

For each of the items below, working in your group, discuss the pros and cons of the different choices of words used to express the same idea. If your group can agree on which option is the most effective in an item, write a short explanation of why you selected that option. If you cannot agree, write a brief discussion of the strengths and weaknesses of the various choices.

1. You work as a supervising nurse in a large hospital. In a formal letter of reprimand for one of your subordinates who has violated hospital policy, which of the following sentences do you think would be the most effective?

   a. Nurse Baker's behavior on December 18 was dreadful.

   b. Nurse Baker's behavior on December 18 was atrocious.

   c. Nurse Baker's behavior on December 18 was unacceptable.

2. The financial aid office at your school has limited funds available for scholarships for needy students. In a letter you write to that office, which of the following sentences do you think would be the most effective?

   a. For the past four years, my family has been struggling financially since my mother lost her job.

   b. For the past four years, my family has been down on their luck since my mother lost her job.

   c. For the past four years, my family has been impoverished since my mother lost her job.

3. As a teacher of a fourth-grade class, you need to write a note to one of your students. Which of the following sentences do you think would be the most effective?

    a. Please ask one of your parents to write a terse note explaining why you are late for school so often.

    b. Please ask one of your parents to write a short note explaining why you are late for school so often.

    c. Please ask one of your parents to write a brief note explaining why you are late for school so often.

4. In an email to your friends telling them how to get to the location for a picnic, which of the following wordings do you think would be the most effective?

    a. After about a half mile, the trail you are following will split. At this point, take the path to the left.

    b. After about a half mile, the trail you are following will divide. At this point, take the path to the left.

    c. After about a half mile, the trail you are following will bifurcate. At this point, take the path to the left.

5. In a letter asking for a refund from a plumbing company, which of the following sentences do you think would be the most effective?

    a. I am writing to complain about the careless work done by the plumber you sent to my house on June 18.

    b. I am writing to complain about the sloppy work done by the plumber you sent to my house on June 18.

    c. I am writing to complain about the negligent work done by the plumber you sent to my house on June 18.

6. In a letter applying for a summer internship at an accounting firm, which of the following sentences do you think would be the most effective choice?

    a. If I am hired as a summer intern at your firm, I will work hard to make your company's relationship with younger customers better.

    b. If I am hired as a summer intern at your firm, I will work hard to ameliorate your company's relationship with younger customers.

    c. If I am hired as a summer intern at your firm, I will work hard to improve your company's relationship with younger customers.

7. You want to carry a sign supporting your candidate Maggie Sloan when you go to a political rally. Which of the following would be the most effective wording for your sign?

    a. Maggie Sloan has what it takes to be mayor.

    b. Maggie Sloan is eminently qualified to be mayor.

    c. Maggie Sloan will be an outstanding mayor.

8. In your position as executive chef at an upscale restaurant, you are writing a letter to a newly hired cook. Which wording do you think would be the most effective?

   a. Before beginning work with us, please carefully look over the following policies.

   b. Before beginning work with us, please carefully read the following policies.

   c. Before beginning work with us, please carefully peruse the following policies.

9. In a cover letter for a job as a manager at a large department store, which of the following sentences do you think would be the most effective?

   a. In my job at Walmart last summer, I became an expert at handling customers.

   b. In my job at Walmart last summer, I became an expert at customer service.

   c. In my job at Walmart last summer, I became an expert at dealing with customers.

10. In an email to your brother, who is coming to work in the same office where you have been working, which of the following would be the most effective wording?

   a. It is important that you respect the limits on personal messages sent over the office's email system.

   b. It is important that you respect the parameters on personal messages sent over the office's email system.

   c. It is important that you respect the boundaries on personal messages sent over the office's email system.

13.6 Tutorial

Figurative Language

Figurative language uses figures of speech, such as similes, metaphors, and personification, to convey information and ideas in more creative and powerful ways than ordinary language. For example, instead of writing "My professor spoke extremely rapidly," you could use a simile, "My professor talked *as* fast as an auctioneer." By comparing your professor's speech to that of an auctioneer, you create an image for readers that helps them to understand just how quickly your professor talks. Or you could use a metaphor and say, "My professor's words were rapid-fire bullets that ricocheted off the classroom walls." Her words were not literally bullets, but this description conveys the idea that they were fast, loud, and strong. Personification involves attributing human characteristics or emotions to an inanimate object or something non-human, as in this example: My computer is a malevolent intelligence determined to see me fail.

Similes

If someone writes, "When he finally sat down to write his essay, Marcos spent fifteen minutes arranging the items on his desk like a dentist preparing his tools before beginning a root canal," he or she is using a simile. Similes make comparisons using the words *as* or, as in this case, *like*. Similes are effective because they use something most of us are familiar with—in this case, the careful arrangement of a dentist's tools—to explain something we don't know about—how carefully Marcos arranges everything on his desk before beginning writing. Similes are also effective because they are often clever, playful, or even funny—but not always. In this example, the comparison suggests that Marcos is about to embark on a serious project; this is a root canal job, not a cleaning. However, overused, worn-out similes have the opposite effect. Try to avoid such hackneyed similes as *ate like a pig, mad as a wet hen*, or *slept like a log*. Try to make fresh, new comparisons in your writing.

Metaphors

A metaphor is a figure of speech that is much like a simile, except that instead of saying X is *like* Y, a metaphor asserts that X *is* Y. Here's an example: "The IRS *is a vulture* circling my meager savings and preparing to swoop down on them." When you use a metaphor like this, you are comparing two dissimilar items that share one characteristic. Although there is not a literal connection, you are making an imaginative one in order to create a memorable image in your reader's mind. In this example, the writer is comparing the IRS to a vulture, suggesting that just as that bird will circle its prey endlessly until it tires or dies, the IRS will never give up, and your savings cannot be protected from it.

Here's another example. In *The Stuff of Thought: Language as a Window into Human Nature*, Steven Pinker writes, "A verb is the chassis of the sentence. . . . It is a framework with receptacles for the other parts—the subject, the object, and various oblique objects and subordinate clauses—to be bolted onto." He doesn't mean a verb literally *is* a chassis. He means that, in a sentence, the verb plays a role much like the role the chassis plays for a car.

One word of caution about metaphors: Once you introduce one into your writing, do not change your mind and switch to a different metaphor as the following example does.

> During the Great Recession, my family became *a ship tossed by violent seas*, but luckily we didn't get *too far over our skis* and do anything foolish.

This writer starts with a metaphor about a ship in rough seas, but switches to a metaphor about skiing, which is confusing for the reader.

Personification

An example of personification appeared in the opening paragraph: "My computer is a malevolent intelligence determined to see me fail." Note that this writer is treating her computer as though it is alive, personifying this inanimate object by suggesting it has the human traits of intelligence and malevolence, or ill will. "My bathroom scale is telling me I need to go on a diet" is another example of personification.

Writers use personification to help readers relate to objects, animals, ideas, or other things, bringing them to life and making them easier to understand or care about. When a journalist talks about a "fire swallowing a forest whole," the reader gets a sense of the enormous destructive power of the flames and the feeling that they are almost alive, choosing their prey. When a novelist writes that "the wasted moon peered through the ragged clouds, too weak to throw a shadow or to reveal the fallen child," she creates a sense of foreboding; the moon, like the child, is weak and powerless.

It is wise to use personification sparingly to make a point, to add depth or color to your writing, or to engage readers with a subject they might not usually relate to.

When to Use Figurative Language

Using figurative language like similes, metaphors, and personification can be fun, both for the writer and for the reader. It can also be powerful and clever. You will most often find it used in works of fiction, such as novels, poems, and plays. Used sparingly in academic papers, it can help readers understand something they aren't familiar with by comparing it to something they are familiar with, help them to perceive something from a different perspective, or bring a dry topic to life. However, figurative language is not always appropriate. In most business writing and in some academic writing, it may seem flowery or pretentious. Also, given the content, it might not be appropriate. In the hard sciences, for example, a lot of writing is very technical, and specific formats must be followed.

There is no formula to help you decide whether or not to use figurative language, but it helps to think about your audience, to consider the context in which you are writing, and even to see what other writing for that audience in that context looks like.

13.7 Tutorial

Using a Dictionary to Understand Words

Writers sometimes find themselves unsure about a word they are thinking about using. One solution to this hesitation is to look the word up in a print dictionary or an online one, such as **dictionary.com** or **merriam-webster.com**. The entries there can help you with spelling, determining the word's part of speech, pronunciation, meaning(s), word origin, and usage. For many words, the dictionary will also suggest synonyms, words with similar meanings that might even more precisely express what you want to say. In an online dictionary, if you click on each of the listed synonyms, you will be taken to a definition of that word, making it easier to decide which word best fits the meaning you are trying to express.

Below is an annotated sample entry from *The American Heritage Dictionary of the English Language* for the word *periodic*.

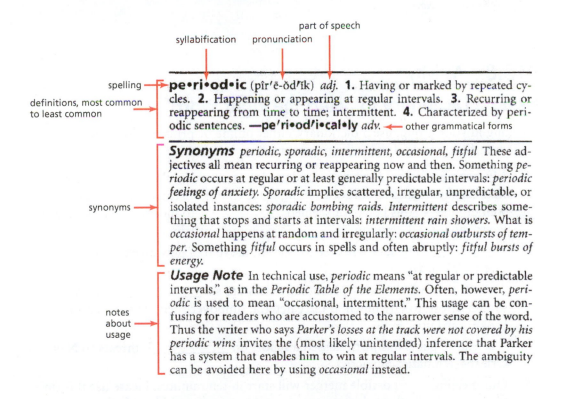

On the next page is a definition from the *Merriam-Webster Online Dictionary*.

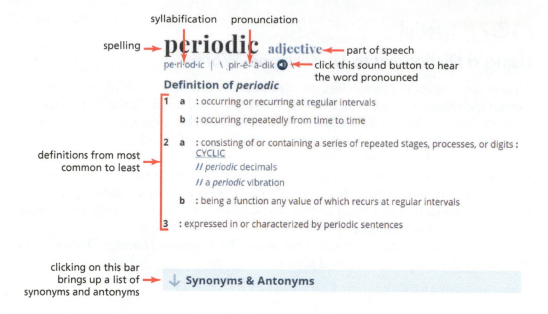

syllabification   pronunciation

spelling → **periodic** *adjective* ← part of speech

pe·ri·od·ic | \ pir-ē-ˈä-dik 🔊 ← click this sound button to hear the word pronounced

Definition of *periodic*

1 a : occurring or recurring at regular intervals

   b : occurring repeatedly from time to time

2 a : consisting of or containing a series of repeated stages, processes, or digits : CYCLIC

     // *periodic* decimals

     // a *periodic* vibration

definitions from most common to least →

   b : being a function any value of which recurs at regular intervals

3 : expressed in or characterized by periodic sentences

clicking on this bar brings up a list of synonyms and antonyms →

↓ **Synonyms & Antonyms**

13.8 Activity

Using a Dictionary to Select the Right Word

Working in your group, use a dictionary, either online or print, to decide which word is the best fit for each of the following examples.

1. My math professor seems to be under a lot of stress. In class today, he couldn't find his glasses and he forgot to bring his textbook. Because he is usually so well organized, this behavior seemed _____ to most of us. (odd, bizarre, weird, abnormal, unnatural)

2. _____ not sure whether we should move to a new apartment in the fall. (We're, Wear, Were)

3. Two of the students in my psychology class are so _____ that they cannot afford to buy lunch in the cafeteria. (impoverished, destitute, poor, broke, hard up)

4. A scientific panel has just released a report on _____ threats to New Orleans. (climatic, climactic)

5. Our meeting on a possible merger will start in ten minutes. Please use this time to _____ these documents so you have a general idea of what we are proposing. (read, skim, peruse, study, review)

6. When you are ready for your interview, simply _____ down the hall to the conference room. (proceed, precede)

7. As soon as I met my fiancé's father, I realized that he was _____. (moneyed, rich, affluent, loaded)

8. The three young boys _____ asked their grandmother if they could have a glass of milk. (respectively, respectfully)

9. I am hoping that the new windows we had installed will _____ our problem with high heating bills. (ameliorate, mollify, solve, reduce)

10. Since my sister has been studying public speaking, she has become much more _____ than she used to be. (verbose, articulate, wordy, garrulous)

13.9 Activity

Determining the Meanings of Confusing Words

This is an activity for you to work on individually, not in a group. When you've finished, you'll have a list of the words that you have found confusing with their correct meanings. Take your time with this activity; do just a few each day.

Listed below are groups of words that some writers confuse. First, read through the list and cross out the words you are sure you know. Then go to work on the remaining words. Look them up in a print dictionary or an online one, and write an explanation of the differences in meaning next to each group. You'll notice there are a few words that are already crossed out. These are not words in formal English, so you should not use them when you want to be formally correct.

accept	except	_____
adapt	adopt	_____
adverse	averse	_____
advise	advice	_____
affect	effect	_____
aggravate	annoy	_____
agree to	agree with	_____
all right	~~alright~~	_____
all together	altogether	_____
allusion	illusion	_____
a lot	~~alot~~	_____

already	all ready		_____
among	between		_____
amoral	immoral		_____
amount	number		_____
angry at	angry with		_____
ante-	anti-		_____
anxious	eager		_____
anyone	any one		_____
assure	ensure	insure	_____
awhile	a while		_____
beside	besides		_____
between	among		_____
bring	take		_____
capital	capitol		_____
censor	censure		_____
cite	site	sight	_____
climatic	climactic		_____
coarse	course		_____
compare to	compare with		_____
complement	compliment		_____
conscience	conscious		_____
continual	continuous		_____
could have	~~could of~~		_____
couldn't care less	~~could care less~~		_____
council	counsel		_____
desert	dessert		_____
different from	different than		_____
disinterested	uninterested		_____
elicit	illicit		_____
emigrate	immigrate		_____
eminent	imminent		_____
everyone	every one		_____

explicit	implicit		_____
farther	further		_____
fewer	less		_____
hanged	hung		_____
hopefully	hopeful		_____
imply	infer		_____
in	into		_____
its	it's		_____
lie	lay		_____
passed	past		_____
precede	proceed		_____
principal	principle		_____
quotation	quote		_____
raise	rise		_____
respectfully	respectively		_____
sensual	sensuous		_____
sit	set		_____
sometime	some time	sometimes	_____
supposed to	~~suppose to~~		_____
their	there	they're	_____
then	than		_____
to	too	two	_____
try to	~~try and~~		_____
used to	~~use to~~		_____
wear	we're	where	_____
weather	whether		_____
whose	who's		_____
would have	~~would of~~		_____
your	you're		_____

TOPIC 14
Thinking While Writing

Very often, the difference between mediocre writing and excellent writing is the quality of the *thinking* that went into the writing. In this Topic you will explore strategies to make your writing more effective by thinking more broadly and deeply about your subject and thesis.

Navigating Topic 14

The tutorials and presentations listed below provide information about strategies for thinking while writing, and each contains, or is followed by, an opportunity to apply the skills you have just learned. You can work through the entire Topic on your own, learning about all the strategies and practicing them; work on items you've been assigned by your instructor; or choose just the ones you find helpful.

Introduction to Thinking While Writing

This Topic begins by asking you to write a short paper about something interesting about you, and then, in groups, you will look at the papers you and your classmates wrote to see what makes some of the papers more interesting than others. Next, there is advice about how to make your writing more interesting by avoiding obvious topics and thinking carefully about your subject, which is followed by writing assignments related to campus parking. Three narrated presentations demonstrate strategies for thinking deeply and thinking broadly, after which you have the option to revise your essay based on what you've learned.

14.1 Writing

One Interesting Thing about You

Write a one-page essay on one interesting thing about the kind of person you are. Your instructor is the audience for this assignment. He or she will be reading these papers to get to know each of you in the class but also to begin a discussion of how to make your writing more effective. Remember this essay should be around one page long; don't take on too much. Please provide concrete examples to back up what you write about yourself.

14.2 Activity

Class Discussion on Interesting Writing

For this activity, you are going to make use of the papers you and your classmates wrote for the writing activity One Interesting Thing about You (14.1), which asked you to write about one interesting thing about the kind of person you are.

Your instructor will make a numbered list of all the thesis statements in your papers and will organize the class into groups, giving each group a copy of the list. Each group's task is to read over these statements and select the five that seem most likely to produce *interesting* papers. Remember that the assignment was to write about "one *interesting* thing about the kind of person you are."

Study the five you select and attempt to come up with some ideas about what makes a thesis statement interesting. Groups will report out after about twenty minutes.

14.3 Tutorial

Avoid Proving the Obvious

An effective essay argues something interesting and thoughtful. It does not argue something everyone already agrees with. Essays that are written to prove statements like the following are unlikely to be either interesting or thoughtful.

- Drunk driving is a terrible thing.
- Communication is important to a good relationship.
- Child abuse should not be tolerated.
- We should not tolerate racism.
- America must protect itself against terrorism.

Each of these statements is true, but none of them is likely to result in a very good essay. Why not? Because almost everyone already agrees with these statements. They belabor the obvious. They argue a point that is not arguable because almost no one disagrees with them.

To avoid wasting your time making an argument that most people would already agree with, you might want to try this trick. Picture yourself standing in front of your class, reading your thesis out loud and then asking whether anyone disagrees. If you cannot picture more than one or two hands being raised, then you need to find a more interesting thesis.

14.4 Tutorial

Use Thinking to Find an Interesting Thesis

Here are two examples showing how two students have thought their way to a thesis that isn't obvious, that makes a point that everyone doesn't already agree with, and that shows they've really given some thought to their topic. In each of these examples, the basic strategy is the same: simply thinking harder about the topic.

Example 1: Thinking about Helping Children "Get Ahead"

In a sociology class, students were asked to write about some aspect of "parenting." Charlene, a single mother with two young daughters, Carrie and Angel, decided on a draft thesis that it is important for parents to do everything they can to help their children "get ahead." She wanted her daughters' lives to be more comfortable and more successful than hers. She wanted to give them "every advantage" so they wouldn't be "left behind."

Charlene started writing about how she bought books and a computer for Carrie and Angel; enrolled them in a preschool program that she could barely afford; and, when her daughters were old enough for elementary school, moved to a neighborhood in her city that was known for the quality of its schools even though she had to take a second job in order to afford the rent.

As she thought she was almost finished with her essay, she saw a news report on television that bothered her greatly—a report that many wealthy parents had spent millions of dollars to hire a company that would get their children into highly competitive universities. This company bribed athletic coaches to write letters about the children's athletic ability when they had not actually participated in any sports. The company also had contacts inside testing companies that allowed them to alter the children's scores on various tests. They even hired people to take college placement tests for the children.

Charlene was shocked. She knew these parents thought they were simply doing everything they could to help their children "get ahead," but they had clearly gone too far. Charlene began to rethink her essay. While she still thought parents should try to help their children "get ahead," she now recognized that there were also dangers to this approach.

The admissions cheating scandal she had seen on the news illustrated one danger, but Charlene wondered if there were others. She thought about parents she knew who were so eager to help their children that they did their children's homework for them. She thought about a friend of hers who was so determined that her son would get straight A's that she wouldn't allow him to try out for the school play because it would take too much time away from his school work. She thought about parents who put so much pressure on their children that they developed stress-related psychological problems.

After all this thinking, Charlene had arrived at a much more thoughtful and interesting thesis: while it is important for parents to help their children be successful, it is also important to avoid the dangers that can arise when this parenting approach goes too far.

Example 2: Thinking about Drunk Driving

In a criminal justice class, students were asked to write about a current criminal justice issue. One student wrote a wonderful paper about drunk driving that didn't just belabor the obvious. He argued that, while drunk driving is certainly a problem, we are placing all our attention on preventing drunk driving when more people in America are killed each year as a result of speeding. He reported that in 2011, 9,878

Americans died as a result of drunk driving, while 10,001 died in accidents caused by speeding. He wasn't arguing that drunk driving isn't a major problem; he was arguing that speeding is a slightly larger problem that people do not appear to be as upset about. There are no Mothers Against Speeding organizations. No one is tying ribbons on their door handles to protest speeding.

Each of the essays discussed above became more effective when the writer found something interesting and thoughtful to say after thinking more deeply about the topic.

One Word of Caution.   Sometimes when students are told to write something that is not obvious, something that everyone doesn't already agree with, they go to the opposite extreme. They write a paper with a thesis that no one could ever agree with and that they have no chance of proving in any reasonable way: "Unicorns really do exist" or "The president is a literal zombie." This kind of farfetched thesis is not what is being suggested here. Instead, you are simply being asked to write a paper that argues something that is not obvious, something that results from doing some real thinking about your topic.

14.5   Writing

Who Should Get Reserved Parking?

Write a short paper, about a page, in which you propose who should get reserved parking spaces at your college or university. Be sure to provide evidence to support your assertions. The audience for this assignment is other students in your class.

14.6   Activity

Thinking about Reserved Parking

The writing assignment for Who Should Get Reserved Parking? (14.5) asked you to do the following.

> Write a short paper, about a page, in which you propose who should get reserved parking spaces at your college or university. Be sure to provide evidence to support your assertions. The audience for this assignment is other students in your class.

Here is what one student, Alex, wrote in response to this assignment:

At this time of year, it is terribly difficult to find a parking place at the college. Several times I have been late to class because I've been driving around looking for a place to park. It would be great to have a reserved parking place, but after discussing this with several of my classmates and thinking about it for a long time, I have decided that the college should provide reserved parking places to the disabled, the faculty, and the college president.

The disabled deserve reserved parking because their lives are hard enough as it is. If disabled students have the courage to attend college, we should do everything possible to make their lives easier. Some disabled students simply could not make it to class if they had to park in the distant lots and make their way in a wheelchair. This should be the highest priority for reserved parking.

If the faculty were not here, there wouldn't be a college. They play the most important role at the college. They teach the classes. If a faculty member doesn't make it to class, then twenty or thirty students suffer. This is why I think faculty should have reserved parking places.

Being the president of a college is a very prestigious position. I know our president worked for more than thirty years before she was promoted to president. If someone has worked his or her way to this position, we should recognize that accomplishment by providing reserved parking.

In conclusion, reserved parking at this college should be given to the disabled, faculty, and the president.

In groups, discuss Alex's paper. What do you think of the *thinking* that went into this essay? Do you think the writer of this paper would want people who work for buildings and grounds to have reserved parking? Why do you think the writer didn't include them? After about ten minutes, the groups will report out.

14.7 Presentation

Thinking about Alex's Paper

To watch this presentation that discusses the thinking that went into Alex's paper in Thinking about Reserved Parking (14.6, p. 410), go to *Achieve for The Hub*, Topic 14, and open Unit 14.7.

14.8 Presentation

Thinking Deeply

To watch this presentation that discusses the deeper thinking that could go into Alex's paper in Thinking about Reserved Parking (14.6, p. 410), go to *Achieve for The Hub*, Topic 14, and open Unit 14.8.

14.9 Presentation

Thinking Broadly

To watch this presentation that discusses the broader thinking that could go into Alex's paper in Thinking about Reserved Parking (14.6, p. 410), go to *Achieve for The Hub*, Topic 14, and open Unit 14.9.

14.10 Writing

Revising Your Reserved Parking Paper

In Who Should Get Reserved Parking? (14.5, p. 410), you wrote a short paper proposing who should get reserved parking spaces at your college. For this assignment, you are going to revise that paper based on what you've learned about thinking deeply and broadly.

TOPIC 15
Revising

Because effective revision is so important and takes time, be sure you schedule enough time for a rigorous review once you finish drafting a paper or other piece of writing.

Navigating Topic 15

The tutorials listed below provide information about strategies for revising. You can work through the entire Topic on your own, learning about all the strategies and practicing them; work on items you've been assigned by your instructor; or choose just the ones you find helpful.

Introduction to Revising

For most writers, revising begins almost as soon they start writing. They are constantly rereading and making changes as they go, but once they have a complete draft, they do a major revision. Revising is what turns average writing into excellent writing. It involves taking a hard look at every element of an essay from the thesis and introduction to the organization of ideas, types of support, and concluding words. Although some revising goes on throughout the process of writing, the most important revision work takes place after a draft has been completed.

Topic 15 provides information about and strategies for revising for audience, purpose, assignment, thesis, unity, support, organization, and coherence. It also discusses using backward outlining as a revision strategy, and it concludes with suggestions for how to make an essay more interesting, along with a revision checklist.

15.1 Tutorial

Revision Basics

When you are ready to revise, you want to be able to stand back from what you've written and view it objectively. Often it is easier to do this if you let some time pass between when you finish a draft and when you start revising it, ideally at least a day or two. However, if you finish your draft late the night before it's due, go to bed and revise it in the morning when you're fresh. If you don't have even that much time, at least get up and have a cup of coffee or take a walk around the block before you start revising. The important thing is to give yourself enough time to switch roles from being the writer of the draft to being an objective reader who can find ways to improve it.

Before you begin revising, it's always a good idea to get some feedback from others. Sometimes your instructor will schedule class time for peer review, a process that allows students to receive feedback on a draft from other students (see Peer Review [8.4, p. 322] for details). Even if no peer review sessions are planned, ask a friend, a brother or sister, or even another student in your class to read over your paper and let you know what works and what could use some improvement.

It's also important to recognize the difference between revision and editing. *Revision* is when you to look at the big issues in what you have written. Does it have a clear thesis? Is it unified? Does it provide enough evidence to support the points it makes? Is it organized effectively? *Editing* is when you look at the sentence-level issues like grammar, punctuation, spelling, and word choice. These are two different activities, and it is best not to try to do them both at the same time. Revise first, and when that is finished, you can more effectively edit for correctness (for more details, see Topic 16: Editing [p. 435]).

Some writers prefer to print out a copy of their draft and revise by marking up that copy and later transferring the changes to the draft on the computer. Others prefer to do their revising directly on the computer. Use whichever approach works best for you.

15.2 Tutorial

Revising for Assignment, Audience, and Purpose

When you are ready to start revising, it's a good idea to read your draft over quickly to refresh your sense of the essay as a whole and then to ask yourself these questions.

1. **What was the assignment your instructor gave for this essay?** What exactly were you asked to do? Does your essay include everything the assignment calls for? Is it the right length? (For more details, see Reading an Assignment [9.1, p. 326].)

2. **Who is the audience for this essay?** Is there more than one? What do they already know? How technical can, or should, you be? Are they likely to agree or disagree with you? Have you written in a style, with a voice, that is appropriate for that audience? (For more details, see Thinking about Audience [9.4, p. 328].)

3. **What is your purpose for writing this essay?** Is it to persuade, explain, express feelings or thoughts, or entertain? Is your purpose to request something, to recommend something, to reassure the audience, or to summarize something? Does the draft you have written really address that purpose? (For more details, see Thinking about Purpose [9.6, p. 331].)

15.3 Tutorial

Backward Outlining

Below is a draft of an essay that will be used throughout this Topic to illustrate the revision process. On the right is a backward outline of the essay. To create the backward outline, the writer simply read each paragraph and jotted down a brief summation of the main point in that paragraph. In this example, these brief statements of each paragraph's main point are displayed to the right of the essay itself. Most writers actually write these statements on a separate sheet of paper or in a separate Word document.

A backward outline like this can be used to improve thesis and unity (see Revising for Thesis and Unity [15.4, p. 419]), ensure logical organization (see Revising for Organization [15.5, p. 421]), and ensure sufficient and appropriate support (see Revising for Support [15.6, p. 423]).

Hard Work and Getting Ahead

1　It has often been said that "in America, if you work hard you will get ahead." This idea is what most people mean by the American Dream. I disagree with this idea. Before I disagree, however, it's probably a good idea to pin down exactly what it is I am disagreeing with.

1. Background

2　When people express this belief in getting ahead in America, I don't think they believe that *everyone* who works hard gets ahead. Surely, they recognize that some people work very hard and, nevertheless, end up living out their lives in grinding poverty. Also, I don't think they believe that everyone who gets ahead worked hard. Surely, they also recognize that some people inherit a fortune or win the lottery and do not need to work much at all. So, I am assuming that advocates of the "hard-work-equals-getting-ahead philosophy" really mean that, even if it isn't true for everyone, it is *generally* true—true for most people. This is what I disagree with. I believe that most Americans, even if they work hard, will not get ahead. I don't believe that the American Dream really exists for most Americans.

2. Introduction with thesis: most Americans, even if they work hard, will not get ahead

3　Young people who grow up in poverty usually don't have the kinds of connections that help them get a good job. Their parents, too often, do not have the kinds of jobs in large corporations or offices where they can help their kids meet people who might hire them. Furthermore, they seldom have older brothers

3. Lack of contacts and familiarity with business behavior

or sisters who can introduce them to people who can give them advice about how to move up in the world. Sometimes, when they do get a job interview at a place where they have a chance of advancement, they are simply unfamiliar with the protocol for such meetings.

4   Another important reason many Americans can't work their way out of poverty, can't achieve the American Dream, is our unequal education system. Funding for schools is based on property taxes paid in each local school district. School systems located in poorer areas are underfunded because the property in that area is of much lower value than property in wealthy suburbs. As a result, funding for schools in poorer neighborhoods will be much less than funding for schools in rich neighborhoods. Bruce Biddle and David Berliner, writing for the Association for Supervision and Curriculum Development website, point out that "a few students from wealthy communities or neighborhoods within generous states attend public schools with funding of $15,000 or more per student per year, whereas some students from poor communities or neighborhoods within stingy or impoverished states attend schools that must make do with less than $4,000 per student per year." Lower funding leads to school buildings that are often dilapidated, textbooks in short supply, and teachers who are paid lower salaries than their counterparts in wealthier areas. In many cases, the most effective teachers in poor schools leave after a few years for the higher salaries in wealthy schools. Things then become even more unequal. Those who went to the better schools do much better on tests and get into the better colleges and universities. The kids from the poor schools are lucky if they get into a regional state university.

4. Funding for our education system favors kids from wealthy families

5   To be fair, however, even though many students from truly wealthy families are sent to private schools where they have beautiful surroundings, the best teachers, small class sizes, and lots of guidance and counseling, they have problems, too. Lots of these kids have grown up in families that put a lot of pressure on them to succeed, so they experience significant stress and frequently have many psychological problems. Depression, bipolar syndrome, and even suicide are common among these students.

5. Wealthy kids go to private schools but feel a lot of stress

6   The belief that all it takes to "get ahead" is hard work results in people thinking that if they haven't gotten ahead, it's their fault. They didn't work hard enough. In fact, there are many causes why, despite hard work, many don't get ahead—an education system that doesn't treat them fairly, the struggle to find the right balance of time and money, a personal crisis, or a personal mistake. It takes more than hard work to get ahead in America. It takes luck or being born into a middle-class family.

6. Belief that hard work = getting ahead leads those born in poverty to blame themselves and not work to change the system

7   I want to be clear about what I mean by "hard work" and "getting ahead." Working hard doesn't have to involve physical labor. In this essay, when I talk about hard work, I mean working as many hours per week as is physically possible, sometimes even at two full-time jobs. It also means that the hard worker works hard at his or her job. They don't goof off, they don't take a lot of breaks, and they seldom call in sick. I also want to clarify what I mean when I talk about "getting ahead." You don't have to be very rich to have gotten ahead. What I mean by getting ahead is doing a little better than your parents did—making a higher salary, living in a nicer house, and having a better education.

7. Defining terms: hard work and getting ahead

8   Sometimes these young people give up on college and decide just to try to make it in the workplace. Starting in jobs that don't require a college education, they find, no matter how hard they work, that they just can't get a promotion. Often they work more and more hours—60 or 70 a week—and they are barely keeping themselves above water.

8. Many who attempt college give up and then discover they will never make a decent living in the jobs available to non-college grads

9   Finally, sometimes young people's chances of "getting ahead" are eliminated because they make a mistake. Seeing how impossible it is to succeed, despite hard work, they decide to try to beat the system by doing something illegal. They steal something, start dealing drugs, get mixed up with a gang, or get hooked on drugs themselves. Suddenly, all their hopes of getting ahead have evaporated.

9. Some young people make a mistake that gets them in trouble and makes it difficult to get hired in a decent job

10   The idea that in America if you work hard, you'll get ahead is both untruthful and harmful. It is untruthful because it ignores the many societal conditions that make it unlikely that people born into poverty will be able to get ahead, and it is harmful because it encourages people to think that if they haven't gotten ahead, it's their own fault and, therefore, they should not question an inequitable system.

10. Conclusion: the idea that in America, if you work hard, you will get ahead, is both untrue and harmful

15.4   Tutorial

Revising for Thesis and Unity

One of the most important revision steps is checking to see whether your draft essay has a clear thesis, whether the thesis at the end of the essay is the same as it was at the beginning—of course, expressed in different words—and whether everything in the paper supports that thesis. (For more details, see Thesis Statements [10.5, p. 346] and Unity [12.1, p. 377].)

Using a Backward Outline to Check on Thesis and Unity

This is the backward outline created in Unit 15.3 (p. 415), which lists the main points in the essay paragraph by paragraph. The two versions of the thesis are underlined.

1. background
2. intro with thesis: <u>most Americans, even if they work hard, will not get ahead</u>
3. lack of contacts and familiarity with business behavior
4. funding for our education system favors kids from wealthy families
5. wealthy kids go to private schools but feel a lot of stress
6. belief that hard work = getting ahead leads those born in poverty to blame themselves and not work to change the system
7. defining terms: hard work and getting ahead
8. many who attempt college give up and then discover they will never make a decent living in the jobs available to non-college grads
9. some young people make a mistake that gets them in trouble and makes it difficult to get hired in a decent job
10. conclusion with restated thesis: <u>the idea that in America, if you work hard, you will get ahead is both untrue and harmful</u>

A backward outline like this makes it easy to check for thesis and unity. The thesis appears in the second paragraph: "most Americans, even if they work hard, will not get ahead." But in the concluding paragraph (10), the thesis is stated this way: "the idea that in America, if you work hard, you will get ahead is both untrue and harmful." In the process of writing the paper, the author came up with an idea that wasn't there when she wrote the second paragraph, so the restated thesis in paragraph 10 adds the idea that the belief that working hard will lead to success is actually harmful.

To ensure that the paper has a single clear thesis, the writer needs to either revise the thesis statement in paragraph 2 or the one in paragraph 10. If the writer changes paragraph 10 by deleting the assertion that the belief that working hard will lead to success causes harm (and perhaps eliminates paragraph 8, which supports that idea), the paper would be unified around a single thesis. However, the idea about "harm" is the most original idea in the essay, so the paper will be stronger if the writer leaves paragraph 10 as it is and inserts the idea of the harm done by that belief to the thesis in paragraph 2. In addition, the writer will need to add more support to paragraph 8, providing evidence that this "harm" really occurs, perhaps even adding two or three new paragraphs.

When the thesis at the end of a draft of an essay is different from the thesis at the beginning, it's usually the result of the writer having done some thinking. In the process of writing the draft, thinking about the topic, and finding evidence, it is not unusual for a writer to end up with a thesis that differs from the original one. Because this difference results from *thinking* about the topic, the thesis at the end, as in this essay on getting ahead, is usually more thoughtful than the one the writer started with, in which case changing the original thesis to agree with the final one is the preferred option.

Now take a look at item 5 in the backward outline above: "wealthy kids go to private schools but feel a lot of stress." The writer, maybe because she has friends at private schools or has read about the issue, included the idea that kids from rich families are under a lot of psychological stress. But it doesn't belong in this paper: this is a paper arguing that it's not true that hard work will lead to "getting ahead," so the paragraph is not relevant and should be deleted.

If you think it will work for you, use backward outlining to help you find and revise problems with thesis and unity. Even if you decide not to use this method when revising, you will still need to make sure your draft essay has a single clear thesis and that everything in the essay supports that thesis.

15.5 Tutorial

Revising for Organization

The tutorial on backward outlining in Unit 15.3 (p. 415) ended with an outline of a draft essay. In Unit 15.4 (p. 419) that outline was modified to eliminate problems with thesis and unity. Below is the backward outline after those revisions were made.

1. background

2. intro with thesis: the belief that most Americans, if they work hard, will get ahead is untrue and even harmful

3. lack of contacts and familiarity with business behavior

4. funding for our education system favors kids from wealthy families

5. ~~wealthy kids go to private schools but feel a lot of stress~~

6. belief that hard work = getting ahead leads those born in poverty to blame themselves and not work to change the system

7. defining terms: hard work and getting ahead

8. many who attempt college give up and then discover they will never make a decent living in the jobs available to non-college grads

9. some young people make a mistake that gets them in trouble and makes it difficult to get hired in a decent job

10. conclusion: the idea that in America, if you work hard, you will get ahead is both untrue and harmful

Now it is time to look at these items and see if there is a way of ordering them that will make the argument easier for the reader to follow. The first thing you might notice is item 7, a paragraph that defines the key terms *hard work* and *getting ahead*. It's a good idea to make sure the reader will understand what the writer means by these terms, but why wait until the seventh paragraph to define them? Moving them up to be closer to the introductory material so they become the third item seems advisable.

In the revised outline below, the definition paragraph that was item 7 has been moved to item 3. Now, paragraphs 1, 2, and 3 are in the right place as introductory material, and paragraph 9, the conclusion, is where it belongs. But what about paragraphs 4 through 8? Are they in the most effective order? Actually, they don't seem to be in any particular order at all. The writer could try arranging them from most important to least, but it's difficult to decide which is most or least important, so chronological order seems like it would work better. Organizing the paragraphs in terms of *when* what they describe would affect an individual—moving from those things that happen to children, to those that impact college students, and finally to those that affect people in the workplace—makes sense. That's what the following revised outline does.

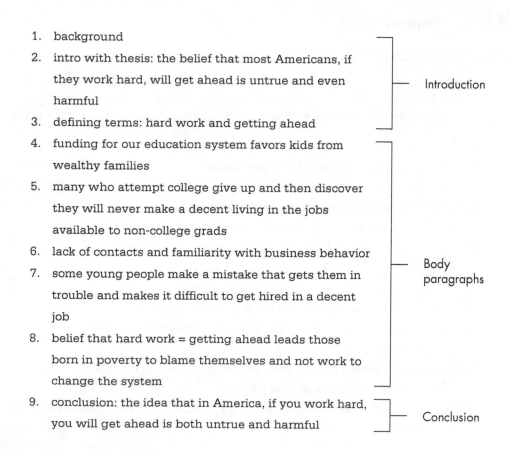

1. background

2. intro with thesis: the belief that most Americans, if they work hard, will get ahead is untrue and even harmful

3. defining terms: hard work and getting ahead

— Introduction

4. funding for our education system favors kids from wealthy families

5. many who attempt college give up and then discover they will never make a decent living in the jobs available to non-college grads

6. lack of contacts and familiarity with business behavior

7. some young people make a mistake that gets them in trouble and makes it difficult to get hired in a decent job

— Body paragraphs

8. belief that hard work = getting ahead leads those born in poverty to blame themselves and not work to change the system

9. conclusion: the idea that in America, if you work hard, you will get ahead is both untrue and harmful

— Conclusion

Now the body paragraphs are in a logical order. Although paragraph 8 has no logical position in the chronological ordering, it is really interesting. Its assertion that the belief that everyone who works hard will get ahead is actually harmful is a thoughtful idea, but it doesn't fit in the chronological order of the other body paragraphs, so putting it last—just before the conclusion—seems like a good solution.

That's how you can use backward outlining to revise the organization of an essay.

15.6 Tutorial

Revising for Support

The tutorial on backward outlining in Unit 15.3 (p. 415) ended with an outline of a draft essay. In Unit 15.4 (p. 419) that outline was modified to eliminate problems with thesis and unity, and in Unit 15.5 (p. 421), it was reorganized to make the writer's argument easier to follow. Below is the backward outline after those revisions were made. In addition, the writer has made notes (in blue handwriting) of places where she will need more evidence to support her assertions.

1. background
2. intro with thesis: the belief that most Americans, if they work hard, will get ahead is untrue and even harmful
3. defining terms: hard work and getting ahead

         Introduction

4. funding for our education system favors kids from wealthy families *Lots of evidence for this point, so I could add some more.*
5. many who attempt college give up and then discover they will never make a decent living in the jobs available to non-college grads *Here I have a little evidence. I should add my brother's experience or my friend Josie's. Perhaps I can find some actual statistics about this.*
6. lack of contacts and familiarity with business behavior *In this paragraph, I state very general opinions with little evidence to back them up. Need more development here.*

         Body paragraphs

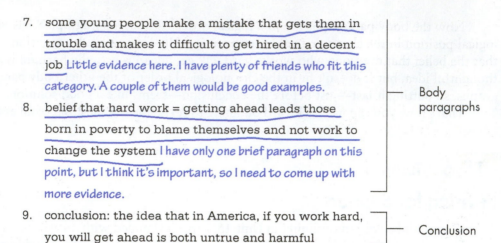

7. some young people make a mistake that gets them in trouble and makes it difficult to get hired in a decent job *Little evidence here. I have plenty of friends who fit this category. A couple of them would be good examples.*

8. belief that hard work = getting ahead leads those born in poverty to blame themselves and not work to change the system *I have only one brief paragraph on this point, but I think it's important, so I need to come up with more evidence.*

— Body paragraphs

9. conclusion: the idea that in America, if you work hard, you will get ahead is both untrue and harmful

— Conclusion

Topic 11: Developing Ideas (p. 355) discussed different approaches for providing support to back up the opinions you express in an essay with facts, expert opinion, examples, and narratives. When revising, you need to read your draft essay carefully, identifying each place you assert an opinion and asking yourself whether you could provide more evidence to support that opinion.

The underlined items in the outline above are all assertions of the writer's opinions. That's not a problem; making an argument always involves expressing the writer's opinions. However, it would be a problem if any of these opinions appear in the essay without adequate support or evidence. At this point, the writer, having identified the five opinions she asserted in the essay, evaluated the evidence she had provided to support each of them and made notes about where she needed to add more support and what that might consist of. She then revised her essay, as shown below. The new support she added is underlined. Note that the author has included in-text citations for the sources she has added and provided a works cited list at the end of her essay.

Hard Work and Getting Ahead

1   It has often been said that "in America, if you work hard you will get ahead." This idea is what most people mean by the American Dream. I disagree with this idea. Before I disagree, however, it's probably a good idea to pin down exactly what it is I am disagreeing with.

2   When people express this belief in getting ahead in America, I don't think they believe that *everyone* who works hard gets ahead. Surely, they recognize that some people work very hard and, nevertheless, end up living out their lives in grinding poverty. Also, I don't think they believe that everyone who gets ahead worked hard.

Surely, they also recognize that some people inherit a fortune or win the lottery and do not need to work much at all. So, I am assuming that advocates of the "hard-work-equals-getting-ahead philosophy" really mean that, even if it isn't true for everyone, it is *generally* true—true for most people. This is what I disagree with. I believe that most Americans, even if they work hard, will not get ahead. I don't believe that the American Dream really exists for most Americans.

3   Before going any further, I want to be clear about what I mean by "hard work" and "getting ahead." Working hard doesn't have to involve physical labor. In this essay, when I talk about hard work, I mean working as many hours per week as is physically possible, sometimes even at two full-time jobs. It also means that the hard worker works hard at his or her job. They don't goof off, they don't take a lot of breaks, and they seldom call in sick. I also want to clarify what I mean when I talk about "getting ahead." You don't have to be very rich to have gotten ahead. What I mean by getting ahead is doing a little better than your parents did—making a higher salary, living in a nicer house, and having a better education.

4   Another important reason many Americans can't work their way out of poverty, can't achieve the American Dream, is our unequal education system. Funding for schools is based on property taxes paid in each local school district. School systems located in poorer areas are underfunded because the property in that area is of much lower value than property in wealthy suburbs. As a result, funding for schools in poorer neighborhoods will be much less than funding for schools in rich neighborhoods. Bruce Biddle and David Berliner, writing for the ASCD (Association for Supervision and Curriculum Development) website, point out that "a few students from wealthy communities or neighborhoods within generous states attend public schools with funding of $15,000 or more per student per year, whereas some students from poor communities or neighborhoods within stingy or impoverished states attend schools that must make do with less than $4,000 per student per year." Lower funding leads to school buildings that are often dilapidated, textbooks in short supply, and teachers who are paid lower salaries than their counterparts in wealthier areas. In many cases, the most effective teachers in poor schools leave after a few years for the higher salaries in wealthy schools. Sean Reardon at Stanford University, in "School District Socioeconomic Status, Race, and Academic Achievement," has concluded that "the variation in academic achievement among school districts is very large; students in some districts have scores more than 4 grade levels higher than others." Further, Reardon concludes, "This variation is

very highly correlated with the socioeconomic characteristics of families in the local community" (12). Things then become even more unequal. Those who went to the better schools do much better on tests and get into the better colleges and universities. The kids from the poor schools are lucky if they get into a regional state university.

5   Sometimes these young people give up on college and decide just to try to make it in the workplace. In fact, the *Washington Post* reports that more than half of students who start college drop out within six years (Salingo). Starting in jobs that don't require a college education, they find, no matter how hard they work, that they just can't get a promotion. Often they work more and more hours—60 or 70 a week—and they are barely keeping themselves above water. For example, my brother Matt gave up the first semester he attended Hightower Community College and went to work full time as a clerk in a Radio Shack. A year later he was still making minimum wage, so he asked for a raise only to be told that he would not get any raises until he completed an AA degree. Having built up $7,000 in credit-card debt, he took a second job driving for Uber. Three years later he's still in debt and working sixty hours a week. For people in my brother's situation, when a crisis hits, they are completely wiped out. If Matt became sick or was laid off by Radio Shack, he would have no choice but to file for bankruptcy. For people like Matt, hard work doesn't pay off.

6   Young people who grow up in poverty usually don't have the kinds of connections that help them get a good job. Their parents, too often, do not have the kinds of jobs in large corporations or offices where they can help their kids meet people who might hire them. My brother Matt and I grew up in a family where both our parents had low-level jobs in a hotel. When Matt started looking for a job, they didn't know anyone who could help him. Furthermore, these young people seldom have older brothers or sisters who can introduce them to people who can give them advice about how to move up in the world. Sometimes, when they do get a job interview at a place where they have a chance of advancement, they are simply unfamiliar with the protocol for such meetings. My friend Josie was invited for a job interview at a large corporation. When she arrived wearing a casual sweater and pair of slacks, she discovered that everyone was wearing business suits and dresses. She never heard again from that corporation.

7   Finally, sometimes young people's chances of "getting ahead" are eliminated because they make a mistake. Seeing how impossible it is to succeed, despite hard work, they decide to try to beat the system by doing something illegal. They steal something, start dealing drugs, get mixed up with a gang, or get hooked on drugs

themselves. My best friend, Althea, was doing well in high school until her junior year. She started dating a guy who was known for dealing drugs. Soon she joined him in the business. A few months later, they were both arrested, and now Althea has a felony on her record, making it unlikely anyone will hire her for a good job. The guy I was dating in my sophomore year was caught shoplifting in his senior year making it unlikely he'll ever reach his goal of going to law school. All it takes is one mistake, and these kids' hopes of getting ahead have evaporated.

8   The belief that all it takes to "get ahead" is hard work results in people thinking that if they haven't gotten ahead, it's their fault. They didn't work hard enough. My father is a perfect example of this. When he was in his thirties and still working cleaning up rooms in a hotel, he gradually began to see himself as a failure. He blamed himself for not having gotten ahead in America. A few years later, when I started college, I tried to get him to take a few classes too. However, he was so convinced he was a failure that he simply couldn't imagine going back to school. In fact, there are many reasons why, despite hard work, many don't get ahead—an education system that doesn't treat them fairly, the struggle to find the right balance of time and money, a personal crisis, or a personal mistake. It takes more than hard work to get ahead in America. It takes luck or being born into a middle-class family.

9   The idea that in America if you work hard, you'll get ahead is both untruthful and harmful. It is untruthful because it ignores the many societal conditions that make it unlikely that people born into poverty will be able to get ahead, and it is harmful because it encourages people to think that if they haven't gotten ahead, it's their own fault and, therefore, they should not question an inequitable system.

(**NOTE:** Always start the works cited list on a new page.)

Works Cited

Reardon, Sean. "School District Socioeconomic Status, Race, and Academic Achievement." Stanford Center for Educational Policy Analysis, Apr. 2016, https://cepa.stanford.edu/sites/default/files/reardon%20district%20ses%20and%20achievement%20discussion%20draft%20april2015.pdf.

Salingo, Jeffrey. "Why Do So Many Students Drop Out of College? And What Can Be Done About It?" *The Washington Post*, 8 June 2018, https://www.washingtonpost.com/news/grade-point/wp/2018/06/08/why-do-so-many-students-drop-out-of-college-and-what-can-be-done-about-it/?utm_term=.b2a90fd8aa04.

Revising for Coherence

Writers provide coherence in their writing in three ways: implementing a logical organization, repeating key words and phrases, and using transitional expressions. (For more details, see Practice Ordering Ideas [12.7, p. 384] and the tutorial Coherence [12.8, p. 384].)

To revise for the use of key words and phrases, you need to identify them in your essay. Below is the essay "Hard Work and Getting Ahead." As you read, it quickly becomes clear that "working hard," "getting ahead," and "American Dream" are key words or phrases. These words and phrases and others that stand in for "hard work" and "getting ahead" are highlighted in blue. Whether you do this highlighting or not (and you could do it with a highlighter on a paper copy of your draft), once you have decided what your key words and phrases are, you need to check to see whether you have used them and other phrases that stand in for them throughout your paper. In the essay below, note that "hard work" and "getting ahead" are repeated throughout the essay, reminding the reader that these are key ideas. However, "American Dream" is used just three times, all in the first four paragraphs. Noticing this, the writer needs to look for places to use "American Dream" more often in paragraphs 5 through 9 so the reader is reminded that "American Dream" is a key concept.

Transitional expressions are like road signs that help readers understand where they are going, what's coming up next, and how the parts of the essay relate to each other. When the writer of this essay circled all the transitional expressions she could find, she was happy to see she had done a good job with this aspect of coherence. However, she also discovered several places where a transitional word or expression needed to be added to help ideas flow smoothly together. These places are underlined.

Hard Work and Getting Ahead

1   It has often been said that "in America, if you work hard you will get ahead." This idea is what most people mean by the American Dream. I disagree with this idea. Before I disagree, however, it's probably a good idea to pin down exactly what it is I am disagreeing with.

2   When people express this belief in getting ahead in America, I don't think they believe that *everyone* who works hard gets ahead. Surely, they recognize that some people work very hard and, nevertheless, end up living out their lives in grinding poverty. Also, I don't think they believe that everyone who gets ahead worked hard. Surely, they also recognize that some people inherit a fortune or win the lottery and

do not need to work much at all. (So,) I am assuming that advocates of the "hard-work-equals-getting-ahead philosophy" really mean that, even if it isn't true for everyone, it is *generally* true—true for most people. This is what I disagree with. I believe that most Americans, even if they work hard, will not get ahead. I don't believe that the American Dream really exists for most Americans.

3   Before going any further, I want to be clear about what I mean by "hard work" and "getting ahead." Working hard doesn't have to involve physical labor. In this essay, when I talk about hard work, I mean working as many hours per week as is physically possible, sometimes even at two full-time jobs. It (also) means that the hard worker works hard at his or her job. They don't goof off, they don't take a lot of breaks, and they seldom call in sick. (In addition,) I want to clarify what I mean when I talk about "getting ahead." You don't have to be very rich to have gotten ahead. What I mean by getting ahead is doing a little better than your parents did—making a higher salary, living in a nicer house, and having a better education.

4   (Another) important reason many Americans can't work their way out of poverty, can't achieve the American Dream, is our unequal education system. Funding for schools is based on property taxes paid in each local school district. School systems located in poorer areas are underfunded because the property in that area is of much lower value than property in wealthy suburbs. (As a result,) funding for schools in poorer neighborhoods will be much less than funding for schools in rich neighborhoods. Bruce Biddle and David Berliner, writing for the ASCD (Association for Supervision and Curriculum Development) website, point out that "a few students from wealthy communities or neighborhoods within generous states attend public schools with funding of $15,000 or more per student per year, whereas some students from poor communities or neighborhoods within stingy or impoverished states attend schools that must make do with less than $4,000 per student per year." Lower funding leads to school buildings that are often dilapidated, textbooks in short supply, and teachers who are paid lower salaries than their counterparts in wealthier areas. In many cases, the most effective teachers in poor schools leave after a few years for the higher salaries in wealthy schools. Sean Reardon at Stanford University, in "School District Socioeconomic Status, Race, and Academic Achievement," has concluded that "the variation in academic achievement among school districts is very large; students in some districts have scores more than 4 grade levels higher than

others." Further, Reardon concludes, "This variation is very highly correlated with the socioeconomic characteristics of families in the local community" (12). <u>When it comes time to go to college</u>, things become even more unequal. Those who went to the better schools do much better on tests and get into the better colleges and universities, <u>but</u> the kids from the poor schools are lucky if they get into a regional state university.

5   <u>Making the problem worse</u>, sometimes these young people give up on college and decide just to try to make it in the workplace. In fact, the *Washington Post* reports that more than half of students who start college drop out within six years (Salingo). Starting in jobs that don't require a college education, they find, no matter how hard they work, that they just can't get a promotion. Often they work more and more hours—60 or 70 a week—and they are barely keeping themselves above water. For example, my brother Matt gave up the first semester he attended Hightower Community College and went to work full time as a clerk in a Radio Shack. A year later he was still making minimum wage, so he asked for a raise only to be told that he would not get any raises until he completed an AA degree. Having built up $7,000 in credit-card debt, he took a second job driving for Uber. Three years later he's still in debt and working sixty hours a week. For people in my brother's situation, when a crisis hits, they are completely wiped out. If Matt became sick or was laid off by Radio Shack, he would have no choice but to file for bankruptcy. For people like Matt, hard work doesn't pay off.

6   <u>Another contributing factor in this sad situation is that</u> young people who grow up in poverty usually don't have the kinds of connections that help them get a good job. Their parents, too often, do not have the kinds of jobs in large corporations or offices where they can help their kids meet people who might hire them. My brother Matt and I, <u>for example</u>, grew up in a family where both our parents had low-level jobs in a hotel. When Matt started looking for a job, they didn't know anyone who could help him. Furthermore, these young people seldom have older brothers or sisters who can introduce them to people who can give them advice about how to move up in the world. Sometimes, when they do get a job interview at a place where they have a chance of advancement, they are simply unfamiliar with the protocol for such meetings. My friend Josie, <u>for instance</u>, was invited for a job interview at a large corporation. When she arrived wearing a casual sweater and pair of slacks, she

discovered that everyone was wearing business suits and dresses. She never heard again from that corporation.

7   (Finally,) sometimes young people's chances of "getting ahead" are eliminated because they make a mistake. Seeing how impossible it is to succeed, despite hard work, they decide to try to beat the system by doing something illegal. They steal something, start dealing drugs, get mixed up with a gang, or get hooked on drugs themselves. For instance, my best friend, Althea, was doing well in high school until her junior year. She started dating a guy who was known for dealing drugs. (Soon) she joined him in the business. (A few months later,) they were both arrested, and now Althea has a felony on her record, making it unlikely anyone will hire her for a good job. Another example is the guy I was dating in my sophomore year. He was caught shoplifting in his senior year, making it unlikely he'll ever reach his goal of going to law school. All it takes is one mistake, and these kids' hopes of getting ahead have evaporated.

8   The belief that all it takes to "get ahead" is hard work results in people thinking that if they haven't gotten ahead, it's their fault. They didn't work hard enough. My father is a perfect example of this. (When) he was in his thirties and (still) working cleaning up rooms in a hotel, he (gradually) began to see himself as a failure. He blamed himself for not having gotten ahead in America. (A few years later,) when I started college, I tried to get him to take a few classes too. (However,) he was so convinced he was a failure that he simply couldn't imagine going back to school. In fact, there are many causes why, despite hard work, many don't get ahead—an education system that doesn't treat them fairly, the struggle to find the right balance of time and money, a personal crisis, or a personal mistake. It takes more than hard work to get ahead in America. It also takes luck or being born into a middle-class family.

9   The idea that in America if you work hard, you'll get ahead is both untruthful and harmful. It is untruthful because it ignores the many societal conditions that make it unlikely that people born into poverty will be able to get ahead, and it is harmful because it encourages people to think that if they haven't gotten ahead, it's their own fault and, therefore, they should not question an inequitable system.

(**NOTE:** The works cited list always starts on a new page.)

Works Cited

Reardon, Sean. "School District Socioeconomic Status, Race, and Academic
  Achievement." Stanford Center for Educational Policy Analysis, Apr. 2016, https://
  cepa.stanford.edu/sites/default/files/reardon%20district%20ses%20and
  %20achievement%20discussion%20draft%20april2015.pdf.

Salingo, Jeffrey. "Why Do So Many Students Drop Out of College? And What Can Be
  Done About It?" *The Washington Post*, 8 June 2018, https://www.washingtonpost
  .com/news/grade-point/wp/2018/06/08/why-do-so-many-students-drop-out
  -of-college-and-what-can-be-done-about-it/?utm_term=.b2a90fd8aa04.

15.8 Activity

Backward Outlining Applied

Backward Outlining (15.3, p. 415) is a tutorial that explains how to do backward
outlining. Units 15.4 (p. 419), 15.5 (p. 421), and 15.6 (p. 423) explain and show how
you could use a backward outline to improve the thesis, unity, organization, and
support of a draft essay.

For this activity, make a backward outline of a draft of one of your essays and
then use it to revise the thesis, unity, organization, and support of the essay.

15.9 Tutorial

Reviewing Options for What to Include in an Essay

At its most basic, the content of an essay consists of these three components:

- An introduction

- Body paragraphs that provide support for the thesis

- A conclusion

These three components can make a perfectly satisfactory essay, but there are
many other components that can make your essay more interesting, more convincing, and more appealing to the reader, as outlined below. When revising an essay,
ask yourself whether the inclusion of any of these components would improve your
essay.

Ways to Make Essays More Interesting

1. **Add more arguments.** Just because you've come up with three reasons that support the position you have taken in your thesis, there is no reason to stop thinking. Most essays can be made more convincing if they include more reasons, more arguments, to support the thesis.

2. **Provide definitions of key terms.** If there are several words or phrases that are central to your argument, you may want to use a paragraph near the beginning of your essay to explain how you will be using them. For example, if you're writing about juvenile delinquency, you may want to explain what that term will mean in your discussion. It's not that you think your reader has never heard of the term; it's just that it has a wide range of meanings, and you want to make clear what you mean when you use the term. Does it, for example, include juveniles who commit murder? How about juveniles who spray paint graffiti?

3. **Recognize negative effects.** Your thesis may be a good idea, and you may have presented a number of positive outcomes that will result from it, but it is often a good strategy also to admit that there are some negative outcomes that may result. Recognizing these can add to your credibility. They demonstrate that you are knowledgeable enough to be aware of these negatives and honest enough to admit they exist. Of course, it is a good idea if you can also explain why these negatives are less serious than they appear or how they can be mitigated.

4. **Recognize what opponents may say.** Closely related to recognition of negative effects is the recognition of opponents' arguments, especially if those arguments are well known. Summarize them as objectively as you can and then answer, rebut, or counter them.

5. **Include some history of the topic you're writing about.** How long has it been an issue? What positions have others taken about it?

6. **Make suggestions for implementation.** If you are trying to convince your reader to agree with you about some issue, it can be a great idea to include some advice, toward the end of the essay, about what steps will be needed to implement the change you are proposing.

7. **Make a call to action.** Even stronger than advice about implementation is a call to action, urging the reader not just to begin implementing some change, but to actually commit to some cause.

8. **Include background about who you are and/or why you decided to write about the topic.** Especially if it makes you a more credible author or demonstrates you are an author with a particular viewpoint, it can be very helpful to take a paragraph or two to give the reader some information about who you are and why you are writing about the topic.

15.10 Tutorial

A Revision Checklist

Use the following checklist to ensure that the next time you are revising an essay, you think about every single issue that might require revision.

Assignment, Audience, and Purpose

☐ Does the essay meet the requirements of the assignment?

☐ Is the style of the essay appropriate for the anticipated audience?

☐ Is the essay likely to accomplish the purpose of the essay?

Title and Introduction

☐ If your instructor expects a title, have you supplied one that captures the essence of your essay?

☐ Does your introduction provide useful background information?

☐ Does your introduction include a clear statement of your thesis?

☐ Does your introduction make your reader eager to read your paper?

Thesis

☐ Does your essay have a clear thesis?

☐ Is the thesis at the end of the essay the same as the thesis at the beginning?

☐ Does your thesis assert something interesting and thoughtful?

☐ Do you avoid proving the obvious?

Support, Organization, and Unity

☐ Does everything in the essay support the thesis?

☐ Do you provide convincing evidence to support every assertion in the essay?

☐ Are the main points of the essay organized in a logical order?

☐ Are related ideas in your essay grouped together?

☐ Do you provide transitional phrases to assist the reader in following your argument?

☐ Do you answer arguments you can imagine someone who disagrees with you raising?

Conclusion

☐ Even though worded differently, does the thesis in the conclusion make the same statement as the thesis in the introduction?

☐ Did you avoid introducing any new ideas in the conclusion?

TOPIC 16
Editing

Despite questions being raised about the insistence that everyone write in a single standard version of English, it is still the case that being able to write in conformity with the rules of Standard Written English can be extremely beneficial in college and in the workplace.

Navigating Topic 16

In this Topic, you and your classmates are going to learn those pesky grammar rules in a new way. Instead of *The Hub* giving you a set of rules, you will be given examples of sentences without errors and similar sentences with errors. Working in groups, you will examine these sets and discover the underlying grammar rules for yourselves. Knowledge gained in this way, by discovering it for yourself, stays with you longer than knowledge that is simply spelled out for you. In addition, you will learn this information, these writing conventions, in your own language, expressed in a way that makes sense to you and that is easier for you to remember.

To make what you learn truly useful, you need to have a place where you record it. I suggest that you open and save a Word document in which you record everything you learn as you work on Topic 16. Alternatively, you could use a notebook or journal to record this information.

The grammar topics are listed below. Your instructor will probably organize the class into groups to work on these together. However, if you want to, you can explore the ones that interest you on your own. You should also be aware that a more traditional presentation of grammar rules is available at *Achieve for The Hub* through the search function.

Punctuating to Avoid Fragments, Run-Ons, and Comma Splices   438

Using Apostrophes to Show Possession and to Indicate Contractions   458

Ensuring Subject-Verb Agreement   469

Thinking about Grammar

To begin this topic, you will do a little thinking about the concept of grammar in a very general way in Units 16.1 and 16.2.

16.1 Activity
Good and Bad English

You've probably heard people talk about "good English" and "bad English." You may have even used these terms yourself. In this activity, you are being asked to think about the meaning of the terms *good English* and *bad English*.

Working in groups, you will discuss the following questions.

1. What is the difference between "good" English and "bad" English?
2. Why do people consider "bad" English "bad"?
3. Who speaks and writes mostly in "good" English?
4. Why should someone want to become proficient in "good" English?

After about fifteen minutes, your group will be asked to report out its response to each of the questions.

16.2 Presentation
The Grammar in Your Head

To watch a presentation that discusses grammar and how much you already know about it (even if you don't think you know anything), go to *Achieve for The Hub*, Topic 16, and open Unit 16.2.

Punctuating to Avoid Fragments, Run-Ons, and Comma Splices

Punctuation is used to divide sentences into their major parts. Because there is no punctuation in spoken English, the proper use of punctuation sometimes proves difficult for students when they are writing.

What Is a Sentence?

In the past, you may have been taught this traditional definition of a *sentence*:

> A sentence is a group of words containing a subject and a verb and expressing a complete thought.

If that definition works for you, of course, continue to use it. But it doesn't work for all students—especially the "complete thought" part.

Using a Test Frame

If the traditional definition above does not work for you, try this "test frame" devised by Rei Noguchi, a linguist and English teacher who taught for years at California State University, Northridge:

> A sentence is a group of words that makes sense when placed on the line below:
>
> They refused to believe the idea that _____

Here's how it works. If you have written a group of words and are not sure whether they are a sentence or not, you place the words on the blank line in the test frame and then read the entire sentence, beginning with "They refused to believe," out loud. If that sentence "makes sense," then the group of words is a sentence. If it doesn't "make sense," your group of words is not a sentence.

For example, imagine you have written, "The woman running after the bus." Now you are not sure whether that group of words is actually a sentence, so you place it on the blank line in the "test frame" and then read it out loud: "They refused to believe the idea that the woman running after the bus." Clearly that sentence doesn't "make sense," so your original group of words is not a sentence.

Here's another example. You have written, "She placed it in her refrigerator." To see whether that group of words is a sentence, you place it on the black line in the test frame and then read the entire sentence out loud: "They refused to believe the idea that she placed it in her refrigerator." That sounds fine, so the original group of words is a sentence.

One caution: This method of identifying sentences does not work for questions or commands, as the following examples demonstrate.

Question: Did you finish the homework? (This is a complete sentence.)

They refused to believe the idea that <u>did you finish the homework?</u>

Command: Turn off the lights when you come to bed. (This is a complete sentence.)

They refused to believe the idea that <u>turn off the lights when you come to bed.</u>

Activity: Is This a Sentence?

Working in groups, decide whether each of the following is or is not a sentence, using the test frame to make your decision. On the line before each number, enter an S for *sentence* or an N for *not a sentence*.

_____ 1. The woman smoking a cigarette in the parking lot.

_____ 2. I found it in the back seat of my car.

_____ 3. The teacher who gave me a D last semester in math.

_____ 4. When Jorge learned that he had been promoted to manager.

_____ 5. The children cried.

_____ 6. Lashawn knew the answer.

_____ 7. The only question that I missed on the exam.

_____ 8. If Tawanda answers the phone and starts laughing.

_____ 9. Dogs bark.

_____ 10. Saving money is not easy.

16.4 Activity

Fragments

A fragment is usually considered a serious grammatical mistake. The following pairs of items are labeled as either fragments or sentences, with the fragments printed in blue. In Tutorial 16.3 (p. 439), you learned what a sentence is. Now, working in your group, study each of these paired examples and then write a definition of the term *fragment*.

Sentence	✓ I saw the damage to my car.
Fragment	✗ When I saw the damage to my car.
Sentence	✓ I had been studying for a math test.
Fragment	✗ The math test I had been studying for.
Sentence	✓ I love vegetables like Brussels sprouts, broccoli, and asparagus.
Fragment	✗ For example, Brussels sprouts, broccoli, and asparagus.
Sentence	✓ Because Lin was late for class, he had to sit in the front row.
Fragment	✗ Because Lin was late for class.
Sentence	✓ The woman wearing a purple sweater is my psychology teacher.
Fragment	✗ That woman wearing a purple sweater.

NOTE: Write your definition of a *fragment* in a notebook or online file for future reference.

16.5 Activity

Correcting Fragments

The following items include fragments. There are usually several ways to correct a fragment. Working in groups, first identify and underline any fragments in each item and then revise the item so that the fragment is eliminated.

1. When I learned Liz was going to be late. I was furious. She has not been on time for a single meeting this year.

2. The fact that Kayla was promoted. Made me determined to work even harder this year. I am going to get the same kind of promotion if I can.

3. The woman who rode to work on her bike and changed clothes in the women's room. She turned out to be a friend of Courtney's. Now she drives a BMW to work every day.

4. I have saved money out of my check every week for two years. Meaning I now can afford a vacation in Europe. When I return in three weeks. I expect to have some money left over.

5. The teacher in the red blouse and the grey skirt. She is the one who gave me an A in physical education. There was only one reason I got an A. The fact that I was never absent or late.

6. The car Sylvester was driving. It used to belong to L'Tanya. He does not know that it was badly damaged in an accident.

7. The binoculars I borrowed from Ms. Patel and then lost on my camping trip. They cost more than a hundred dollars. I will have to pay her back over the next six months.

8. Until Maria learns I won't be pushed around. I will continue to refuse to work with her. She is just too bossy.

9. To hunt for a cat for three weeks and not find him. That was almost more than I could bear. I had given up looking for him, and he just walked into the backyard.

10. The doctor whom Linda has been going to and who also treated my mother. He has an office on Pratt Street. I have an appointment with him next week.

16.6 Activity

What Is an Independent Clause?

In the following sentences, the independent clauses have been underlined. Working in groups, use what you have already learned about sentences to study the following sentences and figure out what an independent clause is. Working together as a group, write a definition of an *independent clause*. Then write an explanation of the difference between an independent clause and a sentence.

1. The phone rang, and my dog started barking.
2. When it rains, my knees ache.
3. Javier tried to solve the puzzle.
4. Raelyn laughed out loud when she heard the news about Earl.
5. Mark graduates in June, and his sister graduates next year.
6. Because of the snow, the parade was cancelled.
7. Paola is buying a new car this afternoon.
8. Riding a bicycle in the city can be dangerous.
9. Jayla made a salad, and Dion roasted a chicken.
10. If Sarah comes to class tomorrow, I will invite her to the party.

16.7 Activity

Run-Ons and Comma Splices

Run-ons and comma splices are serious errors that many teachers find very problematic. In this unit, you will learn to recognize these two errors. In Correcting Run-Ons and Comma Splices (16.8, p. 444), you will learn how to correct them.

In the following groups of sentences, the versions that are run-ons and comma splices are printed in blue. The correct versions are printed in black. Working in your group, study these examples. Then, as a group, write definitions of a *run-on* and a *comma splice*.

Group 1

Correct	✓ I used to live in Seattle. I worked at Boeing.
Run-On	✗ I used to live in Seattle I worked at Boeing.
Comma Splice	✗ I used to live in Seattle, I worked at Boeing.

Group 2

Correct	✓ Matt walked out of the meeting without saying a word. He was angry at the decision the group had made.
Run-On	✗ Matt walked out of the meeting without saying a word he was angry at the decision the group had made.
Comma Splice	✗ Matt walked out of the meeting without saying a word, he was angry at the decision the group had made.

Group 3

Correct	✓ Deon made a delicious lasagna. His wife made an avocado salad.
Run-On	✗ Deon made a delicious lasagna his wife made an avocado salad.
Comma Splice	✗ Deon made a delicious lasagna, his wife made an avocado salad.

Group 4

Correct	✓ All flights to Denver were cancelled. There was a terrible ice storm.
Run-On	✗ All flights to Denver were cancelled there was a terrible ice storm.
Comma Splice	✗ All flights to Denver were cancelled, there was a terrible ice storm.

NOTE: Write your definition of a *run-on* in a notebook or online file for future reference.

NOTE: Write your definition of a *comma splice* in a notebook or online file for future reference.

Correcting Run-Ons and Comma Splices

In Run-Ons and Comma Splices (16.7, p. 442), you learned to recognize run-ons and comma splices within four groups of sentences. In this activity, you will learn how to correct them.

Each of the following groups of sentences begins with a run-on and then a comma splice. These errors, shown in blue, are followed by five correct sentences representing a variety of methods to correct run-ons and comma splices. There are more ways for correcting these errors, but the ones here should give you an idea of the range of options.

Working in your group, make a list of at least five ways to correct run-ons and comma splices. Then see if you can think of one or two additional ways to do so.

Group 1

Run-On	✗	I lived in Seattle in 2008 I worked at Boeing.
Comma Splice	✗	I lived in Seattle in 2008, I worked at Boeing.
Correct	✓	I lived in Seattle in 2008. I worked at Boeing.
Correct	✓	I lived in Seattle in 2008; I worked at Boeing.
Correct	✓	When I lived in Seattle in 2008, I worked at Boeing.
Correct	✓	While living in Seattle in 2008, I worked at Boeing.
Correct	✓	I lived in Seattle in 2008; at that time, I worked at Boeing.

Group 2

Run-On	✗	Matt walked out of the meeting without saying a word he was angry at the decision the group had made.
Comma Splice	✗	Matt walked out of the meeting without saying a word, he was angry at the decision the group had made.
Correct	✓	Matt walked out of the meeting without saying a word. He was angry at the decision the group had made.
Correct	✓	Matt walked out of the meeting without saying a word; he was angry at the decision the group had made.
Correct	✓	Matt walked out of the meeting without saying a word because he was angry at the decision the group had made.

Correct	✓ Angry at the decision the group had made, Matt walked out of the meeting without saying a word.
Correct	✓ Matt was angry at the decision the group had made; as a result, he walked out of the meeting without saying a word.

Group 3

Run-On	✗ Deon made a delicious lasagna his wife made an avocado salad.
Comma Splice	✗ Deon made a delicious lasagna, his wife made an avocado salad.
Correct	✓ Deon made a delicious lasagna. His wife made an avocado salad.
Correct	✓ Deon made a delicious lasagna; his wife made an avocado salad.
Correct	✓ While Deon made a delicious lasagna, his wife made an avocado salad.
Correct	✓ While Deon's wife made an avocado salad, he made a delicious lasagna.
Correct	✓ Deon made a delicious lasagna; meanwhile, his wife made an avocado salad.

Group 4

Run-On	✗ All flights to Denver were cancelled there was a terrible ice storm.
Comma Splice	✗ All flights to Denver were cancelled, there was a terrible ice storm.
Correct	✓ All flights to Denver were cancelled. There was a terrible ice storm.
Correct	✓ All flights to Denver were cancelled; there was a terrible ice storm.
Correct	✓ All flights to Denver were cancelled because there was a terrible ice storm.
Correct	✓ Because there was a terrible ice storm, all flights to Denver were cancelled.
Correct	✓ There was a terrible ice storm; as a result, all flights to Denver were cancelled.

NOTE: Record at least five ways to correct a run-on or comma splice in a notebook or online file for future reference.

16.9 Activity

Correcting Fragments, Run-Ons, and Comma Splices

In Unit 16.5 (p. 441), you learned to correct fragments, and in Unit 16.8 (p. 444), you learned to correct run-ons and comma splices. In this activity, you will put all that you learned together. In the following sentences, correct all the errors, which include fragments, run-ons, and comma splices.

1. I am getting a blister on my thumb, I will have to quit playing soon.
2. When she made a chocolate cake for my mother. She forgot to add any sugar.
3. The man wearing a plaid jacket. He is my math teacher.
4. When Aryelle opened the newspaper. She saw a picture of her old boyfriend.
5. There was no money in my account, the bank honored my check anyway.
6. Odelia's brother has done many stupid things. Such as getting four tickets for speeding. He also is in trouble for bouncing checks.
7. Because Jordan drank fourteen cans of beer. We had to carry him home.
8. Anthony is trying to run two miles every morning. To lose ten pounds in the next three months.
9. The management at my apartment building does a great job. For example, having the parking lot plowed every time it snows. In addition, they keep the lawn in great shape.
10. I have never been to Las Vegas, I have no intention of going now.
11. The picnic has been called off let's all get together at Rab's house.
12. My father made a phone call, then he drove away without saying a word.
13. I hoped to get a part in the play. Even though I knew my chances were not very good. I thought the director might need an actor with a southern accent.
14. When Dexter got to the parking lot. He realized he had left his book in the classroom.
15. I wanted chocolate chip I got mocha chocolate.
16. I am experiencing some physical problems as I reach my fifties. My knees bother me a lot. Also, shortness of breath when I try to run.
17. Gus ran as hard as he could, he came in third.
18. The cake is delicious I cannot eat another bite.
19. Jessica lost fourteen pounds on her diet, I lost only six.
20. Peaches bought a new computer. Using the money she had won in the lottery.

16.10 Activity

Punctuating Independent Clauses 1

In the following pairs of items, the sentence in black is correct, and the sentence in blue has an error. Study these sentences and figure out which grammar rule they all demonstrate.

Pair 1

✓ Chin lives in Overlea, and his brother lives in Parkville.

✗ Chin lives in Overlea and his brother lives in Parkville.

Pair 2

✓ Drew bought a laptop, but he has not learned how to use it.

✗ Drew bought a laptop but he has not learned how to use it.

Pair 3

✓ Kyesha went to the ocean, and it rained every day.

✗ Kyesha went to the ocean and it rained every day.

Pair 4

✓ Maria works at a bakery, but she is looking for a second job.

✗ Maria works at a bakery but she is looking for a second job.

NOTE: Don't record anything in your notebook or online file until you have completed Unit 16.12 (p. 448).

16.11 Activity

Punctuating Independent Clauses 2

In the following pairs, the sentence in black is correct, and the sentence in blue has an error. Study these sentences and figure out which grammar rule they all demonstrate.

Pair 1

✓ Hector opened his biology book and started to study.

✗ Hector opened his biology book, and started to study.

Pair 2

    ✓ Mary opened the door and let a strange cat into the house.

    ✗ Mary opened the door, and let a strange cat into the house.

Pair 3

    ✓ Oklahoma is a great place to work and to raise children.

    ✗ Oklahoma is a great place to work, and to raise children.

Pair 4

    ✓ My mother has worked hard all her life but has not gotten ahead as a result.

    ✗ My mother has worked hard all her life, but has not gotten ahead as a result.

NOTE: While the second sentence in Pair 4 illustrates the "official" rule, many people disregard the rule and use a comma before the *but* anyhow.

NOTE: Don't record anything in your notebook or online file until you've completed Unit 16.12.

16.12 Activity

Punctuating Independent Clauses 3

Now here are all the sentence pairs from Units 16.10 (p. 447) and 16.11 (p. 447). Sentences printed in black are correct; those printed in blue are incorrect. Study them carefully and figure out what the grammar rule is for these kinds of sentences. You may want to refresh your memory of what an "independent clause" is before you work on these (see Unit 16.6 [p. 442]).

Pair 1

    ✓ Chin lives in Overlea, and his brother lives in Parkville.

    ✗ Chin lives in Overlea and his brother lives in Parkville.

Pair 2

    ✓ Drew bought a laptop, but he has not learned how to use it.

    ✗ Drew bought a laptop but he has not learned how to use it.

Pair 3

   ✓ Kyesha went to the ocean, and it rained every day.

   ✗ Kyesha went to the ocean and it rained every day.

Pair 4

   ✓ Maria works at a bakery, but she is looking for a second job.

   ✗ Maria works at a bakery but she is looking for a second job.

Pair 5

   ✓ Hector opened his biology book and started to study.

   ✗ Hector opened his biology book, and started to study.

Pair 6

   ✓ Mary opened the door and let a strange cat into the house.

   ✗ Mary opened the door, and let a strange cat into the house.

Pair 7

   ✓ Oklahoma is a great place to work and to raise children.

   ✗ Oklahoma is a great place to work, and to raise children.

Pair 8

   ✓ My mother has worked hard all her life but has not gotten ahead as a result.

   ✗ My mother has worked hard all her life, but has not gotten ahead as a result.

NOTE: Record the grammar rule these items demonstrate in a notebook or online file for future reference.

16.13 Activity

Punctuating Independent Clauses 4

The sentences you have been working on in Units 16.10 (p. 447), 16.11 (p. 447), and 16.12 (p. 448) all used the conjunctions *and* or *but*. These are the most frequently used of the *coordinating conjunctions*, but there are others. Here's the complete list.

You might want to use the word FANBOYS, which is spelled with the first letter of all seven, to remember them.

For

And

Nor

But

Or

Yet

So

In the following sentence pairs, the black sentences are correct; the blue ones contain an error. Study these to see whether these five additional conjunctions follow the same grammar rules as *and* and *but*.

Pair 1

✓ In New York most people ride the subway to work, or they take a bus.

✗ In New York most people ride the subway to work or they take a bus.

Pair 2

✓ For breakfast I usually have a bowl of cereal or some scrambled eggs.

✗ For breakfast I usually have a bowl of cereal, or some scrambled eggs.

Pair 3

✓ Negotiations are going to continue all night, for the union has announced a strike for tomorrow morning.

✗ Negotiations are going to continue all night for the union has announced a strike for tomorrow morning.

Pair 4

✓ Nathan studied all weekend for the midterm test in his biology class.

✗ Nathan studied all weekend, for the midterm test in his biology class.

Pair 5

✓ There is an accident on the Expressway this morning, so I am driving through the city.

✗ There is an accident on the Expressway this morning so I am driving through the city.

Pair 6

    ✓ My daughter has grown so tall that she needs a new bed.

    ✗ My daughter has grown, so tall that she needs a new bed.

Pair 7

    ✓ I have applied for more than a dozen jobs, yet I have not been invited for a single interview.

    ✗ I have applied for more than a dozen jobs yet I have not been invited for a single interview.

Pair 8

    ✓ We haven't yet received any word from our daughter in Brazil.

    ✗ We haven't, yet received any word from our daughter in Brazil.

Pair 9

    ✓ The new café in my neighborhood doesn't serve espresso, nor does the café near my work.

    ✗ The new café in my neighborhood doesn't serve espresso nor does the café near my work.

Pair 10

    ✓ Neither the textbook for my math class nor the website explains how to factor polynomials.

    ✗ Neither the textbook for my math class, nor the website explains how to factor polynomials.

NOTE: Record in a notebook or online file whether the five additional conjunctions in the preceding examples follow the same grammar rules as *and* and *but*.

16.14 Activity

Punctuating Introductory Elements 1

In the following pairs of sentences, the black versions are correct; the blue versions include an error. Study these to see what punctuation rule they illustrate.

Pair 1

   ✓ When it rains, my knees ache.

   ✗ When it rains my knees ache.

Pair 2

   ✓ Because I sprained my ankle, I cannot play tennis this weekend.

   ✗ Because I sprained my ankle I cannot play tennis this weekend.

Pair 3

   ✓ If I miss the bus, I will have to wait for an hour.

   ✗ If I miss the bus I will have to wait for an hour.

Pair 4

   ✓ Running after the bus, Jamey sprained his ankle.

   ✗ Running after the bus Jamey sprained his ankle.

Pair 5

   ✓ In the third drawer from the top, I found my iPhone.

   ✗ In the third drawer from the top I found my iPhone.

Pair 6

   ✓ To open a bank account, Susan had to fill out more than a dozen forms.

   ✗ To open a bank account Susan had to fill out more than a dozen forms.

NOTE: Don't record anything in your notebook or online file until you have completed Unit 16.15.

16.15 Activity

Punctuating Introductory Elements 2

The following pairs of sentences demonstrate one additional complication to the punctuation rule you worked on in Unit 16.14 (p. 451). Study them to determine what this complication is. Again, the black sentences are correct; the blue ones have an error.

Pair 1

   ✓ When I graduate will be a time for celebrating.

   ✗ When I graduate, will be a time for celebrating.

Pair 2

   ✓ Being unemployed can produce much anxiety.

   ✗ Being unemployed, can produce much anxiety.

Pair 3

   ✓ To let the dog out without a leash was a big mistake.

   ✗ To let the dog out without a leash, was a big mistake.

Pair 4

   ✓ In the top drawer of my dresser is a collection of mismatched socks.

   ✗ In the top drawer of my dresser, is a collection of mismatched socks.

Pair 5

   ✓ Taking five courses this semester has been very stressful.

   ✗ Taking five courses this semester, has been very stressful.

NOTE: What complication to the punctuation rule you identified in Unit 16.14 do these items illustrate? Record your answer in a notebook or online file.

16.16 Activity

Editing an Essay for Punctuation 1

Proofread the following essay and correct any errors you find. These errors will be in the following categories:

- Fragments
- Run-on sentences
- Comma splices
- Errors punctuating two independent clauses joined by *and, but, or, for, so, yet,* or *nor*
- Errors punctuating introductory elements

In some cases, you will be able to correct errors by simply adding or deleting punctuation; in other cases, especially when editing fragments, you may need to do a little rewording of the sentence.

Anticipation Can Kill the Moment

I don't remember my last day of college. It's an odd thing to admit but I don't remember such a major milestone in my life. I don't recall any tearful goodbyes to my favorite professors. Any solemn "see you laters" to my friends and classmates. The whole day is a blank. All the celebration and sadness that I would imagine happened is simply missing from my memory.

For a while, I wondered why this was. After four years of late nights in the library or early mornings working in the dining hall the final day was a dark spot in my memory. All the anticipation of four years of learning, and training for the real world, and I don't remember what I had for breakfast, or if I slept in. It's funny how the most important of days seems to slip by like that, they seem so brief in comparison to the time spent waiting for them. You might miss them if you blink slowly.

What I came to realize, is that many days that held significance in my life were equally blank. My high school graduation, for one. That day was nothing but a commencement speech, as far as I know. Another important day that I can't remember, was my first date, I can't remember picking up my date, taking her home, or anything in between. Similarly, I can't remember the last playoff game I played in high school. I know we lost but I don't know how that happened.

Thinking about all of these days I realized that the thing I remember most about graduating college was fear, I had felt it creeping up on me for the entirety of my final semester. Looking over my shoulder as I filled out job applications and hoped for something to turn up. There's nothing like realizing, after four years of relative safety, that there is nothing standing between you and adulthood. No more years of school, no more time to prepare for jobs, no one to depend on but yourself after you cross the stage. Like all the most important moments in life it's a plunge that has to be taken. A band-aid that has to be ripped off in order to move forward.

So it was for all the other important days I feel I've missed, I remember feeling that fear or anticipation, but not the event itself. I spent so much time worrying about it during the buildup. For my first date, I remember sweating over how much Axe body spray to use, what clothes to wear, and whether the girl liked me or not. For the baseball game I simply wondered if I would play, and for how long, and if we could win it. For graduation my thoughts focused on the future, rather than on the moment I was in. I wondered about where I would work, or if I could even find a job. Worried that I might fail if I ventured out into the world. The anticipation, it seems, killed the moment.

16.17 Activity

Editing an Essay for Punctuation 2

Proofread the following essay and correct any errors you find. These errors will be in the following categories:

- Fragments
- Run-on sentences
- Comma splices
- Errors punctuating two independent clauses joined by *and, but, or, for, so, yet,* or *nor*
- Errors punctuating introductory elements

In some cases, you will be able to correct errors by simply adding or deleting punctuation; in other cases, especially when editing fragments, you may need to do a little rewording of the sentence.

New or Used?

Among the hardest choices of adult life is what kind of car to buy, there are seemingly millions of options to choose from. Whether it's got leather or velour seats, compact or SUV, or any of the dizzying array of colors that manufacturers conjure up. It's not just the looks or the brand that matter while searching there are also seemingly endless places to buy a car, from local shops with a scattering of used vehicles to massive dealerships with parking lots full of options. But underlying all of this is whether to buy new or used and as each has its perks, this can further complicate car buying.

Of course, the first and most important thing to do in a car search is to decide what kind of car you want. This means narrowing down the brands, the makes, and models that you could imagine yourself owning. If you tend to do a lot of sporting activities. Maybe consider a hatchback or an SUV for some extra storage space. If you have a long commute every day, maybe look at compact cars that get good gas mileage. It's essential to think long and hard about what your lifestyle will require, and then to look for that type of car in a brand you trust.

Then you have to make the hard decision of whether to buy new or used. Without a doubt, a new car will be more expensive. No matter how hard you haggle it will end up being thousands of dollars more than older, used models with some mileage on them. In exchange for this upfront cost, though, the car should (theoretically) last for many years, and will include all of the latest technology available. You may also be able to get a warrantee. Which will guarantee free repairs on certain parts of the vehicle for tens of thousands of miles—some brands will even dole out a lifetime warrantee for their vehicles but this is rare. You also have the guarantee that the car has never been in an accident, never had coffee spilled on the seats, and has never had a shaggy dog shed fur all over the rugs.

A used car, sadly, can't always give you that guarantee. Firstly, there's the possibility of a sleazy used-car salesman who sells you an old junker with a promise and a trustworthy smile and the junker breaks down in a cloud of steam and bitter feelings mere weeks later. Many car shops will try to take advantage of first-time car buyers. Selling damaged and even dangerous cars to unsuspecting drivers for new-car money. This often happens in private deals (i.e., a person sells their car to another person without a dealership or auto shop in the middle), but can also happen at less-than-reputable used car lots. A bad deal like this will not always result in injury or a broken-down vehicle, but may simply be a rip-off, used cars are often sold for more than they're worth, which is why it's important to use price-comparison tools like Kelley Blue Book for background research.

Although the consequences of a bad deal can be dire buying a used car means you also have the opportunity to get more than you pay for. Some people buy cars for thousands of dollars less than what they're worth, simply because the owner is trying to get rid of the vehicle at any cost, and a substantial discount in insurance costs. You also avoid the immediate and steep drop in the car's value, which hits the moment you drive a new car off the lot. With a used car you're on the benefiting end of that price drop, and you might end up with a car that's been so well taken care of that it might as well be new. Even last year's model, with practically new features and very few miles on the odometer could be several thousand dollars cheaper used than it was new. To get these deals, is not easy, you have to ask around, this will only work if you have a dealer or another seller whom you trust, who you know won't take advantage of you.

There are a number of different factors that could decide whether you buy new or used, in the end, it will always come down to what you need. If you want a warrantee and a literal carload of new gadgets then maybe a new car is the right way to go. If you want something tried and tested for a bargain price, and are willing to risk some extra maintenance costs in the long run, then a used car might be a better fit. But regardless of which is the right choice for you, it always pays to ask around and find a dealer or a seller who can deliver on your needs. More important than whether you buy a new or a used vehicle will always be whether you trust the person selling it to you.

Using Apostrophes to Show Possession and to Indicate Contractions

Apostrophes can be troublesome because they have two completely different uses in English: to show possession and to indicate contractions.

16.18 Tutorial

Apostrophes 1 (Possessives)

The most common use of apostrophes is to show possession, and most everyone knows that possession is similar to ownership. When you write about "Maggie's car," you mean the car that Maggie owns. When you talk about "my mother's house," you mean the house that your mother owns. However, the use of apostrophes to show possession is much broader than just "ownership." Look at this example:

> We saw Picasso's painting of three musicians in the Museum of Modern Art.

The word *Picasso* is possessive, but Picasso doesn't own that painting; the Museum of Modern Art owns it. Picasso made it. Here are two more examples of a possessive being used to indicate something that someone made:

> Shana's essay was almost five pages long.
>
> Donna's risotto was judged to be the best in the entire city.

Up to this point, you've seen possession used to express two relationships: when someone owns something and when someone has made something. The following sentences contain possessive words expressing other relationships. Working in your group, study each set of sentences and record a brief statement of the kind of relationship being represented by the possessives.

Set 1

> Miguel's arm was fractured in the accident.
>
> My car's windshield is cracked.
>
> My school's roof was damaged in the storm.

Kind of relationship: _____

Set 2

LaDawn's sister was hired at the restaurant where I work.

Chris's mother will graduate from college this semester.

Kyle's niece is getting married this weekend.

Kind of relationship: _____

Set 3

Max's forgetfulness has caused him many problems.

Lizzie's thoughtfulness makes her a great friend.

I really enjoy Gillian's sense of humor.

Kind of relationship: _____

Set 4

Jake was not aware of the college's policy on withdrawing from classes.

Toyota's logo looks like a T made out of circles.

Milano's menu is mostly Italian dishes, but there are some American items too.

Kind of relationship: _____

Set 5

Many of today's students are working at least twenty hours a week.

A one-hour's delay would have caused us to miss our connection in Chicago.

This year's tomatoes are larger than ever.

Kind of relationship: _____

NOTE: The possessive word always appears in front of the word being possessed.

16.19 Activity

Apostrophes 2 (Possessives)

Working in your group, underline or highlight the possessive words in the following sentences. Every sentence may not have a possessive word, and some may have two.

1. Marcella's umbrella is bright red.
2. Today's special is meatloaf and mashed potatoes.
3. I grabbed my boss's hand and shook it forcefully.
4. My professor's absence policy was stricter than the college's policy.
5. Several dogs were barking as I walked up the sidewalk.
6. I have often observed my professor's compassion for students.
7. I was very impressed with the soprano's voice.
8. My bicycle's tire was flat.
9. Yesterday's snow was completely melted by this morning.
10. Craig's book's cover had a large coffee stain.

16.20 Activity

Apostrophes 3 (Possessives)

The following groups of sentences demonstrate one rule about the use of apostrophes. Again, the black sentences are correct; the blue ones have an error. Study these examples and figure out the grammar rule they illustrate.

Group 1

✓ Mariel's laptop was stolen from her car.

✗ Mariels laptop was stolen from her car.

✗ Mariels' laptop was stolen from her car.

Group 2

✓ Greg's car is a Volkswagen.

✗ Gregs car is a Volkswagen.

✗ Gregs' car is a Volkswagen.

Group 3

✓ Jan was sitting in her teacher's car.

✗ Jan was sitting in her teachers car.

✗ Jan was sitting in her teachers' car.

Group 4

✓ I found someone's purse in the restroom.

✗ I found someones purse in the restroom.

✗ I found someones' purse in the restroom.

NOTE: Record the grammar rule these items demonstrate in a notebook or online file for future reference.

16.21 Activity

Apostrophes 4 (Possessives)

The following groups of sentences demonstrate a second rule about the use of apostrophes. Again, the black sentences are correct; the blue ones have an error. Study these examples and figure out the grammar rule they illustrate.

Group 1

✓ These two students' essays are excellent examples.

✗ These two students essays are excellent examples.

✗ These two student's essays are excellent examples.

Group 2

✓ My grandparents' house is more than a hundred years old.

✗ My grandparents house is more than a hundred years old.

✗ My grandparent's house is more than a hundred years old.

Group 3

✓ The two candidates' speeches were long and boring.

✗ The two candidate's speeches were long and boring.

✗ The two candidates speeches were long and boring.

Group 4

✓ Three chairs' cushions were stained when Aris spilled a glass of wine.

✗ Three chairs cushions were stained when Aris spilled a glass of wine.

✗ Three chair's cushions were stained when Aris spilled a glass of wine.

NOTE: Record the grammar rule these items demonstrate in a notebook or online file for future reference.

16.22 Activity

Apostrophes 5 (Possessives)

The following groups of sentences demonstrate a third rule about the use of apostrophes. This grammar rule affects only a small group of words, but it's the one that causes students the most trouble. Again, the black sentences are correct; the blue ones have an error. Study these examples and figure out the rule they illustrate.

Group 1

✓ The children's coats were soaking wet, but they didn't seem to mind.

✗ The childrens coats were soaking wet, but they didn't seem to mind.

✗ The childrens' coats were soaking wet, but they didn't seem to mind.

Group 2

✓ The men's names were Jose and Juan.

✗ The mens names were Jose and Juan.

✗ The mens' names were Jose and Juan.

Group 3

✓ My wife asked the server where the women's room was.

✗ My wife asked the server where the womens room was.

✗ My wife asked the server where the womens' room was.

Group 4

✓ The two deer's footprints were clearly visible in the mud.

✗ The two deers footprints were clearly visible in the mud.

✗ The two deers' footprints were clearly visible in the mud.

NOTE: Record the grammar rule these items demonstrate in a notebook or online file for future reference.

Apostrophes 6 (Contractions)

While the most common use for apostrophes is to indicate possession, they are also used to form contractions. Contractions are formed by combining two words into one and leaving out one or more letters. Note that the apostrophe is placed where the letter or letters have been left out, not at the place where the two words are joined.

is not → isn't

she will → she'll

I am → I'm

we had → we'd

can not → can't

Contractions are not appropriate in formal writing. When deciding whether contractions are appropriate in a particular piece of writing, it's a good idea to ask the person you are writing for. Some teachers think apostrophes are inappropriate in college essays; others think they are fine.

Activity: Practice with Contractions

Form contractions with each of the following pairs of words:

they are	it is
he is	who is
could not	are not
had not	did not
you are	have not

Contractions versus Possessive Pronouns

Students frequently create errors in their writing because they confuse contractions and possessive pronouns, especially the ones that are spelled quite similarly. Study the following examples and try to figure out when to use the version with an apostrophe and when to use the one without an apostrophe. The sentences in black are correct. The ones in blue include an error.

After you've studied these examples, write a paragraph in which you explain how to decide when an apostrophe is needed with pronouns like these and when it is wrong to use an apostrophe with them.

Pair 1

✓ I hope it's not too late to sign up for the trip to Washington.

✗ I hope its not too late to sign up for the trip to Washington.

Pair 2

✓ Jill watched as her dog hid its bone under the bed.

✗ Jill watched as her dog hid it's bone under the bed.

Pair 3

✓ I hope you're coming to the movie with us.

✗ I hope your coming to the movie with us.

Pair 4

✓ Juanita saw your sister in the supermarket.

✗ Juanita saw you're sister in the supermarket.

Pair 5

✓ Jamard's parents are selling their house and moving to Florida.

✗ Jamard's parents are selling they're house and moving to Florida.

Pair 6

✓ They're making a new movie about Alexander Hamilton.

✗ Their making a new movie about Alexander Hamilton.

Pair 7

✓ I wonder whose car that is parked in front of my house.

✗ I wonder who's car that is parked in front of my house.

Pair 8

✓ Tamira knows who's driving to the beach this weekend.

✗ Tamira knows whose driving to the beach this weekend.

NOTE: Record the apostrophe rule these items demonstrate in a notebook or online file for future reference.

16.25 Activity
Editing an Essay for Apostrophes 1

The following essay has errors involving apostrophes. Working in your group, edit the essay to correct these errors.

The Death Penalty

Were all familiar in America with the justice system. Due to the large police presence around the country, its virtually certain that, in some way or another, every single person in the country has had an interaction with law enforcement at some point. Most of us get a speeding ticket here and there, but for the worst offenders—murderers, serial rapists, and the like—the penalty goes all the way up to and including death. The United States is one of the only developed nation's in the world to still allow the death penalty, which raises the question: why? In many cases, the death penalty is not only an inhumane way to treat violence in society, but it can also come out to be more expensive and more time-consuming than comparable rehabilitation programs.

While the death penalty certainly instills fear in many criminals, its never been enough to deter every one of them from committing a heinous crime like murder. So then the question remains, why continue? It solves nothing to kill a murderer—if anything, it only serves to remind us that, as Gandhi once said, "An eye for an eye leaves the whole world blind." It also helps to remember that revenge is not the same as justice, and its' not worth pursuing if the real goal is to prevent future crimes. Families of a murderers' victims may desire to kill the person as payment for their loss, but in reality they only become a little more like the criminal, and in the process another life is taken.

Another more calculating reason to forgo the death penalty is it's extraordinary cost. While an actual execution may not be very expensive, according to a number of recent studies imprisoning death row inmates can be upwards of fifty percent more expensive than for the general prison population.

And then theres the appeal process; most inmates are in a legal fight for their lives right up until the day that theyre killed. That means thousands of hours of legal work for public defenders and prosecutors as inmates work their way through the endless appeals of the American justice system, and those hours are billed directly to the taxpayer's. This compares to roughly two hundred hours of appeals on average for a general population inmate.

And while the drugs often used to execute prisoners are usually cheap, that has not been so in the last couple years. Ohio, Texas, and Oklahoma are just a few of the states that have experienced shortages of the drugs used for lethal injections, which has driven up they're price. Other states' have even considered bringing back the firing squad, although human right's groups are unlikely to be impressed by that proposal.

And then there are the cases where the police, or a prosecutor, or some other office along the way gets it wrong. These are cases where innocent people are sent to their death for crimes they didn't commit. According to a 2014 study, roughly one in twenty-five inmates sentenced to death is innocent—and yet not all of them are able to make their case before their execution is carried out. This amounts to murder by the justice system rather than justice for the victims.

Whether its the cost or the issue of human rights', the death penalty is a holdover from an older era that we could do without. Most countries in the world have done away with it already, leaving the United States as one of only fifty-eight nations that still allow it. Some US states have even banned the practice, such as Massachusetts, New York, and New Mexico. Meanwhile, other states have gone to increasing lengths to keep killing their worst criminals. But rather than trying to erase the problem of violent crime, what we as a society should be doing is working to treat the causes of violence. Treatment, early intervention, and better policing are all more effective ways to try to keep violent crime from occurring—and any of them is more humane than trading life-for-life.

Editing an Essay for Apostrophes 2

The following essay has errors involving apostrophes. Working in your group, edit the essay to correct these errors.

Cooking in the Digital Age

We have a tradition in my family: every Christmas, my mom makes about a dozen small fruitcakes and sends them out to all our relative's households. Some go to New York to my moms sister, some to my dads' family in California, and one travels south to Florida. Its a tradition that weve repeated every year since I was just a little kid.

Every Thanksgiving, after the turkey had been eaten and the leftovers' stashed away for the next week of meals, my mom and I would break out the bowls and measuring cups, the fake maraschino cherries and the candied fruit chunks—and the dreaded figs—and set to work. The fruitcakes would be assembled, the batter would be sampled, and salmonella would be warned of. Then came the wrapping: in order to make a fruitcake properly, it had to sit wrapped in a bourbon-soaked gauze for roughly a month, which not only preserves it but also adds a little zip from the bourbon.

This is the tradition. Every Christmas we cut up the cake and enjoy a few slices (people may cringe, but its' the only genuinely good fruitcake in the known world). It's been this way for decades, ever since my mom got the recipe from my grandmother. But this kind of cooking and passing down of recipes' is falling out of fashion. Since the advent of the internet, family recipes have taken a backseat to quick and easy meals found online, leading more and more young cooks to start at they're phone or they're computer rather than at a cookbook.

A prime example of this trend is Buzzfeed. You might have heard of their news service or social media commentary, but Buzzfeed is also known for it's series of tasty videos. These show time-lapse video's of someone making a certain recipe, often something exotic like a cheeseburger with buns made of fried mac and cheese. The videos are entertainment (and believe me, their as entertaining as they are mouth-watering), but theyre also meant to be instructive. Some episodes will have a guest chef come and teach a new cooking technique, or theyll have a Buzzfeed employees parent come and make their family recipe.

This has become the new norm. The internet is a vast reference book for those who seek tips or recipes or just want to dream about something juicy. Other outlets have gone a similar route to Buzzfeed, and they're videos now take up a great deal of space on everyones' Facebook feed. Its a "thing" for this generation to try out these videos, too; I myself am guilty of using a Buzzfeed recipe to make a "pizza bread boule." (Yes, it's exactly what you're picturing.)

New studies' are showing, however, that millennials are coming into the real world without real-world skills like cooking. In answering the question why that is, the internet cooking craze may be part of the reason. It used to be that you learned a few recipes from someone at home and learned to improvise from there. But now its click, scroll, and read; some site's will even tell you what you can make from the leftover ingredients you find at the back of your fridge. Its' no longer solely a family experience—cooking has become both incredibly accessible and harder to learn properly at the same time.

There are pros and cons to this new way of doing things. On the one hand, not everyone can learn to cook or has someone at home to teach them. For those people, the internet is a welcome helper in the kitchen, where the endless combinations' of ingredients can be an overwhelming place to start. But whats lost are the traditional recipes like my moms' fruitcake, which is not something that will make it's way into a Buzzfeed video anytime soon. Learning to cook at home is learning to cook properly, to improvise and to figure out what combinations work, and to create your own recipes. That creativity may not make it to this generation—though at least well always have mac and cheese buns.

Ensuring Subject-Verb Agreement

Subject-verb agreement errors can greatly diminish the effectiveness of your writing; luckily, they are not that difficult to correct.

16.27 Activity

Subject-Verb Agreement 1

In the following pairs, the sentence in black is correct, and the sentence in blue has an error. Study these sentences and figure out the grammar rule they demonstrate.

Pair 1

✓ One student rides a motorcycle to school.

✗ One student ride a motorcycle to school.

Pair 2

✓ Two students ride motorcycles to school.

✗ Two students rides motorcycles to school.

Pair 3

✓ A tree grows in Brooklyn.

✗ A tree grow in Brooklyn.

Pair 4

✓ Many trees grow in Brooklyn.

✗ Many trees grows in Brooklyn.

Pair 5

✓ Marcia's mother lives in California.

✗ Marcia's mother live in California.

Pair 6

✓ Marcia's parents live in California.

✗ Marcia's parents lives in California.

NOTE: Record the grammar rule these items demonstrate in a notebook or online file for future reference.

Subject-Verb Agreement 2

In the following sentence pairs, the sentence in black is correct, and the sentence in blue has an error. Study these sentences and figure out the grammar rule they demonstrate.

Pair 1

✓ An essay is due on Friday.

✗ An essay are due on Friday.

Pair 2

✓ Four essays are required in this course.

✗ Four essays is required in this course.

Pair 3

✓ He is my cousin.

✗ He are my cousin.

Pair 4

✓ They are my best friends.

✗ They is my best friends.

Pair 5

✓ A car was parked in my driveway.

✗ A car were parked in my driveway.

Pair 6

✓ Two cars were parked in my driveway.

✗ Two cars was parked in my driveway.

Pair 7

✓ A police officer was waiting on my porch.

✗ A police officer were waiting on my porch.

Pair 8

✓ Two police officers were waiting on my porch.

✗ Two police officers was waiting on my porch.

NOTE: Record the grammar rule these items demonstrate in a notebook or online file for future reference.

16.29 Activity

Subject-Verb Agreement 3

In the following sentence pairs, the sentence in black is correct, and the sentence in blue has an error. Study these sentences and figure out the grammar rule they demonstrate.

Pair 1

✓ A friend of my parents lives in Denver.

✗ A friend of my parents live in Denver.

Pair 2

✓ A box of cookies was left on my doorstep.

✗ A box of cookies were left on my doorstep.

Pair 3

✓ One of my friends was in a car accident.

✗ One of my friends were in a car accident.

Pair 4

✓ The box of crayons was on sale for ninety-nine cents.

✗ The box of crayons were on sale for ninety-nine cents.

Pair 5

✓ High levels of water pollution are a threat to health.

✗ High levels of water pollution is a threat to health.

Pair 6

   ✓ Many songs on the top-ten list are ballads.

   ✗ Many songs on the top-ten list is ballads.

NOTE: Record the grammar rule these items demonstrate in a notebook or online file for future reference.

16.30 Activity

Subject-Verb Agreement 4 (Indefinite Pronouns 1)

In the following pairs, the sentence in black is correct, and the sentence in blue has an error. Study these sentences and figure out the grammar rule they demonstrate.

Pair 1

   ✓ Everyone in my math class is going to pass.

   ✗ Everyone in my math class are going to pass.

Pair 2

   ✓ Someone is waiting in your office.

   ✗ Someone are waiting in your office.

Pair 3

   ✓ Anyone with a question is invited to attend the meeting.

   ✗ Anyone with a question are invited to attend the meeting.

Pair 4

   ✓ Each of the puppies was adorable.

   ✗ Each of the puppies were adorable.

Pair 5

   ✓ Either of those sweaters is a good match with that skirt.

   ✗ Either of those sweaters are a good match with that skirt.

Pair 6

   ✓ One of these bicycles was stolen.

   ✗ One of these bicycles were stolen.

Pair 7

    ✓ Neither of these jobs offers medical insurance.

    ✗ Neither of these jobs offer medical insurance.

NOTE: Record the grammar rule these items demonstrate in a notebook or online file for future reference.

Indefinite Pronouns 1

You probably noticed that the subject in each of the preceding sentences is a pronoun; in fact, it is a special kind of pronoun known as an *indefinite pronoun*. Below is a list of common indefinite pronouns. Note that these indefinite pronouns are *always singular*. In Activity 16.31, you will encounter other indefinite pronouns that are not always singular.

Always singular			
anybody	everybody	neither/either	one
anyone	everyone	nobody	somebody
anything	everything	no one	someone
each	much	nothing	something

16.31 Activity

Subject-Verb Agreement 5 (Indefinite Pronouns 2 and 3)

In Unit 16.30 (p. 472), you encountered a group of indefinite pronouns that are *always singular*. Here they are again:

Always singular			
anybody	everybody	neither/either	one
anyone	everyone	nobody	somebody
anything	everything	no one	someone
each	much	nothing	something

Indefinite Pronouns 2

In the following sentence pairs, the subjects are all indefinite pronouns, but these are quite different from the ones you were working with in Activity 16.30. As usual, the sentences in black are correct; the sentences in blue have an error. Study these and figure out the grammar rule for this group of indefinite pronouns.

Pair 1

✓ Both of my brothers are going to work in my mother's restaurant for the summer.

✗ Both of my brothers is going to work in my mother's restaurant for the summer.

Pair 2

✓ Many of the patients in this hospital are from other states.

✗ Many of the patients in this hospital is from other states.

Pair 3

✓ A few of the houses in my neighborhood were damaged by the hurricane.

✗ A few of the houses in my neighborhood was damaged by the hurricane.

Pair 4

✓ Several of my favorite songs are by Beyoncé.

✗ Several of my favorite songs is by Beyoncé.

NOTE: Record the grammar rule these items demonstrate in a notebook or online file for future reference.

There are sixteen pronouns in English that are always singular (see p. 473). The four listed in the box below are the only pronouns in English that are always plural.

Always plural	both	few	many	several

Indefinite Pronouns 3

There is a third group of indefinite pronouns that function in a third way. Study the following groups of sentences, in which those in black are correct and those in blue have an error. Figure out what the grammar rule is for this group of indefinite pronouns. What determines whether the indefinite pronouns in this group are singular or plural?

Group 1

✓ All of my cookies are gone.

✗ All of my cookies is gone.

✓ All of my cake is gone.

✗ All of my cake are gone.

Group 2

✓ Some of my relatives are living in Florida.

✗ Some of my relatives is living in Florida.

✓ Some of my essay is about Florida.

✗ Some of my essay are about Florida.

Group 3

✓ None of the children were absent today.

✗ None of the children was absent today.

✓ None of the lecture was about grammar.

✗ None of the lecture were about grammar.

NOTE: Record the grammar rule these items demonstrate in a notebook or online file for future reference.

Earlier in this activity, you were introduced to the sixteen pronouns that are always singular. Following that, you encountered four pronouns that are always plural. Now you have discovered the six pronouns, listed in the box below, that are sometimes singular and other times plural.

Singular or plural	all any	more most	none	some

16.32 Activity

Editing an Essay for Subject-Verb Agreement 1

Proofread the following essay and correct any errors you find. These errors will all involve subject-verb agreement. To correct these errors, you will need to change the subject so it agrees with the verb or change the verb so it agrees with the subject.

Staying Fit

Something millions of people struggle with, particularly in the United States, is staying physically fit. There are myriad reasons people worry about their weight, ranging from poor diet to not enough exercise. Because this is such an issue for so many people, it have garnered an enormous number of solutions. Some solutions is based in science and research; however, many more are urban myths or are only meant to sell some product and do nothing to help weight loss or muscle growth.

Weight loss is perhaps the most common reason people diet. Millions of Americans is considered overweight or obese, and the number are rising steadily every year. For these millions, the first answer to their weight problems seem simple: eat less. This has given rise to fad "fasting diets," among other calorie-counting methods. The logic seems sound: if you eat fewer calories, your body will search for more and will begin to burn off whatever fat it has stored already. But recent studies has shown that this is not always the case. Your body often responds the opposite way, storing more fat in anticipation of a longer period without food. So while overeating can lead to weight gain, undereating can also result in weight gain.

Another common weight loss idea is that "cleansing" will help. Hundreds of people do juice cleanses, during which each of them spend a week or two drinking nothing but juices. A carton of these juices are shipped as self-contained diets. In one sense, this is not a bad idea—the juices are healthy enough, and they keep one from eating too much else in the way of calories. However, the fat will not simply melt away in a few weeks as some commercials claim. And other cleanses are completely worthless; many are based on supplement pills, seaweed, kelp, or other substances that a company, like GNC, sell to unsuspecting buyers. They sound healthy, but they can't do what they advertise.

There are also fad workouts that are said to cure obesity. You've probably seen the commercials for P90X or Crossfit; they feature men and women who have the most chiseled muscles a person can get and tell people watching that they, too, could look like this if they join the program. Companies like Bowflex tries to sell new workout machines on a similar premise: working out will make you more fit in a few weeks. Recent studies has shown, however, that working out actually doesn't cause the body to burn a significant number of calories when compared to not working out. The body needs an average of 2,000 calories a day just to do the things we all have to do: breathe, talk, walk, and perform other bodily functions. Workouts burn only an extra few hundred calories, meaning that you can cancel out all your sit ups and deadlifts with one slice of pizza.

Which brings us to the only way to really lose weight: balance. Weight loss solutions is all about the panacea for obesity. But one size will never fit all when it comes to weight loss. There are too many factors—everyone's metabolism is different, everyone's genes will only allow them to be so thin or so broad, and men and women carry fat differently. The most important thing to do to lose weight is to find what works for one's own body. This means eating right and avoiding too much processed food and added sugar, and eating vegetables and fruit for nutrients and fiber. It doesn't have to mean counting calories and working out for two hours a day—it just means finding your balance.

16.33 Activity
Editing an Essay for Subject-Verb Agreement 2

Proofread the following essay and correct any errors you find. These errors will all involve subject-verb agreement. To correct these errors, you will need to change the subject so it agrees with the verb or change the verb so it agrees with the subject.

Do We Exist? How Do We Know?

"I think, therefore I am." It's a statement meant to answer the age-old question, "How do we know we exist?" The question of consciousness have bothered philosophers since time has been recorded, asking us to wonder whether or not our world is real, whether or not we are real, and how we can prove it. Though the subject has been probed by many over time, it's only recently that we've seen attempts at a scientific answer. But despite the influx of modern study and thought, an absolute answer still eludes us.

First, a rough definition: Merriam-Webster defines consciousness as "The state of being characterized by sensation, emotion, volition, and thought."

In other words, each of us experience the state of being alive, mentally present, and aware of ourselves. For the sake of not muddying the waters here, we'll leave animals out of this and say that humans are the only beings who fully experience this state (although certain primates and even elephants have been shown to have some basic understanding of self). This is, as far as we can tell, what sets us apart from the rest of the animal kingdom. It's our greatest advantage and the source of all the thought, art, science, and history that we knows today.

Although it was the French philosopher René Descartes who first coined the phrase, "ego cogito, ergo sum" (usually translated to English as, "I think, therefore I am") in the mid-1600s, the idea of higher cognition and the self had already been in existence for millennia. But the focus of early philosophers were often more on the soul than on the mind; for example, Judeo-Christian ideology hones in on the idea of "free will," a gift supposedly given to man by God to separate him from the animals and to allow him to create his own destiny. Similarly, Egyptian and Greek theologies tell of a soul that remains conscious after death, traveling to the underworld to (potentially) live on.

But in modern times, everyone have developed modern perceptions of reality. The age of computers have given rise to a theory that everything we see, the entire universe around us, including our own minds, are all part of an advanced computer simulation being run by a more evolved race of beings. While it may sound like science fiction, it's hard to argue with some of the points the theory makes about our reality. They are perhaps best summarized by the character Morpheus in the first movie of the *Matrix* trilogy: "If real is what you can feel, smell, taste and see, then 'real' is simply electrical signals interpreted by your brain." An advanced enough computer, or artificial intelligence (AI), could (theoretically) hijack the senses the mind relies on and replace the real world with a simulated alternative—or create humans and place us in what we call Earth. What we perceive as consciousness could be no more than an ordered array of 1's and 0's, generated by a hyper-advanced version of Sim City. How would we know the difference?

Stranger still may be the idea of "panpsychism." According to the Stanford Encyclopedia of Philosophy, followers of this theory holds that everything in the world possesses its own brand of consciousness. From humans to animals, all the way down to the grains of sand that cover the beach, everything have some kind of experience. What it's like to be a rock, most of us can never say, but this odd theory tells us that because a rock exists, it has an experience. It may not be able to think like a human, and it most certainly can't tell us what it's like to be itself, but it has the most basic level of consciousness possible. For followers of this odd field, that's enough to say it has some parts of a mind, just not enough to rival our own.

Each of these theories—the soul, the simulation hypothesis, panpsychism—have never been completely proven—and maybe they never will be. Maybe one day neuroscience or some other field will give us the answer to what consciousness is. At the moment, however, scientists can't even agree on exactly when consciousness arises in human beings. It will undoubtedly take more time and further study to discover the origin of human thought. For now, we may just have to accept that Descartes was right: the best way to know that we exist is that we can wonder about whether we do.

Avoiding Pronoun Reference and Agreement Errors

Pronouns are extremely useful words, but errors with them can detract significantly from the effectiveness of your writing.

16.34 Activity

Pronouns and Antecedents

A *pronoun* is a word that takes the place of a noun. In each of the sentences in the following activity, a pronoun is printed in blue. The noun that the pronoun is taking the place of—is standing in for—is called its *antecedent*.

Identifying Antecedents

Working together with your group, identify the antecedent for the pronoun in blue in each of these sentences. Pay particular attention to the last two. They are a little different, but perfectly correct.

1. Our state senator has announced that **he** will retire at the end of next year.
2. Before my sister could finish dinner, **she** remembered to call me.
3. This lasagna will taste great after **it** is baked for an hour.
4. The jury members told the judge **they** wanted to continue deliberating all weekend.
5. My grandparents knew that **they** would be invited to my graduation.
6. Kristin bought a computer from her uncle. **He** fixed it when it broke down.
7. My cousins had a party for the young man who moved in next door. **They** invited everyone in the neighborhood.
8. The book I was reading was about ancient Greece. **It** started with the earliest settlements on the island of Crete.
9. When **she** arrived at work, Imani was surprised to find the office closed.
10. Because **they** live in Hawai'i, my parents don't have any winter clothes.

The pronouns in these sentences work just the way pronouns are supposed to work. Each one is clearly taking the place of a specific noun, its antecedent. Notice that in 6, 7, and 8 the antecedent is actually located in a previous sentence. In 9 and 10, the pronoun comes earlier in the sentence than its antecedent. These are all perfectly correct.

16.35 Activity

Vague Pronoun Reference 1

In Pronouns and Antecedents (16.34, p. 479), you saw the way a pronoun takes the place of a noun, its antecedent. The next set of sentences is a little different. Working in groups, try to identify the antecedent for the pronouns in blue in these sentences. If you cannot identify an antecedent, be prepared to explain why not.

1. Mr. Nowak sent a package to my father when **he** received a promotion.
2. Maria told Christine that **she** had passed the final exam.
3. When Isaiah shook George's hand, **he** never looked at **him**.
4. Helen's brothers never came to see her parents while **they** were on welfare.
5. After Juanita paid the salesclerk, **she** whistled.

This problem—having more than one possible antecedent for a pronoun—is known as *vague pronoun reference*. Revise each of the sentences above to correct this problem.

16.36 Activity

Vague Pronoun Reference 2

In Vague Pronoun Reference 1 (16.35, p. 480), you discovered one kind of error with pronoun reference—a pronoun that has two possible antecedents. In this section, you will discover another. Working in groups, try to identify the antecedent for the pronouns in blue in these sentences. If you cannot identify an antecedent, be prepared to explain why not.

1. In Hawai'i, **they** all live near the ocean.
2. Scott bought a pair of skis, but he has never even tried **it** before.
3. By early April the dogwoods had flowered, and by the middle of May, **they** had fallen to the ground.
4. In New York City, **they** were much friendlier than I expected.
5. At the Department of Motor Vehicles, **they** told me I needed to get a new title to my car.

This problem—a pronoun that simply has no antecedent—is another form of *vague pronoun reference*. Revise each of the sentences above to correct this problem.

16.37 Activity

Vague Pronoun Reference 3

The sentences in this activity are different from any that you've seen so far. Working in groups, try to identify the antecedent for the pronouns in blue in these sentences. If you cannot identify an antecedent, be prepared to explain why not.

1. Actually visiting Jerusalem was something of a disappointment for Sarah. She had dreamed about the trip since she was a child. **This** is what was so disappointing to her.
2. I bought these shoes at Ward's during the spring sale. **This** is why they were so cheap.
3. I got my résumé typed on a word processor, and after three interviews, I was hired as a data processor for the Social Security Administration. I really appreciated Maxine's help with **this**.

4. The sky was beginning to get darker, and I had missed the last bus to Washington. **This** was making me very worried.

5. My mother wants to take us to Portland, and my father is hoping that we come to his house in Boston. **This** seems like a very nice offer.

This problem—using the pronoun *this* to refer back to some general idea that is hard to identify—is yet another form of *vague pronoun reference*. Revise each of the sentences above to correct this problem.

16.38 Tutorial

Pronoun Agreement

Units 16.34–16.37 explain the concept of pronoun reference, the idea that a pronoun stands for or takes the place of a noun (or occasionally another pronoun), which is called the *antecedent* for that pronoun. Those units also explained that it should always be completely clear what noun or pronoun is the antecedent of each pronoun.

This unit will introduce an additional rule about the use of pronouns. In the following sentences the black versions are correct, and the blue versions contain an error. Study these examples and determine what this additional grammar rule is.

✓ My brother lives in California, but he is coming to visit this weekend.

✗ My brother lives in California, but they are coming to visit this weekend.

✓ My mother owns a convertible, but she never puts the top down.

✗ My mother owns a convertible, but he never puts the top down.

✓ When Bernie Sanders ran for president, he surprised everyone.

✗ When Bernie Sanders ran for president, they surprised everyone.

✓ If people in America work hard, they expect to get ahead.

✗ If people in America work hard, he expects to get ahead.

✓ When my father was in high school, he got straight A's.

✗ When my father was in high school, she got straight A's.

NOTE: Record the grammar rule these items demonstrate in a notebook or online file for future reference.

You probably noticed that in each of the blue sentences, there is a problem involving the pronoun and its antecedent. They don't match up correctly. In some cases, the pronoun is singular and the antecedent is plural; in other cases, it's the other way around and the pronoun is plural and its antecedent is singular. In still others, the pronoun is male, but the antecedent is female, or the other way around. We call this matching of pronouns and their antecedents *agreement*. Pronouns must *agree* with their antecedents in number (singular or plural) and gender.

The errors in the blue sentences above are easy to see. Almost nobody would write those sentences. They are being used simply to introduce the principle of pronoun agreement. In the next group of sentences, however, the blue versions contain errors that are not quite so obvious, errors that some students actually make.

✓ I admire women who can stand up for themselves.

✗ I admire women who can stand up for herself.

✓ My Macintosh was much less expensive than I expected it to be.

✗ My Macintosh was much less expensive than I expected them to be.

✓ Janice is one of those women who will make names for themselves.

✗ Janice is one of those women who will make a name for herself.

In these pairs of sentences you can see that ensuring that pronouns agree with their antecedents can be a little tricky. The third pair is especially difficult. Note that the sentence is saying that there are a number of women who will make names for themselves, so *themselves* refers to *women*, not *Janice*.

A Note about "Singular" *They*

Take a look at the following sentences. As usual, the black sentences are correct, while the blue sentence has an error.

✓ When a student takes an exam, he or she should read the questions carefully.

✓ When a student takes an exam, they should read the questions carefully.

✗ When a student takes an exam, they should read the questions carefully.

Note that the second and third bulleted sentences are identical, but one is black and one is blue. They are marked this way because there is some disagreement about the use of *they* in these sentences. For many years, grammarians have insisted that *they* can only be plural, but, despite the grammarians, the English language, like all languages, is constantly changing. These days, most people find that *he or she* is a little awkward, but they don't want to use just *he* because it ignores the fact that students are just as likely to be female. To avoid being awkward or sexist, they use *they* as a singular pronoun. This change in the language is widely—but not universally—accepted today.

For those writers (and readers) who have accepted the use of *they* as singular, the second bulleted sentence is correct. In deciding whether you are going to use *they* as a singular as well as a plural pronoun, you should think carefully about your audience. If your audience is your instructor in an English class, you might want to ask him or her (or should that be *they*?) if it is permissible to use *they* as a singular pronoun. The following examples illustrate the same issue.

✓ A voter in this country should mark his or her ballot carefully.

✓ A voter in this country should mark their ballot carefully.

✗ **A voter in this country should mark their ballot carefully.**

✓ A member of a jury must make up his or her own mind about the guilt or innocence of the accused.

✓ A member of a jury must make up their own mind about the guilt or innocence of the accused.

✗ **A member of a jury must make up their own mind about the guilt or innocence of the accused.**

You may be surprised to learn that writers have been using this "singular" *they* for hundreds of years. Chaucer used it and so did such respected writers as William Shakespeare, Jane Austen, Thomas Huxley, and Daniel Defoe. The rule that *they* could be used only with a plural antecedent was first announced in the eighteenth century and became widespread in the nineteenth century.

Gender-Neutral Pronouns

In the twenty-first century, a new set of rules is being proposed: the use of *gender-neutral pronouns*. In an age in which it has become widely accepted that the two genders—male and female—do not apply to everyone, an age in which we are becoming aware that people may be transgender or non-binary, various new pronouns have been suggested. Most popular of these new pronouns are those represented by *ze* and *hir*. They correlate with traditional pronouns like this:

Ze talked.	I emailed *hir*.	*Hir* car is blue.	*Ze* talks to *hirself*.
He talked.	I emailed *him*.	*His* car is blue.	*He* talks to *himself*.
She talked.	I emailed *her*.	*Her* car is blue.	*She* talks to *herself*.

While this set of non-gendered pronouns grew out of the LBGTQ community, it turns out they are also useful when a pronoun is needed to refer to an antecedent that has no gender or whose gender is unknown: *someone, angels, robots,* and genderless creatures in science fiction.

Agreement and Indefinite Pronouns

You know that a pronoun must agree with its antecedent in two ways: the pronoun must be singular or plural to match its antecedent, and the pronoun must be male or female (or non-gendered) to match its antecedent. However, many students have difficulty with the idea of pronoun agreement when the antecedent is not a noun but an indefinite pronoun. The following chart lists the most common indefinite pronouns and indicates whether they are singular or plural.

Always singular	anybody anyone anything each either	everybody everyone everything much	neither nobody no one nothing	one somebody someone something
Always plural	both	few	many	several
Singular or plural	all any	more most	none	some

The indefinite pronouns that are always singular are a little confusing because words like *everyone* and *each* seem to be standing for a number of people, and so seem to be plural. That's the hard part. Even though they *seem* to be plural, all the pronouns in the first row of the chart are *always* singular.

In the second row of the chart, the pronouns seem to be plural, and they are, so they're not so hard.

In the third row, singular or plural, things are a little trickier. These pronouns are singular if they are followed by a prepositional phrase ending in a singular noun. They are plural if they are followed by a prepositional phrase ending in a plural noun. Here are some examples that show how this works:

- Most of the songs are from the sixties. (*most* is plural because *songs* is plural)
- Most of the music is from the sixties. (*most* is singular because *music* is singular)
- Some of the books were damaged in the flood. (*some* is plural because *books* is plural)
- Some of the test was very easy. (*some* is singular because *test* is singular)
- Any of the beers in this bar are organic. (*any* is plural because *beers* is plural)
- Any of the wine on this list is too expensive for my budget. (*any* is singular because *wine* is singular)

16.39 Activity

Correcting Pronoun Errors

Working in your group and using what you learned in Units 16.34–16.38, edit the following sentences. All errors will involve vague pronoun reference (16.34–16.37) or pronoun agreement (16.38).

1. When young children are read to, he or she is beginning to learn to read.
2. Before she had time to sit down, Joy Reed asked Melania Trump a question.
3. In New York City, they are voting in a special election this Tuesday.
4. The clerk agreed to refund my father's deposit before he had even asked for it.
5. In this election, they are spending millions of dollars on advertising.
6. Regina paid too much for her microwave, and she really doesn't like to microwave food. This is why she tried to sell the microwave on Craig's List.
7. Reggie and Joshua got into a huge argument last night, so this morning he called to apologize.
8. The football team had committed themselves to playing on Sundays.
9. When a customer wants help with a purchase, they shouldn't have to wait fifteen minutes.
10. A politician has to make promises that sometimes they can't keep.

16.40 Activity

Editing an Essay for Pronoun Errors 1

The following essay contains errors involving vague pronoun reference and pronoun agreement. Working in your group, edit the essay to correct these errors.

Voter Registration

Most countries around the world today are democracies. It's the first time in history that that can be said; the number of democracies only surpassed other forms of government in the twentieth century, making it the dominant method of choosing leadership. But this means that each nation has to choose their representatives, and that means there needs to be a method for doing so: voting. In the United States, a single day each year is set on which people vote for their representatives. But in order to get to the voting booth in the first place, citizens must navigate the voter registration laws in his or her home state. In some places, these processes are so arduous that it is difficult or impossible for people to vote—meaning that some people in this democracy are effectively denied a voice.

The United States has been a democracy since the late 1700s when it won its independence from Great Britain. At the time it was one of the only democracies in the world—and perhaps *the* only one. But while other modern democracies have developed over the last 200 years, the United States has done relatively little to adapt to the changing times. It is an embarrassment. We still use paper ballots, we still bubble in the name of the person we vote for, and we still have to register ourselves to vote.

In some countries, the registration process is streamlined. In Estonia, for example, voter registration is automatic. They send a voter identification card to each citizen and even allows it to be used to vote online because it wants people to vote. This not only makes voting more convenient—as it can literally be done from the comfort of one's own home—but also increases voter turnout. When voting is easier, and even encouraged by policies like automatic voter registration, voter turnout rises dramatically.

Other countries have tried a different approach. Australia, for one, has mandatory voting. The fine is about $20 if you don't cast a ballot, and if you think they won't find you, you'll find you're mistaken rather quickly. The government cross-references addresses, tax records, and any other data about each citizen to ensure that everyone votes or pays their fine. This ensures that the country has a virtually 100% voter turnout each year, ensuring every citizen has a voice in their government.

A more relaxed approach to this process is taken in Sweden, where voting is not compulsory but registration is. Once citizens hit 18, he or she is immediately registered to vote. The same goes for immigrants, who are also registered the moment they become citizens. In Sweden, they really want everyone to vote.

These countries compare starkly with the United States. Each American state has their own registration process, and the wait times to be processed can be weeks or even months. When an American mails in their registration forms, they can take weeks to process them and issue voter ID cards.

Americans also don't get the day off from work to vote; in many countries, Election Day is a national holiday. This is another problem that needs immediate attention. In America, many people can't afford to miss time at their job and therefore won't be able to vote. There is also the issue of voter identification: some states now require a photo ID to vote, and this has become a problem for many low-income, elderly, and minority voters, who do not have easy access to identification. That process, too, costs money and can take weeks to carry out.

Compared to many other countries, America has a very complex voting process. Registering can be slow and arduous, and the process of voting itself can be equally so. Many other countries have set better examples and moved into the twenty-first century with their election practices. Though America has one of the oldest democracies around, it is not the most evolved; with some time and some clear guidance from overseas, however, it one day might be.

16.41 Activity
Editing an Essay for Pronoun Errors 2

The following essay has errors involving vague pronoun reference and pronoun agreement. Working in your group, edit the essay to correct these errors.

Wildlife Refuges

It's easy to forget that wildlife refuges exist; we never really see them, as they occupy a space that most humans never set foot in. Their purpose is to shelter animals from human beings and give them respite from pollution and development. But they also provide access for people who want to see the outdoors as it is meant to be: untouched and undisturbed.

The National Wildlife Refuge System (NWRS) was founded over a hundred years ago by President Theodore Roosevelt as a means to preserve certain wildlife species. He ordered Ethan Hitchcock, his Secretary of the Interior, to start work on refuges before he had even been sworn in. At the time, they had been over-hunting animals and driving many species to dangerously low levels, threatening their survival. The creation of the wildlife refuges not only stabilized many of those populations but also created a massive network where scientists could continue making gains on conservation work. Since then, the refuge system has grown to include hundreds of refuges across the country, protecting thousands of animal species and millions of acres of land. This is why the system of wildlife refuges is so important.

While the refuges' original intent was to preserve wildlife for the sake of sustainable hunting and resource conservation (i.e., fur, feathers, and other products taken from animals), they have evolved into a haven for species protected by the Endangered Species Act. And they have also become test sites for conservation work, places where universities and other interest groups can study animal and plant life. This allows them an undisturbed habitat, where they can test new conservation methods and habitat management techniques.

Refuges are essential territory for biologists, but they're also beneficial for the public. They're a great place to go hunting—and with some species, like turkey or deer, it's essential for some of those herds (or flocks) to be culled. A periodic cull controls populations, allowing for greater competition and biodiversity among species. However, in some refuges, the hunters outnumber the biologists, and they don't respect the other's rights.

Another benefit the public gets to enjoy is the trails and other maintained areas where they can walk and enjoy nature. They provide free, curated access to the outdoors that can be hard to find elsewhere. Some of the best trails in the country are on refuges, and they're free and open to the public at all hours of the day.

Wildlife refuges aren't places we think about very often—in fact, people could be driving through a refuge and not even know it. But despite their place on the periphery, they are essential sites for study and research. They provide easy access to nature not only for those who want to conserve it, but also for people who simply enjoy it. They know how important these refuges are. For access to the outdoors, there is no better place.

Combining Sentences in Interesting Ways

The exercises in this section will give you the opportunity to explore the flexibility of language, discover the many options for expressing a single idea, and the chance to practice the grammar conventions covered earlier in this Topic.

16.42 Tutorial

Sentence Combining

Most students find sentence-combining activities to be fun, perhaps because there are no *correct* answers. The following activities give you a series of short, simple declarative sentences and ask you to combine them into one longer and more complex sentence. They invite you to be inventive, to be playful, and to experiment with different combinations. The only rule is that the one sentence you come up with must include all the information that was in the original short sentences. Of course, you will also need to make sure your sentences are grammatically correct.

Here's an example of how this works:

Short Sentences

Daris is a student in my English class.

Daris gave me a ride this morning.

My car broke down on the interstate.

16.43 Activity

Sentence Combining 1

Below are five sets of short, simple sentences. Working with your group, combine each set into one longer and more complex sentence. Make sure your one sentence contains all the information from the set of short sentences.

Set 1

The man is wearing a green sweater.

The man is my uncle.

The man is wearing a red hat.

The man is smoking a cigar.

Set 2

Javier climbed onto his bicycle.

Javier's bicycle was bright green.

Javier grasped the handlebars.

Javier placed his feet on the pedals.

Javier smiled.

Set 3

We went for a hike.

We hiked around Lake Delafield.

It started to rain.

We took shelter in a cabin.

The cabin belonged to Professor Starr.

Set 4

April was sweating profusely.

She clenched her teeth.

April struggled to open the door to her Volkswagen.

Her struggle was desperate.

Set 5

Jasmine had been rude.

Jasmine realized it.

Jasmine made a U-turn.

Jasmine drove back to school.

Jasmine apologized to her teacher.

16.44 Activity

Sentence Combining 2

Below are five sets of short, simple sentences. Working with your group, combine each set into one longer and more complex sentence. Make sure your one sentence contains all the information from the set of short sentences

Set 1

The price of gas has reached three dollars a gallon.

Gerard Bisset's car is seven years old.

Gerard Bisset is my next-door neighbor.

Gerard Bisset is going to buy a Prius.

Set 2

I left my computer in the Parkside Restaurant.

My computer is a Macintosh.

My computer is a laptop.

I had dinner in the Parkside Restaurant last night.

I am not worried.

Set 3

My grandfather was a truly generous man.

My grandfather gave away all his money.

My grandfather left our family impoverished.

Set 4

Benjamin Cardin is a senator from Maryland.

Benjamin Cardin wrote a bill.

The bill would provide more Pell Grants to students.

Benjamin Cardin will be interviewed on Channel 13 tonight.

Set 5

I was listening to my favorite Beethoven symphony.

My favorite Beethoven symphony is the Eroica.

I noticed a woman walking into the room.

She was a woman I did not want to talk to.

She had dumped me for another guy last year.

16.45 Activity

Sentence Combining 3

Below are five sets of short, simple sentences. Working with your group, combine each set into one longer and more complex sentence. Make sure your one sentence contains all the information from the set of short sentences.

Set 1

I like a good cappuccino.

A cappuccino is coffee with lots of warm milk.

A cappuccino usually has whipped cream on top.

I also like a good cold beer.

Set 2

I read a novel this weekend.

The novel was about a totalitarian state.

The novel's title was *1984*.

It was written by George Orwell.

Set 3

I was sitting by a beautiful stream.

I was reading a book.

A woman walked up.

The woman sat down near me.

She was reading the same book I was.

Set 4

I need to go shopping.

I am out of coffee.

I am out of bread.

I am out of eggs.

I am out of money.

I can't go shopping.

Set 5

My daughter started the first grade last week.

She loves going to school.

Two of her best friends are in her class.

Her teacher seems to be very nice.

Her teacher is Ms. Williams.

16.46 Activity

Sentence Combining 4

Below are five sets of short, simple sentences. Working with your group, combine each set into one longer and more complex sentence. Make sure your one sentence contains all the information from the set of short sentences.

Set 1

That man is wearing a bright purple sweater.

That man is wearing an orange shirt.

That man is playing a harmonica.

That man was here yesterday.

I think that man is a busker.

Set 2

Angelique took a deep breath.

She walked to the end of the diving board.

She was wearing a black one-piece swimming suit.

She paused for a full minute.

She launched herself into the air.

She entered the water with almost no splash.

Set 3

Asher was planting irises in his garden.

It started to rain.

Asher refused to stop.

He got all his irises planted.

He got soaking wet.

Set 4

I was waiting for the elevator in the science building.

My English professor walked up.

My English professor was carrying a box of test tubes.

I looked at her more closely.

I discovered she wasn't my English professor.

Set 5

The dancers were waiting for the music to begin.

Their faces looked excited.

Their smiles looked artificial.

They had rehearsed well.

They were ready to perform.

16.47 Activity

Sentence Combining 5

Following are five sets of short, simple sentences. Working with your group, combine each set into one longer and more complex sentence. Make sure your one sentence contains all the information from the set of short sentences.

Set 1

I live in the city.

I am used to lots of noise.

I am used to cars honking.

I am used to the sirens of fire engines.

I probably couldn't sleep in the country.

Set 2

I made a risotto.

Risotto is one of Donna's favorite dishes.

Donna grilled chicken.

We drank some wine from Italy.

The wine was a Chianti.

Set 3

At first the crowd was silent.

Then a roar erupted.

People stood up.

People stamped their feet.

Bono came out again.

Bono took a bow.

Set 4

Arun was studying chemistry.

The phone rang.

Arun answered the phone.

It was his girlfriend.

Arun forgot about chemistry.

Set 5

I applied for a job at the new steak house.

I have an AA degree in culinary arts.

I worked for four years in my parents' restaurant.

My parents owned an Italian restaurant.

I was offered a position as sous chef.

Language and Computers

Here, at the end of Topic 16, you will explore using computers to edit your writing.

16.48 Activity

Computers and Editing 1

Paragraph 1, below, has nine grammar errors that have been underlined. Paragraph 2 is identical to Paragraph 1 except the errors have been corrected. You may want to compare each of the nine underlined errors in Paragraph 1 with the corresponding corrections in Paragraph 2 to make sure you understand what the errors are.

Paragraph 1

Lots of problems for the work force have been solved by the minimum wage. The work force actually has a <u>Government</u> backing the<u>m, and</u> saying <u>its</u> not fair to pay someone pennies when it takes quarters to survive. Before the minimum wage was en<u>acted bus</u>inesses could pay their employees anything they wanted, sometimes leaving their employees without the money to buy simple necessities such as food, w<u>ater cloth</u>ing, or shoes. This was a very unfair system, exploiting the workers, who had no way to defend themselves. Many of these workers didn't even have a <u>choice, ma</u>ny had families that they supported. If <u>you</u> decided to leave your current job to find a better paying one, <u>you</u> never knew how long it was going to take to find one. Spending every penny they earned just to surv<u>ive, le</u>ft no savings to rely on while they looked for a new job.

Paragraph 2

Lots of problems for the work force have been solved by the minimum wage. The work force actually has a <u>government</u> backing the<u>m and</u> saying <u>it's</u> not fair to pay someone pennies when it takes quarters to survive. Before the minimum wage was enacted, businesses could pay their employees anything they wanted, sometimes leaving their employees without the money to buy simple necessities such as food, water, clothing, or shoes. This was a very unfair system, exploiting the workers, who had no way to defend themselves. Many of these workers didn't even have a choice. Many had families that they supported. If they decided to leave their current job to find a better paying one, they never knew how long it was going to take to find one. Spending every penny they earned just to survive left no savings to rely on while they looked for a new job.

Activity: Testing Grammar Checkers

When you're ready to do this activity, type Paragraph 3, below, into a word processor and then run the computer's grammar checker to see what it locates as errors. Compare the grammar checker's list of errors with those in Paragraph 1. How good a job did the grammar checker do?

Paragraph 3

Lots of problems for the work force have been solved by the minimum wage. The work force actually has a Government backing them, and saying its not fair to pay someone pennies when it takes quarters to survive. Before the minimum wage was enacted businesses could pay their employees anything they wanted, sometimes leaving their employees without the money to buy simple necessities such as food, water clothing, or shoes. This was a very unfair system, exploiting the workers, who had no way to defend themselves. Many of these workers didn't even have a choice, many had families that they supported. If you decided to leave your current job to find a better paying one, you never knew how long it was going to take to find one. Spending every penny they earned just to survive, left no savings to rely on while they looked for a new job.

16.49 Tutorial

Computers and Editing 2

Microsoft Word has one simple tool that can be very useful when you are editing your writing: the Find function, usually found on the Edit menu. As you are writing this semester, keep track of the grammar, punctuation, and word choice rules that you have trouble with most often.

When you have finished writing and revising your essay, use the Find function to search for each of the problematic terms. Here's one student's list:

to, too, two

its, it's

's, s'

your, you're

This student first used Find to search for every place she had written *to*. As the computer found each one, she checked to see if it was used correctly. Then she searched for *too* and checked each of those. Next, she searched for *two* and checked each of those. Then she did the same for each of the other terms on her list.

As you saw in Unit 16.48 (p. 497), the computer is not so good at deciding whether something you have written is grammatically correct, but it is infallible at finding every instance of a word or phrase. So I recommend that you use the Find function to locate every place you've used a word or phrase from your list, but then use your own understanding of the rule involved, as you've learned it in this topic, to decide whether you've used the word or phrase correctly.

TOPIC 17

Titles, Introductions, and Conclusions

Topic 17 discusses three brief but important parts of an essay—the title, the introduction, and the conclusion—and provides strategies for ensuring these three components enhance the effectiveness of your essay.

Navigating Topic 17

The tutorials below provide information about how to write titles, introductions, and conclusions, and each is followed by an opportunity to apply the skills you have just learned. You can work through the entire Topic on your own, learning about all the strategies and practicing them; work on items you've been assigned by your instructor; or choose just the ones you find helpful.

Introduction to Titles, Introductions, and Conclusions

Topic 17 opens with a discussion of options for titles, then provides different ways to write an introductory paragraph, and closes with a discussion of strategies for concluding an essay effectively and avoiding several common mistakes.

17.1 Tutorial

Titles

The first thing a reader sees in your essay is the title, so it's important. But coming up with one is probably best left to the end of the writing of the essay. At that point, you'll have a clear idea of what the essay is about and what you want to bring to the reader's attention in the title.

Options for Titles

In coming up with a title, as with everything else you write in an essay, you want to think about the audience you are writing for and the purpose for which you are writing. (For more information, see Thinking about Audience [9.4, p. 328] and Thinking about Purpose [9.6, p. 331].) What will be most effective with your reader? How can you best convey the gist of your paper and indicate your purpose? Of course, there are no easy or automatic answers to these questions. You will need to decide which will work best with the person or people you expect will read what you have written. Here are some useful options.

Option 1: Announce Your Topic or Thesis

At its most straightforward, Option 1 means you simply announce the topic you will be discussing:

> "Genetically Modified Organisms"
>
> "Immigration Policy"
>
> "Global Warming"

Notice that these titles tell the topic of the paper, but do not give a hint about what the writer will say about the topic.

A variation on Option 1 is to announce not just your topic, but your thesis.

> "Tax Cuts for the Rich Do Not Trickle Down to the Rest of Us"
>
> "Children Are Being Separated from Their Parents at the US Border"
>
> "The Next Five Years Are Our Last Chance to Reverse Global Warming"

Option 2: Capture Your Reader's Attention

If the goal in Option 1 is to announce your topic or your thesis, the goal in Option 2 is entirely different. Under Option 2, the goal is to capture the readers' attention, to make them want to read what you have written, to entice them to read your essay. Wit and whimsy can help here, so you can say something startling or puzzling.

> "Unbelievable Development"
>
> "This Doesn't Add Up"
>
> "Until Hell Freezes Over"

Be aware, though, that these puzzling or enticing titles can backfire. Encountering a title that is obviously trying to tease a reader into reading can actually put them off: "I don't like being teased, so I'm not going to read this." The most flagrant and least successful example of this type of title that some students have resorted to over the years is "Sex." Then the first sentence of the paper admits the ruse: "Now that I have your attention, I'd like to talk about gun safety."

Option 3: Entice First; Announce Second

The third option is really a combination of the first two. You start with one of those puzzling, enticing phrases, then you add a semicolon, and then you add a straightforward statement of your topic or your topic and your stance about that topic.

> "Until Hell Freezes Over: The Next Five Years Are Our Last Chance to Reverse Global Warming"
>
> "Unbelievable Development: Children Are Being Separated from Their Parents at the US Border"
>
> "This Doesn't Add Up: Tax Cuts for the Rich Do Not Trickle Down to the Rest of Us"

Option 3 might seem like the obvious best choice since it combines the advantages of the first two options. However, it can also lead to long and somewhat clumsy titles. As it turns out, these two-part titles are most commonly used for very scholarly works, especially book-length works.

Now that you know some basic options available to you for a title, you can combine this knowledge with your understanding of your audience to come up with a title for any writing you do.

17.2 Activity

Writing Titles

Working in your group, select one of the following essay options and come up with at least three different titles for it. Be ready to share your writing in about fifteen minutes.

1. An essay for a class in political science in which you will argue that America's right to free and fair elections is threatened by various political acts of the party in power

2. An article to be published in your local newspaper proposing ways to make it safer for bicyclists on public roads

3. An essay for a class in nursing or another health field in which you argue for changes in how nurses or health-care workers are educated

4. A letter to your local congressional representative in which you argue for the need to lower the cost of going to college

5. A letter to the Secretary of Education in which you suggest improvements in the requirements or procedure involved in applying for financial aid

17.3 Tutorial

Introductory Paragraphs

Because getting started on a piece of writing can often be the hardest part, writing the introductory or opening paragraph can sometimes have a paralyzing effect. In this unit you will read about some options that should help you avoid this kind of paralysis. When you do get started, remember to think about who will read what you're writing. Who is your audience? Then write the kind of introduction that will be most effective with that audience. (For more information on audience, see Thinking about Audience [9.4, p. 328].) You will also want to keep in mind your topic and the purpose for which you are writing (see Thinking about Purpose [9.6, p. 331]).

Elements of a Good Introduction

Regardless of which option you choose for organizing your introduction, certain elements are almost always included:

- **A hook.**   A statement, an example, a fact, or a quotation that catches the reader's attention.

- **Background information or history.**   An explanation of the context in which you are arguing your position. What has happened leading up to your proposal? What problems exist that make your proposal necessary? What solutions have been suggested in the past, and why did they fail?

- **Establishment of *ethos*.**   It's important to convince your audience that you can be trusted, that you know what you're talking about, and that you will not exaggerate or dissemble. (For more information on *ethos*, see Three Types of Appeal [11.6, p. 372].)

- **A thesis.**   The position you are taking—the point you are making, your stand on your topic—is your thesis and is customarily stated in an introductory paragraph. (For more information on thesis, see Thesis Statements [10.5, p. 346].)

Types of Introductory Paragraphs

There are many way you can start an essay. Here are several different strategies you can use.

Problem to Solution

One highly effective option for an introductory paragraph is to identify a problem, providing some evidence that the problem exists, offering some discussion of the history of the problem, and finally suggesting a solution to the problem, which becomes the thesis of the essay.

> Americans have always prided themselves on their rugged individualism. We know how to take care of ourselves. We don't need any help, especially from the government. As a result, we have been slow to adopt a system of universal health care. Today we are the only industrialized country in the world not to provide health care for all its citizens. As a result, compared to other industrialized countries, we have the highest infant mortality rates and the lowest life expectancy. It is clear that, when it comes to health care, we need to "get over" our rugged individualism and adopt universal health care.

State Your Support First

It can also be effective to start your introductory paragraph with examples of your evidence, especially if that evidence is powerful. After a brief statement of some of your evidence, you can then end the paragraph with your thesis.

> The United States is the only advanced industrialized nation in the world that does not offer universal health care. If we adopted such a system, there would be less illness, less suffering, and less early mortality for American citizens. Surprisingly, studies show that under universal health care costs would go down as more people receive preventive care. It is time for the United States to adopt a system of universal health care.

Start with an Example or Quotation

Many writers find it effective to begin their opening paragraph with a quotation or a personal example.

> Last year I was laid off, which meant, in addition to having no job, I had no health insurance. There was no way I could afford to see my doctor for the regular physical I have had every year for the previous fourteen years, so I had no idea that I had gall stones. As a result, in the middle of the night, with extreme pain in my right shoulder and back and horrific vomiting, I ended up having major emergency surgery to remove my gall bladder. Had those stones been detected by a simple chest x-ray, a normal part of my annual physical, my gall bladder could have been removed by laparoscopic surgery, a much simpler procedure. Too many Americans are in the same position I was in: unable to afford preventative care because they have no insurance and, as a result, needing much more dangerous and expensive emergency treatment. Something is seriously wrong with health care in this country. In fact, the United States is the only advanced industrialized nation in the world that does not offer universal health care. If we adopted such a system of health care, there would be less illness, less suffering, and less early mortality for American citizens. Surprisingly, studies show that under universal health care costs would go down as more people receive preventive care. It is time for the United States to adopt a system of universal health care.

Start by Exploring Your Evidence

A less straightforward but more interesting way to write an opening paragraph is to forget about the thesis for the time being, and open instead with a paragraph that dives into your most compelling evidence. Then, after a paragraph or more exploring this evidence, provide a clear statement of your thesis.

> The United States is the only advanced country in the world that does not provide universal health care. As a result, Americans have worse health outcomes than the rest of the world in many categories. For example, life expectancy in the United States is 79.3 years, lower than the life expectancy in thirty other industrialized countries. One study has shown that out of 100,000 Americans, 112 will die each year from preventable diseases. In the twelve other countries in the same study, the highest number of preventable deaths was 84. Infant mortality is measured as the number of deaths within one year per 1,000 live births. Infant mortality in the United States is 5.8; the average rate for eleven comparable countries is 3.4. Why is it that the country with the strongest economy, the highest standard of living, and the greatest gross domestic product in the world has such low health outcomes?

After this strong opening paragraph, the writer could include a paragraph stating the thesis and the primary reasons that support it.

State Your Thesis and Support

The most straightforward way to open an essay is to state your thesis and the primary reasons that support the thesis.

> The United States should adopt a system of universal health care for three reasons. First, universal health care will mean less illness, less suffering, and less infant mortality for American citizens. Second, universal health care will actually result in lower overall costs for health care as everyone will receive preventive care. Third, we are the only advanced industrialized nation in the world that does not offer universal health care.

You may have been taught to write an introductory paragraph this way in the past. However, this is not usually very effective either at capturing the reader's interest or providing context for the discussion to follow. It is too predictable and lacks imagination. Whenever you can, use one of the more creative options listed above.

17.4 Activity

Writing Introductory Paragraphs

Working in your group, select one of the following essay topics and write an introductory paragraph for it. It's okay to select the same essay you chose for Writing Titles (17.2, p. 503). Be ready to share your writing in about fifteen minutes.

1. An essay for a class in political science in which you will argue that America's right to free and fair elections is threatened by various political acts of the party in power

2. An article to be published in your local newspaper proposing ways to make it safer for bicyclists on public roads

3. An essay for a class in nursing or another health field in which you argue for changes in how nurses or health-care workers are educated

4. A letter to your local congressional representative in which you argue for the need to lower the cost of going to college

5. A letter to the Secretary of Education in which you suggest improvements in the requirements or procedure involved in applying for financial aid

17.5 Tutorial

Closing Paragraphs

Like guests who take forever to say goodbye and be on their way, a closing paragraph that goes on too long can make readers groan and roll their eyes, and it can leave them feeling much less enthusiastic than they had felt as they were reading the essay. To choose the most effective strategy for your conclusion, be sure you remember who your audience is and what your purpose is for writing. For more information, see Thinking about Audience (9.4, p. 328) and Thinking about Purpose (9.6, p. 331).

Strategies for Effective Conclusions

In the final paragraph of your essay, you want to wrap things up tidily and leave readers remembering the gist of what they have read. Here's a list of ideas to help you accomplish this:

1. Restate your thesis in a fresh and memorable way.
2. Close with a witty, funny, or moving statement.
3. Remind readers of the most powerful facts, examples, or other evidence you have presented.
4. End with a powerful quotation.
5. Conclude by urging readers to take whatever action you have been arguing for.

Examples of Effective Conclusions

This is an introduction from Introductory Paragraphs (17.3, p. 503) that starts with an example. It is followed by two possible conclusions.

Last year I was laid off, which meant, in addition to having no job, I had no health insurance. There was no way I could afford to see my doctor for the regular physical I have had every year for the previous fourteen years, so I had no idea that I had gall stones. As a result, in the middle of the night, with extreme pain in my right shoulder and back and horrific vomiting, I ended up having major emergency surgery to remove my gall bladder. Had those stones been detected by a simple chest x-ray, a normal part of my annual physical, the gall bladder could have been removed by laparoscopy, a much simpler surgery. Too many Americans are in the same position I was in: unable to afford preventative care because they have no insurance and, as a result, needing much more dangerous and expensive emergency treatment. Something is seriously wrong with health care in this country. In fact, the United States is the only advanced industrialized nation in the world that does not offer universal health care. If we adopted such a system of health care, there would be less illness, less suffering, and less early mortality for American citizens. Surprisingly, studies show that under universal health care costs would go down as more people receive preventive care. It is time for the United States to adopt a system of universal health care.

One effective conclusion for an essay starting with the preceding introduction could be this one:

Our society will be more humane and more healthy, and the costs of health care will be reduced, if we move to a system of universal health care. It is important that you add your voice to this movement and support candidates who will work for universal health care. No one should have to undergo an emergency surgery for gall stones.

In this conclusion, the writer summarizes the main points of his argument and then urges the reader to support the cause of universal health care. The paragraph ties the entire essay together by reminding the reader of the writer's emergency surgery.

Here is another effective conclusion for the same introductory paragraph that uses a different strategy:

Dr. Bruce Viadeck, author of more than 150 articles on medical issues has pointed out that "we used to say that the United States shared with South Africa the distinction of being the only industrialized nations without universal health insurance. Now we don't even have South Africa to point to" (16). We are now the only industrialized country in the world that doesn't guarantee health care to all its citizens. This must change.

This writer has decided to use a powerful quotation—one that points to our unique failure as a nation to provide universal health care—to drive home the point of the essay and then concludes with a terse statement that sums up the point of the essay.

Concluding Strategies to Avoid

One way to ensure you draft a strong concluding paragraph is to avoid doing any of the following.

1. Don't bring up anything new, such as an argument or evidence you have not previously discussed.
2. Don't announce what you have done. Don't write things like "In this essay, I have . . ." or "I have proved . . ."
3. Don't include an overused and obvious phrase like "In conclusion . . ." or "As I have said . . ."
4. Don't apologize by saying something like "Even though I am not an expert . . ."
5. Finally, check the "fresh and memorable" way you have restated your thesis. Make sure that even though it is worded differently, it is still making the same point as the thesis you stated earlier in the paper.

17.6 Activity

Writing Conclusions

Working in your group, select one of the following essay topics and write a conclusion for it. It's okay to select the same essay you chose for Writing Titles (17.2, p. 503) or Writing Introductory Paragraphs (17.4, p. 506). Be ready to share your writing in about fifteen minutes.

1. An essay for a class in political science in which you will argue that America's right to free and fair elections is threatened by various political acts of the party in power
2. An article to be published in your local newspaper proposing ways to make it safer for bicyclists on public roads
3. An essay for a class in nursing or another health field in which you argue for changes in how nurses or health-care workers are educated
4. A letter to your local congressional representative in which you argue for the need to lower the cost of going to college
5. A letter to the Secretary of Education in which you suggest improvements in the requirements or procedure involved in applying for financial aid

TOPIC 18
Writing Strategies

The strategies discussed in this Topic are useful in many different writing situations—essay assignments, reports, summaries, fiction and nonfiction writing, book and movie reviews, lab reports, and more—but the focus here is on writing essays. Writers will sometimes write essays that use a single one of these types of writing: an elaborate extended definition might be a three- or four-page essay, for example, or an explanation of the multiple causes of a complex event like the Great Recession of 2008 could easily be an essay all by itself. More commonly, however, although an essay or article may have one overall organizing principle, such as argument, cause and effect, or classification, it will also include several different strategies in order to present information effectively. For example, after an introductory paragraph in an argument essay, a writer might use definition to explain how she will be using several key words. A little later, she might use narration to provide background information about the topic. Further on, she might include a comparison of two possible solutions to the problem being addressed. This weaving back and forth among the various strategies can result in a sophisticated argument that convincingly presents and supports its position.

Navigating Topic 18

The tutorials listed below provide information about these strategies, and each contains, or is followed by, an opportunity to apply the skills you have just learned. You can work through the entire Topic on your own, learning about all the strategies and practicing them; work on items you've been assigned by your instructor; or choose ones you would find helpful.

Introduction to Writing Strategies

This Topic explores several different writing strategies: argumentation, description and observation, narration, process, comparison and contrast, cause and effect, definition, classification, summary, proposal, and reflection. For each strategy, you will find advice about when it might be useful, examples, advice for using it effectively, and an opportunity to practice using it.

Argumentation

An argument is a piece of writing that takes a position on an issue, provides various types of evidence to support that position, and acknowledges and addresses valid counterarguments.

18.1 Tutorial

What Is an Argument?

An argument is simply a piece of writing that takes a position on an issue and provides evidence to support that position. In fact, it is sometimes suggested that all writing is argument.

In college courses, argument essays are typically three or four pages long, but sometimes, especially if they involve significant research, they can be much longer. They can also be much shorter: an argument could be as short as a single paragraph. The crucial factor is that an argument takes a position on an issue.

The following sections explore many of the features of effective arguments.

18.2 Activity

What Are the Features of Effective Arguments?

Working in your group, make a list of the features necessary for an effective argument. To help you get started, one feature is *an argument takes a position and expresses it in a clear and arguable thesis.*

18.3 Tutorial

The Features of Effective Arguments

In order to be effective, an argument should meet the following criteria.

- **It takes a position.** The primary feature of an effective argument is that is takes a stand, a position, on an issue about which reasonable people may disagree. This position is clearly stated as a thesis, usually near the beginning of an essay. (For more information, see Thesis Statements [10.5, p. 346].) Keep in mind that the point of an argument is not simply to state something that is true; the point is to convince the reader that it is true.

- **It provides support for that position.** This support can take many forms: examples, statistics, facts, reasons, expert opinion, and more. Remember that an argument has to convince the reader, so ask yourself whether you think your reader would be convinced by the evidence you have provided. If not, what kinds of additional support do you need to incorporate? (See Topic 11: Developing Ideas [p. 355] for more on types of support and how to find them.)

- **It provides necessary background information.**   Sometimes this information explains why the issue is important, or it might define important terms or provide some history of how the issue has evolved over time.

- **It responds to opposing arguments.**   An effective argument acknowledges that not everyone agrees with the position the essay has taken. The essay will summarize opposing arguments fairly and politely and then will explain why they are not convincing. Perhaps the evidence supporting the opposition is flawed in some way. Perhaps the opposing argument has overlooked important parts of the argument. Perhaps the opposing argument makes some valid points, but these do not outweigh the arguments in the essay.

18.4 Tutorial

Thinking about Audience and Purpose

Before starting any writing task, most people find it helpful to think about their audience and purpose. Thinking about your audience will help you to write in an appropriate style, determine what technical terms you will need to explain, decide how much background information or history to include, and what tone to use. It will also help you to select the kind of evidence that your audience will find most convincing. For more information about audience, see Thinking about Audience (9.4, p. 328).

Thinking about your purpose—what you want to achieve as a result of your writing—will focus your work and help you to decide how to organize and present your argument. For additional details on purpose, see Thinking about Purpose (9.6, p. 331).

18.5 Tutorial

How to Answer Counterarguments

In most cases, when writing an argument, your audience is not those who agree with you. Why would you try to convince those who already agree with you? Instead, your argument will be most effective if it is aimed at those who are undecided on the issue you are addressing. They can be convinced. What about those who are totally opposed to your position? Some of them may be persuadable, but most of your energy should be aimed at the middle group—those whose minds are not made up and therefore might be open to a different point of view.

Your arguments to support your thesis, supported by reasoning, evidence, and facts, should work well with the undecided group. But think for a moment about why they might be "undecided." In many cases, they are undecided because they are aware of counterarguments, arguments that oppose the position you are supporting. At first glance, it might seem that your best strategy is to ignore these counterarguments. Why bring up arguments that undermine your position? You can always hope your audience isn't aware of these arguments.

Here's the problem with that strategy. If you ignore them, your audience may conclude you are either not well informed or you are biased or not fair-minded. Ignoring counterarguments will make your writing less effective.

Identifying and Refuting Counterarguments

You can develop a list of counterarguments in three ways.

1. Conduct good research, which will probably unearth some of these arguments.
2. Talk to someone (or several people) who disagrees with your position and listen carefully to the arguments he or she makes.
3. Imagine yourself in an argument with someone who holds the opposite position from yours. What arguments would he or she be making?

Once you have identified counterarguments, you need to refute them—prove them to be inaccurate, false, or weak—using any one of several strategies.

- Challenge the authenticity of the evidence, the data supporting the opposing view, if you have reason to suspect it is inaccurate or untrue.

- Produce evidence supporting your position that is stronger than the evidence supporting the opposing view.

- If an opposing view relies on pathos (an appeal to emotion, not facts), point out that the opposing view is based primarily on emotion and not on solid evidence.

- Critique the character or expertise of people making the opposing view if there is evidence that they are not reliable, truthful, or certified experts in the field.

- Point out that the negative consequences that will result from the opposing position outweigh any positive results.

- If an opposing point cannot be refuted, concede it and argue that your other points far outweigh that one opposing point.

18.6 Writing

Answering Counterarguments

The reasons for refuting counterarguments and strategies for doing so are discussed in How to Answer Counterarguments (18.5, p. 514).

Your instructor will assign this activity as part of the process of writing one of the essays that conclude each reading/writing project in Part 1 of *The Hub*.

Assignment. Write a short paper—less than a page—in which you state several of the arguments that opponents of your position might take and then write your answer to each of these counterarguments.

18.7 Tutorial

Three Types of Appeal: *Logos, Ethos,* and *Pathos*

As long ago as the fourth century BC, the Greek philosopher Aristotle identified three types of argument, which he named *logos, ethos,* and *pathos*. These three strategies are usually referred to as appeals. Think about a politician *appealing* for your vote or a nonprofit *appealing* for donations. In this sense, to appeal is to attempt to persuade by adopting a strategy likely to succeed with the audience.

- **Arguments based on *logos*** appeal to the head. They are based on evidence, reasoning, and logic. In fact, the English word *logic* is derived from *logos*. Arguments based on *logos* often make use of facts, quotations from experts, statistics, survey and poll results, interviews, and charts and graphs. Usually these kinds of factual evidence are tied together by sound reasoning which can explain the causes, the results, the benefits, or the side effects of the factual evidence.

- **Arguments based on *ethos*** have the goal of winning the reader's confidence in the writer. To accomplish this, writers include information that establishes their credibility or expertise by mentioning their credentials, awards they have won, or honors they have received. They also make clear the values and beliefs that underlie their arguments. Another way of gaining the reader's confidence is to write in a way that is clearly fair, a way that avoids mean-spirited personal attacks or distortions of the truth, and that recognizes it is possible for reasonable people to disagree about an issue.

- **Arguments based on _pathos_** appeal to the readers' feelings, to their heart. Frequently, writers appeal to their readers' hearts by telling a story, especially a moving one, that includes, for example, details about the suffering of people enduring an oppressive political regime, the injustices a certain group is experiencing as a result of societal bigotry, or the sacrifices parents or family members are making to care for an ill child or ailing elder.

Sometimes writers are hesitant to use and readers are alienated by emotional arguments, but they also can be extremely effective, especially when writers think about their audience and only use emotional arguments that are likely to succeed with that audience. Sometimes a purely logical argument, especially one with an avalanche of factual evidence, can overwhelm or bore the reader. And, if writers spend too much time explaining how many honors they have received and how much they are committed to their values, they may discover they have alienated their audience.

The most effective writing is often a combination of all three types of argument—logical, ethical, and emotional. In the following essay, written by an older student in one of my classes a few years ago, the writer skillfully weaves all three appeals together to make his point. Included below is just the body of Kevin's essay; in its final form, it would also include a works cited list.

Gifted and Talented Programs: More Harm Than Good?

KEVIN TURNER

1   My granddaughter called me a couple of years ago with big news. "I've been selected for gifted and talented," she announced with excitement and joy in her voice. I shared her joy; I was elated to hear how excited she was as she got ready for the sixth grade. But I also felt a contradictory emotion: I felt guilty for feeling such elation. I had for years had serious reservations about gifted and talented programs and any other programs that separate kids according to our perceptions of their abilities.

Kevin begins his essay with an appeal to the reader's feelings by discussing his own feelings (_pathos_).

2   I want to be clear. There are good arguments on both sides of this issue. Those who support "gifted and talented" programs have some powerful reasons for their support.

In this paragraph, he tries to win the reader's confidence by demonstrating he understands both sides of the argument (_ethos_).

3   Some point out, for example, that our society needs to provide challenging curricula to the most talented students, those who will grow up to lead the country, to discover new treatments for diseases, and to produce art and music that challenge our souls. In a gifted and talented program, these students can be challenged to think more deeply and more creatively. They can experience the thrill of learning concepts they never thought they could understand. They can hone their thinking, writing, and speaking skills as they challenge and are challenged by other top students. Our nation will benefit in the future from the "gifts" and "talents" of these students.

Using reasoning, here Kevin argues that students will benefit from these programs and so will the nation (*logos*).

4   A second argument for "gifted and talented" programs is that bright students, like my granddaughter, are too often bored in traditional classrooms with a range of students from those struggling to understand the material to those ready for more challenging material. A conscientious teacher will usually "teach to the middle," which means those students at the "top" will seldom be challenged and will frequently be bored. It was disheartening when my granddaughter told me one summer that she hated reading because the books she was assigned in school were too easy.

Again, an appeal to logic or reasoning (*logos*).

5   My daughter was overcome with joy and pride that her daughter would be in the "gifted and talented" program. She, like most parents, wants what's best for her child. I understand that and love seeing her excitement about her daughter's success. So, I have tried, unsuccessfully so far, to explain to her why I have such reservations about the program.

In this paragraph, the author combines an appeal to feelings (joy and pride) with more effort at showing he is being fair (*pathos* and *ethos*).

6   I point out that our system for identifying these bright students is seriously flawed. A multiple-choice test of arithmetic skills or reading

Here Kevin uses logic to argue that the system for judging students is unfair (*logos*).

comprehension doesn't measure a student's "gifts" or "talents." It, more likely, measures the child's socioeconomic background. Those who grow up in families struggling with poverty are less likely to have access to books. Those whose single mothers have to work two jobs are less likely to have had the experience of learning to add and subtract at home. When they are tested for entrance to a selective program, sometimes as early as the age of four or five, the test will favor children from more affluent homes.

7   This bias is exacerbated in many large cities where wealthier parents are paying for tutoring services to make sure their children get into "gifted and talented" kindergartens. According to Leslie Brody, writing in *The Wall Street Journal*, a tutorial service in New York "charges $100 to $400 an hour for private sessions" and clients can receive "15 to 40 hours of tutoring over four to six months," resulting in fees of thousands of dollars (Brody).

In this paragraph, he is using facts combined with reasoning (*logos*).

8   Because the testing system favors children from more affluent families, the demographics of the students who qualify for "gifted and talented" kindergarten in New York City are heavily skewed against Black and Latinx students. According to "Making the Grade II," a 2019 report by the New York School Diversity Advisory Group, Latinx children made up 41% of all kindergartners in New York City in 2018, but were only 10% of the students judged to be qualified for the "gifted and talented" programs. Black children were 24% of all kindergartners but only 8% of those who qualified for "gifted and talented" kindergarten (26).

More facts and logic to argue that there is racial bias in gifted and talented programs (*logos*).

9   To me, the most compelling reason to oppose "gifted and talented" programs is that they undermine the American Dream, the idea that in

this country everyone who is willing to work hard can achieve success. <u>The illusory state of that dream is manifest in the enormous gap between the wealthy and the rest of us. In 2019, a report by the Federal Reserve Board entitled "Introducing the Distributional Financial Accounts of the United States" presented shocking statistics about the wealth gap in America. "In 2018," according to the Fed's report, "the top 10% of U.S. households controlled 70 percent of total household wealth, up from 60 percent in 1989." The report also notes that "the bottom 50% of the wealth distribution experienced . . . a fall in total wealth share from 4 percent in 1989 to just 1 percent in 2018" (Batty et al. 26). Not only has there been a large gap between the wealth of the top 10% and everyone else, but that gap is growing wider.</u>

10   Many factors contribute to this gap, but it is hard to deny that one factor is programs like "gifted and talented." <u>Whatever gaps exist when four- and five-year-olds arrive in kindergarten are exacerbated by a system that results in mostly children from affluent backgrounds being placed into a program designed to help them advance faster.</u>

11   <u>I fully recognize that those who support "gifted and talented" programs have good arguments to support their position. I completely understand the pride and joy of parents like my daughter when her daughter was accepted into such a program. I don't blame parents for wanting what's best for their children. And I recognize that programs for bright students have produced very talented scientists and entrepreneurs, very</u>

More facts and logic to argue that gifted and talented programs exacerbate the wealth gap and undermine the American Dream (*logos*).

Here he uses reasoning to argue his point (*logos*).

Again, Kevin assures the reader of his fairness, his recognition of the arguments on the other side (*ethos*).

creative artists and composers, and very productive engineers and architects, all of whom contribute greatly to making America the richest and most powerful nation on Earth. Those are positive results of our educational system, at least partially as a result of programs like "gifted and talented."

12   However, those same programs also contribute to the vast and growing gap between the wealthy and the rest of us in our society. Having to choose between these two goals, I have decided that I would rather live in a country in which wealth is more evenly distributed, a country in which the American Dream is a reality, even if that country is less rich and less powerful.

Kevin ends with a reasoned explanation of why he comes down where he does on this issue (*logos*).

Rogerian Argument: A Different Way of Arguing

Up to this point, the discussion has focused on a certain kind of argument, sometimes called "classical argument." In classical argument, the writers (or speakers) are trying to convince their audience to agree with their view, their position, or what they are proposing. This is the way most of us construct arguments most of the time.

But it is not the only way to argue. The psychologist Carl Rogers has proposed an alternative. Instead of viewing the goal of an argument to be to "win," to convince the reader to agree with your position, the goal of Rogerian argument is to reach common ground, to come to agreement. Rogerian arguments tend to avoid staking out an "either/or" analysis but to search instead for areas of "both/and." Instead of viewing the rhetorical terrain as offering either a "win" or a "loss," Rogerians try to find grounds on which the writer and the audience can both "win." Rogerian arguments show respect for the views of those who disagree and seek to understand the reasons for their disagreement.

The following chart illustrates the typical organization for a classical and a Rogerian argument.

Classical Argument	Rogerian Argument
1. Introduction with thesis statement	1. Introduction pointing out a problem and how both writer and reader are affected by the problem
2. Background information	2. An attempt, in neutral and respectful language, to present the reader's position
3. Evidence and argument	3. A presentation, again in fair and reasonable language, of the writer's position
4. Response to opposing views	4. A closing paragraph in which the writer suggests where the reader could move toward the writer's position and why
5. Conclusion	

In most academic and business writing, the classical form of argument is expected, but, when thinking about your audience, you may identify situations in which the Rogerian argument format would be more effective. It is often used in tense situations to get people from opposing sides of an issue to better understand each other's positions and, perhaps, find some common ground.

Description and Observation

Writers use description to provide readers with a vivid picture of a person, a thing, or a place. Description is an important element of observations, writing assignments that ask you to provide a detailed description of an event, room, person, place, or performance.

18.8 Tutorial

Strategies for Writing Descriptions and Observations

This tutorial starts with a discussion of basic description and then discusses how you can use descriptive writing in an observation.

Writing Descriptions

It is important when writing descriptions to provide concrete details—the color, shape, size, or appearance of people, places, and things—but it is also possible to enhance a description by including sensory details about smell, taste, touch, or sound (see Using Concrete Language to Bring Writing to Life [13.3, p. 394]). Descriptions are usually easier for readers to process if they are organized in a logical order—for example, from bottom to top, left to right, or near to far. Refer to Coherence (12.8, p. 384) for a discussion and examples of types of logical organization.

The following is a well-written description of a character in the novel *The Magician's Assistant* by Ann Patchett.

> Mr. Howard Plate was big like his sons, with hair that might have been red when he was their age and now was that colorless sandy brown that red hair can become. But it was his face that drew attention, the way it was fine on one side and collapsed on the other, as if he had been hit very hard and the shape of the fist in question was still lodged beneath his left eye. It had the quality of something distinctly broken and poorly repaired. The bad light cast by the living room lamps threw a shadow into the cave of his cheek, where a random interlacing of scars ended and began. (pp. 205–206)

Writing Observations

Many writing situations call for an observation, or a detailed description of something—an event, a room, a person, a place, or a performance—a type of writing that can be useful in many situations, as shown in these examples:

1. An organization you belong to has asked you to visit a room to see if it is appropriate for a guest speaker your group invited to give a lecture.

2. You and your neighbors have become concerned about a dangerous intersection and want to propose to your local government that steps be taken to make it safer.

3. You have become frustrated by the amount of time it takes to purchase your textbooks at the campus bookstore at the beginning of the semester.

Each of these situations calls for a written document, perhaps a proposal, and that document will include some description.

How to Prepare for and Write an Observation

Here are some guidelines for writing a useful, focused observation.

1. Before visiting the site you are going to observe, you need to make some decisions:
   - What is the purpose of the observation?
   - What kinds of information will be useful for that purpose?

- How much time will you need for the observation?
- Will the time of day or the day of the week make a difference in what you will observe?

2. When making the actual observation, you will need to take careful notes. One good system for doing this is to use a double-entry notebook or pad of paper. Draw a line down the center of the page. On the left, record the actual details you see; on the right, record your thoughts or reactions to those details.

3. The most important feature of an observation is the presence of clear, concrete detail, detail that supports the purpose of the observation.

The two paragraphs below are descriptions of a lecture hall that the writer is observing as a possible site for a guest lecture. The highlighting indicates the different focus in each paragraph.

Paragraph 1

The Humanities Lecture Hall seats 175 people in chairs that provide pull-up desks for taking notes. The lights over the seating area can be dimmed leaving the stage brightly lit. The lectern on the stage has a microphone built in and a small light to illuminate the speaker's notes. The room is equipped with a powerful projector and a large screen that are controlled from the lectern.

Paragraph 2

The Humanities Lecture Hall is an attractive room whose walls are covered by beautiful walnut panels. The seats are covered in an attractive red, yellow, and blue material. The American and state flags hang on either side of the stage. The carpeting in the room is a red and yellow pattern which matches the seat coverings.

Both paragraphs contain concrete details, but the details in paragraph 1 will be helpful to the group trying to decide whether to book the lecture hall, while the details in paragraph 2 will not. The writer of paragraph 1 focused on details relevant to the hall as a possible site of a guest lecture: the number of seats with pull-up desks, the quality of the lighting, the presence of a well-equipped lectern, and easy access to a screen and projector. The writer of paragraph 2 seems to have forgotten the purpose of the observation and instead has focused on details of the hall's decoration.

It is important to organize your written observation in a logical fashion. Notice that paragraph 1 is organized spatially, beginning by reporting on the seating area, then moving to the speaker's lectern, and ending with the projection system available to the speaker.

Sometimes, instead of organizing an observation spatially, it will be more useful to organize it temporally—that is, according to time. Paragraph 3 was written as part of a letter urging improvements in the college bookstore's procedures during the first week of classes. Note the highlighted time-related phrases that help organize the observation for the reader.

Paragraph 3

I observed the check-out procedures at the bookstore on the first day of classes this semester, September 3, 2019, from 8:00 in the morning when the bookstore opened to noon. At 8:00, 43 students were in line waiting for the bookstore to open. In the first half hour, I was surprised to see that only two of the four cash registers were available for use. Employees, who I believe could have been staffing the other two registers, were actually unpacking boxes of books and placing them on the shelves. At 9:00, I asked twelve students as they purchased their books how long they had waited to be checked out. All twelve reported they had arrived at the bookstore at 7:30 and had gotten in the check-out line at about 8:15. Each hour for the remainder of the morning, I questioned twelve students about their wait time to be checked out. At 10:00, the bookstore opened the other two cash registers. The twelve students I questioned at that time had been waiting in the check-out line for an hour and a half or more. At 11:00, the twelve students had waited more than two hours. Again, at 12:00, the twelve students had waited more than two hours.

18.9   Writing

Describing/Observing a Person, Place, Thing, or Event

In a short paper—less than a page is plenty—complete one of the following assignments.

1. **Describe one of the following.**   Be sure to provide plenty of concrete and sensory detail and to organize your description in a logical order.
   - Your kitchen
   - Your bedroom
   - The place where you work
   - Someone in your family
   - Your favorite possession

2. **Observe one of the following situations.** Decide on the kinds of information that would be useful to find out in order to achieve the stated purpose and the best time of day to make your observations.

- **Situation:** A family tradition

    Purpose: What makes it successful?

- **Situation:** Everyday use of cell phones

    Purpose: The impact of cell phones on face-to-face interactions

- **Situation:** A live performance you have attended

    Purpose: Why was it a success or a failure?

See Using Concrete Language to Bring Writing to Life (13.3, p. 394) for more on types of descriptive language, and see Coherence (12.8, p. 384) for examples of types of logical organization.

Narration

Human beings have been telling stories since the beginning of time. Narration is just a technical name for telling stories, and it is one of the most common and most useful writing strategies. Narration can not only make your writing more interesting, but it can also provide persuasive support for your thesis.

18.10 Tutorial

Strategies for Writing Narratives

Normally when we write narration, we organize the content in chronological order—*first this happened, then this*—and so forth. Occasionally, writers may want to vary from this strictly chronological order. For example, a writer might tell the end of a story first and then go back to the beginning to explain how that ending came about. Seldom are narratives written to stand alone; more commonly, they are one part of a larger piece of writing.

So, if you were writing an essay arguing that your city needs to invest in safer bike lanes, your essay would probably contain facts and statistics about safety and the annual number of accidents involving bikes. However, you might also include a narrative about the time you were badly injured when a car struck you as you were riding across an intersection even though you had the right of way.

If you were writing an essay arguing that the federal effort to aid Puerto Rico after Hurricane Maria was inadequate, you would want to report on the damage to the island, the number of lives lost, and the effects on people and institutions of months without electricity. You would also want to report on how the amount of federal assistance to Puerto Rico compared to the assistance provided to Florida after Hurricane Michael and to the Carolinas after Hurricane Florence. But in addition to all this factual information, you might want to narrate the story of your mother's struggle to survive Maria with the highway to her village washed away and no electricity for more than six months. Narration can be a powerful way to provide support to your thesis.

Features of Effective Narrative Writing

In the book *The Immortal Life of Henrietta Lacks*, Rebecca Skloot mixes scientific reporting with the telling of very human stories. Below she narrates the events that occurred when Henrietta Lacks's cancer cells were first delivered to a lab at Johns Hopkins Hospital, where they would start their journey toward playing a major role in medical research.

Excerpt from Chapter 4, "The Birth of Hela"

Mary followed Margaret's sterilizing rules meticulously to avoid her wrath. After finishing her lunch, and before touching Henrietta's sample, Mary covered herself with a clean white gown, surgical cap, and mask, and then walked to her cubicle, one of four airtight rooms George had built by hand in the center of the lab. The cubicles were small, only five feet in any direction, with doors that sealed like a freezer's to prevent contaminated air from getting inside. Mary turned on the sterilizing system and watched from outside as her cubicle filled with hot steam to kill anything that might damage the cells. When the steam cleared, she stepped inside and sealed the door behind her, then hosed the cubicle's cement floor with water and scoured her workbench with alcohol. The air inside was filtered and piped in through a vent on the ceiling. Once she'd sterilized the cubicle, she lit a Bunsen burner and used its flame to sterilize test tubes and a used scalpel blade, since the Gey lab couldn't afford new ones for each sample.

Only then did she pick up the pieces of Henrietta's cervix—forceps in one hand, scalpel in the other—and carefully slice them into one-millimeter squares. She sucked each square into a pipette, and dropped them one at a time onto chicken-blood clots she'd placed at the bottom of dozens of test tubes. She covered each clot with several drops of culture medium, plugged the tubes with rubber stoppers, and labeled each one as she'd labeled most cultures they grew: using the first two letters of the patient's first and last names.

After writing "HeLa," for *Henrietta* and *Lacks,* in big black letters on the side of each tube, Mary carried them to the incubator room that Gey had built just like he'd built everything else in the lab (37–38).

This narrative illustrates many of the features of effective narrative writing.

1. *The author is using narrative to make a point.* By detailing all the steps Mary took to prepare to work with the HeLa cells, Skloot is illustrating the great care taken to sterilize the work space before culturing them and the process involved. Good narrative is usually shaped to convey a particular point of view or to make a point.

2. *Skloot uses transitional expressions or time-related phrases throughout to help the reader keep track of the sequence of events (highlighted in blue).* Narratives are usually organized in chronological order—now one event happened, then this, and so on. However, they can jump around, for instance, first telling what is occurring now, and then providing the backstory, what happened before this event.

3. *There is at least one human character with a name, Mary, to provide human interest.* Narratives usually center around a person or persons.

4. *The narrative is filled with concrete details that help us see the lab and that establish Skloot's expertise as a writer.* She knows the names of things.

The passage is repeated below, this time with these vivid concrete details highlighted.

Excerpt from Chapter 4, "The Birth of Hela"

Mary followed Margaret's sterilizing rules meticulously to avoid her wrath. After finishing her lunch, and before touching Henrietta's sample, Mary covered herself with a clean white gown, surgical cap, and mask, and then walked to her cubicle, one of four airtight rooms George had built by hand in the center of the lab. The cubicles were small, only five feet in any direction, with doors that sealed like a freezer's to prevent contaminated air from getting inside. Mary turned on the sterilizing system and watched from outside as her cubicle filled with hot steam to kill anything that might damage the cells. When the steam cleared, she stepped inside and sealed the door behind her, then hosed the cubicle's cement floor with water and scoured her workbench with alcohol. The air inside was filtered and piped in though a vent on the ceiling. Once she'd sterilized the cubicle, she lit a Bunsen burner and used its flame to sterilize test tubes and a used scalpel blade, since the Gey lab couldn't afford new ones for each sample.

Only then did she pick up the pieces of Henrietta's cervix—forceps in one hand, scalpel in the other—and carefully slice them into one-millimeter squares. She sucked each square into a pipette, and dropped them one at a time onto chicken-blood clots she'd placed at the bottom of dozens of test tubes. She covered each clot with several drops of culture medium, plugged the tubes with rubber stoppers, and labeled each one as she'd labeled most cultures they grew: using the first two letters of the patient's first and last names.

After writing "HeLa," for *Henrietta* and *Lacks,* in big black letters on the side of each tube, Mary carried them to the incubator room that Gey had built just like he'd built everything else in the lab (pages 37–38).

You can, of course, use narration at any point in an essay where it will help support your thesis, but you should also consider using narration as a way of opening or concluding your essay.

18.11 Writing

Narrating an Event

For this assignment, you are going to write a short piece of narration, a page would be plenty, in which you tell the story of an event you have experienced. Don't take on too much—don't try to tell the story of your first *year* in college; pick an event you can narrate in a page.

Choose one of the following to write about.

1. Your experience registering for classes for the first time
2. The first time you met someone you are now in a relationship with
3. What you do when you first wake up on a typical morning
4. A time when you were pulled over by a police officer
5. A time when you were really surprised
6. A time when you learned a lesson
7. A topic of your own choice

Be sure your story makes a point, includes many concrete and sensory details to illustrate it, and uses transitional expressions or time-related phrases to organize it. (See Using Concrete Language to Bring Writing to Life [13.3, p. 394] and Coherence [12.8, p. 384] for discussion and examples of types of logical organization.)

Process

Strategies for Process Writing

When writers find themselves needing to explain how to do something or how something works, they often use process writing. Process writing is usually organized chronologically: *First*, you do this. *Next* you do that. In process writing, it is important to keep your audience in mind. How much detail do you need to explain the process so your reader will understand it? Can you use technical terms? If so, do you need to provide definitions of them? Are you writing for a general audience or for people already familiar with your subject?

▲ Figure 1   Peter Adams

How to Do Something

The following paragraph explains how to chop an onion.

> To chop an onion, you first need a little terminology. The sort of messy end of the onion, where there are hairy strands left from the root, is called the root end. The opposite end is called the stem end. You need to identify this root end of the onion before doing any cutting. Now cut the onion in half making sure your cut passes through the root end, leaving half of the root end on each half. For now, you can set aside one of the two halves. Next, cut away the stem end (not the root end) and then peel away and discard the outer layer or two of the onion. Your next step is to make a series of slices lengthwise, being careful not to slice through the root end. Now make three or four horizontal slices starting at the stem end and stopping before you reach the root end. Finally, make a series of cuts at a 90 degree angle to the horizontal cuts, and watch as the beautiful uniform diced pieces of onion appear.

Of course, many times explaining a process will be clearer if you present it as a numbered list. Illustrations can help as well.

1. To chop an onion, you first need a little terminology. The sort of messy end of the onion, where there are hairy strands left from the root, is called the root end. The opposite end is called the stem end. You need to identify this root end of the onion before doing any cutting.

2. Now cut the onion in half making sure your cut passes through the root end, leaving half of the root end on each half. For now, you can set aside one of the two halves.

3. Next, cut away the stem end (not the root end) and then peel away and discard the outer layer or two of the onion.

4. Your next step is to make a series of slices lengthwise, being careful not to slice through the root end (Figure 1).

5. Now make three or four horizontal slices starting at the stem end and stopping before you reach the root end (Figure 2).

6. Finally, make a series of cuts at a 90 degree angle to the horizontal cuts, and watch as the beautiful uniform diced pieces of onion appear (Figure 3).

▲ Figure 2   Peter Adams

▲ Figure 3   Peter Adams

How Something Works

While explaining how to do something (as in the example above) is the most common use for process writing, the same chronological organization can be used to explain how something works, as the following paragraph illustrates.

How Impeachment of the President Works

The impeachment process begins in the House of Representatives, when any member files charges. These charges are forwarded to the Judiciary Committee, which investigates, usually by holding hearings and listening to witnesses. If a majority of the committee agrees, Articles of Impeachment are submitted to the full House for consideration. If a simple majority of those present and voting agrees, the House appoints managers to present the impeachment charges to the Senate. The Senate conducts a trial based on the impeachment charges. In the case of presidential impeachment, the Chief Justice of the Supreme Court presides. Conviction by the Senate requires a two-thirds vote by those present and results in removal from office.

18.13 Writing

Explaining a Process or How Something Works

Write a short paper—around a page—in which you either explain a process for doing something or explain how something works using one of the following topics.

Explaining a Process

1. How to attach a word-processed document to an email
2. How to find a movie you want to watch, download it, and watch it
3. How to use an application like Google Maps to download directions to someplace you would like to go
4. How to request an incomplete grade for a course
5. How do to another task of your choosing

Explaining How Something Works

6. How a constitutional amendment is passed
7. How a recall of a product is processed
8. How the Most Valuable Player for the American or National Baseball League is selected
9. How the winner of the Nobel Peace Prize is determined
10. How something else of your choosing is done

Comparison and Contrast

Writers often compare and/or contrast two items, people, places, or ideas in order to identify differences or similarities between them, make a recommendation about one of them, explain how they produce different outcomes, or justify different treatments of them.

18.14 Tutorial

Strategies for Writing Comparison and/or Contrast

When you *compare*, you discuss similarities; when you *contrast*, you focus on differences. It is often useful to compare and/or contrast things: two buildings, two cities, two proposals, two ideas, even two people. For instance, if you were recommending which of two candidates for a job should be hired, your recommendation could be based on comparing their qualifications and work experiences. If you were trying to explain why two approaches to the same problem produced such different results, it might be useful to contrast the methods and research involved in designing both.

It is also possible to do both—to discuss the similarities and the differences between two or more subjects. For example, if you were trying to explain why two patients should receive quite different treatments for apparently similar illnesses, you might compare and contrast their symptoms, physical conditions, and histories, as well as the possible treatment options. Although comparing and/or contrasting two items can be very useful, comparing and/or contrasting more than two is, of course, also perfectly valid, but more difficult. Whether you are focusing on similarities or differences or both, it is important to discuss all the points of similarity or difference for both, or all, subjects, giving equal attention to each.

There are two commonly used ways of organizing comparison and/or contrast writing: the point-by-point method and the subject-by-subject method. While the examples given below are paragraphs, it is also possible to use these methods for organizing longer pieces of comparison and/or contrast writing, even for entire essays, as noted in the text that follows the examples.

Point-by-Point Method

Read the following paragraph in which Timothy Noah compares two writers who had a profound influence on how Americans view opportunity and upward mobility.

The writers were Horatio Alger Jr. and James Truslow Adams. Alger wrote *Ragged Dick* (1868), *Luck and Pluck* (1869), and other dime novels for boys about getting ahead through virtue and hard work. To call these books popular would be an understatement: fully 5 percent of all the books checked out of the Muncie, Indiana, public library between November 1891 and December 1902 were authored by Alger. Adams was a more cerebral fellow who wrote books of American history, one of which (*The Epic of America*, 1931) introduced the phrase "the American dream" to our national discourse. Writing at the start of the Great Depression, Adams envisioned not "a dream of motor cars and high wages merely," but rather "a dream of a social order in which each man and each woman shall be able to attain to the fullest stature of which they are innately capable, and be recognized by others for what they are, regardless of the fortuitous circumstances of birth or position." Born a half century apart, neither Alger nor Adams could claim to have risen from the bottom. Both were born into well-established families whose American roots dated to the early seventeenth century. Alger could trace his lineage to three Pilgrims who in 1621 sailed to Plymouth Plantation on the *Fortune*, the second English ship to arrive there. Adams—no relation to the presidential Adamses—was descended from a man who arrived in Maryland in 1638 as an indentured servant and within three years possessed 185 acres. Alger's father was a Unitarian minister, Adams's a stockbroker. Both fathers were men of good breeding and education who struggled to make ends meet but were able—at a time when well over 90 percent of the population didn't finish high school—to obtain higher education for their sons. Alger went to Harvard, and Adams went to Brooklyn Polytechnic and, briefly, Yale. Both sons initially followed their fathers into the ministry and finance, respectively, before becoming full-time writers.

To understand the point-by-point method of organization, let's analyze how Noah's paragraph is organized using Chart 1 (p. 535). Noah basically tells us that there are five ways that the lives of Horatio Alger and James Adams were similar. He then addresses each point for both subjects. His first point is that both Alger and Adams were influential writers. Then he says they both came from well-established families. He observes that while both men's fathers were well-educated, they struggled financially. He next reports that despite these financial struggles, both men's fathers were able to get their sons into good colleges. Finally, he notes that both men initially entered their fathers' professions, but then became writers.

In an essay, a writer could discuss the same points listed here in greater detail, taking each one and writing a paragraph about each subject in relation to that point. For a more in-depth essay, she might write several paragraphs that discuss the two subjects in relation to each point made about them.

Chart 1: Point by Point

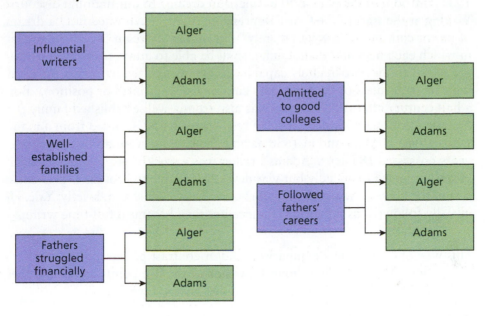

Subject-by-Subject Method

To illustrate the second method of organizing a comparison and/or contrast paragraph, the subject-by-subject method, let's look at a different arrangement of Noah's paragraph.

The first of these two writers was Horatio Alger Jr. who wrote *Ragged Dick* (1868), *Luck and Pluck* (1869), and other dime novels for boys about getting ahead through virtue and hard work. To call these books popular would be an understatement: fully 5 percent of all the books checked out of the Muncie, Indiana, public library between November 1891 and December 1902 were authored by Alger. Born in 1832, Alger could not claim to have risen from the bottom. He was born into a well-established family whose American roots dated to the early seventeenth century and could trace his lineage to three Pilgrims who in 1621 sailed to Plymouth Plantation on the *Fortune*, the second English ship to arrive there. Alger's father, a Unitarian minister, was of good breeding and education and struggled to make ends meet but was able—at a time when well over 90 percent of the population didn't finish high school—to obtain higher education for his son, who went to Harvard. Alger initially followed his father into the ministry, before becoming a full-time writer. Similarly, James Truslow Adams was a more cerebral fellow who wrote books of American history, one of which (*The Epic of America*,

1931) introduced the phrase "the American dream" to our national discourse. Writing at the start of the Great Depression, Adams envisioned not "a dream of motor cars and high wages merely," but rather "a dream of a social order in which each man and each woman shall be able to attain to the fullest stature of which they are innately capable, and be recognized by others for what they are, regardless of the fortuitous circumstances of birth or position." Born a half century after Alger, Adams was also from a well-established family. No relation to the presidential Adamses, Adams was descended from a man who arrived in Maryland in 1638 as an indentured servant and within three years possessed 185 acres. Adams's father was a stockbroker who, like Alger's father, struggled financially but was nevertheless able to provide higher education for his son. Adams went to Brooklyn Polytechnic and, briefly, Yale. He initially followed his father into finance but then became a full-time writer.

This way of organizing a comparison and/or contrast paragraph first makes all five points about Alger and then shows how each of the five points equally applies to Adams. Chart 2 shows how the subject-by-subject method works.

Chart 2: Subject by Subject

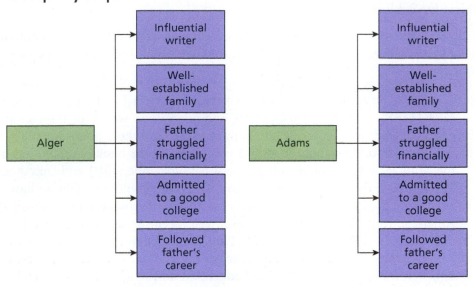

In an essay, a writer could take several paragraphs to discuss the points about Alger and several more to discuss the same points, in the same order, about Adams. He might add paragraphs between the two discussions and again after them analyzing what the writer learned about the similarities between the two subjects and the conclusions he reached about them.

Comparing and/or Contrasting Two Items

Write a short paper—no more than a page—in which you compare two items from one of the listings below. Once you make your choice, you might do a little brainstorming to see how many points of similarity or difference you can come up with for the two. This should help you decide which of the two ways of organizing—point-by-point or subject-by-subject—will work best.

1. Two places you have lived
2. Two candidates for political office
3. The cuisine of two cultures
4. Two vacation spots you have visited
5. Two careers you are considering
6. Three sports you like to play or watch (Comparing and/or contrasting *three* items is more demanding. Try this one if you are feeling up for a challenge.)

Cause and Effect

It is often useful in understanding the world around us to explore what were the causes of something that has happened or to explore what will be the effects of taking a certain action.

Strategies for Writing Cause and Effect

Very often in our complex world, things happen that leave us wondering why. A train derails and scores of people are injured. Why did the train derail? What were the *causes* of the accident? A bad signal? Weather conditions? Operator error? A combination of these factors? What were the consequences, or *effects*? Were passengers injured? Did toxic chemicals spill from a tanker? Were people living close to the accident site impacted?

On the other hand, sometimes institutions consider making changes, and we want to know what will happen if they do. Your city is thinking about closing several schools, for example. What will happen if they do? What will be the *effects*? Will students have to travel further to get to class? Will class sizes increase? Will teachers lose their jobs? Or will there be benefits, such as new buildings with modern equipment, smaller classes, and easier access for low-income students? In thinking about why the city might be considering closing schools, you might think about *causes*: the outdated buildings that cost more to maintain than they are worth, the classrooms designed for a different teaching model than the one now in use, or the lack of public transportation for students coming from other parts of the city. In both cases, you are thinking about causes and effects. It is one important way we understand the world, and it is one useful writing strategy. Sometimes, as in the examples below, the cause-and-effect strategy is used to organize a single paragraph, but quite often it is used to organize longer pieces of writing, including, at times, entire essays.

Causes and effects occur in many combinations. One cause can lead to a single effect or multiple effects: a windstorm can cause significant tree damage and little else, or it can bring down trees, which block roads and fall on power lines, cutting off electricity. Several causes can lead to one effect or several different effects: only attending some classes, doing little studying, and not preparing for a test can lead to an F, but together they can also lead to a failing overall grade, academic suspension, and having to repeat a semester of study. Causes and effects can also occur in related chains, with a cause leading to an effect leading to a cause and so on: you leave early for a job interview and slip on the ice the landlord has not yet salted and sprain your wrist; the ER is busy, so you do not get seen for over two hours and arrive late for your appointment; you have not had time to review your notes or organize your thoughts, so you go in feeling unprepared; you receive a call later that day saying you did not get the job. If only you had not left early that morning.

One word of caution: You should not assert that a cause-and-effect relationship exists when you are not sure that an event, or series of events, has resulted in a particular effect or effects. For example, you wore your "lucky" jeans to school today and you got an A on a test. You may be tempted to argue that your A on the test was caused by the "lucky" jeans, even though there was probably no connection. So, as you think about your topic, be careful to check that there is in fact a direct causal relationship between the events and results you discuss.

The following paragraph asserts that three causes resulted in one effect, that the candidate lost the election. The diagram that appears after the paragraph represents how the effect was the result of three different causes.

> My candidate for Congress lost the election even though everyone thought she would win. Now that the race is over, we can see that she assumed she would have strong support in the city, so she didn't really campaign very hard there; she ended up losing the city vote by 8 percent. She also didn't start fundraising until two months before the primary and never had sufficient money to pay for enough television ads. In addition, her decision to support restrictions on the use of fertilizers because they damage the water supply cost her heavily among rural voters.

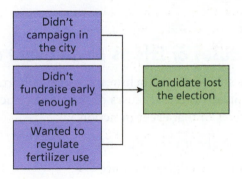

Now let's look at a paragraph that analyzes the effects of a particular action or cause.

The company where I work has decided to allow its employees to work on flextime, which means we can choose whether to work from 8:00 to 4:00, from 9:00 to 5:00, or from 10:00 to 6:00. This flexible scheduling has greatly improved employee morale. In addition, people are not constantly leaving the company for a different job the way they were before flextime. The number of applications for job openings has also doubled. Most important to management, productivity is up 18 percent over a year ago.

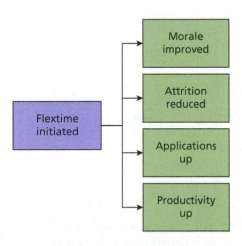

In this example, one cause, allowing flextime, resulted in four positive effects: improved morale, reduced attrition, increased applications for job openings, and improved productivity.

18.17 Writing

Explaining the Causes or Effects of an Event or Action

Choose from one of the subjects listed below and write a short paper—less than a page—in which you explain either the causes of the event or action you have identified or the results or effects of that event or action.

- A decision you made about your education
- A time you had to make a difficult choice
- A time someone helped you in a significant way
- A mistake you made
- A time you experienced bad luck

Definition

Providing a definition of a key word or phrase is a useful strategy, especially in the beginning of an essay. It will ensure that the reader understands how you are using that word or phrase. It is also possible to use the definition strategy to structure longer sections of text. In fact, sometimes an entire essay can be effectively used to provide an extended definition.

18.18 Tutorial

Strategies for Writing Definitions

In this unit, you will learn how to write simple definitions, usually a paragraph or two in length, and extended definitions, which can sometimes be as long as an essay.

Simple Definitions

If you write an essay that makes use of a word or phrase that is important to your argument but may not be familiar to your reader, it is probably a good strategy to provide a definition of that term near the beginning of the paper. You may even need to define more than one term.

Before discussing *how* to define a word, it may be useful to think for a minute about *why* you might want to define it. The first and most obvious reason is because you are using a word that your reader is unlikely to be familiar with. For example:

- You are writing for a general audience about economic issues and want to use the term *arbitrage*.

- You are writing about bird watching to an audience not familiar with birds and you use the term *raptor*.

- You are writing about medical issues to an audience of nonmedical professionals and you need to use the term *keratosis*.

A second reason you might want to define a word you are using is to ensure your readers understand your particular definition of the word. For example, if you will be using the term *juvenile delinquency* in a paper, you may decide to define it because you want to make clear exactly what you mean by it. You might explain, "In this essay, I will be using the term *juvenile delinquency* to refer to serious criminal acts, not misdemeanors and not minor vandalism, performed by people under the age of eighteen." Note that you are not trying to suggest that your way of defining the term is the only correct way to define it; you are merely making clear that *in this essay* this is how you will be using the term.

Defining a word at the most basic level consists of two steps:

1. Placing the word in a broad category
2. Identifying the features of the word that distinguish it from other members of that broad category

This process can be quite straightforward:

A dermatologist is a doctor who specializes in treating ailments of the skin.

Baseball is a sport played with bats and balls on a diamond-shaped field.

Other times it becomes a little more complicated:

A bird is an animal that has feathers and can fly.

The problem here is that kiwis, ostriches, and emus are all birds that don't fly. A more careful definition could be this:

A bird is an animal that has feathers and wings.

Notice that this definition also solves the problem raised by bats and flying insects. They don't have feathers.

The definitions above are fairly brief; each is just a sentence. But in college writing it is often useful to provide a more extended definition, as here:

A raptor is a bird that hunts and feeds on living animals or carrion. Raptors typically have a hooked beak, strong legs, and feet with sharp talons. Common species of raptors include hawks, eagles, owls, and falcons. Most raptors have excellent eyesight. Birds with long straight beaks like herons and egrets are not considered raptors.

Note that after the one-sentence definition, this writer has included other information about what is and what is not a raptor.

Extended Definitions

Sometimes defining a term is both complicated and important. For example, defining exactly what *plagiarism* is can be important to students who need to understand the concept in order to avoid any violation of the rules prohibiting it. Many instructors include a lengthy definition of the term in their syllabi. Many writing textbooks devote pages to explaining and giving examples of what is and what is not plagiarism. In an extended definition, after giving a concise definition of a term, you might include examples of what does and what does not fit the definition, reasons for defining the term just the way you have, and even an explanation of the word's history.

Guidelines for Writing a Definition

Depending on the term you are defining and your reason for defining it, you may use some or all of the following strategies for writing a definition.

- Place the term in the broad category to which it belongs.

- Explain the features that most examples of the term possess.

- Explain how it is different from other members of that category.

- Give examples of the term.

- Explain what the term is *not*: providing contrasting examples can help develop a clearer picture of your meaning.

- Use language and examples with which your audience is likely to be familiar.

- Discuss the origin of the term and how its definition has changed over time.

- Begin with a straightforward statement: A(n) _____ is a(n) _____ that has _____.

Do not do the following:

- Begin with a phrase like any of the following:

    - My definition of _____ is _____.
    - _____ means _____.
    - _____ means different things to different people.
    - _____ is when _____.
    - _____ is something that _____.

- Use the word being defined in the explanation of what it means.

18.19 Activity

Revising Definitions

Below are six definitions. Working in your group, use the guidelines at the end of Strategies for Writing Definitions (18.18) to revise each one to make it more effective.

1. A **recession** means a lot of people are out of work because companies are laying off workers. Recessions can be mild or strong and may even lead to depressions. Also, recessions can be caused by governments spending more money than they have.

2. My definition of the term **medical clinic** is a place where people go when they are sick or injured. Clinics are located in cities and in smaller towns. They always have at least one doctor and many additional support staff.

3. **Obscenity** is something vulgar or disgusting such as a word or event or act.

4. A **socialist** is someone who supports socialism.

5. A **catastrophe** is when something truly terrible happens.

6. A **lie** means a statement that is far from the truth.

18.20 Writing

Providing Simple or Extended Definitions

Write a simple definition of four of the words or phrases in the following list or an extended definition—at least a page—of one of them.

- lie
- art
- fake news
- delayed gratification
- fact

- freedom of speech
- happiness
- word (This one is quite hard; give it some extra time and effort.)
- success

Classification

When writing about a large, complex topic, it is frequently useful to break it down into smaller parts, or categories, that are easier to understand, and then use the information about the parts to help explain the whole.

18.21 Tutorial

Strategies for Writing Classification

Many times, writing about a complex topic can be made easier and more effective if the topic is divided into smaller parts, especially if the parts call for different treatments or different responses. This strategy is often used to write a paragraph or two in a longer essay, but it is sometimes used to organize an entire essay.

At its simplest, classification divides things into just two categories: books are either fiction or nonfiction, athletes are either professional or amateur, and living things are either animal or vegetable. But often it is more helpful to divide things into several categories. Automobiles are either gasoline fueled, diesel fueled, electric, or hybrid. Nonflowing bodies of water can be oceans, seas, lakes, ponds, bays, gulfs, or fjords. Literature traditionally consisted of prose, poetry, or drama, but many today would add at least biography, autobiography, and creative nonfiction. Food can be classified according to the country of origin: Italian food, South African food, Chinese food, and so forth.

Classification is a particularly useful strategy if you want to say something different about the items in different categories within one larger topic. The paragraph below, for instance, divides victims in a mass casualty incident (the larger topic) into three categories and explains how different treatment is allocated to each of these categories.

In a mass casualty incident such as an earthquake, hurricane, or terrorist attack, when medical personnel first arrive on the scene, patients are divided into three categories: those who will die regardless of treatment (Group 1), those who may live if treated quickly (Group 2), and those who will live even if not treated (Group 3). Because doctors' primary responsibility is to save lives, when the victims are many and the providers are few, all resources are focused on Group 2. When more medical personnel and resources become available, palliative care (reduction of pain and suffering) is administered to Group 1. When resources are plentiful, Group 3 will also be treated. During this time, patients are constantly monitored in case their condition changes and they need to be moved to a different group.

Guidelines for Effective Classification

Use classification:

- When you are writing about a complex subject and breaking it down into a small number of categories will make it easier for the reader to understand the content.

- When each of the categories requires a different treatment or response.

Once you decide to write a classification, consider the following guidelines.

- **Select the categories according to a consistent principle of classification.** For example, it would be inconsistent to classify mattresses as twin, double, queen, king, and foam: the first four categories relate to size while the last one refers to content. Choose a principle of classification that is suitable for your purpose and includes most, if not all, items that would be considered important parts of the larger topic you are discussing.

- **Make sure the categories make sense and serve a purpose.** Classifying students as pursuing certain disciplines such as science and technology, liberal arts, social sciences, and business allows a college to specify different required courses for each category. Classifying students according to the number of brothers and sisters they have does not serve any useful purpose in this context.

- **Make sure the categories are able to accommodate all possible examples.** Classifying students according to their method of traveling to college using the categories bus, subway, car, truck, and motorcycle would not account for students who walk to school or ride a bicycle.

- **Decide how to classify examples that fit into more than one category.** If you classify literary texts into fiction, poetry, and drama, where do you place a play that is written in poetic form? One solution would be to add a category labeled *mixed*.

- **Give some thought to the most effective order of presentation of your categories.** One order might be to present the categories with the most members first and those with fewer members last. Another order could be to present the categories that need attention urgently first and those that need attention less urgently later.

18.22 Writing

Breaking a Topic into Categories

Write a short paper—a half page is plenty—in which you break one of the following topics into smaller categories. State the principle of classification you chose and why.

1. Types of government
2. Sports
3. College courses
4. Diseases
5. Bosses
6. Professors
7. Historical military conflicts
8. Games

Summary

Being able to write an effective summary in which you concisely restate the main points of a reading, novel, movie, lecture, textbook passage, or other longer piece of content will help you in many college courses as well as in the workplace.

18.23 Writing
What Makes a Good Summary?

You probably have a sense of what it means to write a summary. You write something short that briefly states the main content of something longer that you have read.

For this assignment, you will try your hand at summary writing. Your instructor will assign a text for you to read. After you've read it and perhaps made some notes, write a short paper—a half page is plenty—in which you summarize the text.

18.24 Activity
Analyzing Summaries

Your instructor will distribute to each group a set of summaries that were submitted for a recent assignment. Your group's task is to read over the summaries and make two lists: one of what you found that worked well in one or more of the summaries and one of the weaknesses or mistakes you found in one or more of the summaries. After a half hour or so, the groups will report out on their lists.

18.25 Tutorial
Strategies for Writing a Summary

Being able to write a summary is a crucial skill in college and beyond. After reading a complex article or chapter, you may find it helpful to write a paragraph or so in which you record the main ideas from what you read. After listening to a lecture or a discussion, you may want to take a few minutes to summarize the most important points, which can help with your understanding of the class and your memory of it. After watching a movie, a play, or even a YouTube video, you may want to summarize the experience for later recall.

In the workplace, you may be asked to interview a candidate for a job and write a summary of what you learned from the interview. In your first job, it would not be unusual for you to be asked to investigate a complex topic like whether an office should switch to digital record keeping or not and to write a summary of your findings.

The ability to gather together a complex body of information and ideas and present the most important points in a coherent, concise piece of writing is an important skill. In a summary of a written text, it is often, but not always, possible to locate the author's main point (often referred to as a *thesis*) and the ideas that support it. But many times, texts, especially excerpts from longer pieces, do not include a single clear thesis. In these cases, it is up to you as the reader to figure out what you think the major idea or ideas are. In summarizing an event, a batch of data, or a visual image, it will almost always be up to you to decide what the main points are.

Writing a Good Summary

Before writing a summary, carefully read the text. Annotate as you read, and review your notes as you prepare to write. Be sure that you understand what the writer is saying and how his or her ideas connect to each other. Reread or ask for help if you do not, as you cannot write an effective summary unless you fully comprehend what the writer is saying.

As you write, keep in mind the following guidelines for writing a good summary.

1. **A good summary should be much shorter than the text or content being summarized.** It should be usually a quarter to a third of the length of the original if it is a short text (e.g., 1–3 pages). It could be longer if you are summarizing an entire novel, a movie, or a large amount of information.

2. **A good summary should include only the major ideas from what is being summarized.** For a longer piece, it would include the thesis and the major supporting ideas. A good summary does not include less important supporting details.

3. **A good summary should be written in your own words.** Restate or paraphrase key terms, concepts, or ideas. Use quotations very sparingly, if at all, and if you do, use quotation marks. Do not simply plug your own words into the structure of the text you are summarizing. Summarize using your own structure.

4. **A good summary should not include your own ideas or opinions.** Summarize what you have read or observed and do not include your own ideas, opinions, or information from other sources.

5. **A good summary should clearly state the source that is being summarized.** The introductory sentence should note the author and title of a reading (or, for example, the director and title of a movie) and should use appropriate in-text citation (see MLA In-Text Citations [23.2, p. 652] or APA In-Text Citations [24.2, p. 688] for details).

Summarizing Baldwin

Below you will find James Baldwin's essay "On Being 'White' . . . and Other Lies." For this assignment, write a summary of the essay. If you need to refresh your understanding of what makes a good summary, refer to Strategies for Writing a Summary (18.25, p. 547).

On Being "White" . . . and Other Lies

JAMES BALDWIN

James Baldwin (1924–1987) is best known as the author of six novels including *Go Tell It on the Mountain* (1953) and *Giovanni's Room* (1956). He also wrote essays that explored race, racism, homophobia, the immigrant experience, and whiteness. "On Being 'White' . . . and Other Lies" first appeared in the magazine *Essence* in 1984. In this essay he's questioning the racial category "white" by pointing out it was only invented as a category when Europeans came to America.

1 The crisis of leadership in the white community is remarkable—and terrifying—because there is, in fact, no white community.

2 This may seem an enormous statement—and it is. I'm willing to be challenged. I'm also willing to attempt to spell it out.

3 My frame of reference is, of course, America, or that portion of the North American continent that calls itself America. And this means I am speaking, essentially, of the European vision of the world—or more precisely, perhaps, the European vision of the universe. It is a vision as remarkable for what it pretends to include as for what it remorselessly diminishes, demolishes or leaves totally out of account.

4 There is, for example—at least, in principle—an Irish community: here, there, anywhere, or, more precisely, Belfast, Dublin and Boston. There is a German community: both sides of Berlin, Bavaria and Yorkville. There is an Italian community: Rome, Naples, the Bank of the Holy Ghost and Mulberry Street. And there is a Jewish community, stretching from Jerusalem to California to New York. There are English communities. There are French communities. There are Swiss consortiums. There are Poles: in Warsaw (where they would like us to be friends) and in Chicago (where because they are white we are enemies). There are, for that matter, Indian restaurants and Turkish baths. There is the underworld—the poor (to say nothing of those who intend to become rich) are always with us—but this does not describe a community. It bears terrifying witness to what happened to everyone who got here,

▶

and paid the price of the ticket. The price was to become "white." No one was white before he/she came to America. It took generations, and a vast amount of coercion, before this became a white country.

5   It is probable that it is the Jewish community—or more accurately, perhaps, its remnants—that in America has paid the highest and most extraordinary price for becoming white. For the Jews came here from countries where they were not white, and they came here, in part, because they were not white; and incontestably in the eyes of the Black American (and not only in those eyes) American Jews have opted to become white, and this is how they operate. It was ironical to hear, for example, former Israeli prime minister Menachem Begin declare some time ago that "the Jewish people bow only to God" while knowing that the state of Israel is sustained by a blank check from Washington. Without further pursuing the implication of this mutual act of faith, one is nevertheless aware that the Black presence, here, can scarcely hope—at least, not yet—to halt the slaughter in South Africa.

6   And there is a reason for that.

7   America became white—the people who, as they claim, "settled" the country became white—because of the necessity of denying the Black presence, and justifying the Black subjugation. No community can be based on such a principle—or, in other words, no community can be established on so genocidal a lie. White men—from Norway, for example, where they were Norwegians—became white: by slaughtering the cattle, poisoning the wells, torching the houses, massacring Native Americans, raping Black women.

8   This moral erosion has made it quite impossible for those who think of themselves as white in this country to have any moral authority at all—privately, or publicly. The multitudinous bulk of them sit, stunned, before their TV sets, swallowing garbage that they know to be garbage, and—in a profound and unconscious effort to justify this torpor that disguises a profound and bitter panic—pay a vast amount of attention to athletics: even though they know that the football player (the Son of the Republic, *their* sons!) is merely another aspect of the money-making scheme. They are either relieved or embittered by the presence of the Black boy on the team. I do not know if they remember how long and hard they fought to keep him off it. I know that they do not dare have any notion of the price Black people (mothers and fathers) paid and pay. They do not want to know the meaning, or face the shame, of what they compelled—out of what they took as the necessity of being white—Joe Louis or Jackie Robinson or Cassius Clay (aka Muhammad Ali) to pay. I know that they, themselves, would not have liked to pay it.

9   There has never been a labor movement in this country, the proof being the absence of a Black presence in the so-called father-to-son unions. There are, perhaps, some niggers in the window; but Blacks have no power in the labor unions.

10   Just so does the white community, as a means of keeping itself white, elect, as they imagine, their political (!) representatives. No nation in the world, including England, is represented by so stunning a pantheon of the relentlessly mediocre. I will not name names—I will leave that to you.

11   But this cowardice, this necessity of justifying a totally false identity and of justifying what must be called a genocidal history, has placed everyone now living into the hands of the most ignorant and powerful people the world has ever seen: And how did they get that way?

12   By deciding that they were white. By opting for safety instead of life. By persuading themselves that a Black child's life meant nothing compared with a white child's life. By abandoning their children to the things white men could buy. By informing their children that Black women, Black men and Black children had no human integrity that those who call themselves white were bound to respect. And in this debasement and definition of Black people, they debased and defamed themselves.

13   And have brought humanity to the edge of oblivion: because they think they are white. Because they think they are white, they do not dare confront the ravage and the lie of their history. Because they think they are white, they cannot allow themselves to be tormented by the suspicion that all men are brothers. Because they think they are white, they are looking for, or bombing into existence, stable populations, cheerful natives and cheap labor. Because they think they are white, they believe, as even no child believes, in the dream of safety. Because they think they are white, however vociferous they may be and however multitudinous, they are as speechless as Lot's wife—looking backward, changed into a pillar of salt.

14   However—! White being, absolutely, a moral choice (for there are no white people), the crisis of leadership for those of us whose identity has been forged, or branded, as Black is nothing new. We—who were not Black before we got here either, who were defined as Black by the slave trade—have paid for the crisis of leadership in the white community for a very long time, and have resoundingly, even when we face the worst about ourselves, survived, and triumphed over it. If we had not survived and triumphed, there would not be a Black American alive.

15   And the fact that we are still here—even in suffering, darkness, danger, endlessly defined by those who do not dare define, or even confront, themselves—is the key to the crisis in white leadership. The past informs us of various kinds of people—criminals, adventurers and saints, to say nothing, of course, of popes—but it is the Black condition, and only that, which informs us concerning white people. It is a terrible paradox, but those who believed that they could control and define Black people divested themselves of the power to control and define themselves.

Proposal

In school, in your neighborhood, or in your workplace, if you want to innovate, to correct injustices, to improve efficiency, or, generally, to make things better, you need to be able to write an effective proposal.

18.27 Tutorial

Strategies for Writing a Proposal

If you want to innovate, to correct injustices, to improve efficiency, or, generally, to make things better, you need to be able to write an effective proposal. For example, you might want to do one of the following.

- Sway your English teacher to give more time for revising essays.
- Prompt your local government to provide more lighting in your neighborhood.
- Convince the place you work to provide more employee parking.
- Persuade the federal government to improve the FAFSA application.

Each of these would require that you write a proposal.

How to Write a Successful Proposal

A proposal must have two essential components: an argument that there is a problem and a proposed solution to that problem. To fully explain both, you need to do the following.

1. **State the problem.**   You need to state clearly what the problem you are addressing is and present evidence to support the idea that it is a problem. You might give examples of how the problem has affected people or even how it could affect the audience you are writing for. It is also useful to provide background information about the problem. What is the history of the problem? What attempts have been made to address it in the past? With what results? What are the causes of the problem? Is it getting worse? Sometimes this background information works best at the beginning of the proposal, but more often, it is more effective after you've explained what the problem is.

2. **Present a solution.**   You need to provide a clear statement of the solution you are proposing. What is it? Who would have to do it? How much would it cost? How would it work? Once you've clearly explained your solution to the problem, you need to present evidence that it is feasible, that it is a realistic proposal. Then you need to present evidence that, once enacted, your proposal

will solve the problem or, at least, reduce the severity of the negative effects the problem causes.

3. **Address objections to your solution.** You need to think about why some people might object to your proposed solution and explain how their objections are not valid. Point out that it won't cost as much as they claim. Clarify that the negative side effects can be avoided. If they argue that your solution has already been tried and found to be ineffective, explain why it wasn't tried correctly or how the situation has changed so that now it will be effective.

   Sometimes those who oppose a solution don't criticize the proposed solution, but instead argue that a different solution would be more effective. You need to find out about any alternative solutions and evaluate them so that you can confidently argue that other solutions won't work, won't work as well, or will have too many harmful side effects.

4. **Make a strong argument.** You will want to close your proposal with a strong argument for immediate action on your proposal.

In the following proposal, LaShawna Williams includes each of the components suggested above.

A Proposal to Substitute a Discussion Board for the Chat Room

1   Dear Professor Jenkins, I want to bring to your attention a problem that is causing many students great difficulty. Your requirement that we join a chat room on line for an hour every Sunday afternoon at 5:00 is having consequences you may not be aware of.

Clear statement of the problem

2   Many of us work on weekends to support our going to school. I am a cook at a restaurant on Saturdays and Sundays. I have to arrive by 3:00 to begin my prep work for dinner. I try to access your chat room on my cell phone at 5:00, but often we are simply too busy. I know that four of my classmates are having similar conflicts with their Sunday jobs.

Examples of how the problem is causing harm

3   While I can use my cell phone to access the chat room, three of my classmates that I know of don't own cell phones and, of course, don't own computers. They depend on computers in the

writing center or in the library to access your website. The problem is that the library and writing center are not open on Sundays.

4 When we registered for your class, the schedule indicated the class meets on Monday, Wednesday, and Friday from 10:15 to 11:05. We built our class schedules and our work schedules around these times. Now we learn that we also are required to participate in the class chat room every Sunday afternoon, creating considerable hardship.

Background information about the problem

5 I would like to propose a solution to this problem which will still allow you to interact with us and read our thoughts about the readings in the course online, but will not cause the hardships for many of us that the Sunday afternoon chat room is causing. I propose that, instead of the chat room at a certain hour on Sundays, you establish a discussion board that we are required to post on at least six times each week.

Clear statement of the solution

6 There is a discussion board available in Blackboard, so there is no expense to the college, to you, or to the students. We could have the same kind of conversations you are calling for in the chat room, but there would not be a specific time we had to join the conversation. Just like with a chat room, you will be able to monitor the conversation, ask us questions, clear up misunderstandings, and evaluate our performance. Last semester, I was in a class that required us to participate in a discussion board, and it was quite successful. There was much more participation by the class than we are getting in the chat room.

Evidence the solution is feasible and will address the problem

7 I know that you have announced that if we miss three chat room conversations, we can write an extra essay and be graded on that. This, however, is not nearly as good a solution as the discussion board I am proposing. First, it feels more like punishment than participation. Second, it means

Argument that the proposed solution is superior to an alternative solution

we do not benefit from the experience of being part of a discussion.

8   I urge you to announce at our next class meeting that we are switching to the discussion board format instead of the Sunday chat room.

Strong argument for immediate action

Thanks for considering my proposal,
LaShawna Williams

18.28   Writing
Making a Proposal to Solve a Problem

Think of a problem at your school, at your workplace, or in your town or city. Then think of a solution to that problem. Finally, think of the person to whom you could write to propose a solution.

Write a proposal to that person. One or two pages would be plenty, but if you need more to make your case, a longer paper is fine too. Refer to Strategies for Writing a Proposal (18.27, p. 552) for more information on how to write a successful proposal.

Reflection

Reflective writing asks you to think back, to "reflect," on an experience—an essay you have written, a major change in your life, a time when you weren't successful at something you wanted to do—and to examine how you now think and feel about that experience.

18.29   Tutorial
Strategies for Writing a Reflection

Reflective writing is different from most writing you do in college. It asks you to examine your feelings. It asks you to think about the effects an experience has had on you. What have you learned? How have you changed? How will you be different in the future?

Reflective writing is useful in many ways. After you've been working on a project for days or even weeks, it can be very helpful to take a minute to think back over the time you spent on that project: What did you learn? What mistakes did you make? What did you do really well? It can also be useful to examine your feelings about the experience. Do you feel satisfied? Eager to get on to the next project? Disappointed? Relieved? How will you be different in the future as a result of this experience? How can you benefit from the experience going forward? What mistakes will you know how to avoid in the future?

In this course you are asked to reflect on your experience writing essays, but the process of writing down your reflections can be helpful in many other situations as well: you can reflect on a reading, a group activity, or a video. After you have a job interview, it can be very useful to write a short reflection about the experience. When a relationship ends, reflection can be a big help in getting over it and moving on. Even after making a mistake in your life—breaking a law, doing something cruel or thoughtless to someone, or cheating on some task at work or at school—reflective writing can help you learn and move on from these experiences.

18.30 Writing

Reflecting on an Important Experience

Think of an experience you have had in the past couple of years. This could be a project you worked on in school or it could involve a job, a program you volunteered for, a family event of some kind, or an athletic endeavor. Almost any experience that you can remember fairly clearly will work, but it should not have been a quick event that was over in a few minutes. Try to pick something in which you invested considerable time and effort. Then write a short paper—a page or so—reflecting on this experience.

- **Report on what you learned.**   What were the most important or most useful ideas you encountered? What mistakes did you make? Was there some part of the experience that you are proud of? Do you have any regrets?

- **Describe how you now feel about the experience.**   Are you disappointed? Satisfied? Proud? Relieved? Eager to get on with some new experience?

- **How will you be different in the future?**   What did you learn that will make a difference for you in the future? How will you be different?

Weaving Strategies into a Strong Essay

After discussing the writing strategies covered in this topic separately, in this final section you will see how they can be woven together into a powerful essay.

18.31 Tutorial

Using Multiple Writing Strategies in an Essay

In this Topic a series of writing strategies have been discussed that are most often woven together to create a coherent and convincing essay. Although you might be writing a predominantly cause-and-effect, comparison/contrast, process, or argument essay, you will find that you need to use other strategies to flesh out your paper. Before you start drafting, consider your subject, audience, purpose, and assignment. Then review the strategies discussed in this Topic and think about which strategy, or strategies, would work best for your assignment. If you are making an argument, for example, you might consider including the following.

- a paragraph or two defining one or more terms critical to that argument

- a narrative paragraph that provides some historical context for the issue

- a lengthy description of a place important to the argument

- several paragraphs that strengthen the overall argument by focusing on the positive effects that would result from taking the action proposed in the thesis

18.32 Activity

Identifying Multiple Writing Strategies in an Essay

The process of weaving various writing strategies together in a longer essay is a very effective way to organize a compelling essay, as Steven Pinker does in the excerpt below, which comes from his introduction to a book on language. The several references to later chapters refer to the rest of the book.

Working in your group, identify as many different writing strategies used by Pinker in this excerpt as you can.

Words and Worlds

STEVEN PINKER

Steven Pinker, an experimental psychologist, was born in Montreal, Canada. He earned a bachelor's degree in experimental psychology from McGill University and a doctorate from Harvard. He has taught at Stanford and MIT and is currently the Johnstone Family Professor in the psychology department at Harvard. After early research on language development in children, he went on to focus on the cognitive, genetic, and neurobiological underpinnings of language. He has authored ten books and received nine honorary doctorates.

1   On September 11, 2001, at 8:46 A.M., a hijacked airliner crashed into the north tower of the World Trade Center in New York. At 9:03 A.M. a second plane crashed into the south tower. The resulting infernos caused the buildings to collapse, the south tower after burning for an hour and two minutes, the north tower twenty-three minutes after that. The attacks were masterminded by Osama bin Laden, leader of the Al Qaeda terrorist organization, who hoped to intimidate the United States into ending its military presence in Saudi Arabia and its support for Israel and to unite Muslims in preparation for a restoration of the caliphate.

2   9/11, as the happenings of that day are now called, stands as the most significant political and intellectual event of the twenty-first century so far. It has set off debates on a vast array of topics: how best to memorialize the dead and revitalize lower Manhattan; whether the attacks are rooted in ancient Islamic fundamentalism or modern revolutionary agitation; the role of the United States on the world stage before the attacks and in response to them; how best to balance protection against terrorism with respect for civil liberties.

3   But I would like to explore a lesser-known debate triggered by 9/11. Exactly how many events took place in New York on that morning in September?

4   It could be argued that the answer is one. The attacks on the building were part of a single plan conceived in the mind of one man in service of a single agenda. They unfolded within a few minutes of each other, targeting the parts of a complex with a single name, design, and owner. And they launched a single chain of military and political events in their aftermath.

5   Or it could be argued that the answer is two. The north tower and south tower were distinct collections of glass and steel separated by an expanse of space, and they were hit at different times and went out of existence at different times. The amateur video that showed the second plane closing in on the south tower as the north tower billowed with smoke makes the twoness unmistakable: in those horrifying moments, one event was frozen in the past, the other loomed in the future. And another

occurrence on that day—a passenger mutiny that brought down a third hijacked plane before it reached its target in Washington—presents to the imagination the possibility that one tower or the other might have been spared. In each of those possible worlds a distinct event took place, so in our *actual* world one might argue, there must have been a pair of events as surely as one plus one equals two.

6   The gravity of 9/11 would seem to make this entire discussion frivolous to the point of impudence. It's a matter of mere "semantics," as we say, with its implication of picking nits, splitting hairs, and debating the number of angels that can dance on the head of a pin. But this book is about semantics, and I would not make a claim on your attention if I did not think that the relation of language to our inner and outer worlds was a matter of intellectual fascination and real-world importance.

7   Though "importance" is often hard to quantify, in this case I can put an exact value on it: three and a half billion dollars. That was the sum in dispute in a set of trials determining the insurance payout to Larry Silverstein, the leaseholder of the World Trade Center site. Silverstein held insurance policies that stipulated a maximum reimbursement for each destructive "event." If 9/11 comprised a single event, he stood to receive three and a half billion dollars. If it comprised two events, he stood to receive seven billion. In the trials, the attorneys disputed the applicable meaning of the term *event*. The lawyers for the leaseholder defined it in physical terms (two collapses); those for the insurance companies defined it in mental terms (one plot). There is nothing "mere" about semantics!

8   Nor is the topic intellectually trifling. The 9/11 cardinality debate is not about the facts, that is, the physical events and human actions that took place that day. Admittedly, those have been contested as well: according to various conspiracy theories, the buildings were targeted by American missiles, or demolished by a controlled implosion, in a plot conceived by American neoconservatives, Israeli spies, or a cabal of psychiatrists. But aside from the kooks, most people agree on the facts. Where they differ is in the *construal* of those facts: how the intricate swirl of matter in space ought to be conceptualized by human minds. As we shall see, the categories in this dispute permeate the meanings of words in our language because they permeate the way we represent reality in our heads.

9   Semantics is about the relation of words to thoughts, but it is also about the relation of words to other human concerns. Semantics is about the relation of words to reality—the way that speakers commit themselves to a shared understanding of the truth, and the way their thoughts are anchored to things and situations in the world. It is about the relation of words to a community—how a new word, which arises in an act of creation by a single speaker, comes to evoke the same idea in the rest of a population, so people can understand one another when they use it. It is

▶

about the relation of words to emotions: the way in which words don't just point to things but are saturated with feelings, which can endow the words with a sense of magic, taboo, and sin. And it is about words and social relations—how people use language not just to transfer ideas from head to head but to negotiate the kind of relationship they wish to have with their conversational partner.

10   A feature of the mind that we will repeatedly encounter in these pages is that even our most abstract concepts are understood in terms of concrete scenarios. That applies in full force to the subject matter of the book itself. In this introductory chapter I will preview some of the book's topics with vignettes from newspapers and the Internet that can be understood only through the lens of semantics. They come from each of the worlds that connect to our words—the worlds of thought, reality, community, emotions, and social relations.

11   Let's look at the bone of contention in the world's most expensive debate in semantics, the three-and-a-half-billion-dollar argument over the meaning of "event." What, exactly, is an event? An event is a stretch of time, and time, according to physicists, is a continuous variable—an inexorable cosmic flow, in Newton's world, or a fourth dimension in a seamless hyperspace in Einstein's. But the human mind carves this fabric into discrete swatches we call events. Where does the mind place the incisions? Sometimes, as the lawyers for the World Trade Center leaseholder pointed out, it encircles the change of state of an object, such as the collapse of a building. And sometimes, as the lawyers for the insurers pointed out, it encircles the goal of a human actor, such as a plot being executed. Most often the circles coincide: an actor intends to cause an object to change, the intent of the act and the fate of the object are tracked along a single time line, and the moment of change marks the consummation of the intent.

3 Reading

Students in college, particularly students in English courses in college, can expect to be required to read challenging texts regularly. Part 3 is a collection of advice, activities, readings, and videos that will help you as you encounter these college-level texts.

TOPIC 19
Active Reading

Active reading means engaging with a text, teasing out what an author is saying, and thinking critically about the ideas being presented.

Navigating Topic 19

The presentations and tutorials listed below provide information about active reading strategies. You can work through the entire Topic on your own, learning about all the strategies and practicing them; work on items you've been assigned by your instructor; or choose those ones you would find helpful.

Introduction to Active Reading

Topic 19 begins with two presentations on concepts that are essential to being a successful active reader: the first emphasizes that reading is thinking, and the second describes how effective readers use a process that involves pre-, during, and after-reading strategies. It then provides information on remembering what you've read, purposes for reading, and how to construct meaning from texts.

19.1 Presentation

Reading Is Thinking

To watch this presentation, which discusses the importance of thinking, questioning, and extracting meaning from a text as you read, go to *Achieve for The Hub*, Topic 19, and open Unit 19.1.

19.2 Presentation

The Reading Process

To watch this presentation, which discusses the different strategies effective readers use before, during, and after reading to get the most out of a text, go to *Achieve for The Hub*, Topic 19, and open Unit 19.2.

19.3 Tutorial

Optimizing Your Reading

Reading takes concentration, so it makes sense to read when and where you can focus best. This differs from person to person. Some people need the absolute quiet of a library carrel, while others read most effectively listening to music or sitting in a coffee shop. The following are some suggestions for optimizing your reading.

- **Find the right place for you to read.** If even the smallest noise distracts you, find a quiet place where you won't be disturbed. This could be the library, a secluded bench on campus, or your apartment or dorm room when your roommates are in classes. If you do better when there's some background sound, play music, try a lounge in your dorm, or go to a coffee shop.

- **Try to read in the same place and at the same time.** Block out time on your calendar for reading and list your assignments and their due dates. Developing a routine of reading in the same place at the same time will help you to focus and become a more concentrated reader.

- **Choose times to read when you are most alert.** Some people find they can concentrate best in the morning while others prefer to read in the evening. Whatever time works best for you, plan to read your most difficult assignments first, when you have the most stamina and focus.

- **Avoid distractions.** In today's world, you are always connected to other people via smart phone, email, instant messenger apps, Facebook, Instagram, SnapChat, Twitter, and WhatsApp. In order to concentrate, you need to turn all social media off. Resist checking for messages, updates, or breaking news until after you've finished reading.

- **Break reading assignments into chunks.** Reading assigned in college can sometimes be dry or difficult to read. Break an assignment into manageable chunks, maybe the content between two major headings, and stop after each section to check that you've understood what you've read. Write a brief summary of the main points or create a diagram or timeline that helps you to organize what you've learned. For challenging readings, break the text into even smaller parts and reread if necessary.

- **Build in breaks and reward yourself for completing assignments.** At the end of a long section or several smaller ones, take five minutes to stretch your legs or get coffee. Reward yourself for completing an assignment by going for a walk, eating lunch with a friend, or checking your social media.

19.4 Tutorial

Remembering What You've Read

Many readers worry that they won't be able to remember what they have read. A wonderful teacher named Cris Tovani has written a book called *I Read It, But I Don't Get It*. In it she describes the experiences of many readers who struggle to read a book, an essay, or a chapter in a text but who, when they finish, don't remember what they read and, therefore, have concluded that they are not good readers.

David Bartholomae and Anthony Petrosky in an influential book about reading and writing, *Facts, Artifacts, and Counterfacts*, point out that a reader who literally memorized an entire text and could recite it back word for word might not have actually understood the text. One can imagine a computer that could read a text out loud, word for word, but no one would claim that the computer had actually "read" the text.

For now, you should be less concerned about "remembering" the text. Instead, think of reading as an act of thinking, of understanding, of comprehending, of engaging with the text. Approached this way, the point of reading is not to remember everything you read, but to understand the important ideas you learned and the conclusions that you developed during the process of reading. Topic 20: Reading Strategies (p. 573) provides a number of techniques that will assist you in doing this more effectively, such as annotating, keeping a journal, summarizing, and playing the believing and doubting game.

19.5 Activity
Purposes for *Your* Reading

Not only do writers have a purpose for their writing, but readers usually read with a purpose.

Working in your group, make a list of the different kinds of reading the members of your group do. Then list what the purpose is for each different kind of reading, as illustrated in the following chart.

Kind of Reading	Purpose for Reading
A letter from a friend	To learn what they are doing, thinking
A recipe for something you plan to cook in the future	To make a shopping list of ingredients

19.6 Tutorial
Purposes for Reading

We read for many different purposes: to find out when the next bus leaves campus, to find a recipe for a special meal, to locate sources for a research paper, to learn what's happening in the world of politics, or to solve a mystery in a crime novel. A list of some of the many purposes we have for reading might look like this:

- Reading to learn new information
- Reading to understand a difficult concept
- Reading to evaluate and critique different perspectives on a topic
- Reading for practical purposes (e.g., how to change brake fluid or build a set of shelves)
- Reading for a class assignment
- Reading to find specific information in a book, article, or online text
- Skimming to get a general sense of a text
- Scanning to find specific information (e.g., the date of a historical event)
- Reading for pleasure

The way we read is often determined by the purpose for which we are reading, and these variations in purpose require the use of different reading techniques, as can be seen in the following examples.

1. You are reading an email to determine the location of an important sales meeting. You scan the document looking for the conference room number.

2. You are reading a novel for pleasure. You read attentively but in a relaxed manner, savoring the pleasure of the experience.

3. You are reading a letter from a company to which you have applied for a job. You read fairly quickly, skimming the document to find the place where the company says whether you are invited for an interview or not.

4. You are reading a textbook about the causes of the War of 1812 in preparation for a test. You read slowly with great focus, annotating the text, making notes to help you understand and remember the details, summarizing important events, and creating and answering questions you think your instructor might ask.

5. You are previewing a challenging article in a scholarly journal before you dive in for a detailed read. You read the abstract, title, headings, and first and last paragraphs; note the name of the author; review any graphic aids, such as charts and graphs; and consider how difficult the article will be to read and how much time you will need.

6. You are reading a half dozen articles on global warming to see if any of them discuss the effect of rising sea levels in Florida, a topic you are writing about. You preview each and then skim through those that sound promising, looking for more specific information.

Notice how your reading techniques will change depending on your purpose. It's a good idea, before you start reading anything, to think for a minute about the purpose of your reading and to adjust your approach to match that purpose.

19.7 Tutorial

Constructing Meaning

Sometimes the meaning of a text is fairly obvious. Sometimes authors state what they mean to say in the first paragraph, even in the first sentence. But at other times, writers aren't so direct. Sometimes the reader has to construct the meaning by reading carefully, weighing the evidence, evaluating the reasoning, and comparing what the text says with the reader's own experiences.

For example, two groups of students read a section of Rebecca Skloot's book *The Immortal Life of Henrietta Lacks* that describes Lacks's experience going to Johns Hopkins Hospital in Baltimore for treatment of what turned out to be cervical cancer.

The book tells us that Lacks was admitted to the "colored" ward of the hospital, her tissues were used for medical research without her permission or knowledge, and, after her death, her surviving husband and children were tricked into signing an agreement to allow the hospital to perform an autopsy on her body. On the other hand, the book tells us that Hopkins was founded to provide health care for the poor, that Hopkins provided Lacks all the therapy for cervical cancer that medicine at that time had at its disposal, and that Hopkins didn't make any money from Lacks's cells.

Asked to write a brief statement summing up what the passage said about Johns Hopkins Hospital, the students in the first group wrote, "Johns Hopkins was a racist organization." The students in the second group wrote, "The good that Hopkins did for medical science far outweighed the racism it was also guilty of."

When asked why the two groups had arrived at such different "meanings" from the text, a woman in the second group, made up of four African American women, after much hesitation, volunteered an observation: "Group 1 is all white. I think they were afraid that if they didn't come down hard on the racism, we black students would jump all over them." At this point, one of the women in the first group suggested that the women in the second group were all studying to be nurses. It turned out three of the four were in the nursing program.

The point here is not that one group or the other had the "right answer." The point is that the meaning of a text is not something lying quietly on the page waiting to be discovered and underlined. The meaning of a text is something to be constructed by the reader. When readers carefully and thoughtfully read a text, weigh the evidence given, examine the assumptions underlying the text, evaluate the reasoning, and compare it all with their own experiences and thoughts, they are able to *construct* a meaning from the text.

The kind of reading that will allow you to engage with a challenging text and construct a meaning after reading that text is what we mean by active reading. In Topic 20: Reading Strategies (p. 573), you will be introduced to a number of different strategies to help you read this way.

19.8 Activity

Constructing Mike Rose's Meaning in "'Grit' Revisited"

Read the following excerpt from Mike Rose's blog. When you've finished reading it, working with your group, decide what the passage means. What is Rose saying? What's his point? Write your group's decision about the meaning of the essay in a sentence or two.

A word of warning: The meaning of this excerpt is fairly subtle. You will need to pay attention to details, weigh the evidence, and do some thinking in order to decide what the passage means.

"Grit" Revisited: Reflections on Our Public Talk about Education

MIKE ROSE

1   One of the many frustrating things about education policy and practice in our country is the continual search for the magic bullet—and all the hype and trite lingo that bursts up around it. One such bullet is the latest incarnation of character education, particularly the enthrallment with "grit," a buzz word for perseverance and determination. . . .

2   In a nutshell, I worry about the limited success of past attempts at character education and the danger in our pendulum-swing society that we will shift our attention from improving subject matter instruction. I also question the easy distinctions made between "cognitive" and "non-cognitive" skills. And I fear that we will sacrifice policies aimed at reducing poverty for interventions to change the way poor people see the world.

3   In this post, I would like to further explore these concerns—and a few new ones—by focusing on "grit," for it has so captured the fancy of our policy makers, administrators, and opinion-makers.

4   Grit's rise to glory is something to behold, a case study in the sociology of knowledge. If you go back ten or so years, you'll find University of Pennsylvania psychologist Angela Duckworth investigating the role of perseverance in achievement. This idea is not new in the study of personality and individual differences, but Duckworth was trying to more precisely define and isolate perseverance or persistence as an important personality trait via factor analysis, a standard statistical tool in personality psychology. Through a series of studies of high-achieving populations (for example, Penn undergraduates, West Point cadets, Spelling Bee champions), Duckworth and her colleagues demonstrated that this perseverance quality might be distinct from other qualities (such as intelligence or self-control) and seemed to account for between 1.4 to 6.3 percent of all that goes into the achievements of those studied. (Later studies would find several higher percentages.) These findings suggest that over ninety percent of her populations' achievements are accounted for by other personal, familial, environmental, and cultural factors, but, still, her findings are important and make a contribution to the academic study of personality—and support a commonsense belief that hard work over time pays off.

5   It is instructive to read Duckworth's foundational scholarly articles, something I suspect few staffers and no policy makers have done. The articles are revealing in their listing of qualifications and limitations: The original studies rely on self-report

questionnaires, so can be subject to error and bias. The studies are correlational, so do not demonstrate causality. The exceptional qualities of some of the populations studied can create problems for factor analysis. Perseverance might have a downside to it. The construct of perseverance has been studied in some fashion for over a century.

6   But Duckworth and her colleagues did something that in retrospect was a brilliant marketing strategy, a master stroke of branding—or re-branding. Rather than calling their construct "perseverance" or "persistence," they chose to call it "grit." Can you think of a name that has more resonance in American culture? The fighter who is all heart. The hardscrabble survivor. *True Grit*. The Little Train That Could.

7   Grit exploded. *New York Times* commentators, best-selling journalists, the producers of *This American Life*, Secretary of Education Arne Duncan, educational policy makers and administrators all saw the development of grit as a way to improve American education and, more pointedly, to improve the achievement of poor children who, everyone seemed to assume, lacked grit.

8   I'll get to that last part about poor kids in a moment, but first I want to ask some questions few policy makers are asking. What is an education suitable for a democracy? What kind of people are we trying to develop? What is our philosophy of education? With these questions in mind, let's consider some items taken from the two instruments Duckworth and colleagues have used in their studies. The items are listed under grit's two subscales, the factors that comprise grit:

Consistency of Interests Subscale:

- New ideas and projects sometimes distract me from previous ones.
- I have been obsessed with a certain idea or project for a short time but later lost interest.
- I often set a goal but later choose to pursue a different one.

Perseverance of Effort Subscale:

- Setbacks don't discourage me.
- I finish whatever I begin.
- I have achieved a goal that took years of work.

These items are answered on a five-point scale:

- Very much like me
- Mostly like me

▶

- Somewhat like me

- Not much like me

- Not like me at all

9   Let me repeat here what I've written in every other commentary on grit. Of course, perseverance is an important characteristic. I cherish it in my friends and my students. But at certain ages and certain times in our lives, exploration and testing new waters can also contribute to one's development and achievement. Knowing when something is not working is important as well. Perseverance and determination as represented in the grit questionnaires could suggest a lack of flexibility, tunnel vision, an inability to learn from mistakes. Again, my point is not to dismiss perseverance but to suggest that perseverance, or grit, or any quality works in tandem with other qualities in the well-functioning and ethical person. By focusing so heavily on grit, character education in some settings has been virtually reduced to a single quality, and probably not the best quality in the content of character. The items in the grit instruments could describe the brilliant surgeon who is a distant and absent parent, or, for that fact, the smart, ambitious, amoral people who triggered the Great Recession. (Macbeth with his "vaulting ambition" would score quite high on grit.) Education in America has to be about more than producing driven super-achievers. For that fact, a discussion of what we mean by "achievement" is long overdue.

10   But, of course, a good deal of the discussion of grit doesn't really involve all students. Regardless of disclaimers, the primary audience for our era's character education is poor kids. As I and a host of others have written, a focus on individual characteristics of low-income children can take our attention away from the structural inequalities they face. Some proponents of character education have pretty much said that an infusion of grit will achieve what social and economic interventions cannot.

11   Can I make a recommendation? Along with the grit survey, let us give another survey and see what the relationship is between the scores. I'm not sure what to call this new survey, but it would provide a measure of adversity, of impediments to persistence, concentration, and the like. It, too, would use a five-point response scale: "very much like me" to "not much like me." Its items would include:

- I always have bus fare to get to school.

- I hear my parents talking about not having enough money for the rent.

- Whenever I get sick, I am able to go to a doctor.

- We always have enough food in our home.

- I worry about getting to school safely.

- There are times when I have to stay home to care for younger brothers or sisters.

- My school has honors and Advanced Placement classes.

- I have at least one teacher who cares about me.

12   My guess is that higher impediment scores would be linked to lower scores on the grit survey. I realize that what grit advocates want is to help young people better cope with such hardship. Anyone who has worked seriously with kids in tough circumstances spends a lot of time providing support and advice, and if grit interventions can provide an additional resource, great. But if as a society we are not also working to improve the educational and economic realities these young people face, then we are engaging in a cruel hoax, building aspiration and determination for a world that will not fulfill either.

13   The foundational grit research primarily involved populations of elite high achievers—Ivy League students, West Point cadets, National Spelling Bee contestants—and people responding to a Positive Psychology website based at the University of Pennsylvania. It is from the latter population that the researchers got a wider range of ages and data on employment history.

14   I was not able to find socioeconomic information for these populations, but given what we know generally about Ivy League undergraduates, West Point cadets, etc., I think it is a safe guess that most come from stable economic backgrounds. (In one later study, Duckworth and colleagues drew on 7–11 grade students at a "socioeconomically and ethnically diverse magnet public school" where 18% of the students were low-income—that's some economic diversity, but not a school with concentrated disadvantage.) It is also safe to assume that the majority of the people who are interested in Positive Psychology and self-select to respond to an on-line questionnaire have middle-class employment histories with companies or in professions that have pathways and mechanisms for advancement. So the construct of grit and the instruments to measure it are largely based on populations that more likely than not are able to pursue their interests and goals along a landscape of resources and opportunity. This does not detract from the effort they expend or from their determination, but it does suggest that their grit is deployed in a world quite different from the world poor people inhabit.

15   It is hard to finish what you begin when food and housing are unstable, or when you have three or four teachers in a given year, or when there are few people around who are able to guide and direct you. It is equally hard to pursue a career with consistency when the jobs available to you are low-wage, short-term and vulnerable, and have few if any benefits or protections. This certainly doesn't mean that   ▶

people who are poor lack determination and resolve. Some of the poor people I knew growing up or work with today possess off-the-charts determination to survive, put food on the table, care for their kids. But they wouldn't necessarily score high on the grit scale.

16 Personality psychology by its disciplinary norms concentrates on the individual, but individual traits and qualities, regardless of how they originate and develop, manifest themselves in social and institutional contexts. Are we educators and policy makers creating classrooms that are challenging and engaging enough to invite perseverance? Are we creating opportunity for further educational or occupational programs that enable consistency of effort? Are we gritty enough to keep working toward these goals without distraction over the long haul?

TOPIC 20
Reading Strategies

Being able to understand, question, connect, and respond to texts is crucial to success in college and beyond. The strategies discussed in this Topic are tools you can use to deepen your reading comprehension.

Navigating Topic 20

The tutorials for this Topic are shown below, and each contains, or is followed by, an opportunity to apply the skills you have just learned. You can work through the entire Topic on your own, learning about all the strategies and practicing them; work on items you've been assigned by your instructor; or choose those ones you would find helpful.

Introduction to Reading Strategies

In this Topic, different strategies are presented to help you read challenging texts: activating schema, previewing, annotating, keeping a reading journal, dealing with difficult language, reading as a believer and doubter, and creating graphics to understand complex texts.

20.1 Tutorial

Activating Schema

"Activating schema" sounds quite intimidating. In fact, all it means is connecting what you already know to new information you are about to learn. After previewing a text (discussed in Unit 20.2, p. 575), take a few minutes to think about what you already know about the topic of the reading. Whatever the topic, you probably have some information about it based on your own experiences, books or articles you've read, TV shows or movies you've watched, radio news or podcasts you've listened to, or social media you follow. For example, if you're reading a chapter on infectious diseases for a health class, you might think of recent news items about outbreaks of measles in New York City, the flu epidemic at your college last year that knocked you out for a week, or the hygiene precautions you have to take at your food service job to prevent the transmission of bacteria and viruses.

Thinking about what you already know about a subject has two significant benefits: it can make new information easier to understand, and it can help you to remember what you learn because you can connect it to information with which you are already familiar.

As you preview, ask questions and try to answer them. Take the titles and sub-titles of chapters and ask yourself what you already know about the issues they will discuss. In a chapter on human populations in an environmental science text, for instance, there might be headings for the number of people the earth can support, factors that influence the size of human populations, the slowing population growth in China, and the increasing population growth in India. What have you heard, read, or seen about population growth and its effects on the environment? Brainstorm a list of everything you already know. Think about news items or documentaries you've watched that talk about decreasing natural resources, increasing pollution, and animal extinctions related to population growth and human activities. When reading a chapter in an economics text that talks about the positive and negative impacts of businesses moving into or out of communities, think about your personal experiences. Maybe you live in an economically depressed area that people are leaving because they cannot find work. What has that meant for your town or city? Or maybe you live somewhere like Seattle, which has become one of the fastest-growing cities in the country, leading to housing shortages and significantly higher rents. Taking a few minutes to think about what you already know will make you a more effective reader and improve your retention of new information.

Activity: Activating Your Schema for Dishonest Numbers

Working in your group, take a look at Daniel Levitin's article "Dishonest Numbers: Evaluating the Accuracy of Statistics" (4.7, p. 141). First decide what the article is about. What topic does it discuss? Then activate your schema by discussing what you already know about that topic.

20.2 Tutorial

Previewing a Text

The tutorials Thinking about Audience (9.4, p. 328) and Thinking about Purpose (9.6, p. 331) discuss how writers can benefit from an awareness of the purpose and the audience for their writing. Similarly, readers are better prepared to understand a text if they start with an awareness of who the writer is and who the writer's audience is. In addition, readers benefit from being aware of the writer's topic and purpose.

When you set out to read a book, an article, an essay, a blog, a web page—when you set out to read any text—your strategy may be simply to dive in, to start reading at the beginning and plow your way through to the end. With the limited time in most of our busy lives, simply diving in can seem like the quickest way to get something read.

Most experienced readers, however, have found that taking a few minutes before diving in to get a sense of what it is they are about to read actually saves them time and makes their reading more effective. This does not mean you need to spend hours previewing and predicting; just a few minutes will be very helpful when you start to read. Four steps for effectively previewing a text are given below. Every text is different, so not all of the steps will apply to all texts, but consider as many of them as you can.

Step 1: Preview the Text

Preview the text by doing the following.

- Take a look at the title.
- If the text is a book, look over the front and back covers and the table of contents, if there is one.

- If the text has headings for different parts, read them.

- If the text starts with an abstract or executive summary, read it.

- Skim any introductory material.

- Read the opening paragraph.

- Read the first sentence of each paragraph if the reading is quite short; read the first paragraph under each heading if the passage is longer.

- Read the final paragraph.

- Take a look at any illustrations, charts, tables, or videos if the text is online.

- Note how the author uses font design (bold, italic, or underlined) and color to signal meaning or relationships (e.g., bolding a word often indicates that a definition is to follow or that the word is a key term and important to know).

- Look to see if there are citations, endnotes, or a works cited list.

- Check to see how long the text is.

- Try listing everything you can remember without looking back at the text.

Step 2: Analyze the Rhetorical Situation

As long ago as classical Greece—300 BC or so—thinkers have been aware that four important components exist for every text: the *author* of the text, the *audience* for the text, the *topic* the text is about, and the *purpose* of the text. You don't need to remember the term *rhetorical situation*, which is made up of these four elements, but thinking about author, audience, topic, and purpose should be part of your previewing and predicting process.

1. **Author.**   Besides the name of the author, what else can you learn about him or her? What evidence is there that the author really has some expertise about the subject? What biases might the author have? Is the author part of an organization? A corporation? What else has the author written?

2. **Audience.**   Whom does it appear that the author intended to be the reader or readers of this text? Whom was he or she addressing? Were there other, secondary, audiences?

3. **Topic.**   What is this text about?

4. **Purpose.**   What does it appear that the author intended or, at least, hoped would happen as a result of this piece of writing? What did the author want the effect of this text to be on its audience?

Step 3: Predict What the Text Is About

If you take a few minutes to think about a text after you preview it, you will gain important information that will help you read it more effectively. While not every text will reveal answers to all of the following questions, every text will provide answers to some of them.

1. Based on your preview, can you predict what position, if any, the author takes on the subject?

2. Based on the headings, what kind of information do you think the author is going to provide in each section?

3. How is the text organized? Is it presenting an argument? Does the author discuss the causes and/or effects of an event? Is it comparing or contrasting people, ideas, or things? Recognizing how authors organize their writing can provide clues to what they might discuss and can help you predict their main idea(s) about the subject.

4. Does the author seem to make any assumptions about the subject? How might this affect the conclusions he or she reaches?

5. Does the author appear to be biased? How might this affect his or her writing on the subject?

Step 4: Think about Yourself in Relation to the Text

As well as previewing, considering the rhetorical situation, and predicting what a particular text might be about, ask yourself some questions about the topic and your reasons for reading about it. Any background information, or prior knowledge, you already have about a subject will help you read more effectively. If the topic is immigration, for example, do you have friends, relatives, or family members who recently came to the United States? Were your grandparents immigrants? What have you read, heard, or seen on the topic of immigration recently?

Actively thinking about what you already know has several benefits: it gets you thinking about what you're going to read, it helps you understand the text better as you read, and it assists you in remembering what you have read because you can connect the new information you learn to what you already know. In addition, knowing *why* you are reading will focus your attention and help you identify the most relevant points made by the writer.

Here are some useful questions you can ask yourself:

- How much do I already know about the topic?

- Have I had any experiences that are related to this topic? Do I know anyone who has?

- Have I read other texts (newspapers, articles, textbooks, novels) about this same topic?

- Have I seen any movies, documentaries, YouTube videos, or TV programs about this topic or heard about it on the radio or in podcasts?

- How do I feel about the text's stand on the topic?

- What is my purpose for reading this text?

- How similar or different am I from the intended audience for the text?

- How difficult will the text be to read?

- How much time will I need to read it?

There's lots to think about here, and all this is supposed to happen before you even start reading! Most students are really pressed for time, and it probably seems like doing all this "previewing" is just too time-consuming, but give it a try. You might not always have time to run through all these questions, but you can do some of them. After a couple of trial runs, you'll find out which are most useful to you, and for longer readings for which you have more time, you should be able to do most of these.

In the long run, you'll find that previewing will actually save you time because it will make the process of reading easier. You will get more out of the reading because you will have prepared yourself to be an engaged reader.

20.3 Activity

Previewing *The Stuff of Thought*, Steven Pinker

The tutorial Previewing a Text (20.2, p. 575) introduced the idea of previewing a text and predicting what it might be about. You may want to review that material before beginning this activity.

Here you will be putting previewing and predicting skills into practice using content from the cover and back page of Steven Pinker's bestseller *The Stuff of Thought*, reproduced below. Following that are a brief biography of Pinker, the title page and table of contents from the book, and an excerpt from the Preface.

Working in your group, study these materials as you would if you were previewing the book before starting to read it. Then answer as many of the following questions as you can.

1. What do I know, or what can I learn, about the author?
2. What do I know, or what can I learn, about the publisher of the text?

3. What audience was this text intended for? How similar or different am I from this audience?

4. What is the purpose of this text? What does it seem the author hopes to accomplish by it?

5. How well does what I know match what the writer seems to expect the reader to know?

6. What assumptions lie behind the argument in the text?

7. What do the chapter headings suggest about the content of the book?

8. How long is this text?

9. How difficult will this be to read?

10. Does it seem that I will agree or disagree with the text?

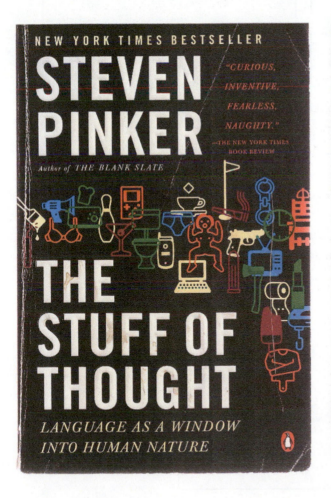

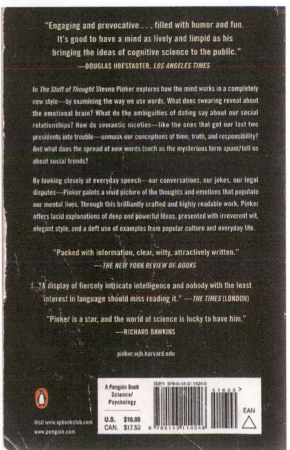

ABOUT THE AUTHOR

Steven Pinker is the Johnstone Family Professor of Psychology and Harvard College Professor at Harvard University. He is the author of seven books, including *The Language Instinct, How the Mind Works, Words and Rules,* and *The Blank Slate.* He lives in Boston and Truro, Massachusetts.

STEVEN PINKER

The Stuff of Thought

*Language as a Window
into Human Nature*

PENGUIN BOOKS

CONTENTS

PREFACE

1 There is a theory of space and time embedded in the way we use words. There is a theory of matter and a theory of causality, too. Our language has a model of sex in it (actually, two models), and conceptions of intimacy and power and fairness. Divinity, degradation, and danger are also ingrained in our mother tongue, together with a conception of well-being and a philosophy of free will. These conceptions vary in their details from language to language, but their overall logic is the same. They add up to a distinctively human model of reality, which differs in major ways from the objective understanding of reality eked out by our best science and logic. Though these ideas are woven into language, their roots are deeper than language itself. They lay out the ground rules for how we understand our surroundings, how we assign credit and blame to our fellows, and how we negotiate our relationships with them. A close look at our speech—our conversations, our jokes, our curses, our legal disputes, the names we give our babies—can therefore give us insight into who we are.

2 That is the premise of the book you are holding, the third in a trilogy written for a wide audience of readers who are interested in language and mind. The first, *The Language Instinct*, was an overview of the language faculty: everything you always wanted to know about language but were afraid to ask. A language is a way of connecting sound and meaning, and the other two books turn toward each of those spheres. *Words and Rules* was about the units of language, how they are stored in memory, and how they are assembled into the vast number of combinations that give language its expressive power. *The Stuff of Thought* is about the other side of the linkage, meaning. Its vistas include the meanings of words and constructions and the way that language is used in social settings, the topics that linguists call semantics and pragmatics.

* * *

3 As in my other books on language, the early chapters occasionally dip into technical topics. But I have worked hard to make them transparent, and I am confident that my subject will engage anyone with an interest in what makes us tick.

> Language is entwined with human life. We use it to inform and persuade, but also to threaten, to seduce, and of course to swear. It reflects the way we grasp reality, and also the image of ourselves we try to project to others, and the bonds that tie us to them. It is, I hope to convince you, a window into human nature.

20.4 Activity

Previewing a Website

The tutorials Thinking about Audience (9.4, p. 328) and Thinking about Purpose (9.6, p. 331) explain how a *writer* can benefit from awareness of his or her audience and purpose for writing. Similarly, a *reader* is better prepared to understand a text if he or she starts with an awareness of who the writer is, the audience for whom he or she is writing, and his or her subject and purpose.

The tutorial Previewing a Text (20.2, p. 575) suggested that when you need to read a text—an article, a book, a chapter, even a website—you should preview it first, which will save you time and make your reading more effective.

Now you're going to apply some of those same previewing techniques to the website **mesotheliomabook.com**. In your group, examine the website and then analyze the rhetorical situation.

1. **Examine the website.**
   - What is the site called?
   - Who is the owner and/or sponsor of the website? Is it a commercial site (.com)? A nonprofit site (.org)? An educational site (.edu)? A governmental site (.gov)?
   - Who is the author of the information you are reviewing?
   - What appears to be the purpose of the site? To provide information about mesothelioma, to sell a product, to raise money, to make a political statement, or something else?
   - How current is the site?
   - Are there any illustrations, charts, tables, or associated videos?

2. **Analyze the rhetorical situation.**
   - **Author.** You don't simply want to find out the name of the author. What else can you learn about him or her? What evidence is there that the author really has some expertise about the subject? What biases might the author have, and how can you tell? Is the author part of an organization? A corporation? What else has the author written?

- **Audience.** Whom does it appear that the author intended to be the reader or readers of this text? Whom was he or she addressing? Were there other, secondary, audiences?
- **Topic.** What is this website "about"? What seems to be its main focus? Does the author take a stand on this focus?
- **Purpose.** What does it appear that the author intended or, at least, hoped would happen as a result of this piece of writing? What did the author want the effect of this text to be on its audience? How can you tell?

20.5 Activity
Previewing Other Students' Essays

For this activity, you will need a draft of a paper you are working on. Your instructor will organize the class into pairs. Then do the following.

1. Exchange draft essays with your partner.
2. Read the title or any headings in the paper and the first paragraph. Do not read the entire essay.
3. Predict what the rest of the essay will be like.
4. If your prediction is not accurate, work with your partner to figure out why it isn't. Did your partner write a title and/or first paragraph that did not fit well with the rest of the paper, or did you misunderstand the title and/or first paragraph?

20.6 Tutorial
Annotation Explained

Effective readers often read with a pencil (or pen) in hand. As they read, they are also writing—right on the text itself. The very process of writing while reading, called *annotation*, almost automatically increases how carefully and thoughtfully you read. Annotating while reading helps you to slow down and think about what you are reading, to decide whether you agree or not with the writer, to ask questions, and to think of examples from your own experience in addition to those in the text. It is a powerful tool for improving how well you understand a text and can be extremely helpful when you return to the text later.

Careful readers often use a highlighter to mark the sections of the text they are annotating. If you like to use a highlighter as you read, don't stop, but try to avoid two common errors: highlighting too much of the text or too little. Too much results in highlighting that is almost useless; it indicates that everything is important, so it's hard to distinguish what are the most significant points the author is making. Too little highlighting can indicate the reader found little of interest in the text, which can result from not understanding the text, or missed some of the main points. Ideally, you want to highlight just the main points, and sometimes important supporting details, so that you can easily find this information later when you are working on an essay or studying for an exam.

Some readers use different colors of highlighting to indicate different kinds of information: for example, blue for important facts, yellow for the main points in the text, and pink for words the reader doesn't know.

Some Reasons to Annotate

Annotations can be used for many different purposes, both alone and in conjunction with highlighting:

1. To mark something important
2. To comment on something you disagree with
3. To mark a reference to another text or book that you'd like to read
4. To add a thought of your own
5. To paraphrase a complicated sentence or short passage to ensure you understand it
6. To mark something you don't understand
7. To mark something you want to think about
8. To question the logic of a section of the text
9. To mark a powerful example
10. To add an example of your own to support the writer's argument
11. To add an example of your own that refutes the writer's argument
12. To summarize a section of text
13. To make a connection to another section of the text
14. To make a connection to something else you have read
15. To make a connection to something you have experienced
16. To remind yourself to follow up on something later

Activity: Explaining Annotations

Below is a text annotated by a thoughtful reader. Next to each annotation is a letter in a yellow circle. Working in your group, explain the reason for each of these annotations.

Prologue: The Woman in the Photograph

A Look this up

There's a photo on my wall of a woman I've never met, its left corner torn and patched together with tape. She looks straight into the camera and smiles, hands on hips, dress suit neatly pressed, lips painted deep red. It's the late 1940s and she hasn't yet reached the age of thirty. Her light brown skin is smooth, her eyes still young and playful, oblivious to the tumor growing inside her—a tumor that would leave her five children motherless and change the future of medicine. Beneath the photo, a caption says her name is "Henrietta Lacks, Helen Lane, or Helen Larson."

B was the original photo in color?

C is she African-American?

No one knows who took that picture, but it's appeared hundreds of times in magazines and science textbooks, on blogs and laboratory walls. She's usually identified as Helen Lane, but often she has no name at all. She's simply called HeLa, the code name given to the world's first immortal human cells—*her* cells, cut from her cervix just months before she died.

D Can cells really be immortal?

E

Her real name is Henrietta Lacks.

I've spent years staring at that photo, wondering what kind of life she led, what happened to her children, and what she'd think about cells from her cervix living on forever—bought, sold, packaged, and shipped by the trillions to laboratories around the world. I've tried to imagine how she'd feel knowing that her cells went up in the first space missions to see what would happen to human cells in zero gravity, or that they helped with some of the most important advances in medicine: the polio vaccine, chemotherapy, cloning, gene mapping, in vitro fertilization. I'm pretty sure that she—like most of us—would be shocked to hear that there are trillions more of her cells growing in laboratories now than there ever were in her body.

There's no way of knowing exactly how many of Henrietta's cells are alive today. One scientist estimates that if you could pile all HeLa cells ever grown onto a scale, they'd weigh more than 50 million metric tons—an inconceivable number, given that an individual cell weighs almost nothing. Another scientist calculated that if you could lay all HeLa cells ever grown end-to-end, they'd wrap around the Earth at least three times, spanning more than 350 million feet. In her prime, Henrietta herself stood only a bit over five feet tall.

F wonder why Henrietta is called by her first name, Defler by his last

I first learned about HeLa cells and the woman behind them in 1988, thirty-seven years after her death, when I was sixteen and sitting in a community college biology class. My instructor, Donald Defler, a gnomish balding man, paced at the front of the lecture hall and flipped on an overhead projector. He pointed to two diagrams that appeared on the wall behind him. They were schematics of the cell reproduction cycle, but to me they just looked like a neon-colored mass of arrows, squares, and circles with words I didn't understand, like "MPF Triggering a Chain Reaction of Protein Activations."

I was a kid who'd failed freshman year at the regular public high school because she never showed up. I'd transferred to an alternative school that offered dream studies instead of biology, so I was taking Defler's class for high-school credit, which meant that I was sitting in a college lecture hall at sixteen with words like *mitosis* and *kinase inhibitors* flying around. I was completely lost.

"Do we have to memorize everything on those diagrams?" one student yelled.

Yes, Defler said, we had to memorize the diagrams, and yes, they'd be on the test, but that didn't matter right then. What he wanted us to understand was that cells are amazing things: There are about one hundred trillion of them in our bodies, each so small that several thousand could fit on the period at the end of this sentence. They make up all our tissues—muscle, bone, blood—which in turn make up our organs.

Under the microscope, a cell looks a lot like a fried egg: It has a white (the *cytoplasm*) that's full of water and proteins to keep it fed, and a yolk (the *nucleus*) that holds all the genetic information that makes you *you*. The cytoplasm buzzes like a New York City street. It's crammed full of molecules and vessels endlessly shuttling enzymes and sugars from one part of the cell to another, pumping water, nutrients, and oxygen in and out of the cell. All the while, little cytoplasmic factories work 24/7, cranking out sugars, fats, proteins, and energy to keep the whole thing running and feed the nucleus—the brains of the operation. Inside every nucleus within each cell in your body, there's an identical copy of your entire genome. That genome tells cells when to grow and divide and makes sure they do their

F — wonder why Henrietta is called by her first name, Defler by his last

G — can't follow this, why was she in college

H — like the way she said this

I — [star marking]

J — cute

K — can sugar be plural?

jobs, whether that's controlling your heartbeat or helping your brain understand the words on this page.

All it takes is one small mistake anywhere in the division process for cells to start growing out of control, he told us. Just *one* enzyme misfiring, just *one* wrong protein activation, and you could have cancer. Mitosis goes haywire, which is how it spreads.

important

"We learned that by studying cancer cells in culture," Defler said. He grinned and spun to face the board, where he wrote two words in enormous print: HENRIETTA LACKS.

what is culture?

20.7 Activity

Annotating a Text

In Annotation Explained (20.6, p. 583), you read how and why effective readers annotate the texts they are reading. For this activity, your instructor will provide a text for you to annotate. Listed below are some of the most common purposes for annotations.

1. To mark something important
2. To comment on something you disagree with
3. To mark a reference to another text or book that you'd like to read
4. To add a thought of your own
5. To paraphrase a complicated sentence or short passage to ensure you understand it
6. To mark something you don't understand
7. To mark something you want to think about
8. To question the logic of a section of the text
9. To mark a powerful example
10. To add an example of your own to support the writer's argument
11. To add an example of your own that refutes the writer's argument
12. To summarize a section of text
13. To make a connection to another section of the text
14. To make a connection to something else you have read
15. To make a connection to something you have experienced
16. To remind yourself to do something later

20.8 Tutorial

Keeping a Reading Journal

If all you want from reading a text is a general sense of what it is about, then a good strategy would be to read quickly, not pausing to think or analyze what you've been reading. But at other times, you will have a different motive: you will be reading because you want to really understand what the text has to say. For this kind of reading, many people find it helpful to slow down and take notes on what they're reading, and one good approach to this kind of reading is to record your thoughts in a reading journal.

Whether you use a notebook, a composition book, or just a plain piece of paper, all you need to do to turn it into a reading journal is draw a line down the center of the page. If you want, you can label the left side something like "Ideas from Text" and the right side "My Thoughts about the Ideas." If you want to do this journaling on a computer, just open a Word document and insert a table with two columns.

A brief excerpt, "Words and Worlds," from an extremely interesting but challenging book by Harvard psychology professor Steven Pinker, *The Stuff of Thought*, appears below. This is not a book you can read quickly and get much out of. It requires slow, deliberate reading and thinking, the kind of reading assisted by keeping a reading journal, so it will be used to illustrate what a reading journal looks like. Following the excerpt, you will find one student's writing journal for this text. The numbers in the writing journal correspond to the numbered underlined passages in the text.

Words and Worlds

STEVEN PINKER

1   On September 11, 2001, at 8:46 A.M., a hijacked airliner crashed into the north tower of the World Trade Center in New York. At 9:03 A.M. a second plane crashed into the south tower. The resulting infernos caused the buildings to collapse, the south tower after burning for an hour and two minutes, the north tower twenty-three minutes after that. The attacks were masterminded by Osama bin Laden, leader of the Al Qaeda terrorist organization, who hoped to intimidate the United States into ending its military presence in Saudi Arabia and its support for Israel and to unite Muslims in preparation for a restoration of the caliphate.

2   9/11, as the happenings of that day are now called, stands as **1** the most significant political and intellectual event of the twenty-first century so far. It has set

off debates on a vast array of topics: how best to memorialize the dead and revitalize lower Manhattan; whether the attacks are rooted in ancient Islamic fundamentalism or modern revolutionary agitation; the role of the United States on the world stage before the attacks and in response to them; how best to balance protection against terrorism with respect for civil liberties.

3   But I would like to explore a lesser-known debate triggered by 9/11. Exactly how many events took place in New York on that morning in September?

4   It could be argued that the answer is one. The attacks on the building were part of a single plan conceived in the mind of one man in service of a single agenda. They unfolded within a few minutes of each other, targeting the parts of a complex with a single name, design, and owner. And they launched a single chain of military and political events in their aftermath.

5   Or it could be argued that the answer is two. The north tower and south tower were distinct collections of glass and steel separated by an expanse of space, and they were hit at different times and went out of existence at different times. The amateur video that showed the second plane closing in on the south tower as the north tower billowed with smoke makes the twoness unmistakable: in those horrifying moments, one event was frozen in the past, the other loomed in the future. And another occurrence on that day—a passenger mutiny that brought down a third hijacked plane before it reached its target in Washington—presents to the imagination the possibility that one tower or the other might have been spared. **2** <u>In each of those possible worlds</u> a distinct event took place, so in our *actual* world one might argue, there must have been a pair of events as surely as one plus one equals two.

6   The gravity of 9/11 would seem to make this entire discussion **3** <u>frivolous to the point of impudence</u>. It's a matter of mere "semantics," as we say, with its implication of picking nits, splitting hairs, and debating the number of angels that can dance on the head of a pin. But this book is about semantics, and I would not make a claim on your attention if I did not think that **4** <u>the relation of language to our inner and outer worlds was a matter of intellectual fascination and real-world importance</u>.

7   Though "importance" is often hard to quantify, in this case I can put an exact value on it: three and a half billion dollars. That was the sum in dispute in a set of trials determining the insurance payout to Larry Silverstein, the **5** <u>leaseholder</u> of the World Trade Center site. Silverstein held insurance policies that stipulated a maximum reimbursement for each destructive "event." If 9/11 comprised a single event, he stood to receive three and a half billion dollars. If it comprised two events, he stood to receive seven billion. In the trials, the attorneys disputed the applicable meaning of the term *event*. The lawyers for the leaseholder defined it in physical terms (two

▶

collapses); those for the insurance companies defined it in mental terms (one plot). There is nothing "mere" about semantics!

8   Nor is the topic intellectually trifling. The 9/11 cardinality debate is not about the facts, that is, the physical events and human actions that took place that day. Admittedly, those have been contested as well: according to various conspiracy theories, the buildings were targeted by American missiles, or demolished by a controlled implosion, in a plot conceived by American neoconservatives, Israeli spies, or a cabal of psychiatrists. But aside from the kooks, most people agree on the facts. Where they differ is in the *construal* of those facts: how **6** the intricate swirl of matter in space ought to be conceptualized by human minds. As we shall see, **7** the categories in this dispute permeate the meanings of words in our language because they permeate the way we represent reality in our heads.

9   **8** Semantics is about the relation of words to thoughts, but it is also about the relation of words to other human concerns. Semantics is about the relation of words to reality—the way that speakers commit themselves to a shared understanding of the truth, and the way their thoughts are anchored to things and situations in the world. It is about the relation of words to a community—how **9** a new word, which arises in an act of creation by a single speaker, comes to evoke the same idea in the rest of a population, so people can understand one another when they use it. It is about the relation of words to emotions: the way in which words don't just point to things but are saturated with feelings, which can endow the words with a sense of magic, taboo, and sin. And it is about words and social relations—how **10** people use language not just to transfer ideas from head to head but to negotiate the kind of relationship they wish to have with their conversational partner.

10   A feature of the mind that we will repeatedly encounter in these pages is that **11** even our most abstract concepts are understood in terms of concrete scenarios. That applies in full force to the subject matter of the book itself. In this introductory chapter I will preview some of the book's topics with vignettes from newspapers and the Internet that can be understood only through the lens of semantics. They come from each of the worlds that connect to our words—the worlds of thought, reality, community, emotions, and social relations.

11   Let's look at the bone of contention in the world's most expensive debate in semantics, the three-and-a-half-billion-dollar argument over the meaning of "event." What, exactly, is an event? **12** An event is a stretch of time, and time, according to physicists, is a continuous variable—an inexorable cosmic flow, in Newton's world, or a fourth dimension in a seamless hyperspace in Einstein's. But **13** the human mind carves this fabric into discrete swatches we call events. Where does the mind

place the incisions? Sometimes, as the lawyers for the World Trade Center leaseholder pointed out, it encircles the change of state of an object, such as the collapse of a building. And sometimes, as the lawyers for the insurers pointed out, it encircles the goal of a human actor, such as a plot being executed. Most often the circles coincide: an actor intends to cause an object to change, the intent of the act and the fate of the object are tracked along a single time line, and the moment of change marks the consummation of the intent.

*   *   *

12   The 9/11 cardinality debate highlights another curious fact about the language of thought. In puzzling over how to count the events of that day, it asks us to treat them as if they were objects that can be tallied, like poker chips in a pile. The debate over whether there was one event or two in New York that day is like a disagreement over **14** whether there is one item or two at an express checkout lane, such as a pair of butter sticks taken out of a box of four, or a pair of grapefruits selling at two for a dollar. The similar ambiguity in tallying events is one of the many ways in which space and time are treated equivalently in the human mind, well before Einstein depicted them as equivalent in reality.

13   As we shall see in Chapter 4, the mind categorizes matter into **15** discrete things (like a *sausage*) and continuous stuff (like *meat*), and it similarly categorizes time into discrete events (like *to cross the street*) and continuous activities (like *to stroll*). With both space and time, the same mental zoom lens that allows us to count objects or events also allows us to zoom in even closer on what each one is made of. In space, we can focus on the material making up an object (as when we say *I got sausage all over my shirt*); in time, we can focus on an activity making up an event (as when we say *She was crossing the street*). This cognitive zoom lens also lets us pan out in space and see a collection of objects as an aggregate (as in the difference between *a pebble* and *gravel*), and it allows us to pan out in time and see a collection of events as an iteration (as in the difference between *hit the nail* and *pound the nail*). And in time, as in space, we mentally place an entity at a location and then shunt it around: we can *move a meeting from 3:00 to 4:00* in the same way that we move a car from one end of the block to the other. And speaking of an *end*, even some of the fine points of our mental geometry carry over from space to time. **16** *The end of a string* is technically a point, but we can say *Herb cut off the end of the string*, showing that an end can be construed as including a snippet of the matter adjacent to it. The same is true in time: the *end of a lecture* is technically an instant, but we can say *I'm going to give the end of my lecture now*, construing the culmination of an event as including a small stretch of time adjacent to it.

▶

14   As we shall see, **17** language is saturated with implicit metaphors like EVENTS ARE OBJECTS and TIME IS SPACE. Indeed, space turns out to be a conceptual vehicle not just for time but for many kinds of states and circumstances. Just as a meeting can be moved from 3:00 to 4:00, a traffic light can go from green to red, a person can go from flipping burgers to running a corporation, and the economy can go from bad to worse. Metaphor is so widespread in language that it's hard to find expressions for abstract ideas that are *not* metaphorical. What does the concreteness of language say about human thought? Does it imply that even our wispiest concepts are represented in the mind as hunks of matter that we move around on a mental stage? Does it say that **18** rival claims about the world can never be true or false but can only be alternative metaphors that frame a situation in different ways? Those are the obsessions of Chapter 5.

Ideas in the Text	My Thoughts about the Ideas
1. 9/11 was the most significant event of this century so far	That "so far" seems very ominous. It implies that worse events are ahead of us.
2. in each of those possible worlds	This is hard to follow. I think he's saying that because, in our imaginations, either plane could have been prevented from striking its target, we are forced to consider, even in the actual world where both towers were struck, that there were two events.
3. frivolous to the point of impudence	I guess that's _very_ frivolous.
4. the relation of language to our inner and outer worlds was a matter of intellectual fascination and real-world importance	Hmmm. Inner and outer worlds? The world in our minds and the world we actually live in?
5. the leaseholder of the World Trade Center	Was the leaseholder just renting the towers? Odd. I would expect the person with the insurance would be the owner.
6. the intricate swirl of matter in space	I don't get this. Is he talking about some kind of nebula or something? What does this have to do with anything?

Ideas in the Text	My Thoughts about the Ideas
7. the categories in this dispute permeate the meanings of words in our language because they permeate the way we represent reality in our heads	These "categories in this dispute" I think refers to whether there was one event or two. What does he mean about the way we represent reality in our heads?
8. semantics is about the relation of words to thoughts	I think words simply stand for thoughts. The word "chair" stands for the thought we have of a thing that is a chair
9. a new word, which arises in an act of creation by a single speaker	Interesting. I wonder how a new word gets into the language spoken by millions of people?
10. people use words to negotiate the kind of relation they want to have with others	Interesting. I wish he had said more about this.
11. even our most abstract concepts are understood in terms of concrete scenarios	I wonder what he means by this.
12. an event is a stretch of time	So far, so good. I get this. Makes sense.
13. the human mind carves this fabric into discrete swatches we call events	Still okay, although I don't see why he decides to call time a fabric.
14. whether there is one item or two in an express checkout line	A great example of how hard it is to count the number of events.
15. the mind classifies things into discrete things (like a *sausage*) and continuous stuff (like *meat*)	Isn't this the same as the distinction between count and non-count nouns?
16. the end of a piece of string compared to the end of a lecture	The end is technically the end, except when it also includes stuff just before the end.
17. language is saturated with implicit metaphors like EVENTS ARE OBJECTS and TIME IS SPACE	This seems to be a major point.
18. rival claims about the world can never be true or false but can only be alternative metaphors that frame a situation in different ways	So here's the answer to the World Trade Center legal argument, but he doesn't tell who actually won in court!

Dealing with Difficult Language

Readers frequently have difficulty when they are reading and bump into a word or phrase that they don't know. The most common strategy for dealing with an unfamiliar word is "to look it up in a dictionary." Now this is not a bad strategy; in fact, sometimes it is very good advice, but "looking it up in a dictionary" is only one of a number of available strategies.

In fact, in many situations it is not the best strategy. When you interrupt your reading to consult a dictionary, it's easy to lose track of the meaning of the text you've been reading. If you encounter a number of unfamiliar words that you look up, you can end up having read an entire passage with little idea of what it meant. To avoid these interruptions to the flow of your reading, you can first use one or more of the following strategies when you encounter unfamiliar words or phrases.

- Derive the meaning from context.
- Analyze the parts of the word.
- Back up and reread the passage.
- Keep reading to see if the writer explains the difficult passage.
- Decide the word is not important and just keep reading.

If all else fails, or if knowing a precise definition of a word is crucial to understanding a text, use a dictionary.

Use Context Clues

Suppose you came across the following sentence in something you were reading:

> She grabbed her portmanteau, which she had packed the night before, and left for the train station.

Chances are, you are not familiar with the word *portmanteau*, but, from the rest of the sentence, it would not be hard to guess that it must be some kind of a suitcase. It is often possible to work out the meaning of a word by carefully reading not only the sentence in which it appears but those that immediately precede or follow it. Basically, you infer from the information provided what a word or term means.

There are several other strategies like this that you can use to figure out the meaning of a word from its context. Authors often include words with similar or opposite meanings close to more challenging words to provide clues to their meanings; textbook authors place important terms in bold or italics and follow them with definitions; and writers often use punctuation to indicate they are about to provide a definition or explanation of a term, introducing it with a colon, setting it off with commas or dashes, or placing it in parentheses.

By the way, figuring out the meaning of a word from its context often gives you only a general sense of the word. For instance, using the example above, a *portmanteau* is actually a large suitcase, usually made of leather, and opening into two halves of equal size. You would never figure out all that detail from the context, but in most cases recognizing that it was a type of suitcase would be all you needed to understand what you were reading.

Use Word Parts

Another strategy that can be useful in figuring out what an unfamiliar word means without "looking it up" is to break it into its parts. Consider the following sentence:

> Karina's essay was filled with polysyllabic words.

If you are unfamiliar with the word *polysyllabic*, you may be able to figure out its meaning by breaking it into parts. You've probably encountered the prefix *poly-* in other words. Do you remember what a polygon is? It's a two-dimensional figure with many sides. How about polygamy? It means being married to multiple partners. By now, it seems clear that *poly-* means *many*, and as the second half of the word is fairly close to *syllable*, a polysyllabic word is apparently a word with many syllables.

Being familiar with word parts, the building blocks of words, can be useful, especially if you are studying in the sciences. Words can contain one or more of the following parts: roots, prefixes, and suffixes. Roots are the core of words and carry their basic meaning. Prefixes are added to the beginning of root words to change their meaning; for example, adding the prefix *un-* to the word *happy* creates *unhappy*, which means the opposite of the original word. Suffixes are placed at the ends of root words and can change their part of speech; for example, adding *-less* to the root word *clue* changes the word from a noun to an adjective, *clueless*. Suffixes can also change the root word's tense; for example, adding *-ed* to the root word *raid* changes it from the present to the past tense, *raided*.

No one expects you to memorize word parts, but if you do a quick search of the internet you will find all sorts of charts listing roots, prefixes, and suffixes with their meanings, which you can download or print out for easy reference. Many scientific terms are built from word parts, and familiarizing yourself with the most common ones, such as *bio-*, *geo-*, *mono-*, or *-itis*, can help you to make sense of terms as you read.

Reread the Passage

Another strategy when you encounter a word or phrase that you don't understand is to back up and reread the passage. Sometimes the meaning will become clearer on a second reading.

Keep Reading

A different strategy is to keep reading. Often writers, realizing they have used a term some readers may not know, will explain the term in the next sentence or even later in the same sentence.

Decide the Word Is Not Important

Sometimes it is perfectly acceptable to decide that a word is not going to be important, at least in the text you're reading, and you can move on without worrying about what it means. Suppose you were reading a mystery novel and came across this sentence:

> The murdered woman was wearing a cerise sweater.

Does it matter what color *cerise* is? Probably not. You will likely be able to follow the action of the novel just fine even though you're not sure of the color of the woman's sweater. But what if, later in the novel, you find out that a suspect had tiny fragments of cerise-colored thread under his fingernails? Now does it matter what color *cerise* is? Actually, it does not. It is important to remember that the victim's sweater was cerise, but it doesn't really matter what color that is. (By the way, *cerise* is a bright or dark red. It comes from the French word for *cherry*.)

Use a Dictionary

Some readers are interested in expanding their vocabulary when they read. If you fit into this group, it is probably still better not to interrupt your reading to look up words unless knowing the meaning of a particular word is crucial to understanding the text. Instead, underline or circle each word whose meaning you guess at from the context. After you've finished reading the text, you can go back, look up all the words you marked, and write their definitions either in the margin beside them or in a log you keep of new words. (Note that online dictionaries are quick and easy to use and provide lots of useful information, including the option to hear how a word is pronounced. It's worth bookmarking a site, such as dictionary.com or merriam-webster.com, for easy reference.)

Decoding Difficult Language

Here is a list of six strategies that you can use when you encounter words you are not familiar with. These strategies are discussed in detail in Dealing with Difficult Language (20.9, p. 594).

1. Derive the meaning from context.
2. Analyze the parts of the word.
3. Back up and reread the passage.
4. Keep reading to see if the writer explains the difficult passage.
5. Decide the word is not important and just keep reading.
6. Look the word up in a dictionary or on your phone.

Your instructor will assign a reading that includes some challenging words. Working in your group, identify the words you have difficulty with. Make a list with three columns as shown in the following example. Then use one or more of the six strategies to figure out the meaning of each word. Save using a dictionary as a last resort.

Challenging Words	Meaning of Words	Strategy or Strategies Used
multifarious	having many parts	word parts
laminated	made of thin layers bonded together	dictionary
restitution	giving back something that had been wrongfully taken away	general context

20.11 Tutorial

Believing and Doubting

The believing and doubting game is an approach to engagement with a text that was developed by Peter Elbow at the University of Massachusetts. It's a wonderful way for getting us, as readers, to engage more deeply with a text.

At its heart, the believing and doubting game simply asks you to read a text two different ways. It asks you to read it once as a "believer," someone who agrees with the author and is reading because you want to understand exactly what the author's point is and why the author came to that conclusion. Then it asks you to read the text a second time from the point of view of a skeptic, someone who doubts that the central argument of the text is correct. This time you are reading to find flaws in the argument, weaknesses in the logic, and reasons to refute the conclusions. Many readers find this approach leads them into a deeper understanding of the text.

One way to use this approach is to write two short—less than a page—summaries of a text. In the first, you write as a believer, someone who agrees with the author, and you focus on the points you agree with. In the second, you write as a doubter, someone who is trying to explain why you disagree with the argument.

20.12 Activity

Reading as a Believer and Doubter

In Believing and Doubting (20.11, p. 597), you read about a strategy that helps you to think deeply about a text as you read it. Now you will try out this approach to engaging with a text using an article supplied by your instructor.

Read the article once as a believer, someone who is in agreement with the author. Don't allow any doubts or disagreements to creep in while you read as a believer. Then write a "believer's summary" in which you summarize the article briefly, emphasizing the points you agree with. Try to limit this summary to a half page.

When you've finished that, read the article again, this time as a doubter, someone who disagrees with the author. Then write a second brief summary in which you focus on the points you disagree with. Again, a half page is plenty.

20.13 Tutorial

Creating Timelines and Family Trees

When reading longer and more complicated works, it is sometimes helpful to keep track of what you're reading and thinking by using creating graphic organizers, such as timelines and family trees.

Timelines

If you're reading a narrative text, one that is telling a story or describing how events happened over time, it may be helpful to create a timeline. Here's an example of what such a timeline might look like.

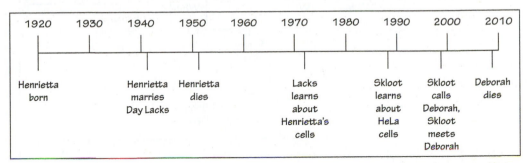

1920   1930   1940   1950   1960   1970   1980   1990   2000   2010

Henrietta
born

Henrietta
marries
Day Lacks

Henrietta
dies

Lacks
learns
about
Henrietta's
cells

Skloot
learns
about
HeLa
cells

Skloot
calls
Deborah,
Skloot
meets
Deborah

Deborah
dies

The student who constructed it was reading *The Immortal Life of Henrietta Lacks*. Early in the book, she learned that the main character, Henrietta Lacks, was born in 1920. Realizing that this book was going to cover events that took place over a number of years, she decided to construct a timeline in which she could post the major events in the story. She marked Henrietta's birth in 1920 at the left end of the timeline and 2010, the date the book was published, at the right end. Then she made a vertical mark for every ten years. As she read the book, she marked major events on the timeline.

The student did all this on a piece of plain paper, although she might have created a similar graphic using a computer. A timeline like this is especially helpful when you are reading a text that doesn't present information in chronological order but skips backward and forward in time, as *The Immortal Life of Henrietta Lacks* does.

Family Trees

If you are reading a text—especially a full-length book—with lots of characters, creating a family tree can help you keep their names straight and see the relationships between the different family members. *The Immortal Life of Henrietta Lacks* includes seven generations of one very large family, so making a family tree seemed to be a good strategy to another student. Here is his tree.

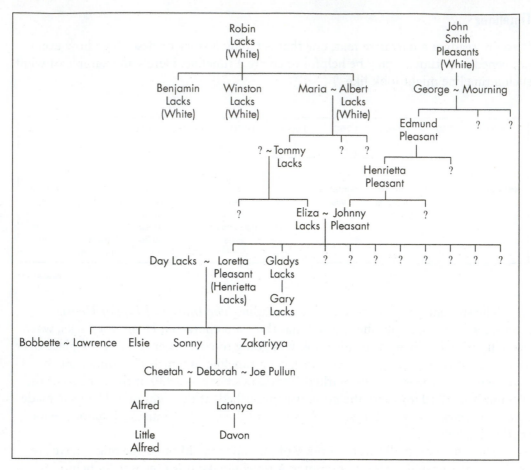

Peter Adams

These family trees can be very messy. Sometimes you discover that you haven't left yourself enough room for all the branches of a family, so you have to start over on a blank sheet. Often, there are several families who interact with each other, so you have to find a way to match up the generations and who married whom. Despite their potential messiness, though, in a book with lots of characters, family trees can be extremely helpful in keeping track of everyone.

TOPIC 21
Critical Reading

Being a critical reader means reading thoughtfully—evaluating the assertions in a text, the support for those assertions, the assumptions underlying them, and the expertise and reliability of the author.

Navigating Topic 21

The tutorials for critical reading are listed below, and each is followed by an opportunity to apply the skills you have just learned. You can work through the entire Topic on your own, learning about all the strategies and practicing them; work on items you've been assigned by your instructor; or choose those ones you would find helpful.

Introduction to Critical Reading

In this Topic, you will learn ways to evaluate the author and source of a text, distinguish between facts and opinions, make inferences, and recognize assumptions and biases, all important critical reading skills.

21.1 Tutorial

How to Evaluate the Author and Source of a Text

As you preview, read, and think about what you have read, two crucial factors to keep in mind are the author and the source. Evaluating them is something you usually do when previewing a text (see 20.2, p. 575), but as you dive into reading and as you pause at various points to think about what you have read, you should keep in mind what you have learned about the author and the source of the text.

Evaluating the Author

For most texts you read, the author's name will appear at the top of the text or, sometimes, at the end. Occasionally, there will be a brief biography. But sometimes there will be no biographical information. In these cases, or even if there is a biography, it is a good idea to take a few more minutes to search for the author on Google or another search engine and see what you can learn about him or her.

To evaluate authors, look for evidence of their expertise:

- Do they have a credential or degree that indicates they are qualified to discuss the topic?

- Have they published other relevant works?

- Have they won any awards?

- Does their job give them access to relevant knowledge?

- Do other authors you have been reading refer to them?

If the source reveals little or no information about the author, this may be an indication that he or she is not really an expert.

Evaluating the Source

If the text you're about to read is a chapter or an article in a book, take a look at who edited or published the book. If the article is in a journal or magazine, look into who publishes the journal or magazine and what other articles appear in it. If the text is on a website, see what you can learn about who owns the website. All this information about the source of the text will help you better understand and evaluate it. As you evaluate sources, ask these questions:

- Has the publisher, print or digital, published or posted material by other authors whom you recognize as having expertise in the subject? If yes, it increases the source's credibility.

- Is the source sponsored by a reputable organization—a university, a major foundation, or a government agency? If so, that adds to its credibility and that of the writers it publishes.

- Does the source provide references or documentation to support the legitimacy of the content it is providing? If it does not, be wary.

- Does the source appear to publish material that seems biased? If yes, that doesn't mean you should ignore it, but do be aware of the bias if you use the material.

- Is the content in the source current? For many subjects, especially those relating to science, technology, medicine, and other rapidly changing fields, information becomes outdated quickly, so you want to make sure the source is providing the most current data.

- Is the source well-written and the content presented in a logical, well-organized fashion? This question relates more often to online sources. Anyone can post information on the internet. Legitimate, professional sources take time to edit their content, check the credentials of the writers whose work they host or present, and provide a well-organized homepage. If the content is inaccurate or poorly written, if links are broken, if navigation is difficult, and if you cannot find out information about the publisher, look for more reliable alternatives. If it is not possible to learn much about the publisher of a text or owner of a website, that may be an indication that the source is not reliable.

21.2 Activity

Evaluating the Author and Source of a Text

For a college essay on the controversy over vaccinations for children, working in your group, search for each of the articles listed below (typing their titles into your browser), and evaluate the author and source for each of them. Be prepared to report out on what you learned about both the author and the source for each one. (If you cannot find a site using its title, there is an updated list of URLs available at https://bit.ly/33IIHtf.)

1. "Vaccines: The Myths and the Facts," no author given
2. "Childhood Vaccines: Tough Questions, Straight Answers," Mayo Clinic Staff
3. "MMR Vaccination and Autism," Andrew J. Wakefield

21.3 Tutorial

Distinguishing among Facts, Statements Most Experts Agree On, and Opinions

The activity Evidence and Assertions (11.2, p. 357) illustrates the relationship between facts (evidence) and opinions (assertions) from the point of view of the *writer*. It is also important that *readers* recognize this relationship and are able to distinguish between facts and opinions. It's even more important for readers to recognize that many ideas that are expressed as if they are facts are merely opinions masquerading as facts.

What Are Facts?

Exactly what is a fact? How can you recognize what is factual in what you read? It has often been said that facts are not arguable. Facts are statements that have been proven to be true. Facts are what the experts agree is true. Some factual statements satisfy these definitions without any difficulty. The capital of California is Sacramento. Mt. Everest is the highest mountain in the world. English 101 is a required course at most colleges.

But sometimes statements that appear to be facts need to be carefully stated. For example, "Water boils at 212°" would seem to be a fact, but those who live at high elevations like Denver know that water boils at a lower temperature at higher elevations. The *fact* is "Water boils at 212° at sea level." The statement that "Native Americans' primary food source was the bison" needs to be examined carefully. It turns out to be true for Native Americans in the Plains states but not true in many other parts of what came to be the United States.

It's also the case that what were considered to be facts can change. As recently as the early 2000s, it was a fact that there were nine planets in our solar system. However, in 2006, the International Astronomical Union decided that Pluto is not a planet; it is too small. Today, the fact is that there are eight planets in our solar system. For years, scientists have agreed that the earliest members of the human genus to use stone tools were *Homo habilis*, who evolved around 2.8 million years ago.

But in 2015, stone tools and fossils of early humans were discovered in Kenya that are 3.3 million years old. So the facts about when humans began using tools have also changed.

As a reader, you should carefully examine and think deeply about statements that authors clearly intend that you will accept as facts. Make sure the "fact" is worded carefully so that it is true and that it is currently considered a fact, that experts haven't learned new information that modified what used to be factual.

How Do We Decide Whether the Experts Agree?

On the one hand, there are issues, such as whether boys should be allowed to play football because of the risks of concussion and whether tax cuts for the wealthy will "trickle down" and benefit everyone, about which experts disagree. Statements where there is significant disagreement among experts cannot be considered to be facts. On the other hand, it is unreasonable to insist that something is not a fact unless there is 100 percent agreement about it by every expert in the world; statements about which the vast majority of experts agree can safely be understood to be facts.

Where should we draw the line? How great must the agreement be in order for something to actually be considered a fact? Perhaps the answer to these questions is that, as a reader, you could accept opinions on which a great many experts agree as evidence, just not quite as strong as actual facts. You may also find it useful to investigate the experts who don't agree. Are they legitimate experts? What reasons do they give for their disagreement? Do you find their reasons to make sense?

A word of caution, however: Do not confuse the generally agreed on opinions of a large number of experts with the many statements cluttering the current public discourse that are not agreed to by most experts. Fake news, exaggeration, hyperbole, and even outright lies are not the same as the well-reasoned, evidence-based opinions of experts in a particular field.

How Should Readers Respond to Conclusions, Claims, and Opinions?

It is a *fact* that college tuition has gone up faster than inflation for years, and it is a *fact* that the cost of textbooks has increased dramatically. Further, it is a *fact* that other fees at colleges have gone up at a steep rate. But it is *not* a fact that college is too expensive. That last statement is an *opinion*. It is based on facts, but it is an assertion that someone might make after thinking about the facts, which doesn't make it a fact. Someone else might look at the same set of facts and reach a different conclusion. Still others might know of a different set of facts that could be used to argue that college is not too expensive.

There is, of course, nothing wrong with writers making assertions of their opinions, but as a critical reader, you need to make sure that such assertions are actually supported by convincing evidence. When reading a text that makes an assertion followed by factual evidence or a text that presents a series of facts and then makes an assertion based on those facts, it's a good idea to stop and think about the conclusions the authors have reached. Do they seem reasonable? Could the same facts lead to a different conclusion? Are enough facts presented to justify the conclusion? These kinds of analysis can lead to a more insightful reading of the text, and being able to distinguish between facts and opinions is essential to this kind of analysis.

Finally, some alternative vocabulary. You've been reading about the differences between facts and opinions. What about *conclusions, assertions,* and *claims*? These terms are usually used to mean the same thing as *opinions*. In any case, as a reader, if you encounter statements that you would consider fitting any of these categories, you should carefully examine the evidence provided to support them.

21.4 Activity

Recognizing Facts, Statements Most Experts Agree On, and Opinions

Distinguishing among Facts, Statements Most Experts Agree On, and Opinions (21.3, p. 604) discussed the difference among (1) facts, (2) statements about which almost all experts agree, and (3) opinions (sometimes called *conclusions, claims,* or *assertions*). It is important for readers to be able to distinguish among these three types of statements because opinions without factual evidence to support them should be given little credence.

Working with your group, decide whether the following statements are facts, statements about which almost all experts agree, or opinions.

1. The cost of health care is increasing too much.
2. The cost of health care has risen every year for the past forty years.
3. More Democrats support gun safety laws than Republicans.
4. More lives are lost to speeding drivers every year than to drunk drivers.
5. Every parent should have their children vaccinated against childhood diseases.
6. Immigration takes jobs away from American workers.
7. A lower percentage of immigrants are arrested for criminal behavior than the percentage of American citizens.

8. Completing a college degree improves the chances of economic success in America.

9. Medical costs are too high in America.

10. Women in government are less likely to support going to war than men.

21.5 Activity

Evaluating Evidence

Distinguishing among Facts, Statements Most Experts Agree On, and Opinions (21.3, p. 604) discussed the difference between facts, statements most experts agree on, and opinions. Here, you're going to think about evaluating the facts or evidence a writer provides to support his or her opinions.

Imagine that your college needs to know, on average, how many students eat in the cafeteria each week. This information will be used for budgeting purposes. Below are reports written by three different student employees who were assigned this task. Working in your group, read each of the three reports, evaluate the evidence that supports the assertion made in each one, and decide which report is most convincing.

Report 1

At this college, on average, 1,578 students eat in the cafeteria each week. To arrive at this number, I sat in the cafeteria each day for a week and counted the number of students in the cafeteria. Below are my totals for the week. The cafeteria is closed on weekends.

Monday: 310

Tuesday: 330

Wednesday: 301

Thursday: 349

Friday: 288

Report 2

At this college, on average, 1,316 students eat in the cafeteria each week when classes are in session. To arrive at this number, I sat in the cafeteria each day for a week in September, December, January, and March and counted the number of students in the cafeteria. Below is my data for each month.

September		December		January		March	
Mon.	310	Mon.	285	Mon.	192	Mon.	301
Tue.	330	Tue.	301	Tue.	186	Tue.	244
Wed.	301	Wed.	280	Wed.	228	Wed.	289
Thu.	349	Thu.	338	Thu.	199	Thu.	260
Fri.	88	Fri.	275	Fri.	165	Fri.	143
Totals	1,578		1,479		970		1,237

I arrived at the figure of 1,316 students each week by averaging the four weekly totals I had observed.

Report 3

At this college, an average of 845 students eat in the cafeteria each week when classes are in session. At first, I thought I would sit in the cafeteria for a week at several different times during the academic year and count the number of students in the cafeteria. Then I realized two things: first, to do this would be extremely time-consuming and boring, and, second, it would be inaccurate. Not all students in the cafeteria are eating; many are there simply to do homework while waiting for their next class.

Faced with this realization, I asked the cafeteria manager if the cash registers recorded the number of students who paid for food each week. When she said, "Yes," I asked if she could give me a copy of those weekly totals for a year. She said, "Sure." All I had to do was average the weekly totals she gave me to arrive at an accurate average number of students who ate in the cafeteria each week when classes were in session.

Below are the totals produced by the cash registers for one complete year:

January	Week 1	764	March	Week 1	928
	Week 2	770		Week 2	919
	Week 3	759		Week 3	908
	Week 4	803		Week 4	Spring break
February	Week 1	965	April	Week 1	889
	Week 2	971		Week 2	891
	Week 3	954		Week 3	868
	Week 4	949		Week 4	860

May	Week 1	869
	Week 2	858
	Week 3	840
	Week 4	No classes
June	Week 1	No classes
	Week 2	619
	Week 3	625
	Week 4	625
July	Week 1	618
	Week 2	611
	Week 3	No classes
	Week 4	623
August	Week 1	629
	Week 2	622
	Week 3	618
	Week 4	609
September	Week 1	980

	Week 2	985
	Week 3	976
	Week 4	969
October	Week 1	962
	Week 2	965
	Week 3	957
	Week 4	956
November	Week 1	950
	Week 2	954
	Week 3	948
	Week 4	946
December	Week 1	943
	Week 2	941
	Week 3	931
	Week 4	No classes
	Total	36,327

Average weekly total: 36,327 ÷ 34 = 845

21.6 Tutorial

How to Make Inferences

We all make inferences every day. We look out the window and infer from the gray sky and looming clouds that it's going to rain. We encounter backed up traffic on a usually quiet road and think about possible causes: an accident, roadwork, or maybe dangerous driving conditions if there is snow or freezing rain. To make these inferences, we use clues in what we see or hear and draw conclusions about them based on our knowledge and previous experiences.

Writers do not always directly state their point. Sometimes they rely on the reader to piece together their message from the information they provide. To make an inference when you read a text, you have to think about what you already know about the subject, notice the details and language the writer uses, add up the facts he or she provides, and combine all these to come up with an idea of what the text means.

Guidelines for Making Inferences

- Carefully read the text and make sure you understand the main ideas and details the writer presents.

- Consider the author's purpose for writing. Who might be his or her audience?

- Look for details that provide clues to what the author is saying, especially any that seem unusual.

- Look at everything the author has said and think about what point these facts and details, taken together, seem to be making. Why were these specific details included and not others?

- Evaluate the author's choice of language. What is the overall tone of the text? What does this suggest to you?

- Think about what you already know about the subject. Does what the writer says fit with the information you already have? Have you had experiences that would help you understand his or her point?

- Finally, once you have made your inference, reread to check that it fits all the evidence in the text. Consider whether other conclusions could be made based on the evidence. Is there additional evidence in the text or from other sources that would confirm your hypothesis or cause you to revise it?

Making an Inference

Let's look at an example, a text written by a young college professor about a class he is teaching:

> Before I could even get to my classroom, I had to pass through a metal detector and wait as a heavy metal gate slammed shut behind me and another one opened in front of me. When I arrived in my classroom, right away I saw that only about a dozen of my twenty students were there. I asked where everyone else was, and one young man replied, "Eight of us are on 'lock down.'"

To make an inference about this passage, you first have to read it carefully. Then you should notice details like the *metal detector*, the *heavy metal gates*, and the fact that eight students are on "*lock down*." When you add up these details, you realize he's in a prison. But he's a professor, so what's he doing in prison? Ah, he's teaching a class to inmates. You've made an inference. The text didn't exactly say the professor is teaching in a prison, but by noticing the details, connecting them to what you already know, and thinking about them, you inferred that he must be teaching a class in a prison.

So that's what's meant by making an inference—reading a text, noticing the details, and, using your own knowledge, coming up with meaning that wasn't directly expressed in words but nevertheless can be inferred.

21.7 Activity

Making Inferences

Working in your group, see what inferences you can make from reading each of the two passages below.

Passage 1: Excerpt from *Better: A Surgeon's Notes on Performance*

This passage comes from Dr. Atul Gawande's book about what is involved in providing good patient care.

> In 1847, at the age of twenty-eight, the Viennese obstetrician Ignac Semmelweis famously deduced that, by not washing their hands consistently or well enough, doctors were themselves to blame for childbed fever. Childbed fever, also known as puerperal fever, was the leading cause of maternal death in childbirth in the era before antibiotics (and before the recognition that germs are the agents of infectious disease). It is a bacterial infection most commonly caused by *Streptococcus,* the same bacteria that causes strep throat—that ascends through the vagina to the uterus after childbirth. Out of three thousand mothers who delivered babies at the hospital where Semmelweis worked, six hundred or more died of the disease each year—a horrifying 20 percent maternal death rate. Of mothers delivering at home, only 1 percent died. Semmelweis concluded that doctors themselves were carrying the disease between patients, and he mandated that every doctor and nurse on his ward scrub with a nail brush and chlorine between patients. The puerperal death rate immediately fell to 1 percent—incontrovertible proof, it would seem, that he was right. Yet elsewhere, doctors' practices did not change. Some colleagues were even offended by his claims; it was impossible to them that doctors could be killing their patients. Far from being hailed, Semmelweis was ultimately dismissed from his job.

Passage 2: Excerpt from *Outliers: The Story of Success*

This passage is an excerpt from Malcolm Gladwell's book, which explores some of the complex factors that contribute to the success of people like Bill Joy, who created

UNIX and Java computer languages; Bill Gates, founder of Microsoft; and John Lennon of *The Beatles*.

Exhibit A in the talent argument is a study done in the early 1990s by the psychologist K. Anders Ericsson and two colleagues at Berlin's elite Academy of Music. With the help of the Academy's professors, they divided the school's violinists into three groups. In the first group were the stars, the students with the potential to become world-class soloists. In the second were those judged to be merely "good." In the third were students who were unlikely to ever play professionally and who intended to be music teachers in the public school system. All of the violinists were then asked the same question: over the course of your entire career, ever since you first picked up the violin, how many hours have you practiced?

Everyone from all three groups started playing at roughly the same age, around five years old. In those first few years, everyone practiced roughly the same amount, about two or three hours a week. But when the students were around the age of eight, real differences started to emerge. The students who would end up the best in their class began to practice more than everyone else: six hours a week by age nine, eight hours a week by age twelve, sixteen hours a week by age fourteen, and up and up, until by the age of twenty they were practicing—that is, purposefully and single-mindedly playing their instruments with the intent to get better—well over thirty hours a week. In fact, by the age of twenty, the elite performers had each totaled ten thousand hours of practice. By contrast, the merely good students had totaled eight thousand hours, and the future music teachers had totaled just over four thousand hours.

21.8 Tutorial

Recognizing Assumptions and Biases

As discussed in How to Make Inferences (21.6, p. 609), it is important to look beyond the words in the texts you read for a deeper level of meaning. Careful reading can help you to accurately infer from clues in a text the unstated assumptions and biases of the author. Recognizing the assumptions and biases authors bring to what they write, as well as the ones you bring to the text as you read what they say, will help you to better understand, evaluate, and comment on the written material you encounter in college.

Assumptions

All of us make assumptions. In most parts of America, if you want to ask someone where the nearest gas station is, you don't start by asking, "Do you speak English?" Even though there are many people in America, even many American citizens, who don't speak English, when we approach someone on the street to ask directions, we *assume* they speak English.

When we walk into a store to buy a hot dog and a Coke, most of us *assume* that we can pay with a credit card. When we sign up for a course in a college, we *assume* that the course will be taught by someone with some expertise in the subject. When our doctor prescribes a medicine for us to take, we *assume* that the medicine is safe and may alleviate the problem we are taking it for. We assume all the time. There's nothing wrong with making assumptions; in fact, they make modern life possible.

However, when you are reading, it is often a good idea to take a few minutes to ask yourself what assumptions lie behind the text, not because there is something inherently "wrong" with assumptions, but because you need to decide whether you agree that the assumptions the author of the text is making are reasonable, whether or not you share them. For example, maybe you are reading an article by an author who believes in mandatory sentencing for drug offenders and bases his argument for increased government funding to build more prisons on it. If you believe that drug treatment programs are a more effective response to substance-related crimes, you might not accept this writer's assertions because you do not agree with his basic assumption. However, before dismissing his ideas, you should look for the evidence he uses to support his argument and compare it with the evidence you are basing your ideas on.

Understanding the assumptions underlying an argument and deciding whether you share these assumptions will help you decide whether you agree with the conclusions reached by the writer.

Recognizing Your Own Assumptions

In addition, it is important to be aware of one's own assumptions. We all have ways of thinking about the world that we learn from our families, communities, or religious and political institutions. These ways of thinking can be so familiar that we don't even recognize that we have them. We don't question them. But in order to fully evaluate the assumptions of an author, a reader must also be aware of and evaluate his or her own assumptions about the topic being discussed. Maybe you disagree with a writer because he or she is not supporting what you believe to be true. Are you sure your assumptions are correct? What evidence do you have to support them? Once you become more aware of the assumptions that underpin your thinking, you will be better able to recognize and evaluate those of the people you read.

Biases

Sometimes it is suggested that we should not read or rely on writers who are biased. We should look for writers who are even-handed and present both sides of an argument equally. In reality, the situation is more complicated than that. First, almost everyone is biased. It's next to impossible to find a writer who isn't. The fact that a writer is producing a piece of writing with a thesis means he or she has a bias in favor of that thesis. Second, we as readers often are not aware of an author's bias unless we make it a priority to be aware of it. We should read any given piece of writing "with a grain of salt," questioning the writer's assertions and evaluating skeptically the evidence presented.

Here are three ways to identify a writer's bias:

1. Investigate the author's biographical information, either located with the article or available on the internet. If the author works for an organization with a known bias or writes regularly for publications with a known bias, that can be a good indication of his or her bias.

2. Look for evidence of bias in the text itself. Does the writer use "loaded language"? For example, does the writer label those who disagree with his or her position as "immature," "stupid," or "narrow-minded"? Does the writer use demeaning adjectives to describe those with alternative viewpoints, adjectives like "so-called," "self-proclaimed," or "ill-informed"? Or does the writer use "loaded" verbs, such as "spewed," "would have you believe," and "whined"?

3. Ask yourself if the writer demonstrates an awareness that there are reasonable arguments on other sides of the issue. If not, this can indicate bias and a point of view that does not encompass all the relevant information on the subject.

Evaluating Your Own Biases

Just as with assumptions, it is important to be aware of your own biases in order to identify and evaluate the biases of writers. For instance, are you prejudiced in favor of or against particular groups of people, politicians, institutions, books, movies, and so on? Would your particular biases make it hard for you to entertain opposing views? Can you put your point of view aside so that you can fairly assess a different perspective, weighing the evidence provided to see if the alternative argument has merit?

21.9 Activity

Recognizing Assumptions and Biases in Three Passages

Working in your group, analyze any assumptions or biases in the following passages. Be prepared to report your group's analysis after about a half hour.

1. **Gun Control. Now.**

Sutherland Springs, Texas. Las Vegas. Orlando. Sandy Hook. Columbine. Red Lake, Minnesota. Essex, Vermont. Lancaster. Aurora. Virginia Tech. How many more innocent victims must die at the hands of an antiquated and oft-misinterpreted amendment? Enough.

It's time to stop the violence.

Gun control doesn't have to mean no guns. I'm not suggesting we take guns away. I'm suggesting we put tighter controls on acquiring and owning them.

Gun show loopholes must be stopped. Ammunition should not be sold online. Mandatory wait periods should be enforced, during which time a thorough background check, psychological and medical evaluation, and character references should be completed.

From the MoveOn.org website
https://petitions.moveon.org/sign/gun-control-now-1

2. **Medicare for All**

The U.S. spends more on health care per person, and as a percentage of gross domestic product, than any other advanced nation in the world, including Australia, Canada, Denmark, France, Germany, Japan, New Zealand and the United Kingdom. But all that money has not made Americans healthier than the rest of the world. Quite simply, in our high-priced health care system that leaves millions overlooked, we spend more yet end up with less.

Other industrialized nations are making the morally principled and financially responsible decision to provide universal health care to all of their people—and they do so while saving money by keeping people healthier. Those who say this goal is unachievable are selling the American people short.

Americans need a health care system that works for patients and providers. We need to ensure a strong health care workforce in all communities now and in the future. We need a system where all people can get the care they need to maintain and improve their health when they need it regardless of income, age or socioeconomic status. We need a system that works not just for millionaires and billionaires, but for all of us.

From the Bernie Sanders website
https://berniesanders.com/issues/medicare-for-all/

3. **Stop Animal Abuse**

Every day in countries around the world, animals are fighting for their lives. They are enslaved, beaten, and kept in chains to make them perform for humans' "entertainment"; they are mutilated and confined to tiny cages so that we can kill them and eat them; they are burned, blinded, poisoned, and cut up alive in the name of "science"; they are electrocuted, strangled, and skinned alive so that people can parade around in their coats; and worse.

The abuse that animals suffer at human hands is heartbreaking, sickening, and infuriating. It's even more so when we realize that the everyday choices we make—such as what we eat for lunch and the kind of shampoo we buy—may be directly supporting some of this abuse. But as hard as it is to think about, we can't stop animals' suffering if we simply look the other way and pretend it isn't happening.

Animals are counting on compassionate people like you to give them a voice and be their heroes by learning about the issues they face and taking action. Each of us has the power to save animals from nightmarish suffering—and best of all, it's easier than you might think. If you're ready to join the millions of other compassionate people who are working to create a kinder, better world for animals, please read on to learn how animals suffer in the food, animal experimentation, entertainment, clothing and pet-trade industries. Together, we can make a difference.

From the PETA website
https://www.peta.org/issues/

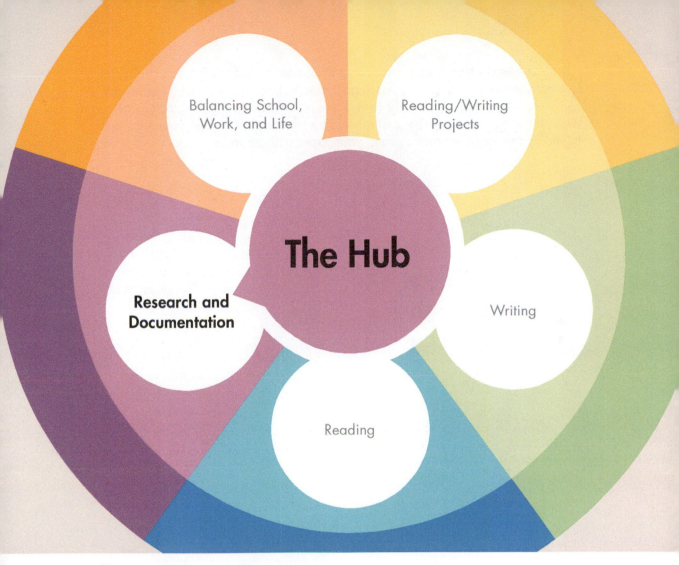

The Hub

Balancing School, Work, and Life

Reading/Writing Projects

Research and Documentation

Writing

Reading

4 Research and Documentation

Locating sources is important to college assignments that ask for a documented paper, usually a longer essay based on research. But often shorter assignments of just a few pages will also benefit from some research. Part 4 is designed to help you with all the writing tasks that call for finding sources that discuss your topic and including information from them in your paper with appropriate documentation.

TOPIC 22
Research

Topic 22 provides information, advice, and suggestions about how to go about doing the kinds of research that are required in many college courses.

Navigating Topic 22

The tutorials listed below provide information about useful research strategies, and each contains, or is followed by, an opportunity to apply the skills you have just learned. You can work through the entire Topic on your own, learning about all the strategies and practicing them; work on items you've been assigned by your instructor; or choose those ones you would find helpful.

Introduction to Research

Topic 22 begins with information on the research process and continues by providing instruction and strategies on how to find and evaluate sources online and in the library, take notes, quote and paraphrase, conduct interviews and surveys, avoid plagiarism, and synthesize sources.

22.1 Writing

Thinking about the Research Process

Think about the last time you had to write a paper that included doing research, or, if you've never been asked to write such a paper, try to imagine yourself writing one. For this assignment, make a list of the steps you took or that you might take if you had to write a paper that included at least some research.

22.2 Tutorial

The Research Process

Below is a list of all the steps that *might* be involved in writing a paper involving research. Of course, not all of these will be involved in every project, but steps 1, 3, 10, 14, 16, 18, 19, 20, and 21 are essential to any research project you work on (and have been underlined in the following checklist), so make sure you complete them. Exactly which steps are necessary in a specific project will depend on many factors: how much time you have, what kind of paper you are asked to write, how much research is expected for the paper, what the assignment is, and more.

Checklist for Steps in the Research Process

Keep in mind that this is a very complete list, and you would use only those steps appropriate for your specific assignment. All of them are useful, though, in different situations, so read through them carefully.

Getting Started

☐ 1. Read and analyze the assignment (see Terms for Writing Assignments [28.2, p. 750] for more details).

☐ 2. Analyze the rhetorical situation (see The Rhetorical Situation [9.3, p. 327]).

☐ 3. <u>Think about how much time you have for the project and set deadlines for each step.</u>

☐ 4. Focus on a topic you are interested in and want to write about. Sometimes it is more appropriate to start with a question about the topic, which will help you focus your research. For example, if the topic is to explore a cause or causes of the Civil War, you might ask, "What was the role of states' rights in the American Civil War?" "How did westward expansion impact the debate on slavery?" "Why did the election of Abraham Lincoln antagonize the southern states?" These questions are sometimes called "research questions."

☐ 5. Brainstorm some tentative ideas about your topic or question (see Invention Strategies [10.1, p. 336]).

Researching Your Subject

☐ 6. Decide what kind of research you are going to do. Online? Library? Both? Interviews? Surveys? Combinations of these?

☐ 7. **Online and library research:** Explore various potential sources in the library or online. You are not yet doing the kind of detailed reading you will need to do later; you are just "browsing around," getting a feel for what kind of sources are out there, and you are thinking about how to narrow, revise, or clarify the topic you plan to research (see Using Brainstorming to Narrow a Topic [10.4, p. 345]). During this exploratory phase, many of the books, articles, or websites you find will include references or links to related sources. Allow yourself to follow links and references that look interesting. Make brief, informal notes about sources that seem particularly interesting. Make sure you record enough information to find these promising sources again. (See Finding Sources Online [22.4, p. 626] and Finding Sources in the Library [22.5, p. 626].)

☐ 8. **Interviews:** If you are going to interview anyone, set up an appointment and make a list of questions. (See Conducting Interviews [22.10, p. 642].)

☐ 9. **Surveys:** If you are going to use a survey, draft the questionnaire, try it out on a few people, and revise it as needed. Decide how you will find people to survey, distribute the surveys, and compile results. (See Conducting Surveys [22.11, p. 644].)

Focusing Your Research

☐ 10. <u>Decide on a focused topic to research and begin thinking about a thesis.</u>

☐ 11. Return to the most promising sources and evaluate them. (See Evaluating Sources [22.6, p. 631].)

☐ 12. When possible, print or copy the resources that seem most useful.

☐ 13. Annotate the copies you made or make notes of those you could not copy. Be sure to include bibliographic information. (See Notetaking [22.7, p. 633].)

Drafting Your Paper

☐ 14. Develop a thesis. (See Thesis Statements [10.5, p. 346].)

☐ 15. Make an outline or informal plan for the paper.

☐ 16. Write a first draft.

☐ 17. Do additional research if needed.

☐ 18. Revise the paper, which might involve writing several drafts. (See Revising [Topic 15, p. 413].)

☐ 19. Check to make sure you have documented all the material you quoted, paraphrased, or summarized with in-text citations. (See MLA In-Text Citations [23.2, p. 652] and APA In-Text Citations [24.2, p. 688].)

☐ 20. Proofread and edit the paper.

☐ 21. Submit the final paper.

22.3 Activity

Choosing Relevant Steps in the Research Process

Below you will find a list of all the steps presented in The Research Process (22.2, p. 620) that *might* be involved in writing a research paper. In that section, it was pointed out that not all of these will be involved in every project. Exactly which steps are necessary will depend on many factors: how much time you have, what kind of paper you are asked to write, how much research is expected for the paper, what the assignment is, and many more. However, this very complete list is worth thinking about before you start a research project, as you can then select just the steps necessary for your project.

Checklist for Steps in the Research Process

Getting Started

☐ 1. Read and analyze the assignment (see Terms for Writing Assignments [28.2, p. 750] for more details).

☐ 2. Analyze the rhetorical situation (see The Rhetorical Situation [9.3, p. 327]).

☐ 3. Think about how much time you have for the project and set deadlines for each step.

☐ 4. Focus on a topic you are interested in and want to write about. Sometimes it is more appropriate to start with a question about the topic, which will help you focus your research. For example, if the topic is to explore a cause or causes of the Civil War, you might ask, "What was the role of states' rights in the American Civil War?" "How did westward expansion impact the debate on slavery?" "Why did the election of Abraham Lincoln antagonize the southern states?" These questions are sometimes called "research questions."

☐ 5. Brainstorm some tentative ideas about your topic or question (see Invention Strategies [10.1, p. 336]).

Researching Your Subject

☐ 6. Decide what kind of research you are going to do. Online? Library? Both? Interviews? Surveys? Combinations of these?

☐ 7. **Online and library research:**   Explore various potential sources in the library or online. You are not yet doing the kind of detailed reading you will need to do later; you are just "browsing around," getting a feel for what kind of sources are out there, and you are thinking about how to narrow, revise, or clarify the topic you plan to research question (see Using Brainstorming to Narrow a Topic [10.4, p. 345]). During this exploratory phase, many of the books, articles, or websites you find will include references or links to related sources. Allow yourself to follow links and references that look interesting. Make brief, informal notes about sources that seem particularly interesting. Make sure you record enough information to find these promising sources again. (See Finding Sources Online [22.4, p. 626] and Finding Sources in the Library [22.5, p. 626].)

☐ 8. **Interviews:**   If you are going to interview anyone, set up an appointment and make a list of questions. (See Conducting Interviews [22.10, p. 642].)

☐ 9. **Surveys:**   If you are going to use a survey, draft the questionnaire, try it out on a few people, and revise it as needed. Decide how you will find people to survey, distribute the surveys, and compile results. (See Conducting Surveys [22.11, p. 644].)

Focusing Your Research

☐ 10. Decide on a focused topic to research and begin thinking about a thesis.

☐ 11. Return to the most promising sources and evaluate them. (See Evaluating Sources [22.6, p. 631].)

☐ 12. When possible, print or copy the resources that seem most useful.

☐ 13. Annotate the copies you made or make notes of those you could not copy. Be sure to include bibliographic information. (See Notetaking [22.7, p. 633].)

Drafting Your Paper

- ☐ 14. Develop a thesis. (See Thesis Statements [10.5, p. 346].)
- ☐ 15. Make an outline or informal plan for the paper.
- ☐ 16. Write a first draft.
- ☐ 17. Do additional research if needed.
- ☐ 18. Revise the paper, which might involve writing several drafts. (See Revising [Topic 15, p. 413].)
- ☐ 19. Check to make sure you have documented all the material you quoted, paraphrased, or summarized with in-text citations. (See MLA In-Text Citations [23.2, p. 652] and APA In-Text Citations [24.2, p. 688].)
- ☐ 20. Proofread and edit the paper.
- ☐ 21. Submit the final paper.

For this activity, working in your group, select one of the following three assignments. Then decide which of the steps listed above you would definitely have to do in order to write the assigned essay.

Assignment 1: Evolution of Thinking on Delayed Gratification

For this assignment, you will write an academic essay suitable for an English composition class in which you discuss the evolution of thinking over the past fifty years about delayed gratification. You will need to explain Walter Mischel's contribution in his famous "Marshmallow Experiment," then explore more recent thoughts on the subject, and, finally, present your own thoughts about the issue. The audience for this essay is your English composition instructor.

You must include information from at least six articles by quoting, paraphrasing, or summarizing relevant passages. When you do this, be sure to provide appropriate citations for any words you quote, paraphrase, or summarize from the websites and to include a works cited list or list of references at the end of your essay.

The essay is due one week from today.

Assignment 2: Freedom of Speech

For this assignment, you will write a ten- to twelve-page academic essay on a topic related to freedom of speech in America. In your essay, you will discuss what freedom of speech means in America through your focus on a specific topic like one of the following:

- The origins of the principle of freedom of speech at the time the country was forming

- Reservations about freedom of speech when it was proposed
- Changes in the principle of freedom of speech over time
- Threats to free speech over the years
- Controversies that have arisen involving free speech
- How the American version of free speech is different from that of other countries
- A topic of your choosing

Think of this essay as writing that would be appropriate in a college course on history, political science, law, or English composition. Your audience for this essay will be your instructor for that course.

Once you've settled on a topic to write about, you will need to do some research. Locate at least six articles or books that discuss your topic. Once you have your articles, write a brief evaluation of each using the questions that follow. Include these evaluations when you turn in your essay.

1. Who was the author(s)? What can you find out about the author(s)? What level of expertise does the author have on the subject?
2. Where was the article published? What kind of journal, book, or website did it appear in, and is that source reliable, accurate, and up-to-date?
3. Does the author or the publisher of the article have a particular bias? Does that bias make the article less valuable as a resource?
4. Who seems to be the audience this article was intended for?
5. Does the article provide convincing evidence to support its thesis?

Be sure to provide appropriate citations for any words you quote, paraphrase, or summarize from the websites and to include a works cited list or list of references at the end of your essay.

This assignment is due in six weeks.

Assignment 3: Taking a Position on the Minimum Wage

For this assignment, you are going to write a three- to four-page essay to convince government officials in your city or state of your position on the minimum wage. You will visit seven websites addressing the issue of raising the minimum wage—five are listed below and two you will find. You will evaluate each of the websites using the questions listed in Assignment 2. Finally, you will recommend what the minimum wage should be in your city or state based on the research you have done. Be sure to provide appropriate citations for any words you quote, paraphrase, or summarize from the websites and include a works cited list or list of references at the end of your essay.

Here are the five websites. Remember: You need to locate two more that also address the effect of raising the minimum wage on employment. You can access these sites by typing their titles into your browser. (If you cannot find a site using its title, there is an updated list of URLs available at https://bit.ly/33IIHtf.)

1. "Increase in Minimum Wage Kills Jobs," Employment Policies Institute
2. "Minimum Wage and Job Loss: One Alarming Seattle Study Is Not the Last Word," Arindrajit Dube, *New York Times*
3. "New Minimum Wage Hikes Set to Kill Jobs in 2018," Brendan Pringle, *Washington Examiner*
4. "The Controversial Study Showing High Minimum Wages Kills Jobs, Explained," Jeff Guo, *Vox*
5. "Study: Seattle's $15 Minimum Wage WORKED," David Pakman, *HuffPost*

22.4 Presentation

Finding Sources Online

To watch this presentation, which discusses how to locate useful and relevant sources through online research, go to *Achieve for The Hub*, Topic 22, and open Unit 22.4.

22.5 Tutorial

Finding Sources in the Library

Research, whether in the library or on the web, has two phases: a "browsing" phase and a "focused" phase. In the browsing phase, you have a general topic you know you want to explore, but you also know that the topic will probably need to be narrowed, focused, or even abandoned. Further, you often have no more than a fuzzy idea about what you are going to argue about the topic or what your thesis will be.

During the browsing phase, you are educating yourself about the topic and getting a feel for the issues, discovering what the main arguments seem to be, and locating "experts," authors referred to over and over in the sources you find. You're not so much looking for material to include in your paper as finding what's out there, although you should be jotting down bibliographic information you come across that looks promising so you can find the source later if you need to.

When you discover a shelf in the library that has a book or two that look useful, explore other books on that same shelf to see if they are also on your topic. When you find an article in a journal that seems important to your topic, look for references to other articles either in a bibliography or perhaps included within the article itself. Again, as you browse, either make notes or make copies of pages so you can locate this material during the focused phase of research.

Once you have a good feel for the topic you have been exploring and have identified the main arguments about it, discovered some "experts," and narrowed, focused, or even revised your topic, you are ready for phase two: the focused phase. At this point, you should have begun to formulate a thesis, with the understanding that it may change considerably as you continue researching and writing.

The second phase is organized around a narrowed topic and a tentative thesis (see How to Use Invention Strategies to Select a Topic [10.3, p. 344] and Thesis Statements [10.5, p. 346]). Now you will be searching the library focusing primarily on two types of materials: books and periodicals (journals and magazines). Because the tools and methods for searching for these two are quite different, we will discuss them one at a time.

Locating Books

The library catalog is your tool for locating books. Today, most libraries' catalogs are computerized, which not only means books are much easier to find but also means you can, in most cases, do your search from home. If you are not familiar with accessing your college's catalog, there are two ways you can become familiar with the process. The first is through a library orientation session. Many college writing classes will schedule a day to meet in the library for such an orientation. Be sure to attend that session. A second way to become familiar is to visit the library and ask a reference librarian to help you get started.

Once you have accessed the library's catalog, you are ready to begin searching for books. The most obvious way into the college's collection of books is to search by *subject* using the topic you have focused on. For example, imagine that you are going to write about the atomic bombing of Hiroshima during World War II, and you have focused on the specific topic of the ethical justification for the bombing. Each college library's catalog web page will look slightly different, but the procedures for locating materials will usually work in a similar way to the following example.

On the search page, begin by choosing to search by title, typing the word "Hiroshima" into the search box, and clicking the Search button.

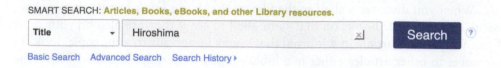

The catalog search engine returns results as follows (only the first two are shown):

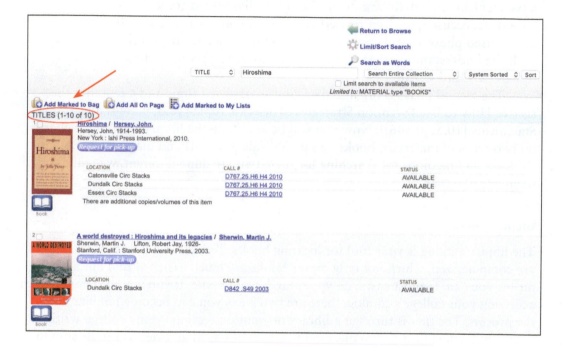

You can see, in the item circled in red, that the library owns ten books with "Hiroshima" in the title. Ten is too many for you to read or even to skim for this assignment, so you need to find a way to narrow down the list. Study the titles to find the books that seem most closely related to your working thesis. Also look for authors who were referred to frequently while you were in the browsing phase.

Locating Articles in Journals and Magazines

It is important that you understand the difference between journals and popular magazines. The following chart will help you with this distinction.

Journals	Magazines
Journals usually have the word *journal* in their title.	Magazines usually do not have the word *journal* in their title.
Articles in journals usually include citations and lists of references.	Magazine articles seldom have citations or lists of references.
Journals are seldom glossy and seldom have full-color illustrations.	Magazines are usually glossy with full-color illustrations.
Journals are usually found in libraries.	Some magazines may be found in libraries, but more often they're available by subscription or at a newsstand.
The authors of journal articles are usually identified by academic credentials.	Magazine articles are usually written by journalists.
Journal articles often begin with a summary or abstract.	Magazine articles usually do not include a summary or abstract.

For most research you do in college, you will be expected to use scholarly sources, although for some topics, some audiences, and some contexts, popular magazines and newspapers may be appropriate.

Most libraries, especially those on college and university campuses, have powerful tools that allow you to locate articles on almost any topic you might want to write about: databases. Many students use Google to search for articles, but there are good reasons why searching using your library's databases is a better choice.

Benefits of Library Databases versus Google

1. **Google will find thousands of articles but does not evaluate the expertise of their authors.** Using Google you'll get a list that includes excellent scholarly articles intermixed with the websites of high school students, blogs by conspiracy theorists, and people trying to sell a gimmick or a cure. Using Google Scholar will produce a list that is more scholarly but doesn't have some of the other benefits of using a library database that are discussed below.

2. **Many of the sources you locate with Google or Google Scholar will charge a fee if you want to access an article.** Most libraries pay a license fee in order for their students to access the sources listed in the databases for free.

3. **When you find articles from a library database that look useful for the paper you are writing, in most cases you can download the paper directly to your computer.** If you later quote from the article, you can cut and paste from the article directly into your paper ensuring that you quote accurately. If you need a paper copy, you can print one from your computer.

4. **Most library databases can be accessed from home.** Sometimes students decide to use Google because they can access it from home, not realizing that they can also access their college library from home. You may want to ask a reference librarian or perhaps your English teacher to show you how to do this.

Many students use Google to search for articles. If you choose to do this, use Google Scholar. Simply open Google, type "Google Scholar" in the search box, and hit Enter. Clicking on the words "Google Scholar" at the top of the page opens the search engine.

Using Library Databases

There are two different types of library databases for periodicals: general and specialized.

General Databases

General databases provide access to a wide range of scholarly journals as well as articles from reputable magazines and newspapers. They can be a good place to start your research if you haven't yet developed your focus or if you have chosen a topic but are not sure what discipline it belongs to. Some of the most widely used general databases are listed below. Your reference librarian can help guide you to the ones that will be most useful for the task you are working on.

- **Academic Search Premier** is a major database that includes general and scholarly sources in the humanities, education, social sciences, computer science, engineering, languages, linguistics, arts, literature, and ethnic studies.

- **JSTOR** provides access to more than 12 million academic journal articles, books, and primary sources; however, JSTOR does not include *current* issues.

- **Lexis/Nexis Academic** provides full-text news, business, and legal publications. It also provides transcripts of television and radio broadcasts and includes national and international sources.

- **ProQuest** includes dissertations and theses, e-books, newspapers, periodicals, historical collections, and governmental and cultural archives estimated to include more than 125 billion digital pages.

Specialized Databases

Specialized databases are preferable once you have a focused topic to search for and when you are confident about the discipline or disciplines where most scholarship on your topic takes place. Most libraries offer large numbers of these specialized databases. Your reference librarian can help guide you to the ones that will be most useful for the topic you are working on. A small sample is listed below.

- **Arts and Humanities Database** covers the arts, archeology, architecture, anthropology, classics, history, philosophy, and modern languages.

- **Medline** includes articles on biomedical and health topics used by health care professionals.

- **MLA International Bibliography** covers scholarship on all aspects of modern languages and literature. More than 70,000 sources are added annually, allowing access to very recent scholarship as well as articles dating back to the 1880s.

- **Social Science Index** covers social science disciplines including anthropology, communication, criminology, economics, education, political science, psychology, social work, and sociology.

22.6 Activity

Evaluating Sources

Two research assignments are listed below. After each assignment, several possible resources (books, blogs, articles, or websites) are listed. Working in your group, view the material provided or visit the website for each of these resources and decide how good a source it would be for a college research paper. Then compile a list of what the group viewed as the strengths and weaknesses of each source you evaluated. The following questions should help you evaluate these sources, as well as others you locate as you research papers.

Questions for Evaluating Sources

- Who is the author(s)? What can you find out about the author(s)? How expert is the author on the subject?

- Where was the article published? (What kind of journal, book, or website?) Who published the book?

- When was the article or book published?

- What can you find out about the organization or company that published it?

- Who seems to be the audience this article or book was intended for?

- Does this article or book add anything new to the argument?

Assignment 1: Exploring Mistakes Made during the Vietnam War

You are writing a research paper for a history class about the mistakes the United States made during the Vietnam War, and you find the following sources. Evaluate them using the questions above. Locate the first three sources using the search terms provided. (If you find that any of the search terms provided do not work, there is a list of URLs available at https://bit.ly/33IIHtf.) Search for the final three sources on Amazon.com, where you can read the back covers.

- An article entitled "The Vietnam War in Hindsight" (Type the entire title into your browser, followed by "Brookings Institute.")

- A book entitled *Against the Vietnam War* (Type "Against the Vietnam War Google Books" into your browser.)

- A blog post entitled "Why Did the U.S. Lose the Vietnam War?" (Type "Why Did the U.S. Lose the Vietnam War? Slate blog" into your browser.)

- A book entitled *Vietnam Insights*

- A book entitled *Vietnam: An Epic Tragedy, 1945–1975*

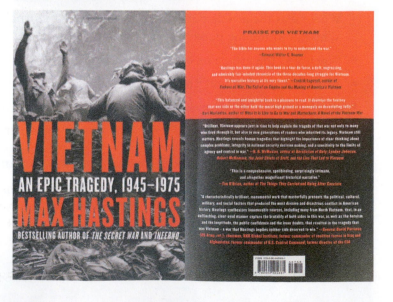

- A book entitled *Argument Without End*

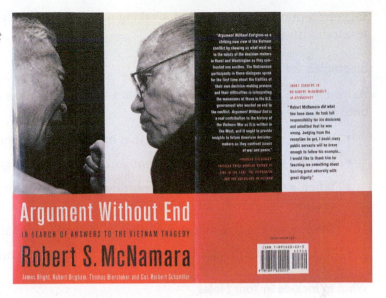

Assignment 2: Evaluating the Affordable Care Act

You are writing a research paper about the Affordable Care Act (Obamacare) and find the following sources. Evaluate them using the questions above. (Locate the sources using the search terms provided. If these search terms do not work, there is a list of URLs available at https://bit.ly/33IIHtf.)

- The official government site for signing up for healthcare provided under the Affordable Care Act (Type "healthcare.gov" into your browser.)

- An article entitled "Why So Many Insurers Are Leaving Obamacare" in *The Atlantic* (Type the entire title into your browser, followed by "The Atlantic.")

- An article entitled "Overwhelming Evidence That Obamacare Caused Premiums to Increase Substantially" in *Forbes* (Type "overwhelming evidence Obamacare premiums Forbes" into your browser.)

22.7 Tutorial

Notetaking

Much of the writing you do in college involves research, whether you are writing a lengthy formal research paper or you are writing a fairly short essay in which you want to include information or perhaps a quotation or two from some experts on your topic. An essential skill for effective research is effective notetaking. This section suggests a number of strategies for taking notes that will help you incorporate research into your writing.

Strategies for Effective Notetaking

As you locate articles, books, and websites with information about your topic, take note of the following:

- When a source has information that may be useful in supporting your thesis
- When a source makes a statement you may want to argue against
- When a source is an expert supporting your position or advocating a position you may want to refute
- When a source is a concrete example that may be useful in your paper
- When a source provides a fact that may be useful in your paper

What to Include in Your Notes

You will want to include four pieces of information in each note you take.

1. A subject heading that indicates what the note is about

2. Information about the source of the note. This information will be important when you construct a works cited list or list of references. It will also make it easier for you to find the source again if you need to. Be sure to record the following:

   a. Title of the source

   b. Name of the author(s)

   c. Name of the translator(s) or editor(s)

   d. Version or edition

   e. Volume and issue numbers for periodicals

   f. Publisher

   g. Date of publication

   h. Page number for print sources or URL for online sources

   Most sources won't include *all* these pieces of information, so include only the elements that are relevant and available for an acceptable citation.

3. A summary, paraphrase, or quotation of the ideas or information in the source. Be sure to indicate in the note what is summary, what is paraphrase, and what is quotation. (See Strategies for Writing a Summary [18.25, p. 547] and Quoting and Paraphrasing [22.8, p. 635].)

4. Your response to the information

How to Record Your Notes

There are at least four ways to record these notes.

1. **On 3 × 5 or 4 × 6 inch cards.** This is a little more labor intensive than digital options. It requires care to make sure quotations are accurate, and it doesn't provide the context for the relevant content or quotation. It does allow for the notes to be arranged in the order they will appear in the paper. Some writers even tack them on a bulletin board to arrange them.

2. **In a paper journal.** This option has all the disadvantages of note cards. In addition, it is not easy to arrange notes in any order.

3. **In a series of word processing documents.** If you are using the library, this requires you to have a laptop. For online sources, it is very convenient and accurate, as online source material can be copied and pasted right into word processing documents. Notes are easy to arrange in order and to organize in files. In most cases, a large chunk of text can be copied and then the part to be used simply highlighted, allowing the writer to see the relevant content or quotation in its original context.

4. **By photocopying each article or page from a book and writing the source information somewhere on that copy.** Photocopying costs money. You do end up with the entire page on which the relevant information or potential quotation appears, allowing you to see it in context. However, it is a little awkward, but not impossible, to arrange this type of material in order.

Each of these options has advantages and disadvantages. You should use the notetaking method that works best for you.

22.8 Tutorial
Quoting and Paraphrasing

The point of doing research is to find sources—books, articles, interviews, reports, studies, or other texts—that include facts, expert opinion, examples, or other forms of support for the thesis you will be arguing in your essay. Once you have located these kinds of support you will include them in your essay in one of three ways: quotations, paraphrases, or summaries. In this unit, we discuss quoting and paraphrasing. Summarizing is discussed in Strategies for Writing a Summary (18.25, p. 547).

Quotations

When you quote a source, you reproduce the words exactly as they appear in the source document, placing them inside quotation marks. Using a quotation is an effective strategy in the following situations:

- When the author's language is particularly powerful or vivid and would not be as effective if paraphrased

- When the author's language is so technical it is important to report it exactly as it was written

- When the author is highly respected and you think his or her exact words will be more convincing than your own

When quoting from a source, accuracy is essential. You must reproduce the source's words exactly, with exceptions that will be discussed below. Short quotations should be incorporated directly into your text. If you are following MLA style, short means four typed lines or less. If you are following APA style, short means forty words or fewer. Long quotations should be set off in block style.

Short Quotation

According to the Chicana writer Gloria Anzaldúa, "Chicano Spanish is a border tongue which developed naturally" (*Borderlands* 77).

Long Quotation

Even though community colleges are often seen as opening the door to higher education for a large number of students who would not have even considered going to college sixty or seventy years ago, it has not always opened that door as widely as we would hope. Rebecca Cox, in her important book *The College Fear Factor*, points this out:

> [T]he community college has also had a winnowing effect, in functioning as an obstacle to students who enter with the intention of transferring and earning a bachelor's degree. The high attrition rates—within individual courses and across various degree programs—suggest that students face barriers that divert them from accomplishing their goals (3).

Framing Quotations

The way you frame the quotations in your essays will make the quotations more effective. This framing (underlined in the following examples) usually, but not always, comes before the quoted material and consists of introductory information that provides context for the quotation that follows.

> Noted sociologist Annette Lareau, in her major study of child rearing in American families, cautions us that she "was struck by how hard parents try, how much effort they put into each day as they pursue their lives" (*Unequal Childhoods* 360).
>
> In her influential book *Grit,* MacArthur fellow Angela Duckworth explains what grit really is: "Grit is about working on something you care about so much that you're willing to stay loyal to it" (54).
>
> So far in this essay, I have given several reasons why change is so difficult to bring about in higher education. Cheryl Hyman, former president of Chicago City Colleges, suggests another reason when she claims that if there is one thing "educators don't want to hear, it's that education should be run more like a business" (*Reinvention* 30).

Note that in the framing material each example includes two pieces of information:

- The name of the person being quoted (Annette Lareau, Angela Duckworth, and Cheryl Hyman)

- Some information to explain why this person has expertise ("Noted sociologist," "MacArthur fellow" and writer of an "influential book," and "former president of Chicago City Colleges")

Sometimes it's also useful to explain in the framing material how the quoted material relates to the essay itself. In the third example, taken from an essay exploring how difficult it is to make changes in higher education, the framing material explains that the quotation from Hyman will provide yet another reason for why it is so difficult.

One additional feature of the materials these authors have chosen to frame their quotations is the verbs they use: *cautions*, *explains*, and *claims*. Notice how much more information these verbs provide than more ordinary verbs that might have been used, such as *says* or *writes*. *Cautions* tells the reader that not only did Lareau write these words but that they say something that calls into question what we might believe about families from different socioeconomic strata. In the second example, *explains* signals that the quotation has something to say that could clear up any confusion the reader might have about grit. Finally, *claims* signals that the writer of the essay is not completely convinced that Hyman is right about faculty attitudes.

Here is a list of more expressive verbs for introducing quotations. Try using some of them the next time you include a quotation in your writing.

Expressive Verbs		
acknowledges	declares	observes
admits	denies	opposes
advises	discusses	points out
agrees	emphasizes	replies
argues	explains	reports
asserts	hypothesizes	responds
believes	implies	reveals
claims	insists	suggests
concludes	interprets	thinks
confirms	objects	

In the previous examples, the framing material was placed in front of the quoted material. The following examples illustrate that this is not the only way of positioning framing material.

> "India is named for the Indus River, along whose fecund banks a great urban civilization flourished more than four thousand years ago," writes historian Stanley Wolpert in the opening chapter of his monumental *New History of India*.

> "Greek drama grew out of religious ritual," argues Moses Hadad in his introduction to *Greek Drama*, "and was presented as part of a religious cult."

Exceptions to Word-for-Word Quoting

This section on quotations began by saying "you reproduce the words exactly as they appear in the source document." However, there are two primary exceptions to this rule: (1) using ellipses to exclude irrelevant words in quoted material and (2) adding words to explain an author's meaning.

Using Ellipses to Indicate Omitted Words. Sometimes you want to include some words from one long sentence, or maybe two adjacent sentences, and not include the words between them that are not relevant to your point. *As long as you do not change the author's original meaning*, it is acceptable to omit some words in a quotation. If you decide to do this, indicate the omission with an ellipsis (three spaced periods). In the following example, unnecessary words have been deleted from the original text by Paul Tough. Note the ellipses this writer has used to indicate where these words from the original have been omitted. He has also maintained the author's original meaning.

Original

"What matters most in a child's development, they say, is not how much information we can stuff into her brain in the first few years. What matters, instead, is whether we are able to help her develop a very different set of qualities, a list that includes persistence, self-control, curiosity, conscientiousness, grit, and self-confidence" (Tough, *How Children Succeed*, xv).

Quotation

Education writer Paul Tough insists that what "matters most in a child's development . . . is not how much information we can stuff into her brain in the first few years. What matters, instead, is whether we are able to help her develop . . . persistence, self-control, curiosity, conscientiousness, grit, and self-confidence" (*How Children Succeed*, xv).

Adding Words of Explanation. Sometimes, it is necessary to add words to quoted text in order to explain what a writer is saying. To add words to the original text, enclose the added words in brackets. Note in the example below how the words in brackets have been inserted into the original text that is being quoted to make its meaning clearer to the reader.

Original

You can trace its contemporary rise, in fact, to 1994, when the Carnegie Corporation published *Starting Points: Meeting the Needs of Our Youngest Children,* a report that sounded an alarm about the cognitive development of our nation's children. The problem, according to the report, was that children were no longer receiving enough cognitive stimulation in the first three years of life, in part because of the increasing number of single-parent families and working mothers—and so they were arriving in kindergarten unready to learn. The report launched an entire industry of brainbuilding "zero-to-three" products for worried parents. Billions of dollars' worth of books and activity gyms and Baby Einstein videos and DVDs were sold.

Quotation

According to education writer Paul Tough, "The [Carnegie] report [*Starting Points: Meeting the Needs of Our Youngest Children*] launched an entire industry of brainbuilding 'zero-to-three' products for worried parents."

Paraphrases

When you use your own words to express an author's ideas fairly and accurately, you are paraphrasing. Being able to express someone else's ideas accurately is one way to ensure that you understand them. Use a paraphrase in these situations:

- To help you think through an author's ideas

- To record ideas that you might want to use in an essay

- To show a reader that you have understood an idea

- When the language in the source is not particularly effective

- When the source language doesn't fit well with your language

When you decide to paraphrase, it is important that you faithfully represent the thought in the source in your own words. Unlike summaries, paraphrases are usually about the same length as the original source, sometimes longer, as you are basically translating someone else's language into your own. You might include a word or two from the original source in quotation marks, but most of the wording should be your own, written in your style. As well as rewording, you might want to reorganize the material you are paraphrasing, breaking complicated sentences in the original into shorter ones. In addition, you must include the name of the author and title of the source in your paraphrase and/or provide an in-text citation.

Reproduced below is the original text from Richard Reeves' *Dream Hoarders*, where he argues that the upper middle class in America is leaving everyone else behind and exploiting a variety of advantages in order to do so. An unacceptable paraphrase follows it. It does not mention or cite the passage it refers to, and it uses much of the language of the original, with just a few words changed. The words that come from the original that are still used in this unacceptable paraphrase are underlined. Because they are not placed inside quotation marks, they are actually plagiarized. (The important topic of plagiarism is discussed in detail in Avoiding Plagiarism [22.13, p. 646].)

Original

Americans have historically lauded education as the great equalizer, allowing individuals to determine their own path in life regardless of background. But if this was ever true, it certainly is not today. Postsecondary education in particular has become an "inequality machine." As more ordinary people have earned college degrees, upper middle-class families have simply upped the ante. Postgraduate qualifications are now the key to maintaining upper middle-class status (11).

Unacceptable Paraphrase

Richard Reeves, from the Brookings Institution, has argued that <u>historically, Americans have</u> praised <u>education as the great equalizer</u>, making it possible for everyone to follow <u>their own path regardless of background</u>. If this was true in the past, <u>it certainly is not</u> these days. College has especially helped to encourage inequality. <u>As more people earn college degrees</u>, the <u>key</u> to getting a job that provides a <u>middle-class</u> lifestyle has become a <u>post-graduate degree</u>.

Below is an acceptable paraphrase. Notice that only a few words from the original text are retained in this paraphrase, and they are placed within quotation marks to make it clear that they are Reeves's words. Notice, also, that just like with quotations, paraphrases are usually framed with material like "In his book *Dream Hoarders*, Richard Reeves from the Brookings Institute makes the point that," which identifies the author, his credentials, and the source of the paraphrased material.

Acceptable Paraphrase

In his book *Dream Hoarders*, Richard Reeves from the Brookings Institute makes the point that in the past Americans considered education to be the best route for people from all levels of society to pursue their choice of career. Whether this was ever true or not, he says that these days higher education "has become an inequality machine," because as more regular people have graduated with bachelor's degrees, wealthier people have now made master's and doctoral degrees necessary requirements for higher-paying jobs (11).

22.9 Activity

Quoting and Paraphrasing Shaughnessy

In this activity, you will use the following short passage from Mina Shaughnessy's book *Errors and Expectations: A Guide for the Teacher of Basic Writing* to practice quoting and paraphrasing. Shaughnessy was teaching at City University of New York in the 1990s and was present as "open admissions" transformed her school and many more, and hers was one of the earliest books to address the teaching of students who arrive in colleges and universities with less-than-college-ready writing skills. The following passage is from the first page of her book:

> Toward the end of the sixties and largely in response to the protests of that decade, many four-year colleges began admitting students who were not by traditional standards ready for college. The numbers of such students varied from college to college as did the commitment to the task of teaching them.

Practice Quoting

In an essay you are writing for an education class, you want to make the point that "open admissions" might have resulted in major transformations at some colleges, but it had little effect at others. Working in your group, write a sentence or two in which you quote from the Shaughnessy passage to make that point.

Practice Paraphrasing

Working in your group, make the point that "open admissions" might have resulted in major transformations at some colleges, but it had little effect at others. Write this in a sentence or two, paraphrasing Shaughnessy's passage.

In both cases, make sure you provide an effective frame for the material you quote or paraphrase.

22.10 Tutorial

Conducting Interviews

When thinking about how to provide evidence to support your thesis in a paper, don't overlook the possibility of interviewing an expert. Quoting the words of someone with direct experience can provide strong support for your argument, as in the following scenarios.

- For an essay on a fairly recent military event, you might interview a cousin or uncle who served in Vietnam, Afghanistan, or Iraq.

- For an essay on civil rights, you might interview someone who took part in the sit-ins in the South in 1960 or the march on Washington in 1963 or a person who has recently experienced a violation of his or her civil rights.

- In making decisions about your program of study and future career, you might interview someone working in the field you are considering.

- In the workplace, you might interview someone in the Human Relations Office for a report or a proposal concerning personnel issues.

- For your marketing or sales department, you might interview customers about their perceptions of your company's products or procedures.

Checklist for Steps for Conducting Interviews

Follow these steps for setting up and conducting an interview.

Scheduling an Interview

- ☐ Identify someone to interview.
- ☐ Once your subject has agreed to be interviewed, establish a time and place for the interview as well as an understanding of how long the interview will last.
- ☐ Send an email or note confirming the time and place.
- ☐ Ask your subject if he or she minds being taped.

Planning for an Interview

- ☐ Write down your questions in advance. Think about what you want to know from the subject and write questions that will produce that information.
- ☐ Prioritize your questions.
- ☐ On the page of questions you plan to use, leave plenty of space after each one to record the subject's responses.
- ☐ Be sure to ask questions identifying the subject and determining his or her exact position, job, or role.
- ☐ Consider including questions that will elicit a story ("Tell me about the time . . .") or allow for an open response "So, how did you feel about . . . ?" Asking questions that produce a simple yes or no answer will not provide you with much information.
- ☐ Make sure you have materials for taking notes.
- ☐ Make sure your recording device is working.

Conducting an Interview

- ☐ Respect the subject's time. Arrive promptly and conclude within the time-frame you established.
- ☐ Note the date, time, and place of the interview.
- ☐ Take notes even if you are also recording.
- ☐ Be careful to distinguish in your notes between quotations, paraphrases, and summaries.
- ☐ If your subject provides useful responses to an early question and you want to continue that line of inquiry, do not feel you must get to all the questions you prepared.

Following Up on an Interview

- ☐ Flesh out your notes as soon as possible after the interview. The longer you wait, the harder it will be for you to accurately recall what was said.

- ☐ If you are not sure of what the person said or meant, contact him or her and ask. It is important that you provide accurate information.

- ☐ Send a thank-you note or email to the interviewee.

22.11 Tutorial

Conducting Surveys

Surveys are a useful way to gather evidence for an essay, but they take some time to construct, to administer, and to interpret. A good place to start is to clearly define what it is you want to learn from your survey. If you were writing a paper about the attention paid to politics by people under 30 years old as compared to those 30–50 years old, conducting a survey to try to measure those differences would be a logical approach.

Developing Survey Questions

Once you know what it is you hope to learn, you can begin writing questions for your survey. These questions will be of two types: questions to determine information about the person completing the survey (respondents) and questions to learn their attitude or behavior about a specific topic or issue.

Questions about Respondents.   For most surveys, you will want to know some basic information about the people you are surveying. What this consists of will vary depending on your focus. In a survey about the attention paid to politics by different age groups, for example, you would certainly need to ask respondents their age. You might also want to know their race, their gender, where they live, and even their party affiliation, although you should bear in mind that the more questions you ask, the more likely it is that fewer people will complete the survey.

Survey Questions.   When you create survey questions, there are some principals you should follow.

1. Keep your survey short. The longer it is, the less likely people are to complete it.

2. Keep in mind that people are less likely to answer questions that request a written response than questions that require yes/no, multiple choice, or ratings answers.

3. Only ask questions directly relevant to your goal. Every question should count.

4. Write questions clearly, so there is no confusion about what you are asking.

5. Only ask one question at a time. Reread your questions to check that you have not asked two questions in one, which can confuse respondents and lead to misleading results. If you have, determine if both are important and, if so, make them into two separate questions.

6. Do not word questions so that they lead people to answer them in a certain way. Questions should be unbiased in order to elicit an accurate response.

7. Include response scales when asking questions. Although asking binary (yes/no, true/false) questions is good for eliciting some kinds of information, using response scales allows people to provide an indication of how strongly they feel about a topic. So if you want to know more about how a person feels about an issue, instead of option (a) below, use option (b).

   a. True or False? Do politicians ever tell the truth?

   b. To what extent do you think politicians tell the truth?

      Not at all/Rarely/Sometimes/Often/Always

8. Test your survey on classmates, friends, or family members before using it. They will help you to spot errors, point out confusing questions, and may suggest corrections or even new questions. Revise based on their feedback.

As an example, for an essay on attention to politics, interview questions like the following are likely to produce useful evidence.

---

1. Circle the item below that most closely represents how often you read a newspaper.

   Never   1–2 times a week   3–4 times a week
   5–6 times a week Every day

2. Circle the item below that most closely represents how often you watch television news.

   Never   1–2 times a week   3–4 times a week
   5–6 times a week Every day

3. Did you vote in the most recent election?

   Yes No

4. What is the last name of the current governor of your state?

   Mitchel Gregory Tomlinson Hernandez Williams

5. Have you attached a political bumper sticker to your car in the past year?

   Yes No

Conducting a Survey

Once you have created your survey, you are ready to go to work on getting it into the hands of respondents. You may just sit down somewhere on campus and ask passersby to fill out the survey. If you have access to a mailing list, you can mail the survey out. If you have access to a list of emails, you can email it out, or you can use an online survey site like SurveyMonkey to host your survey.

To make sure your survey results are credible, you must make sure your survey includes a representative sample of respondents. For example, if you interview students in the parking lot, your sample would not be representative because you are omitting students who take a bus to school. Take these steps to ensure that your survey is representative:

1. Survey as large a group as you can.
2. Think of groups of people who have not been included in your survey and figure out a way to make sure they are included.
3. If you have access to a list of names and emails that is too large, randomize your choice of names by selecting, for example, only every twentieth name.
4. When you have compiled a list, check to see if it is representative, for example, by seeing whether men and women are equally represented.

Finally, you need to compile the results and determine how they fit into your essay.

22.12 Writing

Questions about Plagiarism

As you read Avoiding Plagiarism (22.13), make a list of questions you have about the topic.

22.13 Tutorial

Avoiding Plagiarism

Sometimes plagiarism seems like a very complicated and scary concept, but it doesn't need to be. If you plagiarize, you use the words and ideas of another person without giving them credit; you use them as though they are your own words. In American colleges and universities, plagiarism is considered a very serious academic offense and can result in failing grades or even more serious consequences.

Use Quotation Marks and Document Your Sources

Avoiding plagiarism is really simple: if you use the exact words of another writer, you must place them in quotation marks and provide an in-text citation that links to a works cited or references list; if you use the ideas of another writer you must give him or her credit and document the source. You cannot pretend that someone else's words or ideas are your own.

Hardly anyone has trouble understanding the first part: if you use someone else's words in something you're writing, you must put those words in quotation marks (see Quoting and Paraphrasing [22.8, p. 635] for more details). That part's easy, but then you also must provide a citation—a note in parentheses after the quoted words that tells readers where the quoted words came from so they can find the original source if they're interested. There are several systems for formatting these citations, two of which are discussed in detail in *The Hub*: MLA In-Text Citations (23.2, p. 652) and APA In-Text Citations (24.2, p. 688). Make sure you know which citation system your audience expects.

The definition of plagiarism above also discusses using someone else's *ideas*; that's the part that is sometimes harder to grasp. If, while doing research for a writing project, you read an article or a book in which the author makes a really good point that supports your thesis and if you take that idea and express it in your own words, you must *still* give the author credit for the idea. You must make it clear that the idea you are expressing, even if you express it completely in your own words, is an idea you got from another writer.

When you quote another writer's words exactly, you indicate that the words came from someone else by placing them inside quotation marks, but you don't use quotation marks if you are expressing someone else's ideas in your own words when you paraphrase or summarize. In these cases, you must indicate where the idea came from at the beginning of your paraphrase or summary and include an in-text citation after it that links to a works cited or references list, just as you do when you are quoting. As noted earlier, information on two of these documentation styles, MLA and APA, are available in *The Hub* in Topic 23 (MLA, p. 650) and Topic 24 (APA, p. 687).

Note that these principles apply not only to print sources but also to online sources, handwritten documents, spoken words, and even the words of other students.

Here's another important distinction. It is plagiarism if you use someone else's words or ideas without giving them credit through quotation marks and citations. However, if you make an error in the format of your citation, that is not plagiarism. It may be an error that affects your instructor's evaluation of your essay, but it is not plagiarism.

Synthesis

A well-written essay that uses sources doesn't just present them as a laundry list: "Cunningham says this," "Nguyen says that," and "Marcos says something else." Instead, it weaves them together, points our similarities and disagreements, and compares the methods they use to reach their conclusions. This process of weaving sources into a single conversation, called *synthesis*, can improve the effectiveness of your research.

How to Synthesize Sources

Synthesis is a skill we all practice in our daily lives. Imagine you are looking for a work study job, for example. You might talk to friends and classmates who work in various on-campus venues and ask them what they like and dislike about their jobs, the advantages and disadvantages of each. After thinking about what they all have to say, and taking into account your class schedule, past work experiences, and time limitations, you make a decision that working evenings in the library is your best option. If you're buying a new sound system, you might read *Consumer Reports*, research options on the internet, and talk to friends whose systems you like. Pulling together all this information and taking into account your preferences and needs is how you reach a decision about what to purchase.

In college, synthesis involves researching to locate a variety of sources on the topic you are going to write about, reading them carefully, comparing what they have to say, and then coming to your own conclusion about the issue. In fact, the goal of a research paper is not only to explain what other people have said or think about an issue and how they agree or disagree with each other but to come up with your own ideas about the subject.

In order to synthesize, keep the following in mind as you compare sources.

- What points do different sources agree on?

- What points do different sources disagree on?

- How are the sources different from each other? For example, are they looking at the same or different data, populations, time periods, solutions, and so on?

- How do the different sources support their positions? What types of evidence do they use, and how reliable and convincing is it?

- How do the sources treat the topic? Are they serious, providing significant support for their ideas, or are they expressing personal opinions with little hard evidence to support them?

Once you have a good idea of what your sources are saying, you need to think about what your position is on the issue. Are there sources that support your opinion? Are there ones that do not support your position but make a compelling argument you will need to counter? Once you know what you want to say, use synthesis to create a unified conversation among your sources and yourself.

Examples of Synthesis

Here are some examples of how a writer might synthesize sources in a paper.

1. A writer points out the agreement between two sources, but also acknowledges the differences between their analyses.

   > Slowinski and Smith agree that the current procedure for applying for financial aid is flawed, but they disagree on what the flaws are.

2. A writer points out that two sources agree on some but not all steps to solve a problem.

   > Gomez and Brown agree on three steps that could be taken to curb pollution, but they disagree on the fourth.

3. A writer points out that several sources reached similar conclusions even though the subjects they studied were quite different.

   > Based on studies of three different populations—farm workers in California, college students in Iowa, and hotel employees in the Hilton system—Stevens, Allen, and Crivello reach nearly identical conclusions.

4. A writer, while admitting there is disagreement about solutions to a problem, points to three sources' agreement on what the problem is.

   > Even though they disagree about the solutions we should enact, all three economists I have quoted agree that the extreme wealth gap in America between the very affluent and everyone else is a serious problem.

5. A writer instead of synthesizing two or three sources, synthesizes one source with her own views.

   > Fitzgerald's argument comes to the same conclusion that I have, but for very different reasons.

TOPIC 23

MLA Documentation

In English and in some humanities classes, you may be asked to use the MLA (Modern Language Association) system for documenting sources. These guidelines follow those set forth in the *MLA Handbook*, 8th edition (2016).

Navigating Topic 23

The tutorials listed below provide information about MLA in-text citations, works cited lists, and formatting for papers. You can work through the entire Topic on your own, learning about all the strategies and practicing them; work on items you've been assigned by your instructor; or choose those ones you would find helpful.

Introduction to MLA Style

Rather than thinking of the MLA guidelines simply as rules to be followed, think of them as guidelines for participating in an academic community—a community in which the exchange and extension of ideas require a system. Even though the new guidelines present a system for citing many different kinds of sources, they don't cover everything, and at times you will find that you have to think critically to adapt the guidelines to the source you are using.

Topic 23 provides you with an overview of the MLA style plus guidelines for how to correctly cite and document sources using in-text citations and a works cited list. In addition, it contains information on how to correctly format a paper using MLA style.

Documenting Sources in MLA Style

There are often several possible ways to cite a source in the list of works cited. Think carefully about your context for using the source so you can identify the pieces of information that you should include and any other information that might be helpful to your readers. The first step is to identify elements that are commonly found in works that writers cite.

Author and Title

The first two elements, both of which are needed for many sources, are the author's name and the title of the work. Each of these elements is followed by a period.

> **Author.** **Title.**

Containers

The next step is to identify elements of what MLA calls the "container" for the work—any larger work that contains the source you are citing. The context in which you are discussing the source and the context in which you find the source will help you determine what counts as a container in each case. Some works are self-contained; if you watch a movie in a theater, the movie title is the title of your source, and you won't identify a separate container title. But if you watch the same movie as part of a DVD box set of the director's work, the container title is the name of the box set. Thinking about a source as nested in larger containers may help you to visualize how a citation works. (Also see Figure 1.)

Figure 1: Basic container information

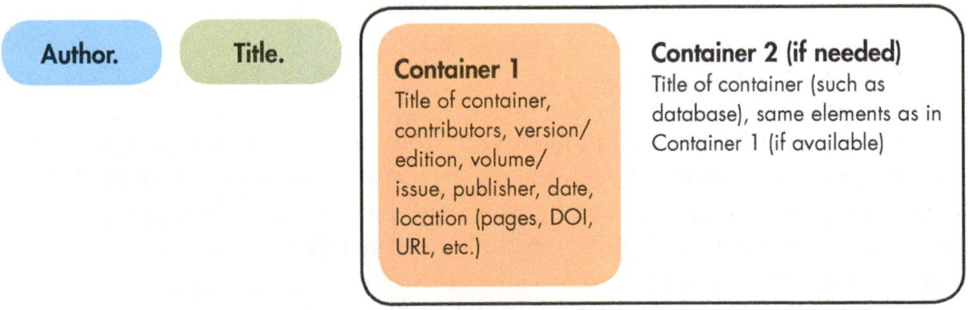

> **Author.** **Title.**
>
> **Container 1**
> Title of container, contributors, version/edition, volume/issue, publisher, date, location (pages, DOI, URL, etc.)
>
> **Container 2 (if needed)**
> Title of container (such as database), same elements as in Container 1 (if available)

The elements you may include in the "container" part of your citation include, in order, the title of the container; the name of contributors such as editors or translators; the version or edition; the volume and issue numbers; the publisher; the date of publication; and a location such as the page number, DOI, permalink, or URL. These elements are separated by commas, and the end of the container is marked with a period.

Most sources won't include *all* these pieces of information, so include only the elements that are relevant and available for an acceptable citation. If your container is itself a part of some larger container, such as a database, simply add information about the second container after the first one. You will find many examples of how elements and containers are combined to create works cited entries on pages in the MLA Works Cited List section. The General Guidelines for the Works Cited List also provide details about the information required for each element.

Works Cited Entry (one container)

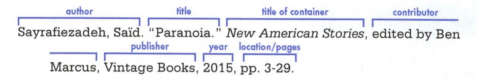

Sayrafiezadeh, Saïd. "Paranoia." *New American Stories*, edited by Ben Marcus, Vintage Books, 2015, pp. 3-29.

Works Cited Entry (two containers)

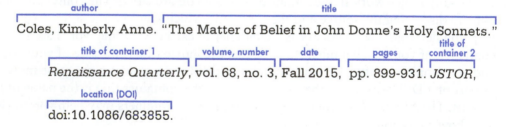

Coles, Kimberly Anne. "The Matter of Belief in John Donne's Holy Sonnets." *Renaissance Quarterly*, vol. 68, no. 3, Fall 2015, pp. 899-931. *JSTOR*, doi:10.1086/683855.

23.2 Tutorial

MLA In-Text Citations

MLA style requires you to supply an in-text citation each time you quote, paraphrase, summarize, or otherwise integrate material from a source. In-text citations are made with a combination of signal phrases and parenthetical references and include the information your readers need to locate the full reference in the works cited list at the end of the text.

A signal phrase introduces information taken from a source; usually the signal phrase includes the author's name. Parenthetical references include at least a page number (except for unpaginated sources, such as those found on the web). The list of works cited provides publication information about the source. There is a direct connection between the signal phrase and the first word or words in the works cited entry.

Sample Citation Using a Signal Phrase

In his discussion of Monty Python routines, Crystal notes that the group relished "breaking the normal rules" of language (107).

Sample Parenthetical Citation

A noted linguist explains that Monty Python humor often relied on "bizarre linguistic interactions" (Crystal 108).

Works Cited Entry

Crystal, David. *Language Play*. U of Chicago P, 1998.

Directory to MLA In-Text Citation Models

Guidelines for In-Text Citations

1. Author named in a signal phrase Ordinarily, introduce the material being cited with a signal phrase that includes the author's name.

Lee claims that his comic-book creation Thor was actually "the first regularly published superhero to speak in a consistently archaic manner" (199).

2. Author named in a parenthetical reference When you do not mention the author in a signal phrase, include the author's last name before the page number(s), if any, in parentheses. Do not use punctuation between the author's name and the page number(s).

The word *Bollywood* is sometimes considered an insult because it implies that Indian movies are merely "a derivative of the American film industry" (Chopra 9).

3. Digital or nonprint source Give enough information in a signal phrase or in parentheses for readers to locate the source in your list of works cited—at least the author's name or title. If the source lacks page numbers but has numbered paragraphs, sections, or divisions, use those numbers with the appropriate abbreviation in your parenthetical citation. Do not add such numbers if the source itself does not use them.

Digital Source without Stable Page Numbers

As a *Slate* analysis has noted, "Prominent sports psychologists get praised for their successes and don't get grief for their failures" (Engber).

Digital Source with Numbered Pages

Julian Hawthorne points out that his father and Ralph Waldo Emerson, in their lives and their writing, "together . . . met the needs of nearly all that is worthy in human nature" (ch. 4).

4. Two authors Name both authors in a signal phrase or in parentheses.

Gilbert and Gubar point out that in the Grimm version of "Snow White," the king "never actually appears in this story at all" (37).

5. Three or more authors Use the first author's name followed by *et al.* ("and others") in either a signal phrase or parentheses.

Similarly, as Belenky et al. assert, examining the lives of women expands our understanding of human development (7).

6. Organization as author Give the group's full name in a signal phrase; in parentheses, abbreviate common words in the name.

> The American Diabetes Association estimates that the cost of diagnosed diabetes in the United States in 2012 was $245 billion.

> The cost of diagnosed diabetes in the United States in 2012 was estimated at $245 billion (Amer. Diabetes Assn.).

7. Unknown author Use the full title, if it is brief, in your text—or a shortened version of the title in parentheses.

> One analysis defines *hype* as "an artificially engendered atmosphere of hysteria" (*Today's* 51).

8. Two or more works by the same author Mention the title of the work in the signal phrase or include a short version of the title in the parentheses.

> Gardner shows readers their own silliness in his description of a "pointless, ridiculous monster, crouched in the shadows, stinking of dead men, murdered children, and martyred cows" (*Grendel* 2).

9. Two or more authors with the same last name Include the author's first and last name in the signal phrase or first initial and last name in the parentheses.

> One approach to the problem is to introduce nutrition literacy at the K–5 level in public schools (E. Chen 15).

10. Indirect source (author quoting someone else) Use the abbreviation *qtd. in* to indicate that you are using a source that is cited in another source.

> As Arthur Miller says, "When somebody is destroyed everybody finally contributes to it, but in Willy's case, the end product would be virtually the same" (qtd. in Martin and Meyer 375).

11. Multivolume work In the parenthetical citation, note the volume number first and then the page number(s), with a colon and one space between them.

> Modernist writers prized experimentation and gradually even sought to blur the line between poetry and prose, according to Forster (3: 150).

12. Work in an anthology or a collection Use the name of the author of the work, not the editor of the anthology, but use the page number(s) from the anthology.

> In "Love Is a Fallacy," the narrator's logical teachings disintegrate when Polly declares that she should date Petey because "[h]e's got a raccoon coat" (Shulman 391).

In the list of works cited, the work is alphabetized under Shulman, the author of the story, not under the name of the editor of the anthology.

> Shulman, Max. "Love Is a Fallacy." Current Issues and Enduring Questions, edited by Sylvan Barnet and Hugo Bedau, 9th ed., Bedford/St. Martin's, 2011, pp. 383-91.

13. Government source Your in-text citation should include the name of the country as well as the name of the agency responsible for the source (as given in the works cited entry). As for an organization as author, use common abbreviations in parentheses.

> To reduce the agricultural runoff into the Chesapeake Bay, the United States Environmental Protection Agency has argued that "[h]igh nutrient loading crops, such as corn and soybean, should be replaced with alternatives in environmentally sensitive areas" (26).

14. Entire work Use the author's name in a signal phrase or a parenthetical citation.

> Pollan explores the issues surrounding food production and consumption from a political angle.

15. Two or more sources in one citation List the authors (or titles) in alphabetical order and separate them with semicolons.

> Economists recommend that employment be redefined to include unpaid domestic labor (Clark 148; Nevins 39).

16. Personal communication or social media source Use the name of the author as given in the works cited list.

> According to @grammarphobia, the expression *if you will* "had a legitimate usage" before it became "empty filler."

17. Literary work Because literary works are often available in many different editions, cite the page number(s) from the edition you used followed by a semicolon; then give other identifying information that will lead readers to the passage in any edition. Indicate the act and/or scene in a play (e.g., 37; sc. 1). For a novel, indicate the part or chapter (e.g., 175; ch. 4).

> In utter despair, Dostoyevsky's character Mitya wonders aloud about the "terrible tragedies realism inflicts on people" (376; bk. 8, ch. 2).

For a poem, cite the part (if there is one) and line(s), separated by a period.

> Whitman speculates, "All goes onward and outward, nothing collapses, / And to die is different from what anyone supposed, and luckier" (6.129-30).

If you are citing only line numbers, use the word *line(s)* in the first reference (e.g., lines 21-22) and the line numbers alone in subsequent references (e.g., 34-36). For a verse play, give only the act, scene, and line numbers, separated by periods (e.g., 4.2.148-49).

18. Sacred text Give the title of the work as in the works cited entry, followed by the book, chapter, and verse (or their equivalent), separated with periods. Common abbreviations for books of the Bible are acceptable in a parenthetical reference.

> He ignored the admonition "Pride goes before destruction, and a haughty spirit before a fall" (*New Oxford Annotated Bible*, Prov. 16.18).

19. Encyclopedia or dictionary entry An entry in a reference work will be listed under the entry's title. Either in your text or in your parenthetical citation, mention the word or entry, enclosing it in quotation marks. Omit the page number if the reference work arranges entries alphabetically.

> The term *prion* was coined by Stanley B. Prusiner from the words *proteinaceous* and *infectious* and a suffix meaning *particle* ("Prion").

20. Visual To cite a visual that has a figure number in the source, use the abbreviation *fig.* and the number in place of a page number in your parenthetical citation: (Manning, fig. 4). If you refer to the figure in your text, spell out the word *figure*. To cite a visual that does not have a figure number in the source, use the visual's title or a description in your text and cite the author and page number as for any other source. Each visual that appears in your project should include a caption with the figure or table number (see p. 673) and information about the source.

21. Legal source For a legislative act (law) or court case, name the act or case either in a signal phrase or in parentheses. Italicize the names of cases but not the names of acts.

> The Jones Act of 1917 granted US citizenship to Puerto Ricans.

> In 1857, Chief Justice Roger B. Taney declared in *Dred Scott v. Sandford* that blacks, whether enslaved or free, could not be citizens of the United States.

23.3 Tutorial

MLA Works Cited List

An alphabetized list of works cited, which appears at the end of your project, gives publication information for each of the sources you have cited.

General Guidelines for the Works Cited List

In the list of works cited, include only sources that you have quoted, summarized, or paraphrased in your project. MLA's guidelines are applicable to a wide variety of sources. At times you may find that you have to adapt the guidelines and models in this section to source types you encounter in your research.

Organization of the List

The elements, or pieces of information, needed for a works cited entry are the following:

- The author (if a work has one)
- The title
- The title of the larger work in which the source is located (MLA calls this a "container")—a collection, a journal, a magazine, a website, and so on
- As much of the following information as is available about the source and the container, listed in this order:
  - Editor, translator, director, performer
  - Version
  - Volume and issue numbers
  - Publisher or sponsor
  - Date of publication
  - Location of the source: page numbers, DOI, URL, and so on

Not all sources will require every element. For more information on identifying and organizing source elements, see Unit 23.1 (p. 651). See specific models in this section for more details.

Authors

- Arrange the list alphabetically by authors' last names or by titles for works with no authors.

- For the first author, place the last name first, a comma, and the first name. Put a second author's name in normal order (first name followed by last name). For three or more authors, use *et al.* after the first author's name.

- Spell out *editor, translator, edited by,* and so on.

Titles

- In titles of works, capitalize all words except articles (*a, an, the*), prepositions, coordinating conjunctions, and the *to* in infinitives—unless the word is first or last in the title or subtitle.

- Use quotation marks for titles of articles and other short works.

- Italicize titles of books and other long works, including websites.

Publication Information

- MLA does not require the place of publication for a book publisher.

- Use the complete version of publishers' names, except for terms such as *Inc.* and *Co.*; retain terms such as *Books* and *Press.* For university publishers, use *U* and *P* for *University* and *Press,* respectively.

- For a book, take the name of the publisher from the title page (or from the copyright page if it is not on the title page). For a website, the publisher might be at the bottom of a page or on the *About* page. If a work has two or more publishers, separate the names with slashes.

- If the title of a website and the publisher are the same or similar, use the title of the site but omit the publisher.

Dates

- For a book, give the most recent year on the title page or the copyright page. For a web source, use the copyright date or the most recent update date. Use the complete date as listed in the source.

- Abbreviate all months except May, June, and July and give the date in inverted form: 13 Mar. 2018.
- If the source has no date, give your date of access at the end: Accessed 24 Feb. 2018.

Page Numbers

- For most articles and other short works, give page numbers when they are available in the source, preceded by *p.* (or *pp.* for more than one page).
- Do not use the page numbers from a printout of a source.
- If an article does not appear on consecutive pages, give the number of the first page followed by a plus sign: 35+.

URLs and DOIs

- Give a permalink or a DOI (digital object identifier) if a source has one. (See item 10.)
- If a source does not have a permalink or a DOI, include a URL (omitting the protocol, such as http://). (See item 9.)
- For a library's subscription database, such as Academic ASAP, that does not provide a permalink or a DOI, include only the basic URL for the database home page. (See the last example in item 9.)
- For open databases and archives, such as Google Books, give the complete URL for the source. (See item 32.)

General Guidelines for Listing Authors

Alphabetize entries in the list of works cited by authors' last names (or by title if a work has no author). The author's name is important because citations in the text refer to it and readers will therefore look for it to identify the source in the list.

1. Single author Give the author's last name, followed by a comma, then give the first name, followed by a period.

> Cronin, David.

2. Two authors List the authors in the order in which the source lists them. Reverse the name of only the first author.

> Stiglitz, Joseph E., and Bruce C. Greenwald.

3. Three or more authors List the author whose name appears first in the source followed by *et al.* (Latin for "and others").

> Lupton, Ellen, et al.

4. Organization or group author When the author is a corporation, a government agency, or some other organization, begin with the name of the organization.

> Human Rights Watch.

> United States, Government Accountability Office.

5. Unknown author Begin with the work's title. Titles of short works are put in quotation marks. Titles of long works are italicized.

> ### Article or Other Short Work
>
> "California Sues EPA over Emissions."
>
> ### Book, Entire Website, or Other Long Work
>
> *Women of Protest: Photographs from the Records of the National Woman's Party.*
>
> ### Television Program
>
> "Fast Times at West Philly High."

6. Author using a pseudonym (screen name) Use the author's name as it appears in the source, followed by the author's real name in parentheses, if you know it.

> Atrios (Duncan Black).

> JennOfArk.

7. Multiple works by the same author Alphabetize the works by title, ignoring the article *A*, *An*, or *The* at the beginning. Use the author's name for the first entry only. For subsequent entries, use three hyphens followed by a period.

> Coates, Ta-Nehisi. *The Beautiful Struggle: A Father, Two Sons, and an Unlikely Road to Manhood.* Spiegel and Grau, 2008.

> ---. *Between the World and Me.* Spiegel and Grau, 2015.

8. Multiple works by the same group of authors Alphabetize the works by title. For the first entry, use the authors' names in the proper form (see items 1–4). Begin subsequent entries with three hyphens and a period. The three hyphens must stand for the same names(s) as in the first entry.

Agha, Hussein, and Robert Malley. "The Arab Counterrevolution." *The New York Review of Books*, 29 Sept. 2011, www.nybooks.com/articles/2011/09/29/arab-counterrevolution/.

---. "This Is Not a Revolution." *The New York Review of Books*, 8 Nov. 2012, www.nybooks.com/articles/2012/11/08/not-revolution/.

Articles and Other Short Works

9. Article in a magazine Use the complete date given in the source.

Butler, Kiera. "Works Well with Others." *Mother Jones*, Jan./Feb. 2008, pp. 66-69.

Leonard, Andrew. "The Surveillance State High School." *Salon*, 27 Nov. 2012, www.salon.com/2012/11/27/the_surveillance_state_high_school/.

Sanneh, Kelefa. "Skin in the Game." *The New Yorker*, 24 Mar. 2014, pp. 48-55.

Sharp, Kathleen. "The Rescue Mission." *Smithsonian*, Nov. 2015, pp. 40-49. *OmniFile Full Text Select*, web.b.ebscohost.com.ezproxy.bpl.org/.

10. Article in a journal Give the volume number and issue number for all journals.

Bryson, Devin. "The Rise of a New Senegalese Cultural Philosophy?" *African Studies Quarterly*, vol. 14, no. 3, Mar. 2014, pp. 33-56, asq.africa.ufl.edu/files/Volume-14-Issue-3-Bryson.pdf.

Coles, Kimberly Anne. "The Matter of Belief in John Donne's Holy Sonnets." *Renaissance Quarterly*, vol. 68, no. 3, Fall 2015, pp. 899-931. *JSTOR*, doi:10.1086/683855.

Matchie, Thomas. "Law versus Love in *The Round House*." *Midwest Quarterly*, vol. 56, no. 4, Summer 2015, pp. 353-64.

11. Article in a daily newspaper

Salsberg, Bob. "Children's Wellness Initiative Unveiled." *Daily Hampshire Gazette*, 30 July 2019, pp. 1+.

Wolfers, Justin, et al. "1.5 Million Missing Black Men." *The New York Times*, 20 Apr. 2015, nyti.ms/1P5Gpa7.

12. Editorial in a newspaper Add the word *Editorial* after the title (and before any database information).

> "Lunar Landing a Shining Moment with Local Ties." *Daily Hampshire Gazette*, 20 July 2019, p. A6. Editorial.

> "The Road toward Peace." *The New York Times*, 15 Feb. 1945, p. 18. Editorial. *ProQuest Historical Newspapers: The New York Times*, search .proquest.com/hnpnewyorktimes.

13. Letter to the editor

> Starr, Evva. "Local Reporting Thrives in High Schools." *The Washington Post*, 4 Apr. 2014, wpo.st/7hmJ1. Letter.

14. Review Name the reviewer and the title of the review, if any, followed by the words *Review of* and the title and author or director of the work or performance reviewed. Then add information for the publication in which the review appears.

> O'Hehir, Andrew. "Aronofsky's Deranged Biblical Action Flick." Review of *Noah*, directed by Darren Aronofsky. *Salon*, 27 May 2014, www.salon.com/2014/03/27/noah_aronofskys_deranged_biblical _action_flick/.

> Spychalski, John C. Review of *American Railroads—Decline and Renaissance in the Twentieth Century*, by Robert E. Gallamore and John R. Meyer. *Transportation Journal*, vol. 54, no. 4, Fall 2015, pp. 535-38.

> Walton, James. "Noble, Embattled Souls." Review of *The Bone Clocks* and *Slade House*, by David Mitchell. *The New York Review of Books*, 3 Dec. 2015, pp. 55-58.

Books and Other Long Works

15. Basic format for a book For most books, supply the author name(s); the title and subtitle, in italics; the name of the publisher; and the year of publication. If you have used an e-book, give the e-reader type at the end of the entry.

> Wohlleben, Peter. *The Hidden Life of Trees*. William Collins, 2016. Kindle.

> Levs, Josh. *All In: How Our Work-First Culture Fails Dads, Families, and Businesses—and How We Can Fix It Together*. HarperCollins, 2015.

16. Author with an editor or translator

Ullmann, Regina. *The Country Road: Stories*. Translated by Kurt Beals, New
Directions Publishing, 2015.

17. Editor

Wall, Cheryl A., editor. *Changing Our Own Words: Essays on Criticism,
Theory, and Writing by Black Women*. Rutgers UP, 1989.

18. Work in an anthology or a collection
Begin with the name of the author of the
selection, not with the name of the anthology editor.

Sayrafiezadeh, Saïd. "Paranoia." *New American Stories*, edited by Ben
Marcus, Vintage Books, 2015, pp. 3-29.

19. Multiple works from the same anthology or collection
Provide an entry for the
entire anthology and a shortened entry for each selection. Alphabetize the entries by
authors' or editors' last names.

Eisenberg, Deborah. "Some Other, Better Otto." Marcus, pp. 94-136.

Marcus, Ben, editor. *New American Stories*. Vintage Books, 2015.

Sayrafiezadeh, Saïd. "Paranoia." Marcus, pp. 3-29.

20. Edition other than the first

Walker, John A. *Art in the Age of Mass Media*. 3rd ed., Pluto Press, 2001.

21. Multivolume work
Include the total number of volumes at the end of the
citation. If the volumes were published over several years, give the inclusive dates of
publication. If you cite only one of the volumes, include the volume number before
the publisher and give the date of publication for that volume.

Stark, Freya. *Letters*. Edited by Lucy Moorehead, Compton Press, 1974-82. 8 vols.

Stark, Freya. *Letters*. Edited by Lucy Moorehead, vol. 5, Compton Press,
1978. 8 vols.

22. Encyclopedia or dictionary entry

"House Music." *Wikipedia*, 16 Nov. 2015, en.wikipedia.org/wiki/
House_music.

Robinson, Lisa Clayton. "Harlem Writers Guild." *Africana: The Encyclopedia of the African and African American Experience*, 2nd ed., Oxford UP, 2005.

23. Sacred text Give the title of the edition of the sacred text (taken from the title page), italicized; the editor's or translator's name (if any); and publication information. Add the name of the version, if there is one, before the publisher.

The Oxford Annotated Bible with the Apocrypha. Edited by Herbert G. May and Bruce M. Metzger, Revised Standard Version, Oxford UP, 1965.

Qur'an: The Final Testament (Authorized English Version) with Arabic Text. Translated by Rashad Khalifa, Universal Unity, 2000.

24. Foreword, introduction, preface, or afterword Begin with the author of the book part, the part title (if any), and a label for the part. Then give the title of the book, the author or editor preceded by *by* or *edited by*, and publication information. If the part author and book author are the same, use only the last name with the book title.

Sullivan, John Jeremiah. "The Ill-Defined Plot." Introduction. *The Best American Essays 2014*, edited by Sullivan, Houghton Mifflin Harcourt, 2014, pp. xvii-xxvi.

25. Book with a title in its title If the book title contains a title normally italicized, do not italicize the title within the book title. If the book title contains a title normally placed in quotation marks, retain the quotation marks and italicize the entire title.

Lethem, Jonathan. *"Lucky Alan" and Other Stories.* Doubleday, 2015.

Masur, Louis P. *Runaway Dream:* Born to Run *and Bruce Springsteen's American Vision.* Bloomsbury, 2009.

26. Book in a series After the publication information, list the series name as it appears on the title page.

Denham, A. E., editor. *Plato on Art and Beauty.* Palgrave Macmillan, 2012. Philosophers in Depth.

27. Republished book After the title of the book, cite the original publication date, followed by the current publication information.

de Mille, Agnes. *Dance to the Piper.* 1951. Introduction by Joan Acocella, New York Review Books, 2015.

28. More than one publisher named If the book was published by two or more publishers, separate the publishers with a slash, and include a space before and after the slash.

> Hornby, Nick. *About a Boy*. Riverhead / Penguin Putnam, 1998.

29. Graphic narrative or illustrated work Begin with the author or illustrator who is most important to your research. List other contributors after the title, labeling their contribution. If the author and illustrator are the same, cite the work as you would cite a book.

> Stavans, Ilan, writer. *Latino USA: A Cartoon History*. Illustrated by Lalo
>   Arcaraz, Basic Books, 2000.

> Weaver, Dustin, illustrator. *The Tenth Circle*. By Jodi Picoult, Washington
>   Square Press, 2006.

Online Sources

30. Entire website If the website does not have an update date or publication date, include your date of access at the end (see the first example in item 31).

> Glazier, Loss Pequeño, director. *Electronic Poetry Center*. State U of New
>   York at Buffalo, 2019, epc.buffalo.edu/.

31. Short work from a website

> Bali, Karan. "Kishore Kumar." *Upperstall.com*, upperstall.com/profile/
>   kishore-kumar/. Accessed 2 Mar. 2016.

> Enzinna, Wes. "Syria's Unknown Revolution." *Pulitzer Center on
>   Crisis Reporting,* 24 Nov. 2015, pulitzercenter.org/projects/
>   middle-east-syria-enzinna-war-rojava.

32. Online book After the book publication information, include the title of the site in italics, the year of online publication, and the URL for the work.

> Euripides. *The Trojan Women*. Translated by Gilbert Murray, Oxford UP,
>   1915. Internet *Sacred Text Archive*, 2011, www.sacred-texts.com/cla/
>   eurip/troj_w.htm.

33. Entire blog Cite a blog as you would an entire website (see item 30).

> Kiuchi, Tatsuro. *Tatsuro Kiuchi: News & Blog*, tatsurokiuchi.com/. Accessed 3
>   Mar. 2016.

> Ng, Amy. *Pikaland*. Pikaland Media, 2015, www.pikaland.com/.

34. Entry or comment in a blog Cite a blog post as you would a short work from a website (see item 31). If you are citing a comment, list the screen name of the commenter, and use the label *Comment on* before the title of the blog post.

> Edroso, Roy. "Going Down with the Flagship." *Alicublog*, 24 Feb. 2016,
> alicublog.blogspot.com/2014/04/friends-in-high-places.html.

> trex. Comment on "Going Down with the Flagship," by Roy Edroso.
> *Alicublog*, 24 Feb. 2016, alicublog.blogspot.com/2016/02/going-down
> -with-flagship.html#disqus_thread.

35. Email

> Thornbrugh, Caitlin. "Coates Lecture." Received by Rita Anderson,
> 20 Oct. 2018.

36. Tweet Give the text of the entire tweet in quotation marks, using the writer's capitalization and punctuation. Follow the text with the date and time noted on the tweet, and end with the URL.

> @John Cleese. "Yes, I am still indeed alive, contrary to rumour, and
> am performing the silly walk in my new app (link: http://www
> .thesillywalk.com) thesillywalk.com." *Twitter*, 30 July 2019,
> twitter.com/JohnCleese.

37. Posting on a social networking site Cite as a short work from a website (see item 31). Use the text accompanying the post as the title, in quotation marks, if such text is available. If the post has no title or text, use the label *Post*.

> kevincannon. "Portrait of Norris Hall in #Savannah, GA—home (for a few
> more months, anyway) of #SCAD's sequential art department."
> *Instagram*, Mar. 2014, www.instagram.com/p/lgmqk4i6DC/.

Visual, Audio, Multimedia, and Live Sources

38. Work of art or photograph Cite the artist's name, the title of the artwork or photograph, italicized; the date of composition; and the institution and the city in which the artwork is located. For works located online, include the title of the site and the URL of the work. For a photograph, use the label *Photograph* at the end if it is not clear from the source.

> Bronzino, Agnolo. *Lodovico Capponi*. 1550-55, Frick Collection, New York.

Hura, Sohrab. *Old Man Lighting a Fire.* 2015, *Magnum Photos,*
www.magnumphotos.com/C.aspx?VP3=SearchResult
&ALID=2K1HRG681B_Q.

39. Cartoon or comic strip

Flake, Emily. *The New Yorker*, 13 Apr. 2015, p. 66. Cartoon.

Munroe, Randall. "Heartbleed Explanation." *xkcd.com*, xkcd.com/1354/.
Comic strip.

40. Advertisement

Ameritrade. *Wired*, Jan. 2014, p. 47. Advertisement.

Toyota. *The Root*. Slate Group, 28 Nov. 2015, www.theroot.com.
Advertisement.

41. Map or chart Cite as a short work within a longer work. If the title does not identify the item as a map or chart, add *Map* or *Chart* at the end of the entry.

"Australia." *Perry-Castañeda Library Map Collection*, U of Texas, 1999,
www.lib.utexas.edu/maps/australia/australia_pol99.jpg.

California. Rand McNally, 2002. Map.

42. Musical score

Beethoven, Ludwig van. Symphony no. 5 in C minor, op. 67. 1807. *Center
for Computer Assisted Research in the Humanities*, Stanford U, 2000,
scores.ccarh.org/beethoven/sym/beethoven-sym5-1.pdf.

43. Sound recording Begin with the name of the person or group you want to emphasize. For a single work from an album or collection, place the title in quotation marks and the album or collection in italics. For a long work, give the title, italicized; the names of pertinent artists; and the orchestra and conductor (if relevant). End with the manufacturer and the date.

Bach, Johann Sebastian. *Bach: Violin Concertos.* Performances by Itzhak
Perlman and Pinchas Zukerman, English Chamber Orchestra,
EMI, 2002.

Sonic Youth. "Incinerate." *Rather Ripped*, Geffen, 2006.

44. Film or video If you cite a particular person's work, start with that name. If not, start with the title of the film; then name the director, distributor, and year of release. Other contributors, such as writers or performers, may follow the director.

> Downey Jnr., Robert, performer. *Avengers: Endgame*. Directed by Anthony
> and Joe Russo, Walt Disney Studios Motion Pictures, 2019.

> Scott, Ridley, director. *The Martian*. Performances by Matt Damon, Jessica
> Chastain, Kristen Wiig, and Kate Mara, Twentieth Century Fox, 2015.

45. Supplementary material accompanying a film Begin with the title of the feature, in quotation marks, and the names of any important contributors. End with information about the film, as in item 44, and about the location of the supplementary material.

> "Sweeney's London." Produced by Eric Young. *Sweeney Todd: The Demon
> Barber of Fleet Street*, directed by Tim Burton, DreamWorks, 2007, disc 2.

46. Radio or television program If you are citing a particular episode or segment, begin with the title in quotation marks. Then give the program title in italics. List important contributors (narrator, writer, director, actors), the network, and the date of broadcast.

> "Free Speech on College Campuses." *Washington Journal*, narrated by Peter
> Slen, C-SPAN, 27 Nov. 2015.

> "Obama's Failures Have Made Millennials Give Up Hope." *The Rush
> Limbaugh Show*, narrated by Rush Limbaugh, Premiere Radio
> Networks, 14 Apr. 2014, www.rushlimbaugh.com/daily/2014/04/14/
> obama_s_failures_have_made_millennials_give_up_hope.

47. Radio or television interview Begin with the name of the person who was interviewed, followed by *Interview by* and the interviewer's name, if relevant. End with information about the program as in item 46.

> Wang, Lulu. Interview by Terry Gross. *Fresh Air*, WNYC, 26 July 2019.

48. Podcast Cite a podcast as you would a short work from a website (see item 31).

> McDougall, Christopher. "How Did Endurance Help Early Humans
> Survive?" *TED Radio Hour*, National Public Radio, 20 Nov.
> 2015, www.npr.org/2015/11/20/455904655/how-did
> -endurance-help-early-humans-survive.

49. Short online audio segment or video Cite a short online audio segment or video as you would a short work from a website (see item 31).

> Fletcher, Antoine. "The Ancient Art of the Atlatl." *Russell Cave National Monument*, narrated by Brenton Bellomy, National Park Service, 12 Feb. 2014, www.nps.gov/media/video/view.htm ?id=C92C0D0A-1DD8-B71C-07CBC6E8970CD73F.

> Nayar, Vineet. "Employees First, Customers Second." *YouTube*, 9 June 2015, www.youtube.com/watch?v=cCdu67s_C5E.

50. Live performance Begin with the title of the work performed and the author or composer of the work. Include relevant information such as the director, the choreographer, the conductor, or the major performers. End with the theater, ballet, or opera company, if any; the theater and location; and the date of the performance.

> Concerto for Trumpet and Orchestra. By Detlev Glanert, conducted by Andris Nelsons, performances by Thomas Rolfs and Boston Symphony Orchestra, Tanglewood Music Center, Lennox, 8 July 2019.

51. Lecture or public address Cite the speaker's name, followed by the title of the lecture (if any) in quotation marks, the organization sponsoring the lecture, the location, and the date.

> Ferrera, America. "My Identity Is a Superpower." *Ted.com*, Apr. 2019, www.ted.com/talks/america_ferrera_my_identity_is_a_superpower _not_an_obstacle.

> Eugenides, Jeffrey. Portland Arts and Lectures. Arlene Schnitzer Concert Hall, Portland, OR, 30 Sept. 2003.

52. Personal interview Begin with the name of the person interviewed. Then write *Personal interview* followed by the date of the interview.

> Freedman, Sasha. Personal interview, 10 Nov. 2018.

Other Sources

53. Government publication Treat the government agency as the author, giving the name of the government followed by the name of the department and agency.

> United States, Department of Health and Human Services. *Keep the Beat Recipes: Deliciously Healthy Dinners*. National Institutes of Health, Oct. 2009, healthyeating.nhlbi.nih.gov/pdfs/Dinners_Cookbook_508-compliant.pdf.

54. Legal source For a legislative act (law), give the name of the act, neither italicized nor in quotation marks, followed by the Public Law number, the Statutes at Large information, and the date of enactment.

> Museum and Library Services Act of 2003. Pub. L. 108-81. Stat. 117.991. 25 Sept. 2003.

For a court case, name the first plaintiff and the first defendant. Then give the law report number, the court name, the year of the decision, and publication information. In a works cited entry, the name of the case is not italicized. (The name of the case is italicized in your in-text citation.)

> Citizens United vs. FEC. 558 US 310. Supreme Court of the US. 2010. *Legal Information Institute*, Cornell U Law School, www.law.cornell.edu/supct/pdf/08-205P.ZS.

55. Pamphlet

> Rainie, Lee, and Maeve Duggan. *Privacy and Information Sharing*. Pew Research Center, 14 Jan. 2016, www.pewinternet.org/files/2016/01/PI_2016.01.14_Privacy-and-Info-Sharing_FINAL.pdf.

56. Dissertation

> Thompson, Brian. "I'm Better Than You and I Can Prove It: Games, Expertise and the Culture of Competition." Dissertation, Stanford U, 2015.

57. Published proceedings of a conference

> Meisner, Marx S., et al., editors. *Communication for the Commons: Revisiting Participation and Environment*. Proceedings of Twelfth Biennial Conference on Communication and the Environment, 6-11 June 2015, Swedish U of Agricultural Sciences. International Environmental Communication Association, 2015.

58. Published interview

> Blume, Judy. "Judy Blume in Conversation with Lena Dunham." Interview by Lena Dunham. *The Believer*, vol. 12, no. 1, Jan. 2014, pp. 39+.

59. Personal letter

> Primak, Shoshana. Letter to the author, 6 May 2019.

23.4 Tutorial

MLA-Style Formatting

The following guidelines are consistent with advice given in the *MLA Handbook*, 8th edition (2016), and with typical requirements for student projects. If you are creating a nonprint project or have formatting questions, it's always a good idea to check with your instructor before preparing your final draft.

Formatting an MLA Project

First page and title page.   The MLA does not require a title page. Type each of the following items on a separate line on the first page, beginning one inch from the top and flush with the left margin: your name, the instructor's name, the course name and number, and the date. Double-space between items; then doublespace again and center the title. Double-space between the title and the beginning of the text.

Margins and spacing.   Leave one-inch margins at the top and bottom and on both sides of each page. Double-space the entire text, including set-off quotations, notes, and the list of works cited. Indent the first line of a paragraph one-half inch.

Page numbers.   Include your last name and the page number on each page, one-half inch below the top and flush with the right margin.

Long quotations.   Set off a long quotation (one with more than four typed lines) in block format by starting it on a new line and indenting each line one-half inch from the left margin. Do not enclose the passage in quotation marks.

Headings.   MLA style allows, but does not require, headings. Many students and instructors find them helpful.

Visuals.   Place tables, photographs, drawings, charts, graphs, and other figures as near as possible to the relevant text. Tables should have a label and number (e.g., Table 1) and a clear caption. For a table that you have borrowed or adapted, give the source below the table in a note like the following:

> Source: Boris Groysberg and Michael Slind, "Leadership Is a Conversation," *Harvard Business Review*, June 2012, p. 83.

All other visuals should be labeled *Figure* (abbreviated *Fig.*), numbered, and captioned. The label and caption should appear on the same line, followed by the source information. Remember to refer to each visual in your text, indicating how it contributes to the point you are making.

Formatting an MLA Works Cited List

Begin the works cited list on a new page at the end of the project. Center the title *Works Cited* one inch from the top of the page. Double-space throughout.

Alphabetizing the list. Alphabetize the list by the last names of the authors (or editors); if a work has no author or editor, alphabetize by the first word of the title other than *A*, *An*, or *The*.

Indenting the entries. Do not indent the first line of each works cited entry, but indent any additional lines one-half inch.

Breaking URLs. If you need to include a URL in a works cited entry and it must be divided across lines, break it only after a slash or a double slash or before any other mark of punctuation. Do not add a hyphen. If you will post your project online or submit it electronically and you want your readers to click on your URLs, do not insert any line breaks.

Sample Pages from Student Writing in MLA Style

The following pages show samples from student writing using MLA style and following typical requirements for student projects.

Basic MLA Format

1"

Writer's last name and page number in upper right corner of each page

Dan Larson

Professor Duncan

English 102

19 April XXXX

Writer's name, instructor's name, course title, and date flush left on first page; title centered

The Transformation of Mrs. Peters:

An Analysis of "A Jury of Her Peers"

½" In Susan Glaspell's 1917 short story "A Jury of Her Peers," two women accompany their husbands and a county attorney to an isolated house where a farmer named John Wright has been choked to death in his bed with a rope. The chief suspect is Wright's wife, Minnie, who is in jail awaiting trial. The sheriff's wife, Mrs. Peters, has come along to gather some personal items for Minnie, and Mrs. Hale has joined her. Early in the story, Mrs. Hale sympathizes with Minnie and objects to the way the male investigators are "snoopin' round and criticizin' " her kitchen (249). In contrast, Mrs. Peters shows respect for the law, saying that the men are doing "no more than their duty" (249). By the end of the story, however, Mrs. Peters has joined Mrs. Hale in a conspiracy of silence, lied to the men, and committed a crime—hiding key evidence. What causes this dramatic change?

Double-spacing throughout

1"

Page numbers in parentheses for quotation from source

The first evidence that Mrs. Peters reaches understanding on her own surfaces in the following passage:

> The sheriff's wife had looked from the stove to the sink—to the pail of water which had been carried in from outside. . . . That look of seeing into things, of seeing through a thing to something else, was in the eyes of the sheriff's wife now. (251-52)

Something about the stove, the sink, and the pail of water connects with her own experiences, and she can imagine Minnie's life.

Title Page

1"

Name, instructor, course, and date aligned at left

Writer's name and page number in upper right corner

David Craig

Professor Turkman

English 219

18 December XXXX

Title centered

Messaging: The Language of Youth Literacy

The English language is under attack. At least, that is what many people seem to believe. From concerned parents to local librarians, everyone seems to have a negative comment on the state of youth literacy today. They fear that the current generation of grade school students will graduate with an extremely low level of literacy, and they point out that although language education hasn't changed, kids are having more trouble reading and writing than in the past. Many adults blame technologies such as texting and instant messaging. But although the arguments against messaging are passionate, evidence suggests that they may not hold up.

The disagreements about messaging shortcuts are profound, even among academics. John Briggs, an English professor at the University of California, Riverside, says, "Americans have always been informal, but now the informality of precollege culture is so ubiquitous that many students have no practice in using language in any formal setting at all" (qtd. in McCarroll). Such objections are not new; Sven Birkerts of Mount Holyoke College argued in 1999 that "[students] read more casually. They strip-mine what they read" online and consequently produce "quickly generated, casual prose" (qtd. in Leibowitz A67). However, academics are also among the defenders of texting and many recognize the power of informal language.

Indirect quotation uses *qtd. in* and author of Web source on list of works cited

Long Quotation

Two social enterprises, Nika Water and Belu, provide perfect examples. Both sell bottled water in the developed world with the mission of providing clean water to impoverished communities through their profits. Both have visionary leaders who define a critical lesson: financial pragmatism will add far more value to the world than idealistic dreams. Nika Water founder Jeff Church explained this in a speech at Stanford University:

> Social entrepreneurs look at their businesses as nine parts cause, one part business. In the beginning, it needs to be nine parts business, one part cause, because if the business doesn't stay around long enough because it can't make it, you can't do anything about the cause.

When U.K.-based Belu lost £600,000 ($940,000) in 2007, it could only give around £30,000 ($47,000) to charity. Karen Lynch took over as CEO, cutting costs, outsourcing significant parts of the company's operations, and redesigning the entire business model; the company now donates four times as much to charity (Hurley). The conventional portrayal of do-gooders is that they tend to be terrible businesspeople, an argument often grounded in reality. It is easy to criticize the Walmarts of the world for caring little about sustainability or social good, but the idealists with big visions who do not follow through on their promises because their businesses cannot survive are no more praiseworthy.

Walmart should learn from nonprofits and social enterprises how to advance a positive environmental and social agenda.

Long quotation indented ½" from left

Visual in Text (Created by Student)

Writer's name and page number in upper right corner

Discussion of findings presented in Fig. 2

My research shows that the popular messaging culture contains at least some elements of its own language (Fig. 2). It also seems that much of this language is new: no formal dictionary yet identifies the most common messaging words and phrases. Only in the heyday of the telegraph or on the rolls of a stenographer would you find a similar situation, but these "languages" were never a popular medium of youth communication. Texting and instant messaging, however, are very popular among young people and continue to generate attention and debate in academic circles.

Messaging is certainly widespread, and it does seem to have its own particular vocabulary, yet these two factors alone do not mean it has a damaging influence on youth literacy. As noted earlier, however, some people claim that the new technology is a threat to the English language.

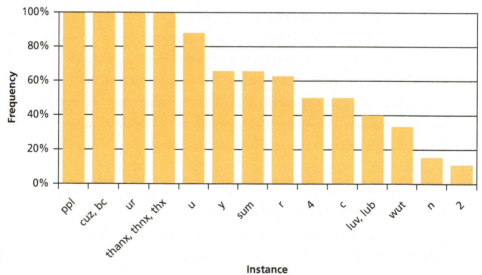

Figure labeled and captioned

Fig. 2. Usage of phonetic replacements and abbreviations in messaging

Visual in Text

The Bechdels' elaborately restored house is the gilded, but tense, context of young Alison's familial relationships and a metaphor for her father's deceptions. Alongside an image of her father taking a photo of their family, shown in Figure 2, Bechdel says, "He used his skillful artifice not to make things, but to make things appear to be what they were not" (*Fun* 16). The scene represents the nature of her father's artifice; her father is *posing* a photo, an image of their family.

Fig. 2. Alison's father posing a family photo
(Bechdel, *Fun* 16)

In that same scene, Bechdel also shows her own sleight of hand; she manipulates the scene and reverses her father's role and her own to show young Alison taking the photograph of the family and her father posing in Alison's place (Fig. 3). In the image, young Alison symbolizes Bechdel in the present—looking back through the camera lens to create a portrait of her family. But unlike her father, she isn't using false images to deceive. Bechdel overcomes the treason of images by confessing herself as an "artificer" to her audience (*Fun* 16). Bechdel doesn't villainize the illusory nature of images; she repurposes their illusory power to . . . reinterpret her memories.

Marginal notes:
Reference to figure in text

Figure number, caption, and source citation

Works Cited List

Title *Works Cited* centered

Works Cited

Gillmor, Dan. *We the Media: Grassroots Journalism by the People, for the People*. O'Reilly Media, 2006.

Glaser, Mark. "NOLA.com Blogs and Forums Help Save Lives after Katrina." *OJR: The Online Journalism Review*, Knight Digital Media Center, 13 Sept. 2005, www.ojr.org/050913glaser/.

List alphabetized by authors' last names (or by title when a work has no author)

Hazinski, David. "Unfettered 'Citizen Journalism' Too Risky." *Atlanta Journal-Constitution*, 13 Dec. 2007, p. 23A. *General OneFile*, go .galegroup.com/ps/.

Jones, Alex S. *Losing the News*: *The Future of the News That Feeds Democracy*. Oxford UP, 2009.

Double-spacing used throughout; first line of each entry at left margin, additional lines indented ½"

Sapin, Rachel. "Credit-Shy: Younger Generation Is More Likely to Stick to a Cash-Only Policy." *The Denver Post*, 26 Aug. 2013, www.denverpost.com/ci_23929523/credit-shy-younger -generation-stick-cash-only-policy.

"The 2006 Pulitzer Prize Winners: Public Service." *The Pulitzer Prizes*, Columbia U, www.pulitzer.org/prize-winners-by-year/2006. Accessed 21 Oct. 2013.

Access date used for a Web source that has no update date

Weinberger, David. "Transparency Is the New Objectivity." *Joho the Blog*, 19 July 2009, www.hyperorg.com/blogger/2009/07/19/ transparency-is-the-new-objectivity/.

Sample MLA Research Project

Benjy Mercer-Golden

Ms. Tavani

ENG 120

28 November XXXX

Name, instructor, course, and date aligned at left

Title centered

Lessons from Tree-Huggers and Corporate Mercenaries:

A New Model of Sustainable Capitalism

Televised images of environmental degradation—seagulls with oil coating their feathers, smokestacks belching gray fumes—often seem designed to shock, but these images also represent very real issues: climate change, dwindling energy resources like coal and oil, a scarcity of clean drinking water. In response, businesspeople around the world are thinking about how they can make their companies greener or more socially beneficial to ensure a brighter future for humanity. But progress in the private sector has been slow and inconsistent. To accelerate the move to sustainability, for-profit businesses need to learn from the hybrid model of social entrepreneurship to ensure that the company is efficient and profitable while still working for social change, and more investors need to support companies with long-term, revolutionary visions for improving the world.

In fact, both for-profit corporations and "social good" businesses could take steps to reshape their strategies. First, for-profit corporations need to operate sustainably and be evaluated for their performance with long-term measurements and incentives. The conventional argument against for-profit companies deeply embedding environmental and social goals into their corporate strategies is that caring about the world does not go hand in hand with lining pockets. This morally toxic case is also problematic from a business standpoint. A 2012 study of 180 high-profile companies by Harvard Business School professors

Robert G. Eccles and George Serafeim and London Business School professor Ioannis Ioannou shows that "high sustainability companies," as defined by environmental and social variables, "significantly outperform their counterparts over the long term, both in terms of stock market and accounting performance." The study argues that the better financial returns of these companies are especially evident in sectors where "companies' products significantly depend upon extracting large amounts of natural resources" (Eccles et al.).

Such empirical financial evidence to support a shift toward using energy from renewable sources to run manufacturing plants argues that executives should think more sustainably, but other underlying incentives need to evolve in order to bring about tangible change. David Blood and Al Gore of Generation Investment Management, an investment firm focused on "sustainable investing for the long term" ("About"), wrote a groundbreaking white paper that outlined the perverse incentives company managers face. For public companies, the default practice is to issue earnings guidances announcements of projected future earnings—every quarter. This practice encourages executives to manage for the short term instead of adding longterm value to their company and the earth (Gore and Blood). Only the most uncompromisingly green CEOs would still advocate for stricter carbon emissions standards at the company's factories if a few mediocre quarters left investors demanding that they be fired. Gore and Blood make a powerful case against subjecting companies to this "What have you done for me lately?" philosophy, arguing that quarterly earnings guidances should be abolished in favor of companies releasing information when they consider it appropriate. Companies also need to change the way the managers get paid. Currently, the CEO of ExxonMobil is rewarded for a highly profitable year but is not held accountable for depleting nonrenewable oil reserves. A new model

First author's name plus *et al.* for source with three or more authors

Shortened title for source with no author

Double-spaced throughout

should incentivize thinking for the long run. Multiyear milestones for performance evaluation, as Gore and Blood suggest, are essential to pushing executives to manage sustainably.

But it's not just for-profit companies that need to rethink strategies. Social good–oriented leaders also stand to learn from the people often vilified in environmental circles: corporate CEOs. To survive in today's economy, companies building sustainable products must operate under the same strict business standards as profit-driven companies. Two social enterprises, Nika Water and Belu, provide perfect examples. Both sell bottled water in the developed world with the mission of providing clean water to impoverished communities through their profits. Both have visionary leaders who define a critical lesson: financial pragmatism will add far more value to the world than idealistic dreams. Nika Water founder Jeff Church explained this in a speech at Stanford University:

> Social entrepreneurs look at their businesses as nine parts cause, one part business. In the beginning, it needs to be nine parts business, one part cause, because if the business doesn't stay around long enough because it can't make it, you can't do anything about the cause.

When UK-based Belu lost £600,000 ($940,000) in 2007, it could only give around £30,000 ($47,000) to charity. Karen Lynch took over as CEO, cutting costs, outsourcing significant parts of the company's operations, and redesigning the entire business model; the company now donates four times as much to charity (Hurley). The conventional portrayal of do-gooders is that they tend to be terrible businesspeople, an argument often grounded in reality. It is easy to criticize the Walmarts of the world for caring little about sustainability or social good, but the idealists with big visions who do not follow through on their promises because their businesses cannot survive are no more praiseworthy. Walmart should learn from nonprofits and social

Long quotation set off by ½" indent

enterprises on advancing a positive environmental and social agenda, but idealist entrepreneurs should also learn from corporations about building successful businesses.

The final piece of the sustainable business ecosystem is the investors who help get potentially world-changing companies off the ground. Industries that require a large amount of money to build complex products with expensive materials, such as solar power companies, rely heavily on investors—often venture capitalists based in California's Silicon Valley (Knight). The problem is that venture capitalists are not doing enough to fund truly groundbreaking companies. In an oft-cited blog post entitled "Why Facebook Is Killing Silicon Valley," entrepreneur Steve Blank argues that the financial returns on social media companies have been so quick and so outsized that the companies with the *really* big ideas—like providing efficient, cheap, scalable solar power—are not being backed: "In the past, if you were a great [venture capitalist], you could make $100 million on an investment in 5–7 years. Today, social media startups can return hundreds of millions or even billions in less than 3 years." The point Blank makes is that what is earning investors lots of money right now is not what is best for the United States or the world.

There are, however, signs of hope. Paypal founder Peter Thiel runs his venture capital firm, the Founders Fund, on the philosophy that investors should support "flying cars" instead of new social media ventures (Packer). While the next company with the next great social media idea might be both profitable and valuable, Thiel and a select few others fund technology that has the potential to solve the huge problems essential to human survival.

The world's need for sustainable companies that can build products from renewable energy or make nonpolluting cars will inevitably create opportunities for smart companies to make money.

No page number for unpaginated online source

In fact, significant opportunities already exist for venture capitalists willing to step away from what is easy today and shift their investment strategies toward what will help us continue to live on this planet tomorrow—even if seeing strong returns may take a few more years. Visionaries like Blank and Thiel need more allies (and dollars) in their fight to help produce more pioneering, sustainable companies. And global warming won't abate before investors wise up. It is vital that this shift happen now.

When we think about organizations today, we think about nonprofits, which have long-term social missions, and corporations, which we judge by their immediate financial returns like quarterly earnings. That is a treacherous dichotomy. Instead, we need to see the three major players in the business ecosystem—corporations, social enterprises, and investors—moving toward a *single* model of long-term, sustainable capitalism. We need visionary companies that not only set out to solve humankind's biggest problems but also have the business intelligence to accomplish these goals, and we need investors willing to fund these companies. Gore and Blood argue that "the imperative for change has never been greater." We will see this change when the world realizes that sustainable capitalism shares the same goals as creating a sustainable environment. Let us hope that this realization comes soon.

Works Cited List

Works Cited

Sources arranged alphabetically by authors' last names or by title for sources with no author

"About Us." *Generation*, 2012, www.generationim.com/about/.

Blank, Steve. "Why Facebook Is Killing Silicon Valley."

    Steveblank.com, 21 May 2012, steveblank.com/2012/05/21/

    why-facebook-is-killing-silicon-valley/.

Church, Jeff. "The Wave of Social Entrepreneurship." Entrepreneurial

    Thought Leaders Seminar, NVIDIA Auditorium, Stanford, 11 Apr.

    2012. Lecture.

Source with three or more authors listed by first author's name followed by *et al.*

Eccles, Robert G., et al. "The Impact of a Corporate Culture of

    Sustainability on Corporate Behavior and Performance." *Working*

    Knowledge, Harvard Business School, 14 Nov. 2011, hbswk.hbs

    .edu/item/the-impact-of-corporatesustainability-on-organizational

    -process-and-performance.

Gore, Al, and David Blood. "Sustainable Capitalism." *Generation*,

    15 Feb. 2012, www.generationim.com/media/pdf-generation

    -sustainable-capitalism-v1.pdf.

Full name of publication given, including article *The*

Hurley, James. "Belu Boss Shows Bottle for a Turnaround." *The Daily*

    Telegraph, www.telegraph.co.uk/finance/businessclub/9109449/

    Belu-boss-shows-bottle-for-a-turnaround.html.

Knight, Eric R. W. "The Economic Geography of Clean Tech Venture

    Capital." Oxford U Working Paper Series in Employment, Work,

    and Finance, 13 Apr. 2010. *Social Science Research Network*,

DOI used if a source has one

    doi:10.2139/ssrn.1588806.

Packer, George. "No Death, No Taxes: The Libertarian Futurism of a

Double-spacing used throughout; first line of each entry at left margin, subsequent lines indented ½"

    Silicon Valley Billionaire." *The New Yorker*, 28 Nov. 2011,

    www.newyorker.com/magazine/2011/11/28/no-death-no-taxes.

Works cited list starts on new page; title centered

TOPIC 24

APA Documentation

The models used in the following tutorials follow the updated guidelines in the *Publication Manual of the American Psychological Association*, 6th ed. (Washington: APA, 2010).

Navigating Topic 24

The tutorials listed below provide information about APA in-text citations, References lists, and formatting for papers. You can work through the entire Topic on your own, learning about all the strategies and practicing them; work on items you've been assigned by your instructor; or choose those ones you would find helpful.

Introduction to APA Style

The following are features of APA style that are represented in the examples in this topic's tutorials:

- Use the state abbreviation with all US cities or the country (not abbreviated) with non-US cities.

- In reference list entries for sources with up to seven authors, use all authors' names. For sources with eight or more authors, use the first six names followed by an ellipsis mark and the last author's name.

- Use the issue number with the volume number only for journals that begin each issue with page 1; use the volume number alone for journals that number pages consecutively through the entire volume.

- Make headings within an APA paper boldface.

24.1 Tutorial

Documenting Sources in APA Style

In most social science classes, you will be asked to use the APA system for documenting sources. APA recommends in-text citations that refer readers to a list of references.

An in-text citation gives the author of the source (often in a signal phrase), the year of publication, and at times a page number in parentheses. At the end of the paper, a list of references provides publication information for the source.

In-Text Citation

Yanovski and Yanovski (2002) reported that "the current state of the treatment for obesity is similar to the state of the treatment of hypertension several decades ago" (p. 600).

Entry in the List of References

Yanovski, S. Z., & Yanovski, J. A. (2002). Drug therapy: Obesity. *The New England Journal of Medicine, 346,* 591–602.

24.2 Tutorial

APA In-Text Citations

APA's in-text citations provide at least the author's last name and the year of publication. For direct quotations and some paraphrases, a page number is given as well.

NOTE: APA style requires the use of the past tense or the present perfect tense in signal phrases introducing cited material: Smith (2005) reported; Smith (2005) has argued.

Basic Format for a Quotation

Ordinarily, introduce the quotation with a signal phrase that includes the author's last name followed by the year of publication in parentheses. Put the page number (preceded by "p.") in parentheses after the quotation.

> Critser (2003) noted that despite growing numbers of overweight Americans, many health care providers still "remain either in ignorance or outright denial about the health danger to the poor and the young" (p. 5).

If the author is not named in the signal phrase, place the author's name, the year, and the page number in parentheses after the quotation: (Critser, 2003, p. 5).

NOTE: APA style requires the year of publication in an in-text citation. Do not include a month, even if the entry in the reference list includes the month.

Basic Format for a Summary or a Paraphrase

Include the author's last name and the year either in a signal phrase introducing the material or in parentheses following it. A page number is not required for a summary or a paraphrase, but include one if it would help readers find the passage in a long work.

> Yanovski and Yanovski (2002) explained that sibutramine suppresses appetite by blocking the reuptake of the neurotransmitters serotonin and norepinephrine in the brain (p. 594).

> Sibutramine suppresses appetite by blocking the reuptake of the neurotransmitters serotonin and norepinephrine in the brain (Yanovski & Yanovski, 2002, p. 594).

Directory to APA In-Text Citation Models

Guidelines for In-Text Citations

1. Work with two authors Name both authors in the signal phrase or the parentheses each time you cite the work. In the parentheses, use "&" between the authors' names; in the signal phrase, use "and."

> According to Sothern and Gordon (2003), "Environmental factors may contribute as much as 80% to the causes of childhood obesity" (p. 104).

> Obese children often engage in limited physical activity (Sothern & Gordon, 2003, p. 104).

2. Work with three to five authors Identify all authors in the signal phrase or the parentheses the first time you cite the source.

> In 2003, Berkowitz, Wadden, Tershakovec, and Cronquist concluded, "Sibutramine . . . must be carefully monitored in adolescents, as in adults, to control increases in [blood pressure] and pulse rate" (p. 1811).

In subsequent citations, use the first author's name followed by "et al." in either the signal phrase or the parentheses.

> As Berkowitz et al. (2003) advised, "Until more extensive safety and efficacy data are available, . . . weight-loss medications should be used only on an experimental basis for adolescents" (p. 1811).

3. Work with six or more authors Use the first author's name followed by "et al." in the signal phrase or the parentheses.

> McDuffie et al. (2002) tested 20 adolescents, aged 12–16, over a three-month period and found that orlistat, combined with behavioral therapy, produced an average weight loss of 4.4 kg, or 9.7 pounds (p. 646).

4. Work with unknown author If the author is unknown, mention the work's title in the signal phrase or give the first word or two of the title in the parenthetical citation. Titles of articles and chapters are put in quotation marks; titles of books and reports are italicized. (For online sources with no author, see item 12.)

> Children struggling to control their weight must also struggle with the pressures of television advertising that, on the one hand, encourages the consumption of junk food and, on the other, celebrates thin celebrities ("Television," 2002).

NOTE: In the rare case when "Anonymous" is specified as the author, treat it as if it were a real name: (Anonymous, 2001). In the list of references, also use the name Anonymous as author.

5. Organization as author If the author is a government agency or another organization, name the organization in the signal phrase or in the parenthetical citation the first time you cite the source.

> Obesity puts children at risk for a number of medical complications, including type 2 diabetes, hypertension, sleep apnea, and orthopedic problems (Henry J. Kaiser Family Foundation, 2004, p. 1).

If the organization has a familiar abbreviation, you may include it in brackets the first time you cite the source and use the abbreviation alone in later citations.

> **First Citation**   (Centers for Disease Control and Prevention [CDC], 2009)
>
> **Later Citations**   (CDC, 2009)

6. Authors with the same last name To avoid confusion, use initials with the last names if your reference list includes two or more authors with the same last name.

> Research by E. Smith (1989) revealed that . . .

7. Two or more works by the same author in the same year When your list of references includes more than one work by the same author in the same year, use lower-case letters ("a," "b," and so on) with the year to order the entries in the reference list. (See item 6 in the reference list section below.) Use those same letters with the year in the in-text citation.

> Research by Durgin (2003b) has yielded new findings about the role of counseling in treating childhood obesity.

8. Two or more works in the same parentheses When your parenthetical citation names two or more works, put them in the same order that they appear in the reference list, separated with semicolons.

> Researchers have indicated that studies of pharmacological treatments for childhood obesity are inconclusive (Berkowitz et al., 2003; McDuffie et al., 2002).

9. Personal communication Personal interviews, memos, letters, email, and similar unpublished communications should be cited in the text only, not in the reference list. (Use the first initial with the last name in parentheses.)

> One of Atkinson's colleagues, who has studied the effect of the media on children's eating habits, has contended that advertisers for snack foods will need to design ads responsibly for their younger viewers (F. Johnson, personal communication, October 20, 2009).

10. Indirect source If you use a source that was cited in another source (a secondary source), name the original source in your signal phrase. List the secondary source in your reference list and include it in your parenthetical citation, preceded by the words "as cited in." In the following example, Satcher is the original source, and Critser is the secondary source, given in the reference list.

> Former surgeon general Dr. David Satcher described "a nation of young people seriously at risk of starting out obese and dooming themselves to the difficult task of overcoming a tough illness" (as cited in Critser, 2003, p. 4).

11. Sacred or classical text Identify the text, the version or edition you used, and the relevant part (chapter, verse, line). It is not necessary to include the source in the reference list.

> Peace activists have long cited the biblical prophet's vision of a world without war: "And they shall beat their swords into plowshares, and their spears into pruning hooks; nation shall not lift up sword against nation, neither shall they learn war any more" (Isaiah 2:4, Revised Standard Version).

12. Electronic source When possible, cite electronic sources, including online sources, as you would any other source, giving the author and the year.

> Atkinson (2001) found that children who spent at least four hours a day watching TV were less likely to engage in adequate physical activity during the week.

Electronic sources sometimes lack authors' names, dates, or page numbers.

- **Unknown author.** If no author is named, mention the title of the source in the signal phrase or give the first word or two of the title in the parentheses (see also item 4). (If an organization serves as the author, see item 5.)

The body's basal metabolic rate, or BMR, is a measure of its at-rest energy requirement ("Exercise," 2003).

- **Unknown date.** When the date is unknown, use the abbreviation "n.d." (for "no date").

    Attempts to establish a definitive link between television programming and children's eating habits have been problematic (Magnus, n.d.).

- **No page numbers.** APA ordinarily requires page numbers for quotations, and it recommends them for summaries and paraphrases from long sources. When an electronic source lacks stable numbered pages, your citation should include information that will help readers locate the particular passage being cited.

    If the source has numbered paragraphs, use the paragraph number preceded by the abbreviation "para.": (Hall, 2008, para. 5). If the source contains headings, cite the appropriate heading in parentheses; you may also indicate the paragraph under the heading that you are referring to, even if the paragraphs are not numbered.

    Hoppin and Taveras (2004) pointed out that several other medications were classified by the Drug Enforcement Administration as having the "potential for abuse" (Weight-Loss Drugs section, para. 6).

NOTE: Electronic files in portable document format (PDF) often have stable page numbers. For such sources, give the page number in the parenthetical citation.

24.3 Tutorial

APA Reference List

In APA style, the alphabetical list of works cited, which appears at the end of the paper, is titled "References." For advice on preparing the reference list, see Preparing the List of References on page 717. For a sample reference list, see the student essay on page 719.

Alphabetize entries in the list of references by authors' last names; if a work has no author, alphabetize it by its title. The first element of each entry is important because citations in the text of the paper refer to it and readers will be looking for it in the alphabetized list. The date of publication appears immediately after the first element of the citation.

In APA style, titles of books are italicized; titles of articles are neither italicized nor put in quotation marks. (For rules on capitalization of titles, see APA-Style Formatting on p. 715.)

General Guidelines for Listing Authors (Print and Online)

In APA style, all authors' names are inverted (the last name comes first), and initials only are used for all first and middle names.

Name and Date Cited in Text

Duncan (2008) has reported that . . .

Beginning of Entry in the List of References

Duncan, B. (2008).

1. Single author

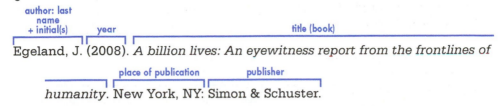

> author: last name + initial(s)   year   title (book)
>
> Egeland, J. (2008). *A billion lives: An eyewitness report from the frontlines of*
>
> place of publication   publisher
>
> *humanity.* New York, NY: Simon & Schuster.

2. Multiple authors List up to seven authors by last names followed by initials. Use an ampersand (&) before the name of the last author. If there are more than seven authors, list the first six followed by three ellipsis dots and the last author's name.

Two to Seven Authors

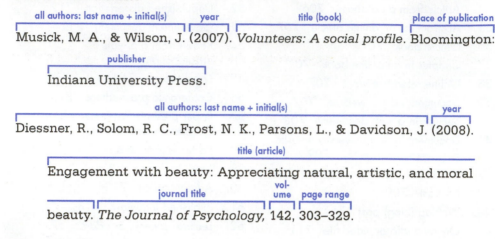

all authors: last name + initial(s) — year — title (book) — place of publication

Musick, M. A., & Wilson, J. (2007). *Volunteers: A social profile*. Bloomington:

publisher

Indiana University Press.

all authors: last name + initial(s) — year

Diessner, R., Solom, R. C., Frost, N. K., Parsons, L., & Davidson, J. (2008).

title (article)

Engagement with beauty: Appreciating natural, artistic, and moral

journal title — volume — page range

beauty. *The Journal of Psychology, 142,* 303–329.

Eight or More Authors

Mulvaney, S. A., Mudasiru, E., Schlundt, D. G., Baughman, C. L., Fleming,
M., VanderWoude, A., . . . Rothman, R. (2008). Self-management in Type
2 diabetes: The adolescent perspective. *The Diabetes Educator, 34,*
118–127.

3. Organization as author

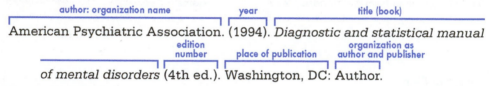

author: organization name — year — title (book)

American Psychiatric Association. (1994). *Diagnostic and statistical manual*

edition number — place of publication — organization as author and publisher

of mental disorders (4th ed.). Washington, DC: Author.

If the publisher is not the same as the author, give the publisher's name as you would
for any other source.

4. Unknown author Begin the entry with the work's title.

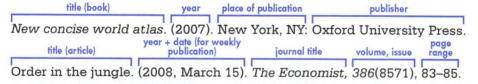

title (book) — year — place of publication — publisher

New concise world atlas. (2007). New York, NY: Oxford University Press.

title (article) — year + date (for weekly publication) — journal title — volume, issue — page range

Order in the jungle. (2008, March 15). *The Economist, 386*(8571), 83–85.

5. Two or more works by the same author Use the author's name for all entries. List
the entries by year, the earliest first.

Barry, P. (2007, December 8). Putting tumors on pause. *Science News, 172,* 365.

Barry, P. (2008, August 2). Finding the golden genes. *Science News, 174,*
16–21.

6. Two or more works by the same author in the same year List the works alphabetically by title. In the parentheses, following the year, add "a," "b," and so on. Use these same letters when giving the year in the in-text citation.

Elkind, D. (2008a, Spring). Can we play? *Greater Good, 4*(4), 14–17.

Elkind, D. (2008b, June 27). The price of hurrying children [Web log message]. Retrieved from http://blogs.psychologytoday.com/blog/digital-children

Articles in Periodicals (Print)

Periodicals include scholarly journals, magazines, and newspapers. For a journal or a magazine, give only the volume number if the publication is paginated continuously through each volume; give the volume and issue numbers if each issue of the volume begins on page 1. Italicize the volume number and put the issue number, not italicized, in parentheses.

For all periodicals, when an article appears on consecutive pages, provide the range of pages. When an article does not appear on consecutive pages, give all page numbers: A1, A17. (See also Online Sources on p. 704 for online articles and articles accessed through a library's database.) For an illustrated citation of an article in a periodical, see Citation at a Glance: Article in a Periodical (APA) on page 698.

APA Citation at a Glance Article in a Periodical

To cite an article in a print periodical in APA style, include the following elements:

1 Author

2 Year of publication

3 Title of article

4 Name of periodical

5 Volume number; issue number, if required

6 Page numbers of article

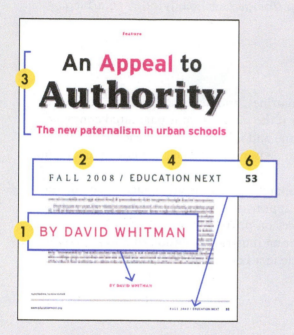

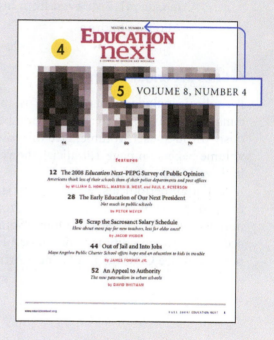

Reference List Entry for an Article in a Print Periodical

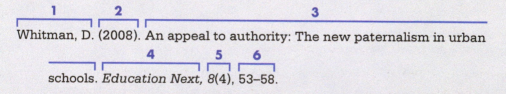

Whitman, D. (2008). An appeal to authority: The new paternalism in urban

schools. *Education Next, 8*(4), 53–58.

Give the year, month, and day for daily and weekly newspapers. Use "p." or "pp." before page(s). For variations on citing articles in print periodicals in APA style, see items 7–16 on the following pages.

7. Article in a journal

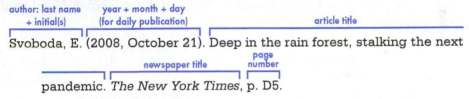

Zhang, L. F. (2008). Teachers' styles of thinking: An exploratory study. *The Journal of Psychology, 142*, 37–55.

8. Article in a magazine
Cite as a journal article, but give the year and the month for monthly magazines; add the day for weekly magazines.

McKibben, B. (2007, October). Carbon's new math. *National Geographic, 212*(4), 32–37.

9. Article in a newspaper

Svoboda, E. (2008, October 21). Deep in the rain forest, stalking the next pandemic. *The New York Times*, p. D5.

10. Article with three to seven authors

Ungar, M., Brown, M., Liebenberg, L., Othman, R., Kwong, W. M., Armstrong, M., & Gilgun, J. (2007). Unique pathways to resilience across cultures. *Adolescence, 42*, 287–310.

11. Article with eight or more authors
List the first six authors followed by three ellipsis dots and the last author.

Krippner, G., Granovetter, M., Block, F., Biggart, N., Beamish, T., Hsing, Y., . . . O'Riain, S. (2004). Polanyi Symposium: A conversation on embeddedness. *Socio-Economic Review, 2*, 109–135.

12. Abstract of a journal article [Abstract]

Lahm, K. (2008). Inmate-on-inmate assault: A multilevel examination of prison violence [Abstract]. *Criminal Justice and Behavior, 35*(1), 120–137.

13. Letter to the editor Letters to the editor appear in journals, magazines, and news-papers. Follow the appropriate model (see items 7–9), and insert the words "Letter to the editor" in brackets after the title of the letter. If the letter has no title, use the bracketed words as the title.

> Park, T. (2008, August). Defining the line [Letter to the editor]. *Scientific American, 299*(2), 10.

14. Editorial or other unsigned article [Editorial]

> The global justice movement [Editorial]. (2005). *Multinational Monitor, 26*(7/8), 6.

15. Newsletter article

> Setting the stage for remembering. (2006, September). *Mind, Mood, and Memory, 2*(9), 4–5.

16. Review Give the author and title of the review (if any) and, in brackets, the type of work, the title, and the author for a book or the year for a motion picture. If the review has no author or title, use the material in brackets as the title.

> Applebaum, A. (2008, February 14). A movie that matters [Review of the motion picture *Katyn*, 2007]. *The New York Review of Books, 55*(2), 13–15.

> Agents of change. (2008, February 2). [Review of the book *The power of unreasonable people: How social entrepreneurs create markets that change the world*, by J. Elkington & P. Hartigan]. *The Economist, 386*(8565), 94.

Books (Print)

Items 17–29 apply to print books. For online books, see items 36 and 37. Take the information about a book from its title page and copyright page. If more than one place of publication is listed, use only the first. Give the city and state (abbreviated) for all US cities or the city and country (not abbreviated) for all non-US cities; also include the province for Canadian cities. Do not give a state if the publisher's name includes it (as in many university presses, for example).

APA Citation at a Glance Book

To cite a print book in APA style, include the following elements:

1 Author
2 Year of publication
3 Title and subtitle
4 Place of publication
5 Publisher

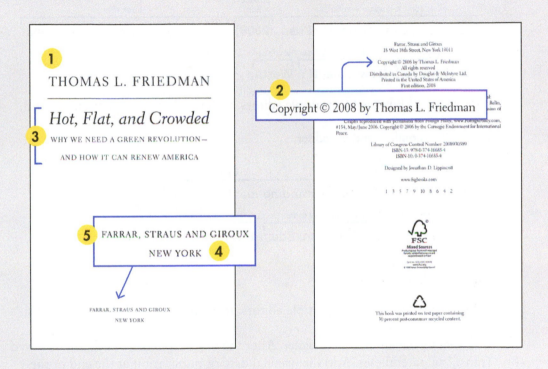

Reference List Entry for a Print Book

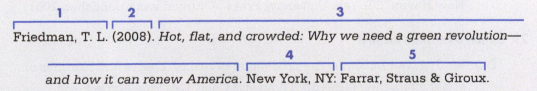

Friedman, T. L. (2008). *Hot, flat, and crowded: Why we need a green revolution—*

and how it can renew America. New York, NY: Farrar, Straus & Giroux.

For more on citing print books in APA style, see items 17–29.

17. Basic format for a book

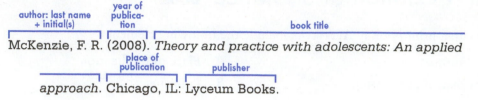

McKenzie, F. R. (2008). *Theory and practice with adolescents: An applied approach.* Chicago, IL: Lyceum Books.

18. Book with an editor

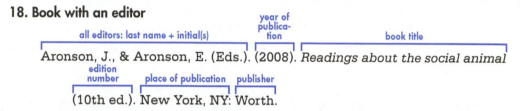

Aronson, J., & Aronson, E. (Eds.). (2008). *Readings about the social animal* (10th ed.). New York, NY: Worth.

The abbreviation "Eds." is for multiple editors. If the book has one editor, use "Ed."

19. Book with an author and an editor

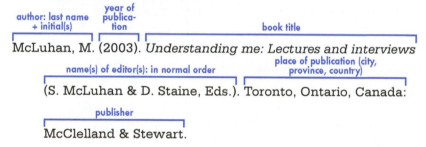

McLuhan, M. (2003). *Understanding me: Lectures and interviews* (S. McLuhan & D. Staine, Eds.). Toronto, Ontario, Canada: McClelland & Stewart.

The abbreviation "Eds." is for multiple editors. If the book has one editor, use "Ed."

20. Book with an author and a translator
After the title, name the translator, followed by "Trans.," in parentheses. Add the original date of publication at the end of the entry.

Steinberg, M. D. (2003). *Voices of revolution, 1917* (M. Schwartz, Trans.). New Haven, CT: Yale University Press. (Original work published 2001)

21. Edition other than the first

O'Brien, J. A. (Ed.). (2006). *The production of reality: Essays and readings on social interaction* (4th ed.). Thousand Oaks, CA: Pine Forge Press.

22. Article or chapter in an edited book or an anthology

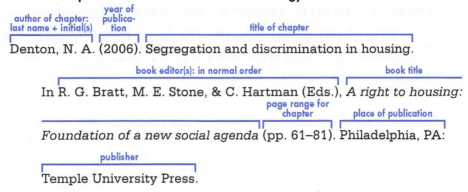

Denton, N. A. (2006). Segregation and discrimination in housing.

In R. G. Bratt, M. E. Stone, & C. Hartman (Eds.), *A right to housing:*

Foundation of a new social agenda (pp. 61–81). Philadelphia, PA:

Temple University Press.

The abbreviation "Eds." is for multiple editors. If the book has one editor, use "Ed."

23. Multivolume work Give the number of volumes after the title.

Luo, J. (Ed.). (2005). *China today: An encyclopedia of life in the People's*
Republic (Vols. 1–2). Westport, CT: Greenwood Press.

24. Introduction, preface, foreword, or afterword

Gore, A. (2000). Foreword. In B. Katz (Ed.), *Reflections on regionalism*
(pp. ix–x). Washington, DC: Brookings Institution Press.

25. Dictionary or other reference work

Leong, F. T. L. (Ed.). (2008). *Encyclopedia of counseling* (Vols. 1–4). Thousand
Oaks, CA: Sage.

26. Article in a reference work

Konijn, E. A. (2008). Affects and media exposure. In W. Donsbach (Ed.), *The*
international encyclopedia of communication (Vol. 1, pp. 123–129). Malden,
MA: Blackwell.

27. Republished book

Mailer, N. (2008). *Miami and the siege of Chicago: An informal history of the*
Republican and Democratic conventions of 1968. New York, NY: New
York Review Books. (Original work published 1968)

28. Book with a title in its title If the book title contains another book title or an article title, neither italicize the internal title nor place it in quotation marks.

> Marcus, L. (Ed.). (1999). *Sigmund Freud's* The interpretation of dreams*: New interdisciplinary essays*. Manchester, England: Manchester University Press.

29. Sacred or classical text It is not necessary to list sacred works such as the Bible or the Qur'an or classical Greek and Roman works in your reference list. See item 11 on page 692 for how to cite these sources in the text of your paper.

Online Sources

When citing an online article, include publication information as for a print periodical (see items 7–16) and add information about the online version (see items 30–35).

Online articles and books sometimes include a DOI (digital object identifier). APA uses the DOI, when available, in place of a URL in reference list entries.

Use a retrieval date for an online source only if the content is likely to change. Most of the examples in this section do not show a retrieval date because the content of the sources is stable; if you are unsure about whether to use a retrieval date, include the date or consult your instructor.

If you must break a DOI or a URL at the end of a line, break it after a double slash or before any other mark of punctuation; do not add a hyphen. Do not put a period at the end of the entry.

APA Citation at a Glance   Article from a Database

To cite an article from a database in APA style, include the following elements:

1 Author(s)

2 Date of publication

3 Title of article

4 Name of periodical

5 Volume number; issue number, if required

6 Page range

7 DOI (digital object identifier)

8 URL for journal's home page (if there is no DOI)

On-Screen View of Database Record

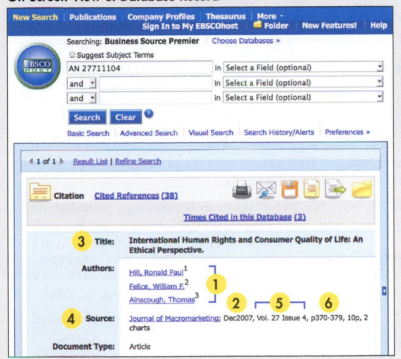

End of Database Record

Reference List Entry for an Article from a Database

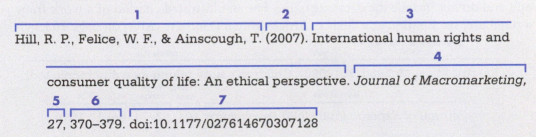

For more on citing articles from a database in APA style, see item 34.

30. Article in an online journal

Whitmeyer, J. M. (2000). Power through appointment. *Social Science Research, 29*, 535–555. doi:10.1006/ssre.2000.0680

If there is no DOI, include the URL for the journal's home page.

Ashe, D. D., & McCutcheon, L. E. (2001). Shyness, loneliness, and attitude toward celebrities. *Current Research in Social Psychology, 6*, 124–133. Retrieved from http://www.uiowa.edu/~grpproc/crisp/crisp.html

31. Article in an online magazine
Treat as an article in a print magazine (see item 8), and add the URL for the magazine's home page.

Shelburne, E. C. (2008, September). The great disruption. *The Atlantic, 302*(2). Retrieved from http://www.theatlantic.com/

32. Article in an online newspaper
Treat as an article in a print newspaper (see item 9), adding the URL for the newspaper's home page.

Watson, P. (2008, October 19). Biofuel boom endangers orangutan habitat. *Los Angeles Times*. Retrieved from http://www.latimes.com/

33. Article published only online
If an article in a journal, magazine, or newspaper appears only online, give whatever publication information is available in the source and add the description "Supplemental material" in brackets following the article title.

Samuel, T. (2009, March 27). Mind the wage gap [Supplemental material]. *The American Prospect*. Retrieved from http://www.prospect.org/

34. Article from a database
Start with the publication information for the source (see items 7–16). If the database entry gives a DOI for the article, use that number at the end and do not include the database name. For an illustrated citation of a work from a database, see Citation at a Glance: Article from a Database (APA) on page 705.

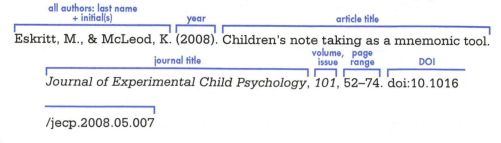

Eskritt, M., & McLeod, K. (2008). Children's note taking as a mnemonic tool. *Journal of Experimental Child Psychology, 101*, 52–74. doi:10.1016/jecp.2008.05.007

If there is no DOI, include the URL for the home page of the journal.

> Howard, K. R. (2007). Childhood overweight: Parental perceptions and readiness for change. *The Journal of School Nursing, 23*, 73–79. Retrieved from http://jsn.sagepub.com/

35. Abstract for an online article

> Brockerhoff, E. G., Jactel, H., Parrotta, J. A., Quine, C. P., & Sayer, J. (2008). Plantation forests and biodiversity: Oxymoron or opportunity? [Abstract]. *Biodiversity and Conservation, 17*, 925–951. doi:10.1007/s10531-008-9380-x

36. Online book

> Adams, B. (2004). *The theory of social revolutions.* Retrieved from http://www.gutenberg.org/catalog/world/readfile?fk_files=44092 (Original work published 1913)

37. Chapter in an online book

> Clinton, S. J. (1999). What can be done to prevent childhood obesity? In *Understanding childhood obesity* (pp. 81–98). Retrieved from http://www.questia.com/

38. Online reference work

> Swain, C. M. (2004). Sociology of affirmative action. In N. J. Smelser & P. B. Baltes (Eds.), *International encyclopedia of the social and behavioral sciences.* Retrieved from http://www.sciencedirect.com/science/referenceworks/9780080430768

Use a retrieval date only if the content of the work is likely to change.

39. Document from a website List as many of the following elements as are available: author's name, publication date (or "n.d." if there is no date), title (in italics), and URL. Give your retrieval date only if the content of the source is likely to change.

Source with Date

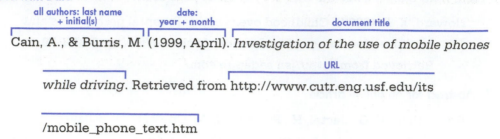

Cain, A., & Burris, M. (1999, April). *Investigation of the use of mobile phones while driving*. Retrieved from http://www.cutr.eng.usf.edu/its/mobile_phone_text.htm

Source with No Date

Archer, D. (n.d.). *Exploring nonverbal communication*. Retrieved from http://nonverbal.ucsc.edu

Source with No Author

If a source has no author, begin with the title and follow it with the date in parentheses.

What causes Alzheimer's disease. (2008). Retrieved from http://www.memorystudy.org/alzheimers_causes.htm

40. Section in a web document

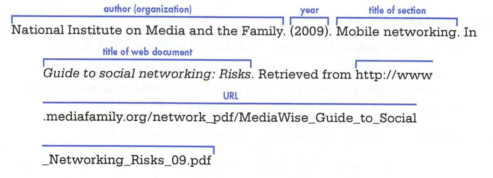

National Institute on Media and the Family. (2009). Mobile networking. In *Guide to social networking: Risks*. Retrieved from http://www.mediafamily.org/network_pdf/MediaWise_Guide_to_Social_Networking_Risks_09.pdf

For an illustrated citation of a section in a web document, see Citation at a Glance: Section in a Web Document (APA) on page 710.

41. Document from a university website or government agency Name the organization or agency in your retrieval statement.

> Cosmides, L., & Tooby, J. (1997). *Evolutionary psychology: A primer*. Retrieved from University of California, Santa Barbara, Center for Evolutionary Psychology website: http://www.psych.ucsb.edu /research/cep/primer.html

42. Article in an online newsletter Cite as an online article (see items 30–32), giving the title of the newsletter and whatever other information is available, including volume and issue numbers.

> In the face of extinction. (2008, May). *NSF Current*. Retrieved from http:// www.nsf.gov/news/newsletter/may_08/index.jsp

43. Podcast

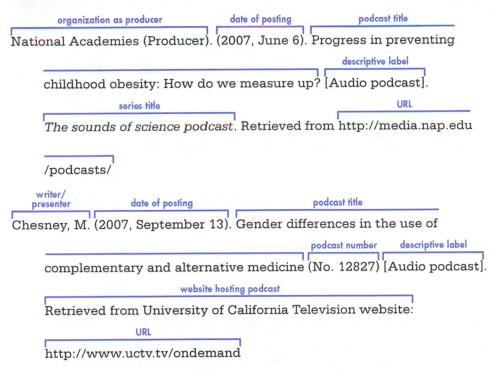

APA Citation at a Glance Section in a Document on a Website

To cite a section in a web document in APA style, include the following elements:

1 Author

2 Date of publication or most recent update

3 Title of section

4 Title of document

5 URL of section

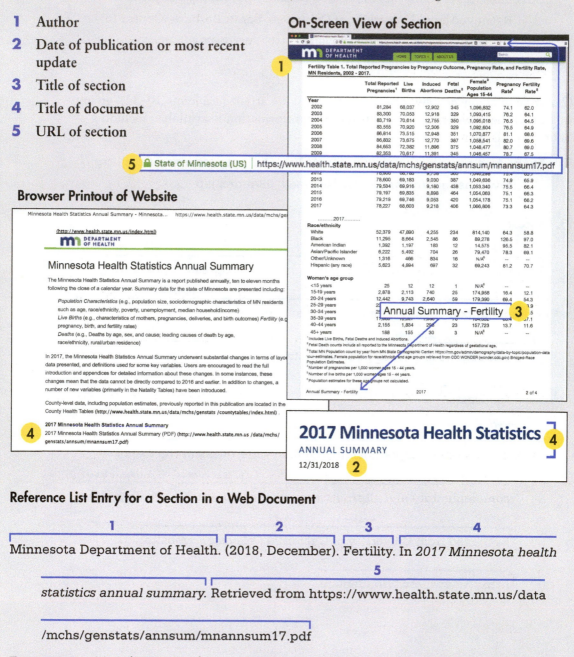

On-Screen View of Section

1 Fertility Table 1. Total Reported Pregnancies by Pregnancy Outcome, Pregnancy Rate, and Fertility Rate, MN Residents, 2002 - 2017.

Year	Total Reported Pregnancies[1]	Live Births[1]	Induced Abortions[1]	Fetal Deaths[2]	Female[3] Population Ages 15-44	Pregnancy Rate[4]	Fertility Rate[5]
2002	81,284	68,037	12,902	345	1,096,832	74.1	62.0
2003	83,300	70,053	12,918	329	1,093,415	76.2	64.1
2004	83,719	70,614	12,755	350	1,095,018	76.5	64.5
2005	83,555	70,920	12,306	329	1,092,604	76.5	64.9
2006	86,614	73,515	12,948	351	1,070,877	81.1	68.6
2007	86,832	73,675	12,770	387	1,058,541	82.0	69.6
2008	84,653	72,382	11,896	375	1,048,477	80.7	69.0
2009	82,353	70,617	11,391	345	1,046,457	78.7	67.5

5 🔒 State of Minnesota (US) | https://www.health.state.mn.us/data/mchs/genstats/annsum/mnannsum17.pdf

2012	78,900	68,783	9,758	359	1,046,298	73.4	65.7
2013	78,600	69,183	9,030	387	1,049,636	74.9	65.9
2014	79,534	69,916	9,180	438	1,053,340	75.5	66.4
2015	79,197	69,835	8,898	464	1,054,063	75.1	66.3
2016	79,219	69,746	9,053	420	1,054,178	75.1	66.2
2017	78,227	68,603	9,218	406	1,066,806	73.3	64.3

.........2017.........

Race/ethnicity

White	52,379	47,890	4,255	234	814,140	64.3	58.8
Black	11,295	8,664	2,545	86	89,278	126.5	97.0
American Indian	1,392	1,197	183	12	14,575	95.5	82.1
Asian/Pacific Islander	6,222	5,492	704	26	79,470	78.3	69.1
Other/Unknown	1,316	466	834	16	N/A[6]	--	--
Hispanic (any race)	5,623	4,894	697	32	69,243	81.2	70.7

Woman's age group

<15 years	25	12	12	1	N/A[6]	--	--
15-19 years	2,878	2,113	740	25	174,958	16.4	12.1
20-24 years	12,442	9,743	2,640	59	179,390	69.4	54.3
25-29 years							
30-34 years			**3** Annual Summary - Fertility				
35-39 years						57.1
40-44 years	2,155	1,834	298	23	157,723	13.7	11.6
45+ years	188	155	30	3	N/A[6]	--	--

[1] Includes Live Births, Fetal Deaths and Induced Abortions.
[2] Fetal Death counts include all reported to the Minnesota Department of Health regardless of gestational age.
[3] Total MN Population count by year from MN State Demographic Center: https://mn.gov/admin/demography/data-by-topic/population-data vour-estimates. Female population for race/ethnicity and age groups retrieved from CDC WONDER (wonder.cdc.gov) Bridged-Race Population Estimates.
[4] Number of pregnancies per 1,000 women ages 15 - 44 years.
[5] Number of live births per 1,000 women ages 15 - 44 years.
[6] Population estimates for these age groups not calculated.

Annual Summary - Fertility   2017   2 of 4

Browser Printout of Website

Minnesota Health Statistics Annual Summary - Minnesota...   https://www.health.state.mn.us/data/mchs/ge

(http://www.health.state.mn.us/index.html)
mn DEPARTMENT OF HEALTH

Minnesota Health Statistics Annual Summary

The Minnesota Health Statistics Annual Summary is a report published annually, ten to eleven months following the close of a calendar year. Summary data for the state of Minnesota are presented including:

Population Characteristics (e.g., population size, sociodemographic characteristics of MN residents such as age, race/ethnicity, poverty, unemployment, median household income)
Live Births (e.g., characteristics of mothers, pregnancies, deliveries, and birth outcomes) *Fertility* (e.g. pregnancy, birth, and fertility rates)
Deaths (e.g., Deaths by age, sex, and cause; leading causes of death by age, race/ethnicity, rural/urban residence)

In 2017, the Minnesota Health Statistics Annual Summary underwent substantial changes in terms of layout, data presented, and definitions used for some key variables. Users are encouraged to read the full introduction and appendices for detailed information about these changes. In some instances, these changes mean that the data cannot be directly compared to 2016 and earlier. In addition to changes, a number of new variables (primarily in the Natality Tables) have been introduced.

County-level data, including population estimates, previously reported in this publication are located in the County Health Tables (http://www.health.state.mn.us/data/mchs/genstats /countytables/index.html) .

4 **2017 Minnesota Health Statistics Annual Summary**
2017 Minnesota Health Statistics Annual Summary (PDF) (http://www.health.state.mn.us /data/mchs/ genstats/annsum/mnannsum17.pdf)

4 # 2017 Minnesota Health Statistics
ANNUAL SUMMARY
12/31/2018 **2**

Reference List Entry for a Section in a Web Document

1 Minnesota Department of Health. **2** (2018, December). **3** Fertility. **4** In *2017 Minnesota health*

5 *statistics annual summary.* Retrieved from https://www.health.state.mn.us/data

/mchs/genstats/annsum/mnannsum17.pdf

For more on citing documents from websites in APA style, see items 30–50.

44. Weblog (blog) post Give the writer's name, the date of the post, the subject, the label "Web log post," and the URL. For a response to a post, use the label "Web log comment."

> Kellermann, M. (2007, May 23). Disclosing clinical trials [Web log post].
>
> Retrieved from http://www.iq.harvard.edu/blog/sss/archives/2007/05

45. Online audio or video file Give the medium or a description of the source file in brackets following the title.

> Chomsky, N. (n.d.). The new imperialism [Audio file]. Retrieved from
>
> http://www.rhapsody.com/noamchomsky

> Zakaria, F. (Host), & McCullough, C. (Writer). (2007, March 6). In focus:
>
> American teens, Rwandan truths [Video file]. Retrieved from
>
> http://www.pulitzercenter.org/showproject.cfm?id=26

46. Entry in a wiki Begin with the title of the entry and the date of posting, if there is one (use "n.d." for "no date" if there is not). Then add your retrieval date, the name of the wiki, and the URL for the wiki. Include the date of retrieval because the content of a wiki is often not stable. If an author or an editor is identified, include that name at the beginning of the entry.

> Ethnomethodology. (n.d.). Retrieved August 22, 2008, from http://en.stswiki
>
> .org/index.php/Ethnomethodology

47. Data set or graphic representation Give information about the type of source in brackets following the title. If there is no title, give a brief description of the content of the source in brackets in place of the title.

> U.S. Department of Agriculture, Economic Research Service. (2009). *Eating*
>
> *and health module (ATUS): 2007 data* [Data set]. Retrieved from http://
>
> www.ers.usda.gov/Data/ATUS/Data/2007/2007data.htm

> Gallup. (2008, October 23). *No increase in proportion of first-time voters*
>
> [Graphs]. Retrieved from http://www.gallup.com/poll/111331
>
> /No-Increase-Proportion-First-Time-Voters.aspx

48. Conference hearing

> Carmona, R. H. (2004, March 2). *The growing epidemic of childhood*
>
> *obesity*. Testimony before the Subcommittee on Competition,

Foreign Commerce, and Infrastructure of the U.S. Senate Committee
on Commerce, Science, and Transportation. Retrieved from http://
www.hhs.gov/asl/testify/t040302.html

49. Email Email messages, letters, and other personal communications are not
included in the list of references. (See Personal Communication in the in-text
citations section [item 9, p. 692] for citing these sources in the text of your paper.)

50. Online posting If an online posting is not archived, cite it as a personal communication in the text of your paper and do not include it in the list of references. If the
posting is archived, give the URL and the name of the discussion list if it is not part
of the URL.

McKinney, J. (2006, December 19). Adult education-healthcare partnerships
[Electronic mailing list message]. Retrieved from http://www.nifl.gov
/pipermail/healthliteracy/2006/000524.html

Other Sources (including Online Versions)

51. Dissertation from a database

Hymel, K. M. (2009). *Essays in urban economics* (Doctoral dissertation).
Available from ProQuest Dissertations and Theses database (AAT
3355930)

52. Unpublished dissertation

Mitchell, R. D. (2007). *The Wesleyan Quadrilateral: Relocating the
conversation* (Unpublished doctoral dissertation). Claremont School
of Theology, Claremont, CA.

53. Government document

U.S. Census Bureau. (2006). *Statistical abstract of the United States.*
Washington, DC: Government Printing Office.

U.S. Census Bureau, Bureau of Economic Analysis. (2008, August). *U.S.
international trade in goods and services* (Report No. CB08-121, BEA08-
37, FT-900). Retrieved from http://www.census.gov/foreign-trade
/Press-Release/2008pr/06/ftdpress.pdf

54. Report from a private organization If the publisher and the author are the same, begin with the publisher. For a print source, use "Author" as the publisher at the end of the entry (see item 3 on p. 696); for an online source, give the URL. If the report has a number, put it in parentheses following the title.

> Ford Foundation. (n.d.). *Helping citizens to understand and influence state budgets.* Retrieved from http://www.fordfound.org/pdfs/impact /evaluations/state_fiscal_initiative.pdf

55. Legal source

> Sweatt v. Painter, 339 U.S. 629 (1950). Retrieved from Cornell University Law School, Legal Information Institute website: http://www.law.cornell .edu/supct/html/historics/USSC_CR_0339_0629_ZS.html

56. Conference proceedings

> Stahl, G. (Ed.). (2002). *Proceedings of CSCL '02: Computer support for collaborative learning.* Hillsdale, NJ: Erlbaum.

57. Paper presented at a meeting or symposium (unpublished)

> Anderson, D. N. (2008, May). *Cab-hailing and the micropolitics of gesture.* Paper presented at the Arizona Linguistics and Anthropology Symposium, Tucson, AZ.

58. Poster session at a conference

> Wang, Z., & Keogh, T. (2008, June). *A click away: Student response to clickers.* Poster session presented at the annual conference of the American Library Association, Anaheim, CA.

59. Map or chart

> Ukraine [Map]. (2008). Retrieved from the University of Texas at Austin Perry-Castañeda Library Map Collection website: http://www.lib .utexas.edu/maps/cia08/ukraine_sm_2008.gif

60. Advertisement

> Xbox 360 [Advertisement]. (2007, February). *Wired, 15*(2), 71.

61. Published interview

Murphy, C. (2007, June 22). As the Romans did [Interview by G. Hahn].
Retrieved from http://www.theatlantic.com/

62. Lecture, speech, or address

Fox, V. (2008, March 5). *Economic growth, poverty, and democracy in Latin
America: A president's perspective.* Address at the Freeman Spogli
Institute, Stanford University, Stanford, CA.

63. Work of art or photograph

Newkirk, K. (2006). *Gainer (part II).* Museum of Contemporary Art, Chicago,
IL.

Weber, J. (1992). *Toward freedom* [Outdoor mural]. Sherman Oaks, CA.

64. Brochure, pamphlet, or fact sheet

National Council of State Boards of Nursing. (n.d.). *Professional boundaries*
[Brochure]. Retrieved from https://www.ncsbn.org/Professional
_Boundaries_2007_Web.pdf

World Health Organization. (2007, October). *Health of indigenous peoples*
(No. 326) [Fact sheet]. Retrieved from http://www.who.int
/mediacentre/factsheets/fs326/en/index.html

65. Presentation slides

Boeninger, C. F. (2008, August). *Web 2.0 tools for reference and instructional
services* [Presentation slides]. Retrieved from http://libraryvoice.com
/archives/2008/08/04/opal-20-conference-presentation-slides/

66. Film or video (motion picture) Give the director, producer, and other relevant
contributors, followed by the year of the film's release, the title, the description
"Motion picture" in brackets, the country where the film was made, and the studio.
If you viewed the film on videocassette or DVD, indicate that medium in brackets
in place of "Motion picture." If the original release date and the date of the DVD
or videocassette are different, add "Original release" and that date in parentheses at

the end of the entry. If the motion picture would be difficult for your readers to find, include instead the name and address of its distributor.

> Guggenheim, D. (Director), & Bender, L. (Producer). (2006). *An inconvenient truth* [DVD]. United States: Paramount Home Entertainment.

> Spurlock, M. (Director). (2004). *Super size me* [Motion picture]. Available from IDP Films, 1133 Broadway, Suite 926, New York, NY 10010

67. Television program List the producer and the date the program was aired. Give the title, followed by "Television broadcast" in brackets, the city, and the television network or service.

> Pratt, C. (Executive producer). (2008, October 5). *Face the nation* [Television broadcast]. Washington, DC: CBS News.

For a television series, use the year in which the series was produced, and follow the title with "Television series" in brackets. For an episode in a series, list the writer and director and the year. After the episode title, put "Television series episode" in brackets. Follow with information about the series.

> Fanning, D. (Executive producer). (2008). *Frontline* [Television series]. Boston, MA: WGBH.

> Smith, M. (Writer/producer). (2008). Heat [Television series episode]. In D. Fanning (Executive producer), *Frontline*. Boston, MA: WGBH.

68. Sound recording

> Thomas, G. (1996). Breath. On *Didgeridoo: Ancient sound of the future* [CD]. Oxnard, CA: Aquarius International Music.

69. Computer software or video game Add the words "Computer software" (neither italicized nor in quotation marks) in brackets after the title of the program.

> Sims 2 [Computer software]. (2005). New York, NY: Maxis.

24.4 Tutorial

APA-Style Formatting

Many instructors in the social sciences require students to follow APA guidelines for formatting a paper.

APA Guidelines for Student Papers

The APA manual provides guidelines for papers prepared for publication in a scholarly journal; it does not provide specific guidelines for papers prepared for undergraduate classes. The formatting guidelines in this section and the sample paper are consistent with typical requirements for undergraduate writing. The samples on the last page show APA formatting for a paper prepared for publication. If you are in doubt about which format is preferred or required in your course, ask your instructor.

Materials and font.　Use good-quality 8½" × 11" white paper. Avoid a font that is unusual or hard to read.

Title page.　APA provides few guidelines for formatting the title page of an undergraduate paper, but most instructors expect students to include one. See the sample student essay on page 719.

Page numbers and running head.　For a student paper, number all pages with Arabic numerals (1, 2, 3, and so on), including the title page, flush right. In the upper-left-hand corner of each page, type a short version of your title in all capitals. On the title page, include the words "Running head" followed by a colon before the paper title. See the Sample APA Research Paper on page 719.

Margins, line spacing, and paragraph indents.　Use margins of one inch on all sides of the page. Left-align the text. Double-space throughout the paper, but single-space footnotes. Indent the first line of each paragraph one-half inch.

Capitalization, italics, and quotation marks.　Capitalize all words of four letters or more in titles of works and in headings that appear in the text of the paper. Capitalize the first word after a colon if the word begins a complete sentence. Italicize the titles of books and other long works, such as websites. Use quotation marks around the titles of periodical articles, short stories, poems, and other short works.

NOTE: APA has different requirements for titles in the reference list. See Preparing the List of References on page 717.

Long quotations and footnotes.　When a quotation is longer than forty words, set it off from the text by indenting it one-half inch from the left margin. Double-space the quotation. Do not use quotation marks around a quotation that has been set off from the text. See page 727.

　　Place each footnote, if any, at the bottom of the page on which the text reference occurs. Double-space between the last line of text on the page and the footnote.

Indent the first line of the footnote one-half inch. Begin the note with the superscript Arabic numeral that corresponds to the number in the text. See page 721.

Abstract.   If your instructor requires an abstract, include it immediately after the title page. Center the word *Abstract* one inch from the top of the page; double-space the abstract as you do the body of your paper.

An abstract is a 100- to 150-word paragraph that provides readers with a quick overview of your essay. It should express your main idea and your key points; it might also briefly suggest any implications or applications of the research you discuss in the paper. See page 720.

Headings.   Although headings are not always necessary, their use is encouraged in the social sciences. For most undergraduate papers, one level of heading will usually be sufficient.

In APA style, major headings are centered and boldface. Capitalize the first word of the heading, along with all words except articles, short prepositions, and coordinating conjunctions. Secondary headings are bolded, capitalized, and aligned flush left. See page 721.

Visuals.   APA classifies visuals as tables and figures (figures include graphs, charts, drawings, and photographs). Keep visuals as simple as possible.

Label each table with an Arabic numeral (Table 1, Table 2, and so on) and provide a clear title. The label and title should appear on separate lines above the table, flush left and single-spaced.

Below the table, give its source in a note. If any data in the table require an explanatory footnote, use a superscript lowercase letter in the body of the table and in a footnote following the source note. Double-space source notes and footnotes, and do not indent the first line of each note. See page 724.

For each figure, place a label and a caption below the figure, flush left and double-spaced. The label and caption need not appear on separate lines.

In the text of your paper, discuss the most significant features of each visual. Place the visual as close as possible to the sentences that relate to it unless your instructor prefers it in an appendix.

Preparing the List of References

Begin your list of references on a new page at the end of the paper. Center the title References one inch from the top of the page. Double-space throughout. For a sample reference list, see page 728.

Indenting entries.   Use a hanging indent in the reference list: Type the first line of each entry flush left and indent any additional lines one-half inch, as shown on page 728.

Alphabetizing the list. Alphabetize the reference list by the last names of the authors (or editors); when a work has no author or editor, alphabetize by the first word of the title other than *A*, *An*, or *The*.

If your list includes two or more works by the same author, arrange the entries by year, the earliest first. If your list includes two or more works by the same author in the same year, arrange the works alphabetically by title. Add the letters "a," "b," and so on within the parentheses after the year. Use only the year and the letter for articles in journals: (2002a). Use the full date and the letter for articles in magazines and newspapers in the reference list: (2005a, July 7). Use only the year and the letter in the in-text citation.

Authors' names. Invert all authors' names and use initials instead of first names. With two or more authors, use an ampersand (&) before the last author's name. Separate the names with commas. Include names for the first seven authors; if there are eight or more authors, give the first six authors, three ellipsis dots, and the last author.

Titles of books and articles. Italicize the titles and subtitles of books. Do not use quotation marks around the titles of articles. Capitalize only the first word of the title and subtitle (and all proper nouns) of books and articles. Capitalize names of periodicals as you would capitalize them normally.

Abbreviations for page numbers. Abbreviations for "page" and "pages" ("p." and "pp.") are used before page numbers of newspaper articles and articles in edited books (see item 9 and item 22) but not before page numbers of articles in magazines and scholarly journals (see items 7 and 8).

Breaking a URL. When a URL or a DOI (digital object identifier) must be divided, break it after a double slash or before any other mark of punctuation. Do not insert a hyphen, and do not add a period at the end.

For information about the exact format of each entry in your list, consult the models in the section APA Reference List on page 693.

Sample Pages from Student Writing in APA Style

On the following pages is a research paper on the effectiveness of treatments for childhood obesity, written by Luisa Mirano, a student in a psychology class. Mirano's assignment was to write a literature review paper documented with APA-style citations and references. Marginal annotations indicate APA-style formatting and effective writing.

Sample APA Research Paper

The running head, which will be used on all pages, consists of shortened title in all capital letters. On the first page, it is preceded by "Running head."

Can Medication Cure Obesity in Children?

A Review of the Literature

Full title, centered

Luisa Mirano

Psychology 108, Section B

Professor Kang

October 31, 2017

Writer's name, instructor's name, date, all centered at bottom of page

Abstract
appears on a
separate page.

Abstract

In recent years, policymakers and medical experts have expressed alarm about the growing problem of childhood obesity in the United States. While most agree that the issue deserves attention, consensus dissolves around how to respond to the problem. This literature review examines one approach to treating childhood obesity: medication. The paper compares the effectiveness for adolescents of the only two drugs approved by the Food and Drug Administration (FDA) for long-term treatment of obesity, sibutramine and orlistat. This examination of pharmacological treatments for obesity points out the limitations of medication and suggests the need for a comprehensive solution that combines medical, social, behavioral, and political approaches to this complex problem.

Can Medication Cure Obesity in Children? A Review of the Literature

In March 2004, U.S. Surgeon General Richard Carmona called attention to a health problem in the United States that, until recently, has been overlooked: childhood obesity. Carmona said that the "astounding" 15% child obesity rate constitutes an "epidemic." Since the early 1980s, that rate has "doubled in children and tripled in adolescents." Now more than nine million children are classified as obese.[1] While the traditional response to a medical epidemic is to hunt for a vaccine or a cure-all pill, childhood obesity has proven more elusive. The lack of success of recent initiatives suggests that medication might not be the answer for the escalating problem. This literature review considers whether the use of medication is a promising approach for solving the childhood obesity problem by responding to the following questions:

1. What are the implications of childhood obesity?
2. Is medication effective at treating childhood obesity?
3. Is medication safe for children?
4. Is medication the best solution?

Understanding the limitations of medical treatments for children highlights the complexity of the childhood obesity problem in the United States and underscores the need for physicians, advocacy groups, and policymakers to search for other solutions.

What Are the Implications of Childhood Obesity?

Obesity can be a devastating problem from both an individual and a societal perspective. Obesity puts children at risk for a number of medical complications, including type 2 diabetes, hypertension, sleep

[1]Obesity is measured in terms of body-mass index (BMI): weight in kilograms divided by square of height in meters. A child or an adolescent with a BMI in the 95th percentile for his or her age and gender is considered obese.

Full title, centered

Mirano sets up her organization by posing four questions.

Mirano states her thesis.

Headings, centered and bolded, help readers follow the organization.

Mirano uses a footnote to define an essential term that would be cumbersome to define within the text.

apnea, and orthopedic problems (Henry J. Kaiser Family Foundation, 2004, p. 1). Researchers Hoppin and Taveras (2004) have noted that obesity is often associated with psychological issues such as depression, anxiety, and binge eating (Table 4).

Obesity also poses serious problems for a society struggling to cope with rising health care costs. The cost of treating obesity currently totals $117 billion per year—a price, according to the surgeon general, "second only to the cost of [treating] tobacco use" (Carmona, 2004). And as the number of children who suffer from obesity grows, long-term costs will only increase.

Is Medication Effective at Treating Childhood Obesity?

The widening scope of the obesity problem has prompted medical professionals to rethink old conceptions of the disorder and its causes. As researchers Yanovski and Yanovski (2002) have explained, obesity was once considered "either a moral failing or evidence of underlying psychopathology" (p. 592). But this view has shifted: Many medical professionals now consider obesity a biomedical rather than a moral condition, influenced by both genetic and environmental factors. Yanovski and Yanovski have further noted that the development of weight-loss medications in the early 1990s showed that "obesity should be treated in the same manner as any other chronic disease . . . through the long-term use of medication" (p. 592).

The search for the right long-term medication has been complicated. Many of the drugs authorized by the Food and Drug Administration (FDA) in the early 1990s proved to be a disappointment. Two of the medications—fenfluramine and dexfenfluramine—were withdrawn from the market because of severe side effects (Yanovski & Yanovski, 2002, p. 592), and several others were classified by the Drug Enforcement Administration as having the "potential for

In a signal phrase, the word *and* links the names of two authors; the date is given in parentheses.

Because the author (Carmona) is not named in the signal phrase, his name and the date appear in parentheses.

Ellipsis dots indicate omitted words.

abuse" (Hoppin & Taveras, 2004, Weight-Loss Drugs section, para. 6). Currently only two medications have been approved by the FDA for long-term treatment of obesity: sibutramine (marketed as Meridia) and orlistat (marketed as Xenical). This section compares studies on the effectiveness of each.

Sibutramine suppresses appetite by blocking the reuptake of the neurotransmitters serotonin and norepinephrine in the brain (Yanovski & Yanovski, 2002, p. 594). Though the drug won FDA approval in 1998, experiments to test its effectiveness for younger patients came considerably later. In 2003, University of Pennsylvania researchers Berkowitz, Wadden, Tershakovec, and Cronquist released the first double-blind placebo study testing the effect of sibutramine on adolescents, aged 13–17, over a 12-month period. Their findings are summarized in Table 1.

After 6 months, the group receiving medication had lost 4.6 kg (about 10 pounds) more than the control group. But during the second half of the study, when both groups received sibutramine, the results were more ambiguous. In months 6–12, the group that continued to take sibutramine gained an average of 0.8 kg, or roughly 2 pounds; the control group, which switched from placebo to sibutramine, lost 1.3 kg, or roughly 3 pounds (p. 1808). Both groups received behavioral therapy covering diet, exercise, and mental health.

These results paint a murky picture of the effectiveness of the medication: While initial data seemed promising, the results after one year raised questions about whether medication-induced weight loss could be sustained over time. As Berkowitz et al. (2003) advised, "Until more extensive safety and efficacy data are available, . . . weight-loss medications should be used only on an experimental basis for adolescents" (p. 1811).

In a parenthetical citation, an ampersand links the names of two authors.

Mirano draws attention to an important article.

Table 1

Effectiveness of Sibutramine and Orlistat in Adolescents

Medication	Subjects	Treatment[a]	Side effects	Average weight loss/ gain
Sibutramine	Control	0–6 mos.: Placebo	Mos. 6–12: increased blood pressure; increased pulse rate	After 6 mos.: loss of 3.2 kg (7 lb)
		6–12 mos.: Sibutramine		After 12 mos.: loss of 4.5 kg (9.9 lb)
	Medicated	0–12 mos.: Sibutramine	Increased blood pressure; increased pulse rate	After 6 mos.: loss of 7.8 kg (17.2 lb)
				After 12 mos.: loss of 7.0 kg (15.4 lb)
Orlistat	Control	0–12 mos.: Placebo	None	Gain of 0.67 kg (1.5 lb)
	Medicated	0–12 mos.: orlistat	Oily spotting; flatulence; abdominal discomfort	Loss of 1.3 kg (2.9 lb)

Note. The data on sibutramine are adapted from "Behavior Therapy and Sibutramine for the Treatment of Adolescent Obesity," by R. I. Berkowitz, T. A. Wadden, A. M. Tershakovec, & J. L. Cronquist, 2003, *Journal of the American Medical Association, 289*, pp. 1807–1809. The data on orlistat are adapted from *Xenical (Orlistat) Capsules: Complete Product Information*, by Roche Laboratories, December 2003, retrieved from http://www.rocheusa.com/products/xenical/pi.pdf

[a]The medication and/or placebo were combined with behavioral therapy in all groups over all time periods.

A study testing the effectiveness of orlistat in adolescents showed similarly ambiguous results. The FDA approved orlistat in 1999 but did not authorize it for adolescents until December 2003.

Side notes:

Mirano uses a table to summarize the findings presented in the two sources.

A note gives the source of the data.

A content note explains data common to all subjects.

Roche Laboratories (2003), maker of orlistat, released results of a one-year study testing the drug on 539 obese adolescents, aged 12–16. The drug, which promotes weight loss by blocking fat absorption in the large intestine, showed some effectiveness in adolescents: an average loss of 1.3 kg, or roughly 3 pounds, for subjects taking orlistat for one year, as opposed to an average gain of 0.67 kg, or 1.5 pounds, for the control group (pp. 8–9). See Table 1.

Short-term studies of orlistat have shown slightly more dramatic results. Researchers at the National Institute of Child Health and Human Development tested 20 adolescents, aged 12–16, over a three-month period and found that orlistat, combined with behavioral therapy, produced an average weight loss of 4.4 kg, or 9.7 pounds (McDuffie et al., 2002, p. 646). The study was not controlled against a placebo group; therefore, the relative effectiveness of orlistat in this case remains unclear.

Is Medication Safe for Children?

While modest weight loss has been documented for both medications, each carries risks of certain side effects. Sibutramine has been observed to increase blood pressure and pulse rate. In 2002, a consumer group claimed that the medication was related to the deaths of 19 people and filed a petition with the Department of Health and Human Services to ban the medication (Hilts, 2002). The sibutramine study by Berkowitz et al. (2003) noted elevated blood pressure as a side effect, and dosages had to be reduced or the medication discontinued in 19 of the 43 subjects in the first six months (p. 1809).

The main side effects associated with orlistat were abdominal discomfort, oily spotting, fecal incontinence, and nausea (Roche Laboratories, 2003, p. 13). More serious for long-term health is the concern that orlistat, being a fat-blocker, would affect absorption of fat-soluble vitamins, such as vitamin D. However, the study found that

For a source with six or more authors, the first author's surname followed by "et al." is used for the first and subsequent references.

When this article was first cited, all four authors were named. In subsequent citations of a work with three to five authors, "et al." is used after the first author's name.

this side effect can be minimized or eliminated if patients take vitamin supplements two hours before or after administration of orlistat (p. 10). With close monitoring of patients taking the medication, many of the risks can be reduced.

Is Medication the Best Solution?

The data on the safety and efficacy of pharmacological treatments of childhood obesity raise the question of whether medication is the best solution for the problem. The treatments have clear costs for individual patients, including unpleasant side effects, little information about long-term use, and uncertainty that they will yield significant weight loss.

In purely financial terms, the drugs cost more than $3 a day on average (Duenwald, 2004). In each of the clinical trials, use of medication was accompanied by an expensive regime of behavioral therapies, including counseling, nutritional education, fitness advising, and monitoring. As journalist Greg Critser (2003) noted in his book *Fat Land*, use of weight-loss drugs is unlikely to have an effect without the proper "support system"—one that includes doctors, facilities, time, and money (p. 3). For some, this level of care is prohibitively expensive. A third complication is that the studies focused on adolescents aged 12–16, but obesity can begin at a much younger age. Little data exist to establish the safety or efficacy of medication for treating very young children.

While the scientific data on the concrete effects of these medications in children remain somewhat unclear, medication is not the only avenue for addressing the crisis. Both medical experts and policymakers recognize that solutions might come not only from a laboratory but also from policy, education, and advocacy. A handbook designed to educate doctors on obesity called for "major changes in some aspects of western culture" (Hoppin & Taveras, 2004, Conclusion section, para. 1). Cultural change may not be the typical realm of medical professionals, but the handbook

Mirano develops the paper's thesis.

urged doctors to be proactive and "focus [their] energy on public policies and interventions" (Conclusion section, para. 1).

The solutions proposed by a number of advocacy groups underscore this interest in political and cultural change. A report by the Henry J. Kaiser Family Foundation (2004) outlined trends that may have contributed to the childhood obesity crisis, including food advertising for children as well as

> a reduction in physical education classes and after-school athletic programs, an increase in the availability of sodas and snacks in public schools, the growth in the number of fast-food outlets . . . , and the increasing number of highly processed high-calorie and high-fat grocery products. (p. 1)

Addressing each of these areas requires more than a doctor armed with a prescription pad; it requires a broad mobilization not just of doctors and concerned parents but of educators, food industry executives, advertisers, and media representatives.

The barrage of possible approaches to combating childhood obesity—from scientific research to political lobbying—indicates both the severity and the complexity of the problem. While none of the medications currently available is a miracle drug for curing the nation's 9 million obese children, research has illuminated some of the underlying factors that affect obesity and has shown the need for a comprehensive approach to the problem that includes behavioral, medical, social, and political change.

References

Berkowitz, R. I., Wadden, T. A., Tershakovec, A. M., & Cronquist, J. L. (2003). Behavior therapy and sibutramine for the treatment of adolescent obesity. *Journal of the American Medical Association, 289*, 1805–1812.

Carmona, R. H. (2004, March 2). *The growing epidemic of childhood obesity*. Testimony before the Subcommittee on Competition, Foreign Commerce, and Infrastructure of the U.S. Senate Committee on Commerce, Science, and Transportation. Retrieved from http://www.hhs.gov/asl/testify/t040302.html

Critser, G. (2003). *Fat land*. Boston: Houghton Mifflin.

Duenwald, M. (2004, January 6). Slim pickings: Looking beyond ephedra. *The New York Times*, p. F1. Retrieved from http://nytimes.com/

Henry J. Kaiser Family Foundation. (2004, February). *The role of media in childhood obesity*. Retrieved from http://www.kff.org/entmedia/7030.cfm

Hilts, P. J. (2002, March 20). Petition asks for removal of diet drug from market. *The New York Times*, p. A27. Retrieved from http://nytimes.com/

Hoppin, A. G., & Taveras, E. M. (2004, June 25). Assessment and management of childhood and adolescent obesity. *Clinical Update*. Retrieved from http://www.medscape.com/viewarticle/481633

McDuffie, J. R., Calis, K. A., Uwaifo, G. I., Sebring, N. G., Fallon, E. M., Hubbard, V. S., & Yanovski, J. A. (2002). Three-month tolerability of orlistat in adolescents with obesity-related comorbid conditions. *Obesity Research, 10*, 642–650.

The list of references begins on a new page. Heading is centered.

The list is alphabetized by authors' last names. All authors' names are inverted.

The first line of an entry is at the left margin; subsequent lines indent ½".

Double-spacing is used throughout.

Roche Laboratories. (2003, December). *Xenical (orlistat) capsules: Complete product information.* Retrieved from http://www .rocheusa.com/products/xenical/pi.pdf

Yanovski, S. Z., & Yanovski, J. A. (2002). Drug therapy: Obesity. *The New England Journal of Medicine, 346,* 591–602.

Sample APA Title Page: Paper for Publication

A running head, which will be used in the printed journal article, consists of a shortened title in all capital letters. On the title page, it is preceded by the label "Running head." Page numbers appear in the upper right corner.

Running head: CAN MEDICATION CURE OBESITY IN CHILDREN?   1

An author's note lists specific information about the course or department and can provide acknowledgments and contact information.

Can Medication Cure Obesity in Children?

A Review of the Literature

Luisa Mirano

Northwest-Shoals Community College

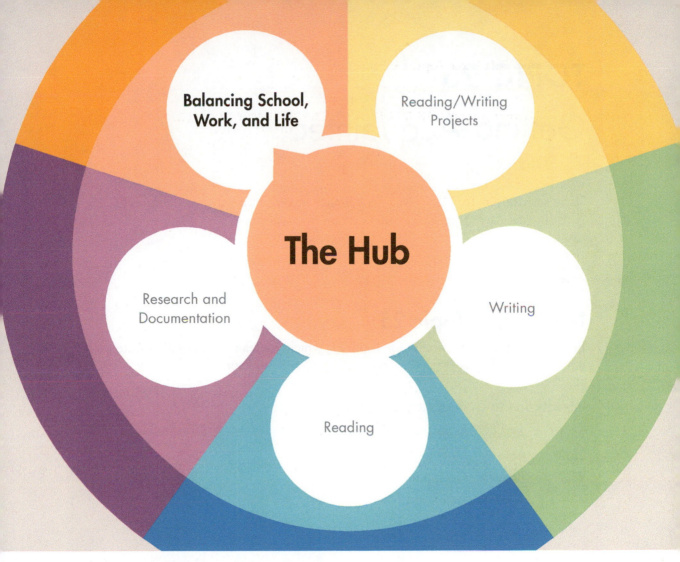

The Hub

Balancing School, Work, and Life

Reading/Writing Projects

Research and Documentation

Writing

Reading

5 Balancing School, Work, and Life

TOPIC 25

Getting Acquainted

The activities in Topic 25 give you a chance to get to know some of your classmates and to get used to participating in group discussions.

Navigating Topic 25

Below is the table of contents for Topic 25, which you can use to easily locate the units you have been assigned to work on by your instructor.

Introduction to Getting Acquainted

The following activities are designed to help you and your classmates get to know each other and get used to working in groups.

25.1 Activity

Interesting Interviews

After the class is organized into pairs, you and your partner will interview each other with the goal of discovering something interesting—an unusual fact, an interesting experience, or a surprising attitude about each other. You might start by asking your partner to tell you three interesting things about him- or herself. You could then select one that you think is the most interesting and ask some follow-up questions about it. Then switch roles. You tell your partner three interesting things about yourself and then answer your partner's questions about one of them. After ten or fifteen minutes, each of you will report to the class on the one interesting thing you learned about your partner.

25.2 Activity

Meet and Greet Bingo

Walk around the room talking to people. For each of the boxes in the chart below (also available as a downloadable PDF in *Achieve for The Hub*), write the name of a person who fits the description in the box. When you've filled in five boxes in a row or in a column or diagonally, take your seat.

Hates to write	Speaks a language other than English	Is good at grammar	Owns a bicycle	Ate breakfast this morning
Plays Words with Friends	Has been out of high school at least ten years	Hated English in high school	Is a vegan	Keeps a diary
Is wearing something purple	Does crossword puzzles regularly	Loves to write	Reads science fiction	Writes poetry

Reads a daily newspaper	Knows where the next Summer Olympics will be held	Knows what haiku is	Has a full-time job	Knows what it means to "86" something
Tweets regularly	Has eaten dim sum	Works in a restaurant	Owns a dictionary	Knows who Matisse is

25.3 Activity

Getting to Know You

This activity is designed to help you get to know some of the other members of this class. Working with the members of your group, figure out the answer to each of the following questions.

1. In the group, who was born in the most interesting place? Where?
2. In the group, who has the most interesting nickname? What is it?
3. In the group, who has the worst boss? What's so terrible about his or her boss?
4. In the group, who is the best cook? What is his or her best dish?
5. In the group, who speaks the most languages? What are they?

Be prepared to share your group's answers with the rest of the class.

25.4 Activity

Two Truths and a Lie

To start, everyone in the group will take a few minutes to think of three statements about themselves, two that are true and one that is a lie. Next each person will tell the group their three statements, and the group will try to guess which statement is the lie. The process continues until everyone has told their three statements.

TOPIC 26
Life Issues

Attending college and trying to cope with the rest of life can sometimes be a challenge. The activities in this Topic are designed to help you develop strategies for balancing school, work, and the rest of your life.

Navigating Topic 26

Below is the table of contents for Topic 26, which you can use to easily locate the units you have been assigned to work on by your instructor or want to review for yourself.

Introduction to Life Issues

These activities are designed to help you think about and problem-solve on issues common to many students: money, renting, health care, child care, time management, and needing a Plan B.

26.1 Writing

Money Matters

At the same time that they are struggling to become more effective writers, many students in developmental writing classes are also struggling to figure out how to pay their bills and put food on the table. Financial pressures are one of the largest sources of stress in the lives of many students.

For this short writing assignment, you will do a little research, a little thinking, and a little writing about one of the financial topics listed below. The plan is that, as the class researches, discusses, and writes about these "financial" topics, many of you will learn things that will help with your financial pressures. At the same time, you should also begin to understand a little about doing research and incorporating the results into your writing.

Researching a Financial Topic

You will need to find some information about your topic. You can do this on the internet, using Google or a similar service, or you can find a book or journal that discusses your topic in the library. For more detailed information, see Research (Topic 22, p. 619).

You are not being asked to do a really thorough research project, just to find *one* piece of information that will be helpful as you write a short essay on one of the financial topics below. At this point in the course, you have probably not had any formal instruction in how to do research, so you're not being asked to give formal citations and lists of references. All you need to do is quote one brief passage—a sentence or more—that you found in your research and that helps to support the argument you are making in your essay. Of course, more than one quotation is fine, but only one is required.

Quoting Sources

Here's a little advice about how to include a brief quotation in your essay. Before the quotation itself, you want to include an introductory phrase that signals to the reader that a quotation is coming and provides a little information about the source of the quotation.

Here are some examples:

- Before being elected president, Senator Barrack Obama pointed out, "One of my favorite tasks of being a senator is hosting town hall meetings."

- One of the world's leading cosmologists, Brian Greene, reminds us that "[t]he ancient Greeks surmised that the stuff of the universe was made up of tiny 'uncuttable' ingredients that they called *atoms*."

- Noted art scholar John Berger suggests that "[i]mages were first made to conjure up the appearance of something that was absent."

Note that in each example, the writer identifies the source of the quotation, explains who the source is, and—using specific verbs like *pointed out, reminds us,* and *suggests*—helps us understand how the quotation was offered.

One more point about quoting: you must be careful to do it accurately. You must quote the words from your source exactly. If you need to change a word or two in the quotation, place brackets around the words or letters you have changed. Take a look at the following example.

Original

My grandparents left Jackson in the late 1940s and raised their family in Middletown, Ohio, where I later grew up.

Quotation

In his best-selling memoir, *Hillbilly Elegy*, J. D. Vance reports that his "grandparents left Jackson [Kentucky] in the late 1940s and raised their family in Middletown, Ohio, where [he] later grew up."

In the quotation, *Kentucky* was added in brackets to clarify where Jackson is, and *I* was changed to *he* (also in brackets) to make the quotation easier to understand.

Activity: Writing about Money

Select one of the questions below and search the internet for credible information to help you answer it. Then, write a short paper—about a page—in which you answer the question. In your paper, quote at least one sentence or phrase that you found in your research that supports your argument.

1. Is a "payday loan" ever a good idea?
2. What are the arguments for taking out a student loan?
3. What are the arguments against taking out a student loan?
4. What are the most important rules associated with a Pell Grant?

5. What rights do consumers have if they are behind in making payments on their credit card?

6. What should I know if I am threatened with eviction?

26.2 Activity
Renting

For this activity, working in your group, brainstorm a list of ideas for how you could lower the amount you are currently paying for rent. After twenty minutes, each group will report out on its list.

26.3 Activity
Health Care

If you or someone you care for became ill, what are your options for getting medical care? Working in your group, brainstorm a list of options for getting medical care. After twenty minutes, each group will report out.

26.4 Activity
Child Care

Working in your group, brainstorm a list of options for child care. List not only what you do but also options that other people you know have done. After twenty minutes, the groups will report out.

26.5 Activity
Time Management: Activity Log

Use the blank chart on page 740 (also available as a downloadable PDF in *Achieve for The Hub*) to keep track of how you use your time for one week. If you are also taking a course called something like "student success" or "first-year experience," a course designed to improve your ability to succeed in college, you may have been asked to complete an activity log in that course. If so, you don't need to do a second one; just use the one you compiled for that course.

Advice for the Specific Columns

1st Column	Enter a three-letter abbreviation for the day of the week.
2nd Column	Enter the time you spent on the activity. Example: 9:00–9:45
3rd Column	Enter a brief description of the activity.
4th Column	Enter a number indicating how important this activity is to you—4 is most important; 1 is least important.

Keep the log for one complete week.

Sample Activity Log

Name: _____

Day	Time	Activity	Priority
Mon.	11:10–12:00	English class	4
Mon.	12:00–1:15	bus home	4
Mon.	1:15–2:30	lunch and video games	1
Mon.	2:30–3:00	walk to Romano's	4
Mon.	3:00–9:00	wait tables	4
Mon.	9:00–10:00	have a beer with friends	1
Mon.	10:00–11:00	work on English paper	4

Activity Log

Day	Time	Activity	Priority

26.6 Activity

Time Management: Analyzing Activity Logs

Working in your group, look at the members' activity logs, one at a time, and then answer the following questions.

1. Are there any surprises in your activity log? Are you spending more time than you thought you were on some tasks? Less time on others?

2. Are there times of the day when you are most productive? Are you working on low-priority activities in these high-productivity times?

3. Are there little stretches of time that you could use to squeeze in small tasks?

4. Are you spending lots of time on low-priority tasks? Doing so can be a sign that you are procrastinating.

5. Are there things you are doing that don't need to be done? Things that can be delayed or cancelled or even done by someone else?

6. Is it possible to do everything you have committed to doing? If so, great. If not, what can you change to make it possible to accomplish everything you need to do?

26.7 Activity

Time Management: Strategies

Working together as a group, make a list of time-management strategies. To get you started, here's one strategy:

Do the hardest task first. Sometimes a difficult task gets pushed to later in the day or even later in the week. Then you spend time dreading it, which makes you less effective at completing other tasks. There's nothing more satisfying than taking on that hard task first, preferably earlier in the day when you are at your most alert, and getting it done.

26.8 Activity

Time Management: Calendars

Most busy people find that they cannot keep themselves organized, they cannot meet deadlines, and they cannot show up on time at events they need to attend without keeping a calendar.

Many versions of online calendars are available, although some people still prefer the old-fashioned calendar in a spiral notebook form. Both forms have their advantages, so you should choose whatever works best for you, but using a calendar is something that will definitely help with organizing your time.

Creating a Calendar

Print and online calendars can be arranged to display a day at a time, a week at a time, a month at a time, or even a year at a glance. Most students find a one-week-at-a-time format works best for them. Here are some suggestions for how to create an effective calendar:

- Set aside time to work on your calendar before the week begins—Sunday evenings work well.

- Start by filling in the times that are fixed: the times you are scheduled to be in class, the times you are scheduled to work, and the hours you will be sleeping.

- Then add any one-time events you know about that are coming up during the week. Your mother's 50th birthday party on Saturday night. The time you've volunteered to babysit your sister's daughter. A house concert you plan to attend.

- Be sure to build in time for studying. Don't just write "9:00–11:00 study." Make a specific plan: "9:00–11:00 Revise essay for English class."

- Don't forget to include travel time and time for household tasks like shopping for groceries or doing the laundry.

- Schedule breaks—time to relax, have a coffee, or talk to a friend on the phone.

Below, you will find a blank calendar for a week. Working with this form (also available as a downloadable PDF in *Achieve for The Hub*), plan out the next week for yourself. While you might normally do this planning on a Sunday, if you start working on some other day—say, Thursday—then just start with Thursday and plan for the next seven days. You should find the Activity Log you created (26.5, p. 738), the analysis of your Activity Log (26.6, p. 741), and the strategies you established (26.7, p. 741) to be helpful as you work on this calendar.

	Monday	Tuesday	Wednesday	Thursday	Friday	Saturday	Sunday
6:00–6:30							
6:30–7:00							
7:00–7:30							
7:30–8:00							
8:00–8:30							
8:30–9:00							
9:00–9:30							
9:30–10:00							
10:00–10:30							
10:30–11:00							
11:00–11:30							
11:30–12:00							
12:00–12:30							
12:30–1:00							
1:00–1:30							
1:30–2:00							
2:00–2:30							
2:30–3:00							
3:00–3:30							
3:30–4:00							
4:00–4:30							
4:30–5:00							
5:00–5:30							
5:30–6:00							
6:00–6:30							
6:30–7:00							
7:00–7:30							
7:30–8:00							
8:00–8:30							
8:30–9:00							
9:00–9:30							

	Monday	Tuesday	Wednesday	Thursday	Friday	Saturday	Sunday
9:30–10:00							
10:00–10:30							
10:30–11:00							
11:00–11:30							
11:30–12:00							
12:00–12:30							
12:30–1:00							

26.9 Activity

Plan B

Most students find going to college stressful. There's the pressure to do all the reading, to do all the homework, and to prepare for tests. But, for many students, there are also the stresses that come from life: financial pressures, family problems, health issues, legal problems.

Much of the time, the stress is manageable even though it's not pleasant. Most students deal with stress by digging down a little deeper, working a little harder, sleeping a little less, and remembering that the semester lasts just fifteen weeks or so. But sometimes the stress becomes unbearable, the student's efforts just grind to a halt, and he or she ends up dropping out of school.

If digging a little deeper and working a little harder is Plan A for dealing with stress, in this activity I want you to think about Plan B. If you felt that all the pressures of school, family, work, and life were approaching the point where you might have to give up on school, what could you do? What changes could you make *before* the stress overwhelmed you?

Activity: Listing Strategies for Coping with Stress

1. Working in groups, make a list of possible strategies that could help you avoid dropping out of school because of stress.
2. Share these strategies with the whole class.

TOPIC 27

Staying the Course

Going to college creates stress and anxiety for some students. The activities in this Topic provide suggestions for how to deal with these kinds of issues.

Navigating Topic 27

Below is the table of contents for Topic 27, which you can use to easily locate the units you have been assigned to work on by your instructor or want to review for yourself.

Introduction to Staying the Course

The activities in Topic 27 are designed to help you think, problem-solve, and develop strategies to address issues commonly experienced by students: questions about why you are in this class, things that worry you, concerns about whether you are "college material," ways to respond to setbacks, and goal setting and planning.

Why Are You in This Class?

For this short writing assignment, you don't need to write an essay or even a paragraph. Just write a list of the reasons why, at this point in your life, you find yourself in this writing class. This list doesn't have to be long; it could even be just one or two reasons. The point is to do a little thinking about why you are in this class.

Thinking about Why Are You in This Class?

1. Your instructor will share with the class a list of all the reasons you and your classmates gave in response to the request to "write a list of the reasons why, at this point in your life, you find yourself in this writing class."

2. After some discussion of that list, your instructor will ask you to study the following chart. Working in groups, what can you learn from this chart about why you might be in this writing class?

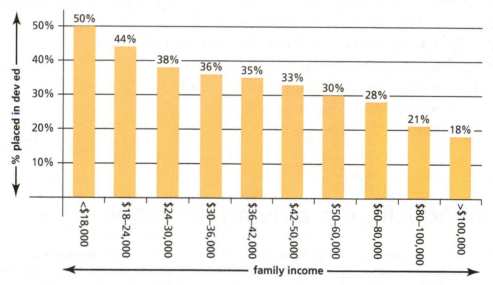

Republished with permission of Russell Sage Foundation from *Economic Inequality and Higher Education: Access, Persistence, and Success*, S. Dickert-Conlin & R. Rubenstein (Eds.) (pp. 69–100). New York, NY: Russell Sage Foundation; permission conveyed through Copyright Clearance Center, Inc.

3. Finally, again working in groups, come up with a list of observations from your life that would explain the conclusion you reached in question 2. In your life prior to enrolling in this class, what can you remember that would have contributed to the conclusions you reached in question 2?

27.3 Activity

What Worries You?

Write down one thing you are worried about on a piece of paper and hand it to your instructor. Don't put your name on it. Anything you are worried about is okay—something about school or work or your relationships or your family or the country or the world. Your instructor will read as many of these as possible to the entire class so the class can discuss them.

27.4 Writing

Who Is "College Material"?

Many students arrive in college with insecurities, doubts about whether they belong, doubts about whether they can succeed. In some cases, they express these doubts by saying something like this: "I'm just not sure I'm 'college material.'"

For this assignment, write a short essay—about a page—in which you discuss the term *college material*. You don't have to answer all of the following questions, or any of them, but they're here to help you think about the term.

1. What does *college material* mean?
2. Where do you suppose that students who wonder about whether they are *college material* learned the term? Who told them there was such a thing as students who are not "college material"?
3. Are you sure you are "college material"? If so, how did you avoid the doubt that comes from wondering whether you are?
4. Do you think anyone is not "college material"? What would put someone into that category? What keeps someone from being "college material"?
5. Do you know anyone who has these kinds of doubts about themselves? Are they "college material," in your opinion? Why do they have these doubts about whether they belong in college?
6. Do people get the idea they may not be "college material" in high school or does that doubt occur once they get to college?

27.5 Writing

Responding to Setbacks

Think about a setback you have experienced—a time you got a low grade in school, a time when you weren't hired for a job you wanted, a time your performance in a sport was publicly bad, or even a time when you learned that someone you loved did not return your affection. Write a short paper—about a page—in which you describe what you learned from that experience.

27.6 Writing

Goal Setting and Planning

Where do you want to be in five years? What do you want to be doing? Where do you want to be living? What kind of car do you want to be driving? How many children would you like to have (if any)? How much education do you want? Write a paragraph in which you answer at least some of these questions.

Activity: Twelve-Month Goals

Now think about what you need to do in the next twelve months to make those goals possible. Make a list of these "Twelve-Month Goals."

You will be discussing these "Twelve-Month Goals" with your group. During this discussion, you should feel free to add to your list, subtract from it, or revise it.

TOPIC 28
College Knowledge

The world of college can be quite different from the world outside. It has its own terminology, procedures, and expectations. The activities in this Topic are designed to help you understand and thrive in this specialized world.

Navigating Topic 28

Below is the table of contents for Topic 28, which you can use to easily locate the units you have been assigned to work on by your instructor or want to review for yourself.

Introduction to College Knowledge

The activities in Topic 28 are designed to help you become more familiar with the language, or terminology, used in college; understand the terms used in writing assignments to indicate the kind of essay an instructor wants you to write; recognize how important it is to ask for help when you need it; and learn what resources are available to you and how to access them.

28.1 Writing

College Terminology

Colleges and universities have a language of their own. Sometimes students new to college run into difficulty because of terms they don't know. The following is a list of such terms.

AA degree	department	plagiarism	transfer
appeal	essay	prerequisite	tutoring
books on reserve	FAFSA	probation	withdrawal
bursar	GPA	program	writing center
certificate	incomplete	registration	
composition	major	school	
dean	office hours	syllabus	

This list will be divided up among several groups of students. Each group will be responsible for writing a paragraph explaining each of the terms it is assigned. Groups should use the knowledge of the individuals in the group to define the terms. If necessary, it's okay for the group to Google a term, but then the definition should be translated into "student-friendly" language. The audience for this writing is next year's new college students. These paragraphs will be compiled into a document suitable to be given out to students.

28.2 Writing

Terms for Writing Assignments

Writing assignments in college frequently use terms like those listed below. In order to complete an assignment effectively, you will need to understand each of these terms and the differences in what they ask you to do.

Activity: Defining Terms

For this short writing assignment, you and your classmates will be compiling a document explaining these terms, which will be handed out to new students.

You will work in groups, each of which will be assigned some of the terms to work on. Each group will write a "student-friendly" paragraph explaining each of its assigned terms. Groups should use the knowledge of the individuals in the group to define the terms. If necessary, it's okay for the group to Google a term, but then the definition should be translated into "student-friendly" language.

agree or disagree	create	evaluate	state
analyze	defend	explain	summarize
argue	define	identify	support
classify	demonstrate	interpret	synthesize
compare	describe	list	
construct	develop	paraphrase	
contrast	discuss	solve	

28.3 Activity

Asking for Help

A website called Academic Tips (**search for "academic tips ask help" to locate the site**) contains great advice about asking for help when you're in college. Working in your group, discuss the tips on asking for help that you find on the Academic Tips website and list some additional tips you would add.

28.4 Activity

Locating Resources

Working in groups, your job for this activity will be to find out where to go on campus for each of the items listed in the chart on page 752 (also available as a downloadable PDF in *Achieve for The Hub*) and provide the following information about each place the group recommends. Of course, you may learn that your college doesn't have an office where you can go for several of these items. If that's the case, just write "Not available" next to those items.

- Location
- Phone number
- Email
- Hours
- Additional services available

		Location	Phone number	Email	Hours	Additional services available
1	Help with financial aid.					
2	Assistance with a disability.					
3	Help with doing research for a term paper.					
4	Advice about a career.					
5	Assistance with writing.					
6	Assistance with technology.					
7	The place to appeal a grade.					
8	A place to safely complain about harassment.					
9	Advice about transferring to a four-year school.					
10	Advice about getting into the Nursing Program.					
11	Help with child care.					
12	A copy of your transcript.					
13	To withdraw from a course.					
14	To look at a book that your instructor has placed on reserve.					
15	To pay your tuition bill.					

What Is Group Work, and Why Are We Doing It?

In this course, you will be doing a great deal of what is known as group work. Your instructor will often divide the class into small groups of three or four students and ask the groups to work on some task. These groups might be asked to answer questions about a reading, make sense out of a seeming contradiction, decide which of several arguments is most compelling, or make a list of ideas or experiences of the members of the group. Each group will regularly be asked to "report out" on what their group's conclusions were. At other times, groups will be asked to produce a written document, usually quite short, to be turned in, or to write their responses on large sheets of paper to be posted around the classroom.

If you're not sure why instructors include group work in the course, here are four important reasons why they do:

1. **Group work almost always involves a process known as *active learning* or *discovery learning*.** In more traditional classrooms, students learned by listening to instructors as they delivered information by means of lectures. In active learning students learn information by solving a problem or studying examples. They *actively* discover information for themselves, and there is considerable research to support the idea that what students learn through active learning stays with them longer that what they learn through lectures.

2. **Group work creates more of a community in the classroom.** Students get to know each other and develop a network of other students whom they can ask for advice or assistance. As a result, they feel more connected to the college and have a greater sense of belonging to a community of peers.

3. **Being able to work well in a group is a skill for which many employers are looking.** Many companies now have staff working together in groups on a wide variety of tasks, such as problem-solving design issues, creating new products, coming up with marketing campaigns, or trouble-shooting bad media coverage. Being able to work well with others, share and delegate responsibilities, brainstorm as a team member, and write joint responses to specific prompts or questions are all skills that prove very useful to students when they look for jobs.

4. **Group work can be fun.** Once students get over any initial anxiety, most find participating in group work much more enjoyable than listening to a lecture.

Tips for Successful Group Participation

Here are some tips to help you participate successfully in group work.

1. **Come to class prepared.**   If a reading was assigned, make sure you have read it. If you were supposed to bring a draft of an essay, make sure you bring it. If you were supposed to do anything else in preparation for the class, make sure you have done it.

2. **Don't be reluctant to participate.**   Everyone feels a little anxiety about expressing their ideas in a group at first, but once you join in, you will find it's easier than you expected. It's certainly more fun and more helpful if you are actively involved.

3. **It is also possible to participate too much, to take up more than your share of time for talking.** Dominating the conversation can be as harmful to the group as not participating. Take the time to listen to and understand the idea expressed by other members of your group in addition to sharing your own thoughts and opinions.

4. **If you have been assigned a specific role or responsibility in the group, be sure to perform that role diligently.**   Sometimes it's easy to get so caught up in the discussion that you forget your assigned role. For example, if you are the note-taker, be sure to come equipped with pen and paper, or your phone or laptop, to listen carefully, and to record what is being said as accurately as possible. This might mean talking less than you would if someone else was taking notes.

5. **Listen carefully to what your classmates are saying.**

6. **Be respectful of everyone's opinions.**   Avoid being judgmental.

7. **The most common problem groups have is when one or two members don't perform their share of the responsibilities.**   Make sure you come to class prepared to participate, that you make your share of contributions to the group's efforts, and that you follow through on any tasks assigned.

Tips for Group Success

Here are some tips to help *groups* be more successful.

1. The group's first task is to make sure every member understands and agrees on the task the group is asked to perform.

2. The group should take a little time to plan how they are going to use the allocated time.

3. The group needs to keep an eye on the clock. If they've used half of their time and are still discussing the first task of three, they need to move along faster.

4. If the instructor hasn't assigned roles to the group members, the group needs to think about taking on roles themselves. If there is to be a written project, who is going to do the actual writing? If the group will be asked to report out at the end of their work, who will do this reporting?

5. Perhaps the most important thing groups need to learn how to do is to settle disagreements. Sometimes a compromise can be reached. Sometimes, a group has to recognize that they cannot agree and, therefore, submit two reports or a primary report and a minority report in response to the assigned task.

6. The most common problem groups have happens when a member or two don't do their share of the work. Groups need to confront this problem directly. It is not an acceptable solution for the other members of the group to do most of the work. The group needs to confront the "slacker(s)" directly and discuss the problem. If it cannot be resolved within the group, then the instructor should be consulted. Learning how to handle the problem of a "slacker" is an important skill that will be beneficial in the workplace.

Acknowledgments

Jaison R. Abel and Richard Deitz. Reprinted by permission from Jaison R. Abel and Richard Deitz, "Do Big Cities Help College Graduates Find Better Jobs?" Federal Reserve Bank of New York, *Liberty Street Economics* (blog), May 20, 2013, http://libertystreeteconomics.newyorkfed.org/2013/05/do-big-cities-help-college-graduates-find-better-jobs.html. The views expressed in this article are those of the authors, and do not necessarily reflect the position of the Federal Reserve Bank of New York or the Federal Reserve System.

American Association of University Professors. "On Freedom of Expression and Campus Speech Codes." *Policy Documents and Reports,* Eleventh Edition, pp. 361–62. Copyright © 2015 American Association of University Professors. Reprinted with permission of Johns Hopkins University Press.

Julian Baggini. "The Nature of Truth." From *A Short History of Truth.* Copyright © Julian Baggini, 2017. Reproduced by permission of Quercus Editions Limited.

James Baldwin. "On Being White . . . and Other Lies." Copyright © 1984 by James Baldwin. Originally published in *Essence* magazine. Collected in *Cross of Redemption* by James Baldwin, published by Pantheon/Vintage. Used by arrangement with the James Baldwin Estate.

Bill Burnett and Dave Evans. Excerpts from *Designing Your Life: How to Build a Well-Lived, Joyful Life.* Copyright © 2016 by William Burnett and David J. Evans. Used by permission of Alfred A. Knopf, an imprint of the Knopf Doubleday Publishing Group, a division of Penguin Random House LLC. All rights reserved.

John Canaday. Excerpt from *What Is Art?* Copyright © 1980 by John Canaday. Used by permission of Alfred A. Knopf, an imprint of the Knopf Doubleday Publishing Group, a division of Penguin Random House LLC. All rights reserved.

Suresh Canagarajah. From "The Place of World Englishes in Composition: Pluralization Continued," *College Composition and Communication,* Vol. 57, No. 4 (June 2006), pp. 586–619.

Copyright © 2006 by the National Council of Teachers of English. Reprinted with permission.

Conference on College Composition and Communication. "Students' Right to Their Own Language." Adopted by the Conference on College Composition and Communication, 1974. http://www.ncte.org/library/NCTEFiles/Groups/CCCC/NewSRTOL.pdf. Reprinted by permission of the National Council of Teachers of English.

Arthur Danto. "Working Towards a Definition of Art." From *What Art Is,* pp. ix–xii. Copyright © 2013 By Arthur Danto. Reprinted by permission of Yale University Press.

Lisa Delpit. "The Silenced Dialogue." Originally published as text in Lisa D. Delpit, "The Silenced Dialogue: Power and Pedagogy in Educating Other People's Children," *Harvard Educational Review*, Vol. 58, No. 3, pp. 280–98. Copyright © 1988 by the President and Fellows of Harvard College. All rights reserved. Reprinted by permission.

Angela Lee Duckworth. Editorial review from the cover of *The Marshmallow Test: Mastering Self-Control* by Walter Mischel. Reprinted by permission.

Albert Elsen. "What Is Art?" From *Purposes of Art*, 4e. Copyright © 1981 South-Western, a part of Cengage, Inc. Reproduced by permission. www.cengage.com/permissions.

Daniel Goleman. Editorial review from the cover of *The Marshmallow Test: Mastering Self-Control* by Walter Mischel. Reprinted by permission.

"Gun Control. Now." https://petitions.moveon.org/sign/gun-control-now-1. Reprinted by permission of MoveOn.org.

Tim Harford. "The Problem with Facts," *FT Magazine*, FT.com, March 9, 2017. Used under license from the Financial Times. All rights reserved.

Anemona Hartocollis and Jacey Fortin. "Should Teachers Carry Guns? Are Metal Detectors Safe? What Experts Say," from *The New York Times*, February 24, 2018. Copyright © 2018 The New York Times. All rights reserved. Used under license.

Rodney A. Smolla. "Speech Overview." Freedom Forum Institute: https://www .freedomforuminstitute.org/first-amendment-center/ topics/freedom-of-speech-2/speech-overview/. Reprinted by permission of the author.

Ashley Stahl. "Six Reasons Why Your College Major Doesn't Matter," from Forbes.com, August 12, 2015. Copyright © 2015 Forbes. All rights reserved. Used under license.

"Stop Animal Abuse." From the PETA website: https://www.peta.org/issues. Reprinted by permission of PETA.

Will Storr. "A Better Kind of Happiness," *The New Yorker*, July 7, 2016. Copyright © 2016 Condé Nast. Reprinted by permission.

Andrew Sullivan. "America Wasn't Built for Humans." Copyright © 2017 by Andrew Sullivan. Used by permission of The Wylie Agency LLC.

Margaret Sullivan. "When Reporters Get Personal." From *The New York Times*, January 1, 2013. Copyright © 2013 The New York Times. All rights reserved. Used under license.

United Nations Geneva Convention. From *International Convention on the Elimination of All Forms of Racial Discrimination.* Copyright © 2016 United Nations. Reprinted with the permission of the United Nations.

University of Chicago. "Report of the Committee on Freedom of Expression: College Policies on Controversial Speakers." Reprinted by permission of the University of Chicago.

University of Colorado Board of Regents. Policy 1.D: Freedom of Expression and Policy 7.C: Academic Freedom, from the University of Colorado Board of Regents Laws and Policies, Adopted September 14, 2018. Reprinted by permission of the University of Colorado Board of Regents.

Jeremy Waldron. From *The Harm in Hate Speech* by Jeremy Waldron, Cambridge, Mass.: Harvard University Press. Copyright © 2012 by the President and Fellows of Harvard College. Reprinted by permission.

Timothy Wilson. Editorial review from the cover of *The Marshmallow Test: Mastering Self-Control* by Walter Mischel. Reprinted by permission.

Index